WIFE TO WIDOW

WIFE TO WIDOW

Lives, Laws, and Politics
in Nineteenth-Century Montreal

BETTINA BRADBURY

UBCPress · Vancouver · Toronto

21 20 19 18 17 16 15 14 13 12 11   5 4 3 2 1

Printed in Canada on FSC-certified ancient-forest-free paper
(100% post-consumer recycled) that is processed chlorine- and acid-free.

Library and Archives Canada Cataloguing in Publication

Bradbury, Bettina, 1949-
  Wife to widow : lives, laws, and politics in nineteenth-century Montreal / Bettina Bradbury.

Includes bibliographical references and index.
Also issued in electronic format.
ISBN 978-0-7748-1951-0

  1. Married women – Québec (Province) – Montréal – Social conditions – 19th century.
2. Married women – Legal status, laws, etc. – Québec (Province) – History – 19th century.
3. Widows–Québec (Province) – Montréal – Social conditions – 19th century. 4. Widows–
Legal status, laws, etc. – Québec (Province) – History – 19th century. 5. Montréal (Québec)
– History – 19th century. 6. Montréal (Québec) – Biography. I. Title.

HQ1453.B73 2011   306.872'3097142809034   C2011-901702-4

Canadä

UBC Press gratefully acknowledges the financial support for our publishing program of the Government of Canada (through the Canada Book Fund), the Canada Council for the Arts, and the British Columbia Arts Council.

This book has been published with the help of a grant from the Canadian Federation for the Humanities and Social Sciences, through the Aid to Scholarly Publications Program, using funds provided by the Social Sciences and Humanities Research Council of Canada.

Printed and bound in Canada by Friesens
Set in Chisel and Bembo by Artegraphica Design Co. Ltd.
Copy editor: Judy Phillips
Proofreader: Theresa Best

UBC Press
The University of British Columbia
2029 West Mall
Vancouver, BC V6T 1Z2
www.ubcpress.ca

To the joys of my life, my daughters, Anna and Emily,

and in loving memory of
my mother, Elespie
and my father, Ian Prior, who outlived her

Contents

Figures and Tables

Tables

Preface and Acknowledgments

In June 1988, I was walking toward the McGill university chapel in Montreal, holding the hands of my five- and eight-year-old daughters, Emily and Anna. My parents walked a few steps behind. John Bradbury, my first husband, had died several weeks earlier. As we walked toward the chapel I was approached by one of my university colleagues. Over John's six-month battle with stomach cancer, I had become accustomed to the discomfort with dying and death that characterize late-twentieth-century Western societies. I had also benefited from enormous support from friends and neighbours. But this was a colleague whom I did not know very well. He was clearly searching for the right words to express his condolences. "I just wanted to tell you," he started, in French, "I just wanted to tell you," he continued, "how lucky you are to be a widow and not divorced." I gulped, thought how glad I was that my parents' French was not fluid enough for them to understand him, thanked him, and filed the story away. Over time it became a good tale for dinner table exchange, sometimes another way to ease the discomfort of those who discovered for the first time that I had lived through a husband's illness and death.

I recount this here, not to embarrass that colleague, should he read the book and remember, but rather because it serves as a reminder of the similarities between the ways divorce dissolves family today as widowhood did more frequently in the past. It also underlines the differences between people's familiarity with death and widowhood in the nineteenth century, and the discomfort of the twentieth and twenty-first centuries. Little about having experienced a husband's death or having been a widow myself helps me to understand the lives of the women I follow here from their marriages through their widowhood to their own deaths. The temporal and cultural distance of close to two centuries is immense. The gap between my place in the 1980s as a privileged, middle-class widow, with my own home and a tenure-track university teaching position, and the social and economic situations of the widows of many classes and ethnicities whom I study here is huge too. I first thought of writing about widowhood as a wife, not a widow – integrating some material into the final chapter of my previous book. Studying working-class families in an industrializing city heightened my sense that widows deserved a study of their own.

This book has been a long time in the making and my debts are enormous and diverse. It is the result of a collective research effort. It would have been·impossible to write without major support from SSHRC and FQRSC; my first thanks go to them. Grants from both agencies, to me and to the Montreal History Group have allowed me to employ many students, who have performed much of the demanding and sometimes tedious work of tracing men and women from their marriages through to their deaths. I could not have done the work without them. Many also shared intellectual insights that helped me better understand nineteenth-century Montreal. To acknowledge their hard and often tedious work, I have used the word "we" in the chapters that follow when I refer to research that was the product of more than my labour. My second set of thanks, therefore go to Hélène Bedard, Marie-Anne Chaput, Alexandre Dessan, Amanda Glasbeek, Peter Gossage, Michel Guenette, Laila Haidarali, Kathryn Harvey, Stephen Henderson, Dan Horner, Darcy Ingram, Evelyn Kolish, Dominique Launay, Valerie Minette, Tamara Myers, Nathalie Picard, Mary Anne Poutanen, René Roy, David Silverman, John Spira, Michelle Stairs, Alan Stewart, Sylvie Taschereau, Steven Watt, Jennifer Waywell, Erica Wien, Sovita Chander, and others. My third set of thanks is to Sherry Olson for making the maps, for helping me track people, for all her careful work on Montreal's past, and much more, and to Robert Sweeny, Mary Anne Poutanen, Jean-Claude Robert, Jean-Marie Fecteau and Nathalie Picard for sharing databases and for their other contributions that have shaped this book. A special thanks to Heather Steel and Jarett Henderson for creating the index. And, many thanks too to the anonymous readers of the manuscript for supportive and helpful suggestions. All mistakes are, of course, my own.

It has been my privilege to get feedback on various versions of these chapters from many colleagues, friends, and graduate students. My fourth set of thanks goes to all of them. I would especially like to thank Kathryn McPherson, Molly Ladd-Taylor, Anne Rubenstein, and Michele Johnson, who generously read the whole manuscript and offered wise suggestions and generous encouragement. To Craig Heron a special thanks for listening to widows' stories over the years, supportive intellectual encouragement and feedback, reading a near final draft, sharing our children, and so much more. Further thanks to all my colleagues in the Montreal History Group, from whom I have learned so much over our many years together: to Lorraine Code and Susan Ehrlich for a stimulating year of reading one another's work, to members of the women's and gender history reading group at York University who have commented on several chapters, and to the former Faculty of Arts at York University for a research leave and other support. I have written and revised parts of this manuscript at home and on sabbatical in Australia and New Zealand. Thanks to the history department at the University of Melbourne for space to work there and to colleagues there, especially Pat Grimshaw for support and feedback. Thanks to Charlotte Macdonald, Rosalba Finnerty, and my sister, Ione, for giving me space to write in New Zealand; to Andrée Lévesque for her friendship and giving me a home base in Montreal; to Nikki Strong-Boag and to all other colleagues, friends, and family who have shared laughter and love, food and wine.

This book has been a long time in the making, and earlier versions of some of the material herein have already been published. A very early analysis of the marriage contracts and the legal issues treated in Chapter 3 was co-authored with Alan Stewart, Evelyn Kolish, and Peter Gossage. It appeared as "Property and Marriage: The Law and Practice in Early Nineteenth Century Montreal," in *Histoire sociale/Social History* 26, 51 (May 1993): 9-39. Some of the material in Chapter 4 appeared initially as "Debating Dower: Patriarchy, Capitalism and Widows' Rights in Lower Canada," in Tamara Myers, et al., eds., *Power, Place and Identity: Historical Studies of Social and Legal Regulation in Quebec* (Montreal: Montreal History Group, 1998), 55-78. Aspects of the practices and laws treated in Chapters 7 and 8 were explored in "Itineraries of Marriage and Widowhood in Nineteenth-century Montreal," in Nancy Christie and Michael Gauvreau, eds., *Mapping the Margins: Families and Social Discipline in Canada, 1700-1975* (Montreal: McGill-Queen's University Press, 2004), 103-40, while an early version of Chapter 9 appeared in Mona Gleason and Adele Perry, eds., *Rethinking Canada: The Promise of Women's History*, 5th edition (Toronto: Oxford University Press, 2006), 73-94, as well as in "Widows at the Hustings: Gender, Citizenship, and the Montreal By-elections of 1832," in Rudolph M. Bell and Virginia Yans, eds., *Women on Their Own: Interdisciplinary Perspectives on Being Single* (New Brunswick, NJ: Rutgers University Press, 2008), 82-113. I first investigated the material used in Chapter 11 on elderly women's use of institutions in "Mourir chrétiennement: La vie et la mort dans les établissments catholiques pour personnes âgées à Montréal au XIXe siècle," *Revue d'histoire de L'Amérique française* 46, 1 (été

1992): 143-75, and in "Elderly Inmates and Care Giving Sisters: Catholic Institutions for the Elderly in Nineteenth Century Montreal," in Franca Iacovetta and Wendy Mitchinson, eds., *On the Case: Case Files and Social History* (Toronto: University of Toronto Press, Toronto, 1998), 129-55. I am grateful to all these publishers for allowing me to reprint material.

WIFE to WIDOW

Introduction

And, I am sure you will also have the imprudence, the lack of reason, tact and intelligence to imagine, in caricature ... on one side of the street a dowered widow "à la loi française," at ease, well dressed and nourished and on the other side a widow "à la loi anglaise" walking the streets with her children in tow, begging for bread and requesting alms because the father had not perhaps seen too clearly.

     – M., letter to the editor, L'Aurore des Canadas, *18 December 1840*

On 18 December 1840, in a letter to the editor of the Montreal newspaper *L'Aurore des Canadas,* "M." brilliantly and sarcastically uses the story of a father approached by his daughter's suitor to assert the superiority of French over English law in its treatment of widows and to underline the arrogance of British claims to a superior civilization. "Dower" is a word little used today. It is frequently confused with a dowry, the property a woman brings into a marriage. "Dower," however, refers to a widow's right to the use of a defined portion of her husband's property after his death. As M. explains in the same letter, a dower means that "after the husband's death the wife will have the use of certain lands and property during her life and that ownership will go to the children, or that before any other creditors she will take for herself and her children certain sums of money."[1]

The full text of this letter foreshadows many of this book's main themes, arguments, and concepts. In it, M. highlights women's transition from wife to widow, reminding us and his readers of death's centrality as the main cause of family dissolution. (Today, a more complex mix of separations, divorce, and death dissolve long-term relationships.) His caricature represents only two potential outcomes of a husband's death: a home, independence, and comfort; or begging, charity, and a life on the streets. I argue here that widows' lives were much more diverse than that. In attributing the poverty or wealth of widows to the differences between French and English law, M. highlights the coexistence of at least two different understandings of the law and of patriarchy among Montreal's citizens of the early nineteenth century. Elsewhere in the letter, he links this essentially domestic question of a woman's claim on her husband's property to major political, legal, and social issues of the period, tying together private familial decisions and public policy. The letter represents and produces different gendered cultural and ethnic identities through differing legal marriage regimes as dualities for political ends in this particular colonial context. In the "colonial order of things," early-nineteenth-century Montreal and the colony of Lower Canada (later Quebec) was a historically specific contact zone in which British colonizers, Canadiens (the conquered French Canadians), and other immigrants sorted out their individual and collective identities and lives, largely separate from the colony's Aboriginal peoples.[2]

Wife to widow. It is this transition that lies at the heart of this book's subject and its structure. I focus here on the lives of women who married and became widows in Montreal, and on negotiations and renegotiations of patriarchy in their individual lives, in the laws that framed marriage and widowhood, and in the politics of the period. I observe this transition and these negotiations at different levels, moving across analyses at the scale of individuals, couples, families, and kin, the institutions of the city, custom, the law, and colonial politics.[3] *Wife to Widow* follows two generations of Montreal women from the time they became wives in the 1820s and 1840s respectively, through their years as widows, to their own deaths in the nineteenth century and beyond. It links narratives of the individual itineraries of their lives with analysis of the laws and customs that framed their rights as wives and widows and the political debates that changed them. I seek to show the ways women interacted with and shaped the city's culture, customs, and institutions, alongside their ongoing but changing exclusion as women from most positions of power and authority, by weaving their lives as wives and widows into the history of the city and society in which they lived. Thus, this book shares with much feminist history the desire to articulate the ties between personal and political issues, and with historians of gender and colonialism the goal of exploring the "broad scale dynamics of colonial rule and the intimate sites of its implementation." Historians of other colonial contexts have focused extensively on interracial sex and relationships or extra-marital sexuality as key sites of intimacy; my interest here is in the institution of marriage and questions of property, wealth, and inheritance within this city in a white settler society with two main groups of colonizing Europeans.[4]

At the heart of *Wife to Widow* are the biographies of the women, who, roughly a generation apart, were married by Catholic priests, Protestant ministers, or Jewish rabbis in Montreal in selected years during the 1820s and the 1840s. So that readers may understand the information that I have pieced together about the women of these two generations of marriages, this introduction first explains my sources and methodology in greater depth. It then explores the different historical contexts in which each generation married and concludes by turning briefly to the concepts and intellectual influences that have shaped my approach.

Two Generations of Women: Building Biographies and Collective Genealogies

The book begins, as my research strategy did, with marriage. To become a widow it was necessary to be recognized as female, marry a male, and outlive him. The biographies of individual women and most of the broader patterns discussed in the chapters that follow are based on the traces my researchers and I have been able to find of the lives of women who married in Montreal between 1823 and 1826 and a generation later, between 1842 and 1845.[5]

These two decades were chosen in part because Montreal censuses exist for 1825 and 1842 that show some characteristics of the city's population at the time of these marriages, and because in 1842 registration of marriage contracts promising widows dowers was first required. Most importantly, these two generations were married on either side of many of the major political, legal, social, demographic, and religious transformations of the period. The couples followed here married before and after the rebellions of 1837 and 1838 and the challenges they reflected regarding the relations between this colony and its metropole, between the conquered French colonizers and English colonizers, and issues of political representation and citizenship in the colony. They became husbands and wives before and after major changes to widows' dower rights were initiated by a Special Council that replaced representative government following the rebellions. Those changes were part of broader changes in the law and jurisprudence of the colony, which incorporated elements of English common law into the Custom of Paris, the body of French law retained for civil matters following the British Conquest. In the 1820s, land transactions were complicated by seigneurial tenure, dower, and other claims on land that left few if any written records. In the years following the 1840s marriages, changes to dower and other laws left land more "liberated from all of these restrictions."[6]

When the couples married in the 1820s, migration from rural areas, Ireland, and elsewhere in the British Isles was relatively slow. By the 1840s, even before the Irish potato famine, the numbers were growing rapidly. In between, in 1832, Irish immigrants brought cholera to the colony. Epidemics shaped family dissolution for both generations. Typhus hit in 1847; cholera returned in the 1850s. The generation who became wives in the 1820s married in an artisanal, commercial city, the retirement place of many of the colony's wealthy fur traders. A generation later, producers were accelerating transformations that would lead to industrialization, steamships were replacing sailing ships, and the earliest railways were attracting attention. The first generation married when the Catholic Church in this French and Catholic colony was in a particularly fragile state. Women of the second generation became wives at a time of significant Catholic and Protestant revival.

M. was one of the pseudonyms used by Charles-Elzéar Mondelet, a Canadien lawyer, politician, and Patriote. In June 1824, this Catholic French Canadian married Mary Elizabeth Henrietta Carter in Montreal's Christ Anglican Church.[7] Charles and Mary were among the first generation of couples whose lives are followed here. Between 1823 and 1826, Catholic priests officiated at the weddings of 584 women with French names – Canadiennes – who were born in the colony of Lower Canada, and 192 Irish women, virtually all of whom were immigrants. A further 560 women, mostly of American, Scottish, English, and Irish origin, were married by Anglican or Presbyterian ministers, the only Protestant denominations allowed at that time to perform marriages in the colony. A generation later, between 1842 and 1845, the numbers marrying in the city reached over 2,800. We sampled half these marriages: they included 508 Canadienne Catholics, 366 Irish Catholics, 575 apparently English-speaking Protestant women, and a few Jewish women. By then, Methodists, Baptists, Congregationalists, and Jews could also register marriages.[8]

Few of these women left diaries or letters that might reveal the joys or anguish of their lives as wives, mothers, or widows. Those that did were usually members of the city's most powerful economic, political, and religious elites. I draw on these at times. Other historians have demonstrated the richness and limitations of family papers for capturing the ways women experienced courtship, marriage, death, and widowhood.[9] I have chosen to make visible a wider range of women by seeking to "recover the traces" they left at key moments of transition in their lives through the documents produced on such occasions. I call this approach collective genealogy. Family demographers have developed family reconstitution as a method in which all records of births, deaths, and marriages are recorded separately then linked together to constitute family histories and genealogies.[10] Other, Quebec historians who have sought to reconstitute families to study questions of demography, inheritance, and family reproduction have done so in small parishes or relatively small towns,[11] by creating massive databases of the population of a whole region,[12] by focusing on a specific occupational grouping,[13] or by focusing on a set of family names.[14] Large-scale family reconstitution is difficult for a city like Montreal, though recent digitization projects make it increasingly feasible.[15]

The collective genealogies and life histories of the women followed here began with their marriages. Having recorded the information available about the couples in those records, we then searched for each spouse's death or remarriage first in indexes, and then in the church registers. In these searches we confronted all the problems a mobile population poses, as well as the challenges of identifying people across different sources with diverse spellings and some with names too common to follow.[16] Readers who have attempted to trace aspects of their own family history will know the frustrations, joys, and chance discoveries that are part of that process. In a city as large as Montreal, with its mobile population, these were not simple tasks. Following Protestants is particularly challenging because their records are sparser. Here I must again acknowledge my deep gratitude to those students who attempted this task, which at times truly seemed to be a mission impossible.

Having established the demographic profiles of those couples who left traces we could follow, we then searched systematically in some sources, selectively in others, and sometimes made serendipitous finds. We searched the files of Montreal's notaries systematically for any marriage contracts the couples made prior to their weddings, and more selectively for inventories of goods, wills, and testaments. Locating wills is challenging because, unlike in common law jurisdictions, there was no probating or central registration of all wills. Wills and testaments could be made either with a notary or, in English style, privately in front of several witnesses.[17] Most have remained in notary's archives. English-style wills had to be proved in court, and alphabetical listings make them easier to find. The process of establishing a tutor – guardians legally responsible for the care of minor children of widows or widowers and who had the authority to represent them in all civil acts – required a meeting of family and friends, held usually before a judge. We consulted these selectively. In connecting the dots in individual women's lives, as well as in determining overall patterns among widows in the city at particular points in time, city directories and censuses taken between 1825 and 1901 were further complementary sources. We identified all information on the Montreal households that included widows and widowers in 1861, and searched selectively for some of the widows of these two generations who were still alive in the 1881, 1891, and 1901 censuses, as well as searching for specific wives, husbands, and widows in city tax records.

To understand the law and politics of the period more broadly, I turned to the formal documents produced by the political and legal systems and their experts. Most important were the digests of jurisprudence, legal case reports, notaries' manuals, statutes, and journals of the Special Council, Legislative Assembly, and Legislative Council, along with reconstituted political debates. The print culture of the period – primarily newspapers and pamphlets – provided evidence of how marriage, widowhood, and death were represented culturally and debated alongside the formal structures of law and politics.

Unrevealing of emotions and sentiment, of little use in weighing romantic love against economic pragmatism, these documents can nevertheless be read productively to reveal much about the power dynamics at play at particular moments. They reveal choices made when daughters became wives, wives became widows, and families resolved issues of widows' claims, tutorship of children, or of declining health and imminent death. The collective genealogies allow a broad picture of demographic and social patterns and practices. To better understand women's lives and the laws and politics of the times, I have built more detailed biographies of some twenty women and woven them throughout the upcoming chapters. Most of these women are unknown. They were the wives and widows of labourers, carters, and craftsmen, the largest groups in this pre-industrial city. Others are known only as the wives of prominent men like Charles-Elzéar Mondelet. Only one – Émilie Tavernier – already features in the historiography in her own right.[18] The women whose individual stories I tell are not "representative" widows – the routes from wife to widow were so diverse that there were no such women. Rather, in their diversity they represent something of the range of practices, experiences, and situations of Montreal wives and widows. I chose some because their lives left particular traces in the archives, others because they faced dilemmas that reveal key practices structuring marriage or widowhood, and some simply because their stories seduced me. As much as possible, they represent a range of ethnicities, religions, classes, and generations.

Collective genealogies are challenging to create. The scratches of evidence of people's lives left in archives are not random. Those used here were produced at moments when men and women formalized decisions they had made, or reported vital events that had occurred, and some male official of the church or state recorded the details. As such, the nature of their traces vary depending not just on the unfolding of their individual lives, or their visibility and power in the society of the time, but also on their cultural practices and the particular demands of the religious, political, legal, or economic institutions with which they interacted. Most left only scratches resulting from the bureaucratic acts recording their marriages, the birth or death of their children, the death of a spouse, or census enumeration. Other actions produced records more like scars – the remaining written evidence of conflicts and tension that erupted into the public domain – "signs of victimization but also of resistance."[19] When things went wrong in families either because of conflict between generations or between husband and wife, some men and women ended up in civil or criminal courts defending their actions or claiming their rights. Others turned to local notaries for help. A few women marched through their times leaving a trail of abrasions and bruises in the archives.[20] A few left more fully formed vignettes and portraits.

In this genealogical tracking, legal, religious, and cultural custom and practices condition what it is possible to know about individuals and influence our certainty about who individuals were.[21] When Scholastique Bissonnet married Louis Ducharme dit Saint Denis in Montreal's Notre Dame Parish church on 10 July 1826, the register indicated that she was a minor and that her mother was her legal tutor. Louis was identified as a joiner who resided in the parish, though was not originally from there. The names of both of their parents were also listed, as required by Catholic rules but not the law.[22] The register also indicated that both of their fathers were dead. A year later, when their son Louis died eight days after his birth, Scholastique's husband was again identified as a joiner. Six years later, when yet another son named Louis died at the age of sixteen months, his father was described as an innkeeper. When Louis himself died in April 1834, leaving Scholastique a widow, the register again indicated that he was an innkeeper but did not identify her name. When men died, Catholic officials only sometimes recorded the names of their widows. When married women or widows died, in contrast, Catholic records nearly always listed the name of their spouses. Not only does this show how married women's identity was linked closely to that of their husbands, it also facilitates successful tracing and makes successfully identifying women easier than successfully identifying men. Catholic registers also normally listed the previous spouse's name when a widow or widower remarried.

The "methodology of family-tree building is a gendered one," as Megan Doolittle has argued, "because it relies so heavily on names to make kinship links."[23] This is true, but naming practices vary across cultures. Catholic practices in Lower Canada offer a stark contrast to the English practices she targets. At his death in 1834, Louis was listed only by his name, as an innkeeper, and as aged thirty. Were it not for Scholastique's remarriage three years later to a shoemaker, when she was identified clearly as the widow of Louis Ducharme, joiner, it would be difficult to be sure that this was her husband. Similarly, the registration of her death in 1895 at the age of eighty-three indicated clearly that she was the widow of her second husband.[24]

This patriarchal lingering identification with a dead husband thus serves to make it pretty easy to successfully trace Catholic women from marriage to their deaths or remarriages. Compare these traces with those left by the Protestant Sarah Young. In 1844, she married Samuel Allen at the Zion Congregational Church, one of the nine Protestant denominations allowed to register marriages by that date. The record indicates that she was a spinster living in Montreal and that he was a labourer. There are no names of parents to aid later identifications, no indication of whether either spouse was widowed. In trying to follow her life, my researchers found two Sarah Allens who died. Both turned out to be infants. They also found a marriage between a Sarah Young and a John Neil in 1856, but this Sarah Young was listed as a spinster, so it was not considered a trustworthy match.[25] Our tracing method, which worked pretty well for Catholics, was much less useful for non-Catholics because they left different tracks.

Sarah Young's itinerary following her marriage would likely have remained unknown, as it did for large numbers of the Protestants whom we sought to follow, had we not turned to the records of the Protestant cemetery.[26] The cemetery was the one place in Montreal that united all Protestants who died or were buried in the city after the early 1860s.[27] The records its officials made included alphabetical indexes of all Protestant deaths in the city. For the early years, they are in bound, handwritten registers and have an index in which the names of all those buried in a year are clustered by the first letter of the dead person's family name. Wives were usually listed by their husbands' names, following English practice. After the new Protestant cemetery opened on Mount Royal in the 1860s, names were listed on alphabetical cards kept in a drawer. In one of the early registers we found mention of a Samuel Allen who died of cholera on 8 July 1854. Upon searching a second source – the names of grave owners – we discovered that the grave in which he was buried belonged to a Mrs. Samuel Allen. Was this Sarah née Young? Possibly. Possibly not. These traces lead readily into false genealogical tracks that turn on themselves so often that they take on the appearance of truth. A third piece of information available at the cemetery is a listing of all the people in a particular grave. There we found buried with Samuel Allen a John Neil who had died in 1878 of a "disease of the heart" at the age of fifty. Thus, the remarriage we had found between the "spinster" Sarah Young and John Neil in 1856 must indeed have been that of Sarah Young, widow of Samuel Allen. The card with Sarah's name and details of her death is bundled in the records next to those of her two husbands. Her card records that she died of cirrhosis of the liver in 1883 at the age of sixty-two.[28]

If I seem to linger unnecessarily over these examples of how we have traced these women's lives it is for three reasons. First, the differences between Protestant and Catholic registers serve as a reminder that seemingly simple bureaucratic acts involve a set of rules and interactions among actors with different power, authority, and traditions that shape their content and categories. This is as true of parish registers as it is of censuses, wills, marriage contracts, and the records of charity workers. Marriage was not just an individual arrangement between husbands and wives, or an agreement between their families. It was a contract sanctioned and recorded by state, church, and community members. Parish registers in Lower Canada were both civil and religious documents. One copy remained with the church, the other had to be deposited with the civil authorities.[29] The law of the colony set out a minimal amount of information that was meant to be recorded. It also required two to four witnesses and the signatures of the literate. The Catholic Church had long demanded more. Protestant churches often provided less. Some of those responsible for recording asked for more details than others. Individuals, family members, and bureaucrats brought their own concerns and cultural traditions into these situations, choosing what they wished to report and how.

Second, these differences have influenced the numbers of Protestants and Catholics whom we have been able to follow from their marriages to the deaths of the first partner. The difficulty of making sure matches interacted with the greater mobility of Protestants to shrink the proportions of Protestants we could trace from marriage through to the death of the first partner. As a result, whereas I know definitely whether the wife or husband died first for over half of Catholic marriages, I have this information for under a quarter of the Protestants.[30] Because of this vast difference in the numbers of marriages where the outcome is known with certainty, some comparisons of Catholics and Protestants are not statistically robust. Yet, the combined information on both populations does provide useful demographic information about the lengths of marriages and of widowhood, the speed of remarriage for men and women, and the ages at which people married and died. This allows me to locate the individual life stories of specific wives within broader patterns.

Third, as mentioned earlier, the biographies based on such searching and on combining the demographic details with information from marriage contracts, wills, censuses, and city directories are the core of the book. The people, processes, and such divergent, culturally determined practices are my focus as much as are statistical patterns. Piecing together the traces that couples left, interrogating the significance of visibility and invisibility in these and other sources, and treating these documents as revealing moments and processes in which new identities and rights were produced ·

rather than just reflected allow me to narrate aspects of the individual life stories of wives and widows and to ponder people's unequal ability to leave traces of their lives and deaths in particular kinds of records.

Here I tell the stories of women who became widows, not of husbands whose wives died first, leaving them widowers. The possibility that wives might become widows was, I argue, a matter of private worry for parents, for husbands, and for wives. It shaped early philanthropic work and entered public policy and debate, as Mondelet's letter reveals. Husbands were as likely to become widowers. Yet, legally, socially, and culturally, widowhood was not the same for men and women. Widowhood was neither imagined, legislated for, nor lived in the same way as was the transition from husband to widower. Wives became widows. M.'s letter captures some of the ways widowhood was represented as a female status and as the concern of fathers or husbands. The protection that Mondelet envisages fathers seeking for their daughters through a dower was a provision that had no equivalent for men in the Custom of Paris.[31]

Both husbands and wives were expected to grieve, yet widows remained publicly linked to their deceased husbands in myriad ways that were not true of men. Both faced challenges if they were widowed with dependent children. But those challenges were of a different order. Widows resumed the legal capacity they had surrendered on marrying. Marriage never stripped husbands of theirs. Women, not men, were imagined slipping from comfort to poverty through the death of their spouse. And, given the few ways women could earn or raise money, their chances of doing so were greater. Mourning customs and expectations were different too. Because of these differences, and because widows are important historically as the largest group of single mothers in the past, they are the main focus here. At times, where relevant and possible, I compare the rights, practices, and experiences of husbands who became widowers.

The Historical Context of These Two Generations

Charles-Elzéar Mondelet concluded his 1840 letter to the editor by suggesting that should his readers wish to talk to the current legislators or even the governor about the importance of preserving widows' dower rights, they would be unlikely to get a sympathetic hearing. This letter was published sixteen years after his marriage, and just two years after reformers, radicals, and Patriotes in the two colonies of Upper and Lower Canada had moved from contesting the authoritarian rule of governors and their Tory supporters in the legislative assemblies and print media to armed conflict and Patriote defeat by the well-organized British-led troops and loyalist volunteers in successive battles in December 1837.[32]

It was nearly a year since exiled, increasingly radical Patriotes crossed the border from the United States, proclaiming the independence of Lower Canada, calling for universal male suffrage, claiming that "all persons including INDIANS, are to enjoy the same civil rights," and seeking voting by ballot and an end to widows' customary dower rights. They had again faced defeat. Mothers lost sons, sisters lost brothers, wives became widows. Repression was particularly harsh after November 1838, when well over eight hundred Patriotes were imprisoned in Montreal's jail. Over one hundred faced charges of treason. Twelve Patriotes were publicly hanged in Montreal. More than fifty were transported to Australia, others exiled to Bermuda.[33] Publication of Patriote newspapers was forbidden and habeas corpus was suspended, along with trial by jury for the accused. The governor suspended the Legislative Assembly of the colony of Lower Canada. From April 1838, successive Special Councils comprising elite men, handpicked by successive governors for their loyalty, had been passing numerous laws, furthering "a single legislative agenda," which Steven Watt argues represented the wishes of Montreal's most anti-French Tories.[34] One of the changes they were considering as Mondelet wrote would transform widows' rights in the colony. Hence his letter.

Reshaping patriarchy was on the agenda of both the predominantly Tory Special Council and the Patriotes. Both sought to reduce widows' claims on men's property, though in different ways. Both in their own ways were rethinking the contract of marriage.[35] The rebellions and the period of authoritarian rule that followed them constituted a significant watershed in Quebec history and in the ongoing negotiations of authority, power, influence, and identity that Britain's conquest of the colony of New France in 1759 had precipitated. As M.'s letter, the demands of the Patriotes, and Allan Greer's work make clear, issues of gender as they intersected with ethnicity, race, culture, and religion were part of these colonial contests and were reshaped in the aftermath of the rebellions.[36]

Growing immigration, especially from the British Isles, fuelled Patriote worries, reshaped the ethnic and religious composition of Montreal, and shaped each generation of marriages differently. Marguerite Paris, Émilie Tavernier, and Caroline Campbell were among the 1,338 women whose marriages were registered in Montreal churches between 1823 and 1826. As world cities went, Montreal was a relatively small town. The census taken by Jacques Viger and his colleague Louis Guy in 1825 recorded just over twenty-two thousand inhabitants.[37] This was about the same size as Cape Town, though there just over half were classified as "slaves," "Hottentots," or "free-blacks." It was double the population of Sydney, New South Wales, where over four out of ten of the inhabitants had been transported

FIGURE 0.1 "Montreal from Indian Camping Ground." This view of Montreal around the time the second generation of couples married positions First Nations men and women outside the growing city. Their clothing and temporary shelters appear primitive in contrast to the houses, smoke, windmills, and church spires that signal the civilization and progress of the not so distant city. | After a lithograph by James Duncan, 1843; T.L. Hornbrook, 1780-1850 (copyist). *Library and Archives Canada, 1934-409-1.*

as convicts.[38] At that time, New York boasted well over sixty thousand people and Edinburgh some eighty-three thousand, whereas the city of London was the world's largest city with over a million. Montreal's inhabitants included Canadiens, the eldest of whom still remembered living in a French colony. Immigrants from the United States, Scotland, England, Ireland, and from a few other parts of Europe and the expanding British Empire had joined them in the years since the Conquest. Some came in the army and stayed. Montreal was home to a very small black community, including descendants of slaves of African heritage who had once worked as house slaves for the city's elite, blacks who had migrated as Loyalists, and African Americans escaping the fugitive slave acts. Their numbers would increase after mid-century as the railroads began to offer work to the men.[39] First Nations men and women were concentrated away from the city. They might visit from the mission village of Kahnawake, across

FIGURE 0.2 "Old Market, Montreal." James Duncan was a prolific sketcher. In this image of the market, the class and ethnicity of sellers and buyers are signalled by their clothing. The background captures the mixture of sail and steam boats that characterized the harbour. | James Duncan (1806-82), *The Duncan Sketchbook*. Watercolour and gouache over black crayon, 1831-34. *Royal Ontario Museum, 951.158.12, ROM2009_10778_7.*

the Saint Lawrence River, or from further away. Visitors noted them walking the city streets; setting up their baskets, moccasins, and other wares to sell near the city market; and camping on the city outskirts, as evoked in this mid-century image in Figure 0.1. They were not welcome as residents.[40]

As Jacques Viger, the city's first modern sociologist, and later its first mayor, attempted to categorize the ethnic identities of its citizens in the 1825 census, he conceptualized three groups: Canadiens, English Canadians, and English and Strangers – or those not born in the colony. His categories showed that when the first cohort of couples married in the 1820s, Canadiens made up over half the population, English and "foreign" newcomers a third, whereas locally born anglophones comprised about 13 percent. Viger's categories blended Montreal's Scots, English, Irish, and Americans, whether they were born in the colony or were more recent arrivals, and hid the city's small Jewish community and its tiny numbers of blacks, Italians, and other Europeans. Montrealers were either Catholic or Protestant, French or English, married or not. Widowhood, so important in the city, and the status his wife had held before their marriage, disappeared, as did more subtle markers of ethnic and religious difference (see Figure 0.2).[41]

A generation later, when the Irish Catholic immigrant Maria Mitchell married the Irish Protestant Thomas Spiers, and the Canadienne Catholic Marie-Louise Genant married the master tailor Pierre-Bernard Decousse, the city's population had nearly doubled, reaching over forty thousand. By then, Montreal had clearly outdistanced Quebec City as the largest city of the colony of Lower Canada, indeed of the colonies of British North America. It was also the colonies' major economic centre. Immigration had boosted the number of non-French-speaking residents so that even before the famine Irish started arriving in 1847, they outnumbered Canadiens. Yet Canadiens remained the largest ethnic group, and their numbers increased as growing numbers migrated to the city from rural areas of the colony. Over upcoming decades, the city's growth continued. In 1871, the census recorded some 107,000 inhabitants. When the last known surviving widow from the two generations studied here died in 1915, the city had over 300,000 residents.

In the early 1820s, when Marguerite Paris and others of the first genera-tion married, demolition of the walls that had separated the old town of Montreal from the suburbs, populated largely by artisans and labourers, was complete. Ambitious plans led to the remodelling of city streets and squares, providing the city with grand new public spaces, which, Robert Sweeny argues, heralded and fostered a new bourgeois order. The pre-industrial, walled town was being transformed into a bourgeois colonial city. A large new courthouse and jail represented the rule of law through their classical architectural style. The streets along the waterfront and stretching out to the suburbs had been widened, facilitating the movement of immigrants, locals, and the wares traded across the Empire and into the west. Land in the city was increasingly concentrated in the hands of a few prominent families: in 1825, close to three-quarters of its households rented their homes.[42] (See Figure 0.3.)

By the time of Sarah Young's marriage in the 1840s, the city was a dif-ferent place. Montreal merchants were adjusting to the effects of Britain's repeal of much of the protection that had encouraged trade through Montreal and colonial ports. The numbers of immigrants, especially Irish Catholics, passing through the city had increased dramatically. Over a thousand British troops were housed in the city's garrison. The wharves had been rebuilt in granite, and the streets along the riverside housed ele-gant new three-storey stone commercial buildings. Nearby was the grand

FIGURE 0.3 "Southwest view, Notre-Dame Street, Montreal." This drawing by John Murray presents a clean and ordered view of Montreal's streets peopled by respectable men, women, and children. | John Murray (1810-68), 1850, engraving, coloured by hand. *Library and Archives Canada, 1970-188-87, W.H. Coverdale Collection of Canadiana.*

new Bonsecours market building. The Catholic hierarchy was aggressively seeking greater control over its flocks, while evangelical Protestants sought to control drinking and increase converts. Montrealers of different religious and political beliefs continued to use violence to settle scores, most notably when a Tory mob, incensed at compensation being offered to Patriotes who had lost property during the rebellions, torched the building housing the Parliament.[43]

In the 1820s, as in the 1840s, the men of the city made livings for themselves and their families as entrepreneurs, merchants, bourgeois, craftsmen, journeymen, labourers, carters, sailors, and soldiers. Montreal was a mercantile city, linked to Great Britain through the export of furs, lumber, and wheat and the import of semi-manufactured and luxury goods. Its merchants included Canadiens; Scots who had long dominated the fur trade; Americans, some of loyalist and some of more recent origin; and Englishmen from various parts of the British Isles, many of whom traded with merchants, even family members, in the colonial metropole. The city's merchants also included large numbers of Canadiens and newcomers who bought and sold at the more local scale of the continent, the colony, or the more immediate region. Merchants large and small were involved in a wide range of economic activities.[44]

Montreal's vibrant artisanal sector involved many Canadiens and growing numbers of craftsmen, skilled workers, and tradespeople from Great Britain and the northern United States, where the Industrial Revolution had long been transforming their crafts. Canadiens and newcomers alike also set up shops both large and small and ran inns, hotels, and taverns. Craftspeople, shopkeepers, and innkeepers sold their products and services to families in the city, to migrants passing through, and to an ever-growing hinterland to the north and south of the city and especially to the expanding areas of settlement in Upper Canada (later Ontario), to the west. Providing this population with professional services as notaries, lawyers, and doctors were Americans, Canadiens, and English and Jewish Canadians. Providing, among other things, the daily labour on construction sites, and the horses and carts that moved people and goods around, were the city's numerous labourers and carters, men of many backgrounds, though Canadiens and Irish Catholics predominated.[45]

Women's employment in the city is harder to capture. Their labour was critical to the running of their husbands' artisanal workshops, and in a few trades – notably the clothing trades – women hired and trained girls as apprentices. Wives often assisted their merchant, shopkeeping, and artisan husbands. They dealt with creditors, orders, and deliveries during the long absences that many merchants' work demanded. Married women, single women, and widows alike opened up their homes or rented spaces to run schools and to teach music, or to house boarders. Young girls, often recently arrived from rural areas or Ireland, were employed throughout the city as domestics. Women were visible in street trades that ranged from hawking wares to prostitution. They were also visible, as Mary Anne Poutanen has shown, among the vagrants who were living on the streets, surviving by stealing, squatting, and selling their bodies. A few were well established in the sex trades and ran profitable brothels. Some did well in this city with its floating population of sailors and garrison of British soldiers.[46] In the 1820s, a very small number of women worked and lived religious lives in the city's Catholic convents. Numbers then were at an all-time low. Recruitment of sisters and priests had been falling for over a century. This would change during the 1840s as Catholic leaders sought growing control over their people's lives.[47]

Over the lifetimes of the survivors of these two marriage generations, Montreal was transformed from a pre-industrial town to a modern, capitalist, cosmopolitan metropolis, from one city in a conquered colony to the largest and most important urban centre in the nation of Canada.[48] Work options for women changed first as industry opened up paid labour in factories, workshops, and the exploitative putting out of the sewing and leather trades, and then toward the end of the century as new possibilities for employment were created in offices and department stores. Only a few of the women who married in the 1820s and 1840s would live long enough to experience all those transformations.

Influences and Debts

This study of women's lives as wives and widows and of the negotiations and renegotiations of patriarchy in their individual lives, in the laws that framed marriage and widowhood, and in the politics of the period has been shaped by many areas of feminist inquiry and historical writing. My approach and analysis has been profoundly influenced by the last two decades of social and cultural history and by the broad shifts in historical and academic writing. The linguistic or cultural turn in history and a range of post-structuralist theories have reshaped thinking in and outside academia over the last two decades about how to understand the present, the past, power, and social change. Cogent critiques of the kind of quantitative study I had initially envisaged – in which data would be collected on individuals, coded, slotted into categories of my making, and then subjected to statistical testing – have pushed historians to think much more carefully about who produced the records we use, why, and to consider the cultural work they performed. Above all, historians have learned to be careful about what they can claim to know from such documents, complicating illusions that there are simple ways of capturing the experiences of people without power in the past.[49] Here I seek to blend the strengths of social history with insights from old and new cultural historians, through biographically focused narratives.[50]

In seeking to make sense of these women's lives I have built mostly on the concepts, methods, and findings of feminist history, family history, legal history, and histories of Quebec and Montreal. Feminist debates have informed the interrelated, widely debated, and diversely deployed understandings of patriarchy, gender, identity, class, and public and private upon which I draw here. Patriarchy was one of the earliest concepts used to understand women's oppression. It has been widely criticized for being ahistorical and essentialist, for ignoring women's agency, and as an inadequate tool for capturing the complex ways class, race, and gender intersect.[51] Yet, like Judith Bennett, I believe it remains a useful concept for some subjects. Adrienne Rich defined patriarchy years ago as "a familial-social, ideological, political system in which men – by force, direct pressure, or through ritual, tradition, law and language, customs, etiquette, education, and the division of labour, determine what part women shall or shall not play."[52] Thinking in this broad way still seems to me to help us understand nineteenth-century women's lives. Patriarchy was equally a cultural system that produced and policed gender difference. It was one axis of power that was constantly negotiated and renegotiated in individual relationships and through legal, political, and institutional changes. Those negotiations were historically specific and diverse, shaped by class, age, religion, ethnicity, sexuality, and other individual characteristics, as well as by gender. In 1986, Constance Backhouse argued that despite some commitment to what family historians have called "companionate marriage" among legislators, the judges in English Canada imposed a "pure patriarchy" that vested authority with the husband. I argue here that nineteenth-century marriage is best understood as companionate patriarchy, and that Montreal couples opted for a range of different versions of companionate patriarchy in their marriages, especially regarding property and authority, depending on their cultural-legal heritage and their class.[53] What couples considered the proper ordering of gender and property relations in marriage changed between these two generations and across the century. Of course, not all marriages were companionate. Some were loving, some respectful, some abusive, and some simply did not work.

Identity, like patriarchy, is used in diverse ways. In this book I use the concept to refer very broadly to cultural meanings produced discursively in ways that usually made particular characteristics and differences seem natural or biological. Identities were expressed culturally as well as negotiated, performed, and reshaped collectively, individually and interrelationally. Gender is one such identity; ethnicity, race, age, sexuality, and class are others. Catherine Hall has argued that "the time of empire was the time when anatomies of difference were being elaborated, across the axes of class, race, and gender. These elaborations were the work of culture, for the categories were discursive, and their meanings historically contingent."[54] In the colonial city of Montreal, Canadiens and newcomers forged new meanings of national, ethnic, and religious identity in relationship to each other. M.'s letter to the editor in 1840 began by claiming that English Montrealers regarded "the law of dower as a residue of barbary and of ignorance." It cleverly poked fun at the English belief that they were the most civilized society because they treated their women better than other nations by showing how badly the English common law treated wives and widows. Another major argument here is that in Lower Canada/Quebec, debates about marriage, widowhood, and inheritance fused with broader conflicts over the merits of French and English law. Montrealers imagined marriage and widowhood through the lenses of the legal cultures linked to their identities as Canadiens or British.

Class too has many meanings and is used in diverse ways by historians. How to designate women's class has occasioned much debate. I use "class" broadly to refer to men's wealth, their status in the community, and their relationship to the means of production as captured in their occupations. I treat wives and widows as sharing their husbands' class position, though not necessarily their wealth. Class was also a cultural category expressed through material culture. A further argument of *Wife to Widow* is that money, property, and class mattered. Different legal regimes framed divergent claims on husbands' estates and family fortunes. Yet, the types and amount of property accumulated during a marriage mattered too. Without family fortunes, inherited in their own right, or accumulated during their marriage and bequeathed by husbands, widows' alternatives were stark.

A husband's death turned a wife into a widow. Both wife and widow were legal, social, and cultural identities. The law forged categories of wives and widows as individuals with widely divergent legal capacities. Customs of mourning intensified the differences between the identities of wives and widows. Custom demanded that widows don a complete outfit of black mourning clothes for up to twelve months. Most men wore only an armband to signify their mourning. Mourning clothes, like names, marked widows with traces of their dead husbands' identities, for months, years, and sometimes for lifetimes. Caroline Scott, who married the notary Thomas John Pelton in 1844, was identified at diverse times after he died as "Mrs. Widow Pelton," "Mrs. C. widow John," and "Pelton, Mrs. Caroline, widow, Thomas J." Traces, Nancy Hewitt has reminded us, drawing on the definition in the *American Heritage Dictionary,* "can be 'a visible mark or sign of the former presence or passage of some person, thing or event'; 'a barely perceptible indication of something.'"[55] Beyond the similarities of such traces and markers, the categories of wife and widow as individual identities and as discursive constructs were diverse. They were lived and produced concurrently with their class, gender, ethnicity, religion, and age. The diversity of widows' situations and of the range of ways they interacted with historical events and shaped the city in which they lived is another main argument of the book.

The idea that men and women occupied and should occupy different spheres was a significant component of gender ideology in most Western nations in the nineteenth century. As an explanatory concept, it has been found wanting. Most historians would now agree that few women lived out their lives in domestic seclusion and that age, ability, class, ethnicity, race, and religion interacted to shape different experiences. Intellectual historians have pointed to the many divergent meanings of "public" and "private" in philosophical, political, religious, and other discourses of the times. I draw here on the rich body of writing that problematizes the question of gender and separate spheres and that seeks to explore the "ragged frontiers" between public and private and the complicated ways in which place and space, from homes through streets and notary's offices to the hustings, were gendered as appropriate for some men and women and not for others.[56]

Within feminist history I build most specifically on the small but growing number of studies of widowhood and "singlehood" that explore aspects of widows' lives in the past.[57] Writing about widows in Canada has focused more on the period of New France or on rural areas than on women in nineteenth-century cities.[58] Most useful have been studies of widows elsewhere that explore provisions in husbands' wills, laws of inheritance, widows as businesswomen, and institutions providing for poor widows, or that offer snapshots of widows' residential situations through census listings.[59] Building on these themes and this work, I insist here on the importance of understanding both marriage and widowhood and of following women across their lives by blending demography with the study of legal, political, and institutional histories. Hence, my debts extend also to the broader literature that explores issues of marriage and property;[60] female poverty, charity, and the work of benevolence;[61] early pensions for widows and mothers;[62] and gender, citizenship, and nation.[63]

In *Wife to Widow*, I seek to contribute both the stories of individual women's lives and an understanding of the different ways they negotiated and reshaped patriarchy across their lives in nineteenth-century Montreal. Feminist historians in Quebec have paid surprisingly little attention to women and gender in the early nineteenth century. Mary Anne Poutanen's important work on prostitutes and vagrants, Janice Harvey's research into women and Protestant charities, and Nathalie Picard's research on voting women are the main exceptions. I am indebted to all three, both for their insights and for sharing data with me that have enriched this study. I build here too on the insights of the Collective Clio, which in what remains the only survey of Quebec women's history, highlighted the significance of the transformations to dower rights and women's loss of the right to vote in this period. I dig deeper into these changes, nuancing the book's argument that capitalist expansion led by the British explains these changes.[64]

In thinking about population movements and legal and political debates about marriage of the period, I found it useful to conceptualize Montreal as a particular colonial space in which the dynamics of race, class, sexuality, gender, ethnicity, and the workings of difference can be fruitfully approached through the lenses of the rich and growing literature on gender and empire.[65] The particularities of Quebec's place in the relations of empire deserves more attention than it has received.

This is a feminist family history. Family historians have influenced my intellectual trajectory, the sources I use, and some of my methodology. In particular, this book joins the growing number of studies that extend the boundaries of family histories beyond domestic and internal familial relations and track the complex interactions among families, family members, kin, and other charitable, social, economic, and political institutions.[66] I build in different ways too on historical demography, studies of marriage and family formation,[67] of household structures and residential patterns,[68] aging and old age,[69] family dissolution, death, and inheritance.[70] A wonderfully rich scholarship in English Canada and especially Quebec explores the dynamics of inheritance. Yet, its focus is largely on the transmission of property in agricultural families. Such research has been critical to understanding the dynamics of settlement as Canadiens moved away from the earliest areas of settlement along the Saint Lawrence River into new agricultural areas. Gérard Bouchard's work in particular has placed the dynamics of family reproduction at the heart of analyses of migration and settlement. His study of the Saguenay provides empirical details that demonstrate how gender operated in these areas.[71] Yet, widows either get little attention in studies of rural areas or appear as helpless victims of family strategies or men's "patriarchy from the grave."[72]

The dominant focus on rural inheritance in Canada has been broken with Peter Baskerville's recent path-breaking study of urban women. In 1987, Carole Shammas and colleagues argued that in the United States too much inheritance literature concentrated on passing on land. They bemoaned the lack of comparable literature on the growth of financial assets and its possible impact on inheritance. Jon Stobart and Alastair Owens have argued cogently for the importance of studies of urban property and inheritance in the British context.[73] Our approaches, sources, and periods are different; still, *Wife to Widow* joins Baskerville's *A Silent Revolution?* in looking at questions of women and inheritance in an urban setting in which moveable property – investments, stock, cash, furniture, luxuries, even clothes were more important for most widows than land.

Inheritance, property, and widowhood are also the subjects of legal history. I am indebted to Quebec legal historians for scholarship that has

helped me understand the transformations of Quebec laws regarding marriage, widowhood, and family property and the changes made to the civil
law over the late eighteenth and early nineteenth centuries. I build also on
writing about the law in other areas of mixed legal jurisdiction.[74] Studies
that explore how the law was practised, used, and transformed by individuals, and the place of legal rituals in family relations and daily life, have
been especially useful to me.[75]

The chapters that follow are structured around the transition that the
women who outlived their husbands made from wife to widow. In making
sense of their lives, general histories of Montreal, dissertations, monographs,
and articles on that city's history, along with the broader literature on families, religion, and institutions in Quebec over this period have also been
invaluable.[76] The chapters explore the unfolding of the couples' marriages
and individual life courses in the city of Montreal rather than proceeding
chronologically, because women lost husbands and husbands lost wives at
all ages, in ways that are closer to the erratic timing of divorces today than
to the dominant, contemporary impact of partners' deaths. Part 1 investigates marriage. Part 2 turns to widowhood. Chapter 1 introduces the
couples who married in Montreal in the 1820s and 1840s, and explores
some of the "entanglement of genealogies of dispersion with those
of 'staying put'"[77] that blended in this particular colonial city. Chapter 2
analyzes how different legal traditions and economic factors influenced
couples' decisions about how to organize property during their marriages,
producing wives with a wider range of legal identities and rights than in
the jurisdictions of the English common law. The following chapter probes
the range of material and physical contributions that women brought to
new households, exploring what Davidoff and Hall called their "hidden
investments" and tracing the geographic, occupational, and professional
trajectories of some of the couples.[78]

In Chapter 4, I turn to the more public discussions that took place about
marriage, and especially widows' right to dower, in the political sphere of
legislative assemblies, councils, and select committees. The critical moment
here was the debate to which M. was contributing as the Special Council
reshaped land registration and widows' dower rights. The final chapter of
Part 1 moves back to the private decisions husbands and wives made as they
imagined how best to deal with the death of one or other spouse before
and after the passage of that law. It returns to those sections of marriage
contracts that dealt with the possibility of widowhood, looks at the provisions made by some husbands and wives who wrote wills, and examines
some of the other ways spouses made provisions for their death and burial.

The chapters of Part 2 turn to the wives who became widows. Chapter
6 investigates the demographies and details of the moments when wives

became widows and looks at those who chose to escape widowhood through remarriage. The following two chapters explore the first year of widowhood, that twelve-month period in which widows are commonly understood to have worn deep mourning and retired from public. I suggest that widows had many tasks to see to, so few could simply stay home and mourn. In Chapter 9, I return to politics, and follow several of the women who had already become widows by the time of the particularly violent by-election in Montreal in 1832 to the hustings. Many widows voted in this by-election. I revisit the details of their voting and the jockeying of nationality, class, ethnicity, and gender produced discursively in newspapers, then in the Assembly's investigation, to re-examine the question of why Patriote politicians sought explicitly to exclude Lower Canadian women from voting soon afterward. One of those voters was Émilie Tavernier, the best known of the women of these two marriage cohorts. Chapter 10 follows her as she threw herself into sheltering poor, senile, and homeless widows, then took the veil and became the Mother Superior of the first female religious order created in Quebec, the Sisters of Providence.

The two final chapters explore diverse itineraries of widowhood, following some of the widows as they patched together livelihoods, as they aged, and then as some of their bodies and brains faltered, and they faced final illnesses and death. The diverse ways these widows, some wealthy, some indigent, survived as widows, stitching together support systems rich, varied, or sparse, highlights the inadequacy of M.'s didactic contrast between English and French widows, between the poor and the comfortable. Only privileged widows well provided for in marriage contracts or wills, or independently wealthy, could rely on support from their dead husbands for the duration of their widowhood. Most had to shape their own patchwork of support, though on the basis of vastly differing personal and material resources. For many wives who became widows, this was not new. Differences of material resources characterized their lives as wives as well as widows. It is to their marriages in Montreal that the next two chapters turn.

PART I

Marriage, Identity, and the Law

1

Marriage Metropole
Mobility and Marriage
in Early-Nineteenth-Century Montreal

On Wednesday, 4 June 1823, Émilie Tavernier married the merchant Jean-Baptiste Gamelin in Notre Dame Church, "one of the most significant monuments of French colonial architecture in Montreal."[1] It was the church that they both attended and had been the parish church for the large Catholic parish of Montreal since it was built in the 1670s.[2] A year later, construction of a new church began. The new Notre Dame Church would remain the only Catholic church registering births, deaths, and marriages until the middle of the nineteenth century. Both spouses were born and raised in the city. There had been members of Émilie's parents' families, the Taverniers and Maurices, in the parish of Montreal since before the Conquest. Her father, Antoine, was born in the city in 1754. Marie-Josephte, her mother, was born at the northeastern end of Montreal Island, in Rivière des Prairies, in 1756.[3] Émilie had dense networks of kin within the city and its suburbs.

Marguerite Paris' family were relative newcomers to the city. Her parents married in Terrebonne, north of Montreal, in the late 1790s. Two children were born there, and two more in the nearby parish of Sainte-Anne-des-Plaines. When Marguerite married, both her widowed mother and deceased labourer father were identified as Montrealers. The family of the man she married on Monday, 12 September 1825, the labourer Joseph Guilbault, also came from northeast of Montreal. He was a relative newcomer to the city. His parents married in 1797 in Mascouche, where one of their children was born. At the time of Marguerite and Joseph's marriage, they were identified as living north of there, in Saint Roch. He had moved to Montreal and was identified as domiciled there.[4]

The man whom Mary Anne Forrest wed in 1845 had arrived in Montreal by more circuitous routes. Both her family history and his were shaped by and part of the complicated webs of empire that accompanied nineteenth-century British colonialism, emigration, and settlement. Her parents, James and Georginna Forrest, married in London in 1818 and migrated to the colony from England some time after that.[5] James Bond Forrest was an officer of the British government. During the rebellions of 1837 and 1838, he worked as a commissary and as paymaster for the British troops. At the time of their wedding he was still working for the government and had settled with his wife and other children in Mile End, then a small community north of the city.[6]

Mary Anne's new husband, Joseph Charles Jourdain, might easily be mistaken for a Canadien, for there had been Catholic Jourdains in Montreal since before the Conquest. Yet, family genealogies reveal that he was of Huguenot origin. His father was a merchant silk dyer, living and working in London, England, at the time of Joseph's birth in 1814. Jourdain initially apprenticed in the silk trade. He left England in February 1833, sailing for over four months on the ship *Esther* to Sydney, New South Wales. Colonial port cities like Montreal or Sydney, as historian Kirsten McKenzie argues, were places where "fortunes could be made and new identities forged," places where the "large proportion of newcomers and itinerant visitors" meant that "residents had a certain degree of licence to reinvent themselves." In New South Wales, Jourdain bounced from job to job, working first as a clerk in the New Commercial Bank, then in the Audit Office, and finally in the Office of the Principal Superintendent of Convicts.[7] Two months after his arrival, a "Mr. C. Jordane" boarded the *Esther* in Sydney. It was bound for the convict colony on Norfolk Island, where convicts had recently seized a government boat full of supplies. Listed with him on the passenger list were convicts, the executioner, and Justice Dowling, fairly recently appointed by the Colonial Office as one of the senior judges of the Supreme Court of New South Wales. This was a work-related trip.[8]

In 1835, Joseph married a woman named Ann Moore, possibly the "Mrs. Moore" listed as a passenger on the boat he had taken to Norfolk Island. Their wedding was registered at Sydney's first established Catholic church, St. Mary's.[9] Sydney offered possibilities for free men like Charles Jourdain. The 1830s were relatively prosperous years in this convict colony. With good luck, good manners, and a dose of acting ability, a newly married couple might hope to secure a respectable place in the "anxious parade of social distinction," and "competitive status assertion" that the Sydney elite sought to police and newcomers to crack. Yet, as Kirsten McKenzie argues, the "danger of slipping back from a position of respectability and status" was ever present.[10] Bad luck and instability as a worker, husband, and provider haunted Jourdain. Within three years of his arrival and one year after his marriage, he fled the colony, spending some time in Lisbon before returning to London. In September 1836, he was listed as an insolvent debtor in the *London Gazette*. The entry enumerated the positions he had held in New South Wales and identified him as "late of No 1. Castle Street, Finsbury Square, Middlesex, gentleman."[11] What happened to him next is unclear. Family genealogies indicate that Ann and Joseph had four children. Yet, I have found no further traces of Ann or the children. At some point after this brush with his creditors Jourdain again moved on. In 1842, a Rolph Thomas published a study in London extolling the potential of settling in Canada. There, he affirmed, "the moderately industrious and sober, however poor, are sure of obtaining not only a plentiful subsistence," but also "many comforts" that in all probability they would "long be strangers" to in the mother country.[12] Canada offered Jourdain the possibility of a new start and some distance from his creditors.

By 1845, Joseph had been in Montreal long enough to court Mary Anne Forrest and convince her she should marry him; long enough too for her parents to decide that this was not a wise match for their daughter.[13] The wedding took place on 13 December. It was recorded in the registers of Christ Anglican Church, the elegant neoclassical cathedral that the Anglican elite of Montreal had built in close and competitive proximity to the Catholic Notre Dame Church.

Early-nineteenth-century Montreal is well known in Canadian history as the heart of the Empire of the Saint Lawrence, the metropolis of the fur trade, as a seigneury run by the Sulpicians, a pre-industrial city with a rich artisanal sector, a centre of entrepreneurship, and as a key site of confluence and conflict among Anglo-Protestant and French Canadian and Irish Catholic cultures and migration patterns.[14] The diverse roots and migration histories of the brides Émilie Tavernier, Marguerite Paris, Mary Anne Forrest, their spouses, and the other men and women who married in Montreal in the 1820s and 1840s suggest the advantage of also considering Montreal as a marriage metropole within a particular colonial contact zone. In this chapter I approach Montreal as a place where men and women from within the city, elsewhere in the colony, North America, the British Empire, and the world became husbands and wives, starting new families, blending genealogies. Some married and moved on. Some made Montreal their home for the rest of their lives. In this historical space, specific local, colonial, continental, trans-Atlantic, and imperial migration routes merged and diverged. In such diasporic spaces, as Avtar Brah has suggested, "genealogies of dispersion" tangled with those of "staying put." Newcomers and long-term residents sorted out new senses of their own identities in relationship to each other. Diverse roots and routes complicated claims of belonging.[15] Ideas of difference, home, religion, faith, and politics required repeated negotiations of meaning and social significance. Marriages re-asserted and transformed identities of gender, religion, class, and culture and shifted the descent lines of family genealogies. Thinking of Montreal as such a diasporic space blends productively with the interest of historians of nineteenth-century empire in the diverse and different contact zones, in webs and networks of empire, and with empirical studies of population movements, ethnicity, and changing rural-urban relationships in Lower Canada.[16]

This chapter serves to introduce readers to Émilie Tavernier, Marguerite Paris, Mary Anne Forrest, and some of the other women and men who married between 1823 and 1826 and between 1842 and 1845 whose stories are followed in subsequent chapters. It explores aspects of the city and colony that their marriages reveal, drawing predominantly on the registrations of the marriages of these two generations by the officiating priests, ministers, and rabbis, complemented where possible by other sources. First it explores the diverse histories of migration and residency that brought marrying Montrealers together. It then looks at the ways husbands and wives were inserted differently within the intersecting "social relations of class, gender, racism, sexuality," religion, "or other axes of differentiation" of this city.[17] I turn then to demographic similarities and differences of the spouses, examining their marital status and ages, and whether their parents were alive when they married. The chapter concludes by looking briefly at disappearances and departures from the city following couples' marriages.

Roots and Routes to Marriage

Montreal marriages united locals, newcomers, and birds of passage. Who would marry in the city was influenced by the custom of marrying in the bride's parish, by both spouses' place of residence, and by migration patterns. The city attracted some betrothed couples from elsewhere in the colony who chose to marry because of strong social and familial networks in the city or its rich array of cultural and religious institutions. Some came seeking a stately church, a minister of their faith recognized as having the right to officiate at weddings, or a well-informed notary. Others hoped for the relative anonymity that a city with a large floating population offered in contrast to small parishes where an unplanned pregnancy or marriage between close relatives could not escape the eye of vigilant priests and local gossips. Catholics seeking to wed a Protestant, or relatives within the forbidden degrees, could exercise the threat of choosing a Protestant minister with much greater potency in this very Protestant city. Dispensations, historian Serge Gagnon has argued, were more freely given in and around Montreal than in the predominantly Catholic parishes of most of the rest of the colony. They increased throughout the 1820s and 1830s.[18]

Marriages were key moments of identity transformation for women as they agreed to the legal and social understandings of what it meant to be a wife. That transition from single woman to wife was shaped by state and church rules, religious rituals, and familial practices. Marriage was a time when spouses, their families, and the broader community negotiated identities of class, gender, cultural affinity, and emotion. Marriage reinscribed gender inequalities in producing husbands and wives with vastly different legal and social power. When Émilie Tavernier, Marguerite Paris, and the other 1,336 women who became wives in Montreal between 1823 and 1826 married, only Catholics, Anglicans, and Presbyterians could officially sanction marriages and keep registers of marriages, births, or deaths. Some 57 percent of the marriages were, like those of the Canadiennes Émilie and Marguerite, registered at the Catholic Notre Dame Church. Nearly 25 percent were officially recognized in the registers of either St. Andrew's or St. Gabriel Street Presbyterian churches, whereas the remaining 19 percent were listed either at Christ Anglican or the small Anglican garrison church, which largely served the local military.

When the second generation of women married in the 1840s, political pressure from Jews, Methodists, and other dissident Protestants had made it legal for Jews and most Protestant denominations to marry their own parishioners and maintain legal registers.[19] As a result, Montreal offered couples a much greater array of churches through which to formalize their marriages. Catholic marriages at Notre Dame made up around 60 percent of those registered, though more of the couples were from Ireland than a generation earlier. The Presbyterians, who were mostly Scots and had dominated the early Protestant community and economy, were becoming one denomination among many – only 16 percent of couples married in their seven churches. Similarly, the proportion marrying in the six Anglican churches of the city had dropped to 14 percent. Among this marriage cohort, a further 5 percent of couples married in one of the three Methodist chapels, 4 percent at Zion Congregational Church, whereas under 1 percent chose to sanction their union at either the First Baptist Church or the Spanish Portuguese Shearith Israel synagogue.

Where did these brides and grooms come from? What were their roots and by what routes had they arrived in Montreal to marry? And whom did they marry? Seen through the different traces left in marriage registers, in which place of residence but not of birth were recorded diligently for Catholics and erratically for Protestants, the couples marrying in Montreal can be crudely categorized in the three solitudes that Sherry Olson and Patricia Thornton have described as characterizing nineteenth-century Montreal: Canadiens – or Catholics with French names; Catholics with non-French names who were mostly Irish; and English Protestants or Jews.

Yet, individual genealogies and choices confound such neat categories. In the 1820s, 43 percent of the brides were Canadiennes. Irish and other non-French Catholics made up some 14 percent of the brides. A further 43 percent of the women, largely of English, Irish, American, and Scottish background and a few Jews, had their marriage sanctioned by a Protestant minister. A generation later, between 1842 and 1845, the percentage of Canadiennes had shrunk to 35 percent, Irish Catholic women made up 25 percent of the brides, and the predominantly English, Irish, and Scottish Protestants and small number of Jewish women made up around 40 percent of those marrying. The shift in Montreal's population to predominantly English speaking, captured in the census of 1842, occurred earlier among the relatively young and very mobile marrying population than in the city as a whole.[20]

Émilie Tavernier and Marguerite Paris were among the roughly eight of every ten Canadienne brides in each cohort whose parents were identified as Montrealers. The categories of information that officials recording Catholic marriages in Lower Canada in this period were required to include had their history in European Catholicism, augmented by local requirements. Registers reflected both civil and ecclesiastical categories.[21] As we saw, the Catholic records of their marriages included the names of both of their parents, the name of the parish that the parents and the marrying couple were from originally, and the parish in which they were living or domiciled in at the time of the marriage.

Other Canadienne brides had moved to Montreal, some with their parents. Many were women who had apparently migrated on their own, with siblings, other kin, or friends, leaving parents, living and dead, behind. Even taking into account the custom of marrying in the bride's parish, a greater proportion of Canadien grooms than brides appear to have migrated to the city before they married, leaving families elsewhere in the colony, hinting at the different mobility possibilities for men and women. Whereas some two of every ten Canadienne brides were not from Montreal, this was true of around four of every ten of the grooms.[22]

These migrations of women and men with parents and siblings and on their own were part of the extra-ordinary mobility along the Saint Lawrence River that the geographer Serge Courville has described as having two major thrusts: north and west into new resource areas; and into the cities, especially Montreal.[23] Brides in each cohort had moved from as far away as the north shore of the Saint Lawrence, east of Quebec City. Most left parishes located in the agricultural regions around Montreal already linked through close economic, cultural, and social ties. These areas would furnish waves of rural Canadien migrants that matched the growing numbers of immigrants from the British Isles. Their fathers were largely listed as being from parishes just north and east of Montreal, especially Saint Roch, Saint Ours, Saint Henry de Mascouche, and Sainte-Anne-des-Plaines, or from the western and northerly parts of the Island of Montreal or the Île-Jésus. They also migrated from the south-shore parishes – from Saint Denis and from parishes west of the city toward the border with Upper Canada. Brides left areas where agriculture, commerce, and inheritance patterns were in transition as families modified their practices in the face of population growth and the growing attraction of Montreal as a market and potential source of work. Some also migrated from the two other main towns of the colony, Quebec City and Trois-Rivières, perhaps choosing Montreal because it seemed to promise greater possibilities of employment as a domestic, in a trade or business, or on the streets.

Most of Montreal's French-speaking Catholic brides and grooms traced their ancestry back to the period of French rule. But Catholicism and a French name also included those of more recent migration from France, Switzerland, and other parts of Europe. The family of Marie-Louise Lacroix, who married the conservative merchant Charles-Séraphin Rodier in 1825, came originally from Alsace. Rodier's grandfather, Pierre Rodier, was a native of the Dauphiné who came to Canada as a soldier during the Seven Years War and remained in Canada after 1759. By the time of the marriage, both families had resided in Montreal for at least a generation.[24] The man whom Charlotte Mount married in February 1823, Jacques-François-Louis Genevay, also had family roots in Switzerland. His father was Swiss, possibly Protestant. Genevay senior served in the militia during the Seven Years War, worked with Governor Haldimand, and was the deputy paymaster general for the District of Montreal prior to his death. He married a French-Catholic Canadienne, Agathe Dumas, and died while Jacques-François was still a young boy. Agathe remarried with another government official, the English Protestant Samuel Dunham Flemming. By the time of her son's marriage she was again a widow. The trail of documents that this young man, his mother, and Charlotte left in the records of notaries shifts between the two languages. They were married in a Protestant church but shortly thereafter purchased a pew at Notre Dame Church.[25] Charlotte Mount came from a prominent family in which intermarriage between Catholic Canadiens and English-speaking Protestants had been frequent.

In the 1820s, and even more so in the 1840s, some of the English-speaking Protestant brides and grooms were born in the colony. A minority were second, even third generation Montrealers.[26] The marriage of Jane Prescott Forsyth and George Gregory in 1823 at St. Gabriel Street Presbyterian Church united the offspring of two prominent former fur traders and members of the North West Company. Their fathers, John

Forsyth and John Gregory, had both arrived in the colony in the 1770s from Scotland. They were of the generation of Montreal-based men who had extended the reach of the fur trade into new areas of the west, where many kept First Nations women as country wives. By the time their children married, Gregory, Forsyth, and their wives had established themselves among Montreal's elite, investing in land and commerce, maintaining elegant homes, entertaining lavishly, acting on grand juries and as justices of the peace, and engaging in politics.[27]

The Molson family's roots in the colony began shortly after the Conquest when John Molson senior set up his first brewery. William Molson's two daughters, Elizabeth Sarah and Anne, who married in 1844 and 1845 respectively, were the third generation of that entrepreneurial beer-brewing family to be born and raised in Montreal. Elizabeth Sarah married a recent Scottish immigrant, David Lewis Macpherson. He had arrived in the city as a sixteen year old from Scotland just nine years earlier, joining older brothers and sisters already established in British North America, and settling into a lucrative partnership in his brother's forwarding company. Anne married her cousin, John Molson, thus retaining wealth in the family. John continued in the family business.[28]

Betsy Rea, who married the merchant John Smith in 1825, was also born in the colony. Her new husband, another immigrant from Scotland, was well established by the time of their marriage. A generation later, their daughter Matilda Caroline maintained the Scottish link when she married the merchant Hugh Allan in 1844. Hugh had been in Canada some eighteen years and was rapidly rising in Montreal's merchant circles, especially in the business of his family – shipping. He was a partner in the company that had "the largest shipping capacity of any Montreal-based firm." His brother Andrew had also come to Montreal from Glasgow to help Hugh in the extensive family business. Hugh was clearly a man with a future.[29]

Caroline Campbell, whose marriage to the American immigrant Oliver Wait was also registered at St. Gabriel Street Presbyterian Church in 1823, had probably lived many of her seventeen years in the city, though she does not seem to have been born there. Her Scottish father, William Campbell, had been in the city long enough to build up a solid hotel business by the time he witnessed the marriage of his young daughter to this upwardly mobile widower with six children from his first marriage.[30] Like Oliver Wait, both Hannah Lyman and John Easton Mills, the successful merchant whom Hannah married in January 1823, had moved to Montreal from the United States. Mills and his brother Ceophas, who married Hannah's sister, Fanny, two weeks earlier, had migrated as young men in the late 1790s, attracted from Massachusetts by the possibilities that the fur trade offered young men. She migrated to Montreal from Vermont in 1816 when she was about sixteen with her family.[31]

Some of the small elite Jewish community had also lived in the colony for several generations. Constance Hannah Hart was born and raised in Montreal. Her father, Benjamin, was a prominent merchant in the city. Her new husband, Adolphus Mordecai Hart, was raised in Trois-Rivières, the colony's third-largest city. His father, Ezekiel, had fought to dismantle the laws that prevented Jews from being elected to the House of Assembly. Adolphus continued the tradition, fighting vigorously as a young lawyer to further expand the rights of Jews in the colony. He also defended several Patriotes following the rebellions. At some time, in the early 1840s, he moved to Montreal, where he set up his legal practice. It was there that he married his cousin Constance. Their union was recorded in December 1844 in the register of the Spanish Portuguese Shearith Israel synagogue, then the city's only synagogue.[32]

The marriage of Norah Deegan and the labourer Patrick Crowe in November 1823 brought together two of the growing number of Irish Catholics migrating to or through Montreal. Most were relative newcomers. Around one in five of the women from Ireland marrying in the Catholic parish and slightly more a generation later appear to have lived in the city for long enough to be identified in the parish records as Montrealers, rather than as simply domiciled there.[33] The record of their marriage describes Norah, her parents, and Patrick as residents of the parish of Notre Dame. His parents, in contrast, appear to have remained in Tipperary. Mary O'Leary, who married the local painter Nicolas Venière in 1824, was listed as domiciled in Montreal, hinting at a more recent migration. Her parents were from County Cork. Whether they were in Montreal or not is unclear.[34] The places of origin in Ireland recorded for these brides and grooms fit the broad patterns of emigration from Ireland that historians have described for the years before the potato famine of 1847 further increased migration. The highest proportion of Irish Catholic brides in the 1820s came from Ulster, the northeastern of Ireland's four provinces.[35] Within Ulster, most came from Antrim, the county that includes Belfast, or from Cavan, the most southerly county. A further third of the women of that generation came from Leinster, the province that stretches down the eastern side of Ireland. Husbands came in more equal proportions from Ulster, Leinster, and Munster provinces, and many more men than women came from Tipperary and Cork in the south. Twenty years later, the women came from pretty well all over Ireland. The proportion from the southwest had increased. Among the brides marrying between 1842 and 1845, the largest numbers came from Munster province, in the southwest, especially from the counties of Tipperary and Limerick, though many still left Ulster and growing numbers were arriving from both Leinster and Connacht. In this period just before the famine, these women and men were already leaving the areas that would increasingly dominate emigration from Ireland.[36] The somewhat different patterns for men and women hint again at the divergent forces and possibilities that gendered decisions to migrate. Like migrants within the colony of Lower Canada, Irish brides and grooms left economies in transformation.[37] They left families who were changing decisions about inheritance to keep family farms intact and adjusting marriage practices.

The numbers of Irish marriages in Montreal certainly support Donald Akenson's argument that there were formidable numbers of Irish Catholics as well as Protestants in British North America prior to the famine.[38] At a broad level, the choices these men and women made also confirm Philippe Beaudoin's suggestion that prior to the famine, the Irish were likely to marry partners from the same province.[39] Yet, Irish migrants appear to have nurtured intimacies at a smaller scale than that of the four provinces. We can imagine some women leaving their local parish with men they already knew, intent, perhaps, on marrying once away from the controlling eye of parents or other kin, or when they had established the basis to support a family. Future partners might also meet at Belfast, Cobh, or the other port towns as they waited to arrange passage. Intimate relations initiated on the docks, on the voyage, while brushing shoulders on Grosse Isle awaiting medical inspection and permission to move on, while travelling toward Montreal, or in the city's churches and on the streets might be consecrated through weddings in Montreal. About half the women from Antrim in the 1820s or from Limerick, Clare, and Roscommon in the 1840s married men from their own county of origin. These were the highest rates of regional endogamy. The vast majority of Irish women married someone from somewhere else in Ireland.

Some couples married while still in motion between a journey and destination. These people on the move provoked anxieties among Catholic Church officials: bigamy was a worry, as was the requirement that parents authorize marriages of men and women under age twenty-one. It was not unknown, Mgr. Plessis reminded the *curé* of a rural parish, for women to leave husbands in Ireland, or for men to leave wives and seek to start a new family in Canada. Authorities struggled with what to do about immigrants who had struck up a relationship on the passage over and sought to marry upon their arrival. In Montreal, where the possibilities that couples who were refused permission to marry in the Catholic Church might turn to a Protestant minister, the dilemma was particularly acute. In response to the challenge that these Irish immigrants posed to upholding local Catholic rules, Catholic leaders requested at the end of the 1820s that Irish bishops provide their compatriots with a certificate of freedom to marry before embarking for North America.[40]

Wives and Husbands: Faith, Ethnicity, and Marriage

The marriages of the Canadiens Marguerite Paris and Joseph Guilbault united two individuals who shared Catholicism, ancestry dating back to New France, French as their language, and their social location in the labouring classes of the pre-industrial colony of Lower Canada. Mary Anne Forrest and Joseph Jourdain arrived in the colony by different routes but both were Protestant and of English ancestry, and claimed a position in the middle classes. Most Montreal marriages were relatively endogamous, as was theirs, uniting men and women of similar classes, status, religious beliefs, ethnicities, and languages. More than nine of every ten Canadien Catholic women and similar proportions of anglophone Protestant women married men who appear to have shared their broad faith and national identity. As committed, engaged Protestants, imbued with the anti-Catholicism that was so central to late-eighteenth- and early-nineteenth-century Britishness, Montrealers like the Molsons or the Smiths were particularly unlikely to marry non-Protestants.[41] Constance and Theodore Hart were typical of most members of the city's small Jewish community in marrying fellow Jews. Most Irish Catholic women married Irish Catholic males. Still, Mary O'Leary was one of the 14 percent of Irish Catholic brides in the 1820s who chose either French Canadian Catholics or Protestants as grooms. Fewer did so two decades later.

Marriages between English Protestants and French Catholics were rarer but occurred (see Figure 1.1). They seem more common among the earlier generations of male English merchants and adventurers whose marriages to Canadienne wives gave them social mobility, prestige, or local connections in the colony. The first wife of Oliver Wait, Caroline Campbell's new husband, was a French Canadian Catholic. Some families among the seigneurial elite of the colony had long histories of marriage across lines of language, religion, and culture, though seldom class. In December 1823, Marie-Louise-Josephte Chartier de Lotbinière married an English Protestant newcomer, Robert Unwin Harwood, at the Christ Anglican Church. She was the daughter of Michel-Eustache-Gaspard-Alain Chartier de Lotbinière, a former member and speaker of the Assembly and the seigneur of Vaudreuil, Rigaud, and Lotbinière.[42] John, the father of her mother, Mary Charlotte Munro, was a Highland Scot who moved to America, married in 1760, fought as a Loyalist, and then settled in Upper Canada. He was a member of the first Legislative Council and, in that capacity, his family had received over ten thousand acres of land.[43] By the 1820s, several of Mary Charlotte's

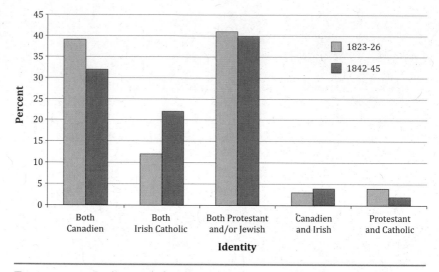

FIGURE I.I   Percentage of marriages within and across the "three solitudes," by religious and ethnic identities of spouses, 1823–26 and 1842–45

Note: 1823–26, $N = 1,338$; 1842–45, $N = 1,455$.

Source: Parish registers, Montreal, all marriages, 1823–26, 50 percent of marriages, 1842–45, BAnQM.

siblings were settled in and around Montreal. Most were married to Canadiens, and many of their offspring also chose Canadien or other off-spring of mixed English-French families as their spouses. These included Charlotte Mount's mother, Christiana Munro, who had married the Montreal doctor Phillip Mount at St. Gabriel Presbyterian Church in Montreal in 1786. The paintings shown in Figure 1.2 of Marie-Louise-Josephte and Robert were made within a year of their marriage. Hers is attributed to the American portrait painter Anson Dickinson.

Marriages that transgressed boundaries of religion were not taken lightly. Serge Gagnon has shown how desperately Catholic *curés* and priests struggled during this period to prevent their parishioners from choosing Protestant ministers or marrying a Protestant. The new religious hybridity of the colony, particularly in and around Montreal, prompted major changes in the policy of a church that for over a century before, and for several decades after the Conquest, had been able to enforce particularly rigid rules regarding mixed marriages, parental consent, and marrying relatives within prohibited degrees because of the homogeneity of the population. In the 1820s, Catholic spouses who chose a Protestant partner had to get a special dispensation from the archbishop in Quebec City. This could take time, and approval was not guaranteed. In the 1840s, Montreal's new bishop, Mgr. Ignace Bourget, secured permission from Rome to bestow

FIGURE 1.2 Marie-Louise-Josephte Chartier de Lotbinière, daughter of a Canadien seigneur and politician Michel-Eustache-Gaspard-Alain Chartier de Lotbinière and Mary Charlotte Munro, married the English, Protestant newcomer merchant from Sheffield, England, Robert Unwin Harwood, in December 1823. He arrived in the colony in 1821. She was twenty years old and he was twenty-five. They may have had these miniatures painted around the time of their marriage. She had them photographed at Notman's studio after she became a widow. | Mrs. Harwood, miniature painting by Anson Dickinson, 1824, copied 1863, William Notman, photographer, silver salts on paper mounted on paper, albumen process. *McCord Museum, Notman Photographic Archives, I-6965.1.* Honourable Mr. Harwood, miniature painting, copied 1863, William Notman, photographer, silver salts on paper mounted on paper, albumen process. *McCord Museum, Notman Photographic Archives, I-6964.1.*

such dispensations himself, thus endowing himself with new power, and likely saving time for couples.[44] At least five other Catholic couples who married between 1842 and 1846 took advantage of this new possibility. Others simply married in Protestant churches.

This was the choice of Maria Mitchell and Thomas Spiers. Years later, her friend Mary Eliza Peters would report that Maria belonged "to the Catholic Church and always did." Yet, there is no indication that she was not a Protestant in the register of Zion Congregational Church, where the ardent temperance minister Henry Wilkes married her to Thomas Spiers in 1845.[45] The marriage worried Mary Eliza Peters' husband. Thomas Prendergast would later explain that he warned Spiers of the pitfalls of marrying someone of a "different religion" when Spiers talked to him of his hope to marry Maria. The couple was not dissuaded.[46] Mary O'Leary, the Irish Catholic immigrant from County Cork, and her groom, the Canadien Montreal painter Nicolas Venière, also turned to a Protestant minister when they sought to marry. Why is unclear.[47] Their nuptials were registered at Christ Anglican Church as celebrated on 7 November 1824. Witnessing their marriage were two anglophones. At some point they had a change of heart. They were living in sin in the eyes of their church. They approached the bishop of Quebec to solicit permission to marry in the Catholic faith. Gagnon reports that to dispense with three banns and marry as they did could be costly. Dispensing with wedding banns meant that their second marriage would receive minimal publicity. In February 1825, they married again, this time at the Catholic Notre Dame Church. Two Canadiens witnessed this second wedding, along with the required Church officials. From then on, all the official moments of their lives – the births of children and their deaths – were recorded by the Catholic Church.[48] A decade later, as the church struggled with the array of possibilities the massive expansion of Protestant faiths offered, it was made much easier to recognize such marriages through a process referred to as "rehabilitation."[49]

Margaret Jamieson and the printer William Moody appear to have reconciled denominational differences between them by having two ministers marry them on the same day. Their 20 December 1842 nuptials were recorded in the registers of St. James Street Methodist and St. Andrew's Presbyterian churches. Over the following years, the births of at least seven children and the death of two were listed at St. Andrew's. When William died in 1861, however, his death was registered at St. Luke's Anglican Church. As historians of religion have shown, specific denominational identities were stable and strongly held by some, frequently changed by others, and fluid or rejected by yet others.[50]

Class, Occupation, and Marriage Partners

Montreal's grooms of the 1820s and 1840s made their living in a wide range of ways, only some of which can be determined from the records generated at the time of their marriages or complementary sources. The superiority of Catholic recording of occupations skews comparisons. Still, allowing for the mobility and the relative age-specificity of the marrying population, the occupations reported and the ethnic division of labour pretty well parallel what other historians of Montreal during this period have found.[51] At the broadest level, men's reported ways of making a living can be grouped into four categories that crudely distinguish the work they performed; their class, prominence, and prestige; their potential wealth; and their family economies.[52]

The largest group in this pre-industrial city made their living in the vibrant artisanal sector or as small shopkeepers or proprietors of inns and taverns. Around 45 percent of the women in the first generation and 40 percent in the second married men in such crafts or small businesses. Here, Canadien grooms dominated, with half working in crafts or small businesses, compared to around four out of ten Anglo-Protestants and just over a third of Irish Catholic grooms, though as Olson shows for the 1840s, in this middling group "cultural differences were woven into a more elaborate segmentation of crafts networks."[53]

Labourers, carters, and other men who made their living on construction projects, in transportation, or other areas of the labour market that required few acknowledged skills were the second-largest group. They made up around 30 percent of the grooms who reported an occupation when they married in the 1820s, and closer to 40 percent two decades later. Many of the men who reported no occupation also probably made their living as casual labourers. In the 1820s, nearly half the Irish Catholic husbands who reported an unskilled occupation were labourers, as were just over a third of Canadiens, but only one-fifth of Anglo-Protestants. Two decades later, Irish Catholic grooms remained more concentrated in unskilled jobs than other husbands; most were labourers, but more were working as carters or in the lower ranks of the army. Most reported no occupation at all.

Relatively few Anglo-Protestant grooms were recorded as labourers. Many of these were common soldiers, serving in the regiments sent to Canada. Montreal's port and garrison filled the city streets, taverns, and public places with sailors and soldiers, offering a clientele for women in the sex trades, and worrying Catholic priests and Protestant ministers who warned the single women of their congregations about the dangers of marriages to dashing soldiers.[54] Decades later, Montreal novelist Rosanna Leprohon would write *Antoinette de Mirecourt, or, Secret Marrying and Secret Sorrowing,* a book now widely read in many Canadian literature courses. Her tale underlined the dangers of secret marriages based on passion through the story of a local Canadienne girl who fell in love and eloped with a handsome but unreliable British soldier.[55] It was set in Montreal soon after the Conquest, yet much about the story better captured the dynamics of early-nineteenth-century Montreal, the city to which Rosanna's parents migrated and in which they married in 1824. Rosanna was the daughter of the Irish Catholic couple Francis Mullins, a merchant from County Cork, and Rosanna Connelly, a schoolmaster's daughter. Between 1842 and 1846, around two hundred women married soldiers in Montreal's churches, despite army rules discouraging marriage among the lower ranks. This was double the number that married men involved in agriculture, the fourth main occupation of grooms.[56] In the 1820s, some 12 percent of the grooms were recorded at the time of their marriage as making their living in agriculture. Two decades later, as the city expanded, this proportion had halved.

Smaller in numbers than the community of craftsmen, shop- and inn-keepers, and unskilled labourers, but powerful in their influence both economically and politically, were the merchants, bourgeois, gentlemen, government functionaries, professionals, and even lower down clerks who might be considered the elite of the city. Economic and political power, prestige, and prominence were concentrated in the hands of a relatively small number of Montreal families of all faiths and origins. After residing there in the 1820s, Edward Talbot described the city's elite as comprising "merchants of large fortune," "civil and military officers," "most professional men in Law, Physic, and Divinity," and some prominent fur traders.[57] Even casting the net more widely to include clerks and others who would not normally have been admitted to the homes of the most prominent of the city but might be seen as part of the broader middle classes, this was a pretty small group.[58] Men reporting such occupations represented around 15 percent of the grooms whose ways of making a living are known in each generation of marriages. Canadiens constituted about a third of the grooms making a living as merchants, professionals, government officials, or clerks in the 1820s. Two decades later, their proportion in this elite/middle-class category had fallen to closer to a quarter. Anglo-Protestants and a few Jewish men, in contrast, made up roughly two-thirds of this group in each cohort, joined in the 1840s by a small group of Irish Catholic men reporting working on the fringes of the elite as merchant tailors, grocers, and clerks.[59]

Marriages across these broad occupational groupings occurred more often than ones traversing differences of religion or language. Boundaries of status and class were more fluid in the colonial context than in Europe's major cities and probably than later in the century. These broad categories hide vast differences of wealth and status, confounding comparisons. In both generations, roughly half the brides married men of similar background to their fathers. Roughly half did not (see Table 1.1). For men, a well-chosen wife might secure upward mobility and social and commercial contacts that could be critical in trades, professions, or business. Wives brought, depending on their particular situation, dowries, capital, labour power, prestige, new social networks, and the ability to produce heirs. A good marriage might provide the basis for success, a spouse wrongly chosen risked just the reverse. What was expected of a good wife varied among these different groups, as did women's expectations of a good husband.

TABLE 1.1 Marriages within and across broad occupational groups, based on cases where the occupations of the husband and of the bride's father are known

Grooms	Wives' fathers				
	Elite and middling	Crafts and shops	Labouring	Agriculture	Number known
Marriages, 1823-26					
Elite and middling	50%	21%	12%	17%	58
Crafts and shops	7%	41%	34%	18%	309
Labouring	2%	21%	59%	18%	233
Agriculture	3%	19%	28%	50%	58
Total both known	55	200	266	137	658
Marriages, 1842-45 (50% sample)					
Elite	46%	31%	10%	13%	48
Crafts and shops	5%	50%	29%	16%	224
Labouring	0%	25%	51%	24%	179
Agriculture	0%	24%	24%	52%	21
Total both known	33	177	167	95	472

Note: "Elite and middling" includes bourgeois, rentier, merchants, professions, ranked army men, public service, and clerks. "Crafts and shops" includes artisans in all trades, including construction and those running small shops. "Labour" includes labourers, carters, lower ranks of soldiers, and male domestics. Cases where occupations were listed for brides' fathers and the grooms in marriage registers, contracts, or other sources.

Source: Parish Registers, Montreal, all marriages, 1823-26, 50 percent of marriages, 1842-45, BAnQM.

Marguerite Paris, who married the labourer Joseph Guilbault in 1825, was a labourer's daughter. Like her, just over half of the daughters of labourers and other unskilled workers in both the 1820s and the 1840s married men with similar occupations to their fathers. A few married farmers, even fewer found grooms among the city elite. The vast majority of those not marrying unskilled workers chose grooms from the crafts community. Most labourers' daughters brought some experience contributing to family coffers, to the care of siblings, and to the domestic labour of households. They might supplement their husbands' incomes by earning cash in a variety of ways, possibly taking in washing or sewing, or seeking domestic work by the day. Adelaide Bebel, who married the labourer Charles Cousineau in 1824, was one of the very few brides to explicitly report an occupation at the time of her marriage. Her skills as a seamstress would help sustain them over the forty-six years of their marriage. Neither she nor Charles was able to sign their own names.

Daughters of craftsmen and shopkeepers also married men of similar class background, though not necessarily from the same trade as their father. Scholastique Bissonnet, who married Louis Ducharme in 1826, was the daughter of a man listed as a sawyer. Louis described himself as a joiner at the time of their marriage. Men who worked as he did in the construction trades were the largest group of craftsmen among the grooms. The vast majority of them were Canadiens. Marie-Amable Papineau's new husband, François Gareau dit Vadeboncoeur, came from the second-largest group of craftsmen represented among the grooms, those working in the city's significant leather-trades sector as shoemakers, tanners, and saddle makers.[60] He was a saddle maker. Her father reported that he was an inn-keeper at the time of their marriage at Notre Dame in January 1826. An innkeeper's daughter's assets might include capital as well as significant social connections that could help a saddler in his trade.

Other grooms worked in trades that produced food, furniture, and clothing for people in the city and beyond. Marie-Louise Genant's new husband was a master tailor when they married in 1843. Her father was a merchant grocer and a bailiff. Both she and Pierre-Bernard Decousse could sign their names. As Joanne Burgess has shown for the leather trades, many artisans did not marry until they had completed their time as a journeyman and could set up shop.[61] Six months prior to marrying, Pierre-Bernard leased a substantial, solid two-storey stone house at the corner of St. Joseph and Little St. James streets for £27 a year. This was well over the amount any labourers or many craftsmen might hope to make in a year, let alone pay in rent.[62] It would serve as both workplace and living quarters. Its location in the heart of the commercial section of the old city suggests that Marie-Louise was marrying well and would likely be secure as a master craftsman's wife. Prospects looked promising too for Rebecca Conegan, a Protestant immigrant from Ireland who could not sign her name. She married Sampson Brady in 1844 at St. Gabriel Street Presbyterian Church. No occupation was listed for him in the register, but within a month of his marriage he had joined with his brother, William Brady, and David Darling to create the Brady and Darling Soap and Candle Manu-factory.[63] The "tallow chandlers" business, and probably their dwelling as well, was located in the predominantly artisanal Saint Lawrence suburb, initially on St. Lawrence Street.[64]

The marriage between the Irish immigrants from King's County, Leinster, Ann Groghan and Thomas Casey, in 1823 united the daughter of an agricultural worker with a man who listed his occupation as labourer. Similarly, Judith Butler, who was described as a farmer's daughter, married William Coonan, the son of a farmer who had found work in Montreal as a labourer. Both came from Tipperary, in the province of Munster in the southwest of Ireland. Social change, Irish migration, the declining number of farmers within the parish, and the vastly different economic situations an occupation in agriculture could mask meant farmers' daughters in these two cohorts were less likely to marry men working in the same sector as their fathers than were women from most other classes.

It was among the city's leading merchants and prominent professionals that parents watched most carefully over their daughters' suitors. In Montreal, as elsewhere, bourgeois men "tended to choose women who were of their own class, or slightly better."[65] Over six of every ten brides whose fathers fell into the broad elite category married men in a similar situation. Matilda Caroline Smith's father, John, was a well-established merchant when she married Hugh Allan in 1844. For Hugh Allan, as for Robert Unwin Harwood, marriage within elite families with long roots in the colony provided local familial and social connections that as newcomers they would otherwise have had to build step by step. Similarly, Édouard-Raymond Fabre's marriage to Luce Perrault cemented his ties with the more prominent Perrault family. Émilie Tavernier's marriage to the relatively affluent merchant Jean-Baptiste Gamelin placed her closer socially to her elite Perrault relatives than to the voyageur, fur-trading, artisanal worlds of her father and brothers. In a few non-Catholic families, marriages with cousins kept wealth within the family. Theodore Hart married his cousin Fanny David in 1842. We saw that his sister, Constance Hannah Hart, also married her first cousin when she became the bride of Adolphus Mordecai Hart in 1844 and that William Molson's daughter Anne married his brother John's son and namesake in 1845.

Marriages to elite women opened up social networks and access to capital for some bourgeois men. Others built upon and secured networks and connections among the families and customers of the city's artisans and small businesses. In the 1820s, about four out of ten daughters of elite and middle-class men married into the crafts, farming, or labouring communities. A generation later, all daughters of merchants, professionals, accountants, or clerks married either elite men or men in crafts and trade. We saw that Caroline Campbell's father was an innkeeper. Oliver Wait's social origins are unknown, but they appear relatively lowly, certainly when compared with the prominent merchants Abner and Stanley Bagg, with whom he worked on several business ventures. He first appears in Montreal records in 1810 when he married Marie Laporte at St. Gabriel Street Presbyterian Church. At that time he was just twenty-one and listed as a farmer. Marie was nineteen. In 1819, he and Abner Bagg subcontracted with another American contractor, Jedediah Hubbell, to level the northern section of Citadel Hill, one of the major projects transforming city space in the period. Over subsequent years, through the birth of several children and the death of Marie in 1823, he worked closely with members of the Bagg family. In the 1820s, Oliver and Stanley Bagg worked together buying up firewood to sell in the city and along with Thomas Phillips and Andrew White secured the contract to excavate the Lachine Canal. The Lachine job has been described as one of the major public works of these times.[66] Work was slow, but this canal that served both as a critical throughway for commerce and a source of water power for Montreal's earliest industrial revolution opened for traffic around the time he married his second wife, Caroline. At the time of their marriage in 1824, he was identified as "canal contractor" and as *ecuyer,* or esquire, a title suggesting new recognition on the fringes of the city elite.

Oliver Wait's choice of an innkeeper's daughter might reflect his and Caroline's shared social origins, well below the society of leading merchants like the Rodiers, Harts, Smiths, and Molsons, or the genteel circles of the Fabres, Rodiers, and Perraults. It is possible too that William Campbell had an extensive network of contacts through the customers of his hotel that might help Oliver Wait in his career. They lived near each other before the couple married. Campbell's St. Mary Hotel was not far from Oliver's farm at St. Mary's current on the eastern reaches of the city, near where the Molsons ran their brewery. Within several years of Oliver and Caroline's marriage, Oliver's name began to appear on the lists of grand jurors alongside those of Hannah Lyman's husband, John E. Mills, the future mayor; Abner Bagg, his ex-partner; and such other eminent wealthy Montrealers as Antoine-Olivier Berthelet.[67]

Many of these elite husbands of the women who married in the 1820s and 1840s are well known to Canadian historians. Their wives, or the significance of marriage in their prominence, are less so. In particular, the men who reached early adulthood and decided to marry in the 1820s were part of the generation that reshaped the city's streets, economy, and society, as well as the law and politics of the colony. Many appear among the merchants, traders, and early industrialists whom Gerald Tulchinsky has argued made up the elite of the city. Some would become involved in the early railway promotion about which Brian Young has written. At least forty of the grooms who married between 1823 and 1826 and thirteen of those marrying between 1842 and 1846 have been deemed sufficiently prominent by the producers of the *Dictionary of Canadian Biography* to merit their own biography, or a mention in that of someone else.[68] These male biographies have been enormously helpful to me in getting a better sense of these men's involvement in Montreal society, culture, politics, and economy. In contrast, only two of the wives, Émilie Tavernier and Anne Molson, and the author Rosanna Leprohon, who, as mentioned above, was the daughter of Mullins and Connelly, have been accorded biographies of their own.[69]

The elite husbands were men whose paths crossed in the city's civic, religious, and charitable associations and in the many business ventures of the merchants. They sat together on grand juries, the Board of Trade, and on the boards of banks and worked separately in denominational and national charities and societies that they and their wives played a part in initiating. Many became involved in banking ventures, in steamships, and later in railroads. Some become significant manufacturers. Some were business and political partners. Others were rivals in love, marriage, business, or politics. They supported each other as candidates for their preferred parties and denigrated their opponents. A few became prominent in city politics as councillors and mayors: Hannah Lyman's husband, John Easton Mills, became mayor of Montreal in 1846; Luce Perrault's husband, Édouard-Raymond Fabre, was chosen as mayor in 1849; Marie-Louise Lacroix's husband, Charles-Séraphin Rodier, was elected mayor in 1858.

This elite was divided in terms of religion, language, politics, the scale of their economic operations, the amount of capital they could command or accumulate, and their capacity to draw on familial ties to further businesses. Bernard, Robert, and Linteau argue that anglophone merchants were most likely to be involved in imperial commerce, whereas the radius of exchange of Canadiens was more frequently within the colony.[70] These elite marriages joined some women to very prominent Anglo-Protestant men whose businesses took place within family networks forged in an imperial and/or trans-Atlantic framework. Robert Unwin Harwood in the 1820s and Hugh Allan and his brother Andrew in the 1840s, as we saw, came to Canada with family connections and capital in England and Scotland respectively. Theirs were trans-national family businesses built with family money.[71]

The combined access to family money, trans-Atlantic familial connections, and business acumen at the heart of empire did not exist for most Canadien merchants. Their family roots were neither in England nor in France, but within the colony. Nor could many other Montreal merchants command such ties. Still, the husbands of both of these cohorts included Canadiens who were successful in trans-Atlantic trade. Among them was Marie-Louise Lacroix's new husband, Charles-Séraphin Rodier. This son of a blacksmith, like many Canadiens of his generation, moved out of the artisanal community into commerce. Rodier began his career as a dry goods merchant on St. Paul Street at least ten years before their marriage. Frederick Armstrong reports that he was the first merchant to import his goods from both England and France, worked with agents in Liverpool and London, and crossed the Atlantic some forty times between 1819 and 1832. He is also typical of most of the merchant elite, both anglophone and francophone, in the wide array of economic ventures in which he engaged and the range of prominent social and political positions that he held. By the time of his marriage, Rodier was a very successful merchant.[72]

Elmire Painchaud married the Canadien sea captain Joseph-Alexis Painchaud in 1844. His father, a captain, shipowner, and merchant had capitalized on his knowledge of the sea to trade with the British Isles since at least the 1820s. By 1828, he owned a 218-ton boat that "took wheat to Liverpool, Cork and Dublin," and transported salt, coal, iron, and Irish immigrants back to Montreal. In 1857, he brought Joseph-Alexis and his other son into partnership as Painchaud and Sons.[73] Still, by the 1850s, their two schooners were insignificant beside the growing number of ocean-going barques and other vessels that would make Hugh Allan's company "one of the largest merchant fleets on the North Atlantic."[74] Unlike the Allans, they captained their family ships. It was in this capacity that Joseph-Alexis Painchaud drowned in a shipwreck in 1860, leaving Elmire a widow.

The vision of such imperial trade as the peak of commerce is shaped by the staples thesis that led so many economic historians and political economists to downplay the dynamism of local trade and production within the colony. Many Anglo-Protestant men and French-speaking Catholic husbands made their living within local economies, and many did so with considerable success. The Molsons are the best known for their brewing and distilling. The Scottish merchant David Handyside, who came to Montreal from Edinburgh with two of his brothers, married Melinda Adams from Vermont in 1824. The three brothers started out as merchants, then set up a distillery.[75] Benjamin Brewster, who married Sarah French in 1823, began in hardware then became involved in the Canada Ocean Steam Navigation Company with two other husbands of these two cohorts – Thomas and Benjamin Workman. He soon shifted his interest to internal investments in banking, railways, and provisioning the lumber camps of Upper Canada. The Workman brothers also gradually focused more of their investments and energy in land and local manufacturing.[76] Both Oliver Wait and Andrew White profited from contracts for the construction of public works, buying and selling firewood, and a range of other activities within the colony.[77]

Canadien merchants in this period engaged in a similar range of activities, though generally they were less successful at securing such major construction contracts as those that crowned the economic ascension of Wait and White. The man whom Julie-Adelaide Gravel married in 1845, Joseph Barsalou, was a Canadien merchant who invested extensively in land as well as in industrial production. He apprenticed as an auctioneer in the late 1830s with the prominent auctioneer, merchant, and politician Austin Cuvillier and went on to form an auctioneering company with

James Benning. In 1860, it was "considered the largest of its kind." He also became involved in a range of industrial ventures, running flour, wool, and soap factories; purchasing the British American Rubber Company in 1866, which Hugh Allan later invested in heavily; and increasingly specializing in investing in urban mortgages.[78]

Émilie Tavernier's new husband, the merchant Jean–Baptiste Gamelin, was typical of Canadien entrepreneurs who traded at the level of the colony. His widowed mother had arranged an apprenticeship for him at the age of sixteen with a Montreal shoemaker. There he would have learned English along with the trade. He could read but never wrote well, and signed official documents with an X. After working as a master shoemaker in the Saint Antoine suburb as a young adult, he began buying up property and having houses constructed to rent out in the city and its suburbs. By 1819, he was established as a merchant, growing apples and making and selling cider. When he and Émilie married in 1823, he had been trading Montreal's famous apples in Quebec City for several years.[79] Luce Perrault's new husband, Édouard-Raymond Fabre, also moved from the crafts community into business. He was a carpenter's son. By the time of their marriage in 1826, he had built on his training as a hardware clerk for Arthur Webster, spent time in Paris getting a working knowledge of the bookseller's trade, and opened what would become Montreal's most prominent bookstore and publishing enterprise.[80]

Diverse Demographies

Marriages between spouses of different marital statuses and ages were more common than unions across differences of religion, language, or even class. Marguerite Paris, Émilie Tavernier, and Mary Anne Forrest were all single when they married. This was true for about 90 percent of the brides in the marriage cohorts of the 1820s and 1840s, compared to 85 percent of the grooms. Marguerite's and Émilie's new husbands were both bachelors, whereas, as we saw, Mary Anne's husband, Joseph Jourdain, had been married before. Overall, among the Catholic couples, for whom this information is more systematically included than for Protestants, around eight of every ten marriages involved a spinster and a bachelor; one out of ten was between a single woman and a widower. Thus, Caroline Campbell's marriage to the merchant widower Oliver Wait, or Margaret Logan's to Wait's partner, the widowed contractor Andrew White, were not particularly unusual in this period of high death rates, when widowers with young children quickly sought new wives.[81] It was rarer for widows to remarry than widowers, as historians of other regions and periods in the Western world have invariably found. Still, at least 10 percent of the brides in the 1820s and rather fewer a generation later were widowed, compared to closer to 15 percent of the grooms. The proportion of marriages involving a widow was double that which Gérard Bouchard found in the predominantly rural Saguenay area, where colonization was just beginning at this time. Widows often moved to cities after husbands' deaths seeking work, sociability, or institutional support. For those hoping to remarry, Montreal and smaller towns like Saint Hyacinthe appear to have offered more potential husbands than the Saguenay.[82]

High death rates thus contributed to unions involving widows, and widowers constituting a small but significant proportion of these urban marriages. High death rates also meant that many of the brides and grooms had lost one or both parents by the time they wed. The possibility of widowhood was well known to most of them. Émilie Tavernier's mother had died when she was four, her father when she was fourteen. Ann Grohan from King's County, Leinster, Ireland, shared with Émilie and many of her fellow countrywomen the experience of losing both parents prior to their marriages. When Caroline Campbell married Oliver Wait, only her father was still alive. Both of his parents were dead. Marguerite Paris' only living parent at the time of her union with the labourer Joseph Guilbault was her widowed mother.[83]

Among the Catholic Canadien brides for whom we have this information, around 20 percent of those marrying in the 1820s had lost their father, 15 percent their mother, and 8 percent both parents prior to their weddings – a striking reminder of death's impact on past family life. Two decades later, the proportion without either parent had nearly doubled. Among Ann Groghan's fellow female immigrants from Ireland, the proportion of orphans was higher. Well over a quarter of the Irish brides in the 1820s had lost their fathers, nearly one in ten had lost their mothers, and just over one in ten had lost both parents. In the 1840s, although the proportions with widowed parents remained similar, those without either parent had increased to 22 percent. Many more Irish women than Irish men marrying in Montreal had only one or no living parents. Philippe Beaudoin's study of Irish marriages in Montreal over the following fifteen years suggests that the trend toward orphaned immigrants would increase dramatically among the post-famine Irish immigrants.[84] Deaths at sea or cholera onboard and on land likely killed some of the parents of these pre-famine Irish. Other women and men surely decided to emigrate following the deaths of fathers, mothers, or both parents in Ireland. Parents' deaths may have left some offspring with few other options. Orphanhoods may also have liberated some young women and men to migrate in these years before the famine began. The shift from family migration out of Ireland to that of individual, young people noted by famine historians perhaps started earlier.[85] Although the death of a parent cannot be disentangled from the changing decisions about inheritance and marriage that have most captured the attention of historians, it deserves some emphasis. The disruption caused by a parent's death and, for some, the sorting out of inheritance that this entailed could shape life decisions.[86]

Deaths, remarriages, and a lack of resources shaped Émilie Tavernier's youth. Her mother died when she was four. As a widower who made his living as a voyageur in the fur trade and had no unmarried older daughters, her father could not raise her. She was sent, as her mother had requested, to live with her more wealthy aunt, Marie-Anne Tavernier Perrault, in her comfortable home on St. Vincent Street in the commercial heart of the old city. Marie-Anne's sick, widowed mother also lived there. Shortly after Émilie's arrival, Marie-Anne's husband died. Émilie remained in this home of widows until she was eighteen, when her brother François' wife died, and she moved into his much more modest home to assist with running his household.[87]

When François remarried a year later, her aging aunt sent Émilie to stay with her daughter, Émilie's cousin, Agathe. Agathe Perrault had married Maurice Nowlan, an Irish Catholic in Her Majesty's 100th regiment during the war of 1812. He died in battle, leaving Agathe a widow after less than two years' of marriage. Émilie's stay there was short. The Perraults sent Émilie to Quebec City when she was nineteen to assist one of her cousins who was having her first baby. Despite her status as something of a poor cousin, she mingled in elite society, attracting the interest of at least one serious suitor and raising speculations about possible marriages. She returned to Montreal when her aunt, Marie-Anne, died in 1822 and moved with Agathe to the home that this cousin and confidante purchased on St. Antoine Street in the western part of the city, not far from where her brother François lived.[88]

Within a year, she surprised her friends and family by announcing her engagement to a neighbour, Jean-Baptiste Gamelin. He was well known to them as a pious, charitable man and a wealthy merchant. Her choice was a surprise in part because she had talked about the possibility of becoming a nun. People's surprise may also have resulted from the knowledge that Jean-Baptiste had been engaged twice before and that he had cancelled the most recent marriage contract just days before the planned wedding. The jilted widow had threatened to pursue him for breeching his promise of marriage. She had relented upon being financially compensated.[89]

Émilie's engagement to Jean-Baptiste was also surprising because, in contrast to her young and wealthy admirers in Quebec City, he was more than twice her age. Demographers have long shown that large age discrepancies between husbands and wives were features of pre-industrial, *ancien régime* societies.[90] They remained fairly common among the couples who married in the 1820s and, to a lesser extent, in the 1840s. Seventeen-year-old Caroline Campbell's new husband, the widower Oliver Wait, was thirty-six years old and nineteen years her senior. Betsy Rea was twenty when she married the thirty-six-year-old merchant John Smith in 1825. Their daughter Matilda Caroline was just sixteen when she married the thirty-four-year-old Hugh Allan in 1844. Constance Hannah Hart was around eighteen when she married in 1844; her Jewish lawyer husband, Adolphus Hart, was thirty. Marrying young was not unusual. Although a traveller's account of observing a thirteen-year-old wife in Montreal is better understood as a thread in British constructions of French Canadian difference as "a most unenterprising race" than as a useful description of marriage age, there were a few brides who must have been close to fourteen when they married.[91] Among those whose age we have been able to calculate, some 15 percent were under seventeen, and over a quarter of the first-time brides were under twenty. Émilie Tavernier was very close to the average age at marriage of just under twenty-three for the brides who were marrying for the first time. Between the 1820s and the 1840s, the average age increased by about half a year. These averages are close to demographers' calculations based on the 1852 census that place Montreal brides' average age at their first marriage at just over twenty-three.[92]

Grooms whose ages we have been able to calculate married at an average age of around 28.5 in the 1820s and 27.9 two decades later. Thus, it was not unusual for women to marry men anything from four to fourteen years their senior.[93] But Émilie's fiancé, Jean-Baptiste Gamelin, was fifty. Such a twenty-seven-year age difference was exceptional even for elite men, who tended to marry later than other classes and among whom wider age gaps were common. The average age difference when both spouses were marrying for the first time was nearly six years in the 1820s. It had dropped to closer to four a generation later, pretty close to the age differences Peter Ward reports for Cornwall, Ontario, around this time.[94]

This was a significant drop in the average gap between husbands and their wives. The decline was general but most marked among crafts and labouring couples. Smaller age differences may signal a move toward more equal, companionate marriages based on mutual affection between spouses of roughly similar age. A flurry of charivaris in Montreal in the years, and indeed the days, leading up to Émilie's marriage may have encouraged men and women to choose spouses of similar age, class, and marital status in order to avoid the rough music and violence that age mismatches like that of Émilie and Jean-Baptiste Gamelin could produce. In 1821, masked, turban-wearing locals and a crowd that was said to reach five hundred protested the marriage of a wealthy widow and a younger gentleman, exhorting a contribution to the recently formed Ladies' Benevolent Society. Just two days before Émilie's wedding on 4 June 1823, the city was shaken by the murder of George Johnson Holt's servant, after "ten or fourteen days" of charivari that followed the merchant Holt's marriage to Caroline Henshaw on 10 April. Reading the Riot Act on 30 May did not silence the rough music. On 2 June, Caroline's brother appears to have sought to defend the still besieged newly wed couple, possibly mistaking John Swails, George's manservant, for one of the belligerent crowd outside their house when he fired. This manslaughter increased the crowd's anger. Montreal's magistrates and justices failed to control them with the watch, constables, soldiers from the garrison, or special constables.[95]

What exactly made the crowd so mad is not clear. This couple was not mismatched in age. Holt was about twenty-seven and Caroline around twenty-four. But she was a widow with at least one child who was marrying a bachelor. This "mismatch," combined with Holt's refusal to pay the crowd, likely made matters worse. For it was said that prominent people often instigated such charivaris and that the monies raised normally went to charitable institutions in the city. Holt was charged as an accomplice to the murder. The charivari and murder left Swails's wife a widow with seven children to support. She remarried quite quickly, to a widower who came as she and Swails did, from Yorkshire. Holt remained in the city. Caroline died in 1834, George in 1842.[96]

Regulations seeking to control charivaris already existed in the city. In the early decades of the century, Montreal's magistrates instigated new regulations against charivaris, along with others against playing on Sundays, playing marbles or cards in the market, and nude bathing in the river. Following Swails's death, some respectable Montrealers agreed to volunteer as special constables should similar situations recur. Some Canadiens blamed foreigners for denigrating a good local custom. George Longmore, a staff corps officer, chose words rather than vigilante justice to comment on charivaris and promote companionate marriage. His 179-stanza poem *The Charivari* depicts a wedding between a bachelor of fifty and a lovely, younger widow; no sooner had they gone to bed than "all at once, as if the house 'twould shatter, there rose a tintinabulary clatter." His poem largely condoned such community-led intervention, explaining that charivaris had become customary, "wen'er a widow wiv'd with bachelor; – or widower with spinster," and that the crowd had been "led to join in sports, which Custom form'd, not spite." Yet, the lesson he imparted in the final stanza was:

Let no one wait, until a *certain age*
That is, – old bachelor, for Hymen's blisses
But think, (If Canada should be the stage,)
Charivari, may hail his wedlock kisses.[97]

Montrealers contemplating marriage may or may not have read the poem. The decline in the age difference between spouses suggests that growing numbers of individuals were following the sentiments that informed his advice.

Marriage ages, as Peter Gossage reminds us, are "sensitive to a wide range of factors, including cultural traditions, social norms, religious pre-scriptions and material circumstances" and "influenced by economic opportunity ... household circumstances, by personal choice, and by family and community pressure."[98] Montreal marriages in the 1820s and 1840s fit within the European pattern of relatively late marriage, especially for men. Women were somewhat younger than in Europe, but not as young as

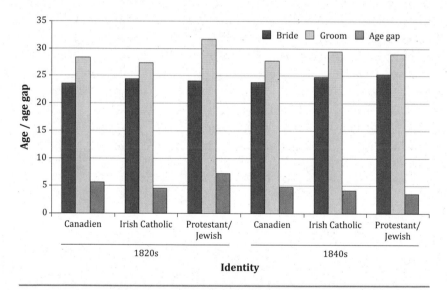

FIGURE 1.3   Average age and age gap at first marriage for Canadien, Irish Catholic, and Protestant and/or Jewish brides and grooms, 1823-26 and 1842-45

Note: Known marriage ages, 1823-26, for brides, $N = 360$, for grooms, $N = 256$; 1842-45, for brides, $N = 375$, for grooms, $N = 298$; ages of both spouses known, 1823-26, $N = 164$, 1842-45, $N = 172$.

Source: Parish Registers, Montreal, all marriages, 1823-26, 50 percent of marriages, BAnQM, linked to information on age in death registrations, obituaries, censuses, and cemetery records, 1823-1915.

brides in Saint Hyacinthe a few decades later.[99] Among grooms of all classes, Anglo-Protestants and the few Jewish males tended to marry later than Canadiens – especially in the earlier period, when the averages were 31.4 and 26.7, respectively. In the 1840s in Montreal, as in other areas studied, Irish Catholic men and women married at a slightly older average age than others – women at 24.1 and men at 29.1 (see Figure 1.3).

Class differences interrelated with ethnicity. Bourgeois, merchant, and elite husbands married at an average of 29.4 in the 1820s, compared to the average of 27.8 among men in the crafts and small shops and 28.5 among labourers. A generation later, when a larger proportion of labouring grooms were Irish Catholics, labourers were delaying marriage until an average of 29.3, compared to 27.7 among men in the crafts and 27.9 among the elite. Daughters from elite families usually married later than women raised in crafts or labouring families. Among those who became brides in the 1840s, elite daughters averaged twenty-five years, compared to around 22.5 for daughters of craftsmen, innkeepers, and day labourers. With little information about women's occupations prior to marriage, little definitive can be said about whether women earning wages or running shops and businesses delayed marrying. The seamstress Adelaide Bebel became a wife at about age twenty-four. The madam Rosalie Paquet was around thirty-two years old when she married in 1843. She had first been arrested for keeping a disorderly house at sixteen in 1827. Over the next twelve years she was arrested at least five more times, often with her husband, Eloi Beneche, or other members of the Beneche family.[100] At the time of her marriage, she was listed in the city directory as running a boarding house on St. Constant Street near Lagauchetière, one of the areas where prostitution flourished. This was the site of virtually all her arrests for keeping disorderly houses during the 1830s and early 1840s. Prior to their marriage, only one bann, rather than the usual three, was read. The register lists her husband as a labourer, though someone has crossed this out, suggesting that Catholic officials were aware of his past involvement in the sex trade.

Rituals and Celebrations

The publicity given to upcoming weddings, their timing, location, and the presence of friends and family varied across faiths and among individuals. Marriage was a sacrament for Catholics. Couples usually met the parish priest some time before the wedding. He probed to determine whether they were relatives within the forbidden degrees and had parental consent or that of their tutors if they were minors. The banns could then be publicized. They had to be read in the current or previous parish church of the future spouses, depending on the length of residency. Three banns were read in the parish church of the spouses on three Sundays prior to the wedding ceremony for six of every ten of these Catholic marriages.[101] Most other Catholic couples had only one or two banns published. Yet, the bishop dispensed with the need for any banns prior to Émilie and Jean-Baptiste's wedding. This was rare among Catholics. Perhaps it was their age difference, or the haste of their decision to marry, that led them to avoid such publicity. Catholic marriages had to be celebrated in church by a competent priest, and at least four male witnesses aged twenty or older.[102]

There was also little publicity prior to Mary Anne Forrest's marriage to Joseph Jourdain. The record of their union indicates that they had secured a marriage licence rather than publishing banns. Marriage licences avoided the publicity of banns and were widely used by Protestants. A little over half of all couples marrying in Anglican churches in these two generations secured a licence, as did nearly three-quarters of those marrying in Presbyterian churches in the 1820s, and about half two decades later. As Mary Anne was marrying Joseph Jourdain against her parents' will, this option likely appealed to them. Usually the groom organized a marriage bond "with one or two people who knew him and who were prepared to guarantee to the Crown that no legal impediment to the marriage existed." The couple could then secure a marriage licence and marry a few days later.[103]

Before going to the Notre Dame church, Émilie and Jean-Baptiste met at her brother's house to write up the marriage contract. Friends and relatives witnessed this document, the details of which are explored in the next chapter. The couple then proceded to the parish church. There, in the presence of Émilie's confessor, the *curé* oversaw the benedictions and reminded them of the sacrament of marriage and their promises to each other as husband and wife.[104] Afterward, their wedding was publicly announced in city newspapers.[105] Protestants might marry in a church or in their homes, Jews at home or in the synagogue. Some marriage ceremonies involved only members of the family and close friends. Others were large events.[106] Abraham Joseph described numerous friends and relatives at the 1839 wedding of Samuel Hort and Emily Hart in Montreal. Festivities afterward were often larger, with dinners and dancing. The Hort-Hart wedding was followed by a sumptuous lunch with "every possible rarity," "champagne in abundance," "the usual quantum of speeches," and an evening dinner with toasts and dancing.[107]

The choice that Émilie and Jean-Baptiste made to marry on a Wednesday was as unusual as their avoidance of banns. Marriages were usually celebrated on Mondays in New France, and this remained the dominant choice in the 1820s as in the 1840s, especially among Canadienne brides and their grooms. In 1823, three-quarters of Canadienne brides were married on a Monday, as were nearly three-fifths of Irish Catholics, but only

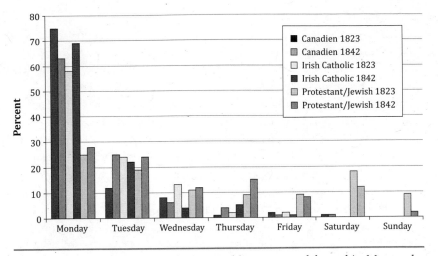

FIGURE 1.4 Days of the week that weddings were celebrated in Montreal, 1823 and 1842

Note: 1823, *N* = 351; 1842, *N* = 329.
Source: Parish Registers, Montreal, all marriages, 1823, 50 percent of marriages, 1842, BAnQM.

around one-quarter of Protestants. Catholic authorities were keen to move wedding preparations and celebrations further away from the weekend to avoid proximity to the Sabbath. Scholars have shown that Tuesdays became increasingly popular in Quebec during the nineteenth century. In 1842, a quarter of Canadienne brides were marrying on Tuesdays, yet Monday remained the favourite choice. Very few married on any other day of the week.[108] Although Protestants also favoured Mondays and Tuesdays, their weddings were spread more evenly over all the days of the week (see Figure 1.4). These nineteenth-century marriages were far from the weekend-focused events they became in the twentieth century. Religious traditions shaped both where and when they were held. This was as true of the time of year as of the time of day. Catholic marriages peaked in the months leading up to the holidays in early spring and between October and November, then dipped dramatically during Lent and Advent, when they were forbidden. Protestant weddings were much more evenly spread across the year, though October and November were also the favourite months.

Departures and Disappearances

Many women became wives in Montreal and then moved on. It was customary for couples to marry in the parish or hometown of the bride, but the law required and custom and pragmatic realities dictated that a woman take up the domicile of her husband — to "follow him wherever he judged appropriate to fix his residence." As a result, for around one in twenty local women who married men with residences elsewhere, marriage initiated a separation from parents, siblings, and other kin in the city. Henriette Berthelet's marriage to the Saint Esprit merchant Horatio Munro meant that she moved to that community some seventy kilometres northeast of Montreal after her wedding. Marie-Anne Lessy de Montenach also left her widowed mother and Montreal some time after her marriage to Colonel John James Whyte of Her Majesty's 7th Hussars, who had been stationed in Montreal. He had attracted local attention when one of her relatives challenged him to a duel because he disapproved of Whyte's conduct toward one of his relatives prior to their marriage.[109] They moved to Ireland, taking up residence in his family seat in Leitrim. John James became a justice of the peace and high sheriff, and the couple were prominent among the gentry. Marie-Anne gave birth to five children, four of whom survived.[110]

Other couples, especially English-speaking Protestants and Irish Catholics, departed disappointed, never having planned to stay, or hoping that other places might offer better opportunities. Their massive mobility parallels what historians have described for other parts of North America, as well as for Montreal. Joanne Burgess found, for instance, that only 9 of 128 non-Canadiens who entered the trade of shoemaking in the city between 1830 and 1831 were still there six years later.[111] The movements of the most prominent women and men are the easiest to follow. Many moved west into the expanding colony of Upper Canada. Elizabeth Molson lived in Montreal as a wife for less than a decade, though in that time David Lewis Macpherson built on the connections his marriage to her had brought him among the city elite and made a fortune in construction contracts, stock manipulation, land speculation, and railway promotion. In 1853, they moved to Toronto. She died there thirty years later, two years before her by then very wealthy, prominent, knighted, politician husband.[112] Christian Fisher and George Monro married in Montreal in 1823 because it was her hometown. They lived out their married lives in his city, Toronto, where this ardent Conservative became mayor in 1841.[113]

Those most likely to stay in Montreal were women who married local men whose parents resided in the city and whose work was unlikely to take them elsewhere. This, of course, was most prevalent among Canadiens, for whom strong family ties in the city and surrounding region, language, and religion made it less likely that they would seek employment and a new life elsewhere. Émilie Tavernier's husband, Jean-Baptiste Gamelin, had little incentive to leave. He owned land in the city and connections that made his trade as a merchant between Montreal and Quebec profitable. She cherished the close connections she had to her brothers, cousins, aunts, and uncles in Montreal. Similarly, Rosalie Paquet and Eloi Beneche's network of familial and other connections through the sex trade linked them intimately to the city.

Although departure or disappearance was the sequence to marriage for over three-quarters of the women who married in Protestant churches, a core of anglophones remained in the city, adding a new generation of children to its population. They included women who married labourers, craftsmen, and small shopkeepers, as well as women married to the upper elite of English-speaking Montreal merchants. Elizabeth Sarah Molson's sister Anne remained there as a wife, living in great comfort after 1860 in the former home of her father-in-law on Sherbrooke Street. Anne Molson worked hard to reshape women's educational opportunities and was influential in having women admitted to McGill University. She died in 1899, some years before her husband.[114] Matilda Caroline Smith remained in the city of her birth, as did her parents. She lived out her married life in the ostentatious mansion Ravenscrag, which Hugh Allan had built for them on the flanks of Montreal. She gave birth to nine daughters and four sons. She died in 1881, one year before her husband.[115] Caroline Scott, who married the notary Thomas John Pelton, remained in Montreal close to her sister and other relatives, even after he moved away to the Eastern Townships.

Marriage was a ritualized moment, heavily invested with sentiment and custom. Individual choice was promoted in romantic literature. Women were advised to choose carefully and to choose well. Mutual appreciation and happiness together, not sexual passion, was presented in guide books, popular advice, and melodramatic tales serialized in newspapers as the best soil in which to cultivate a strong relationship. Newspaper stories warned women of the dangers of "ill assorted" marriages – "that most fatal indiscretion of youth."[116] Usually these chronicled the downhill spiral that resulted when girls married "beneath" themselves. Parents retained a critical role, especially during courtship and the negotiations that preceded some marriages. The higher the stakes, the more likely parents were to observe closely, intervening to foster romance, expressing their discontent, and at times forbidding inappropriate marriages. They were not always successful. Mary Anne Forrest married the widower Joseph Jourdain in 1845, despite her parents' disapproval.

Neither all women nor all men would marry. But the marriages of the majority constantly reinscribed the idea that family formation was based on the heterosexual union of a man and woman, reasserted differences between men and women, and subjected husbands and wives to specific gendered obligations and authority relations. Marriage usually precipitated a forced migration in which brides might move just a few houses along the street, as Émilie Tavernier did; within the neighbourhood, as Caroline

Campbell did; or across cities, colonies, and oceans.[117] As the lawyer Jacques Crémazie explained in a manual written to teach schoolchildren their rights and obligations, the first civil effect of marriage was the right of the husband to oblige his wife to live with him, and follow him wherever he established his domicile. This was one way that gender shaped genealogies of dispersion along with those of staying put.[118]

Marriages were also moments when identities of religion, language, politics, class, and culture were reasserted or negotiated anew. Colonialism, internal migration, and transnational moves brought together different peoples, furthering the possibilities of some genealogical mixings, constraining others. The absence of all but one Aboriginal couple from the marriages registered in Montreal is a reminder of the distancing of Aboriginals not just from the city over the centuries of changing colonial rule but also from the bank of suitable spouses. Intermarriage might continue in the western fur trade, but not in the city whose merchants it had made rich. The Montrealers who married in the 1820s and 1840s were not unusual in mostly choosing spouses who shared their faith, language, class, and culture. Nor were their high rates of geographical mobility unusual in North America. Yet, the impact of endogamy, like that of intermarriage, is historically, culturally, and spatially specific. When like marry like, the boundaries of difference are re-enforced in particular locales. The labourer Thomas Prendergast echoed popular wisdom when he warned the Protestant Thomas Spiers about the danger of marrying Maria Mitchell because she was of a "different religion."[119] Such warnings from friends, family, or religious authorities were part of the local social and cultural dynamics that made it likely that most men and women would choose spouses who shared their faith, culture, and class. In so doing, they contributed to the relative "solitude" of Montreal's main religious and ethnic groups, to what Lord Durham described in his 1839 report as minimal softening of the "animosities of the two races" by "the formation of domestic connexions."[120]

All brides entered a patriarchal institution. They agreed by the act of marrying to their future subordination as wives.[121] Age differences compounded legal and social inequality. The legal aspects of that subjugation for the women who married in Montreal and were domiciled within the colony were framed by the rules of the Custom of Paris, local legislation, and individual decisions negotiated prior to the marriage and throughout it. The next chapter explores the particular patriarchies and authority relations negotiated by these couples.

2

Companionate Patriarchies
Money Matters and Marriage

The law makes you master of the Community.
> — M., letter to the editor, *L'Aurore des Canadas,*
> 18 December 1840

On 14 August 1824, seventeen-year-old Caroline Campbell, her father, and her future husband, Oliver Wait, gathered at her father's inn at the foot of St. Mary's current. William Campbell had asked Notary André Jobin to join them. His fellow notary, Peter Lukin, accompanied him. They met to formalize the material side of Caroline's upcoming life as a wife by making a marriage contract. Speaking for his minor daughter, William agreed that the future spouses' goods should not become community property, shared equally by both spouses, but managed by the husband during the marriage. This was the regime that was created in all marriages under the Custom of Paris unless a different arrangement was specified in a marriage contract made prior to the wedding. Instead, they determined that Oliver should have "exclusive administration, direction and management," and "receive exclusively the use, enjoyment, rents, issues and profits" from all real and personal property Caroline held, or was entitled to, or might receive or accumulate in any way during their marriage. Oliver agreed to apply these "towards the support and maintenance" of the couple and their family "without him being accountable to any other party."[1] Oliver and Caroline had agreed to the arrangement of property that secured Oliver powers as close to the English common law as was possible within the Custom of Paris. Caroline signed, noting her consent to this contract that spelled out her rights and status as Oliver's wife.

Because she was a minor, Caroline's father spoke for her. Still, her consent was necessary for her marriage and her marriage contract to be legal.

Men and women both made the agreement to marry as free, autonomous individuals. Like workers agreeing to labour for an employer, women about to marry agreed to enter a relationship that sanctioned their unequal authority. Yet, unlike the parties to any other kind of contract, as Carole Pateman, Amy Dru Stanley, and other feminist scholars remind us, women were voluntarily agreeing to give up their autonomy and their control over property.[2] They were expected to assume the domicile of their husbands and to remain with them. Frequent notices placed by husbands in Montreal newspapers, as elsewhere, sought the whereabouts of runaway wives and announced that they would not take responsibility for any debts they incurred.[3] Wives could hold no national citizenship other than their husbands'. Their bodies and labour – housework, sex, children – were understood to belong to their new masters, though they might control their own property if this was agreed to in a marriage contract. And their husbands were understood to have the power to discipline them within reasonable limits. As Henry Desrivières Beaubien explained in his 1832 treatise on the laws of the colony, a "husband's power over his wife consists in his right to demand of her all the duties of submission that are due to a superior."[4] In return, husbands were expected to provide for their wives and children according to their means, unless, as Wait had specified, the brides' assets were to be used to this end.

Love, affection, and mutual respect tempered men's powers in many marriages. Some family historians have argued that by these early decades of the nineteenth-century, love was widely understood to be the best basis for marriage. Romantic love and complementary roles for husbands and wives gradually replaced older ideas about the importance of marrying to further family economic or status-related interests.[5] Yet, the spread of romantic sensibilities and the idea of companionate marriage associated with them was uneven and class specific, and its effects were heavily gendered. As Suzanne Lebsock reminds us, such marriages were only as companionate as the husband allowed.[6] Companionate patriarchy, rather than companionate marriage, seems to me to best capture these new understandings about marriage in the nineteenth-century Western world. In Montreal, the mixed legal heritages and the accessibility of notaries offered couples significant latitude to tailor spousal relations of authority and property and hence some aspects of patriarchy in a marriage contract. This chapter explores four versions of companionate patriarchy, authority, and property relations: what I call customary patriarchy, as determined by the law in the absence of a marriage contract; communal patriarchy created when couples actively opted for community property in a marriage contract; liberal patriarchy created when couples decided wives should retain ownership and control over their own separate property; and conservative patriarchy created, as in the case of Oliver Wait, when husbands conserved pretty well as much power over property as husbands in jurisdictions of English common law.

I draw mostly here on the marriage contracts of the couples marrying in the 1820s and 1840s and on the broader jurisprudence as set out in notaries' manuals, legal treatises, and court cases. Marriage contracts, like wills, Margaret Darrow argues, offer a window into beliefs about fairness and "particular kinds of familial order."[7] In making choices about property, men and women imagined their upcoming marriages through sentimental, emotional, pragmatic, economic, and cultural lenses rooted in individual circumstances and diverse national identities linked to the different bodies of marriage law that were part of their legal heritage. Law, contracts, and individual personalities produced marriages with diverse sets of authority relations and wives with different legal identities and property claims, without ever toppling husbands' broadest powers.

Marguerite Paris' Marriage Bargain: Customary Patriarchy

Marguerite Paris and the labourer Joseph Guilbault made no marriage contract prior to their wedding in September 1823. They may have discussed the possibility in the days and weeks leading up to their wedding. Making a contract had been common practice among earlier generations of Canadiens of all levels of wealth, just as it was "deeply embedded" in the French society from which so many of their ancestors had come. Any conversations that Marguerite and Joseph had about their respective financial contributions to the new family they planned to form are hidden from us today. Neither possessed any land. It is unlikely as a labourer's widow that Marguerite's mother, Marguerite Brières, had much to contribute as they started their married life. With few possessions, it probably seemed pointless to pay even the relatively small notary's fee required to make a simple contract.[8] Sweat equity would be this labourer's daughter's major contribution to the new household economy.[9]

By not using a notary to make a marriage contract, Marguerite and Joseph agreed to organize property for their marriage and afterward according to the rules of the Custom of Paris. This customary patriarchy provided that assets they accumulated during their marriage would become part of community property, shared equally by both spouses, but controlled by Joseph during the marriage. Community property included all moveable property such as wages and other revenues, furniture, animals, kitchen utensils, and clothing; any real property such as land, a house, or crops in the field that either spouse acquired by their labour during the marriage; and the income from any properties that the husband or wife inherited or owned before their marriage. Each spouse retained ownership of such inherited real properties, known in the Custom of Paris as *propres,* though any income from them was controlled by the husband during the marriage.[10]

These provisions kept family, heritable, or lineage property out of the shared property created in a marriage. They acknowledged the claims of each spouse and their heirs or family to half the assets accumulated during a marriage. Joseph and other husbands had full management rights over their wives' property. As a result of legislation following the Conquest, both wives and husbands could dispose of their half of the community, as well as their own goods, in a will. Wives who became widows also had the right to use half of their husbands' own property as their dower during their lifetime. Dower then passed to their children or his closest heirs. I return to dower and widows' claims in later chapters.

Common sense to most Canadiens, the concept of community property would also have been familiar to migrants from many parts of Europe, including Scotland, where similar regimes prevailed.[11] But to colonists who migrated from Britain, Ireland, and the United States, it was both foreign and outrageous. England stood apart from the rest of Europe in the extent of power over wives' property that the law placed under the full control of husbands. Most American states and the other colonies of British North America adopted and adapted English common law rules of husband and wife, which gave husbands full ownership of all of their wives' property except land. Until the passage of married women's property acts later in the nineteenth century, this included wives' wages and income, all the assets they brought into a marriage except items like jewellery, and the revenues from any land they possessed. In return, men were obliged to support their wives. Widows had the right to use one-third of their husbands' property for the duration of their widowhood as their dower, if they had not agreed to bar that right when land was sold.[12]

English merchants and other migrants from common law jurisdictions brought with them the presumption that male family heads had relatively unfettered rights to accumulate and decide freely how to dispose of what they saw as their property. As later chapters show, some militantly sought to change many aspects of the Custom of Paris, including dower rights. They publicly articulated their discontent at a law that entitled a wife to "one half ... of the entire personal property of the husband, and one half of the real property which he has acquired during his marriage," and a wife's relations to "claim from the husband one half of the fruits of his labour, although the wife may never have brought him anything."[13]

Canadiens countered such assertions of gender disorder with the argument that their law made "husbands and wives ... partners and joint proprietors of every species of personal property" and acknowledged wives'

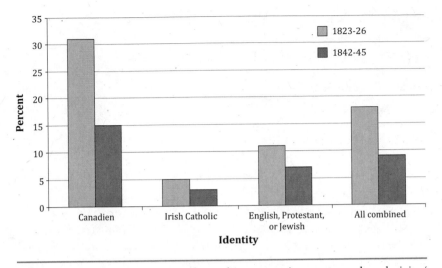

FIGURE 2.1 Percentage of couples making a marriage contract, by ethnicity/religion of grooms, 1823–26 and 1842–45

Note: Actual percentages were probably higher as some couples would have made contracts in men's home parishes outside the Montreal district. Marriages, 1823–26, N = 1,338, contracts, N = 244; marriages, 1842–45, N = 1,445, contracts, N = 128. *Source:* Parish Registers, Montreal, all marriages, 1823–26, 50 percent of marriages, 1842–45, linked to marriage contracts filed with Montreal notaries, BAnQM.

role in saving in order to transmit property to their "children as the fruit of a *mutual collaboration.*"[14] The Custom, they argued, was enlightened and protective, and took much better care of "widows and minors."[15] Thus, Canadien nationalists wove a discourse in which one thread of faithfulness to the community they were reimagining in response to the growing numbers of new colonizers involved protecting the law of their forefathers from assaults by newcomers. As in M.'s letter, they asserted that their law treated wives and widows better than the English did, critiquing British assertions about the superiority of their civilization based on the claim that they treated women more fairly than other races or nations.[16]

Marguerite Paris and Joseph Guilbault were among the majority of couples who did not make a formal marriage contract. Historians have found that between six and nine of all couples among earlier generations of Canadiens did so.[17] Among Canadiens marrying in the 1820s, only three of every ten made a contract; a generation later that proportion had halved. Traditions were changing. Over eight of every ten brides and grooms of all origins marrying between 1823 and 1826 would have their claims on property determined by the law because they had not made an individual contract. Two decades later, this was true for nine of every ten couples marrying in the city.[18] (See Figure 2.1.)

Reasons no doubt varied. Five stand out. First, signing a marriage contract among earlier generations of Canadiens was integrated into the social rituals preceding marriages. Over these two generations, the demands, different sensibilities, and material inequalities of urban life likely diminished this ritualized sociability. Second, for men and women like Marguerite and Joseph, who owned little property, a contract was surely an unnecessary expense and distraction from work and daily demands. Third, some Canadiens understood and accepted the provisions of the law. It is hard to believe that when Marie-Louise Lacroix married Charles-Séraphin Rodier in 1825, they neglected to make a marriage contract through ignorance. As a merchant involved in international trade and a fairly conservative Canadien versed in the tradition of the Custom of Paris, he must surely have decided explicitly that no contract was necessary.[19] Fourth, recently arrived American, English, and Irish immigrants may well have had no idea that such a possibility existed. In the common law jurisdictions from which they came, ante-nuptial agreements were made by lawyers and were more expensive and complicated to have drawn up than marriage contracts. Such settlements were instruments used mostly by an elite minority.[20] Finally, some migrants from other common law jurisdictions may have thought that English rules of marriage and property travelled with them as part of their rights as members of the British Empire. The question of which rules about marital property governed migrants was unsettled in these early decades of the nineteenth century in Lower Canada, throughout the Empire, and indeed in international law. Englishmen were particularly prone to assume that the peculiar powers that the common law offered them as husbands were rights that should accompany them wherever they moved and settled.[21]

Marriage contracts were made to organize property, so it is not surprising that, like Marguerite Paris and Joseph Guilbault, most other couples who were unlikely to have property seldom made contracts, whereas wealthier Montrealers did so. "The relationship between class position and having a contract was direct and dramatic," as my colleagues and I argued when we first analyzed these marriage contracts years ago.[22] In the 1820s, under 5 percent of women who, like Marguerite Paris, married labourers or other unskilled workers benefited from a marriage contract, compared to around 20 percent of the wives of artisans, and about two-thirds of the women who married merchants. Within all classes, more Canadiens drew on longstanding practices and organized marital property with the help of a notary than did the city's English-speaking Protestants, the small number of Jewish

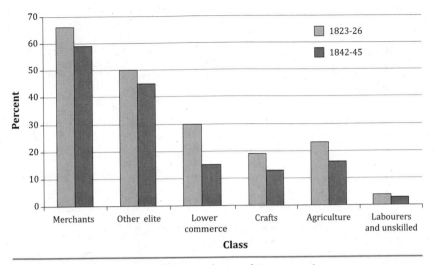

FIGURE 2.2   Percentage of Montrealers making a marriage contract, by husbands' class, 1823-26 and 1842-45

Note: Marriages, 1823-26, *N* = 1,338, contracts, *N* = 244; marriages, 1842-45, *N* = 1,445, contracts, *N* = 128. Actual percentages were probably slightly higher as some couples would have made contracts in men's home parishes outside the Montreal district. *Source:* Parish Registers, Montreal, all marriages, 1823-26, 50 percent of marriages, 1842-45, linked to marriage contracts filed with Montreal notaries, BAnQM.

couples, or Irish Catholics. Among Canadiens, the numbers doing so fell rapidly, especially in the growing ranks of unskilled grooms and men in the city's many crafts and trades (see Figure 2.2).

Class differences continued to be highly significant in the generation marrying in the 1840s. Making a marriage contract remained usual only among the city's elite, especially its merchants. The proportion of all marrying couples making one dropped from 18 to 9 percent; even among Canadiens it halved from 31 to 15 percent. Marriage contracts were becoming the province of the elite, much as marriage settlements were in common law jurisdictions. One contemporary Canadien observed despairingly in the 1830s that the process of making a contract, "as simple as it is, is more unknown among the population of French origin, and is entirely so with several exceptions among those coming from the United Kingdom and elsewhere."[23] Such a statement masks the simple fact that growing numbers of Montrealers had little property to be concerned about and that many newcomers had not yet learned what the provisions of the Custom of Paris would mean for their marriages. It also downplays the possibility that some Canadiens chose not to make a contract either because the legal regime of community goods satisfied them, or because it seemed loyal to use it.

Whether chosen consciously or not, wives and husbands who married in Montreal without a contract were subject to the particularities of the customary patriarchy the law produced. Following their marriage, they would be identified in most legal undertakings explicitly as wives common as to their property. Such wives' legal ownership of half the property accumulated during the marriage acknowledged the partnership so critical to the effective running of farms, small businesses, or workshops in which the wife was "the associate of her husband as well as his companion." This was not an equal partnership. Husbands were recognized as seigneurs "of the moveable and conquests immoveable acquired by him during the marriage of him and his wife." As such they had absolute power to dispose of all the goods they purchased, or any other assets they accumulated during their marriage.[24] They could ruin or increase assets, and, unless they were certifiable as a drunkard or insane, or agreed to separate their goods through the courts, wives had little recourse. They could not even sell the property they inherited or make a legal contract of any kind without their husbands' express permission.

A range of decisions across the nineteenth century confirmed the subordination of wives married in community of goods within the person of their husband. They could sue with their husbands regarding a debt of the community, but not on their own. They could not be subpoenaed to appear without their husbands in court. Nor could they sign a lease without explicit authorization. They could not be held responsible alone for breaking the law. Later in the century, one case decided that a woman who sold liquor from her home regularly on Sundays was not individually responsible, as she was under her husband's control.[25] Yet, in comparison with wives in common law jurisdictions, they did have considerable claims on family property. Some newcomers, as we will see later, sought to write wills to overturn the provisions that the law made, especially those for widows. These were invalid unless their widows accepted their wishes following their husbands' deaths.

Friends, Family, and Making Marriage Contracts

Marriage contracts remained important as the only way to modify or escape community property and to specify the particular rights of wives or husbands over money matters and property. The decisions made by the relatively elite minority making one shaped particular rights and claims for husbands and wives during and after a marriage and produced wives with differing degrees of autonomy and different potential sources of support as widows.

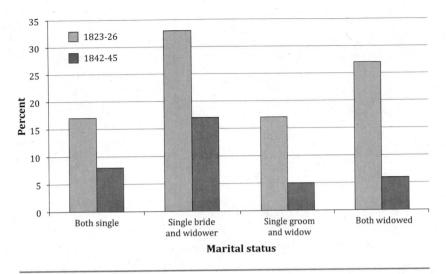

Figure 2.3 Percentage of couples making a marriage contract, by marital status of the future spouses, 1823-26 and 1842-45

Note: Marriages, 1823-26, N = 1,338, contracts, N = 244; marriages, 1842-45, N = 1,445, contracts, N = 128. Actual percentages were probably higher as some couples would have made contracts in men's home parishes outside the Montreal district.
Source: Parish Registers, Montreal, all marriages, 1823-26, 50 percent of marriages, 1842-45, linked to marriage contracts filed with Montreal notaries, BAnQM.

William Campbell, like the fictitious father in M.'s letter, had many reasons to propose that his daughter be protected through the provisions of a contract. At seventeen, Caroline was still a minor and nineteen years younger than Oliver Wait. She was about to become both a wife and a stepmother. William sought assurance that she would be well looked after as a wife and should she become a widow. Oliver Wait had good reasons too. He was a widower with six surviving children from his previous marriage to Marie Laporte. These children's interests had to be seen to, their property rights clarified. He had not made a contract the first time he married. Couples like theirs in which the groom was a widower and the bride a single woman were much more likely to make a marriage contract than two single people or when a widow married a single man.[26] This was partly because more widowers than widows remarried, and they often had children from their first marriage whose interests they sought to protect. The parents of young women who were to become both mothers and wives by marrying may also have insisted on marriage contracts to ensure that adequate provisions were made for their widowhood, especially, when as in the cases of Caroline Campbell and Mary Anne Forrest, they were marrying men who were significantly older and hence more likely to die first (see Figure 2.3).

Wait had other reasons for making a marriage contract. As an ambitious, hardworking trader and contractor, it was important to ensure that no debts from his contracting work would deprive his young second wife and growing children of the assets needed for daily living. He was surely privy to the widely circulating complaints among the anglophone elite about marriage law under the Custom of Paris. He may also have wanted to ensure that her relatives would not benefit from any wealth he accumulated should she outlive him. Such money matters could be seen to only in a marriage contract, and these had to be drawn up by a notary.[27]

There was no shortage of notaries in Montreal. Notaries were key players in the legal system of Lower Canada, as they were in so many European towns. They drew up a wide range of documents, mediating, as Julie Hardwick suggests, between "state and subject, between literate and oral cultures, between an increasingly commercialized economy and producers, consumers, borrowers and lenders."[28] The marriage contracts that we have located for 245 of the couples who married between 1823 and 1826 were made by twenty notaries practising in the city. Two decades later, some forty notaries in the city recorded the wishes of 293 couples. In both decades, most of these professionals had offices in the old part of the city, especially on the main business thoroughfares, Notre Dame and St. James streets. Some Montrealers did most of their business with one particular notary. Others may simply have chosen any notary who was available when needed.

A second notary was required to witness the act, so he too had to be available.[29] Hence, Lukin's presence along with Notary Jobin at William Campbell's inn. Just as it was customary to marry in the parish of the bride, so too was it usual to formalize and celebrate this precursor to marriage in space associated with the bride's family. A few couples and their parents went to the notary's office, but this was rare. Usually notaries left their offices, going to the home of the bride or of someone in her immediate family. A few were called to the groom's home or to the residences of friends of the bride or groom.

Friends and relatives were often invited to share and witness this economic and social ritual. Large gatherings were part of French Canadian family tradition, less so of other groups. Many Canadienne brides would have participated in such events as siblings and cousins. When Émilie Tavernier prepared to marry the apple merchant Jean-Baptiste Gamelin on 4 June 1823, she had attended at least three such occasions. At age twelve she witnessed the first marriage of her brother François. She witnessed again when her brother Julien married, and again when François remarried in 1819, six months after the death of his first wife.[30] It was at the home of this brother that she and Jean-Baptiste signed their marriage contract in the company of his friend, a local merchant; her brother Julien; an aunt on her father's side; and two cousins.[31]

Marie-Louise Genant, the daughter of a merchant grocer, signed her contract with the merchant and master tailor Pierre-Bernard Decousse in 1843 in her home in the presence of her parents, two brothers, two sisters, and a cousin, as well as his maternal uncle, brother-in-law, and a friend. Her transition from minor daughter to wife, and her future rights as a wife and potentially a widow, were thus overseen by some ten relatives and friends, largely from her side of the family, along with the notary. This would later prove to be a problem, for a valid marriage contract required the presence of two notaries.[32]

The gathering to witness the arrangements made between Robert Unwin Harwood and his wife-to-be, Marie-Louise-Josephte Chartier de Lotbinière, was of a similar size (see Figure 1.2 and also Figure 7.2). It took place in the afternoon of 13 December 1823 at the Montreal home of her mother, Mary Charlotte Munro, the widow of the late Hon. Michel-Eustache-Gaspard-Alain Chartier de Lotbinière, described in the contract as "of his life time of Montreal, a member of His Majesty's Legislative Council."[33] The notary that this careful businessman and his bride's prominent family chose was Nicholas Benjamin Doucet, one of the city's most prolific and experienced practitioners. He worked in both English and French, and drew up more marriage contracts for the couples of these two cohorts than any other notary. Fifteen years later, he would build upon his extensive experience, commitment to his profession, and good name to publish a bilingual treatise setting out the articles of the Custom of Paris. Harwood's only witnesses were two friends. Witnessing for Marie-Louise were her mother, who was also her legal tutor, her two uncles, Hugh Munro and Henry Munro, one female cousin and a male friend.[34]

Tradition and the greater likelihood that Canadien Montrealers would have a large, local network of kin meant that there were usually more witnesses present when they signed marriage contracts than when English-speaking couples did so. The ten witnesses, two spouses, and one notary who oversaw Marie-Louise Genant's contract writing was close to the average of eleven witnesses present at Canadien events. Anglophone gatherings were often smaller, averaging about eight.[35] Many factors influenced who was present on such occasions. As we saw, many spouses, like Émilie, had only one or no living parents. Second marriages or those of older couples were frequently simpler affairs. Recent immigrants had fewer kin to call upon. Two friends accompanied Laura Mower and the Montreal grocer John Campbell when they made their marriage contract in Notary Doucet's office at 49 Great St. James Street.[36] Nor did any relatives accompany Joseph Jourdain and Mary Anne Forrest in 1845, probably because of her parents' disapproval of the match. So Mary Anne spoke in her own name, as a *fille majeure usante de ses droits,* as was relatively common among women like her who were over twenty-one and had no family present.[37]

Caroline Campbell may have discussed the provisions of her marriage contract with female relatives prior to signing. As a minor, with no living mother, nor any other women present, she had no chance to consult another female as she signed. Barbara Diefendorf has argued that in early modern Paris, the presence of other family members at such occasions was a significant factor in determining the fairness of the conditions of the match for women.[38] Caroline's voice and presence seem particularly muted in the written contract. In every clause, the notary first described her as "Eleanore," then crossed this out and added "Caroline." Caroline had to inscribe her initials eight times to confirm this name change.[39] Once the document had been read out loud to all present, as was required, she and the others signed their names. The notaries left. Doucet would then have made sure the contract was filed in chronological order and that reference to it was inscribed in the repertory he kept of all the contracts made with him. There were more witnesses at the wedding later in the day. Then Caroline and her father were joined at the inn by Oliver Wait's brother James and his colleague, Andrew White. Caroline was no longer a minor daughter, spoken for by her father. She was Mrs. Wait, Oliver's wife and the stepmother of six children.[40]

As the practice of making a marriage contract became increasingly limited to the elite with property to manage, some such occasions appear more like business arrangements than a family celebration. The space of their production shifted from the home of the future wife or her relatives to the offices of notaries. This was especially true among the anglophone merchant elite. When Betsy Rea married the merchant John Smith in 1825, Notary Doucet came to her home to make the arrangements. When their daughter, Matilda, prepared to marry Hugh Allan in 1844, Betsy and John accompanied the couple to Notary Ross's office.[41] As befitted a man described by his minister as having "little sentiment," Hugh took neither kin nor friends as witnesses.[42]

Shaping Patriarchies: Options, Choices Made, Documents Filed

Before marrying, brides and grooms might consult friends and relatives or notaries about the best provisions to make in a contract. Ludger Duvernay consulted a notary friend, who gave detailed advice, as well as expressing his opinion that the marriage was a bit premature. Amedée Papineau consulted an uncle who was a notary.[43] Notaries met the parties prior to the formal occasion, informing them of their options and listening to their wishes. They then reshaped these into wording that they hoped would hold up in court if necessary. Decisions could be contentious. All we see in the contracts themselves is the way the notary inscribed his understanding of their wishes. The process of recording was highly formulaic.[44] The notary led the parties through a series of steps and questions. All contracts began by indicating that the couple planned to marry. Caroline Campbell and Oliver Wait's states that he "did and dothe hereby promise to take the said Caroline Campbell to be his lawful and wedded wife" and that she promised the same. Theirs has a more secular ring than many, simply stating that "both parties do hereby mutually agree to have their marriage solemnized forthwith in due form of the law."[45] Laura Mower and John Campbell's contract also specified the law rather than religion.[46] Margaret White and William Gay's contract indicates that they planned to marry according to the rites and ceremonies of the Church of Scotland, that of Constance Hannah Hart and Adolphus Mordecai Hart their intention to "lawfully solemnize" theirs in "conformity with the rites and ceremonies" of "the Jewish Faith." Most contracts in the 1820s were handwritten by the notary, though Doucet created a standardized preprinted form that he used for the simplest of contracts during that decade. By the 1840s, more notaries used forms preprinted with the most standard options. Doucet's 1820s printed form assumed a Catholic marriage, stating that the parties would celebrate their marriage in the "Ste. Eglise Catholique Apolostique et Romaine" as soon as one of the parties asked it of the other.[47]

The main provisions on such standardized forms, as in most marriage contracts, detailed how property would be organized. The Custom of Paris offered couples considerable flexibility about how to delineate the ownership of property that each partner brought to the marriage. As long as choices did not violate morality, public order, or the established law of the land, they could introduce whatever clauses were required to fit their particular circumstances. Despite this latitude, there were really only two major questions that had to be answered about property during the marriage and two others concerning what should happen after the death of the first partner. We will return to these latter issues in Chapter 5. The two main questions concerning the period of marriage were, who would own property accumulated during the marriage? And who would own any property or be responsible for any debts that each partner brought into the marriage?

The Custom of Paris recognized three main answers to these sets of questions, producing three divergent ways of imagining marriage and organizing gendered claims on property. Each had very different implications for wives' claims on their own and on their husbands' property, as well as on what they could expect should they become widows. The first was community property. By choosing this regime in a marriage contract, as opposed to accepting the legal regime of community property created without one, couples could make detailed provisions about what would become part of shared property, about debts, and about widowhood. Couples who sought to avoid community had to make this very clear in their contract. Having done so, they had two options. They could opt to keep each spouse's property separate. Or they could reject community property without making any provisions to separate the wife's property from the husband's.

Couples brought their own legal and cultural understandings of marriage, as well as specific pragmatic material interests to these decisions. As John Neilson suggested in 1828, "In spite of all laws," people "will follow their old customs and usages. It requires ages for people to alter their customs."[48] In the 1820s, most couples making marriage contracts followed legal traditions rooted in their respective cultures. Community property was the choice of over nine out of every ten contract-writing Canadien couples. Close to nine of every ten contracts written by English Protestant couples, in contrast, sought to avoid community property. Even more did so a generation later. In the 1820s, four of every ten Anglo-Protestant contracts kept husbands and wives' property separate, often giving wives the authority to manage their own assets. Half may have sought this goal but effectively excluded community property, giving husbands major power over all assets. In the 1840s, nearly nine of every ten chose separate property. Many Canadiens made rather different choices. Around a third opted for separate property. In the 1820s, the tiny number of Irish Catholics making a contract mostly embraced community property. A generation later, most opted for separate property. In their choice of marital regimes, as in their politics, the Irish of the 1840s aligned less with their fellow Catholics and more with English-speaking Montrealers. The reasons for these shifts, their meanings for the couples, the wives and women who later became widows are best grasped by looking in on the details of the decisions that some of these couples made.

Collaborative Patriarchy: Tailoring Community Property

Hermine Legris and Michel Julien, who listed his occupation at the time of their marriage as carpenter, followed Canadien tradition by opting for community property when they met at her mother's home in 1825. As the tutor of her minor children, it was her mother, Angelique Saint Germain, who agreed that her seventeen-year-old daughter could marry. Angelique was separated from Hermine's father, so she might well have learned some of the dangers of shared property from that experience. Yet, the evidence suggests otherwise. The contract is quite simple and a typical Canadien one of the time. It embraced the three main advantages that making a contract in community provided over the legal community created without one. Notary Doucet first set out the provisions for the surviving spouse. He then specified that each spouse would be responsible for any debts incurred prior to their marriage, thus protecting the community against the creditors of either spouse. And third, Doucet noted that Angelique was giving Hermine an advance on her inheritance. She would contribute £37 10s. worth of goods to the marriage. All agreed that these should become part of their community property. Known technically as *ameublissement,* or mobilization, this placed these goods under Michel's administration, and within their shared assets. It augmented the capital available to Michel and provided basic furnishings to set up their household. This decision also meant that none of these assets was protected from creditors, as they would have been had Hermine and her mother decided differently. Nor would they be recognized as Hermine's own property should she become a widow. The proportion of couples making this choice fell between these two generations.[49]

Émilie Monjean and her father sought to avoid such potential dangers in her contract with the master painter Antoine Laurent. Both spouses grew up in the Saint Lawrence suburb and were among the middling ranks of artisans and master artisans who were so prominent in that expanding area of the city. Émilie Monjean was a good match for this twenty-four-year-old artisan. Just four months prior to her marriage, she had purchased land with a house and stable in her own name. Her father, a blacksmith, agreed that he would contribute household furniture and goods, as well as a second piece of property in the Saint Lawrence suburb. Eight years later, these two properties were valued at around £300. In contrast to Hermine and Michel Julien's decision to pool resources, Émilie and Antoine ensured that Émilie's property should remain in her family line. This process, legally referred to as *realisation,* worked in the opposite way to *ameublissement*. It allowed moveable property to be designated as if it had some of the qualities of inherited property. The value of Émilie's belongings, her *propres fictifs* established an obligation against the marriage community for that amount.[50] This was exactly what Ludger Duvernay's cousin advised him to arrange prior to marrying Reine Harnois in 1825. He suggested they have two parties evaluate her property, then recognize that amount as hers in the marriage contract, and hence as outside the community property. She could then control it in her will.[51]

In a city marked by the unpredictability of both death and debt, such clauses ensured that if wives became widows they could claim this amount as their own should they renounce a community in which the debts out-weighed the assets at the time of their husband's death. They also allowed families who owned no immoveable property but had other significant assets to keep such assets in the family. In both the 1820s and 1840s genera-tions, this was an option chosen by around half the wives whose marriage contracts established community property for at least some of their assets, highlighting how even those marrying under this regime sought to keep separate control over capital not embodied in land, including deeds of debt, bank stock, or furniture and household goods, as in Émilie Monjean's case. Such choices made sense as fewer and fewer couples entered marriage owning or expecting to inherit land. Any other wealth they accumulated during their marriage through her labour or his would become part of their shared family assets.[52]

As we saw, over nine of every ten Canadien couples making a marriage contract in the 1820s and over six of every ten a generation later chose community property, thus producing individualized versions of collabora-tive patriarchy, as Émilie and Laurent, and Hermine and Henri did. Its com-monness is reflected on Doucet's earliest standardized form, which only covered this choice in the 1820s, stating: "The future spouses will share all goods and property that they will make during their marriage, following the dispositions of the Custom of Paris, followed in this land."[53] This simple wording suggests that there was something natural, possibly loyal, in mak-ing this choice. Canadien couples from the crafts community continued to opt overwhelmingly for the marriage regime of their ancestors and the one that best reflected the shared work necessary for success. Community property remained the dominant choice of that minority of couples mak-ing a marriage contract in which the husbands were labourers or in crafts, trades, and small businesses. Choosing this regime in a contract explicitly acknowledged that the wife was to be "the associate of her husband as well as his companion."[54] Collaborative patriarchy might recognize wives' con-tributions, yet husbands remained in control of that community and could do with it as they wished (see Figure 2.4).

Avoiding Community: Liberal and Conservative Patriarchies

If the moment of signing a marriage contract allowed some Canadiens to assert their commitment to their own laws and reminded them of the importance of retaining them in a city and colony under British rule, some Scottish and English Montrealers rejected those laws with dramatic flour-ish. Making a contract became a time of asserting Britishness in conjunc-tion with arranging their new identities as husbands and wives. The wording suggests that one of the main reasons for signing the contract was

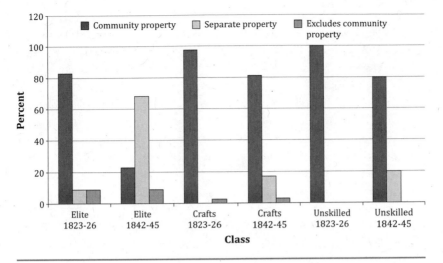

FIGURE 2.4   Choices in the contracts of Canadien grooms of different classes, 1823-26 and 1842-45

Note: Canadien marriages, 1823-26 with a contract, *N* = 166 (elite = 34, crafts = 79, unskilled = 17); marriages, 1842-45, *N* = 77 (elite = 22, crafts = 36, unskilled = 10). Husbands in small commerce and trade, agriculture, or the army have been excluded. *Source:* Marriage contracts filed with Montreal notaries of couples marrying 1823-26, and 50 percent of couples marrying 1842-45, where the groom was Canadien, BAnQM.

to avoid everything about Lower Canadian family law. It is hard not to hear the insistence of a determined father or groom behind the pen of the notary in some of the most flourishing denunciations of community property. John Smith and Betsy Rea's contract made with Notary Doucet asserted that the spouses

> do hereby expressly [sic] declare, stipulate, covenant and agree that a communauté de biens, or communion of Property shall not at any time hereafter by reason of the said intended marriage or on any other pretence whatsoever exist or be between the said John Smith and the said Betsey [sic] Rea – notwithstanding the *Coutume de Paris* and all and every other law, usage or custom of the said Province of Lower Canada, to which and all and every of which the said parties to these present did ... renounce and derogate from, and did declare to be by them renounced and wholly derogated from ... and have no effect whatsoever.

The contract then goes on to state that each spouse was to have the full power to administer his or her own estate, "any law or custom to the contrary notwithstanding."[55] Such notwithstanding clauses, rejecting not just a regime but the whole Custom of Paris, were not necessary to establish separate property. They were rare in Canadien contracts. The same notary, Doucet, drew up the agreement for Émilie Tavernier and Jean-Baptiste Gamelin earlier that year. It simply specified that there would be no community of goods between the future spouses, notwithstanding the laws of the province, from which they were derogating, and that they would separately enjoy all the goods they held that day or might receive in the future through purchase, succession, inheritance, or otherwise.[56] Notary Mondelet's formulation in the marriage contract of Luce Perrault and Édouard-Raymond Fabre was even simpler: "There will be no community of property between the future spouses. They will enjoy their property separately, thus derogating to that effect from the Custom of Paris."[57] Such simple derogations contrast with the florid rejections of the whole body of law by some English-speaking Montrealers.

Notarial caution may have contributed to some of the hyperbolic rejections of the law. In the 1820s, when opting out of community property was relatively uncommon, some notaries made mistakes, or couples voiced their wishes in ways notaries found hard to capture. The profession was not at that point highly regulated. It was learned as a craft in other men's offices. And, as in France when revolutionary changes to laws of inheritance created confusion among notaries and clients alike, the shift in clients' desires left ample space for confusion. As a result, some husbands and wives believed they had established one regime, only to discover later that they had not. This confusion is reflected in the numbers of Protestant and Irish Catholic contracts apparently seeking separate property but effectively only excluding community property.[58]

The most disastrous mistake for wives thinking they were keeping their own property separate was made when a marriage contract excluded community property but did not establish that the wife's own property was to remain separate and under her administration. With such a contract, a wife could not claim her own property against her husband's creditors or reclaim it if she separated from her husband or become a widow. When a Mrs. Simard attempted to assert her rights as a woman married separate as to property in order to recover her goods from her husband's creditors in 1857, Judge Dominique Mondelet, Charles-Elzéar's older brother, acknowledged that marriage contracts could be "written up contrary to the intention of the contracting parties." He and Judges Day and Chabot concurred that if the Simards had "intended to stipulate separation of goods, the principles of the law on the matter have been confused by the Notary, for the contract only contains an exclusion of community between the partners."[59]

In the 1820s, notaries struggled about how to correctly phrase these choices that existed within the Custom yet were so overwhelmingly the choice of English-speaking couples. Over half the contracts written in English effectively excluded community property by specifying that there would be no community property and by giving husbands full administrative powers. We believe that many of these couples hoped, as did Madame Simard, that they were establishing separate property.[60] By mistake – or on purpose – a minority of husbands secured powers as close to the English common law as was possible within the Custom of Paris. Excluding community deprived wives and relatives of claims on any properties and revenues acquired during the marriage, as well as of any goods wives brought to the marriage.

Caroline Campbell, her father, and Oliver Wait appear to have chosen this regime deliberately. Two decades later, Hugh Allan secured similar powers when he married Matilda Caroline Smith. Her parents had also rejected community property when they married in 1825. But John Smith had authorized Betsy to "use and manage" her own individual properties. John, in contrast to his future son-in law, had agreed to pay all household expenses out of his own property. And they had also agreed that "if at any time hereafter the said intended marriage shall be dissolved either by death or otherwise," Betsy could have and take away her bed, wearing apparel, linens, jewels and every other kind of property that belonged to her.[61] In contrast, they agreed to a contract for their daughter that gave Hugh Allan full use of all the profits from her properties. They also agreed that any gifts or property that Hugh gave Matilda during her marriage would be listed in a notarial contract. All else accumulated during the marriage, except the "watch, rings, jewels and all ... clothes, linen and other articles and effects" that she used personally were to be considered his or his heirs.[62] Thus, the man who would become Canada's most successful and richest businessman established an agreement that left his wife with no claim on his accumulated wealth, past or future, except the support he promised her should he die before her.

Would Betsy Rea and John Smith have considered this a fair contract for their daughter? Did she? They were certainly all parties to it. It was already clear that Hugh Allan was a good catch. They were surely keen, as were most parents, to ensure their daughter's happiness and security as a wife, and afterward, should she become a widow. Her marriage contract and Hugh Allan's obvious business acumen certainly seemed to promise that much. The two families would remain closely linked over the following decades. Just four years later, Matilda Caroline Smith's sister, Isabella Ann, married Andrew, Hugh's younger brother.[63] Over twenty years later, when John Smith wrote his last will, he chose both Hugh and Andrew as executors, along with another relative. Still, the contract they agreed to for Matilda Caroline was remarkably different from the way they had imagined money matters within their own marriage.

Although Betsy Rea and John Smith's contract was exceptional in making provisions for the possibility that separation and not death would dissolve their union, it was close to most other English contracts in seeking to give Betsy Rea authority over her own separate property during the marriage. In opting to exclude community property, their daughter and new son-in-law, Matilda and Hugh Allan, were among a shrinking minority in the 1840s. We believe that around one in ten Anglo-Protestant Montrealers meant, as Oliver Wait did, to establish this regime in the 1820s. A further three or four out of ten did so mistakenly, thinking they were choosing separate property. Two decades later, only around one in ten Anglo-Protestant or Jewish couples chose exclusion, whereas the vast majority opted correctly for separate property. Few couples writing their contracts in English chose community. The different contracts of Betsy Rea and her daughter capture the contrast between the two options chosen instead of community property: Betsy's reflects the apparently liberal provisions of contracts establishing that the wife's property should be separate and that she should be allowed to manage it; her daughter's reflects the more conservative ones, closer to the English common law in giving husbands full administrative powers and sometimes control over their wives' property.

Laura Mower appears to have fully grasped the possibilities that separate property offered women. She showed no intention of giving up either her autonomy or her goods to her new husband, the bookseller John Campbell, when they married in 1826. Notary Doucet made it clear that during their marriage John and Laura wished to keep all the property that either partner owned, accumulated, or inherited completely separate. Their contract also specified that each spouse would have the power to manage their own assets as they wished – as if "the said John Campbell and Laura Mower had remained single and the said intended marriage had not taken place, any law or custom to the contrary." Laura's reason for this arrangement was clearer than most. Doucet noted that she was "intending to keep a store and commerce in the retail business." Both agreed that the "said trade and commerce shall be separate, distinct and free." The contract went on to specify that John and John alone would be responsible for all household expenses and would provide all the necessary and decent clothing and other personal necessities for Laura.[64]

Over these two decades, more and more of the couples making contracts opted for the liberal regime of separate property. And as notaries' skill at phrasing this choice correctly increased, growing numbers of contracts

TABLE 2.1   Choices in marriage contracts according to the religion/ethnicity of the groom (%)

	Canadien		Irish Catholic		Protestant or Jewish	
	1823–26	1842–45	1823–26	1842–45	1823–26	1842–45
Community property	93	65	78	22	13	2
Exclude community	4	4	11	11	46	12
Separate wife administers	3	31	11	67	40	83
Separate husband administers	0	0	0	0	1	3
Number of contracts	166	78	9	9	68	196

Note: This table refers to the regimes effectively established, which may or may not have been what the couples intended. All percentages have been rounded up.
Source: Marriage contracts filed with Montreal notaries of couples marrying 1823–26, and 50 percent of couples marrying 1842–45, BAnQM.

established this regime. Among Protestant and Jewish Montrealers, 85 percent established separate property in the 1840s, whereas only around 11 percent chose to exclude community. Among couples where both spouses were French Canadian, the percentage establishing separate property went from three to thirty-three. Among the very small number of Irish grooms who made a contract in the 1820s, seven had opted for community property, one for separation, and one excluded community. A generation later, two-thirds chose separate property. Montreal couples of all origins who made contracts in the 1840s made different choices from those a generation earlier.[65] Commonsense understandings about the proper organization of property and money matters in marriage were changing.

Among Canadien contract makers, the shift to rejecting community property in favour of separate goods was most prevalent among merchants. In the 1820s, Émilie Tavernier was among the minority of less than two in twenty women marrying Canadien merchants who decided to keep the spouses' property separate or exclude community. A generation later, around eight out of ten did so. Even among Canadien grooms in crafts and small trades, the proportion not choosing community property increased over this generation (see Figure 2.4).

Vast differences remained between marriage "*à la loi anglaise*" and "*à la loi française*," but growing numbers of Canadiens were using the flexibility of their law to make choices different from their ancestors. The strongest arguments against English law and English conceptualizations of property and women's rights were voiced during the 1830s by Patriotes and through the Patriote paper *La Minerve* and the patriot press more generally. Articles in the early 1830s disparaged the law of England that placed women "in an inferior position," stressing the "difference between the two legal systems on this subject."[66] Yet, Patriote supporters were among the early couples rejecting community property and opting for the apparently more English choice of separate property. In the 1820s, as we saw, these included Émilie Tavernier and Jean-Baptiste Gamelin. This was also the choice of Luce Perrault and Édouard-Raymond Fabre. And after the rebellions, the Patriote leader, Louis-Joseph Papineau's eldest son, also chose separate property when he married the American Mary Westcott, as did the children of several other Patriotes.[67]

What lay behind this shift? Laura Mower was exceptional in specifying why she wished to keep her property separate. Few couples explained their choices. Some of the reasons can be spelled out. They are ideological and material, diverse and contradictory. First, though not foremost, was the growing critique of women's subordination within marriage in the Western world. The movement for the abolition of slavery expanded in the early decades of the nineteenth century, drawing American and British women into new public activism. Among abolitionists and early promoters of women's rights, condemnations of the institution of slavery fuelled critiques of women's enslavement within marriage. These critiques rippled across the Western world, spread by immigrants, visitors, word of mouth, letters, the press, and popular writing. In England, William Thompson's socialist critique of marriage was published in 1832. Over that decade, some American states and British colonies passed legislation allowing deserted wives to keep their own property separate from returning husbands. A few states legislated to keep all wives' property separate, though without powers of administration. Across the border in New York State, legislation that would have made separate property for women the norm was proposed in 1837, and Sarah Grimké had begun publishing her now famous series of letters in the *New England Spectator*. In these she criticized marriage under the common law for destroying women's independence and crushing their individuality. Shortly after the second cohort of Montreal women signed their marriage contracts in the early 1840s, activist American promoters of woman's rights meeting at Seneca Falls declared that women's subordination within marriage and lack of property rights was one of the main planks of their platform for change in that country.[68]

New ideas about women's rights within marriage circulated widely, gathering both interest and scorn in Lower Canada, as elsewhere.[69] These may have influenced some couples making contracts. Still, in Montreal, as elsewhere, there were much more pragmatic reasons behind husbands' agreements to allow wives and their property some autonomy, as other historians have long shown.[70] Concern about debt and fear of death were powerful factors. Keeping a wife's property separate from her husband's effectively protected her assets from creditors when husbands went bankrupt, thus avoiding the potential loss of furniture and other assets. The years between the 1820s and 1840s were ones of economic uncertainty. Business failure was always a possibility for men making their living as merchants, small traders, and artisans. The severe economic crisis that hit North America in 1837, a further recession in 1843, and the prominence of many cases of bankruptcy must have convinced some Montrealers of the dangers of combining all assets in the one pool created either by men taking over women's property or by shared community property.[71]

The communal principles of community property posed new dangers in the volatile world-capitalist economy into which Montreal was increasingly integrated. The English common law principle that all property belonged to the husband was equally dangerous. In many common law jurisdictions, growing numbers of couples were choosing to make antenuptial marriage settlements in order to secure separate property.[72] Inscribed in the margin of the marriage contract signed in 1826 by Isabella Torrance, daughter of the late Thomas Torrance, a wealthy merchant, and John Stephenson, the son of a snuff and tobacco manufacturer, was the provision that "in case of insolvency of the said John ... or any great derangement of his affairs during the said intended marriage the direction, management and administration shall then and in such case devolve upon and belong exclusively to the said Isabella Torrance, for which purpose she is hereby fully authorized to all intents and purposes."[73]

Debt was a major concern in this contract. Yet, this clause also speaks to a shared confidence in Isabella's administrative capability. So does Robert Unwin Harwood's explicit renunciation of "the right of administering the property of" his future wife and seigneur, Marie-Louise, whom he authorized "from this moment ... to sign, seal and execute any deeds of sale, leases, obligations, deeds of purchase, discharges and all other instruments in writing which (she) ... may think fit, any laws, usage or custom to the contrary notwithstanding."[74] Jean-Baptiste Gamelin agreed to similar powers for Émilie Tavernier when they married. So did the bookseller and Patriote Édouard-Raymond Fabre for Luce Perrault, and Pierre-Bernard Decousse, the master tailor, for Marie-Louise Genant.[75]

Future husbands would not have given such authorizations to women they considered helpless in financial matters. This recognition of a wife's capacity might be rooted in an acknowledgment of individual women's special capacities or intentions. It might also reflect a liberal conception of marriage based on separate property that acknowledged individual abilities and some possibilities for wives. Or it might be read as evidence of faith in women as co-workers in businesses that many historians have argued would be erased as the doctrine of separate spheres and women's natural domesticity took hold.[76] Jean-Baptiste Gamelin knew he would need Émilie to see to business matters when he was away in Quebec City selling his apples. In its broad pattern, this growing willingness to allow wives to retain their property and to exercise some autonomy in its administration fits patterns historians have found elsewhere and diverges from others. Suzanne Lebsock found that in Petersburg, Virginia, couples increasingly specified in marriage settlements that wives should be able to sell their own property.[77] And R.J. Morris argues that in Leeds, England, fathers and husbands were increasingly leaving their daughters and widows separate property over this period, though usually tied up in trusts that allowed the women access only to the revenue.[78]

The liberal patriarchy produced through the choice of separate property gave these women the rights that women in common law jurisdictions would fight for in subsequent decades, making organization to fight for such rights unlikely in this colony. This essentially bourgeois, liberal choice suggested a view of society made up of free individuals, apparently offering women some autonomy if they already owned property. Here, along with the new emphasis on choice in marriage, is evidence of liberalism's growing influence.[79]

Yet, separate property under the Custom of Paris, as under equity law in England and elsewhere, only designated wives' property as separate from that of their husbands and not vice versa. Her separate property included only what she could prove was hers – hence listings in marriage contracts. This was its beauty in protecting specific goods and property from creditors. It retained men's control of income, property, and goods that they brought into or accumulated during the marriage in a society and economy in which husbands were much more likely to augment their separate property than were wives.[80] The economic independence it offered wives was real but constrained. Women who chose to proclaim their status as independent traders, as Laura Mower did, had the greatest degree of legal freedom and might undertake most civil actions without any involvement of their husbands as long as they could prove they were authorized to act. In proposing to take on the legal identity of a married female trader, Laura was taking advantage of the special status of *feme sole* or sole trader that in both the Custom of Paris and the English common law allowed wives to regain some of the rights that marriage automatically eliminated for women.[81] This identity and the rights that went with it were not bestowed on women who simply represented their husbands in trade. Had Laura wished to help John with his bookstore, she could not have claimed to be a trader. Women had to have their own separate trade. Once secured, how-ever, female traders could act autonomously in law and in court for every-thing concerning their own business.[82]

Émilie Tavernier and Betsy Rea; Caroline Scott who married Notary Thomas John Pelton in 1843; and Caroline's sister, Mary Ann, who married the doctor Robert Godfrey a year later; and other women whose marriage contracts established their property as separate and specified that their hus-bands had authorized them to administer that property themselves would find this right increasingly questioned over the decades following their marriages. Quebec wives with separate property had greater powers of administration than wives in England whose ante-nuptial agreements placed their separate property in trusts, managed by men. However, juris-prudence suggests that the apparent autonomy of such general authoriza-tions in marriage contracts was soon whittled away. An 1859 case made this explicit in the published decision that "an action to recover the price of goods sold and delivered to a married women, separated as to property from her husband, will not be maintained without proof that the husband expressly authorized the purchase by his wife." Increasingly, husbands were required to explicitly authorize every civil action a wife separate as to goods made. This might be done in writing or by accompanying them in any act. Either way, their judicial autonomy in civil matters was thus pulled into line with that of the majority of wives married in community prop-erty through the law or contract who always required their husbands' au-thorization to deal with community property.[83]

Excluding community allowed a minority of Montreal couples to get around the community provisions of the Custom of Paris without accord-ing the new wives any of the authority to deal with their own property that the regime of separate property recognized. Caroline Campbell and Matilda Caroline Smith would have no power to control real property of their own, no claim on the considerable wealth their husbands accumu-lated during the marriage. In this option, the closest to the English com-mon law, any moveable property they brought into or received during their marriage in any way except by inheritance would belong to their husband. This was the most draconian choice, the one that suggests a lack of faith in the wife's ability to manage money, and a corresponding natur-alness to men's rights to accumulate.

These particular legal identities of wives mattered. When married women interacted with the business world, they were identified not just as wives but as wives common as to their goods, wives separate as to their goods, or as wives married in exclusion of community. These particularized patri-archies and diverse marital regimes made a difference to the tasks wives could undertake on their own; to what would happen to the income, profits, or sale of property that they owned or helped to accumulate; to their claims on their husbands' property; and to the kinds of legal actions that husbands were required to authorize. The question of whether this identity had been correctly established in a marriage contract could be used by husbands' or wives' creditors seeking a claim over a greater proportion of family property and by wives or children questioning their claims on an estate. Women too could play with uncertainty about the regime that governed their rights as wives when seeking to extract themselves from debtors' claims.

Decisions about whether to make a contract or not – and the contractual agreements made by those who did – reflected, reproduced, and shifted ethnic customs and differences of class and gender, as well as initiating a range of different legal identities for wives, and hence divergent authority relations between spouses. Fewer couples from the generation marrying in the 1840s chose to make a contract than a generation earlier, so most women became wives in community property. Those that made contracts opted increasingly to avoid community property except within the Canadien crafts community. In the 1840s, Canadien merchants and professionals joined anglophone Montrealers in choosing the liberal organization of property that recognized women and their property as separate and independent, and concurrently denied them any guaranteed access to the wealth accumulated during a marriage. The proportions choosing the more conservative regime that excluded community and gave full control to husbands diminished. Separate property was close to the regime rooted in English equity law that became the basis of married women's property rights within all regions of English common law over the nineteenth century. Feminist historians have debated at length how revolutionary this change was for women in English common law contexts. Seen in a different light, from a colony where community property offered wives significant claims on accumulated family assets, it is rather less appealing. Separate property, it should be recalled, did not only keep women's property separate from that of their husbands. It also deemed that all property a woman could not prove as her own belonged to the husband.

Whether arrangements were specified in marriage contracts or not, women's material goods, their domestic labour, and their contacts contributed to family fortunes and to the setting up of households.

3

Marriage Trajectories
Class, Choices, and Chance

Five gold finger rings, two gold lockets, two gold brooches, and two miniature frames, along with five silk, six muslin, and six calico dresses were among the goods listed as Catherine Farquhar's separate property when she married Dr. William Sutherland in 1844. Catherine's clothing and jewellery proclaimed her gentility as a doctor's wife. Her father, William Farquhar, had accumulated considerable wealth over a decade and a half in the grocery wine and spirit trade in Montreal. Their contract specified that he was giving her £88 worth of clothes, candles, and kitchenware as a gift, and a further £456 worth of furniture, furnishings, books, and instruments as an advance on her inheritance. All were to remain her separate property. A piano valued at £50, furniture made of mahogany – the wood that signified status in early-nineteenth-century urban society – twenty-nine dinner plates, and sufficient sliver cutlery, salt spoons, and salt cellars to entertain guests, this critical undertaking "for all who aspired to gentility," were among the contributions that would allow the couple to live in a style that only some professional men could achieve.[1]

They could grace their dining room with a liquor stand and three ladles, and cover their windows with damask curtains. For their bedroom there was a four-poster mahogany bed, a large coloured quilt, and a pair of blankets. The kitchen would house "common" tables and chairs. And their library would be well stocked with books. These included several recent novels – Dickens' 1838 bestseller *Oliver Twist* and Charles James Lever's military tale *Charles O'Malley*, published in 1841. This Anglo-Irish novelist had, like Farquhar's new son-in-law, studied medicine and spent some time in Canada. Such tales of half-pay officers, military manhood, and battles surely fed the culture of Britishness that pervaded post-rebellion Montreal. Ovide and Cicero added classical weight to their collection. Dictionaries, books on surveying and mathematics, and other reference works spoke to the practical interests of middle-class men and women. The many atlases, a globe, and a telescope suggest that this couple shared in the scientific and geographical curiosity of their times. A sleigh and robes, as well as a saddle and bridle, ensured transportation for this doctor who visited the sick throughout the city. Catherine's father helped with more than home furnishings. He provided for his new son-in-law's medical career, equipping him with a range of medical instruments and fifty-two volumes of medical books on surgery, chemistry, dissection, and other subjects.[2]

All women brought what Davidoff and Hall have called hidden investments to the founding of their new family. Most remain hidden. Some are revealed when material contributions such as those of Catherine were listed in marriage contracts or identified in inventories made when a spouse died. These allow glimpses of the "material prominence of the bride's family in the construction of the new household."[3] Contributions varied of course with class, wealth, custom, and individual desires. The assets that women contributed were never only material. Skills, reputations, good health, and connections to kin and to others in the city were commodities that crossed the lines of class, religion, and ethnicity, invaluable for those who possessed them, a potentially dangerous form of penury for those who did not. These are harder to identify. This chapter explores aspects of wives' contributions to the setting up and running of households and traces the trajectories of the lives of the labourer's wife Marguerite Paris, of Émilie Monjean, Hermine Legris, Marie-Louise Genant, and Rebecca Conegan, all of whom married traders, artisans, or small manufacturers, and of Catherine Farquhar, Mary Anne Forrest, Luce Perrault, Constance Hannah Hart, and Caroline Scott, all of whom married men in the middle classes or elite of the city.

Material Beginnings

As a labourer's daughter, Marguerite Paris was surely used to the unstable employment that characterized the life of her new husband, Joseph Guilbault, and other labourers in this pre-industrial, changing commercial city. As a widow's daughter, she had practice contributing to the household economy in any way she could. Such habits and competencies were the sweat equity she brought to the marriage. Perhaps her mother helped set up the new household. Without a marriage contract like Catherine Farquhar's specifying her contribution, this can only be guessed at. It was customary for parents to contribute a bed, mattress, and set of linen as a marriage gift to their daughters. A feather bed, mattress, and its linen was one of the most valuable possessions the couple owned a few years later. Marguerite soon became a mother. In 1826, she gave birth to Marie-Marguerite. A year later, a son was born and named, as was common among Montrealers of all origins and religions, after his father. Little Joseph lived for only a few days. She bore no more children.⁴

With few mouths to feed, luck, and perseverance, Marguerite and Joseph did fairly well for a labouring couple. In the 1820s, it was still possible for some of the city's poorer families to contemplate owning property. Two and a half years after their wedding, they purchased a small house and lot in the southern part of the Saint Lawrence suburb from Joseph Vallée, a Montreal notary, and one of that significant minority of Canadiens who were speculating in land as a way to prosper. The short street on which they took up residence was named after him. Located between St. Catherine to the north and Dorchester to the south, and stretching between St. Phillip and Jeanne Mance streets, its houses were mostly modest, like theirs (see Figure 3.1). All were assessed in the early 1830s as generating between £6 and £13 annually as rentals. Their neighbours were mostly masons, carters, and coopers, although in 1827, Émilie Tavernier and her husband, the merchant Jean-Baptiste Gamelin, purchased a small lot and house, just three houses from theirs. Marguerite and Joseph agreed to pay Notary Vallée £50 and a *rente annuelle* in perpetuity, as was usual in this city where all land still fell within the seigneurial system. Joseph's father helped make this possible by lending them £13.⁵

Their small one-storey house was built of wood and probably had only one room, as was true of many older houses, as well as of the new ones being thrown together in such working-class suburbs of Montreal. Cooking, sleeping, lovemaking, and fighting all took place in such spaces, or spilled out to the streets. It would be valued in 1832 as worth about £100, or an annual rental of just £7, nearly the lowest property value conveying the right to vote in colonial elections. After five years of marriage, Marguerite and Joseph's most valuable possessions were their bed and bedding and their stove, with its pipes, so essential to keeping warm through the long, cold Montreal winters. Their furniture was minimal, possibly brought by one of them when they married or accumulated over the early years of their marriage. In early 1830, they owned four chairs, a table, and two smaller chairs, possibly child-sized. Some cooking equipment, a pair of scales, and a few other items made up most of their other furnishings. Such labourers' homes did not contain enough chairs, china, or utensils to entertain friends or family as the doctor's wife, Catherine Farquhar, could. Marguerite and Joseph were more likely to socialize on the streets, at church, or in the city's taverns.⁶

Women marrying artisans generally contributed more to their new households than did those marrying labourers. Joanne Burgess has shown that Montreal's shoemakers and leather workers were able to marry and establish themselves as heads of households thanks in large part to the

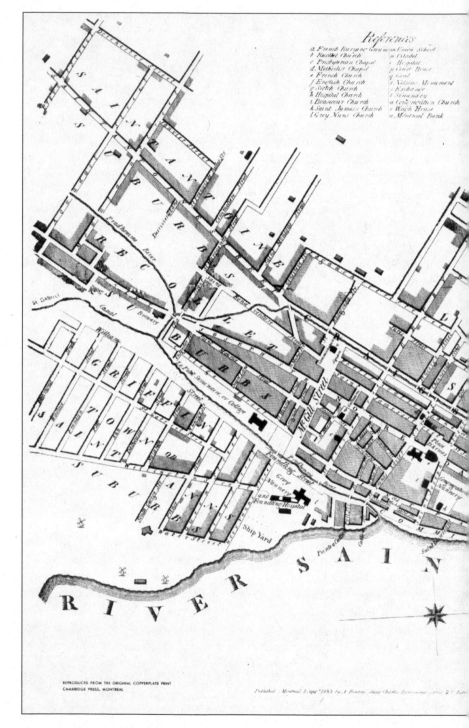

FIGURE 3.1 A plan of the city of Montreal, 1823.

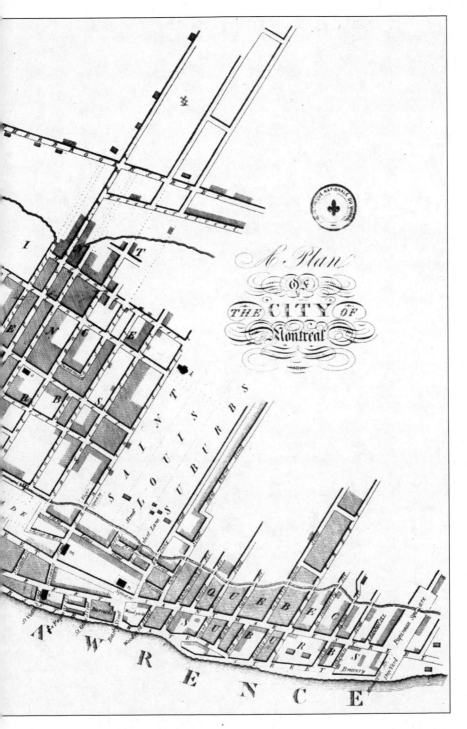

furnishings women brought.[7] Hermine Legris' mother, as we saw, gave her an advance on her inheritance, and she and the carpenter Michel Julien agreed that the £37 10s. worth of furniture and other goods she had inherited would become part of the community property he would administer throughout their marriage. Hermine's contribution included the furniture for one bedroom, two tables, twelve chairs, enough plates and cutlery to serve twelve people, along with one tea service, a stove, and saucepans.[8] Émilie Monjean also used her inheritance from her mother, and the land, house and workshop that she had purchased herself, to enrich the household she set up with the master painter, Antoine Laurent. She contributed bedding, a clock, sideboard, table, armchair, mirror, and curtains, as well as some basic crockery, valued at £51. Such women's contributions ensured that artisanal couples began their married lives with simple furnishings for their bedroom and kitchen, and in Hermine and Michel's case, sufficient crockery to entertain significant numbers of friends and family.[9]

Émilie Monjean and Antoine Laurent set up their home in the house she had purchased on Sanguinet Street, in the Saint Lawrence suburb, about eight blocks east of Vallée Street, where Marguerite Paris and Joseph Guilbault settled. Housing on this north-south street was more mixed than on Vallée. Alongside small properties assessed as potentially generating just £6 annually were others worth up to £40. Theirs was assessed as worth £18 annually by Jacques Viger in 1825, and at £15 in 1832 – more than double the estimated value of Marguerite Paris and Joseph Guilbault's property. Owning real property allowed these two artisanal couples residential stability that was rare and became rarer toward the mid-century. Antoine and Émilie remained in this home throughout their marriage. It too was only one-storey high, made of wood, and possibly had only one room. Yet, the difference between the value of their dwelling and that of Marguerite Paris and Joseph Guilbault, and between their interior furnishings, signals the large social and economic gap between the housing that a master craftsman and his wife could afford and that of an unskilled worker and his wife.[10]

The furnishings that Émilie and Antoine owned ten years after their marriage hint at the modest but respectable lifestyle of this master painter's household. No furniture was made of mahogany or walnut. But they possessed six chairs, all painted green, a folding cherry wood table, a sideboard with leaded glass windows, the mandatory stove and pipes, and a fairly expensive sofa, in addition to the belongings Émilie had brought to the marriage. A gold rimmed mirror hung on one wall. Émilie had a small hand mirror, though the glass had lost its lustre. Perhaps they had owned more at some point. Inventories, the main documents that provide these glimpses of furniture and belongings, never capture everything. As Richard

Bushman reminds historians, portions of the household furnishings were removed for many reasons prior to the deaths that usually precipitated inventory taking. Furthermore, when a couple's marriage created community property, only their shared belongings had to be listed. Émilie and Antoine appear to have lived quite a comfortable life, but they did not prosper. The children Émilie bore died one after another, and Antoine fell ill. Some time during the first eight years of their marriage, Émilie sold one of her lots for £200 in return for an annual payment of 6 percent, which would have brought the couple about £14 annually.[11] Her ownership of land thus provided some stability in times of crisis.

Marie-Louise Genant's contribution to the household she set up with the master tailor Pierre-Bernard Decousse in 1843 was more substantial than that of Hermine Legris, though unlike Émilie Monjean, she had no real property to share. The listing of goods designated as her separate property in their marriage contract suggests that her mother and father, a merchant grocer and also bailiff, provided her with sufficient furnishings to begin her married life comfortably. They set up house in the northeastern part of the old city on Sanguinet Street, southward on the same street as Émilie Monjean, near where it intersected with Craig Street. Pierre-Bernard's tailoring shop was separate from their dwelling quarters (see Figure 3.2). Centrally located at the corner of Little St. James Street and the Place d'Armes, it was just a few blocks southwest of their home. These remained the locations of their home and his workplace for at least the first three years of their marriage, possibly longer.[12]

Pierre-Bernard's relative prominence as a master tailor is captured in the advertisement of his business in the city directory around the time of their wedding (see Figure 3.2). This trade was changing by the time of their marriage. Competition intensified as immigrant tailors set up shop in Montreal. Some masters began taking on more apprentices, increasing the workload for those wives who provided meals, bedding, and domestic labour for live-in apprentices. More began to use apprentices as a daily workforce, teaching some tasks but not always the whole trade.[13] Pierre-Bernard fell ill. The city directory of 1848 is the last to list him as a master tailor. In 1852, he was identified as keeping a tavern in Jacques Cartier Square, the busy, noisy hub that served as a market, home to some of the city's prominent hotels, and a meeting place. Running a tavern was demanding, but it was work that wives and husbands could combine with overseeing young children. By 1852, they had four living children, aged between one and eight. As Pierre-Bernard's illness lingered, much of the work fell to Marie-Louise. The hotels and taverns of the square catered to the crowds who bought and sold at the markets. The inventory made of their goods in 1853, ten years after their marriage, suggests that their tavern at 36 Jacques

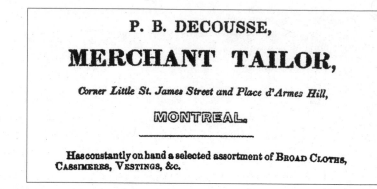

FIGURE 3.2   Marie-Louise Genant's husband announces his wares as a merchant tailor. In February 1843, Decousse rented the two-storey stone house from which he ran his business for £27 a year. He and Marie-Louise were married July that year and set up residence several blocks away, on Sanguinet Street. Such simple "cards" were more visible and expensive than listing a name and address, as less prosperous tailors did. A similar advertisement also appeared a year earlier. | Bibliothèque et Archives nationales du Québec, *Lovell's Montreal Directory,* 1845-46, 263.

Cartier Square was a humble establishment, combining their living quarters with the means to serve drinks to a few customers at a time, and possibly offer casual nighttime shelter. A couple of pine tables, tablecloths, a few chairs, glasses, carafes, several dozen empty bottles, bottles of brandy, flagons of gin, and one and a half gallons of red wine were among the only obvious tools of the tavern trade. In contrast to the one-room home of Marguerite Paris and her labourer husband, the property that Marie-Louise and Pierre-Bernard rented had at least three rooms – a kitchen, a bedroom, and one other room, which may have served as both living room and tavern. A few possessions suggest they began their marriage with greater respectability than Marguerite Paris, or Émilie Monjean and her painter husband: a commode, picture frames, a tablecloth, and an American grandfather clock might all have been used for guests, but they also suggest a different level of material furnishings.[14]

The soap maker Sampson Brady and his new wife, Rebecca Conegan, also established a certain level of gentility in their furnishings over the first seven or so years of their marriage. They made no marriage contract, so there is no way to identify Rebecca's material contributions to the household. It was just a month after their wedding that Sampson Brady formed the "Brady and Darling Soap and Candle Manufactory" in partnership with his brother William and David Darling. Sampson and Rebecca seemed to have first lived at 86 St. Lawrence Street, the address listed for the manufactory in the directory. In 1846, they separated their home and workplace, setting up house at 37 Phillip Street – several blocks west. In 1852, Sampson and Rebecca purchased land close to the factory. By then they had two sons, Sampson and John Morton. Their home had at least three rooms – a kitchen, a bedroom, and one that could have functioned as both sitting and dining room. Here they could receive a small number of guests and lounge in some comfort. In that room they placed six chairs made of mahogany, a fairly valuable dining room table and cover, a sofa, another small table, a card table, an eight-day clock, and a looking glass. The kitchen boasted a large stove, two other tables, six chairs, a rocking chair, a cupboard full of crockery, and carpet for the floor, as well as a washstand and a clothes horse for drying laundry. The bedroom included a good number of quilts, a baby's crib, a French bedstead, and a pine cupboard for storage.[15] These furnishings suggest this illiterate wife and her family lived in some comfort.

The sparsely furnished one-room homes of Montreal's labourers, with sufficient chairs to seat only family members, and their tables made of pine or cherry, or even the better equipped homes of artisans, contrast sharply with the material furnishings with which Catherine Farquhar and her new husband, Dr. William Sutherland, and other members of the professional, merchant, and elite families of the city began their married lives. Whatever debts had led to Joseph Jourdain's insolvency in England, he owned considerable furniture when he married in Montreal. Protecting it from future creditors was clearly on his mind. The marriage contract he and Mary Anne Forrest made in 1845 settled £330 worth of his household goods on her "for her natural life." After his death they were to "revert to the children of their marriage or his heirs or legal representatives." The listing of these goods suggests his aspirations for a middle-class lifestyle as he sought his fortune on a new continent. There was sufficient bedding for several children, as well as for the newly married couple. Bed linen, four bedsteads, two feather beds, four horsehair mattresses, and one four-post mahogany bedstead, along with bed curtains, were valued at £18. There were numerous sofas, tables, chairs, and desks, many of them made of mahogany for the living and dining rooms, and 125 pieces of silver plate. Their floors would be covered with valuable Brussels carpets and rugs, their windows hung with crimson curtains. A mantelpiece clock, reading lamps, plated candlesticks, and a china tea service all spoke to the hopes of respectability and gentility in Mary Anne's new household. More practical were the washstand and the three clothes horses that she might well have hoped would be used by a servant, rather than her. In designating these furnishings, along with "all monies, property and effects now held by her," and any she might get in the future through inheritance as her and her heirs' absolute property, and separate from Joseph's, they effectively placed them out of the reach of future creditors.[16]

Caroline Campbell, whose marriage contract with Oliver Wait gave her no powers over property, seems to disappear into domesticity after their marriage. She was no doubt fully occupied with overseeing his substantial household and farm, and caring for the minor children from his first marriage. Births and departures shifted the dynamics of this blended family over the early years of their marriage. Caroline gave birth to at least four children; three survived their infancy. One stepchild and one of her own children died young. She oversaw the education of the seven minor children from both of his marriages while Wait travelled and administered his contracts. By 1831, several of the children of his first marriage were reaching adulthood. That year, Oliver's two eldest daughters married. One moved with her husband to Upper Canada; Julia Mary and her husband Logan Fuller remained nearby.[17]

Oliver Wait prospered over these years, continuing his move up the lower ranks of Montreal's merchant community, along with his more prominent partner, Andrew White. Oliver owned properties in the city on which he received rent regularly. His long experience buying and selling firewood was recognized in 1832 when he secured a good contract to supply firewood to Her Majesty's fuel yard in Quebec City. That year he was also the main contractor for further canal construction work.[18] Following their marriage, Caroline moved into his two-storey, eight-room, graciously furnished home at the foot of the St. Mary's current, east of the city and close to her father's inn. They lived in bourgeois style. There were twelve chairs in the parlour for guests, a Brussels carpet, and large looking glass. Their dining room furniture was made of mahogany. Guests drank from cut-glass wine and liquor glasses. There were three bedrooms. Oliver and Caroline's bedroom seems to have been on the ground floor. The cradle in it suggests that successive babies slept there with them. Their books reflect Wait's interest in commerce but also suggest that she or he also took an interest in history and the geography of the world. They included the *Dictionary of Trade and Commerce,* a two-volume *History of England,* a *History of the United States,* and a copy of the 1831 publication *The World Displayed,* along with other unspecified titles.[19] They grew a range of crops on their extensive property and employed labourers to help dig the potatoes and reap and take in the crops. They also employed a servant in the house. Oliver kept an impressive stable of horses. He owned at least five kinds of carriages, as well as significant numbers of cows, calves, and pigs.[20]

Luce Perrault and Édouard-Raymond Fabre began their married life in 1826 in a spacious building on St. Vincent Street, in the heart of the commercial and financial sector of the old city owned by her family. Their nine-room living quarters were on the floor above Fabre's book-selling business. This carpenter's son who had married well invested wisely. Over the time of their marriage he accumulated significant assets in newspapers, railways, and telegraph companies. By the mid-1840s, he could afford massive renovations to his business. He boasted to his son that his shop would be as "beautiful as any of the bookstores of Paris," with its facade and furnishings in the French style. They moved house then, setting up northwest of the bookstore at the corner of St. Lawrence and Craig streets. Their new home boasted the familiar bourgeois mahogany furniture and expensive carpets. The sitting room could hold twenty-five people without adding furniture, and their dining table seated ten readily. Luce supported her husband in his politics and profession, hosting receptions of which Édouard-Raymond was very proud. In the 1830s, she was doing so with the assistance of four servants.[21]

Numbers of rooms, chairs, and dining places; whether furniture was painted or made of mahogany; the presence or absence of clocks, maps, paintings, and carriages – these were but a few of the indicators of class and status in the growing city. Legible to locals and visitors alike, these markers of gentility transcended local geographies, part of class cultures expressed with cultural variations across Europe and the Empire.[22] Inherited or purchased, such material trappings of family life were part of couples' expression of selves, family, and class. They could also be lost. Luck, clothes, manners, money, and hard work allowed men like Oliver Wait or Édouard-Raymond Fabre to rise some distance in Montreal society. Bad luck, illness, addictions, shrinking, or changing work possibilities or weak character dragged other men down. Wives' futures were intimately tied to the successes and failures of their husbands. Successes and failures of husbands were linked to their wives' contributions, connections, and health. Wives' capacity to bear children, to manage households, to bring in additional cash, or oversee servants influenced the trajectories of husbands.

Marriage Itineraries

The unfolding of couples' lives after they married and set up their households varied as much as the levels of fortune with which they began. Luck, perseverance, and health interacted with their diverse financial and social situations to shape the choices they could make, and their places in this changing urban society. The relative importance of childbearing and child rearing; making a living; and involvement in church, other religion-based activities or more secular reform, and urban or colonial politics varied too. Hints in a range of sources suggest that many of these marriages were companionate and loving. Others degenerated into disagreement, disappointment, conflict, and sometimes separations that erupt into historical records.

Labouring jobs were available erratically after Joseph Guilbault and Marguerite Paris settled into their home on Vallée Street. Canadien labourers competed for work on the city's major construction projects over these years with the growing numbers of Irish arrivals. Caroline Campbell's husband, Oliver Wait, and Andrew White, who married Margaret Logan in 1823, provided work for many newly arrived Irish labourers on their canal construction projects in the early years of the decade. Wait would later be lauded in *La Minerve* for having also hired many Canadiens. Labourers' wages in the 1820s were less than a dollar a day.[23] Joseph and Marguerite soon had trouble meeting the annual payments on the land they purchased. By 1829, they had missed two years in a row. Nor did they pay the feudal *lods* due to the Sulpicians as the seigneurs of the island of Montreal. After four years of marriage, their financial situation was precarious and their debts were mounting. In 1829, or possibly earlier, Joseph fell ill, and Marguerite began seeking medical help for him. At a time when it was unusual for labourers' families to turn to doctors, she consulted at least three – calling on the assistance of Doctors Nelson, Gosselin, and Berthelot, none of whom sought immediate payment.[24]

When illness prevented husbands from working or led to medical bills, wives intensified their own contributions to daily survival. Marguerite Paris might have drawn on sewing or other skills, sought work as a domestic, taken in washing, bought food at the market and hawked it from door to door, begged or turned to prostitution. Few records of the period capture these kinds of casual work that were so central to labouring family economies. Some labourers' wives definitely turned to prostitution, though there is no evidence that Marguerite did. Norah Deegan, who had married the Tipperary-born Irish labourer Patrick Crowe in 1823, was arrested with him in 1839 and again in 1840 for keeping a disorderly house. The labourer Jacob Abdullah dit Bisserno and his second wife, Catherine Curra or Guillet, were both arrested for prostitution-related offences five years after their marriage. This labourer, who was listed at his first marriage as being from Malta, married for the first time in January 1823. Within six months, his first wife was dead. He married again in 1826, and it was in June 1832 that he and his second wife, Catherine, were both arrested in Montreal.[25] Such partnerships might indicate a collaborative business choice or coercion by the husband. That such forays into prostitution were commonest among the wives of labourers is no surprise.[26] They remind us of the difficulty of managing on the inadequate and irregular wages of casual workers at a time when the state offered no support and charitable

networks were minimal. Prostitution was just one of the more visible re-
sorts, one strand in what Olwen Hufton has called the economy of make-
shifts or expediency that such women forged.[27]

For Rosalie Paquet and Eloi Beneche, prostitution was not something
resorted to in a moment of crisis during their marriage. As we saw, the sex
trade was at the heart of the relationship they developed in the years before
their wedding in 1843. Court records suggest that Rosalie was frequently
arrested but seldom charged for keeping a disorderly house. However, in
1841, she was arrested and sentenced to a month in the new House of
Correction. Perhaps this shook her confidence. By then she was around
thirty and had worked in the sex trade for some fourteen years. When she
married Eloi Beneche in 1843, it had been six years since their first arrest
together. That year, they were both sufficiently prominent in the city to be
identified by their respective names in the city's directories. Rosalie appeared under her own name as running a boarding house on St. Constant
near Lagauchetière Street — at what was likely the location of her brothel.
Eloi was listed as a grocer and as living on Visitation Street, near St.
Catherine, several blocks north and west of the brothel. As an established
madam, with what may well have been a highly lucrative brothel and business, Rosalie did not fade quietly into the identity of her new husband
immediately after their marriage. For the first three years of their marriage,
their separate listings in the directory continued. She then disappeared
from such records.[28]

Labourers' wives were not alone in turning to prostitution. As we saw,
Hermine Legris' marriage began well enough materially, with significant
contributions of furniture from her mother. One child was born in 1831.
Three years later, Hermine was arrested for keeping a disorderly house and
identified as a widow, though Michel Julien would not die until the 1870s.
Hermine gave birth to two other children later in the 1840s. The register
records them as his. Yet, evidence suggests that she and Michel did not live
together consistently for much of this period. Only in 1843 and then again
in 1852 was there a listing for a Michel Julien in the city directory. In 1853,
Hermine was listed separately as Mrs. Julien at 106 St. Joseph Street and as
keeping a boarding house — such designations were sometimes a front for
prostitution. A year later, she was recorded as living in a hotel. For several
years after that, Hermine was identified as living in a house on Lagauchetière, near Sanguinet, pretty close to one of the city's red light districts. In
the 1860s, she moved to St. Felix Street, where she was identified at a range
of addresses and sometimes as Mrs. Julien, sometimes as Widow Julien.
What precipitated these moves and separations, or her self-presentation as
a widow, is not clear. Michel does not seem to have stuck to one trade. At
his marriage he was listed as a carpenter. He appears at various times as a

labourer and a baker in other records. His slipping in and out of sight in the city directories is another indicator of his tenuous hold on the positions of breadwinner and household head. Hermine managed to house her children and succeeded in raising at least three to adulthood. Michel appears to have come and gone as a father, cohabiting again as he reached old age. [29]

The reasons for the deterioration of the marriages of the affluent grocer Charles Smith and Agnes Kirkpatrick, of Maria Mitchell and Thomas Spiers, and of Marie-Adelaide Lamontagne and Luc Dufresne are clearer because they left traces in judicial and other records. Charles Smith and Agnes Kilpatrick married in May 1842. He had a grocery shop on St. Mary Street, near Dalhousie Square. Their household included at least one servant. Soon after their marriage, Charles started beating Agnes. In June 1843, she prosecuted him for assault and battery, describing various acts of violence, including "grievous head injuries." Two domestic servants corroborated her story, graphically describing his brutality and reporting that she was left "disturbed in the head." In July 1845, Agnes died. The death notice placed in the *Montreal Gazette* the next day, likely by Smith, reported only that she died "after a short illness." Agnes was twenty-four. Within two years, Charles had remarried. [30]

Drink was at the root of the problems that Marie-Adelaide Lamontagne, Marie-Anne Gauthier-Landreville, and Maria Mitchell faced with their husbands. Marie-Anne took her labourer husband, Vincent Labelle, to court in July 1837, thirteen years after their marriage, fed up with his "scandalous" and abusive conduct and the blasphemy that he uttered even in front of their children. [31] Marie-Adelaide's husband, the cooper Luc Dufresne, had become an alcoholic by the end of their first decade of married life. Eventually, her brother helped her have him declared incapable of managing his own affairs, but this neither prevented his drinking nor solved the challenges she faced raising four children. Luc's death in 1854, when he was fifty and she forty-nine, may have come as a relief. Thierry Nootens has eloquently evoked the problems that heavy drinking caused for wives like Marie Adelaide, as well as the ways other family members stepped in to assist and to protect property. [32]

Drinking and abuse characterized the marriage of Maria Mitchell and Thomas Spiers from the beginning too. Her friends Thomas and Eliza Prendergast later testified that Thomas began to beat Maria within a month of the wedding. She fled frequently, as so many abused wives did, seeking refuge in their house during the first seven or so years of her marriage. But such flights "did not usually offer more than a temporary reprieve from a malevolent spouse." [33] Eliza reported seeing Thomas beat Maria "six or seven times myself," at the couple's house. Prendergast swore that Spiers was "a constant drinker ... sometimes ... speaking kind of her, and at other times he would beat her until she was nearly dead."[34] At least once she went to the police for assistance. Local newspapers report that in November 1849, "warrants were issued to arrest Michael Higgins and Thomas Spiers on the complaint of their wives for aggravated assault." On that occasion Thomas was arrested and fined the significant amount of "five pounds and costs, or two months in the House of Correction."[35]

By then, Maria had three children. Mary Jane was born in early 1846, some eleven months after their marriage, Priscilla exactly two years later, and Donald shortly after her. In 1852, she gave birth to Sarah. Eliza was born three years later in 1855 and Catherine in 1856. Another child died as an infant over these years. By the time of Sarah's birth, Maria appears to have shut herself off from her friends and was drinking heavily herself. Evidence suggests that she went on a drinking binge two months before her youngest daughter, Catherine, was born, spending fifteen days in jail as a result.[36] Over the years of their marriage, Thomas' pattern of employment was erratic. They moved frequently. He described himself as a grocer when they married. Between 1845 and 1852, he was listed in city directories as in provisioning, as a master sweep, and from 1853 to 1855 as an accountant. In 1858, the *Montreal Witness* reported that he was "well known in this city," having worked at a series of jobs – as inspector of chimneys, delivering messenges for the St. Lawrence and Atlantic Railway, and delivering "circulars and funeral cards."[37] These odd shifts in trade indicate a man failing at what John Tosh describes as integral components of middle-class masculinity. He did not "establish a home," "protect it," or "provide" for his wife or children. Spiers floated in and out of that group of nineteenth-century men who, like Joseph Jourdain, struggled to keep a foothold in the respectable middle classes as small traders, clerks, or accountants. At a time when "the idea that what a man did in his working life was an authentic expression of his individuality" and one of the most "characteristic – and enduring – features of middle-class masculinity," such failure was hard on men's self-respect. Men like Spiers teetered near the edge of the middle classes, of respectability, and of successful manhood, their fortunes determined by social connections, luck, and the vagaries of the economy.[38] Maria bore the brunt of his frustrations.

Yet, Thomas Spiers was well connected as well as well known in the city. He was a Freemason and, despite his own drinking problem, he seems to have been actively engaged in two of the local lodges frequented by some of Montreal's most prominent English-speaking Protestants. Between 1855 and 1858, the city directory listed him as assistant treasurer, then as an assistant tyler, a position that involved guarding the door to ensure that only qualified masons entered, first at the Provincial Grand Lodge of Montreal and William Henry, then at the St. Paul's Lodge. Members of the latter lodge met monthly, except between June and October. Here he rubbed shoulders with some of the city's most prominent men. For many years, the Grand Master of the Montreal and William Henry Lodge was the Anglican and ardently pro-British and Protestant mason William Badgley.[39] "Freemasons assumed that their institution, like the family, would see to the material and emotional needs of its members," explains Jessica Harland-Jacobs. She argues that an idealized notion of a family of men was at the heart of Freemasonry and was deployed to forge a "sense of community and mutual obligation," through their rituals of initiation and integration into the brotherhood.[40]

Thomas' bonds with some of the city's most prominent anglophone Protestant elite as part of "a group of men who pledged to respect, help, and love each other through all circumstances" did not help Maria escape his abuse.[41] Spiers failed at the most central challenge facing the men of his times – that of succeeding in shaping his own home, marriage, life, and livelihood.[42] He transgressed the rules of brotherhood, and failed miserably at negotiating those spaces between home, work, and associational life that John Tosh argues were central to nineteenth-century middle-class masculinities. As his situation deteriorated, he clung to vestiges of respectability – controlling the reporting of his occupation in the city directory as "accountant," rather than publicizing the more menial tasks that other sources indicate as his occupations at the time.[43]

Thomas and Maria's joint drinking accelerated their social decline. Over the first twelve years of their marriage, they slipped from the edges of the middle class to the murky underworld of the taverns and the streets, with the attendant wife abuse and hunger. In this period, Ian Christopher Pilarczyk has argued, wives and husbands could and did charge violent spouses with assault, but "the legal response towards spousal violence was defined neither by consistency nor by severe sentences designed to act as deterrents."[44] Neighbours reported frequent quarrels. Middle-class observers suggested that the children lived lives of hunger and possibly fear. Benevolent visitors later claimed to have stepped in at times, providing clothing and food but failing to prevent the violence from recurring. Protestant Montrealers also arranged to take the children away to the Ladies' Benevolent Society for shelter at least once during the marriage. In August 1857, when Sarah was four, Priscilla eight, and Mary Jane ten, they were taken to the orphanage this society ran, though by whom is unclear. Police records show that their mother was on another drinking binge that month. On 24 August, Maria was arrested in Bonsecours Market for being drunk and disorderly. Less than two weeks after that arrest, a Mrs. Perkins, probably a visitor for the society, took Elizabeth, then aged two, and Donald, aged six, to join their siblings in the orphanage. This was the largest of the two main Protestant institutions, run by relatively elite Montreal women to provide shelter for destitute widows and their children. It specialized in taking children temporarily when their mothers were widowed or deserted, or when families were facing hard times. The majority were discharged to their parents. The Spiers children's stay in the orphanage was relatively short. At the end of September 1857, Thomas came and retrieved them.[45]

That month he also arranged for, or agreed to, the baptism of the three youngest children as Protestants. Whereas Maria and Thomas had married in a Congregational church, and baptized the first three children at Trinity Anglican Church, these three were baptized at the Anglican St. George's Chapel, where the ceremony was performed by W.B. Bond, the minister who was also a regular visitor at the Ladies' Benevolent Society.[46] Thomas may have wanted his children to be raised Protestant, though Prendergast swore later that before his marriage he had said he did not mind. A week after their baptism, Maria was again confined in the jail after she was found drunk on Beaver Hall Terrace. Could her disappointment that Thomas had broken his promise that he would let her take them to "whatever church she thought fit" have pushed her back to the bottle? By this point she probably needed no excuse to drink, though later events would suggest she wanted her children brought up Catholic.[47] Maria lived her wifehood as an abused wife and a drunkard.

The challenges that Rebecca Conegan faced as the wife of the soap maker Sampson Brady were of a different order. The tallow chandler business did well. And, although she seems to have been illiterate, Rebecca kept a tight hand on family finances and carefully saved up money that she considered her own. At some point between their marriage and the early 1850s, she placed the significant sum of £50 in the Montreal City and District Savings Bank. She would later declare that she was "not indebted to any ... person whomsoever."[48] The first children Rebecca bore did not survive long. In 1848, however, she gave birth to a son, whom they named after his father, and a year later she had another boy, John Morton, named after Sampson's brother.

By 1851, however, Sampson was sick and blind, possibly as result of work-related hazards. His partners – his brother, William, and friend David Darling – clearly had a strong sense of the problems Sampson's blindness and incapacity would pose for him, Rebecca, and their young family. They dissolved the partnership and effectively bought Sampson out of the "stock in trade implements, real estate and premises, outstanding debts and other effects and property" that they had co-owned. In return, they arranged to pay Rebecca over £1,800 in generous installments that would allow her to run the household.[49] R.J. Morris describes men moving capital out of high-risk businesses into family property and trusts as a risk-spreading strategy used by the middle classes of Leeds in this period. In Brady's case, this transfer promised security for his family at a time when his ability to provide was severely compromised.[50] Rebecca was able to manage as a mother and the wife of a man who was both ill and blind because he had successfully made the transition to small manufacturer, and the candle factory appears to have been prosperous enough for his partners to offer him sufficient funds to live on. Like Hermine Legris, but for different reasons, Rebecca too found herself as both wife and the effective head of her household.

So did Caroline Scott. The reason for the deterioration of her marriage to the notary Thomas John Pelton is also unclear in retrospect, though at the time whisperings and gossip no doubt spread through the circles of notaries and their clients in the city. Pelton began working as a notary in Montreal in 1837 as a bachelor. Initially, he specialized in preparing protests and obligations covering loans of money for a small, privileged clientele. His work placed him at the hub of the relations of credit among the city's major English-speaking merchants. He worked largely for the Bank of Montreal until 1841, then as a notary for the Montreal City and District Savings Bank between about 1842 or 1843 and 1848, until a "change occurred" and he was replaced just before the bank failed.[51]

Between 1844 and 1846, John Redpath, one of the owners of property reaching up onto Mount Royal purchased from Montreal's leading fur traders, used Pelton as his notary when he was subdividing, converting it to freehold tenure, and selling off lots. In that capacity, Pelton's work was central to the forging of a new elite urban space on the lower slopes of the mountain. Like Edinburgh's New Town, London's West End, or Edgbaston in Birmingham, such elite spaces increased the separation between professional and businessmen's workplaces and their homes, contributing to the understanding that middle-class homes were the domain of women. This new development was not for any elite. Rod MacLeod shows that in the increasingly polarized post-rebellion city, its promoters imagined the new spaces they were developing as both middle class and English speaking.[52]

The ex-fur trader and merchant John Easton Mills, whom Hannah Lyman married in 1823, had also purchased land on the mountain. In 1846, he, like Redpath, began to divide it. By then, his thirty years in business and investing in stock had secured him a sufficient competency to turn to other matters. That year he became the city's fifth mayor. He, Hannah, and the children did not move up to the mountain. They remained in the home they had named Bellaire Cottage, at the head of Genevieve Street, a couple of blocks north and some eight blocks west of his office on St. François Xavier Street in the old city, and not far from city hall.[53]

Over the following years, the mountain slopes became home to many of the city's leading merchants and professionals, and eventually to some of Pelton's own family, as well as to English-speaking elite and professional couples from the two generations of marriages studied here. Couples caught by "mountain fever" usually saw Thomas John Pelton to produce the necessary documents. William Laurie purchased two lots at the fairly standard price of £450 in 1844, two years after his marriage to Maria Laberge. They then oversaw the construction of some of the first terrace housing on what became Mountain Street. The row of seven houses they had built is still known as Mountain Terrace. Annabella Eadie and Margaret Daly married the two Irish Protestants, Thomas and James Workman, during the 1840s. Thomas purchased two mountain lots.[54] Prominent English-speaking Jews also partook of "mountain fever." Theodore Hart purchased two lots from John Redpath using Notary Pelton in 1845. Later he was joined on the slopes by his cousins, Constance and Adolphus Hart.[55]

In the mid-1860s, Catherine Farquhar and Dr. William Sutherland joined the movement of Montreal's Anglo-elite up the hill, taking up residence at 667 Dorchester Street near where it intersected with Beaver Hall Terrace, then the location of the homes of many prominent Scottish and English merchants and professionals. Following their marriage in 1844, they had set up house on St. James Street, the elegant road in the old city, which, according to Robert Sweeny, was fast becoming "the professional street of preference" (see Figure 3.3).[56] They were within minutes' walk from Christ Anglican, the church they attended, and where they registered the births of their children. William's medical skills did not ensure the survival of all their children. Their daughter died at the age of five. One son, William, survived infancy but died at the age of twenty-six. Their third child, Louis, who was born in 1850, was the only one to outlive his parents.[57] Catherine and William retained ownership of the land and buildings they owned in the old city, which gave them a regular income over and above that from William's medical work. Property investment was a strategic professional move and profitable for this doctor, as Sweeny has suggested it was for others of the period. Their property accumulation reflects the ways middle-class families in Montreal, like those studied by R.J. Morris in Leeds, sought to build up their investments during the prime of their lives, in the hope that they would provide a steady income in their later years as a couple, or as widows or widowers.[58]

FIGURE 3.3   Looking east on St. James Street, Montreal, ca. 1869. |
McCord Museum, MP-0000.39.11.

Towering above the residences of the Sutherlands, Workmans, Lauries, and Harts and dwarfing the splendour of the other gracious terrace houses or bourgeois villas that became more and more popular in the years after the 1840s was the mansion Hugh Allan had built for himself, Matilda, and their family in the 1860s. This couple moved several times after their marriage in 1844, starting married life on Craig Street, just north of the old city, then moving closer to his brother on St. Catherine Street, an area that was then at the northern fringes of most urban development.[59] Over the twenty years following their wedding, Allan expanded his family's shipping business; secured the contract to provide the fortnightly mail service linking Montreal and the Canadas to Portland, Maine, and to Liverpool; invested in railways and in mining for gold and coal; and made significant purchases of urban and rural land. The Allan Line ships brought immigrants

Pelton, Joshua, superintendent of the old Protestant
    burying ground, 90 German
Pelton, T J, notary public, conveyancer, &c, 22 St
    François Xavier, house 90 German
Penn, Fred, house Grey Nun
PENNINGTON, MYLES, goods manager, G T Railroad
    office 11 Great St James, house 71 Champ de
    Mars

FIGURE 3.4 Thomas Pelton's listing in the Montreal Directory, 1856–
57. The co-residence of Thomas J. Pelton with his father in 1856–57 hints at
his problems maintaining his clientele as a notary and an independent residence as a husband and father. Note that his name is listed after that of his
father, and they are living at the same address. | Bibliothèque et Archives natio-
nales du Québec, *Lovell's Montreal Directory*, 1856–57, 221.

and manufactured goods to Canada and transported Canada's wheat and
wood back to Great Britain.[60]

Ravenscrag, the Italianate mansion that became their new home in the
mid-1860s, proclaimed his success, status, and power to all Montrealers.
Ornate and pretentious, it boasted thirty-four rooms, each decorated in a
different style. Their estate covered fourteen acres of mountainside above
McGill University. It was splendidly isolated from the bustle of the city
and from potential neighbours. But they were not isolated from workers.
Matilda Smith ran the household and oversaw the children's upbringing
with the assistance of an army of servants, gardeners, and other staff.
She gave birth to nine daughters and four sons. In 1871, their mansion
housed twenty-two people. Eleven were family members; eleven were
staff. Twenty years later, four Allan children still at home were supported
by a resident staff of sixteen, while the coachman and gardener raised their
own families on the estate. Such increases in the proportion of staff, Rod
MacLeod suggests, "can only be explained as an example of conspicuous
consumption."[61]

Thomas Pelton may have aspired to reside on one of these properties
that he played a professional hand in opening up to middle-class Montrealers. He would not do so. He and Caroline Scott began their married
life in 1844 just north of the centre of the old city in a house on Lagauchetière Street, near St. Urbain Street. Pelton's office was five or six blocks
south, on St. François Xavier Street, not far from the offices of other prominent notaries. City directories show frequent moves over the following
twelve years. Sometimes the couple seems to have lived in the same building as Pelton's office. Sometimes their dwelling and his workplace were

separate.[62] They moved house at least six times prior to 1856. Such moves were not unusual for Montrealers, though they were less common among middle-class families like theirs. When the 1856-57 city directory was organized, they had moved in with Thomas' father, Joshua Pelton, on German Street. A year later, they were far north of town in a house on Mile End Road. After 1853, Thomas was no longer listed among the city's notaries, though his residential listing still indicated that he was a notary (see Figure 3.4).[63]

Pelton's disappearance as a practising notary in the pages of the city directories, along with the couple's repeated moves, parallel the decline in his business evident in his notarial files. After 1850, the number of cases he dealt with fell dramatically. Days and sometimes weeks or months went by without any documents produced. By 1858, there is no evidence he still had clients in the city. Montreal notaries varied in the success of their businesses, as did notaries elsewhere.[64] Sickness, depression, or drinking could limit any professional's success. The reasons for Pelton's decline are only partially clear. He was subjected to very public questioning in 1851 when the House of Assembly investigated the money-lending practices of the Montreal Savings Bank. This may have precipitated or accentuated health problems, or ruined his reputation. In 1856, a growing proportion of the very small number of cases in his files was executed in Granby, in the Eastern Townships. Perhaps the family, which by then included five children, moved to the townships for a while. Between 1858 and 1860, there is no mention of them in the city's directories. In 1859 they registered their sixth child's birth at St. George Anglican Church, and in January 1861 Thomas completed the census form for the family. His name appeared that year for the last time in the directory listing.[65]

In mid-1861, Pelton was residing in Knowlton in the Eastern Townships. Caroline remained in Montreal. On 4 June that year, he wrote a moving letter to his eldest daughter, also named Caroline but often referred to in the family as Carrie. He reported sadly that although he had "written to your mother more than a week ago," he had "as yet received no reply." "Surely," he continued, "because circumstances have caused a separation between my dear wife and my self there should be none why I should be made uninformed of the welfare and position of my dear children." Thomas asked his daughter to send news of all the children, about their education and their health. He took pains to assure her that though he was "absent and away from you," "day and night I am always thinking about you all. How are dear Geoff, Charlotte, Maria and my dear little toddling Emma, I fancy I see the latter now, stepping about the sofa where I used to lay down and read, God almighty bless her and you all, do my dear first born write to your old father." He concluded by giving her his address.[66]

This couple apparently dealt with separation genteelly and retained some level of mutual caring. They communicated, if rather irregularly, following their estrangement. In subsequent letters to her daughter, Caroline expressed concern that she had not heard from "your Papa for a week" or "for three weeks," and reported wondering how he was "getting on poor man." She wrote to him and encouraged Carrie to do so. Hinting at problems and past histories that are hidden to us, she conveyed her fear in March 1863 that "things are not all right, it makes me very anxious as usual."[67]

Separations, as Julie Hardwick notes, were among those occasions that entailed "constant negotiation of issues of authority and power on terms that refined the bases of both gender and kinship."[68] Caroline had to re-negotiate her position in the community as a separated wife and take responsibility for her and her children's housing and upbringing. In this, Caroline had many worries but a strong support system. By 1861, Carrie had graduated from normal school and was sending home some of her earnings from her teaching position in Buckingham, near Ottawa. Caroline's relatives assisted her with money, encouragement, and sociability. Her sister, Mary Ann, and brother-in-law, Dr. Robert Godfrey, were specially important. They provided Caroline and her children with emotional support, friendship, and fun, along with dresses for the girls. The cousins moved readily between the two households.

Caroline separated from her husband with evident pain, and possibly on her own initiative. Love and duty meant that most wives remained with their husbands and moved with them if they decided to try their fortune elsewhere. In 1850, the lawyer Adolphus Mordecai Hart left Montreal for the United States, six years after his marriage with Constance Hannah Hart. The visible products of his time there are literary and philosophical rather than legal. He was active in the Democratic Party and engaged in his passion for history and polemics, publishing profusely on a wide range of topics during his six years away. These included histories of paper-money issues in the American colonies before the revolution, of the discovery of the Mississippi Valley, a pamphlet on the liquor question, and a booklet on the reception of Harriet Beecher Stowe's *Uncle Tom's Cabin* in Paris. In the latter, this outspoken liberal crusader for the rights of Jews in Lower Canada and defender of Patriotes expressed his distaste for the hypocrisy behind much anti-slavery agitation, pointing out that many involved would never engage in social interactions with ex-slaves. He drew parallels between the condition of the working-classes of Europe and that of slaves. The treatise mixed realistic assessments of the challenges that racism posed for freed slaves faced with racist assertions that freedom and equality could not apply to the "negro race."[69]

Constance may not have joined her husband initially. David Rome's biography of Hart states that he left Montreal in 1850. That year the birth of their third son, Asher, was registered at the synagogue in Montreal. He did not survive. Their fourth child, Harriet, was born some time in 1852, in Trois-Rivières, Quebec. Adolphus may have travelled back and forth for a while, leaving Constance to care for their growing family in Montreal. At some point she joined him, for their second daughter, Miriam, was born in the United States, around 1855. They returned to Montreal in the late fifties or early sixties. Adolphus resumed his legal practice in the city. Their married life had begun in the old city, first on St.Vincent Street close to Édouard-Raymond Fabre and Luce Perrault, then on the prestigious Beaver Hall Terrace. On their return from the United States, Adolphus set up his office on Notre Dame Street in the old city, as so many lawyers did. They moved their residence onto the slopes of the mountain, settling with their four children into a comfortable home on Durocher Street, between Sherbrooke and Pine, just east of McGill University. The street was home to some of the city's most prominent judges and businessmen.[70] They lived on that street for the rest of their married lives, passing on their shared passion for research, writing, and history to their children.[71]

In 1865, Constance made her own particular claim to domesticity and bourgeois status by publishing a cookbook under the "name" of "A Montreal Lady." *Household Receipts or Domestic Cookery* was a respectable yet unusual undertaking for a wife in this period. Unlike in the most influential manual "of practical domesticity," *Mrs Beeton's Book of Household Management,* published in England just four years earlier, Constance did not offer social advice about cultural etiquette.[72] Nor did she seek to assist newcomers to Canada with the challenges of Canadian cooking as Catharine Parr Traill had eleven years earlier in her *Female Emigrants' Guide.* Her book contained only recipes, commended, she explained, by "women in fashionable circles" in Montreal. Most were very simple. The historian of Canadian cookbooks Elizabeth Driver points out that only ball soup was particularly Jewish, and her recipie mentioned only crackers rather than the matzo meal or crackers normally used for matzo ball soup. Yet this small cookbook made its own modest impact on the history of publishing in Canada. It was, Driver reports, the first such book published in English in Quebec, and the first published in Canada by a Jewish author. It must have filled local needs, for two years later a second edition appeared. By then, Constance and Aldophus' eldest son, Emile, was aged twenty and working in the family business. Gerald was two years younger. At fifteen and twelve, the two girls were still of school age. Constance may have done some of her own cooking, but she had the help of at least one servant. The labour of her Irish Catholic domestic liberated her to pursue her interest in collecting recipes and to engage in charitable works.[73] Adolphus continued to explore issues of inequality and difference and to provoke controversy in writing, in addition to maintaining his law practice. He is considered to have been the author of a pamphlet entitled *The Political State and Condition of her Majesty's Protestant Subjects in the Province of Quebec,* published in 1871, which David Rome reports was so controversial it was "purchased and destroyed by the government."[74]

The Harts benefited from the privilege of family connections, education, and wealth. They had no trouble re-establishing themselves on their return to Montreal. In contrast, the decision of Joseph Jourdain and Mary Anne Forrest to leave Montreal and try their fortune in the United States was rooted in desperation. Jourdain was no more successful in Montreal than he had been in the Australian colonies. He had trouble finding employment. He lacked family connections. His in-laws had little faith in his abilities. Between the time of their marriage in 1845 and their departure in 1855, he was never listed in the directories of the city. Among the few traces of their lives that I have found are records of the birth and christening of their daughter, Elvira, in 1846; the birth and then burial of a son who lived for nineteen months and died in February 1851; and the birth of another daughter, Bertha, four years later.[75]

Shortly after Bertha's birth, Mary Anne and Joseph moved to New York. There, Ernest and Blanche were born in 1856 and 1858 respectively. Mary Anne wrote frequently to her mother. Her letters detail Jourdain's ongoing failure as a provider. In response to pleas to return home, Mary Anne frequently reminded her mother that they left Montreal convinced that Jourdain would never find a suitable "situation" there. Jourdain's inability to secure stable employment persisted. From New York they moved first to Philadelphia and then to the Boston area. Mary Anne's letters chronicle their bad luck and rapid social decline and excuse Jourdain's failures: a prospective employer died suddenly; in 1858, the "panic" ruined many of the clients for whom he was writing advertisements; in 1864, it was the "feeling against Englishmen" that was preventing him from finding work. She represented herself variously to her parents as a victim, a loving daughter, a loyal wife, and a tough mother who would take on anything to provide for her children. Not long after arriving in Philadelphia she reported that they had sold all their furniture except trunks and bedding, for only US$52.50. The furniture that Joseph had gifted to Mary Anne when they married had been valued at £330, or some $990. This cannot have been the first lot of furniture sold to raise money. In 1858, one child nearly died of typhoid fever. Two years later, Mary Anne was "very ill all winter," then had "a very bad miscarriage." Letters described other illnesses and attempts to earn money making shirts. "You will be horror-struck," she wrote in 1864, "when I tell you that I have to work just the same on Sunday as on [a] week day I am worked harder than any Slave in the South, to enable me to have the children in a fit state to attend Church and Sunday School."[76]

As pleas for assistance, these letters were successful, though Mary Anne would argue she was not begging, just expressing "her thoughts and feelings" and her "over burdened heart" to her mother. Her parents sent small sums of money. She always let them know that they arrived at critical moments. At times they sheltered some of the children, and they offered repeatedly to house the family in their home while Jourdain sought work, should the couple decide to return to Montreal. To this request Mary Anne replied that she would rather "die of Starvation here" than deprive her parents of comfort on her behalf.[77]

Mary Anne consistently parried critiques of her husband and his ability to provide. The final letter that remains of this ongoing negotiation of her place as both dutiful daughter and wife seems to respond to a suggestion from her mother that she had put her pride aside, possibly by taking on paid labour. Replying to her "dear mother" in 1864 she wrote:

> I have not put my pride in my pocket I am prouder now than ever. I am too proud to be dependent on my Father while my husband lives, if I can possibly avoid it, and I am proud to think ... that with my own hands I can earn money enough to dress myself and Family respectably ... I will continue on until the fall and then if there is no better prospect for the winter I suppose I must accept my Fathers kind offer, altho I feel as if I should never have a home of my own again. It will be a hard and bitter pill to swallow.[78]

There the collection of letters in the archives ends. Mary Anne never returned permanently to Montreal. Her parents moved to Ottawa, and she remained in the United States at least until Joseph's death there in 1888. When the census was taken in 1881, they were still living in the Boston area. Joseph was by then aged sixty-five and described as a journalist, Mary Anne was fifty-four and "keeping house." In one of the letters written to her mother when the children were young, she had said that she felt she had to "struggle on until the children are able to do something to help me." By 1881, this was happening. The four children from that marriage were all still living with them, and the eldest boy, Ernest, was working as a clerk. Elvira, Bertha, and Blanche, then aged thirty-three, twenty-six, and twenty-two respectively, were described only as "at home."[79]

Mary Anne's story is exceptional in that her mother saved her letters. They leave us with parts of the story of a marriage in which the husband failed to secure work that would allow them to live in the middle-class style in which they had begun their married life. They lived instead "in a very plain way," with Mary Anne's earnings clothing her and the family "respectably." Mary Anne's letters offer no hints about any personal traits that inhibited Joseph's work chances. His experiences underline the insecurities of life on the fringes of the middle classes, adding a North American case to the "considerable anecdotal evidence for the existence of a substantial and insecure group of professionals" and clerical workers that R.J. Morris reports on for England in the same period.[80]

Wives, Husbands, and Civil Society

Constance Hannah Hart's cookbook placed her name in the public world of print, while linking it concurrently to the essentially domestic question of food and its preparation. Other middle-class and elite wives from these two generations of marriages participated in a range of associations and public activities formed through their churches or non-denominational but religiously inspired reform groups, or organized for political ends. As in other North American cities, women's initiatives reshaped much of the provision of early-nineteenth-century charity. Montreal differed from most other North American or British cities in the bifurcation of Catholic and Protestant institutions and the absence of any poor law heritage, with its related public institutions. Of the wives from these two cohorts of marriages, Émilie Tavernier is the best known for her institution building and benevolence. After their marriage, she and her husband, Jean-Baptiste Gamelin, collaborated closely on charitable works, as well as in their business ventures. She assisted him in choosing the apples to purchase and in buying several orchards. When he was away in Quebec City selling apples and seeing to business, she acted as his "deputy husband," as so many women had done in this colony and elsewhere for generations. Both partners were devout Catholics. Both considered generosity to the poor a prime virtue. According to her biographer, Denise Robillard, the poor of the city knew that theirs was a door they could knock on in times of hunger.[81]

In the late 1820s and early 1830s, Émilie was at the forefront of organizing the renewal of lay Catholic responses to the problems of poverty in Montreal. I return in detail to these initiatives in Chapter 10. Working with her in creating an asylum for elderly and poor widows and later orphans were other Catholic women who married, as she did in the 1820s. Among them were her second cousin, Luce Perrault, wife of Édouard-Raymond Fabre; Marie-Louise Lacroix, wife of Charles-Séraphin Rodier; and Mary Carter, wife of the letter writer M. – Charles-Elzéar Mondelet. By the early 1840s, they were joined in this work by women of the younger generation. Marie-Anne Lessy de Montenach and Adelaide Quesnel took part in these initiatives prior to their marriages in the 1840s. Catholic daughters often followed in the footsteps of mothers who had raised them to take an active part working in and building new charitable institutions in the city.

Similarly, women who married in the 1820s were among the first female Protestant Montrealers to initiate and direct this kind of social activism, building and running parallel institutions. Elite Protestant women in 1815 formed the Female Benevolent Society, the first major Protestant charitable endeavour providing aid to women and children, replaced in 1822 by the Protestant Orphan Asylum. The younger generation kept the institutions going. Janice Harvey has shown that many of the women involved were mother-daughter pairs, and that a small group of interlocking bourgeois families, centred especially around the Anglican Ross/McCord/Tylee kin network, dominated the administration of the orphan asylum over the century. Jane Davidson Ross was involved from the beginning, serving on its committees from 1823 until her death in 1860 and drawing in three of her daughters. Mary Jane Ross was active before she married Robert Smith Tylee in 1845 at the age of twenty-six. She remained so afterward.[82] In 1843, when leading members applied for official incorporation, both Catherine Farquhar, who married Dr. William Sutherland a year later, and Susanna Holmes, who had married the merchant John McDonnell in 1824, were named.[83]

Susanna Holmes was also active in the Montreal Ladies' Benevolent Society, the other offshoot of the Female Benevolent Society. Initiated in 1832 to provide help to widows and orphans after the cholera epidemic, at the same time as Émilie Tavernier and other Catholic women created the Roman Catholic Orphan Asylum, it was formally incorporated in 1841. Susanna and Mary Jane Ross Tylee were among the women petitioning for its legal recognition. Working with them were Margaret White, who had married the wholesale grocer William Gay in 1826, and Elizabeth Molson who, as we saw, would marry the merchant and future senator David Lewis Macpherson in 1844. Some wives were active in such associations throughout their married lives. Others were more active once their children were of school age or older. In 1870, the women arranging the incorporation of the Protestant Infants' Home included Annabella Eadie, who had married Thomas Workman in 1845, and Caroline Scott Pelton's sister-in-law, Mary Ann, the wife since 1844 of Dr. Robert Godfrey. Anna and Mary Ann were in their late forties or early fifties at this time, possibly with more time on their hands than when their children were young.[84] In 1891, Mary Ann Scott was one of the "Lady Managers" and her husband was acting as one of the two consulting physicians.[85]

As single women, wives, and widows, these elite Anglo-Protestant Montrealer ladies built and directed that part of the Protestant system of private charity that provided social assistance for needy women and children, whereas men dealt with issues like outdoor relief and the House of Industry. Some, like their Catholic counterparts, were also involved in creating shelters for unwed mothers and their offspring. In these female-run institutions, elite and middle-class women exercised leadership and practised their commitment to Christian charity. As Protestant ladies, they hired other less privileged women as matrons and to perform other tasks. In Catholic institutions, these would eventually become the job of nuns. They visited the poor, attended meetings, and discussed the individual cases of children, coming to know much about working-class life.[86] Protestants and Catholic women alike exercised class power and privilege through assistance.

The women of these two generations were instrumental in forging a legitimate place for middle-class women in the intermediate spaces between the economy, politics, the home, and family. Servants at home made charitable work possible. Denise Robillard cites Romuald Trudeau, who described Canadienne women of his time developing a network of services for the poor and outcast as an essential part of "a nation taking measures to reconquer its civil and political liberty and to root it on solid bases." She suggests helpfully that there was a gendered division of labour in this nation-making project, with men dealing with politics and women building the social network.[87] Yet, such an argument separates politics too neatly from civil society and assumes a gendering of politics as male that was underway yet contested at the time.

Politics shaped men and women's lives in these years when the contours of British colonialism in Lower Canada were so hotly contested. Only men were active politicians. Only men could be elected to the Assembly or named to the Legislative Council or the executive. But political debates took place around family tables, as well as at political meetings and the hustings. Some of the women who married in the 1820s participated in elections as wives, more frequently, as we will see later, as widows. And when men were swept into the most visible political acts of the times – rebellion and repression – the lives of their wives, children, and mothers were affected.

Following the lengthy and tumultuous by-election of 1832 in Montreal West, Patriote and Tory organization intensified.[88] In Montreal, Patriote meetings took place daily in the building on St. Vincent Street that housed Édouard-Raymond Fabre's bookstore and home. The very practical Fabre took on a key role as an organizer, advisor, money raiser, and disseminator of printed information. To this end he purchased the *Vindicator* in 1832, placing it first under the editorship of the fiery Irish journalist Daniel Tracey, and then of of his Irish Catholic friend Edmund Bailey O'Callaghan. It offered information in English that countered the conservative, elite, and Protestant views circulated by the *Montreal Gazette* and the *Montreal Herald,* in the hope of attracting support among the growing numbers of Irish Catholic or liberal English-speaking immigrants in the city. Work, family, and politics intermingled in the different spaces of their building on St. Vincent Street, as they did throughout the city. Luce, his wife, was among the women who created the Club of Patriote Women in 1833. Her family were more fiery and outspoken Patriote supporters than the "sober and ambitious" Fabre. Both of her parents were militant Patriotes. Her brother, Charles-Ovide, friend and confident of Fabre, has been described as the "artisan of the famous victory" of Daniel Tracey in Montreal West in 1832.[89] As political conflict mounted, few Montrealers' lives were untouched by the intense politics of the times. This was especially true of the couples who married in the 1820s. By the 1830s, they were in the prime of their lives, and many were actively involved in reshaping the colony's economic, political, and social institutions.

Women married in the 1820s had husbands, brothers, and other relatives active on both sides of the political spectrum. Édouard-Étienne Rodier was among the radical supporters of the Patriotes who met and discussed their colony's future in Fabre's bookstore. This son of a voyageur was still a law student when he married Julie-Victoire Dumont in 1826. Their early years of marriage were financially precarious. His career was just beginning to flourish when she died in 1829. His remarriage in 1831 to the daughter of a wealthy merchant allowed him to dedicate himself to politics. In 1832, he was elected to the House of Assembly, a position he still held during the rebellions. His fiery, eloquent oratory contributed to building up the Patriote cause. Thousands of Montrealers met in Montreal in late October 1837 to hear him and other Patriote speakers promising to be faithful to their country or die.[90] He argued that the time for trusting the British to resolve local divisions was gone, and called for cannonballs rather than assemblies to solve the divisions between rulers and the Patriotes. In early November 1837, Rodier took part in the bloody clash between the Patriotes and the supporters of colonial rule on the streets of Montreal, and later that month he was part of the group planning to take the British fort at Saint Jean. Émilie Tavernier's brother François was equally passionate and involved. In October 1837, this "old radical" was at the head of one of the three detachments of a thousand Patriote men engaged in military exercises in the Saint Lawrence suburb and the Côte-à-Baron.[91]

In the early 1830s, a few of the English-speaking husbands, especially the Americans and Irish, were also supporters of the Patriotes. They included Oliver Wait, Caroline Campbell's husband. He had been considered a possible candidate for the Patriotes in the Montreal West by-election, though Daniel Tracey was the final choice. Caroline's father, who also supported the Patriote candidates, was an early target of violence in that election.[92] Most others threw their weight vigorously on the side of the governor and the Tory politics of the members of the Legislative Council.

The impact of the rebellions of 1837 and 1838 on many Patriote families was devastating. Luce Perrault's brother, Charles-Ovide, was killed at the Battle of Saint Denis in late 1837. Louis-Joseph Papineau claimed that Luce's mother, Marie-Anne Lamontagne, lauded her children for having acted "not out of ambition, but out of love of their country and hatred against the injustices endured."[93] Fabre's role was prominent, though he did not take part in active fighting. After a brief foray to the earliest battle-grounds to try to persuade his friends Papineau and O'Callaghan to flee to the United States, he went into hiding in the colony for seven months, leaving Luce to manage their household and three children, then aged three to ten. In December 1838, he was arrested and imprisoned. Wives whose husbands fled the colony or were deported or executed experienced longer absences and widowhood. Political absences and anxieties took their toll in many ways. Édouard-Étienne Rodier was separated from his second wife, Elise Beaupré, and his young children for over nine months. She faced severe financial problems and sought to separate her goods from those of her absent husband.[94] The financial and emotional struggles of Ludger Duvernay's wife, Reine Harnois, as she and her sister cared for their children while he was in exile, have been well documented by Françoise Noel.[95] Luce Perrault was pregnant at the time of Fabre's arrest. She had a miscarriage, which Louis-Hippolyte LaFontaine claimed threatened her life and was caused by her anxiety about Édouard-Raymond's imprisonment.[96] Édouard-Étienne Rodier died of exhaustion a year and a half after his return from Vermont, leaving Elise a widow and his daughter fatherless.[97]

In the early 1840s, Fabre threw himself into the campaign to bring the exiles home to their wives and children. He raised funds for their return from the United States or Australia, personally securing gifts from the new governor Sir Charles Metcalfe, along with more likely donors among Montreal's bourgeois Patriotes. Fabre adeptly deployed the gendered language of dependency to make his point. When the colonial secretary's assistant neglected one appeal, he wrote again, "demanding him in the name of the women whose husbands were exiled" to talk to Lord Stanley, the colonial secretary, to determine whether they had to pay their own costs to return. Eventually, the government agreed to pay to reunite these families.[98]

Fabre's career suffered no long-term setbacks after the rebellions. He continued to invest wisely and to expand the operations of the bookshop. He accommodated to the increasingly ultramontane religious atmosphere of the post-rebellion years, publishing more and more religious material. In 1848, he was elected as a city councillor and in 1849 became the sixth mayor of Montreal. Like Hannah Lyman, Luce took on the tasks required of "The Lady Mayoress." Between their wedding day and 1854, Luce gave birth to eleven babies.[99] Only five survived their first year: Édouard-Charles, Hortense, and Hector were born prior to the rebellions, and Gustave-Raymond and Marie-Anne Hectorine were born in 1842 and 1854, respectively. Luce's child-bearing years began nine and a half months after her marriage, when she was around sixteen years old, and continued until she was about forty-two.

Together, this prominent and affectionate couple micro-managed "the establishment of our children."[100] Fabre, as economist in his approach to family matters as he was to business, politics, and running the city, told his sister in Paris that he and Luce were proud that so many friends complimented them on their children; "We spend lots of money for them ... it will be reimbursed five-fold by our contentedness and the good they do with it." When his eldest son, Édouard-Charles, wrote from Paris in the 1840s of his plans to join the church, Fabre insisted that he had hoped his investment would lead Édouard-Charles to take up something more useful to his fellow citizens. Fabre also strongly encouraged his daughter, Hortense, to marry the rising lawyer and future prominent politician George-Etienne Cartier. "Our daughter cost us a lot," he wrote to his sister, "we have made great sacrifices for her education, but we will marry her advantageously, we have known this young man for 12 years, he was always a friend of the house, she will be happy, we are sure, he is certainly one of the leading parties in Montreal, excellent lawyer, and brilliant in business."[101] They married in June 1846. In 1850, Édouard-Charles was ordained. For this liberal son of a master blacksmith who had climbed socially through his own hard work and the connections his wife's family opened up, it was important that his children use their education to contribute to Quebec society and that they continue the family's social ascension, or at least maintain his status.

Women's contributions ranging from bedroom furniture and wooden chairs to sets of silver and mahogany pianos shaped the material comfort of new households in ways appropriate to their class and culture. Types of wood, numbers of rooms, serving places or utensils, the presence or absence of mirrors and of maps or prints and pictures on the walls, or books on the shelves – these were material markers of class difference that transcended Montreal's cultural divides. Personal contacts, connections, good health, and good relations were also significant assets, maintained and nurtured by some wives and some husbands, shattered by or denied to others. Skills at housework, running a household, stretching incomes, or nursing sick family members were other assets that varied among women and were vital to the workings of companionate patriarchies.

Yet, much about the marriage trajectories of these two generations of spouses was a matter of luck and circumstance. Ill health, disease, and debt haunted families of all classes with their menaces of poverty and death. Companionate patriarchy in all its legal varieties worked for some couples, not for others. Illness, drink, men's failures as breadwinners, or incompatibility led to temporary and permanent separations between spouses at all social levels. Husbands nurtured wives. Husbands beat wives. Some women fought back using the law. Maria Mitchell tried once but did not leave Thomas Spiers, despite his violence on many of their shared drinking sprees. Mary Anne Forrest followed Joseph Jourdain to the United States despite his failure as a good provider. Other wives ran away or separated, for diverse reasons. Thus, a minority of wives assumed the position of female family head and alone, or with the support of kin, secured housing and raised their children on their own for short periods or permanently.

Convention, affection, respect, love, children, and the lack of viable alternatives kept most women within the companionate patriarchies of marriage. In homes ranging from one room to large mansions, they bore children, raised and lost children. Although most elite women would have both preached and practised some version of the understanding that the home was women's sphere, and politics and the economy men's, the trajectories of many of these wives show that they also blurred those boundaries, moving among political, social, and domestic activities, appropriate to their class, religion, and culture, and creating and running institutions in the intermediate spaces of charitable activities. The building in which Luce Perrault first raised her family included domestic, social, business, and political spaces. The dinners she oversaw fed the family and fuelled her husband's political engagements. It is to the politics of the period, and to the particular place of debates about property registration, inheritance, and the rights of married women and widows that the next chapter turns.

4

"Dower This Barbarous Law"

Debating Marriage and Widows' Rights

Go see Mr Ogden and Sir James Stuart, or if they fail, the Governor of the Country will explain to you why you are wrong and I, who am for the English law, am right without reason. If you were more loyal, you would understand.

– M., letter to the editor, *L'Aurore des Canadas,* 18 December 1840

When Marie-Louise-Josephte Chartier de Lotbinière married the recently arrived Scottish hardware merchant Robert Unwin Harwood in 1823, they agreed in their marriage contract to keep each spouse's property separate. Marie-Louise also explicitly renounced any claim she might have as a widow to dower. Instead, Robert promised her an annuity of £200 and the use of all their household furniture and carriages should he die first.[1] This provision in their marriage contract prevented her dower rights from complicating any land sales he may have wished to make. It could not prevent other widows' claims to dower from complicating his or other people's land purchases. Robert was called upon to contemplate this aspect of dower when he was invited by Governor Colbourne in 1839 to sit on the Special Council set up to rule the colony following the suspension of the Legislative Assembly and Council after the rebellions.[2] Among the many ordinances these elite and loyal men, so hated by the Patriotes, would pass was the Registry Ordinance. It transformed widows' claims to dower in the colony and married women's legal rights.[3] It was to the special councillors' discussions of dower that M. was referring in his letter to the editor titled "Dower this barbarous law." This chapter examines widows' dower rights under the law and the debates about dower in the years leading up to the consideration of the Registry Ordinance in the Special Council in 1840. The following one explores the individualized provisions that couples made for widowhood, death, and burials in marriage contracts and wills and through joining associations covering the costs of burials.

In assessing these debates, I try to disentangle the threads of public discourses in which posturing about the advantages of the Custom of Paris versus English common law sometimes meshed and sometimes conflicted, with changing understandings of freedom of contract, of property, gender, and power within families. Feminist historians have only briefly discussed the significance of these debates about dower.[4] And Canadian historians have paid little attention to the significance of the Registry Ordinance, and surprisingly little to the rule of the Special Council.[5] Yet, this essentially domestic question about a woman's claim on her husband's property was intimately linked to the major political, economic, cultural, and national issues of nineteenth-century Lower Canada. It was negotiated, debated, and discussed in public and in private. To date, the changes to widows' rights occurring within this ordinance have been presented rather simply in Quebec women's history as part of a broader dismantling of women's rights in the early nineteenth century that included loss of both the right to vote and dower. I want to paint a more complex picture of what was changing, of the significance of the Registry Ordinance, and of its long-term legacy.[6] The political debate has left records in colonial papers, newspapers, pamphlets, journals of legislative assemblies and councils, and in some private papers. I draw largely on these sources here.

Dower in the Custom of Paris

Marguerite Paris' marriage to the labourer Joseph Guilbault meant that if he died first she could claim her right as a widow to dower in addition to her ownership of half the property they accumulated during their marriage. Widows' dower rights varied in different legal regimes. In the common law jurisdictions of the other colonies of British North America, most of the United States, and England, widows' dower rights guaranteed them the use of the rents and profits from a third of their husbands' real property for their lifetime – hence references to a "widow's third." If a husband had not made a will, this property passed to the children after the widow's death. When husbands made wills, widows could opt to take their dower right instead of following their wishes, if this seemed advantageous to them.

Under the Custom of Paris, widows had a larger claim. Unless specified otherwise in a marriage contract, dower gave widows the use of half "the estates which the husband ... possesses on the wedding day," as well as half of any inherited during the marriage.[7] These customary dower provisions, especially in conjunction with the community property created by all marriages unless a contract stipulated otherwise, offered wives and widows a more generous proportion of family assets than under the English common law. In both legal systems, dower rights offered some kind of compensation for wives' inability to control property during the marriage and provided a basis for their support in widowhood.[8] However, many immigrant and labouring husbands possessed little if any such property when they married. For Marguerite Paris and the growing number of other women married to propertyless men, dower was a meaningless right.

As M.'s letter made clear, dower or its alternative could be specified in a marriage contract made prior to a wedding – this was known as a stipulated *douaire* or *douaire prefix*. But wives' right to dower as widows required no written document. Dower existed automatically as a claim on husbands' real property from the moment of marriage. This was known in the Custom of Paris as the customary dower – *le douaire coutumier*. Thus, in the absence of a marriage contract, marriage meant that all of a man's own property was encumbered with a general hypothec or mortgage to ensure his wife's dower, should she outlive him. A widow's dower took precedence over the claims of any other creditors of an estate. And it was not extinguished if land was sold during the marriage. It was to get around this tenacity of dower that laws were passed in most common law jurisdictions over the late eighteenth and early nineteenth centuries that made it easy for wives to relinquish their dower rights during the process of conveyancing.[9] No such provisions existed in Lower Canada.

Dower as Dangerous Terrain: Debating Dower

M.'s sarcastic letter critiqued the concept of civilization that was so central to British justifications of colonial rule. In referring to dower as a barbarous law, Mondelet explicitly pointed to its opposite – civilization. By representing English law as pushing widows onto the streets and French law, with its dower, as providing protection, he was hitting at what was both the heart and the Achilles heel of the favourite British claim to a superior civilization: their supposedly superior treatment of women. Catherine Hall has argued that the British defined and judged "the masculine and feminine characteristics of other peoples" against those "of the one 'truly civilized' society, Britain. And Britain celebrated, in theory at least, the family as the keystone of that civilization, with its manly, independent male heads of households, dignified by their labour and operating in the world of work and politics, and its feminine, dependent wives and mothers, confined to the sphere of home. This superior form of family, with its elevated yet inferior female, was critical to the British legitimation of colonial rule."[10] Patriotes like Mondelet played with such British claims, asserting their own superior treatment of women. British colonizers, in turn, represented French Canada as feudal and priest-ridden.

Dower rights were one of many kinds of "secret encumbrances" that some British merchants tiraded against and sought to eliminate from the 1790s until 1841. To men with common law-rooted conceptions of marriage, dower provisions were outrageous not because they helped widows but because they complicated the easy buying and selling of land. In the public pronouncements of these men, dower assumed the shape of a feudal devil casting the shadow of widow's weeds over the land and freezing up the possibilities of honest and open exchange of land. If the law respecting "the legal consequences of marriage on the property of the parties, remains unaltered, the English will be deterred from settling in the country," J. Stephen asserted to the Select Committee hearings on the Civil Government of Canada, held by the British House of Commons in 1828. In this largely anglophone vision, dower was one element of an outmoded legal system controlled by notaries who kept their documents under lock and key.[11]

Mondelet was reiterating Canadiens' frustration with the elaboration of these "anatomies of difference ... across the axes of class, race and gender" that positioned them as an inferior civilization. He and others contested the representations of Canadiens as backward, feudal, and likely to be led by priests or demagogues because of their Catholicism. The administration must stop "making and supporting distinctions of race in all its administrative or social relations," wrote Louis-Hippolyte LaFontaine to Edward Ellice in 1838.[12] For a while, Canadiens presented their dower as evidence of their better treatment of widows and orphans. In the public and private pronouncements of leading Canadien politicians from the late eighteenth century on and among Patriotes until the mid-1830s, dower shines as a beacon, signalling the enlightened nature of a marriage law that looked after "widows and minors," the powerless members of families most in need of protection. The moderate anglophone John Neilson explained he had not supported a bill to create registry offices because wives and "children would lose their privileges."[13]

These divergent visions of marriage and widows' rights were pronounced in the Legislative Assembly and Council. They were presented to British politicians by the men who appeared before the 1828 Select Committee. And they occupied columns of the city's newspapers. In debates about the law before the mid-1830s, dower seemed to constitute a danger zone, a word difficult to utter without conjuring up different visions of family, gender, and property that divided Canadiens from more recent colonists. Successive governors suggested instituting a system of land registration. Talk of registry offices invariably invoked the question of dower. At least nine bills were introduced in either the Assembly or the Council from 1817 through to 1836. Some were designed by Tories, others by Canadiens and by Patriotes. The clever moderate nationalist Joseph-Rémi Vallières de Saint-Réal proposed a bill in 1823 in the Legislative Assembly that would have led to the public registration of all instruments related to real property.[14] It did not pass in the Legislative Council. Indeed, every attempt between 1785 and the 1830s to introduce some kind of land registry system, to make the ownership of land public in some other way, or to eliminate other kinds of secret encumbrances foundered unless dower was excluded.[15] Registry offices were established only in the Eastern Townships, where land was held under free and common socage rather than the seigneurial system, as was true in Montreal and elsewhere in the colony.[16]

The most militant crusaders for registry offices were the ardent Tories and constitutionalists who opposed the Patriotes. Most prominent was the Montreal fur trader, merchant, and Legislative Council member George Moffatt. This "moral leader" of the English-speaking community and rabid opponent of the French Canadians in the Assembly would later be described privately as "the most pig headed, obstinate, ill tempered brute in the Canadas" by Charles Poulett Thomson, later Lord Sydenham, who became governor after Lord Durham's departure in 1838.[17] During the 1830s, Moffatt began to push doggedly to create registry offices. He backed and probably initiated an 1836 petition to the Legislative Council from Montreal inhabitants seeking registry offices. He was likely behind the Legislative Council's promotion of wider debate on the issue by ordering that 250 copies of the petition be printed in English and French. That year, Moffatt chaired a special committee of the Legislative Council set up to study the question. It sent questionnaires to members of the province's elite soliciting their opinions about the need for a system of registration and the problems caused by dower. The report of his subcommittee seriously misrepresented the diversity of opinions expressed in response to the questionnaires. Many of the respondents voiced their preference for some system of registration and limitation of dower in moderate terms. Some expressed their concern about the need to protect widows. Yet, the report stressed the "numerous instances of fraud and destructive loss" caused by dower. Dower had "been productive of serious injury" and was the "fruitful source of many of the evils complained of."[18] The bill that his committee drafted to make mortgages and hypothecs special and abolish customary dower was passed in the Council. As was usual in these pre-rebellion years when the Assembly and Council were at loggerheads, the Assembly took no action.[19]

Moffatt did not give up. Late in 1837, when discontent and difference had erupted into armed conflict, the Constitutional Association of the District of Montreal – the most vocal opponents of the Patriotes – sent

him and William Badgley to England. Their mission was to encourage the
imperial government to pass bills the association believed were important
for the colony. Both men were keenly interested in making sure a system
of registration became law. Like Moffatt, William Badgley had already contributed to shaping the emerging discourse on registration and dower. In
1836, he published a series of articles, first in the *Montreal Herald* under the
pseudonym of "Civis," and later in a pamphlet under his own name, arguing that registry offices were the best way of ensuring the security of investments in land. More conciliatory than Moffatt in the tone of his public
writing, Badgley suggested that it would be possible to make changes in
ways that respected the principles of the Custom of Paris and did not
interfere with "old prejudices" or disturb "existing rights." He pointed out
that a system of registration for land ownership and mortgages had been
established in France in 1795 and that the customary dower had been abolished there. Similar changes, he concluded, would help "retain Capital" in
the colony and advance and improve the country.[20] Once in England,
Moffatt and Badgley again stressed the need for a good system of land
registration, explicitly linking the barring of customary dower to the abolition of seigneurial land tenure. And they made sure that Lord Durham
knew that Moffatt's bill to abolish customary dower and the elimination of
dower had already passed the Legislative Council. They misleadingly implied that it had received general satisfaction in the province.[21]

As Lower Canada lurched toward open rebellion, and the last shreds of
cooperation between the elected Assembly and the appointed Legislative
Council broke down, Patriotes also embraced the possibility of accepting
the abolition of the customary dower – the dower that existed for Marguerite
Paris and all other women who did not make a marriage contract. Many
also accepted the possibility of some kind of registration system. This shift
in the Patriote position on dower meshes with their willingness to abolish
the vote for women and to transform what Allan Greer has called "the
politico-sexual order." It fits the politics of a largely middle-class group
dominated by professionals, with a sprinkling of merchants, seigneurs, and
landlords, "busily laying the cultural foundations of a capitalist order." And
above all, it fits their embrace of a liberalism that gave primacy to the individual property rights of men and to easy exchange. Dower rights tied up
credit. They inhibited a man's right to accumulate and to freely dispose of
his property, and made it difficult to buy or lend money for land purchases
with certainty. Buying urban land, as Paul-André Linteau and Jean-Claude
Robert argued years ago, was one of the economic pursuits in which elite
Canadien Montrealers were especially successful.[22]

A letter published in the Patriote paper *La Minerve* in early 1836 argued
that the frequency of land sales in the colony made it logical to abolish

customary dower. Its author claimed that most couples marrying without a written marriage contract had no intention of creating such a dower: "The husband does not intend to submit his goods to it, the wife never counts on this clause as a basis for living upon as a widow." In November, another letter argued that dower was causing problems for land purchases in rural areas too, and that the bill proposed in 1836 but blocked by the Legislative Council would have solved existing problems.[23] When, a year later, Patriotes advertised a public meeting to discuss seigneurial dues and dower rights during the rebellions, they were announcing a public platform for the reformulated Patriote vision of social relations. In this, as Greer suggests, husbands and fathers would be in sole possession and full control of property: "Wives and seigneurs should not be allowed to interfere." Greer has suggested that these subjects were secondary to the burning constitutional issues of the time. Yet, dower was not just a private or domestic question. It was a critical political and economic issue. In the emerging Patriote discourse, patriarchy, capitalism, and liberal rights were interwoven public issues.[24] In this they were not far from the position of their opponents. Witness a meeting in Montreal's Place d'Armes around the same time at which James Holmes spoke to a loyalist assembly facing flags announcing "Our two grand objects – Registry Offices and Abolition of Feudal Tenures."[25]

As the Patriotes' composition shifted and radicals replaced the more social conservatives like Papineau, abolishing customary dower was more explicitly linked to other new citizenship claims. When the Montreal Patriote Dr. Robert Nelson issued the radical Declaration of Independence in March 1838, three of the key eighteen resolutions called for the abolition of customary dower, the creation of registry offices, and for making all mortgages special rather than general. Other key demands were universal male suffrage for those over twenty, the same civil rights for all, including Indians, freedom of the press, abolition of seigneurial tenure, and voting by ballot.[26]

By 1838, then, it seems that dower had lost its earlier position as a key rupture point between French and English and between civil law and common law concepts of family and widows' rights. A bourgeois, liberal view of dower dominated among conservatives, radicals, nationalists, and constitutionalists alike. Dower was fused with ancient, outmoded practices, especially the feudal relations of the seigneurial system as a reason for the difficulties of attracting industry and capital to the province. Widows and their rights virtually disappeared from the idea of dower, reconstituted as nothing more and nothing less than an impediment to the circulation of capital and the easy buying and selling of land.[27]

The Registry Ordinance: "A Law That Would Never Have Been Passed by a Free Legislature"

Initially, the men appointed to the Special Council that ruled the colony following the suspension of elected government after the rebellions included equal numbers of anglophones and francophones.[28] In early April 1838, then-governor Sir John Colbourne invited George Moffatt and Dominique Mondelet, the politically moderate brother of M. (Charles-Elzéar Mondelet), to join what was by then a council with twenty members.[29] During his short tenure, Lord Durham chose instead men from his own retinue to avoid councillors with a stake in the virulent local politics.[30] After his departure in November 1838, Governor Colbourne again sought to balance English- and French-speaking councillors, but there were many resignations, especially of Canadiens. In July 1839, Robert Unwin Harwood was informed that the new governor, Charles Poulett Thomson, soon to be Lord Sydenham, wished to appoint him to the Special Council if he had no objections. Harwood replied that he would not "shrink from the responsibility" given the current crisis and the important measures that were to be considered.[31]

There were many reasons why Robert Harwood might have hesitated or refused to accept this onerous appointment. These were familial, personal, and political. He and Marie-Louise were no longer living in Montreal where the Council met. After their marriage in 1823, they had set up house in a building valued at over £400 on St. Hubert Street, in the easternmost part of the old city, near his family hardware business. For six years he continued to work in the business with his brother. The firm prospered, and Robert gradually withdrew from the day-to-day work, hiring a skilled metalworker to run the shop and entrusting him to make improvements to the machinery and act as superintendent. Robert Sweeny describes Harwood as one of the early Montreal merchants to invest in manufacture, divide up the labour process, and initiate technological change.[32]

Harwood's engagement of a skilled mechanic to run his factory was also influenced by family matters. That year, Marie-Louise, by then the mother of several children, turned twenty-five. She was the eldest of three girls. Her father's will had specified that his children were to inherit his three seigneuries once they reached that age. So her birthday precipitated the division of his considerable holdings of seigneurial property. The process of evaluating her father's property was very slow. In 1825, three years after her father's death, the family chose Louis-Joseph Papineau and the lawyer Hughes Heney as tutor and subtutor for her two sisters, who were still minors. The heavy involvement of these men in the Patriote politics of the times had prevented the required evaluation of the properties that had to precede their division among the heirs. In 1829, the family appointed the girls' uncle, Henry Munro, and Paul-Joseph Lacroix instead. By then, the other sisters were also married. The document describing the distribution of the property states that they agreed amicably that each would receive one of their father's three seigneuries.[33]

Marie-Louise inherited the seigneury of Vaudreuil. In most marriages, husbands' careers, capacities, and health significantly shaped the unfolding of women's married lives. In contrast, the trajectory followed by Marie-Louise and Robert Unwin Harwood was shaped by her inheritance. The couple may have maintained a city house, as did so many other seigneurs for whom Montreal was the centre of social and political life. But they soon made the seigneury their primary residence, building a substantial three-storey stone manor house for their growing family. According to John Thompson's short biography, Harwood happily gave up trade and business for the life of a seigneur. He commuted "seigneurial property into freehold tenure" well before other seigneurs and was reputed to be fair and honest. Thus, Harwood was able to lead the life of the English gentry, blending modern business and feudal rights, though he apparently avoided the unpleasant task of taking tenants to court for not paying their seigneurial dues.[34]

Accepting the position on the Special Council would mean travelling over forty kilometres across the Île-Perrot and the western part of the Island of Montreal into the city. He would have to take up residence in town away from his wife and children for the time the sessions lasted, or bring them with him into town.[35] His fellow councillor Edward Hale, who lived even further away in Sherbrooke, complained to his wife, Eliza, frequently about being an "absentee from my snug little home." Contrasting his living situation alone in a hotel "with what it might have been living in my own House with my dear Wife and dear Children," Hale concluded that he had been foolish for accepting to be on the Council.[36] Possibly more daunting for Harwood was the company he would keep. Harwood had never shared the virulent anti-Patriote, anti-French, and often anti-Catholic politics of many of the leaders of Montreal's English-speaking business community. After all, Marie-Louise was both French speaking and Catholic. Yet Harwood's marriage and business acumen had helped place him among that elite, leading to his nomination to the grand jury presiding over criminal cases at several points between 1824 and 1828. There he worked alongside Peter McGill, John Molson, George Moffatt, and other prominent English Protestant merchants. In 1832, Governor Aylmer had appointed him to the Legislative Council of Lower Canada at a time when it was increasingly under attack for blocking Patriote initiatives. Canadiens were in a minority, and the English party was headed by the belligerent George Moffatt and John Richardson, another Montreal merchant. Perhaps the governor hoped that Harwood's moderation would temper the divides of those tumultuous years. But Harwood said very little. John Thompson argues that "as a moderate and youthful member, he had little influence." His tenure was short. By the time the Patriotes sent their Ninety-Two Resolutions to England in 1834, singling out Peter McGill, George Moffatt, and John Molson as among the most problematic members of this council that pretended to be specially appointed "to protect one class of Her Majesty's subjects," he had turned his full attention to the seigneury.[37]

As a moderate liberal with an interest in reform and links through family and friends to the Patriotes, Harwood might well have dreaded further close relationships with McGill, Moffatt, and Molson, all of whom were already members of the Special Council and determined to use the suspension of elected government to push through their favourite policies.[38] Yet, he had already reached out to maintain some level of civility, for these were important, influential men. When he first arrived from Scotland, Harwood had joined the Montreal Masonic Lodge in which George Moffatt, William Badgley, and Peter McGill were all office holders. When he left the city, he had apparently misunderstood the terms on which he could maintain his membership and was expelled for not paying his dues. Early in 1839, he wrote to Badgley expressing both his annoyance at his expulsion and his satisfaction at having "again broken bread" with him "in brotherly peace." This reconciliation may have helped pave the way for his invitation to join Badgley's friends on the Council (see Figure 4.1).[39]

Did Marie-Louise provide any advice for or against accepting the position? Politics were certainly not foreign to her. There were politicians on both sides of her family. Her father, as noted earlier, had been elected to the first Legislative Assembly in 1792 and initiated the equal recognition of English and French as the working languages of that body. Her grandfather on her mother's side, John Munro, was a member of the Legislative Council of Upper Canada. Robert accepted and was formally appointed in early August 1839. He joined the fourth Special Council, the first under the new governor Charles Poulett Thomson, who was elevated to the peerage as Lord Sydenham some months later.[40] Hundreds of repressive and controversial ordinances had already passed. Initially, these dealt with the aftermath of the rebellion, suspending habeas corpus, and legitimating arrests and repression. In subsequent sessions, Brian Young has argued, they developed and passed a series of ordinances that swept "over the whole field of the law of real property"; reshaped the laws surrounding bankruptcy, insolvency, and credit; set up new police forces in the major cities; and began reshaping the administration of justice.[41]

FIGURE 4.1   Robert Unwin Harwood, about twenty years after he sat on the Special Council. Marie-Louise-Josephte Chartier de Lotbinière likely had this image copied shortly after his death in 1863. | Anonymous, copied 1863, silver salts on paper mounted on paper, albumen process. McCord Museum, Notman Photographic Archives, I-7807.0.1.

George Moffatt had hoped that a bill setting up registry offices and abolishing dower that he had drafted would be passed soon after he joined the Special Council. Other members were clearly also expecting to deal with such a project early in their mandate. Friends and relatives lobbied councillors for the new patronage positions that would be required to operate a system of registry offices throughout the colony.[42] But this was a complex subject. There was some concern that it went beyond the councillors' jurisdiction because it involved fees, and the Special Council had no taxing powers.[43] At the time Harwood joined, no new bill had been drafted, and there seemed to be no question of using Moffatt's earlier one. By the time the special councillors turned their attention to the issue of registry offices, their mandate had virtually expired. Late in 1840, a bill drafted by James Stuart was finally introduced. Stuart, "a pillar of the British Party," a brilliant, arrogant, mercurial lawyer with experience as the colony's attorney general, was well versed in both English and French law. Between its introduction on Thursday, 5 November 1840, and Syden- ham's signature of the ordinance on 9 February 1841, it was sent to a subcommittee for amendments, then discussed again on twelve occasions. The Registry Ordinance became law the day before the Union of Upper and Lower Canada was proclaimed. It took effect on the last day of December 1841.[44]

The council sat six days a week except on holidays or when there was no quorum. By the time Harwood joined, many councillors had resigned. These included the political moderate John Neilson, Edward Hale's uncle of the same name, and many francophones. In these closing months, only five francophone appointees were present. Barthélemy Joliette was present the day after the Registry Ordinance was introduced and for the following week, then stopped attending. Joseph-Édouard Faribault attended on only two of the early occasions when the ordinance was discussed then never returned after 22 December. Jules-Maurice Quesnel and Dominique Mondelet attended more regularly. They were present on most of the four- teen days when clauses of the Ordinance were considered.[45]

Like George Moffatt, the men who discussed the ordinance were pre- dominantly Protestant, English speaking, and part of the well-established economic, social, and political elite.[46] The majority were from the genera- tion of elite Montrealers who had made their wealth in the fur trade and other forms of commerce but whose business interests were expanding to include banking, land companies and speculation, shipping, and in some cases industrial production. John Molson was among the second genera- tion of the beer-brewing family. He and the merchants Peter McGill and Samuel Gerrard were, had been, or would be directors of the Bank of Montreal or of some other bank. Many had long sought to anglicize the Custom of Paris. Most had political experience. Harwood and at least five others had been members of the Legislative Council for brief or longer periods over the two previous decades.[47] Several had been members of the Assembly. Most had made their loyalty only too clear during the rebellions. At least four had been members of the Constitutional Association.[48] Paul Holland Knowlton, a lesser merchant, had distinguished himself by captur- ing Wolfred Nelson, one of the Patriotes' military leaders. Charles Dewey Day had prosecuted the arrested Patriotes.[49]

In addition to this business elite there were men of legal training on the Special Council. Edward Hale told his wife that they were frequently at loggerheads with each other. Most important were James Stuart, framer of the registry bill, Charles Dewey Day, and Dominique Mondelet.

Dominique, like his brother, M. – Charles-Elzéar – was nationalist in his politics but had broken with the Patriotes prior to the Montreal West by-election of 1832, when he supported the Tory candidate Bagg over the Irish Patriote candidate, Daniel Tracey. In 1839, Dominique replaced the Patriote sympathizer Joseph-Rémi Vallières de Saint-Réal in the Court of Queen's Bench in Trois-Rivières. He remained distant from the Patriotes and their politics – hence his appeal to the governor. Charles-Elzéar, in contrast, became centrally involved in Montreal Patriote activities leading up to the rebellions, was imprisoned for a while afterward, and successfully defended four Patriotes accused of executing a loyalist Canadien during the rebellions by arguing that theirs was a political rather than a criminal act.[50]

Nearly all these men were married, several for the second time. George Moffatt had taken a First Nations wife in his fur-trading days; later, like so many fur traders, he took a European wife, Sophie McRae. Charles Ogden married for the first time in 1824. His first wife died soon after their marriage, and in 1829 he remarried. Most, like Robert Harwood, had considered dower and made alternative provisions for the possibility of leaving their wives as widows. At forty-two, Robert Unwin Harwood was among the youngest and well below the average age of fifty. The oldest, the Irish-born merchant Samuel Gerrard, was seventy-three. At thirty-four, Charles Dewey Day was the youngest. Harwood stood apart, too, as someone who had relinquished his business ties in Montreal, as a Protestant who had taken a Catholic and partly Canadienne wife, and as someone who had not been involved in the rebellions.[51]

Thus, Harwood's politics, age, marriage, and sensibilities set him apart from most of the other English-speaking councillors, and probably closer to those of Dominique Mondelet. They must have known each other quite well, for Dominique's wife, like Harwood's mother-in-law, came from the large Munro family. Edward Hale's letters to his wife shared much detail about the members of the Council and the policies under discussion. He distinguished between men who were independent as he and Harwood were, who were nearly all "dissatisfied with the goings on," and councillors who were "officers of government," at least one of whom on being told that he had to vote as he was instructed said he would "never sit in the council again."[52]

James Stuart presided over the Special Council and chaired the meetings. According to Edward Hale, he did so wretchedly. Hale complained to his wife that Stuart kept no order "and gets on with nothing at the same time that he is perpetually lecturing us." In contrast to the discussions of the Assembly and Legislative Council, no court clerk or newspapermen recorded the debates surrounding this or any other of the ordinances the Special Council passed. No verbatim reports appeared in the colony's newspapers. The sessions were held behind closed doors. Only the usual sparse recording of amendments and votes that had long appeared in the legislative journals offers formal information about the deliberations. "It is to be regretted," wrote John Bonner in 1852 when he was trying to make sense of the Registry Ordinance, "that we have no accounts of the debates of the Council at its various readings in committee." Thus, "we are compelled to grope through its many obscurities."[53]

The bill creating registry offices and curtailing dower was indeed lengthy, obscure, and complicated, as was its title. This seventy-eight-page piece of legislation set out to create registry offices that would facilitate land sales by rendering all claims on land visible through a system of registry offices that were to be set up throughout the province.[54] In drafting the sections concerning registration, Stuart drew on his wide knowledge of both civil and common law. He borrowed from the new civil code of post-revolutionary France and blended in procedures drawn from English acts setting up registries in York and Middlesex. The ordinance set out the details of the massive infrastructure and bureaucracy that would be required. Key sections addressed widows' dower and married women's rights.[55]

The changes to dower were radical but different from either those proposed by Badgley and Moffatt or those favoured by Patriotes. Stuart's ordinance made three major changes to the law regarding relations between husbands and wives and the rights of widows. The import of these changes and the meaning of the law were debated for decades to come in the Quebec courts. First, dowers promised in a marriage contract would no longer have precedence over other claims to a man's estate unless they were registered.[56] This was a curious provision. For nothing in the ordinance abolished customary dower, the dower that existed without a marriage contract and that Patriotes and constitutionalists alike had been pushing to eliminate or particularize.[57] Instead, the ordinance made it mandatory for husbands or guardians to register any dower stipulated in a marriage contract and to specify how it would be secured. Any other claims that wives might have on their husbands' property because of assets they brought into the marriage as their dowry also had to be registered. Failure to register did not eradicate widows' claims. Rather, dower would no longer rank ahead of other claims.

The councillors disagreed about who should be responsible for registration and on the appropriate penalties for neglecting to register. In what we can reconstruct of their deliberations, the plight of "the helpless widow and orphan," whose husband or guardian might fail to register their claims, was pitted against the desires of capitalists for easy access to information about titles. Moffatt, in particular, pushed constantly to minimize the power of dower. Usually, Day, Molson, and McGill supported him, whereas the remaining francophones, as well as Harwood and sometimes Stuart, dissented. Most councillors were determined to ensure that title could be readily ascertained. Amendments made it a misdemeanour, punishable by imprisonment for up to twelve months or a £500 fine, to knowingly take part in the sale of land subject to any kind of unregistered claim. Husbands would be coerced, if necessary, into learning their new obligation to register any claims their wives might have on their property.[58]

The second change gave women new but circumscribed powers within marriage. The ordinance recognized them as owners of their dower rights in unprecedented ways that, at the broadest level, brought the law in Lower Canada closer to conveyancing methods in common law jurisdictions. In his desire to make the alienation of land as easy as possible, Stuart jettisoned the inviolability of the dower under French law, allowing women to release customary dower rights on any property that their husband wished to sell during the marriage. This was a fundamental shift in the logic of a law that had viewed the dower as essentially children's property a woman could use during her widowhood. By allowing women to release their dower rights on land their husband wished to sell, Stuart was proposing to sever the bonds of protection characterizing the old law and to curtail children's claims. Wives gained a limited freedom to contract – the right to agree to alienate their dower. In setting out how women could do this, he drew on conveyancing rules sorted out in the American colonies that were much simpler than in England. Women could release their dower rights simply by signing to that effect on the conveyancing document.[59]

In contrast, if married women wished to sell their own lands, the new provisions required that they appear before a judge of the Court of Queen's Bench, who was to examine them and ensure they were not being coerced into the sale. Previously, married women had been able to sell, alienate, and mortgage their estates if they had the "authority and express consent of the husband." That was a private decision, subject to minimal outside interference. After the Registry Ordinance, however, their husband's permission was no longer sufficient. This new requirement was borrowed from English conveyancing laws that had long assumed a husband would "kiss or kick" his wife out of her real property if he had a chance. After 1841, wives had to swear before a judge that their consent was free and voluntary and that husbands had not coerced them.[60] Here was a new level of constraint placed on a man's influence over his wife that drew directly from English law.[61] In this way, the new law in this area, as in so many others, grafted elements of English law onto the local practices. Here was further reason for concern among Canadien jurists. For even those who had been in favour of changing elements of the law had been adamant that it should be done in a way that respected French law, rather than imposing English practices.

Unlike the English Dower Act of 1833, this provision was retroactive. Any married woman over twenty-one, regardless of when she had married, was given this new legal capacity. Only Harwood and Dominique Mondelet attempted to curtail this major change to the rights and obligations of all men and women who had married in the colony. Their modest attempt to limit the applicability of this clause to those married after the ordinance came into effect failed.[62]

Harwood agreed with the other men on the third major provision. It limited dower to the property a husband owned at the time of his death. This provision was a logical extension of the clause allowing wives to relinquish their dower rights any time land was sold. It promised to prevent many of the kinds of legal conflicts that had clogged up the courts and for years so bothered those interested in purchasing land. Similar changes were proposed throughout the Western world. The English Dower Act of 1833 went further than Stuart's ordinance in disallowing dower on any land a husband disposed of in his will as well.[63] Yet, in other parts of North America, politicians were reluctant to repeal dower. In Upper Canada, dower still applied to real property husbands had owned over their lifetime, though conveyancing laws made it possible for wives to bar dower when husbands sold their land. Debates about reshaping dower in that colony in the 1840s elicited hot and somewhat raucous debates in which familiar figures of dependent, fragile widows were cast against shrewd, scheming, calculating widows. In many American states, legislators resisted changing dower.[64] Thus, the suspension of elected government in Lower Canada allowed the relatively easy passage of legislation that met considerable resistance in other jurisdictions. After the union of the two provinces, Thomas Lewis Drummond, the Irish-born lawyer and politician who had studied with Charles Dewey Day and also defended Patriots following the rebellions, described the Registry Ordinance as "a law that would never have been passed by a free legislature."[65]

Most of the key clauses of the Registry Ordinance that reshaped women's rights as wives and widows provoked no amendments. Disagreements were about the lengths to which it was possible to go to attain clear title. Lord Sydenham was forced to step in and break a tie vote when George Moffatt proposed that every kind of title or claim had to be registered within twelve months or it would be null and void. As no offices existed outside the Eastern Townships, this would have provoked bureaucratic chaos. Moffatt's subsequent attempt to push creditors' rights at the expense of widows' by allowing a man's debts to be taken out of his widow's dower must have provoked a slight twinge of conscience about defenceless widows. Only five other councillors supported him.[66]

The special councillors would not have argued that widows should fend for themselves. Most, like Robert Unwin Harwood, had provided for the possibility that their wife might outlive them in marriage contracts, wills, or both. Their decisions reflect the understanding that such individual contracts were the best way to determine a widow's subsistence, and that it was imperative that land and the market more broadly be freed up from constraining influences like dower. They had little patience for laws and customs that set out a more generalized marriage bargain and tied up the property of those without the common sense to make such contracts themselves, or which promised too much to widows or offspring. The Registry Ordinance reshaped patriarchy and the marriage bargain in the colony.[67] Contracts and husbands' individual responsibility increasingly replaced older socially guaranteed rights like dower, which had not required any written documents. There were differences among the men but, like a growing number of other men in the colony and elsewhere, they shared the liberal view that men's freedom should be "limited only by voluntary obligations to others or to God."[68]

Registration and Dower Outside and After the Special Council

The letter from Charles-Elzéar Mondelet that was published in *L'Aurore des Canadas* on 18 December 1840 alerted readers that dower was on the agenda of the Special Council without revealing the source of his information. Given the secrecy of proceedings, he had surely been in conversation with his brother, and possibly with Harwood. The letter was published the day before Dominique Mondelet and Harwood sought to prevent the ordinance from being applied retroactively. His final sentence enjoined readers to "Go see Mr Ogden and Sir James Stuart, or if they fail, the Governor of the Country," making quite clear that the letter was explicitly about the Special Council. Telling his brother about the daily agenda was one way Dominique could subvert these proceedings, so detested by Patriotes and even moderate Canadiens like him. Charles-Elzéar deployed reason, wit, and gender to caricature the differences between French and English law, and to laugh at British claims to superior use of reason and a superior civilization. Other public criticism questioned the legitimacy of an ordinance passed by the Special Council. Later critics complained of its class and nationalist bias, alleging it would hurt the poor most and create a new kind of aristocracy.[69]

The most sustained analyses of the ordinance questioned its language and logic without necessarily proposing its reversal. Louis-Hippolyte LaFontaine, former Patriote and future co-premier with Robert Baldwin of the United Province of Canada, set the tone a year later.[70] A pamphlet he published in 1842 explained the new law clause by clause, dismissing it as a scissors-and-paste job, and predicting that it would cause many problems in the courts. He was particularly critical of the section that required wives to appear before a judge if they wished to sell their own land. Prickling with nationalist sensitivity, he suggested that this clause implied that the legislator "acted under the impression that women are better treated by their husbands elsewhere than in Lower Canada." He blamed this mistake on the Special Council asserting that "the customs of the country do not excuse this injurious impression." Using the common method of providing snapshots of domestic life to make a point, he invited his readers to imagine a woman going to see the judge one day and swearing that her husband had coerced her into a sale, then returning a day later to say she was consenting. "You won't know what takes place that night between the husband and wife ... probably new violence and new acts of coercion."[71]

Four years later, Jacques Crémazie was instructed by the Legislative Assembly to examine the functioning of the registry offices. He built on LaFontaine's critiques in a scathing report and also aimed his critique at its origins in the Special Council. Having outlined earlier attempts to introduce legislation and the public's hostility to changes regarding dower, he described the Special Council as a "factory of laws ... cutting vigorously in all the country's institutions." No one, he suggested, imagined that in the last few months of their existence they would intervene in the prickly, complicated, and difficult question of hypothecs, dower, and registration. He identified many shortcomings in the law, arguing that there was major resistance and that registrations had been minimal.[72]

Crémazie attributed people's resistance to the law to their abhorrence of the legislation and to the common Canadien conviction that "with a real legislature one of the first acts would be to repeal all the odious laws imposed by the Special Council, especially the Ordinance."[73] Yet, LaFontaine and the others in the new assembly of the united Provinces of Upper and Lower Canada made no attempts to eliminate it. Subsequent legislation cleaned up Stuart's work rather than reshaping it. Over the next forty years, politicians of diverse stripes whittled away at what remained of widows' dower rights and set out to make it as easy as possible for a married woman to agree to the sale of her husband's land. In 1845, politicians extended married women's power to renounce their dower rights on land their husbands wished to sell to include dowers promised in a marriage contract. The amount of time allowed to register existing dower rights was extended several times.[74]

In 1866, the men who blended the Custom of Paris, existing legislation, and their own ideas to forge the colony's new civil code effectively abolished the customary dower for those marrying after 1 August that year. They also avoided following aspects of the Napoleonic Code of 1804 that would have offered married women greater autonomy and rights. The new code specified that the "right to legal customary dower" in future marriages would be recognized only if the marriage certificate was registered along with a description of the "immoveables then subject to such dower."[75] Subsequent legislation gradually eliminated unregistered dowers for women married prior to codification, though it was not until the mid-1880s that customary dower was completely abolished by a series of bills.[76] One by one what MPP Ross Cuthbert had called the "ingeniously contrived trap doors," the "numberless latent back stairs," and "subterranean alleys" in which rights like dower had been hidden were rendered visible to anyone willing and able to pay the price necessary to consult the new arbiter of land exchange in each district, the registry office.[77]

The debate about widows' rights explored here was one engaged in largely by a male elite. Few women's views filter into the government documents and newspapers of the times, except when men like Mondelet spoke for them. Even then, widows lurk as images and archetypes, their presence frequently as dark and shadowy as their mourning attire. Sometimes represented as requiring protection, sometimes as colluding and scheming, they were inserted into other debates, increasingly featured as obstacles to freedom of contract or clarity of title.

I have found little evidence of women writing to complain of these changes. The public, published investigations, debates, and pamphlets were all apparently the work of men, though the use of pseudonyms may obscure some women's veiled voices. Yet, women continued to claim dower as a right. Individually, they contested challenges to their dower rights in the courts. Sometimes they did so while still married. More often it was after their husbands' deaths. Frequently, they were on the defensive, claiming their entitlement against husbands' creditors, executors, or family, or against landowners, their own sons and daughters, and sometimes their grandchildren. At other times they aggressively pursued claims. Dower did not disappear either from the courts or from widows' potential bases of support with the passage of the Registry Ordinance. Rather, that legislation opened up myriad new problems that ended up in court, as LaFontaine had predicted. Such cases were fairly extensively commented on in the colony's law journals, where they reflected and shaped contemporary jurisprudence, giving us glimpses of how judges were interpreting these laws.[78]

The key issues around which widows ended up fighting underline the changes wrought by the Registry Ordinance. After 1841, these hinged largely around the issues of registration, retroactivity, wives' renunciations of their dowers, and the strength of dower against the claims of other creditors. In the 1840s and 1850s, the reported cases show widows wrestling with the question of registration as creditors sought to get their hands on dowers promised in unregistered marriage contracts and widows tried to negotiate their options within and around the new law. When Widow Panet went to court in 1851 to claim the £1,200 promised as a dower in her marriage contract, the case was rapidly settled and became the basis of most future decisions. The contract had not been registered. Her dower therefore could not be the first claim on her husband's estate, as it would have been before the Registry Ordinance.[79]

The lessons of the new requirement to register were learned quickly by some husbands, widows, and landowners, though not always quickly enough. Some attempted to claim dower on lands long sold, as they had been able to do in the past, some to register retroactively. Mme Mure had married in 1817. Her husband died in 1852. She registered their marriage contract a year later and went to court, seeking to claim the £500 dower and £250 *préciput* she had been promised from the man who had bought the land from her husband in 1819. The purchaser, more canny and aware of legislation than Mme Mure, had registered his deed in 1844. The judges included Charles Dewey Day, who had been on the Special Council when the law was changed, and Charles-Elzéar Mondelet. They ruled against her on the basis of the delay "between the signing and the registration of the contract" and dismissed her action with costs. They agreed that under the new laws the defendant's claim was strongest because he was the first to register it. This precedent-setting case demonstrated that dower had lost the power it once held as a claim privileged before all others.[80] Its strength would be determined henceforth by the technicality of the timing of its registration.

Other reported cases confirm judges' commitment to the sanctity of well-made contracts, though court decisions may have been more varied. When a couple and the notary had clearly specified a dower in a marriage contract and the document had been properly registered, the law reports taught lawyers and other readers that widows' claims would be upheld, even against opponents with excellent lawyers.[81] Here was a further lesson in the importance of contracts over customary rights. Dower had not disappeared. In this version of liberal patriarchy, it had become one contractual right among many.

Debates about dower and registering titles took place around this time across much of the industrializing Western world, as in most British colonies. Everywhere, questions of class and gender and capitalist development were central. In Lower Canada, these issues intersected with questions of national identity, which were frequently linked to different legal heritages. Because the legal attributes of marriage were determined by the Custom of Paris and later the civil code, which worked very differently from the common law, this was always highly charged, disputed territory.

Widows fought individually for dower in the courts, but they seem voiceless in the public arenas of the press and politics. Perhaps the relative silence of women on this issue reflects the fact that dower was important only to certain groups of women. Dower still held promise for the widows of property-owning habitants in rural areas, as it did for some elites. In the land-rich Prairies, women would fight for dower in the early twentieth century precisely to get a claim to land. Yet, for the propertyless, especially the emerging working classes, dower offered little. It was not the Registry Ordinance but migration, economic change, dispossession, and proletarianization that took away widows' dower rights. For working-class wives like Marguerite Paris, ownership of their half of the community of goods offered greater promise than dower rights. Indeed, by the early twentieth century, the Quebec feminist Marie Gérin-Lajoie was suggesting that the distinction between real and moveable property be eliminated to enhance wives' claims on property accumulated during a marriage.[82]

Still, the Registry Ordinance reshaped widows' rights, changed the meaning of many kinds of contracts, shifted common understandings of the rights and relations of husbands and wives, and jammed a wedge of English-based law into the edifice of French civil law in the colony. It made a difference to women who might become widows and whose husbands had property of their own. Prior to 1841, the marriage bargain in Lower Canada meant that men's freedom to dispose of their own real property was constrained by their obligation to provide dower for their widow and offspring. Dower was a socially guaranteed right, with priority over other claims. Afterward and following later legislation, it became just another private contractual agreement, its priority determined by the time of its registration, like any other contract.[83] Husbands gained the new possibility of selling and buying land free of such encumbrances. Propertied men emerged freer to dispose of their real property as they wished.[84] This reshaped patriarchy acknowledged individual male rights to decide whether to be benevolent or not. To achieve this, it also opened up new, but very limited, forms of freedom of contract for wives. It thus placed new emphasis on contracts in general and on that instrument so central to British men's exercise of patriarchy from the grave – the will.

Fifteen years after the Special Council ended its work, Robert Unwin Harwood thought again about the possibility of his own death and of Marie-Louise becoming a widow. It was thirty years since they had made their marriage contract. She clearly would not face the poverty that working-class men might imagine for their widows. They had made pretty generous provisions for her widowhood in their marriage contract and she was a wealthy woman in her own right, the owner of their seigneury. Yet, Robert wished to leave her more and to leave instructions for his children as well.[85] He sat down and set out his final wishes in a last will. It is to the history of wills in Quebec and to such private arrangements and imaginings of death, funerals, and widowhood in marriage contracts, wills, and burial societies that the next chapter turns.

5

Imagining Widowhood and Death
Marriage Contracts, Wills, and Funeral Provisions

The gallant, understanding the father's concern concludes that he will offer a Dower. That is to say that after the husband's death, the wife will have the use of certain lands and property during her life and that ownership will go to the children, or that before any other creditors she will take for herself and her children certain sums of money.

– M., letter to the editor, *L'Aurore des Canadas,* 18 December 1840

M.'s 1840 letter presents the moment before marriage as the proper time for men to imagine that their wives might outlive them and to provide for this by offering a dower. In the early to mid-nineteenth century, contemplating marriage meant imagining its dissolution by death in ways that parallel the possibility of separation and divorce today. An 1874 newspaper article described a marriage ceremony performed in a cemetery with the bride and groom positioned on opposite sides of a grave. Another reported on a wedding in which the bridegroom had not left the church before being solicited to purchase a lot in the local cemetery.[1] Like Mondelet's letter, such tales capture the coupling of marriage and its dissolution by death in the popular imagination.

This tight bonding of these two critical life cycle moments was rooted in the demographic realities of the times. This chapter begins by briefly looking at the omnipresence of death and widowhood in people's lives, their correspondence, and the public imagination. It then explores some of the different ways Montrealers made formal provisions for their deaths, starting with those made in marriage contracts, then turning to wills, and ending with a brief overview of some of the growing number of ways Montrealers, worried more about leaving debts than assets, made preparations for their deaths, focusing especially on the new Catholic prayer groups that promised members commemorative masses and a decent funeral. It engages with M.'s solicitation to his readers to "imagine" widowhood as an outcome of marriage that was shaped by decisions made long before a man's death and probes his caricature of the difference between English and French ways of envisaging of widowhood.

Death's Omnipresence

In early-nineteenth-century Montreal, reminders of death's unpredictability were inescapable. Montrealers of all backgrounds watched siblings, grandparents, and neighbours die, joined friends and families at deathbeds, attended funeral services, and accompanied processions. Many spouses had lost one or both parents long before they married. Letters from friends and family elsewhere registered demographies of deaths, births, and marriages far away. Invitations to funerals, death notices, novels, poems, and sermons, like the rumble of carts carrying the dead to the cemetery, warned Montrealers to be prepared.[2] An 1846 newspaper article entitled "On the Thoughts of Death" advised: "In the morning, imagine thou shalt not live till night: and when evening comes, presume not to promise thyself the next morning. Be therefore always prepared, and live in such a manner, that death may never find thee unprovided."[3] More secular stories of sudden deaths, or dying wives and husbands, transmitted a similar message – death might dissolve marriages at any time. Men and women should prepare themselves both spiritually and materially.[4]

In the papers and letters of nineteenth-century Montrealers, illness and death form recurrent themes. Mary Westcott, who in 1846 married Amedée Papineau, son of the Patriote leader Louis-Joseph, wrote frequently to her father in New York State. Fear of death when friends were ill was a frequent theme. In one letter she described the death of a young Mrs. Cuvillier, mother of three little children. "As my circle of acquaintance enlarges, how frequent does death enter it. I meet the gay and strong and the next thought of them comes with the black edged note, calling for a convoy to place them in the lonely grave. Oh! That we were all prepared for death."[5] The chance of death at any age held a place in the public imagination, popular culture, religious and legal practice, and daily life that is difficult for many of us who live in the Western world today to grasp. We associate death largely with old age. This situation is new historically, and a privilege of Western developed countries.

In imagining the transition from marriage to the grave, from wife to widow, questions of property were hard to avoid. The widespread understanding that adequately supporting wives was a measure of manhood among the middle and working classes included the desirability of supporting widows should the man die first. Writing to her father on 21

February 1847, Mary Westcott reported that the funeral held for Joseph-Rémi Vallières de Saint-Réal, the early proponent of registry offices and modifications of widows' dower rights, was the "grandest" ever seen in Montreal. When he died he had been the chief justice of the Court of King's Bench for the Montreal district for five years and the first Canadien to hold that position. Mary described him as their "fellow boarder," for he resided in the same luxury hotel – Donegana's – where she and Amédée took up residence after their marriage. Mary had few kind words to say about this brilliant, eloquent nationalist – but never Patriote – politician. She was not impressed by the pomp of his funeral nor by his profligate lifestyle. He "lived most extravagantly." Worse, he had "left his wife with *nothing,* sad change for her, widowhood of poverty, or at least *comparative* poverty." To this young, American-raised, middle-class wife, the dead judge displayed the worst of aristocratic values.[6]

The political elite of the colony considered the public poverty of his widow sufficiently deplorable that they provided her with an annuity of £200 on the recommendation of the governor general. The wording of the act downplayed Vallières de Saint-Réal's failure as a provider, lauding his "high Scholastic and Literary attainments," contributions as chief justice, "encouragement of Science and the Arts, and his eminent position as a public man." His public performance of engaged citizenship was the rationale for the support provided to his widow. Only in the last clause did the legislation refer to the "destitution of his Widow and his aged Mother."[7]

Most ordinary male citizens would not imagine the state providing in any way for their widows, though the individual widows of some soldiers might receive pensions, and other widows of state officials petitioned the Legislative Assembly fairly frequently for assistance. Indeed, by the 1850s, one enterprising Montreal lawyer was advertising that he would assist soldiers and their widows and children in pursuing pension claims.[8] Broader state provision for poor widows who were also mothers was achieved in some Canadian provinces nearly seventy years later, after Canada's early feminists campaigned for pensions for needy mothers. In Quebec it took ninety more years.[9]

Provisions for Widowhood in Marriage Contracts

The marriage contract that Marie-Louise-Josephte Chartier de Lotbinière and Robert Unwin Harwood made prior to their marriage followed Mondelet's advice in making provisions for widowhood. However, as reported in the previous chapter, it did not follow his advice by offering her a dower. Along with rejecting community property, it made clear that she was renouncing any claim as a widow to dower. Instead, Robert promised her an annuity of £200 and the use of all household furniture and carriages

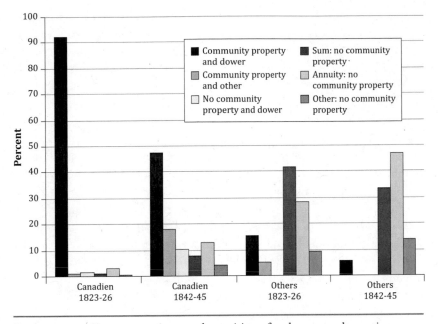

FIGURE 5.1 Property regimes and provisions for dower or alternatives promised to potential widows in marriage contracts, Canadien husbands and other husbands

Note: Canadien marriages with a contract, 1823-26, $N = 166$; 1842-45, $N = 78$. Other marriages (Irish Catholics, Protestants, Jews) with a contract, 1823-26, $N = 77$; 1842-45, $N = 51$.
Source: Marriage contracts filed with Montreal notaries of couples marrying 1823-26, and 50 percent of couples marrying 1842-45, BAnQM.

should he die first."[10] In using their contract to renounce dower, their decision paralleled those of most English-speaking Montrealers making a marriage contract in the 1820s, as well as in the 1840s. Rejecting dower, sometimes with the same flourish they used in rejecting community property, was an additional component of the liberal patriarchy that most embraced (see Figure 5.1).

When wives rejected dower in a marriage contract, grooms usually promised some alternative. These varied. The notary Thomas John Pelton chose the most frequent alternative. In their 1843 contract, he promised Caroline Scott a lump sum of £100 should she outlive him. The Jewish lawyer Adolphus Mordecai Hart promised Constance Hannah Hart ten times that amount. A lump sum was the promise made by about half the English-speaking husbands during the 1820s, and around a third two decades later. These promises ranged from £10 and £6,000.[11]

John Campbell, the bookseller, promised Laura Mower an annuity of £50 instead of dower should she become a widow. Like Marie-Louise, she would also retain ownership of her own separate property, as well as any profits that she made from her independent trading should she outlive him. Campbell mortgaged all his property to secure his promise and gave Notary Doucet the necessary power to effect his wishes.[12] Such annuities were the second most frequent alternatives to dower offered by husbands whose contracts were written in English. John Smith, a much wealthier merchant than John Campbell, promised Betsy Rea an annuity of £60 in 1823, adding that she should also take her own bed, bedding, and wearing apparel should she outlive him. Two decades later, Hugh Allan promised their daughter, Matilda Caroline Smith, five times that amount as an annuity. Caroline Campbell and her trader-merchant husband, Oliver Wait, also rejected dower, asserting, as some anglophones did regarding community property, that this was "notwithstanding the Custom of Paris." In its place, Oliver promised that should Caroline outlive him, but not otherwise, she would receive the annual legal interest on £830 6s. 8d. in current money, to be paid immediately upon his death and in half-yearly payments of £25 until she died. Specifying interest on a sum of money rather than an annuity became more popular in the 1840s, when close to a third of those writing in English offered such a possibility in the case of widowhood.[13]

In private marriage contracts, as in public pronouncements, Montrealers who were of English, Irish Protestant, Scottish, and American origin saw dower as something to avoid in the 1840s, as in the 1820s. The small number of Irish Catholics making a contract, in contrast, made decisions closer to Canadian Catholics. In the 1820s, seven of the nine Irish Catholic husbands offered a dower. A generation later, only two of nine did so. Renouncing dower was part of English-speaking Montrealers' opposition to the Custom of Paris, community property, and its particularly generous dower. These were similar choices to some of their peers in England, who used wills to instruct their trustees to make specific provisions for their widows "in full satisfaction and discharge of any dower." As historian R.J. Morris observes, barring dower did not exclude a widow from benefiting from her husband's property. Rather, it ensured that she did so "on terms set by the husband and also ensured that there was clear title to the property in the event of a sale."[14]

Thus, the dominant anglophone choice among the minority making marriage contracts concentrated control over most property in the husband's hands by avoiding the regime of community property, barring dower, and promising a lump sum, an annuity, or interest on capital to the widow. In contrast, most Canadiens who made contracts in the 1820s sought to place a significant proportion of family property in the survivor's hands, regardless of which spouse died first. The generation marrying between 1823 and 1826 modified but followed the preferences of earlier generations, crafting particularities within the broad collaborative patriarchy established as the basis of their marriages. Hermine Legris and the carpenter Michel Julien made choices that were fairly typical of Canadiens marrying in the 1820s, and especially of those from the community of craftspeople in which they circulated. In addition to choosing community property, Michel promised Hermine a dower, stipulated as worth £50. It would be taken from the property he owned that had remained outside the community, or from his share of the community property. She could use it, but had to pass on the equivalent to their children. They also promised that the surviving spouse could take £25 worth of goods as their *préciput* from their shared community property prior to its division. This combination of a dower and a *préciput,* usually set at half the value of the dower, was customary and widely used among Canadiens. In addition, they specified that the surviving spouse should have the use of all their shared property unless they remarried.[15] Such provisions making donations of family property to the surviving spouse, with or without conditions – for example, if there were no children or if the spouse did not remarry – were most common in the crafts community.

Émilie Monjean and the master painter Antoine Laurent imagined a similar bundle of provisions. He promised her a dower of £2,400 old currency, or about £100. They agreed that each could take a *préciput* of half that amount, as was usual, and that the survivor could take ownership of the community property if they had no children.[16] In this Canadien imagining of widowhood, rooted in the world of the craftspeople of the city, the survivor would have control over most of the couple's property, especially if left without children. The contribution of wives to accumulation during the marriage was recognized and rewarded, and the potential disruption of dividing up family assets delayed.

Luce Perrault and Édouard-Raymond Fabre, the prominent Patriote bookseller, and Émilie Tavernier and the merchant Jean-Baptiste Gamelin were, as we saw, among the minority of Canadiens not choosing community property in marriage contracts made during the 1820s. Yet, neither of these Patriote-affiliated couples rejected dower when they imagined that the wife might die first. Édouard-Raymond promised Luce a significant dower of £1,000, one of the highest amounts offered in these two marriage cohorts. Jean-Baptiste Gamelin promised Émilie Tavernier a dower of £500.[17]

Among the generation of Canadien couples who married after the Registry Ordinance, this attachment to dower dwindled, as it had among Patriote politicians. The proportion of Canadiens renouncing dower in a marriage contract increased dramatically from well under one in ten in the 1820s to over four out of ten two decades later (see Figure 5.2). This shift

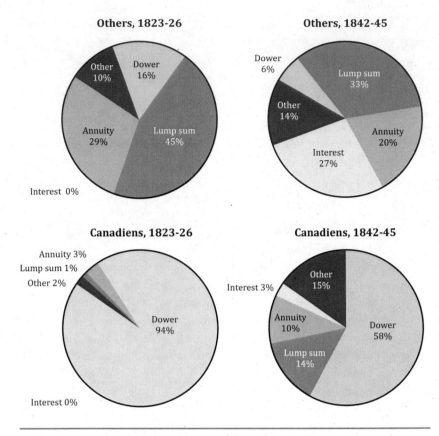

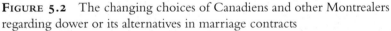

FIGURE 5.2 The changing choices of Canadiens and other Montrealers regarding dower or its alternatives in marriage contracts

Note: Canadien grooms with contracts, 1823-26, $N = 166$, 1842-45, $N = 78$; Other (Irish Catholics, Protestants, and Jews), 1823-26, $N = 77$, 1842-45, $N = 51$.
Source: Marriage contracts filed with Montreal notaries of couples marrying 1823-26, and 50 percent of couples marrying 1842-45, BAnQM.

away from dower, like the choice of separate property, was most pronounced among the city's elite of merchants, professionals, and government officials. Over three-quarters chose community property and a dower in the 1820s, whereas nearly one in ten opted for separate property and also stipulated a dower. Two decades later, only around one in three chose dower, often in conjunction with rejecting community, whereas around six out of ten rejected dower. In its place, the Canadien elite, like their Anglo counterparts, provided annuities, lump sums, or interest on a specific sum.

In contrast, among the shrinking proportion of Montreal's mostly Canadien crafts couples making a marriage contract, dower along with community property remained the dominant choice, though a growing proportion opted for annuities, lump sums, or some other alternative. Marie Genant and her master tailor husband Pierre-Bernard Decousse blended old and new ways in their 1843 contract, rejecting community property, not mentioning dower, yet providing for a £50 *préciput* for the survivor. They agreed that the survivor should continue to use all the goods both owned at the time of the other spouse's death and care for them as a "good father of family." Should the remaining spouse remarry, this property was to be returned to the survivor's heirs.[18] Thus, Marie and Pierre-Bernard sought the advantages of separate property, while retaining the logic of community property.

In these provisions for widowhood, formalized a day or so before marriages and inscribed in notarial contracts, Montrealers articulated visions of the proper ways widows should be provided for that drew on cultural practices rooted in different legal systems and in divergent class and economic realities. Dower, a *préciput,* and community property, the lynchpins of Canadien choices, were modified by those who saw economic and familial advantages in different options. Most spouses whose understandings of marriage and property derived from the English common law assimilated their rejection of elements of the Custom of Paris to assertions of their own difference as British and Protestant citizens. But even those sympathetic to the evident fairness of provisions for wives and widows in the Custom, whether they were Canadiens or newcomers, began to reject community property and especially dower in the face of the changes leading to and wrought by the Registry Ordinance, disastrous business cycles, the widespread evidence of bankruptcies, and the declining significance of real property as a basis of wealth.

In so doing, they asserted the possibility that a new, bourgeois sense of property rights and obligations within marriage could be accommodated within the Custom of Paris. In this ultimately bourgeois and liberal view of property, family, and gender, the right of individual men to choose how to dispose of their own property overrode the law's older prescription of the proper proportion of accumulated or inherited wealth that should be made available to a man's widow or children. Designated amounts, increasingly specified as annuities, lump sums, or interest on a sum, rather than dowers, superseded the customary claims that widows had on half a man's own property.

The amounts these husbands contracted to provide from the grave should they die before their new wives are best viewed as guesstimates, approximations of what they hoped their property could generate at some unknown future point in their lives. The value of the sums offered drew on long-standing traditions blended with aspirations for their futures as providers, husbands, and fathers; anticipated inheritances; and immediate financial exigencies. They reflected both a man's sense of what he might be worth and a woman's parents' sense of how their daughter should be provided for should she become a widow. However these amounts were specified, they were usually imagined in round figures. Dowers ranged from £300 to £24,000 old currency or between £12 and £1,000, annuities from as low as £4 to nearly £500 yearly. Lump sums, as we saw, varied between £10 and £6,000.

Dowers offered by men from the crafts community and construction trades clustered at four amounts: £300, £600, £1,000, or £1,200 old currency – which translated to £12 10s., £25, £42, and £50. Better established skilled workers and master craftsmen offered dowers closer to £100. The master painter Michel Julien's promise to Hermine Legris of £50 was thus a relatively generous dower in his community, reflecting perhaps the good bargaining skills of her separated mother, and recognizing her significant contribution to the household. Most dowers promised by merchants and professionals were double those of craftsmen. Most clustered between £200 and £500, the amount that Jean-Baptiste Gamelin promised Émilie Tavernier. Édouard-Raymond Fabre's £1,000 promise stood out as exceptionally generous among this generation.[19]

Dower had one advantage over lump sums or annuities, as M. pointed out clearly in his letter of 1840. The widow could take the specified sum of money, or lands and property of that value, "before any other creditors," for "herself and her children." The disadvantage of dower, as many feminist historians have long argued, was that it gave widows only the right to use that property, not to own or dispose of it. Once they died, it passed to their children. When husbands offered an annuity or interest upon a specified sum, they were frequently offering something very similar. Widows could not dispose of the capital. It too would either go to men's heirs or be disposed of in wills. The advantage of dowers, annuities, or interest was that as long as the man's estate was sufficient, they provided a regular, predictable income. In contrast, lump sums, the most common alternative to dower, offered widows the liberty of dealing with their own investments and spending money as they wished. They gave significant autonomy and demonstrated trust in wives' financial skills. Some feminist historians analyzing wills have interpreted the discretion that similar provisions offered as the most favourable way husbands could provide for widows. Others have suggested the dangers and disadvantages of full control. Managing a lump sum bestowed both autonomy and risk. It left widows more vulnerable to creditors and to fortune seekers than did a dower or annuity.[20]

No one of type of provision was intrinsically better than another. Much more important for most wives was the amount they could count on receiving to live on should their husband die first. The dower of £1,000 that Fabre promised Luce Perrault in 1826 would produce a similar standard of living as the £1,000 lump sum that Adolphus Mordecai Hart promised Constance Hannah Hart. The £50 that the merchant Oliver Wait promised Caroline Campbell would receive annually from his investments was unquestionably a more stable basis of widowhood than the £100 lump sum that Notary Pelton promised Caroline Scott.[21] What would work best for particular widows depended on situations that could seldom be predicted when they married. Whether they would receive what they were promised and what it would be worth should they become widows were unknown when such contracts were signed.

Writing Wills in Montreal "À la loi anglaise" and "À la loi française"

Fifteen years after his time on the Special Council and over thirty years after making a marriage contract, Robert Unwin Harwood again imagined how he would like Marie-Louise to live should she become a widow. It was 1854. He was fifty-six years old and apparently "in perfectly good health." But cholera was again spreading through the ports of the Empire. He sat down and handwrote a last will and testament, asserting his love and affection for her, then enumerating his final wishes.[22] Austin Cuvillier suggested in 1828 that English Lower Canadians made wills to provide for inheritance matters, whereas Canadiens generally made marriage contracts. Samuel Gale more carefully explained that a husband's freedom to dispose of his property in a will depended on provisions in marriage contracts. Without a marriage contract avoiding community property, he explained, "he cannot dispose of a very considerable portion of his property."[23] As we saw, newcomers imbued with common law understandings of family and property learned to make marriage contracts. Canadiens also made wills.

Wills were recognized in the Custom of Paris, as they were in many European codes, though they were seldom the major instrument for transferring property. Louise Dechêne estimated that some quarter of Montreal's inhabitants in the seventeenth century made a will. Prior to the Conquest, the rules of succession required the equal division of most property among legitimate children.[24] Succession rules, along with those governing marriage in the Custom of Paris, placed familial interest over that of the individual. In France, regional codes varied dramatically in the liberty of men and women to make wills and in the amount that could be bequeathed. Following the Revolution, equal inheritance was required, and wives' control over their property was severely restricted. The Napoleonic Code, like the laws and customs of many European states, continued to restrict the amount that could be disposed of in a will, guaranteeing children's rights to a certain proportion of their parents' estates.[25]

In Lower Canada/Quebec, inheritance law was changed in the opposite direction. Englishmen at home and in the colonies proclaimed freedom of willing as an essential component of their superior civilization, their manliness, and their Britishness. As Susan Staves has argued, the British had increasingly come to believe that "the husband rather than society was the right judge of the proper provisions for his wife – not only during marriage" but also following his death.[26] An 1847 British treatise on inheritance asserted that "the ability ... to transmit our property to those who occupy the chief place in our affections ... is indispensable to the advancement of society in wealth and civilization."[27] These ideas spread rapidly in those colonies where male settlers encountered legal impediments to this right. "In England, a man can do as he likes with his property," asserted a British settler in the Cape colony, in southern Africa, in 1866, as he bemoaned the provisions of Roman Dutch law.[28]

The Quebec Act of 1774, which mostly sanctioned the Custom of Paris as the basis for civil matters, responded early to this very male and particularly British claim by offering Quebec residents the right to make a will "notwithstanding any law, usage or custom to the contrary." This, legal historian André Morel has argued, eliminated the idea that children had a rightful claim on a significant portion of family goods, allowed spouses to privilege each other, and muddied the distinction the Custom made between inherited goods and those accumulated during a marriage. He suggests it "made the testator judge without appeal."[29] The Quebec Act of 1774 also made it clear that wills and testaments could follow either British or customary format, hence legitimating a mixture of practices.

By the turn of the nineteenth century, the arrival of growing numbers of settlers from common law regions, along with uncertainty about what the previous law had allowed to be disposed of in a will, led to new legislation. In 1801, legislation clarified that freedom of willing applied to both men and women, including married women, though it did not leave husbands with power over all property accumulated in a marriage, as English common law did. Evelyn Kolish has suggested that the only restriction on freedom of willing was the clause that specified that a will could not prejudice "the rights of the survivor or the customary or settled dower."[30] This ignores the dominant community property regime that continued to acknowledge wives' rights to half the property built up during a marriage, unless arranged otherwise in a marriage contract. Still, wider freedom of willing, combined with the growing choice of separate property in marriage contracts and, after 1840, the new restrictions on widows' dower, enlarged the power of men to dispose of property by contract. These laws diminished the older guarantees for widows and children that were so central to the Custom of Paris and Canadien understandings of marriage. Inheritance law, like dower, became one of the gendered symbols that fuelled the production of oppositional ethnic communities and nationalisms in early-nineteenth-century Quebec.[31] Then and since, Canadien responses have stressed the superior morality of their law, pointing to the dangers inherent in the possibility that men could disinherit one child, leave their widow penniless or, worse, give all their property to a mistress.[32]

Oliver Wait decided to make a will, as did many Montrealers, while cholera raged through the city in 1832. The epidemic was in its third month when Notary Arnoldi and two witnesses came to his home on the morning of 12 August. He was not well. As we saw, Oliver's fortune had grown with his family. Perhaps as he realized that his second wife was about to become a widow, he decided that the £50 annually that he had promised her in their marriage contract was insufficient to maintain her and his seven minor children at a standard that would reflect well on his capacity as a good provider. His will stands out for the number of missing provisions. Perhaps Oliver's weakness or fear of catching cholera may have made Arnoldi careless. For Oliver Wait named no executor, made no mention of funeral arrangements, and failed to specify that his debts should be paid. These were the most usual opening clauses of wills. It did clearly specify that Oliver wanted Caroline to receive a further £50 annually.[33] Because their marriage contract had excluded community property and given Oliver full control not only over all he accumulated but also over the revenues from her separate property, his promises would make a significant difference to her standard of living should cholera kill him.[34]

In choosing to make a will with a notary, Oliver was opting for the testamentary practice rooted in the Custom of Paris. He might also have chosen to write a will in the English fashion. For, in Lower Canada, will making, even more than writing marriage contracts, could follow the practices of "la loi française" or "la loi anglaise."[35] Wills conforming to the Custom of Paris were usually written by a notary. They required the presence of one or two notaries. When only one notary attended, as in Oliver's case, two other witnesses were required. Women, including wives, could make wills, but it was not until 1915 that they could act as witnesses.[36] Witnesses had to be male, over twenty, civilly and mentally capable, and not among those who would benefit from the will's provisions. Normally, notaries prepared a client's will following an initial consultation, then returned and went over the clauses again, as with marriage contracts. It seems unlikely that this had occurred in Wait's case. For the will to be valid, the notary was obliged to read it and reread it to those assembled, noting this in the act. This Notary Arnoldi did. He then took Oliver's will back to his office and, as was usual, made sure that it was properly filed.[37]

The Custom of Paris also recognized wills that were handwritten in the testator's own hand, rather than by a notary. Known as holograph wills, these could be written alone. They required neither a signature nor witnesses. This was Robert Harwood's choice in 1854. During this period, they were relatively rare. Usually holograph wills were proved in ways similar to English-style wills, though jurists argued that this was not required in the Custom of Paris.[38]

Like Oliver Wait, Charlotte Mount's husband, Jacques-François-Louis Genevay, was ill when he made his will. It was just four years since their marriage. Unlike Wait, he did not call a notary or ask his wife to do so. Instead, he wrote his will at home in English form in English. Jacques-François-Louis transcribed his last wishes in the presence of the Montreal physician and surgeon John Stephenson, as well as a medical student and a law student. All four signed the document. His marriage contract with Charlotte had promised that if she outlived him, she should receive lodging in any house he might own at the time of his death, the use of a furnished bedroom, clothing, and £100, paid in installments four times over the year from the day of his death. He too sought to make better provisions for his wife than those of their marriage contract as he contemplated the reality of her becoming a young widow. His will promised that after his debts had been paid, Charlotte should inherit all he had. Genevay then named Notary Thomas Bedouin and the bilingual Montreal lawyer Hugh Heney as his executors.[39]

Nicholas Charles Viadiger, the law student who witnessed Jacques-François-Louis' will, may have offered advice as he formulated his final wishes. However, such English-style wills had to be written and signed by the testator. Literacy was therefore a critical skill. Genevay clearly knew that such a will required three witnesses. Later, to "assimilate" Lower Canadian law to that of England, this number was reduced to two.[40] Such wills might be passed on to a lawyer, or occasionally a notary, held within the family, or filed secretly with a man's papers. To enact their clauses, they had to be proved. This required that executors appear in court before a justice of His Majesty's Court of King's Bench, who verified the identity of the testator by taking depositions from witnesses. The process was more expensive and time-consuming than for notarial wills, which allowed executors to act on their provisions immediately after the testator's death. It also required that executors assume control of the deceased's assets and manage them – often a demanding and cumbersome responsibility.[41]

This range of ways of making wills may have confused some Montreal residents. Yet, this diversity of choice and the ease with which a notary could be used expanded the possibilities of will making to a broader range of the colony's population than in other parts of the British world. Wives' rights to make wills was clear. The ready presence of notaries allowed the illiterate and those lacking confidence in their knowledge of the law to receive advice and make wills. Notarial wills were relatively cheap to make, and simple to execute.

The different ways wills were written, filed, and executed makes it difficult to search for specific wills and to estimate the proportions of Montrealers who made one. We have found some wills made by men and women who married in the 1820s or 1840s by searching systematically through the rough alphabetical listings of probated and holograph wills, and by both systematic and serendipitous searches in notaries' files.[42] English-style wills are easier to locate because of the proving process. Overall we have located wills drawn up by seventy-seven men of these two cohorts when they were husbands, by thirty-four wives, thirteen widows, and seven widowers. Small as these numbers are, reading the wills and relating them to other information about their makers reveals clues about who made which kinds of wills, when people chose to write their wills, and about their contents. Wills, like marriage contracts, show us something of men's and women's ideas about gender, family, justice, and property. Yet, because they were usually written some years into a marriage, and in times of illness, they reveal more about intimate and individual desires than do most marriage contracts. I return to some of the provisions, as well as to the wills that widows made, in later chapters.[43]

Most writers of English-style and holograph wills were merchants, professionals, and "gentlemen," the men most likely to write wills in common law jurisdictions.[44] John Smith wrote down his final wishes this way, as did his son-in-law, Hugh Allan. The doctor William Sutherland wrote several English-style wills as he imagined and reimagined how Catherine Farquhar should live her life if she became a widow. That such literate, elite Montrealers of English, Scottish, and American origin chose to write wills in ways that fitted their cultural and legal roots is hardly surprising. In one of the few works that looks at wills and testaments made in Montreal, Claude Champagne argues that, between 1777 and 1825, British and Canadien Montrealers each followed their own traditions. Unfortunately, he limited his study to probated wills and hence captured only English-style and a few holograph wills. He did not investigate whether English Montrealers wrote notarial wills. From the 1820s on, they were clearly doing so in fairly large numbers. Over three of every five wills we have located written in English by husbands from these two generations were made with a notary.[45] Two days after Oliver Wait wrote his will with the assistance of Notary Arnoldi, William Gay called on Notary Blackwood to draw up his final wishes. Gay had married Margaret White in 1826. She was the daughter of Wait's colleague Andrew White, from White's first marriage. Caroline and Oliver were customers at Gay's well-stocked grocery store. These young couples may well have been friends. Perhaps the illness of this close acquaintance pushed Gay into acknowledging his own potential demise and the importance of making arrangements in addition to those established in the marriage contract. So might his father-in-law's death from cholera.[46]

Using a notary offered these fairly prominent literate, and in some cases, sick men the hope that their wills were well drafted. English-speaking butchers, coopers, furriers, clockmakers, painters, plasterers, and a few labourers also embraced the advantages notarial wills offered, in some cases because they could not write themselves. Apart from Genevay, whose ethnic identity is hard to pin down, all Canadien husbands whose wills we have found made either notarial or holograph wills. And so did wives of all ethnicities.[47]

English-speaking Montreal wives seem to have embraced the advantages of notarial wills more than English-speaking husbands if the people whose wills we have located are at all representative. Seven of the nine wives whose wills we have found that were written in English chose a notary, as did all the francophone wives. Nearly half of these female testators were unable to sign their names.[48] Montreal's residents of British origin, especially men in crafts and trade, women, and those unable to write, thus joined Canadien will writers in taking advantage of the guidance and assistance possible when writing wills following the practices of the Custom of Paris with a notary.

Many factors lay behind people's decision to prepare a will and the moment they chose to do so. The most obvious catalysts were epidemics and illness. Nearly one-third of these husbands' wills indicated that they were sick.[49] Some were on their deathbeds.[50] It was John Campbell's illness in 1836 that led him or Laura Mower to call Nicholas Doucet to their home on St. François Xavier Street. The will describes John as in a sickly state but of sound and disposing mind, memory, and understanding. This phrase was fairly standard, and important. Any suggestion that testators were not in full control of their faculties could invalidate the will. John cannot have seemed perilously close to death, for Notary Doucet and the witnesses helped Laura designate her final wishes before recording those of John.[51]

The decision to make a will at the same time, and their contents, evoke a spirit of joint decision making and understanding of partnership and conjugal property that contrast the image of the solitary husband making a will to dispose of his own property in the way he saw best. Laura Mower and John Campbell were not unique in making such mutual wills. As the cholera epidemic raged around them in 1832, this was the choice of Marie-Louise Asselin and her carpenter husband, Louis Gauthier. In 1849, Marie-Anne Séné and her husband, the joiner Antoine Hurtubise, made a similar choice twenty-six years after their marriage. Three-quarters of the wills we have found made by wives were mutual wills, and this was true of both English- and French-speaking wives.[52] Most were made by couples whose marriage created community property in which they had a mutual interest, but as Laura Mower's situation shows, this was not always the case. We have found none made by members of the English-speaking elite.

These mutual wills fit a pattern found in earlier times in New France, occasionally in American states, and in some European jurisdictions where marriage law gave women greater access to property within and after marriage and where versions of community property dominated.[53] Historian Margaret Darrow has argued that such reciprocal wills became common in the southwestern part of France, after the revolutionary period had drastically changed local property rules concerning marriage and inheritance closer to those of the Custom of Paris. "Shortly after marriage, husband and wife would go together to the notary's office to make their wills, setting up identical legacies in life rights or assigning each other" the small portion of family property that post-revolutionary law allowed them to bequeath as they wished.[54] In Lower Canada/Quebec, spouses were free to dispose of much more property. The timing of their writing seems more serendipitous.

Provisions for Widowhood in Wills

The provisions of these mutual wills were usually identical. Laura Mower and the bookseller John Campbell, who were childless when they wrote theirs but would later have four children, promised all to each other with no restrictions. In the sparse language typical of such notarial wills, John bequeathed all he had to Laura, as she did to him – "to have and to hold the said by herself her heirs and assigns for ever, without any account to be by my said wife rendered to any person." Each also appointed the other as executor. In contrast to most wills, neither mentioned God. The carpenter Louis Gauthier and Marie-Louise Asselin promised all their goods to each other, with the proviso that if there were children, the surviving spouse would have the use of only their half. It the spouse remarried, he or she

TABLE 5.1   Bequests in last wills located for husbands who married in Montreal, 1823-25 or 1842-45, combined

	All to spouse to own		All to use		Half or more to spouse		All or most to children		Income, sum, other		N
	N	%	N	%	N	%	N	%	N	%	
Class/occupation											
Elite	7	25	10	34	4	14	1	4	7	25	29
Crafts and trades	14	41	14	41	2	6	0	0	4	12	34
Unskilled	0	0	2	100	0	0	0	0	0	0	2
Other	0	0	4	33	1	8	4	33	3	25	12
Ethnicity/religion											
Husband Canadien	11	32	18	53	2	6	0	0	3	9	34
Husband Irish Catholic	2	40	1	20	2	40	0	0	0	0	5
Husband Protestant or Jewish	8	21	11	29	3	8	4	11	12	32	38
Cohort of marriage											
1823-26	14	24	23	40	6	10	3	5	12	21	58
1842-45	7	37	7	37	1	5	1	5	3	16	19
Will made at same time as spouse or individually?											
Mutual will	10	42	12	50	0	0	2	8	0	0	24
Individual will	11	21	18	34	7	13	2	4	15	28	53

Source: Last wills located for couples marrying in Montreal, 1823-1826, and 50 percent of couples marrying 1842-45, Montreal notaries, probated wills, BAnQM.

would lose that right.[55] Such mutual wills stand out from others in their parallel timing and provisions, and in being rather more likely to promise all the property to the spouse who died first to use or own outright. Otherwise they vary little from most others.

The provisions of the husbands' wills that we have found imagined three broad property arrangements for widows (see Table 5.1); those of wives envisaged only two. The dominant choice among husbands was to give the widow the use of pretty well all their property for her lifetime and to make the children their heirs. This was the way the merchant Charles-Séraphin Rodier imagined Marie-Louise Lacroix managing when he wrote a will in December 1831, six years after their marriage. It was the choice of around five out of every ten Canadien husbands, of one of the five Irish Catholics, and of around three of every ten men who wrote their wills in English. A third of elite husbands whose wills we have found and around four of every ten men in trades and crafts or agriculture chose this option. It was also the wish of nearly six of every ten wives of all ethnicities and faiths.

Minor variations on this provision fitted the particularities of family histories. The cooper Jean-Baptiste Bergevin balanced the claims of the children from his first and second marriage when he wrote his will in 1848, just six years after his marriage to Euphrosine Mitresse Sansfaçon. He bequeathed all the tools and materials of his cooperage to his only son from the first marriage, on the condition that he continue to pay the debts still owing on Jean-Baptiste's first wife's funeral arrangements. Euphrosine was to have the use of his lot "planted with fruit trees," in the Saint Lawrence suburb and the house he had built for her on it. After her death, this property was to pass to the children from their marriage in equal parts.[56] In these imaginings of widowhood, widows or widowers continued to benefit from the revenues and use of the full family estate, large or small. Widows could use these assets to raise, nourish, and support their children but could neither sell their spouses' part of that property nor dispose of it in a will.[57]

As his sight failed and illness rendered him "weak in body," the soap and candle manufacturer Sampson Brady decided to take advantage of Notary Smith's presence to set out his final wishes. Immediately after the contract was drawn up in which his business partners bought him out of their business in return for paying him and his wife an annuity, Sampson organized his final wishes. He promised Rebecca the use of all his estate during her lifetime for her own support and the support and education of their "beloved children" but on one condition. Rebecca was to renounce all claims against his estate that resulted from the "community of property existing between her and me." Thus, Sampson sought to reproduce the common law understanding that property accumulated during a marriage belonged to the husband alone, while allowing Rebecca the full use of it as a widow and passing it on in equal parts to his two sons. She and other wives whose husbands sought to use their wills to overturn community property would be able to choose the most favourable option if they became widows.[58]

The second most frequent choice among both husbands and wives in the wills we have located was the one that historians have interpreted as the most generous. John Campbell, Jacques-François Genevay, and Eloi Beneche promised all or nearly all they owned outright to their spouses. This was the wish expressed by nearly half the craftsmen, a third of the men in commerce, and a quarter of the elite. It was chosen by a third of Canadien husbands, two of the five Irish Catholics whose wills we have located, and about one in five English Protestant husbands (see Table 5.1). It was also the choice of around one in three Canadien and English-speaking wives. Many but not all of the spouses choosing this option had no children at the time they wrote their wills.[59]

These two main choices that placed the whole estate that remained at a husband's death in his widow's hands for life or until remarriage were most commonly made by wives of all classes and by husbands who were craftsmen or working as small traders. They differ little from the choice of the majority of husbands in the predominantly Canadien wills that Gérard Bouchard has studied in the Saguenay region where, he reports, the majority gave all to their wives either for life or outright.[60] Such provisions were less common choices of the merchant and professional elite.

A jumble of provisions characterized the third group of testators. Like Brady's attempt to foil the provisions of the law, they were united by the logic of liberal patriarchy that deemed that a man should do as he wished with his property. All offered their widows less than the full use or ownership of their estate for life or widowhood. A few sought to leave their wives the equivalent of at least half of their estate, respecting the spirit of equally shared property of the Custom of Paris. Others promised an income as Oliver Wait did for Caroline, or a specific sum of money, a house to live in, a room, furniture, or other goods.[61] Most such bequests would rank low on Suzanne Lebsock's scale measuring men's trust in their wives. In her examination of wills written in Petersburg, Virginia, she argues that wills reflect men's "respect for the wife's capacity to manage property in an intelligent, responsible way." On her "discretion scale," men trusting their wives with the full use of their entire property and also naming them their executors exhibited "major discretion." At the other end were men who offered only the life use of all or a portion of an estate and did not trust their wives as executors. The Montreal men most likely to make their wives executors were the same ones who bequeathed their full estates to them.[62] Yet, Lisa Wilson, in particular, has questioned whether absolving a widow of responsibility for the onerous tasks of the executor represented a lack of faith in a wife's abilities.[63] I return to the question of executors in later chapters. For now it is sufficient to know that around half the husbands' wills we have located named their spouse as the only executor; a few more made her co-executor. Assigning this job to their future widow was more frequent among men in the crafts than in the elite, among Canadiens than English Protestants, and among men who married in the 1840s rather than the 1820s.

Robert Harwood used his will to augment the promises he had made Marie-Louise in their marriage contract. One farm was to go to one of their sons. Otherwise he left all the property, real and personal, that he owned at the time of his death "to my dear wife whose many virtues and great qualities I have had so many proofs of." His will carefully expressed his "full confidence" that she would then dispose of his property in the best interests of their ten children. To them he left his "blessing," articulating his hope that they would "remain to be good and kind to their mother, and affectionate to each other and that they will avoid all disputes or quarrelling amongst themselves, but on the contrary aid and assist each other and they will not but find themselves much more happy and prosperous individually."[64]

Like Harwood and Oliver Wait, Dr. William Sutherland sought to augment the promises of his marriage contract as he imagined his wife outliving him. Between 1873 and 1874, shortly after his and Catherine's move up the hill and the death of their twenty-six-year-old eldest son, he made an English-style will and several codicils. These stand out for the detailed way he sought to micro-manage his future widow's economic viability, social stature, and behaviour. Recall that their marriage contract had served mostly to establish separate property and to identify Catherine's father's significant contribution of furniture, books, and instruments. It had barred dower but offered no alternative support should she become a widow. The will that he handwrote on 24 March 1873 made bequests to a wide range of female relatives, as well as to the Montreal General Hospital and the Montreal Lying-in Hospital, the main institutions where he had worked. He promised Catherine the use of one of his two houses rent-free, as well as an income of £600 or nearly $2,000 annually in quarterly payments as long as she continued to provide a suitable domestic situation for his surviving son. She was to "furnish and supply my son with good and reasonable board and lodging including lights, fuel, washing and attendance in her own establishment" until he reached the age of twenty-five or married. Should any conflict arise between them, he suggested they should cease co-residence and make "an amiable division of the furniture." Yet, he also insisted that "any such estrangement would be scandalous and that therefore every effort to maintain harmony or to induce reconciliation between mother and son should be made."[65] If their co-residence ceased, Sutherland wanted his wife's independence maintained, but she was no longer to live rent-free, and the allowance would fall to £500. He made his only son, Louis, his main heir.[66]

As Dr. Sutherland contemplated his own death, he sought to provide Catherine with material security, stability, and shelter, as well as moral oversight, rather than autonomy. Catherine would be well provided for. But well she should, for as will be recalled from Chapter 3, Catherine's father had contributed over £500 worth of goods to their marriage, including elegant mahogany furniture, silver cutlery, and damask curtains, as well as medical books to the setting up of their household and of his medical practice.[67] He was pretty sure the annuity could be paid readily from the rents coming in from his two properties but left instructions about what to do if this was not the case. Sutherland was clearly a man with an intimate knowledge of his own stocks, other investments, and real estate. He was in his late fifties when he wrote this will. Catherine was still in the prime of her life and possibly quite capable of dealing with financial matters. William spared her any such worries. He proposed two merchants and his son as his executors.

Dr. Sutherland kept thinking of new ways he would like to use his property and imagining different needs Catherine might have as a widow. Six months later, he added a codicil in which he specified in dollars that the amount she was to receive annually should increase to $3,000 until their son left home, when it was to drop to $2,400. William also specified that Catherine should be given a further $300 per year for dress money and that should she require "a new carriage," she could secure one with the "estate money."[68] Such concern about how their wives would manage as widows, and pride in or anxiety about their ability to provide for them from the grave, was surely evidence of ongoing love, affection, and responsibility. It was also part of these men's patriarchal control over their own separate property and their wives' persons. Such elite, bourgeois males displayed their liberal belief in individualism and their concern to ensure not just their widows' economic viability but also their social stature and behaviour.

Wealthy Montrealers like Dr. Sutherland imagined their widows living in a degree of comfort that few ordinary Montrealers could aspire to. When John Smith wrote his final will in 1868, forty-seven years after his marriage to Betsy Rea, five of his six daughters were married, including Matilda Caroline, who had married Hugh Allan in 1844, and Isabella Ann, who married his brother Andrew. His will sought to equalize the inequalities caused among the daughters by the wealthy matches these two had made. At seventy-nine, John chose his business-savvy sons-in-law as two of his executors and sought to minimize disruption for Betsy following his death. The executors were to provide her with $3,000 a year, in four equal payments to support her and their remaining single daughter.[69] Thus, John Smith imagined his wife sustaining their current standard of living as a widow. In 1868, $3,000 was about ten times the income that labourers, shoemakers, or any workers earning $1.25 a day might realistically hope to earn. Forty years later, when Canadians were asked about their incomes for the first time in a Canadian census in 1901, wage-earning female single parents, mostly widows, listed an average annual income of $203.[70]

Such wills stand out for the precision of men's imaginings about how their wives should live as widows. There is both control and concern in the determination that wives should have access to their clothes, their jewellery, good carriages, an adequate income, and often the family home. This male Montreal elite stands out also for the confidence it displays in predicting its own capacity to generate income from the grave. Men who promised their wives ownership or use of their estate or of shared community property seldom made any predictions about its worth. This, as other historians have noted, is a frustrating characteristic of many wills.[71] In contrast, Oliver Wait, John Smith, and William Sutherland, like Smith's son-in-law, Hugh Allan, imagined their widows' future in exact amounts of money. In 1832, Oliver Wait was sure he had sufficient capital to generate both the £50 promised in the marriage contract and the additional £50 of his will. John Smith was certain in 1868 that his investments could readily provide Betsy with $3,000 a year. Hugh Allan surely knew he could readily provide the more meagre $1,000 annuity he promised John's daughter when he wrote his will in 1880. These were men who had successfully combined the earning of income from trade or business with good investments that were producing predictable rents, dividends, or interest. They had reached the later stages of the middle-class property cycle, in which income from investments or real estate was already equally or more important than monies earned from businesses or professions. These men were "gentleman," a title that in this context reflected their status as "men at the end of their life cycle, who had retired from active business and lived on an independent or rentier income."[72]

Provisions for Funerals and Burials: Collective Imaginings and Solutions

When Charles-Séraphin Rodier, the merchant who later became a lawyer and then mayor of Montreal, wrote a will in 1831, he named Marie-Louise Lacroix as his executor and stated that he trusted to her wisdom regarding all the decisions about his funeral. Forty-five years later, when they were both over eighty and much wealthier, he decided that the task of executor was better left in the hands of a notary. He still wanted her to take charge of the funeral.[73] Eloi Beneche left the madame, Rosalie Paquet, with similar instructions in his will. His began, as roughly half the wills of Catholic husbands did, by recommending his soul to God as a Christian and Catholic and begging him humbly to pardon his wrongs and to accept him among the blessed in heaven. After the usual request that his debts be paid and any wrongs righted, he voiced his trust in Rosalie to see to the details of his funeral, masses, and the requiem to be said after his death. Marie-Aimée Cliche has proposed that notaries recommended such clauses.[74] Formulaic phrasing and preprinted forms certainly support this suggestion, though some of the details chosen suggest testators had their own ideas. Specific wishes ranged from minimal to stipulations about every detail of funeral services, burials, and memorial masses. The latter were most common among Catholics.

In virtually every will we have found, as was conventional in other jurisdictions, the first two clauses requested a decent burial and that debts be paid before other bequests. Most men and women who wrote wills could afford a respectable funeral and burial. Less privileged Montrealers knew from experience that once debts were paid there might be no money for a decent burial. To imagine accumulating the capital to generate revenues for widows and children following their death was out of the question for unskilled workers and many men in the crafts community who frequently had trouble making ends meet on their incomes while alive and healthy. Even within the crafts community and middling classes, debt and bankruptcy meant many might die with estates in which debts outweighed assets. This does not mean, however, as Peter Stearns suggested in his study of working-class culture in France, that the working-class made no provisions for aging and death. He is on surer footing when he argues that they fought "more for provisions for their wives than for their own persons."[75]

The fear of a pauper's burial, without a proper service or individual grave, or of death in an institution whose corpses were used for training medical students haunted Montrealers, as it did the citizens of so many nineteenth-century locations.[76] Such fears were fuelled by experiences within their own families, among friends, and by gossip, rumours, and newspaper stories. Local papers published graphic stories about bodies snatched from graves, body parts found on church steps, and avaricious parents who sold dead children's bodies to anatomists.[77] The prevalence of poverty and death and this discursive environment provided fertile soil for the growth of associations offering diverse ways to finance funerals, to support widows and orphans, or to pray for the souls of the departed.

When the eight-year-old son of the carpenter-turned-carter François Lemay and Rose Galipeau died in April 1833, this couple from the Saint Lawrence suburb scraped together 4s. 6d. for his burial. There were no special candles and no special service, but they were able to afford a proper child's burial and did not depend on the parish council to cover the costs, as many other parents at the time did.[78] Perhaps the minimalist funeral troubled them. In the 1850s, when Catholic parishes began creating groups to meet and pray for the dead, as well as making small contributions toward the costs of family funerals, François and Rose joined a prayer union. Historian René Hardy reports that these prayer unions were aimed explicitly at the poor and promised to secure them a decent funeral through the pooling of contributions. They offered Catholic members the security of knowing they would receive a decent funeral and burial and prayers for the salvation of their souls.[79]

More of the Catholic men and women who married in the 1820s and were still alive by the 1850s would have joined such prayer societies than made a marriage contract or a will. The records of the fabrique of the parish of Notre Dame show that Hermine Legris and her baker husband, Michel Julien, became members.[80] Information we collected in the fabrique's records on who paid for the funerals of the Catholic spouses who married in the 1820s and were buried in Montreal suggests that these groups expanded rapidly after the 1850s. Around four of every ten of the wives and husbands of that generation were buried with the financial and spiritual support offered by such groups.[81] In 1852, François Lemay died. The parish records note that he was sixty-eight years old. The prayer union paid the £1 9s. 6d. that secured him the decency of a simple service and burial, surely a relief to Rose Galipeau as she faced her first days as a widow.[82] She maintained her own membership.

Church authorities and parish finances benefited too. Pooling the costs of funerals also saved money for parishes, which had long provided free burials for the poor. These prayer unions were among the growing number of religious associations, confraternities, and institutions created or revived after the rebellions by Catholic authorities seeking to reinvigorate their Church and shape their parishioners' lives and spirituality. Saving one's soul, as historian Louis Rousseau indicates, played a key role in many of these.[83]

Working-class Montrealers also created their own mutual benefit societies, forging, Martin Petitclerc suggests, an original form of popular resistance in the context of capitalist transition that was rooted in communal solidarity and contrasted with bourgeois initiatives. By the 1860s, a wide range of Catholic, Protestant, and work-based benevolent societies and other groups dealt in some way with providing for funerals and offering assistance during times of sickness or support for widows and orphans.[84] Like the prayer unions, and in contrast with the individualized provisions of marriage contracts and wills, these associations spread the costs of funerals and assistance during illnesses and following a breadwinner's death. As Petitclerc points out, they shared in the collective risk that lies at the basis of insurance. They also often provided their members with class, social, and religious solidarity and sociability.[85]

As in other North American and European cities, craftsmen and men in particularly dangerous professions were at the forefront of the move to forge benevolent societies. Montreal pilots, who plied the dangerous waters of the Saint Lawrence; carpenters; joiners; and other craftsmen created their own benevolent associations starting in the 1830s. By the 1850s, such "large and increasing numbers of all classes" were associating in order to provide "for themselves and their families ... and for the relief of widows and orphaned children" that legislators considered their incorporation critical to controlling possibilities of fraud. Legal regulation and incorporation renders many groups visible that had been operating informally. In the late 1860s and early 1870s, they expanded to include civil servants, artists, and other professionals, all keen to ensure that their widows and children would not be left unprovided for and to secure some support in times of illness.[86]

Whereas workers and some professional groups forged their own institutions, other groups were created by prominent Montrealers. Established elites sought ways to assist and regulate newcomers or poorer citizens who shared their ethnicity and religion but not their privilege. Charles Wilson, an apothecary, who had married the wealthy Ann Platt in 1823, joined with the Patriote and mayor, Wolfred Nelson and other prominent Montrealers in 1854 to incorporate the British American Friendly Society of Canada. By the 1860s, members of Montreal's diverse non-Catholic population had created a range of national and other societies to assist immigrants and help with disease, deaths, and widowhood.[87] Some of the husbands from both cohorts of marriages were involved in seeking the incorporation of friendly societies. All of these initiatives forged new forms of association, sociability, and solidarity. They were also powerful instruments for proselytizing and for regulating behaviour and practices. For Protestants, as for Catholics, they were part of what Quebec historian Jean-Marie Fecteau refers to as the shift from "statutory Christianity to Christianity of association." Such initiatives, he insists, must be seen as part of the way "liberalism constructed social relations" in ways that prevented questions about the "tensions present in capitalist societies," and left dealing with poverty especially to "civil society and private initiatives."[88] When legislators explicitly spoke to the importance of such groups in encouraging "habits of providence and forethought among all her majesty's subjects," they were referring mostly to male family heads. And they were conveniently ignoring the reality of many workers' lives that made putting even tiny amounts of money aside on any regular basis impossible.[89]

Slowly, insurance companies offered similar possibilities but without the collective mutuality and support. Montreal's financial elite initiated the earliest local ones in the 1840s and 1850s. Their incorporation acts echo the descriptions of the benefits of benevolent societies, claiming they would encourage prudence and help promote the prosperity of the province, as well as "enabling persons of limited capital to provide from their yearly income for the support of their families in the event of their decease." When the clerk John McMillan married Elizabeth Smith in November 1844, they made no marriage contract. In the 1850s, he had steady work with the merchant firm Nelson and Wood. In May 1853, he took out a life insurance policy on his own life for the amount of £250, specifying that it was for the sole benefit of his wife and children.[90]

By the 1860s, there were several life insurance companies to choose from. Elite husbands of each generation invested in them and sometimes directed them. In 1865, legislation made it very clear that men could insure their lives for the benefit of their wives and children, and that such policies could be taken out either in their own names or those of their wives. Furthermore, echoing the older privileges of dower, such policies were free from the claims of creditors. This could have been a boon to widows inheriting estates where the debts outweighed the assets. However, over subsequent years, this protection was whittled away as successive bills allowed the use of life insurance policies as collateral for loans and made it possible for the insured to use their will to leave the policy to only one of the named beneficiaries. In these ways, insurance companies took the idea of mutual assistance and turned it into a business, creating a new and different form of family property. They offered marrying couples new ways of imagining how to provide for the possibility of widowhood, but freedom of willing spread into the world of life insurance, making it possible for men to give all to their children rather than their widow unless the insurance in favour of the wife had been promised in a marriage contract.[91]

It took no great act of imagination to contemplate the dissolution of one's marriage through death in nineteenth-century Montreal. Death was familiar. Widowhood was common. Funerals were public events and cogent reminders. It was the timing and cause of death that was unpredictable. To imagine the death of a husband was to contemplate a household left without its dominant breadwinner and family head. Montrealers dealt with this possibility in provisions in marriage contracts and in wills, as well as by joining a range of different societies that offered support toward funerals and widowhood.

Husbands exercised "patriarchy from the grave" through the provisions of their marriage contracts and wills as several Canadian historians have suggested. Yet, the documents produced by these urban families suggest that few of the men envisaged their widows living in attics, totally dependent on children, or deprived of all resources, as some authors have suggested was true for rural widows.[92] Legal documents crafted particularized versions of patriarchy that differed from the customary patriarchy of the Custom of Paris, building on the ways money matters were organized for the duration of their marriage.[93] Across this period of economic and social change, and in this city with its mixture of peoples, these particularized patriarchies varied with couples' class, ethnicity, and cultural and legal traditions.

Montreal husbands imagined their own deaths, burials, and the possibility that their wives might outlive them in three main ways. Marguerite Paris and her labourer husband, Joseph Guilbault, were typical of the vast majority who subscribed deliberately or not to the customary patriarchy of the law. If she outlived him, she would become the legal owner of half their goods, the other half belonging eventually to any surviving children. Joseph, like a growing number of Montrealers, did not own any property when he married or inherit any during his marriage. If he had, Marguerite could have anticipated having the right to use half that property or the revenues from it as her dower, until this was changed with the codification of the law in 1866. After the Registry Ordinance became law in 1841, wives could agree to reject this right if the husband wished to sell such land. Yet, labourers like Joseph, along with the many Montreal artisans and working-class men who allowed the law to sort out property questions, were likely more worried about dying in debt and burial in a pauper's grave than about designating an heir or paying to inscribe their final wishes. These were the Montrealers who in growing numbers joined mutual benefit associations, prayer groups, and other institutions that ensured a decent funeral, burial, and sometimes economic support for widows and children.

The communal patriarchy chosen most often by Canadiens and couples from the crafts community who made marriage contracts balanced the material needs of urban widows or widowers against the claims of children and reflected the spirit of the Custom of Paris' property provisions. The primary goal was to keep family property together after a spouse's death. This was sought by choosing community property, making mutual donations, stipulating a dower for the widow, or making bequests, often in mutual wills. Some husbands envisioned trusting their wives with full ownership of the property as widows. More offered only the use of it until remarriage or death, after which it would pass to their children, usually in equal parts. In this, their overall goals varied little from the patterns of transmission among the rural families in Quebec and much of Europe, who have received greater attention than urban families. This communal patriarchy was more generous to potential widows than the law or than husbands in many common law jurisdictions in terms of the proportion of an estate they would get to use or own. However, its worth depended on its value and state when the man died.[94]

The third cluster of provisions built upon the more liberal, individualistic version of companionate patriarchy, often rooted in the rejection of community property during the marriage. These husbands sought full control over property accumulated during the marriage. Many had learned to do this by making a marriage contract either excluding community property or establishing separate property and offering an annuity or lump sum to avoid dower. Failing to have made such a contract, some Montreal men sought to use their wills to overturn the community property regime, demanding that widows relinquish that right, even while making pretty generous bequests. English-speaking Montrealers often combined this particular version of masculinity with a locally-induced assertion of Britishness based on florid rejections of the Custom of Paris in contracts and wills. Still, a growing proportion of Canadien husbands, especially among the merchant elite, also negotiated some version of this more liberal patriarchy by opting for separate property, rejecting dower, and promising alternatives.

Most liberal patriarchs sought to maintain wives' standards of living as widows, though they might fall short of the law's provision of half. Most also sought to give equal amounts to all their children. As elsewhere, primogeniture had little place in wills: support for widows and roughly equal division for children was the norm.[95] Some explicitly incorporated their hopes about how their wives should live as widows, specifying, as William Sutherland did for Catherine Farquhar, their rights to specific houses, to carriages, and to clothing for mourning and after. In this elite and predominantly English Canadian and urban imagining of widowhood, widows continued to display their dead husbands' class position and success as a provider through their housing, carriages, and clothing.

In Mondelet's letter signed as M., it was the French custom of dower, agreed to in a marriage contract, that would ensure that a widow walked the streets "well dressed and nourished," whereas English law left the widow "walking the streets with her children in tow, begging for bread and requesting alms." English and French Montrealers did make rather different provisions for widows. The distinctiveness of the bodies of law and custom that were part of their heritage shaped men's and women's imaginings, as did their economic situation and their emotional ties to each other. Yet, Montrealers of all origins blended elements of the Custom and the common law. The desire to keep one's widow off the streets was largely a shared one, rooted in individual sentiment and understandings of men's ongoing responsibility as breadwinners. Imagining one's widow well dressed and nourished, however, was within the realm of the possible for only a small proportion of husbands. The understanding that men should continue to provide from beyond the grave was more widespread than the acknowledgment that many could not.

When couples married, wrote marriage contracts, joined benevolent associations or other religious groups offering ways of covering the cost of funerals, or purchased life insurance, they seldom knew for sure which spouse would die first. Some wills, in contrast, were written by men and women close to death. Husbands' deaths made widows of wives, initiating the diverse itineraries of widowhood that are studied in the second part of this book. Its first chapter explores the timing and demographies of death and widowhood among these two generations of couples.

PART 2

Individual Itineraries of Widowhood

6

Diverse Demographies
Death, Widowhood, and Remarriage

Monsieur, my daughter is quite well off at home with me, she needs for nothing, you take her, but after five, six or more years, you die, leaving perhaps, 5 or 6 children.

– M., letter to the editor, *L'Aurore des Canadas,* 18 December 1840

The signature on Oliver Wait's will is large, the writing shaky (see Figure 6.1). His scraggly inscription looks different from the crisp letters of his signatures on other documents produced as he traded firewood, secured government contracts, or agreed to the organization of property in his marriage contract with Caroline Campbell. Notary Arnoldi noted that he was "sick of body but of sound mind and memory."[1] Oliver died later that day. He died at home, as did most people during the nineteenth-century who were lucky enough to avoid accidental deaths on the streets, at work, or at leisure. Usually only the poorest Montrealers died in the Hôtel-Dieu or the General Hospital. A minority even of the elderly spent their final years in any kind of institution.[2]

Death and widowhood might be imagined and prepared for when marrying or even earlier. Funerals and property provisions could be described in marriage contracts and in wills, discussed in conversation, or provided for by joining benefit and burial societies. Yet, it was only over their dead spouse's body that men and women knew for sure they would become a widow or a widower. This chapter explores the demography of death, widowhood, and remarriage through the individual experiences of women of the two generations that had married in the 1820s and 1840s. It begins with the days and hours leading up to women's widowhood, probing household dynamics during final illnesses and contemporary ideas about dying. It then zeros in on husbands' deaths, examining where

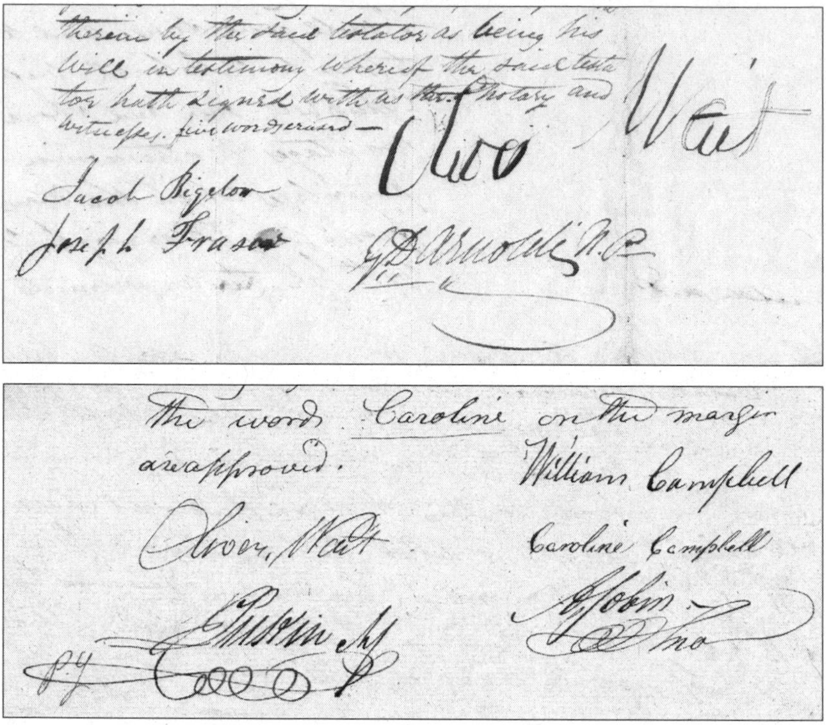

FIGURE 6.1 Oliver Wait's signatures on his will, 1832, and marriage contract, 1824. | Extract from the will of Oliver Wait, Notary George Dorland Arnoldi, 12 August 1832, act no. 1363. Centre d'archives de Montréal de Bibliothèque et Archives nationales du Québec, CN601, S7. Extract from the marriage contract between Caroline Campbell and Oliver Wait, Notary André Jobin, 14 August 1824, act no. 3481. Centre d'archives de Montréal de Bibliothèque et Archives nationales du Québec, CN601, S215.

possible their causes, contexts, and timing. In the third section I review the demography of these marriages, considering how long they lasted and the ages of widowhood. The final section looks briefly at women who rejected widowhood by remarrying.

Other historians have analyzed family papers to describe the increasingly romantic understandings about what constituted a "good death" in the nineteenth century and the rituals that drew family and friends around the bodies of the dying and the dead.[3] Such documents are usually limited to a small, literate elite. I have turned instead to parish registers, wills, religious prescriptions, inventories of assets following a death, obituaries, and coroners' reports. Shards of information from such sources, read in conjunction with writings about nineteenth-century death, offer glimpses of the minutes, hours, and days leading up to a husband's death, of some of the causes, the ages of the dying men, and of the lives of those women who remarried.

Households of Illness and Death

Charlotte Mount and Jacques Genevay lived for some, possibly all, of their short marriage with Jacques' twice-widowed mother, Agathe Dumas. Jacques and his mother struggled to keep creditors at bay. The estate of his grandfather on his mother's side was not fully settled when he married in 1823. Two years later, Jacques sold a lot and house, but the annual installments of £500 were not to start until 1831. In September 1826, he and his mother failed to pay around £90 owing on a promissory note. Later that month, he arranged to repay some debts for construction materials, brandy, and cash loans once assets were available from his dead grandfather's estate. In early October, the Montreal clothing merchants Gibb and Company took Jacques and his mother to court to secure payment of two bills totalling about £28. Two days later, mother and son procured the services of John Samuel McCord as their attorney in order to sort out how they would pay £3,000 owing the Bank of Montreal.[4] Bills to lawyers mounted as they sought to delay the payment of diverse debts. Bills to doctors mounted too as they dealt with Jacques' "lingering illness." His signature on 1 February 1827 was wobbly. By the 24th, when Dr. Stephenson and the medical and law students witnessed his will, he, Charlotte, and his mother clearly knew he would die soon.[5]

Debt and death hung over the household and over the future of Charlotte and her mother-in-law. Despite their debts, Charlotte and Agathe spared no expense in caring for Jacques. Young Dr. Stephenson was one of the city's most prominent English-speaking doctors. His union with Isabella Torrance, daughter of a wealthy merchant, had taken place just a year earlier. Stephenson had trained at the University of Edinburgh medical school, then apprenticed with a leading city doctor on his return to Montreal. In 1827, he had been on the staff of the Montreal General Hospital for five years. He and his colleagues there were leading efforts to professionalize medicine in Montreal. When Genevay's debts were tallied, he owed Dr. Stephenson £70. A further £11 was owing to Dr. Berthelet. Eighty-one pounds was among the highest debt to doctors listed in the inventories we have found made following deaths of these two generations of couples.[6] The elite families whom the British historian Pat Jalland studied in England in the nineteenth century consulted a minimum of one doctor as family members approached death, even though they understood the limited ability of medical knowledge to cure most diseases. She suggests they sought reassurance and comfort for the dying from doctors rather than miraculous cures. Doctors could also be witness to a testator's soundness of mind.[7] Jacques died later on the day Dr. Stephenson called and he wrote his will.

Among the two dozen inventories made following a husband's death that we found for women who married between 1823 and 1826 and became widows, at least seven had debts that were clearly to doctors. Many were explicitly for the final illness of their husband.[8] These were not limited to prominent middle-class families, or even to the families of skilled artisans or men running inns, taverns, and small businesses. Despite the cost, the labourer's wife Marguerite Paris turned to Doctors Nelson, Gosselin, and Berthelot as she sought to nurse Joseph Guilbault through his final illness. They were never paid. Clearly, some doctors were willing to assist Montreal's sick and dying, even when their chances of being paid were slim.[9]

The best assistance for the dying, contemporary British doctors argued, was comfort and a "little tender nursing" by anyone other than a pauper nurse.[10] Some Montreal women worked as sick nurses. Occasionally, they listed their occupation in city directories or reported it to census takers. Usually, their work is hidden. Scattered mentions of small sums owing to women in inventories made following a final illness hint at the presence of sick nurses and women skilled in laying out bodies. Both the Grey Nuns and the Sisters of Providence visited the Catholic sick and dying in their homes.[11] The main caregivers were usually the women of the family. Nineteenth-century women's diaries and letters show mothers, aunts, and unmarried sisters moving between households to help in times of sickness. When Caroline Scott Pelton's daughter Maria was very sick, two of Caroline's married sisters spent several days with them. This was a great relief to Caroline, she told her daughter Carrie, for she had "enough to do with one thing and another, not to say anything of the anxiety about Maria."[12] Men too were anxious when children and wives were sick. Some contributed to the care and nursing of loved ones.[13] Yet, when wives were ill or dying, most men were obliged to continue earning, so daughters or other relatives stepped in. When husbands were ill, their most likely nurse was their wife.

Caregivers at the bedsides of the sick and dying might compete for space with notaries, witnesses, doctors, and those bringing spiritual comfort. Some wills indicate that sick husbands were lying in bed in a room on the first floor of their homes as they arranged their final wishes, suggesting how some households were rearranged to accommodate the demands of caring and the stream of friends, family, officials, and visitors that incipient deaths precipitated. When Oliver Wait explained his final wishes in 1832, Caroline Campbell opened up her home to Notary Arnoldi, as well as to the two witnesses.[14] As Rosalie Paquet's husband, Eloi Beneche, lay dying in February 1846, Notary Vallée found him in a room overlooking Lagauchetière Street, probably in the house on St. Constant where Rosalie had been arrested so often between 1831 and 1840 for keeping a disorderly house. They had called a master cabinetmaker and master carpenter from the Saint Lawrence suburb to witness his final wishes.[15] Eloi died six days later. In Jacques Genevay's case, as we saw, his doctor, a medical student, and a law student served as witnesses, while probably also dispensing medical care and legal assistance.

For most of Montreal's Catholic, Protestant, or Jewish husbands and wives, faith, spiritual support, and their spiritual state were critical elements of dying well. All shared the understanding that a good death included "solemn farewells and pious advice to spouse, children, and servants, the resolution of worldly affairs, and the public reading of the will," preferably at home and surrounded by family and friends. Dying alone was to be avoided in all faiths. Death notices and obituaries of the husbands of these two generations who died before their wives sometimes reported that the death occurred at home. When Betsy Rea's husband, John Smith, died in 1878, the notice specified that it occurred at their home at 102 Alexander Street.[16]

Yet, in this religiously divided city, contrasts infused the meanings and practices around dying and death. Theological differences shaped who was sought at the bedsides of the dying. The Evangelical model of the "good death" that Pat Jalland and others have argued was influential among most Protestants of the Victorian period stressed the importance of rapidly settling worldly affairs to minimize distraction from the spiritual, the message of hope in Christ's resurrection, and the desirability of "uplifting last words and joyful signs of grace." Books and tracts published in the 1820s and 1830s suggested good "death bed thoughts" and appropriate final words, and offered narratives of good deaths. Montreal Protestant newspapers published melodramatic stories in which women's piety and pleas were expected to convince dying or surviving husbands who had strayed from religious lives to change their ways and embrace God and goodness. The elite, conservative, Anglican Montrealer and lawyer John Samuel McCord, a contemporary of the men and women who married in the 1820s, took copious notes about death. He transcribed sermons, stories, and accounts of "good deaths," into a "Theological Commonplace Book." These books, available for purchase, included printed subheadings such as "Mourning," "Deathbed," "Death," and "Sudden" so that individuals could record edifying stories or practices.[17]

In this Evangelical good death, Protestant clergymen might visit the dying, providing spiritual succour. But with the exception of Anglicans, their presence was a minor component of the good death, compared to

FIGURE 6.2   Notre Dame Street, near McGill Street, Montreal, 1806. The reproduction of this early-nineteenth-century design in 1879 evoked more than simpler times in a pre-industrial city. It followed articles on the difficult place of francophones and Métis in the west and discussions of the place of Native peoples and Canadiens in the new country, and served as a reminder to readers of the Conquest and of how things had changed. Note the priest and his assistants in the lower right-hand corner, carrying the sacraments. John Lambert, artist, 1810. | Republished in *L'Opinion Publique,* 9 January 1879, 3. From the collection of the Bibliothèque et Archives nationales du Québec.

the centrality of priests for Catholics. As Genevay lay dying, Charlotte, his mother, and his wide circle of "faithful friends" could hold his hand, console him, and nurse him in the worst moments of his illness. Catholic nuns might have provided spiritual guidance and support, though in the 1820s their numbers were small. But, just as women could not witness wills or provide notarial expertise, neither could they provide the final sacraments so essential to the good Catholic death. For Catholics, it was crucial to call a priest once there was any possibility that a family member might die. Death rituals, writes Louis Rousseau, were the most important of nineteenth-century Catholic rites. Only a very small number of saints were expected to go directly to heaven, and an equally small group of unrepentant sinners to hell. Most people would spend time in purgatory. As a result, the issue of eternal salvation played a key role in ordinary people's

FIGURE 6.3 "Her Last Sacrament." This 1878 image of a deathbed scene conforms to many of the dominant representations of death. Family members are present, grieving. The dying woman appears lucid and ready to receive the final sacraments from the priest. Priests, doctors, and notaries writing wills might mingle with the dying, though this turn-of-the-nineteenth-century scene suggests the more quiet family scenes that would increasingly be favoured as deaths were pushed out of sight. | *Canadian Illustrated News,* 19 October 1878, 18, 16: 253. Library and Archives Canada, 4428.

consciousness and in official discourses. Correct rituals at the time of death, combined with the continued prayers of the living, could hasten the journey to heaven. Because only priests could perform all the required final rites, the families of the dying did their best to secure their presence.[18]

Priests attending to the dying walked or travelled by carriage. They were accompanied by an assistant, specially attired for the occasion, carrying the final sacraments in a special container hidden under a cloth (see Figure 6.2). These practices became more elaborate and romanized after the 1840s as Montreal's new bishop, Bishop Bourget, sought to reshape and unify Catholic rituals to fit the "emotive, expressive, external and popular" religiosity he promoted. Lanterns and other decorative elements were added to new rules that choreographed rituals more closely and promoted Roman practices around deaths.[19] The procession to the bedside of the dying was ritualized and public. Its codes were understood by Catholic friends and neighbours, who could join in and follow the sacrament into the death chamber to offer prayers and support. Once in the house, the *curé* placed the viaticum on a table and blessed the sick person and the room. This makes the wisdom of rearranging households to accommodate these and other visitors clearer. Priests might return several times during an illness. However, if the patient appeared to be on the verge of death, all the elements of the final sacraments were combined – confession, absolution, administration of the viaticum, the Eucharist, and the anointment of the patient with holy oil – the extreme unction. As with the writing of a will, the final sacrament was meant to be delivered to someone in full control of their faculties (see Figure 6.3).[20]

The drama and tension of some deathbed scenes is palpable. Waiting until a final illness to write a will was risky for husbands or wives who wanted to be clear about how their property should be distributed. Witnesses might be unwilling to assist or unavailable. Those wishing to write out their own will in English fashion might lose the strength or the mental capacity to do so. In one 1869 case, the will of a man who died while dictating his wishes was declared invalid, despite the presence of two witnesses. Catholic Montrealers could not be sure to find a priest in time for the final sacraments. Before mid-century, there were hardly enough Catholic *curés* and priests in Montreal to serve all the dying, particularly in times of epidemics. Nor did they always come when requested. Rousseau suggests that those most likely to be visited lived closest to the church.[21] Furthermore, the dying and their families could not always judge when death was near, and many deaths were sudden ones, leaving little time to notify a priest. Jean-Baptiste Bergevin, as we saw in the previous chapter, left Euphrosine Mitresse Sansfaçon very detailed instructions about his funeral in his will. He also expressed his hopes for the afterlife. The first clause of his July 1848 will recommended his soul to God, asking him to pardon his sins and to place him among the happy in heaven when he left this world. Jean-Baptiste had taken care of his material and religious wishes, but he could not control the manner of his death. He died suddenly of apoplexy on 9 December 1848, five months later. Euphrosine and other family members may or may not have had time to call a priest for the final sacraments.[22] This worry added a particular tension to Catholic deaths, a spiritual parallel to the material concern about completing a final will while lucid.

Historians who have examined the ideas about dying and the good death have relied largely on sources that describe ideal rather than actual deaths, or that capture deaths narrated in written family records.[23] Such sources tend to locate death in beds within family homes and to freeze the family around the bedside of the dying person. This was also common in visual depictions of deathbed scenes. Yet, poverty and accidents, along with other sudden deaths, made such final moments impossible for many. Coroners' reports capture the other end of the spectrum – suspicious and sudden deaths. Men died at work. Construction workers died after falling off planks or when walls they were building or buildings they were demolishing crushed them. Labourers slipped and drowned as they carried cargo down gangplanks. Ships' carpenters fell overboard. As mentioned earlier, Elmire Painchaud's husband, Joseph-Alexis Painchaud, drowned in a shipwreck in 1860 while captaining a family boat. Carts ran over carters, citizens, and children alike, sometimes killing them. Later, railway workers fell from carriages and died. Leisure was also sometimes the site of death. Men, women, and children drowned in the Saint Lawrence or the Lachine Canal while bathing. They fell off boats and out of canoes. They fell out of bed and were found dead the next morning, or they drank too much and fell off chairs, into ponds, or simply fell asleep outside and did not wake up. Strokes and heart attacks could strike anywhere and anytime. Adolphus Mordecai Hart was in the middle of pleading a case in court in 1879 when he suffered the stroke that killed him.[24]

Death notices occasionally announced whether someone had managed to die a good death. Jean-Baptiste Bergevin's sudden death "of an attack of apoplexy" was announced in the newspapers. Other mentions of sudden deaths suggest family members were robbed of the chance to say goodbye and to provide support to the dying. In contrast, when Marie-Louise Letourneau's husband since 1824 died in 1852 at the age of fifty-two, the family described Joseph Lecour's death as "gentle and calm," as befitted someone whose humble and honest life was that of a true Christian.[25] Such explicit mentions of good, "Christian" deaths were rare, and more common in death notices and obituaries that followed women's, rather than men's, deaths.[26] The narratives of men's lives submitted by survivors tended to stress their secular roles as fathers, husbands, and citizens. Women's final illnesses and deaths, in contrast, elicited more commentary and became occasions to extol their virtues as Christians and as patient sufferers. Even such brief death notices conveyed moral and religious lessons, producing several versions of masculinities and femininities. When Marie-Adelaide Maillou died four months after her marriage to the joiner, Louis Audet-Lapointe, the notice explained that her death followed "a short and painful illness of four days, which she suffered as a true Christian and with the greatest resignation to the wishes of God." Longer than most, it claimed for her the life of an engaged Catholic woman. "The poor lose in her a perfect model of charity. Her gentleness attracted the friendship of all who knew her, because one can say that she was gifted with all the social virtues and was an ornament of her sex."[27]

Cramped homes, the scant resources of the city's poorer citizens, and old age made caring for sick and dying husbands or wives impossible for some spouses. Lacking domestic help and often co-resident children, support during lingering illnesses likely were beyond their physical and financial means. Adelaide Bebel was in her seventies when her labouring husband, Charles Cousineau, fell ill in 1871. Perhaps she had cared for him herself for a while. Eventually, he went to the Hôtel-Dieu, where the cloistered sisters provided nursing assistance to so many of the city's poor and dying. It was there that he died, at the age of seventy-nine.[28]

Epidemics

By the time of Oliver Wait's death from cholera in August 1832, newspaper reports suggest that well over a thousand people had died in Montreal.[29] The epidemic hit the city just three weeks after the violent 1832 Montreal West by-election, to which I return in a later chapter. Cholera in 1832, typhus in 1847, and cholera again in 1856 meant that one major demographic feature of the lives of the couples marrying in the 1820s and 1840s was the impact of epidemics. A second was the unpredictability of when death would hit. These are the twin themes of this and the following section.

Cholera's spread from Asia into Europe was reported in the colony's newspapers. Politicians attempted to prepare for the pandemic's potential arrival. Legislation in early 1832 set up a quarantine station at Grosse Isle for immigrants and provided for local medical boards.[30] These provisions proved woefully inadequate from the moment the first Irish immigrant died on the Montreal wharves on 7 June. Curious residents walked down to the wharves to observe the body of the disease's earliest victim. Montrealers noted its impact in their diaries and letters. Alexander Hart, Theodore and Hannah's uncle, described thirty-four corpses passing his home in one day, and noted that the Board of Health was using twelve carts to carry away the dead, who were interred "without prayers." Elites studied cholera's impact and developed structures of regulation to contain its spread. Benjamin Workman, who had married Margaret Manson in June 1823 and was the owner and editor of the *Canadian Courant* during the epidemic, published sociological comments on its impact and his opinions about how it should be dealt with. Later, his older brother, Joseph, wrote a dissertation on the subject.[31] In mid-June, his paper suggested that a "panic of almost indescribable nature" appeared to have "taken hold of the whole body of citizens and ... deprived them of their presence of mind."[32] That same month he reproduced the translation of an article from *La Minerve* reporting that "women with terror on their countenances, and many of them weeping were to be seen on every street ... carts with coffins containing dead bodies, each occupied with four or five persons, were passing frequently." This gendered interpretation located fear, terror, and grief resolutely among women. In August, the *Courant* reported that cholera hit males more than females, the poor more than the wealthy: "Although its footsteps can be traced through all ranks of life, yet its lowest blows have fallen among the labourers."[33]

The first of the husbands who married in the 1820s to die during the cholera epidemic were indeed labourers and men from the artisanal community. On 11 June, the labourers André Juneau and John McKee both died. Marie-Amable Papineau's husband, the saddler François Gareau, died on 18 June, leaving her a widow after five and a half years of marriage. On 21 June, the labourer Antoine Desormier, who had married Agathe St. Jean in 1824, died, leaving her a widow at the age of thirty. Contact with the sick and dying, or with their bedding or clothing, exposed those nursing cholera patients to the disease. A month later, Agathe was also dead. Cholera turned women quickly from wives into widows and husbands into widowers. Cramps, terrible diarrhea, nausea, and fever led quickly to shivering, dehydration, and collapse as the patient's body turned cold and bluish. Death might occur within hours of the first symptoms.

Joseph Workman later described Montreal's upper classes as flattering "themselves on a happy exemption from its ravage" before discovering that "cholera's carnival was not complete and the devastations were now extended beyond the habitations of the indigent and homeless."[34] By July, non-labouring or artisanal men were also dying. Andrew White's second wife, Margaret Logan, became a widow on 6 July. The record of his death suggests he had been working as an undertaker, a position that placed this trader, and former partner of Oliver Wait, in the front line of risk.[35] He died after only "a few hours of illness." The will he wrote earlier that day described him as "in perfect health." At the age of forty-eight, Margaret became a widow and the single mother of a young daughter scarcely seven years after their 1823 marriage. On the same day, Caroline Campbell's father, William, died.[36] By August, when Oliver Wait wrote his will, there could be little consolation in the belief that only the poor died of cholera. Caroline Campbell became a widow at the age of twenty-five. Ten days later, on 22 August, William Gay, the husband of Margaret White, who was Andrew White's daughter, also died. Margaret White joined Margaret Logan, her stepmother; Caroline Campbell; Marie-Amable Papineau; and many other Montreal spouses widowed by the cholera epidemic. Margaret was only twenty-three and, like Caroline, had lost both husband and father to the disease.

Cholera cut like a scythe into the lives of the couples who married during the 1820s, killing husbands and wives who had been married for less

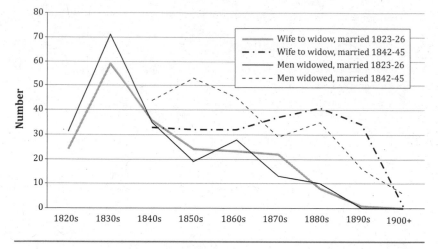

FIGURE 6.4   Number of husbands and wives known to have been widowed, by decade, marriages of the 1820s and 1840s compared

Note: Couples in which the husband definitely died first, so she is a widow, 1823-26, *N* = 197, 1842-45, *N* = 210; couples in which the wife definitely died first, leaving the husband a widower, 1823-26, *N* = 206, 1842-45, *N* = 227.

Source: Montreal all marriages, 1823-26, and 50 percent of couples marrying 1842-45, for whom the date of the death of the first partner has been located in a death registration, necrology, obituary, or cemetery records.

than a decade. The dead were buried hastily. Officials scrambled to record their names. The usual information offered by relatives about the deceased's age, cause of death, occupation, and name of spouse was often missing. Deaths of those who fled the city were not always listed in local death and burial records. Hence, it is often difficult to be certain about whether a particular husband or wife died during the epidemic. We know that at least twenty-two of the women who married between 1823 and 1826 became widows during the three hot summer months that cholera raged in the city. Ten more probably did, but lack of detailed information makes it hard to be sure. Were more reliable information available, the real figures and proportions would no doubt be higher. And, despite the argument that women were more susceptible than men, similar numbers of men appear to have become widowers. Dramatically high numbers of women who married in the 1820s and whose husbands' deaths we have definitely identified became widows in the 1830s, especially in 1832. Similar numbers of men lost their wives (see Figure 6.4).

Cholera's arrival among Irish immigrants gave Canadien nationalists new ammunition in their growing critiques of colonialism and colonial policies.[37] The bishop Jean-Jacques Lartigue privately linked the murders of two Canadien men on 21 May following the by-election with cholera as two prongs in British policy seeking to reduce the Canadien population. Marie-Louise Lacroix's husband, the moderate Charles-Séraphin Rodier, articulated this view publicly in a speech in August. As we saw, he was already a very successful merchant, on the brink of retiring early and changing to a career in law. "When I see my country in mourning and my native land nothing but a vast cemetery, I ask what has been the cause of these disasters," he said. "The voice of my father, my brother and my beloved mother, the voices of thousands of my fellow citizens respond from their tombs. It is emigration. It was not enough to send among us avaricious egotics without any spirit of liberty than that which can be bestowed by a simple education of the counter, to enrich themselves at the expense of Canadians, then endeavour to enslave them, they must rid themselves of their beggars and cast them by the thousands on our shores ... they must do still more, they must send us in their train pestilence and death.[38] For the correct and conservative Rodier, these were strong words.

The plight of the immigrants and the dangers of cholera led other Montreal elites, both Canadien and English speaking, to promote changes in local government and to seek to cleanse their city of some of the worst features of poverty and disease. Men married in the 1820s were drawn into the drama of its unfolding in many ways other than as victims. Workman, as we saw, commented in the columns of his newspaper. Dr. John Stephenson became one of the citizens at large on Montreal's first Board of Health, as did Rev. Henry Esson, who had married Maria Sweeny in 1823, and become a widower in 1826. Wives and widows of this cohort were involved too, for, as we saw in Chapter 3, the epidemic stimulated the creation of the Ladies' Benevolent Society, the Roman Catholic Orphan Asylum, and other female-led charitable associations. Protestant and Catholic women alike visited the sick in the city, seeking to aid widows and orphans.[39]

This Board of Health's ability to police sanitary matters was limited, and citizens were increasingly critical of its inability to deal with the epidemic. Frustrated elite Montrealers formed their own Citizens' Committee for Sanitary and Emigrant Purposes at a meeting held on 22 June at the Montreal courthouse. Its goal, as Mary Carter's husband, Charles-Elzéar Mondelet, explained at the group's founding meeting, was to "restore the shaken confidence and courage of the public." Some of the city's leading merchants and professionals were involved. They included George Moffatt, then the leading spokesperson for Montreal's businessmen in the Legislative Council. This new committee oversaw the provision of shelter for immigrants on land of the Grey Nuns, away from the wharves. They secured funding for widows and orphans from the government and became vigilantes for cleanliness in the homes of the city's poorer citizens. The sanitary committees they set up in the city's wards allowed citizens to "take management of affairs into their own hands," as Benjamin Workman explained in his paper. These local committees named up to thirty local men as "health wardens," authorizing them to enforce sanitary regulations and ferret out "nests of abominations."[40]

The Health Board, these sanitary committees, and their wardens targeted the poor as those they understood most likely to spread cholera. They prosecuted Irish men who kept pigs or harboured too many people in their homes. Their ambitions about surveillance were large. In the mostly business area of the West ward, they advocated that some thirty-six members visit assigned streets at least three times a week to report. In the East ward, according to the *Canadian Courant,* some zealous wardens turned their firehoses onto the houses of refractory inhabitants, soaking them from attics to cellars. Workman's paper lauded their activities, arguing that volunteer health wardens did "more in a week towards cleansing our city" than those employed by the Board of Health. Not everyone welcomed this scrutiny of their domestic spaces. When a warden called at the home of Laura Mower and John Campbell, the bookseller, an argument ensued. John ordered the warden out of the house, and a few days later wrote to the *Courant* to complain of the warden's grossly improper behaviour.[41]

Laura and John survived the scourge of 1832. So did Marie-Louise Lacroix and Charles-Séraphin Rodier, Isabella Torrance and John Stephenson, Benjamin Workman and Margaret Manson, and Mary Carter and Charles-Elzéar Mondelet, all members of the elite who played some role in forging structures of surveillance and support, or commenting on the epidemic. Their diverse interventions and those of their fellow citizens left legacies that shaped the lives and deaths of other Montrealers over the following decades. The massive voluntary organization of the elite to police the cleanliness of the poor built on existing patterns of charitable visiting and shaped future reform initiatives in which both men and women would be involved. The rapid forging of action-oriented groups was not new, but it contributed to the reservoir of experiences that would be called on again as the city's and colony's residents lurched toward rebellion. The involvement of doctors, including John Stephenson, in health boards, and the new respect for their expertise, led to new integration of medical knowledge into governance and regulation at the municipal and colonial levels that reshaped future urban government.[42] But these initiatives did not prevent future epidemics.

In 1847, typhus hit Montreal. Hannah Lyman's husband, John Easton Mills, had been elected as mayor a year earlier in a hotly contested municipal election. Over the decades since his marriage, his politics had shifted. In the Montreal West by-election of 1832, he had voted for Stanley Bagg, the Tory candidate. In the lead-up to the rebellions of 1837 and 1838, he like so many other merchants was a strong Tory supporter and a member of the Constitutional Association.[43] In 1846, however, he ran as the reform candidate in the controversial process of selecting a new mayor that pitted him against the Tory incumbent James Ferrier. Mills had been at the forefront of many ventures that were transforming the economy of Montreal and the colony. In addition to subdividing land on the mountain and running his own bank, he served on the first administrative council of the Montreal City and District Savings Bank at the request of the new Catholic bishop, Ignace Bourget. He was closely associated with the new world of railways as a director of the Montreal and Lachine Railroad, incorporated in 1846, and as an investor in the St. Lawrence and Atlantic Railroad. When he became mayor in 1846 he was nearly fifty, wealthy, and well respected in the world of business.[44]

Within a year of Mills's election, the Irish potato famine's devastating impact was being reported in the colony's papers. More immigrants were anticipated in the spring. Mills was president of the city's Immigration Commission, as well as mayor. In March 1847, when the first immigrants arrived after the spring thaw, it was clear that there was "ship fever" on board. Mills and his council built on lessons learned during the 1832 cholera epidemic. They had temporary wooden sheds built near the wharves to serve as hospitals and to prevent the sick from moving around the city. These were busy, overcrowded, dangerous places, insufficient for the numbers of sick. Like cholera, the disease spread from the riverside through the city, carried, some would say, by Irish children who escaped from the sheds to beg for food. Fear of typhus spread virulently too.[45]

It was a hard time to be mayor. Some Montrealers wanted to refuse the immigrants entry to their port or to move them far from the city. They organized aggressively and voiced their indignation publicly. Mills parried their critiques, calling for humanity and showing it. He personally oversaw the arrangements being made for the sick and worked among them, as did many other Montrealers. Grey Nuns and Sisters of Providence nursed the sick and dying, losing many of those exposed. Catholic priests who could understand English went to hear the final confessions of the dying and caught the disease. And, despite the danger, prominent notables also visited. Lord Elgin, who had taken up his position as governor general of the colony at the end of January, made his first visit to Montreal that summer and visited the sheds. Bishop Bourget also visited, fell sick, then recovered.[46]

Like cholera, typhus turned wives into widows and husbands into widowers, killed widows and widowers, and left children orphaned. At 11 a.m. on Friday, 2 November, Hannah Lyman became a widow. John Mills had been ill for a few days with typhus contracted while he worked with the sick immigrants in the sheds. Among those visiting him during this painful illness was Rev. Henry Wilkes. When a few days later he delivered the address at Mills's very public funeral, he used the occasion to remind those present of the impossibility of knowing the timing of death. Mills's life and his final days became teaching tools in the eulogy. Mills had not complained, questioned, or blamed God. Rather, "our deceased friend expressed his felt need of ... salvation and his conviction that only in Christ could it be found." This good death by a wealthy man who understood that wealth was not as important as faith could teach others about how to live and die well.[47] Hannah Lyman became a widow at the age of forty-eight. She had borne John eight children. Three sons died young. John's death left her a widow with four minor children between the ages of two and fifteen, and one married daughter. John had been too busy to make a will. Nor had they made a marriage contract. He left a considerable fortune.[48]

Seven years later, in late July 1854, Louis-Joseph Papineau described to his friend, and old Patriote comrade Côme Séraphin Cherrier, the pain he felt at having to send his condolences to Luce Perrault. Édouard-Raymond Fabre died of cholera on 16 July that year. Expressing his wish that his friend would be the last victim of cholera, Papineau mourned the shrinking circle of his true Montreal friends who were still alive. The cholera epidemic that peaked in 1854 was not as devastating as earlier ones. And the city was better equipped to quarantine its victims, some of whom they housed in special wards in the hospitals. Fabre had been elected as Montreal's mayor in May 1849, two years after Mills's death from typhus on the job. Prior to that he had spent a year as a councillor and as president of the city's finance committee. In these capacities he had been brilliant at cutting the city's deficit and dismal at articulating any long-term vision. Shortly after his election, cases of cholera were again reported in the city. When his second mandate ended in 1851, he was relieved to be free of the mayor's job. He continued as a councillor and president of the local health bureau, then ran again unsuccessfully for the mayor's position in 1854. It was after this election, and possibly while visiting hospitals, that he likely contacted the cholera that killed him in July that year.[49] Luce became a widow in her early forties. As we saw in Chapter 3, their three eldest children were already well established, but the two youngest were still under ten years old.

Other Deaths

Papineau's wish was fulfilled. Cholera did not return to Montreal. The three major epidemics of 1832, 1847, and 1854 took their toll on the marriages of the 1840s, as well as those of the 1820s. Such demographic disasters largely disappeared in the West between 1854 and the flu epidemic following the First World War. For the men and women who survived these years, death in an epidemic was no longer likely. Epidemics were one characteristic of the demographic regime in the years before significant public health initiatives and antibiotics began to link death in the West more definitively to old age. The second major demographic characteristic of the nineteenth century was the wide range of diseases and natural and unnatural causes that killed men and women, as well as children, of all ages. Some of the marriages of couples wed in the 1820s and 1840s lasted only a few months, some a few years. The longest lasted over sixty years. Wives were especially likely to die during their child-bearing years, men more erratically. When cholera hit in 1832, roughly one in six of the wives from the 1820s marriages for whom we know for sure when their husband died, were already widowed. And because deaths in childbirth were common, especially among young women, this was true of even more husbands – around one in five were already widowed when cholera hit the city.[50] Causes of death were not required and rarely recorded in parish registers, though they did appear in cemetery and fabrique records. The unsystematic information from these and other sources suggests some of the causes of their deaths, though even recorded causes are often not very revealing. When James McIntyre fell on the floor at the baker's shop where he worked in the Saint Anne suburb in 1834, the coroner referred to the death as resulting from the "visitation of God." The same explanation was used when Anna Taylor's husband the painter, Charles Gall, died after complaining of pain in his chest in August 1847. He was, the coroner explained, of a "feeble constitution."[51]

Some causes are clearer than others. The moments of Frances Swift's and Maria Mitchell's widowhood burst into the public record because they were brutal, sudden, and reported in local newspapers. Robert Watson, Frances' husband, was a flour inspector. They took up residence in the Recollet suburb after their marriage in November 1824. Just over two years later they were both at home, conversing with their minister. Frances left the room. A Mr. Cameron entered, engaged in conversation, then shot Robert. Frances returned to find her husband dying. The newspaper lamented the death of this "peaceful, honest and universally respected citizen." Of the young woman widowed after such a brief marriage, the newspaper report said little except that it was suspected that Mr. Cameron waited for her to leave the room before firing.[52]

Maria Mitchell did not witness her husband's death either. The day he died, they were both drinking again. And, once again, Thomas beat Maria, this time until she was "perfectly insensible, from the effects of blows and liquor." Thomas then slit his own throat. At the coroner's inquiry that followed, some said he did so out of remorse, believing he had killed his wife. Others argued that the action was premeditated. In contrast to Frances Swift, whose plight as a widow slips from the public eye, Maria's life entered a period of intense scrutiny, as we will see in Chapter 8.[53]

Chronic illnesses rarely generated such public records. Among the small number of husbands' whose cause of death was identified in records we have located, tuberculosis, other pulmonary problems, and heart diseases were among the leading causes listed. Accidents, paralysis, apoplexy, and dropsy were other reasons listed frequently. Among the men who lived past fifty, old age, senility, and debility were the most commonly cited causes.[54]

Demographies of Marriage and Death

Within three years of their wedding, Émilie Tavernier had given birth to three children: two had died, and her husband, Jean-Baptiste Gamelin, was sick. Émilie nursed him carefully, but on 1 October 1827 he died. He was fifty-four. The twenty-seven-year age difference between these spouses surely meant they may have expected that she would outlive him, though the risks of childbirth countered such probabilities. Still, they can hardly have expected their marriage to last only four years. He left Émilie a widow at the age of twenty-seven, with one young surviving son to raise.[55] The marriage of the madam Rosalie Paquet to Eloi Beneche lasted just three years. Married at thirty-two, she was a widow at thirty-five. Beneche died six days after leaving her all he had in the will drawn up in February 1846.[56] Marguerite Paris became a widow after just four years as a wife when her labourer husband, Joseph Guilbault, died in 1829. She had one surviving daughter. Charlotte Mount also became a widow after four years of marriage and while in her twenties. She was childless. Scholastique Bissonnet's marriage to the innkeeper Louis Ducharme lasted nearly twice as long. He died in 1834, eight years after their wedding, leaving her with two small children to console and support while she mourned his death.

Émilie Tavernier, Rosalie Paquet, Marguerite Paris, Charlotte Mount, and Scholastique Bissonnet were widowed after brief marriages. Rebecca Conegan dealt with her husband's illness and blindness for some time before Sampson Brady died in November 1852. He was thirty-six years old. Their marriage had lasted eight years. She became a widow at about thirty-two. Young Sampson and John Morton Brady were four and three years old respectively. Hannah Lyman, as we saw, was forty-eight, yet still had children under five, when John Mills died of typhus. Their marriage had lasted twenty-four years, very close to the average of twenty-three years for the couples who married in the 1820s. The deaths of the elite and professional husbands of Constance Hannah Hart, Marie-Louise-Josephte de Lotbinière, Marie-Louise Lacroix, Betsy Rea, and Catherine Farquhar came after longer marriages. Constance was fifty-three and had been married for thirty-five years when Adolphus Mordecai Hart had his stroke in 1879. Marie-Louise and Robert Unwin Harwood remained man and wife for forty years, spending most of their married life on the seigneury she inherited, while continuing to use Montreal as an urban base. In 1863, some nine years after he had written his will, Robert died of tongue cancer, at the age of sixty-five. Dr. William Sutherland, as we saw, lived long enough to change his mind several times about what Catherine Farquhar should receive after his death. In 1875, he died of lung disease, five months after adding the codicil to his will that promised her $300 extra per year for dress money, and a new carriage, if she needed one.[57] In the precise counting of life that characterized middle class tracking of time, he was recorded as fifty-nine years and three months old. Their marriage began in 1844 and lasted thirty-one years. Joseph Jourdain, so unlucky in his professional life, lived until 1888. He and Mary Anne Forrest never returned to the place of their marriage. He died in the United States in his mid-seventies after thirty-six years with the wife whose parents had so disapproved of their union. Marie-Louise Lacroix became a widow at eighty-one when Charles-Séraphin Rodier died at the age of eighty in 1876, of "debility." They had been married for fifty-one years.

Long marriages were not limited to the city's elite. Indeed, on average, marriages seem to have been longest among couples in the artisanal world. Of all the women married in the 1820s who outlived their husbands, the last we know of to become a widow was Marie-Anne Descarie. Her husband, Charles Turcot, was identified as a saddler when they married, though by the time of his death at the age of ninety in 1891 he was described as a rentier. Their marriage had lasted sixty-six years. She became a widow at the age of eighty-one. Despite the challenges of illness and poverty that the city's labourers and casually employed faced, some survived well into old age. Adelaide Bebel had been married for forty-seven years when her labourer husband, Charles Cousineau, died in 1871 at the age of seventy-nine. Adelaide was about seventy-two. Hermine Legris joined her as a widow a year later when her sometimes husband, Michel Julien, died at the age of seventy-two. She was about sixty-four. At his death, Michel was listed as a labourer. The records of his burial at the fabrique of the parish of Notre Dame described him as dying of heart disease. The parish record of his death simply noted the cause as old age.

As these widows' experiences suggest, the irregularity of death's impact led to widely divergent marriage lengths and ages of death and widowhood. These make average measures of age at death or widowhood or of the length of marriages useful only as very broad indicators of difference and change, especially given the variability of Protestant and Catholic records. Overall, the average length of marriages broken by a husband's death rose from around twenty-three to twenty-seven years between these two generations. Among couples where the husband worked in a craft or skilled occupation it rose from twenty-five to closer to twenty-nine years. Among husbands in the elite or in a profession it rose from twenty-two to over twenty-six, among unskilled workers from twenty-one to twenty-five. In both generations, the longest average marriages among the couples in which the wife became a widow were those where men worked as artisans and craftsmen. Marie-Anne Séné's marriage with the joiner Antoine Hurtubise lasted twenty-six years, the average for artisanal, crafts couples of the first generation. And, at fifty, Marie-Anne was very close to the average age at which women of that class became widows. The shortest marriages on average were those among those in shops, inns, and other lower echelons of commerce: Marie-Louise's eighteen-year marriage with Pierre-Bernard Decousse, tailor turned innkeeper, was a couple of years short of the average of around twenty we have found among that relatively small group. Marriages in the professions and elite fell between the two. At twenty years, Caroline Scott's marriage to the notary Thomas John Pelton fell about six years short of the average for those who married as she did in the 1840s and outlived their husbands.

There were only minor variations in the average ages of death on the basis of class, ethnicity, or religion among those couples whom we have been able to trace from their marriages to widowhood and the death of the first partner, as well as establish their ages. The husbands who married between 1823 and 1826 died at an average age of about fifty-nine and a half. Those who died before their wives were close to an average age of fifty-four. Men of that generation who outlived their wives averaged close to seventy at their deaths, after marriages averaging just under twenty-one years. Men who married in Montreal between 1842 and 1846 lived a bit longer, dying at an average age of close to sixty-one. Those who left a widow died on average at fifty-six; those who outlived their wives reached an average of around sixty-eight.

The dangers of childbirth meant that the women of these two marriage cohorts died younger on average than the men, and there was less evident improvement in women's life expectancy. The average age at death for women for whom we have been able to determine age reliably remained similar for each generation, at just over fifty-six and a half. The gap between those dying as wives and as widows was greater than that between men who died before or after their wives. Wives whose deaths left their husbands widowers died at an average age of forty-four in the 1820s marriage cohort and forty-six two decades later. Women who became widows died at closer to an average age of seventy in both generations.

Escaping Widowhood: Men, Women, and Remarriage

The Irish immigrant Mary O'Leary's Canadien husband, Nicolas Venière, died in June 1829. He had been married before. At his death he was forty-five years old. Over their brief marriage, Nicolas seems to have made his living as an inn or tavern keeper, a grocer, and a painter. Mary was a wife for less than five years. Her widowhood was brief. Six months after Nicolas died, she remarried. Her second husband, another Canadien, Joseph Cadotte, was a merchant tanner. He resided on the Côte Notre-Dame-des-Neiges, one of the neighbourhoods on the fringes of the city where Joanne Burgess has described shoemakers and tanners living and plying their trades.[58] Although Cadotte was a widower with four children, whose future claims on his property from his first marriage might have concerned him, the couple did not make a marriage contract before marrying. However, within three weeks of his and Mary's marriage, both made wills, treating them essentially as marriage contracts. She promised that all she had should go to her new "beloved" husband. Joseph made his four children his main heirs. Should Mary again become a widow, he offered her clothing, linen, a furnished bedroom, and an annual payment for the duration of her widowhood. The amount of the latter was not mentioned, but it was intended instead of a dower.[59] For Mary, widowhood was a very brief interlude between two marriages.

That this young, childless, and probably quite poor widow would remarry is not surprising. Demographers and historians studying widows' remarriages in modern times in most of the Western world have found that young and poor widows were the widows most likely to marry again. They have also found that men consistently remarried at much higher rates, as well as more quickly than women.[60] So Mary O'Leary's second husband, Joseph Cadotte, was not unusual in seeking a new wife to assist him in raising his four children.

The relationship between gender, age, and remarriage is direct and dramatic among the men and women of these two generations whose age we have been able to determine. The influence of class or wealth seems more ambiguous. Half of the women who married in the 1820s and became widows in their twenties remarried. The proportion dropped rapidly with age to 44 percent of those in their thirties, 16 percent of those in their forties, and close to zero among women widowed in their fifties or older. A lower proportion of widows who had married in the 1840s appear to have remarried, possibly because they were widowed slightly older, possibly as

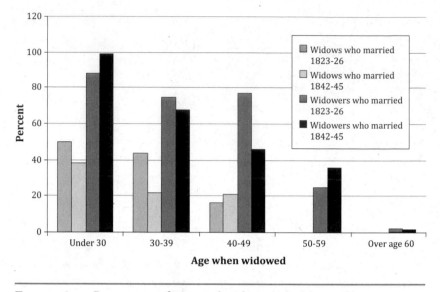

FIGURE **6.5**   Percentages of Montreal widows and widowers known to remarry, for those whose age at widowhood can be determined

Note: 1823-26, known to be widows, *N* = 292, ages known, *N* = 135; 1842-45, known to be widows, *N* = 271, ages known, *N* = 140; 1823-26, known to be widowers, *N* = 253, ages known, *N* = 93; 1842-45, known to be widowers, *N* = 279, ages known, *N* = 108.

Source: Montreal all marriages, 1823-26, and 50 percent of couples marrying 1842-45, linked to remarriages, death registrations, necrologies, obituaries, censuses, and/or cemetery records.

industrialization and urban expansion increased the income-generating possibilities for them and their children, or possibly because we were less successful in identifying their remarriages. Still, a decline in rates of remarriage is consistent with studies of this period by demographers and historians.[61] (See Figure 6.5.)

Overall, around three out of ten of the women who married in the 1820s and became widows definitely remarried, whereas we have found remarriages for only two out of ten of those who married in the 1840s. In contrast, at least four out of every ten widowers of both generations remarried. And the men of these two marriage cohorts remarried at dramatically higher rates than widows whatever their age when their wives died. These rates parallel those that the historians Gérard Bouchard and Peter Gossage have calculated for the mostly rural Saguenay region and the small industrial town of Saint-Hyacinthe respectively.[62]

Youth was the major distinguishing feature of the widows who remarried. Neither class, religion, ethnic identity, nor clauses in wills or marriage contracts that limited a widow's rights should she remarry appear to have had a major influence. Clauses in husbands' wills limiting their claims should they remarry seem to have had little influence. No single motive, as Kirsten Wood has observed, explains widows' decisions about whether to remarry or not. Love, poverty, lust, pregnancy, or a desire to provide a father figure for children might have led some to seek suitors or to respond favourably to overtures. "Practical and emotional factors" might combine to make an offer irresistible, Wood suggests.[63] A bad marriage, relief at being independent, a lack of suitors, or satisfying relationships with children or with other women might explain remaining widowed. Montrealers are said to have disapproved when the young, eligible widow Émilie Tavernier spurned suitable suitors, preferring instead her work helping elderly, decrepit widows.

Speed of Remarriage

Mary O'Leary's remarriage as a young, poor widow was not unusual. The speed at which she remarried was. Custom, etiquette, and the law decreed that women should not remarry in the first year following their husbands' deaths. As we will see in further detail in the next chapter, over these first twelve months, widows were meant to wear deep black mourning clothes to signify their grief and their ongoing loyalty to their dead spouse. For family members and neighbours, expectations of loyalty might mingle with concern about widows' "potentially unfettered sexual longing."[64] Such cultural anxieties made young, attractive widows the subjects of pity, lust, surveillance and critique for their callousness, as evoked in the 1874 sketch below of a young widow choosing one suitor over another (see Figure 6.6).

Remarriage might quell surveillance and gossiping, or sanction pregnancy. O'Leary was one of a small minority of women who defied gendered mourning conventions, rushing from widow back to wife in less than a year. Victoire Dufrêne had already lost one husband when she married the baker Gabriel Laurent-Lorty in October 1823. He died in December the following year. Within six months of his death she remarried again with a shoemaker. Marie-Amable Papineau remarried just three weeks less than a year after François Gareau died of cholera in 1832. This was not her last remarriage. A second widowhood followed, then a third marriage, a third widowhood, then a fourth marriage. She had been sixteen when she married Gareau. She was only forty-five and had outlived three husbands when she died in 1855. Two sons from her first marriage witnessed the registration of her death, and someone arranged for notice of her death to be published in *La Minerve*. It made no mention of earlier husbands.[65] Such multiple marriages fit readily into circulating stereotypes of women who killed husbands to gain their fortunes or their own freedom as "black

MONTREAL WEST *log.* : Never mind, Tom, I'll be a widow again bye and bye, and then perhaps you'll have better luck.

JILTED.

FIGURE 6.6   "Jilted by a young widow." The caption reads "Montreal West: 'Never mind, Tom, I'll be a widow again bye and bye, and then perhaps you'll have better luck.'" Reflecting a broader genre of marriage humour, this caption both renders it normal for young widows to remarry and casts them close to the notion of a black widow for doing so. | Artist unknown. *Canadian Illustrated News,* 19 December 1874, 10, 25: 385. Library and Archives Canada, Record 1695.

widows." Yet, most of the repeated and rapid remarriages occurred among women whose husbands had been labourers or craftsmen and who left them as young widows, usually with small children to raise. Their financial needs surely outranked any financial gains from hasty remarriages. Rapid remarriage seems more common among the women who married in the 1820s than a generation later. The growing grip of more romantic understandings of marriage alongside a hardening sense that speedy remarriage was improper for women might have influenced this change. In various measures, poverty and loneliness, love and lust pushed and pulled these young, working-class widows from one husband's bed to another, from one man's rule to another, from wife to widow to wife again. Men remarried even more quickly, but the reasons and reactions were different.

Gender differences in the duration of widowhood and the timing of remarriage are captured in the histories of Susanna Holmes and her second husband. As we saw in Chapter 3, her first husband, the merchant John McDonnell, died in 1836. They had been married twelve years, and she was widowed at the age of thirty-four. Two daughters, Susan and Ann Martha, had survived infancy. Her own resources, which she had kept separate when they married, along with the provisions of McDonnell's will, should have left her in some degree of comfort as a widow. She owned the building in which they lived on Notre Dame Street. John had promised that should the revenues from it fall below the usual £100 annually, his executors should pay her the difference. The combined promises of their marriage contract and his will gave her a lump sum of £3,000, £500 of which he instructed should be used to pay off the mortgage on the Notre Dame Street property. The remainder would have generated a further £150 a year. And he left her all their household furniture.[66]

Thus, Susanna Holmes apparently had no financial need to remarry. Yet, her money and her social standing also made her a desirable catch. Her brothers, James, Andrew Fernando, and Benjamin, were all prominent men, engaged in business and medicine in the city. McDonnell had named them as his executors, and they likely maintained close links with their younger sister in that capacity, as well as supportive siblings.[67] It was just such a wealthy widow that George-Etienne Cartier's brother Sylvestre had in mind when, only partially facetiously, this country doctor argued that a government post or a rich girl or widow were his only hopes professionally.[68]

Susanna Holmes married Rev. Henry Wilkes in September 1839. Clergymen were poorly paid and largely dependent on the contributions of their congregations. Concern about how their widows and children would survive led Presbyterian ministers in the 1840s and the Congregationalists several decades later to establish widows and orphans funds. But Wilkes was a widower, not a widow. And he had been a businessman prior to his theological training, so he may have had more resources than most.[69] Still, Susanna's financial independence must have been part of her appeal. When they married, Wilkes was actively promoting Congregationalism in Canada. He had returned from taking his theological degrees and ordination in Edinburgh in 1836. While there he had actively recruited Congregational ministers for Canada. He returned to Montreal as a delegate of the Colonial Missionary Society, which sought to establish Congregational

churches in the colonies. That year he took up his post as the pastor of
Zion Congregational Church and quickly emerged as Canada's leading
Congregationalist. An excellent speaker, temperance crusader, and "zealous proselytizer," he would later have close ties with the British and Foreign Bible Society, which sought to convert francophone Catholics, and
hence attracted the ire of the Catholic hierarchy.[70] Wilkes' first wife died
shortly after giving birth in 1838. They had two daughters. Few widowers
could balance work, their own domestic care, and the raising of children.
Wilkes' aggressive religious crusading and busy life was impossible to conciliate with caring for their two little daughters. Wilkes' solution was one
among many. He sent the two girls to Brantford, Upper Canada, to live
with his mother. He resided with a fellow temperance crusader and his
family in Montreal.[71]

Even this highly visible minister waited only a year to remarry. He must
have courted Susanna as he mourned his previous wife. Susanna had been
a widow and single mother to Susan and Ann Martha for three years when
she became a wife again in 1839 at his church. They immediately formed
a blended family. His biographer describes his "home circle" as "enlarged
by the addition of two step-daughters." Susanna was now the mother of
four young girls. She and Henry had three more children, but only one
lived past infancy.[72] Although Henry Wilkes' involvement in the history of
Congregationalism and temperance in Canada is well known, not much
has been written about either of his wives. His biographer reports that
Susanna was "spoken of by those who knew her, as a woman of ability and
piety ... and active, as far as domestic duties allowed her, in every good
work." Susanna came from a strongly Anglican family, yet seems to have
switched readily to the Congregationalism of her second husband. After
her remarriage, she threw herself into charitable work, especially, as recounted in Chapter 3, the Protestant Orphan Asylum. However, as she
approached her mid-forties, Susanna's health declined. She had given birth
to seven children, and had lost three. Her health was a source of worry for
several years. Summers at health spas in Vermont brought no noticeable
change.[73]

As she struggled with illness, and as her children from her first marriage
approached adulthood, Susanna contemplated what she should do with her
own property. Property, historian Kirsten Wood has argued, was a "bone of
contention in widows' remarriages."[74] In December 1847, she donated the
property that she owned in the old city to her daughters, Susan and Ann
Martha. The deed carefully specified that this property was for them and
their heirs. It was to remain their separate property if they married, under
their "sole and exclusive control and management, independent of and
unauthorized by their said husbands." If they wished to sell it, the proceeds

were also to remain theirs, otherwise the concerns of the "giver would be frustrated." Susanna made no mention of her second husband's children, nor of their child in this deed. She treated property as if it should remain in the family line, and drew on current practices that prevented it from falling into husbands' hands. As a remarried widow, she ensured that her daughters had assets of their own. This was no free gift, however. Susan and Ann Martha were required to assume responsibility for paying the interest on the sum of over £2,000 borrowed when the land was purchased in 1835.[75] Susanna's desire to ensure that this property was protected "from the misfortunes or misappropriation" of future husbands might be read as evidence of her feminist analysis of the dangers of male power. As a mother of daughters and a former widow, she knew the importance of having property of her own. Yet, similar clauses were widespread in men's wills in Montreal, as we saw in Chapter 5, as they were in England and the United States. They were part of the widespread shift to liberal, individualized understandings of property and patriarchy within marriage. They fed into the growing acceptance that some separate property for wives was a wise way to avoid the complete loss of family property during bankruptcies and business failure.[76]

By early September 1850, Susanna was seriously ill. "In spite of the best medical skill, and the tenderest care, and nursing," she died "after three weeks of suffering." Downplaying the significance of her work for the Protestant Orphan Asylum and trivializing her contributions as wife, mother, and manager of their household, her husband's biographer suggested that the words "she passed quietly away" were a "fitting record of the termination of an unobtrusive but useful Christian life."[77] Even with servants, marriage to such an energetic, crusading minister would have been demanding, pushing most women into the background. Henry Wilkes buried Susanna on 27 September after a funeral that began at their home on Beaver Hall Terrace, proceeded to the new Zion Congregational Church which had opened on St. Radegonde Street in 1846, and then to the Protestant cemetery. The notice of her death in the *Gazette* invited friends to attend and specified that no funeral cards would be sent.[78] After her death, Wilkes moved out of the home he had shared with Susanna and set up house on Bleury Street. One of Susanna's daughters stepped into her role, taking care of their son and the two girls from his first marriage. Within two years, Wilkes took a third wife.

Wilkes was typical of men in moving rapidly after his wives' deaths from widower to husband again. Neither custom, the church, law, nor gossip placed restraints on men's remarriages as heavily as they did on women's. A few men remarried within several months of their wives' deaths. Catherine Martin died on 11 September 1848. She had married the joiner Joseph Charland six years earlier. He remarried a month later, on 16 October. Rosalie Collard died on 10 February 1863, after forty years of marriage. Within two months, her husband, Pierre Plouff, a navigator, had remarried. At least twenty-two of the men from these two marriage cohorts who outlived their wives remarried in under a year, and unlike among women, such relatively rapid remarriages were equally common in each of the marriage cohorts. Early in the century, Bishop Lartigue advised that such speedy remarriages should be allowed, as long as the "man wanting to remarry" had the means to pay for the funeral of his first spouse.[79]

Most men remarried within the three years following their wives' deaths; widows were more likely to wait for four or more years. Rebecca Conegan remained a widow for one year and four months after Sampson Brady died, blind and ill. In March 1854, this widow of a small manufacturer and mother of two young children married Henry Benallick at Montreal's Unitarian Church. The ceremony was witnessed by several members of his family and several male and female friends. For the blacksmith Henry Benallick, marriage to this illiterate but propertied widow who likely still had substantial assets after her short widowhood was surely a step up. Their marriage lasted for over thirty years. Widowed first in her early thirties, Rebecca became a widow again in her late sixties, in 1887.[80]

Susanna Holmes was typical of bourgeois widows, who usually waited longer than poorer widows to remarry when they did so. Greater economic security, greater familial supervision, stronger senses of the propriety of demonstrating loyalty to dead husbands, and higher stakes all permitted them leeway and choice that most poor widows could simply not afford. As historian Kirsten Wood suggests, there were powerful incentives for wealthy widows to remain single.[81] There were also men keen to find a wealthy wife. As we saw, the cholera epidemic of 1832 left Margaret White without a husband or father. Their wills left her wealthy. She moved cautiously. William Gay had left her the use of their substantial dwelling and well-stocked shop on St. Paul Street in the eastern part of the commercial city when he died in 1832. She did not remain there long. Caring for children, ill health, or the growing tendency of those bourgeois women who could afford it to withdraw from family shops and businesses may have influenced her decision to move a few years after his death.[82] So might the death at the age of seventeen months of the child she must have been carrying at the time Andrew died. She and the children boarded for a while in a house belonging to another Montreal grocer and trader, James Carswell, the family friend who was made co-tutor to her children after William's death.[83]

After seven years as a widow, she married again. Her new husband, John Birss, held property close to that of Carswell. Birss paid off some £190 that

Margaret owed Carswell for her board and lodging, and soon put Gay's store up for rent. She and Birss had one child together. Two years after her remarriage, she was unwell. Notary Gibbs came to her house to write her will. Her first request was that her debts to her second husband for the money he had paid for her board while a widow along with some other debts, which amounted to close to over £150, be paid off. She also wanted him to receive £500 from her assets. The rest of her belongings of all kinds were to be divided equally among the three children from her first marriage and the child she had with Birss. She entreated her "dear Husband" to take "fatherly care" of all the children, and begged them to "hearken to" his counsel. She concluded by clearly asserting her trust in the way John would look after all the children, requesting that he and her friend Joseph Ross be appointed their tutors. Yet, she did not name her husband as her executor. For that role she chose Stanley Bagg, the prominent merchant who had been the Tory candidate in the violent 1832 by-election that had preceded her first husband's death. Three men witnessed the will, including her long-time friend and former landlord, James Carswell. As a wife and a remarried widow and mother, she balanced the requirement of her first husband's will that all his goods go to her and then equally to their children, with the desire to give to her second husband and to recognize the present and future needs of her children from both marriages. As a woman who owned her own separate property, she was able to achieve this balance.[84]

Margaret White wrote this last will shortly after normal government resumed in the colony, and shortly after the new Registry Ordinance became law. The same day, either she or the notaries decided that it was important to have it properly registered. So, after completing her will, she signed a second document in which she declared that this was her last will and that "authentic copies" of it were to be registered.[85] A month later she died. Margaret had become a wife at seventeen and a widow at twenty-three. Her widowhood lasted seven years. Her second marriage lasted only two and a half. She died at the age of thirty-two. Her stepmother, the widow Margaret Logan White, outlived her by over thirty years. She never remarried.

Widowhood came suddenly upon some women, slowly on others. Epidemics, violent deaths, suicides, sudden heart attacks, or accidents at work or play left little time to prepare. Such deaths catapulted women from wife to widow and men from husband to widower with little or no warning. Lengthy illnesses and suffering disrupted family routines but offered time for goodbyes, time to seek to put spiritual and material matters in order, and, for some women, time to learn the role of family provider.

Final illnesses and the desire of the dying to settle spiritual and material matters drew other Montrealers into their homes. Some came in official capacities as witnesses and notaries. These had to be men. Other men passed through the homes of the sick and dying providing medical and religious care, professional tasks also largely closed to women. Female relatives, offspring, friends, and neighbours might help care for the dying, provide emotional and religious support, offer food, and dress the dead body.

The timing of the dissolution of marriages by death was as unpredictable as that of separations and divorces today. Women became widows in their teens or twenties after just months or a few years of marriage. Others remained wives for twenty, thirty, even forty years, facing widowhood only in their old age. World-wide epidemics hit each of these two generations of marriages hard, accentuating but not explaining the irregularity of death's impact. In this premodern demographic regime, average ages of death or lengths of marriage serve only as the broadest indicators of difference.

In Montreal, as in other places historians and demographers have studied, men were more likely to remarry than women. Marriages involving major age differences, or a widow marrying a single man – as when the young widow, Caroline Henshaw, married George Johnson in 1823 – produced community responses like charivaris as we saw in Chapter 1. Yet men's remarriages evoked few cultural archetypes to parallel those applied to women. Oversexed widows seeking sex in or outside the marriage bed, merry widows with similar goals, widows scheming to find rich husbands, black widows plotting the deaths of successive husbands to enrich themselves fuelled circulating discourses that reiterated gender difference. Pragmatic remarriages agreed to for convenience and shelter found little place in these constructions. Most remarrying widows were quite young. Their age was part of what made them attractive to new spouses but also of what propelled them into remarriage. Older widows who inherited income or lump sums through provisions in marriage contracts or wills were not only better armed to avoid remarriage if they wished but also less likely targets of men seeking a wife.

Most widows did not remarry. Some no doubt embraced their new independence, especially if they had sufficient assets to live upon. Kirsten Wood suggests that "more women dreamed of re-uniting" with their husbands in heaven than of finding a new one.[86] Husbands' deaths left some women pregnant, some with young children, others with children who were married or employed, and still others old, sick, and alone. The transition from wife to widow raised a host of emotional, material, legal, and social issues. Custom and law required newly widowed women's ongoing involvement with professionals, merchants, family, and friends as they arranged for their mourning clothes and for funerals, organized death notices

and obituaries, acted as executors of wills, arranged the listing of possessions and tutorship of minors, and determined whether to accept or reject
family property or bequests in wills. It is to these tasks, normally undertaken within twelve months and a day of a spouse's death, that the next
chapter turns.

In the Shadow of Their Husbands
The First Days of Widowhood

Scholastique Bissonnet dressed in a modest but respectable black mourning outfit when her husband died in April 1834, thanks to £4 10s. loaned
to her by her widowed mother, Angelique Lahaie. The chenille gloves and
crape mourning attire that she and her two young children wore cost
about half the amount that she paid for the funeral, a final mass for Louis
Ducharme, and his burial. These came to over £8. She also owed Ludger
Duvernay £1 for a death notice placed in *La Minerve* the day of her husband's death. With her widowed mother's help, Scholastique was able to
proclaim her bereavement publicly in the black clothes she wore, inform
her fellow Montrealers about his death in the newspaper, and give Louis
Ducharme a decent burial and funeral. In 1826, when they married, he had
reported he was a joiner. When he died they were running an inn. He was
identified as an innkeeper.[1]

Dr. William Sutherland, who, as we saw, imagined every detail of how
his wife, Catherine, would live as his widow, also specified that she should
receive £40 for mourning clothes. His son was to receive £20 and servants
either £5 or £2 10s. depending on the length of time they had worked for
the family.[2] Thus, Dr. Sutherland ensured that his whole household could
dress in mourning clothes that reflected his status. Catherine Farquhar
began her widowhood in February 1875, with ten times the amount that
the artisan's widow Scholastique had borrowed for her widow's weeds forty
years earlier. Wealth, more than the intervening years, determined these
vastly different expenditures.

As dead husbands' bodies awaited burial, Scholastique, Catherine, and
most other widows clothed their bodies in dull, black mourning attire.
Their dress and accessories signalled to the world that they were widows
engaged in a particularly European and female version of grieving. In stepping into them they performed and reiterated the gendered meaning of

FIGURE 7.1 "The Young Widow." This sketch from 1873 ties the young widow closely back to her marriage through the wedding veil she holds, and represents her in a way that matches obituary descriptions of widows as "inconsolable." Here her dark clothing, her pose, and her lack of attention to the little boy at her side, who is virtually hidden in the black material of her dress, also suggest a widow immoblized by her grief and unlikely to be acting on legal or other matters. | Artist unknown. *Canadian Illustrated News,* 12 July 1873, 8, 2: 28. Library and Archives Canada, Record 3864.

widowhood through "a stylized repetition of acts."[3] Their black clothes evoked their past status as wife, their ongoing identification with their dead husband, and their new legal status as widows. These three elements structure this representation of a young woman, widowed around the time of Dr. Sutherland's death: the link backward to her marriage through the wedding veil she is holding; her apparent absorption in the memory of her husband that leaves the young child ignored at her side; and the black clothing of widowhood. It suggests an inconsolable widow, immobilized in her bereavement (see Figure 7.1).[4] Material historians, the main researchers to turn their attention to mourning paraphernalia and dress, have re-enforced this impression with graphic descriptions of the discomfort of the fabrics used, and by depicting widow's weeds as a "chrysalis of gloom."[5] Some historians have presented similar images of the first year of a woman's widowhood, conveying the impression that the early period of mourning and bereavement was one of withdrawal from the public and retreat into the family, with funerals and business matters acting as temporary distractions from grieving.[6]

In this and the following chapter, I seek to complicate this picture of widows' retreat into the private space of home, family, and private grieving. In the moments and hours following their husbands' death, there were mourning clothes to secure, bodies to clean and dress, friends and family to notify and receive, funeral services to organize, burial plots to be selected, and bodies to bury. All these tasks were usually seen to within five days of death. Such matters did not allow most widows to focus exclusively on their grief, even when others oversaw arrangements. This chapter lingers on these early days of widowhood. It follows Scholastique and some of the other widows as they dealt with three main matters: mourning clothes; death notices, obituaries, and funeral invitations; and funerals and burials. Here I make no attempt to gauge women's grief as they grappled with these early days of widowhood. That would require different sources and different sensibilities. I draw mostly on what it is possible to determine about mourning clothes and funerals from newspapers, inventories of couples' goods, and church and cemetery records. The chapter returns to particular widows, especially Scholastique Bissonnet and Marie-Louise Genant, both widows of innkeepers; Hannah Lyman and Luce Perrault, two of the widows of successful businessmen who were also mayors; Constance Hannah Hart, widow of the Jewish lawyer and writer Adolphus Mordecai Hart; Émilie Monjean, the saddler's widow; and Marguerite Paris, widow of the labourer Joseph Guilbault. Their different cultures, religious beliefs, and levels of wealth give us some idea of the diversity of the material, social, and religious cultures of mourning dress and funeral customs. Gender and class, religious and ethnic customs and rituals, family fortunes, and individual foibles interacted to shape women's first days of widowhood.

Widows' Mourning Clothes

No images have captured the mourning clothes that Scholastique Bissonnet donned. Nor is it likely that her dress survived long. A painting was beyond the reach of this innkeeper's widow, and when her husband died in 1834, photography was in its infancy. Catherine Farquhar, in contrast, may well have had her photo taken in her widow's weeds after Dr. Sutherland died in 1875. She had the financial means to do so. And more and more Montreal women of her class were having their photographs taken, especially at the fashionable William Notman's Studio. It was there that Marie-Louise-Josephte Chartier de Lotbinière went, within months of Robert Unwin Harwood's death in 1863, in her black mourning dress and white widow's cap to have her new status as a widow captured on camera. At the same time, she arranged to have the miniature paintings made when they married photographed (see Figure 7.2 and Figure 1.2). Historians of material culture have turned to paintings, photographs, fashion magazines, etiquette manuals, and surviving nineteenth-century mourning outfits to describe mourning fashions. Mourning was one of the few and first acceptable occasions for the purchase and display of non-essential items. Today, suggests Mary Louise Kete, "only marriage comes close to the role mourning once held in terms of the production and reproduction of social status."[7] This is a useful analogy. Yet, the artefacts and photographs of women in mourning that have survived leave a very bourgeois view of mourning dress.

There are paintings or photos of a few of the women from the 1820s and 1840s marriages who became widows. Not surprisingly, all come from the city's relatively elite families. Émilie Tavernier and Jean-Baptiste Gamelin commissioned a painting of themselves shortly after their marriage, as Marie-Louise-Josephte de Lotbinière and Robert Unwin Harwood had done. Another survives of Émilie that was painted sixteen years after her husband's death and shows her still wearing black clothing and a white cap. When Luce Perrault, Édouard-Raymond Fabre's widow, died in the early twentieth century, the article recounting her death reproduced a photograph of her, apparently still wearing her widow's clothing (see Figure 12.5). The images of Marie-Louise-Josephte, Émilie, and Luce, all Canadienne women who married in the 1820s but had their images painted or photographed at vastly different points in time, suggest that some women of their generation wore remarkably similar clothing whenever their husbands died. Even for wealthy women, historians' arguments that trends in mourning attire followed fashion more generally need to be tempered with sensitivity to the ways age, differing interest in fashion, and consumption may have shaped sartorial decisions. Émilie Tavernier's clothing projected modesty and practicality (see Figure 7.2).

For Maria Mitchell, Marguerite Paris, and many of the widows of labourers and artisans, purchasing new and fashionable clothing was out of the question at the very moment that they had to assume responsibility for supporting themselves and often their children. Yet, mourning mattered, as

FIGURE 7.2 Bourgeois Canadienne widows: Émilie Tavernier, 1843 (right), and Marie-Louise-Josephte Chartier de Lotbinière, 1863 (above). Émilie Tavernier married the merchant Jean-Baptiste Gamelin in 1823 and was widowed in 1827. Sixteen years after Jean-Baptiste Gamelin's death, her dark clothing and white cap suggest that she was still in mourning. Marie-Louise-Josephte Chartier de Lotbinière married the merchant and manufacturer Robert Unwin Harwood in 1823. Robert Unwin Harwood died on 16 April 1863. She had this image of herself in her widow's clothing taken later that same year and had copies made of earlier paintings of the two of them. | *Madame Gamelin,* by Vital Des Rochers, 1843. Original painting conserved in the Museum of the Sisters of Providence, Montreal. "Mrs. Harwood. 1863," William Notman, photographer. McCord Museum, Notman Photographic Archives, I0-7626.1.

did proper funerals. Even Maria Mitchell, the Irish Catholic reputed to be a "habitual drunkard," whose husband killed himself after beating her brutally in March 1858, was glimpsed on the streets of Montreal dressed in mourning clothes three months after his death.[8] Clothes donned when children died might be reused, dresses dyed black, or money or clothes borrowed from kin or friends, as Scholastique Bissonnet did.

Between the 1820s and 1830s – when Émilie Tavernier, Charlotte Mount, Caroline Campbell, Scholastique Bissonnet, and some of the other women who had married in the 1820s became widows – and the later century, fashions changed dramatically. For widows who could afford them and sought to be fashionable, mourning clothes followed trends, differing mostly from other garments in their colour, lack of sheen, and accessories. Early in the century, widows with the means and desire to keep abreast of fashion wore the low-cut, high-waisted neoclassical dresses that were in vogue. The long-sleeved, high-necked, large-skirted dresses of the later Victorian period that hid most of women's bodies were much more confining and required many more yards of fabric. Trim and accessories multiplied among those who could afford the expenses, especially after Queen Victoria's widowhood intensified the cult and culture of mourning for women throughout the Empire and beyond.[9]

The crape "(always spelt with an 'a' to indicate mourning crape)," that Scholastique used, possibly as trim over a black dress, or perhaps for the whole dress, was the fabric most frequently employed for mourning attire.[10] It was a dull-looking gauze with a texture so stiff that it could not be worn over softer fabrics like velvet or satin. Uncomfortable, impractical, even dangerous, it became synonymous with mourning. It stained easily. Its colour rubbed off on women's skin as they sweated. It smelled. Late in the century, crape veils were said to shed a "pernicious dye" into women's nostrils, and the mingling of tears and dye to cause eye infections, even blindness.[11] Bombazine and dull black silk were other widely used options. These too were frequently trimmed with crape.[12] Dull black gloves, black jewellery, a black feather fan, a mantle or cloak, a crape mourning bonnet for outside, a widow's cap for inside the house, and handkerchiefs with black borders were other components of respectable grieving in the first year of widowhood. These were financially possible for only some widows. As the pictures of Émilie and Marie-Louise and Luce Perrault show, white remained acceptable, especially as trim on bonnets or for collars or cuffs.[13] Mourning clothes served, as an article in *Harper's Bazaar* suggested late in the nineteenth century, both as a "shield to the real mourner" and a "curtain of respectability to the person who should be a mourner but is not."[14] They locked widows' bodies into their husbands' shadows for at least a year, while publicly announcing their mourning.

Some older widows chose to wear mourning for the remainder of their lives. Queen Victoria made this more fashionable. But Quebec politics produced their own versions of loyal widows. Robert Roquebrune's memoirs recounted visiting the widow and daughter of François-Marie-Thomas Chevalier de Lorimier, one of the Patriotes hanged following the rebellions of 1838. Lorimier practised as a notary in Montreal between 1829 and his death. He married in 1832, and he and Henriette Cadieux had five children. Two girls survived infancy. In July 1838, this ardent Patriote had told a friend he was "ever ready to spill my blood on the soil which gave me birth in order to upset the infamous British Government – top branches, roots and all." He was taken prisoner after the failed Patriote assaults in 1838, moved to the Montreal Prison, and in January 1839 faced a court martial. Henriette and his lawyers sought to stay his execution without success. He and four others were hung for treason on 15 February 1839. Lorimier mounted the scaffold steps proclaiming, "Long live Liberty! Long live Independence!" and asserting that he was leaving his young children and wife, "who have only my industry for their support," in the hope that his compatriots would learn what they could expect from the British government.[15] In these last words, Lorimier played on the sentiments attached to widowhood to turn the British colonizers into widow makers.

Thus, Henriette's widowhood symbolized the conflict between British colonizers and Canadiens. Poor, with her two daughters to raise, she left Montreal and settled in L'Assomption. It was there, years later, that the young Roquebrune met Henriette and one of her daughters. He recounted that the two women "always wore deep mourning: black dresses and black veils," and that people treated them "with marked deference," as "persons who have been especially singled out to be the victims of a great misfortune." Nearly half a century after her husband's death, $1,000 was raised for Henriette "by way of reparations from the nation." When Henriette died, he reports, "her funeral was made the occasion for a patriotic" display in which the events of 1837 and 1838 were memorialized.[16]

Scholastique's loan of £4 10s. from her mother for her mourning attire is recorded because the Custom of Paris allowed widows to claim the costs of mourning from their husbands' assets. In marriages like hers that created community property, this was taken from their husband's half of their shared goods. The details appear in the listing of their property made two weeks after she became a widow. In marriages like Catherine Farquhar's where each spouse's property was kept separate, mourning clothes were a claim against the husband's assets. In this way, the law underscored women's obligation and their right to represent their deceased spouse in a way that displayed their loss and their new status as widows. When wives died, in

FIGURE 7.3 Widow Narcisse Vézina Dufault (top right) and her children, ca. 1875. | Courtesy of Estelle Brisson, Private collection.

contrast, widowers had to pay for their mourning clothes out of their own property. And the conventions of etiquette requiring widows to wear black for a year and a day asked much less of men when their wives died. Some donned black mourning capes, but over the early decades of the century, these were increasingly replaced with a simple black arm band.[17] Nor were widowers expected to publicly exhibit their mourning for as long as widows, or to cease working.[18] Culture and etiquette thus allocated excessive space for women's grieving and little for men's.

The amount widows could claim for mourning was meant to be reasonable in relationship to their husband's wealth.[19] Scholastique's £4 was close to the mourning claims of other wives of craftsmen whose husbands died in the 1830s and 1840s. This represented over thirty days' wages for a labourer paid at the going daily rate of two to three shillings.[20] It was a significant outlay even in the artisanal community. Given the debts that Marguerite Paris and her labouring husband Joseph Guilbault owed doctors and others, she had every reason to claim any costs she had incurred for mourning clothes following his death in 1829. Yet, she did not.[21] Such widows were more likely to borrow mourning clothes than to have them made by the city's dressmakers, as wealthier women did. Rebecca Conegan spent twice the amount Scholastique Bissonnet had for her outfit after the blind soap and candle manufacturer Sampson Brady died in 1853. This too was a modest outlay. After the ex-soldier and bank employee William Radenhurst died in 1830, Sarah Walker paid over £16 for mourning apparel. Charlotte Mount would later claim that the mourning outfit she donned following the death of her young indebted husband had cost her £60.[22] Widows' clothing publicly and concurrently proclaimed their bereavement and their class status. The few images of non-elite widows project the challenges they faced as widows, as in the mid-1870s image of the widow Narcisse Vézina Dufault and her children (see Figure 7.3).

For women left with little or no assets or cash, or with heavy debts and few other resources, respectable mourning clothes, ensuring a decent burial, and avoiding the poor ground were among their earliest challenges as a widow. Scholastique borrowed from her mother. Marie-Noflette Charland was helped by another Montreal innkeeper after her husband, the innkeeper Joseph-Henri Letourneau, died in 1834. François Benoit lent her £2 9s. 4d. to pay the dry goods merchant G.D.N. Ducondu for the black crape, gloves, and ribbon that formed part of her mourning outfit.[23] Ducondu and other Montreal shopkeepers advertised mourning fabrics in the newspapers. Discretely embedded in a long list of fabric and other merchandise was M. Laframboise's announcement in *La Minerve* in 1827 that his shop on St. Paul Street carried black veils, black bombazine, "black crape and black gloves for funerals ... at very moderate prices." McDunnough, Muir and Company's 1861 advertisement was less discreet in its announcement of a separate department for "MOURNING GOODS."[24] (See Figure 7.4.)

As the century advanced and an "ever multiplying array of commodities" were presented as "essential components of the 'respectable funeral,'" merchants placed larger and more prominent advertisements for mourning

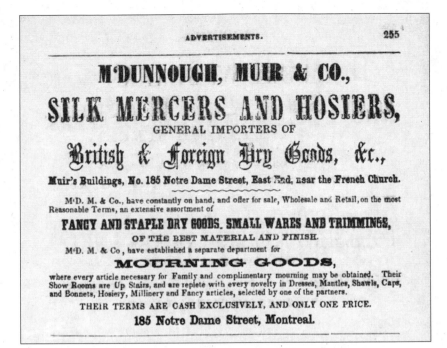

ADVERTISEMENTS. 255

M'DUNNOUGH, MUIR & CO.,
SILK MERCERS AND HOSIERS,
GENERAL IMPORTERS OF
British & Foreign Dry Goods, &c.,
Muir's Buildings, No. 185 Notre Dame Street, East End, near the French Church.

M'D. M. & Co., have constantly on hand, and offer for sale, Wholesale and Retail, on the most Reasonable Terms, an extensive assortment of

FANCY AND STAPLE DRY GOODS, SMALL WARES AND TRIMMINGS,
OF THE BEST MATERIAL AND FINISH.

M'D. M. & Co, have established a separate department for

MOURNING GOODS,

where every article necessary for Family and complimentary mourning may be obtained. Their Show Rooms are Up Stairs, and are replete with every novelty in Dresses, Mantles, Shawls, Caps, and Bonnets, Hosiery, Millinery and Fancy articles, selected by one of the partners.

THEIR TERMS ARE CASH EXCLUSIVELY, AND ONLY ONE PRICE.

185 Notre Dame Street, Montreal.

FIGURE 7.4 Advertisement for mourning goods. | Bibliothèque et Archives nationales du Québec, *Lovell's Montreal Directory,* 1861, 255.

fabrics in the print media of the city (see Figure 7.4). In 1863, Gagnon, Watson and Co. took out a full-page advertisement in the city directory announcing its "extensive and recherché stock" of ready-made clothing and fabrics. A boxed section entitled "MOURNING GOODS" in large print announced "Bombainze, Crape, Crape Collars," and other mourning gear.[25] Such advertisements solicited the custom of grieving customers, while reminding others that they might require such goods at any time. Widows' purchases of fabric and other mourning items, and their engagement of dressmakers to make their outfits, wove them into the city's economy as consumers. Those who borrowed from friends, circulating dresses and other mourning paraphernalia, sustained an informal economy of exchange that allowed for proper mourning among the penniless.

A widow's right to take the money for her mourning outfits from her husband's assets or community property could be challenged. Notary Smith's formulation that Rebecca Conegan had been allocated the £10 for her mourning outfit with the "agreement" of the subtutor hints at disagreements that might arise over such disbursements or a widow's loyalty.[26] Occasionally, disagreements went to court. In an 1872 case, a widow who had remarried sued the children from her first marriage for the $50 she spent on mourning clothes, along with a dower she had been promised in her marriage contract with their father. Judge McKay found both claims sound but noted in his private papers that "to come now and ask for the mourning" smelled of "indelicacy." He reduced her claim for clothing costs to $20, recognizing her right but punishing her for making the claim following remarriage. When, in 1891, a widow Dessaint contested the decision of her children's tutor, who had refused to repay the cost of her mourning clothes and some other funeral-related expenses, the court upheld such widows' rights, making clear that these held whether their marriage created community or separate property.[27]

Infidelity cancelled widows' right to wear clothes paid for by their dead husband, as it did their right to dower. The Custom of Paris considered a widow adulterous if she had deserted her husband or committed adultery during the marriage and not been forgiven prior to his death. It also deemed that "even one single act of fornication" as a widow, "above all in the year of mourning," eliminated her claim to dower or the cost of mourning clothes. Remarriage within a year was treated as adultery.[28] Mary O'Leary, Victoire Dufrêne, and Marie-Louise Dufresne, all widows who remarried within less than a year, forfeited this right. Marie-Louise Dufresne remarried nine months after the death of her first husband, the mason Pierre Mallette. On the inventory of the goods she had shared with Mallette that she and her new husband, labourer Charles Renaud, arranged to have made after their marriage, Notary Labadie recorded that she would not be allowed anything for her mourning from her husband's part of the community because she had remarried in under a year. The law penalized her for this infidelity to her husband's memory. The costs of the clothing she wore to mourn her first husband's death became her own expense, quite possibly assumed by her new husband. The meagre £1 3s. 7d. paid for her first husband's funeral remained a legitimate claim.[29]

Death Notices, Funeral Invitations, and Obituaries

Scholastique Bissonnet, a friend, or family member arranged to report her husband's death in *La Minerve*. The death notice was short and simple. It announced that "Louis Ducharme, innkeeper," had died at the age of thirty in Montreal. His funeral and burial occurred two days later.[30] News of deaths circulated through the tolling of bells and the interlocking circuits of friendship, kin, and the print media, usually leaving minimal records for historians.[31] In the Saguenay region, deaths were announced by knocking on the doors of neighbours and family: two knocks for male deaths, three for females.[32] In cities, fellow workers or members of mutual benefit societies or prayer groups would quickly spread the news and prepare to visit or to participate in the funeral.[33]

Throughout the century, some middling and wealthier families sent funeral invitations to those they hoped would attend. The wording was usually simple, stating where and when the funeral was to be held and noting the route the procession would follow. Increasingly, such hand-delivered invitations were complemented or replaced by notices in the newspapers.[34] These placed the news of the death in the public domain, by their very presence there asserting the deceased's membership in the wider urban community. Such notices announced the deaths of elite and middling people, as well as of some Montrealers of modest means, like Scholastique's husband and several Irish Catholic labourers. There was no mention of the death of Marguerite Paris' labourer husband, Joseph Guilbault, in any of the newspapers we have consulted. Nor did many widows of labourers pass on the news of a death in this way.[35]

Montreal newspapers usually printed very simple notices of deaths like that for Scholastique's husband, Louis. Many combined news of the death with a public invitation to the funeral. Cursory as most notices were, the conventions of their writing were highly structured, as Mushira Eid has argued in her research into such notices across time and cultures. The ways the deceased was named reflected and reproduced differences of gender, class, and ethnic identity.[36] Most announcements of the deaths of artisans, owners of small businesses, or, later in the century, skilled workers evoked only the age, occupation, and sometimes the place of residence of the deceased. When Laura Mower's husband died in 1836, the notice in *La Minerve* reported simply that "Mr John Campbell, bookseller," had died in Montreal on the previous night. Immigrants were often identified with their country, city, or parish of origin. The Irish Catholic immigrant James Barker was described as "a native of the County Monaghan, parish of Tyholand, Ireland."[37] Neither the Campbell notice nor that for Louis Ducharme mentioned the widows or children left behind. In contrast, after Leocadie Paris' husband, the carriage maker Louis-Joseph Gauthier, died in 1857, the death notice reported that he had long looked death in the face, died after an honourable career, and that his death hit his wife and several children hard.[38] Similarly, the notice that Marie-Louise Genant or her friends or family arranged for Pierre-Bernard Decousse in 1852 mentioned that he had died after a long illness and that he left his wife and four children to deplore his loss. It went on to invite friends and family to the funeral.[39] Such brevity was not limited to the crafts or trades community. When Charles-Séraphin Rodier died, the notice identified him as a member of the Legislative Council for the district of Lorimier and invited relatives and friends to attend the funeral.[40] There was no mention of Marie-Louise, his wife of fifty-one years. Cryptically, such notices reminded readers of selected characteristics of men's lives or deaths that those surviving him wished known.

When husbands died before their wives, it was exceptional for death notices to name the widow who survived him. Even mentioning that men were survived by a spouse, children, or both was rare.[41] Men's identities were usually evoked through the categories of age, profession, and occasionally their public involvement, seldom as fathers, husbands, or family heads. Their widows disappear, possibly effaced at their own request, and effectively absent in the brief narrative offered of their late husbands' lives. In contrast, when newly widowed men announced their wives' deaths in the city's newspapers, they invariably named themselves. David Handyside was typical. When his wife died in 1848, after twenty-four years of marriage, the notice in the *Montreal Gazette* read simply: "On 12th inst, aged 47, Melinda Adams, wife of David Handyside, esq." Men of the 1840s marriage generation who outlived their wives sometimes added a term of endearment. "Beloved wife" was the most common.[42] Thus, husbands linked their deceased wives' identities firmly to their own when announcing their deaths, though the Canadien custom of retaining family names spilled over into English custom in Montreal, preserving dead wives' links to their birth families in ways that were rare in English jurisdictions.[43] Less frequently they were also identified as mothers or daughters.[44]

Obituaries offering longer assessments of the deceased's life were rare. Usually published after the funeral, they constituted a very public reckoning of the character, citizenship, and political loyalty of fairly prominent citizens.[45] That published about Caroline Campbell's socially ascendant husband, Oliver Wait, epitomizes the interlocking assessment of the familial, financial, and political aspects of his life that constituted the narrative stuff of the male version of this genre. A short death notice appeared in *La Minerve* the morning after his death from cholera. Three days later, an obituary in the same Patriote paper lauded this English-speaking Protestant contractor as a man who had lived in Lower Canada for a long time and whose entrepreneurial character had contributed to its improvement. It spoke positively of his employment of many Canadiens on his public projects, highlighted his contributions as an active worker for Daniel Tracey during the bloody 1832 by-election, and reported that he had been considered as an alternative to Tracey as the Patriote candidate for Montreal West. Having assessed his economic and political contributions, the obituary then noted that he left a significant fortune to divide among his large family and that he had died as a good Christian with the reputation of being a good man. Caroline's individuality as a newly widowed woman was submerged within his "large family."[46]

Oliver Wait's death from cholera was sudden. His burial was rapid. It took a few days for this obituary to appear. Jacques-François Genevay, in contrast, had been ill for a long time. Oliver Wait was well into middle age, with married children, as well as a young second wife and minor offspring when he died. Jacques was only twenty-six years old. He and Charlotte Mount had no living offspring. His obituary appeared before his body was buried. More than these differences of age and family status explain the divergent life narratives recounted in their respective obituaries. Whereas Wait's spoke to his citizenship, Genevay's stressed the loss to loved ones and the sociability of this man who died young. "Lost in the flower of his youth to his dear wife, tender mother and a large circle of faithful friends that his eminently sociable qualities and excellent heart had united around him, he courageously made the sacrifice of a life." Here, perhaps, was what Charlotte and his mother penned even before his anticipated death.[47] This obituary harnesses the popular deployment of sentiment, that mode of writing that was increasingly characterizing fiction, didactic literature, and popular poetry that evoked homes and families under conditions of loss. Mary Louise Kete has suggested that we think about such modes of expression as "sentimental collaboration," in which the exchange of sympathy establishes "the ground for participation in a common cultural, or intellectual project," facilitating "a collaborative effort against loss."[48]

The community being called on to collaborate in the commemoration of Jacques-François was that of family and friends. The obituary that followed John Easton Mills's death from typhus while mayor enjoined the whole city to collaborate. The *Courier* reported that "the family will issue no funeral invitation," described the funeral route, and asserted that it had no need to "state that it is the duty of every good citizen to pay the last tribute of respect to a gentleman who not only held the highest civic office, but must also have endeared himself to hundreds amongst us by his amiability in private life." Virtually every major newspaper of the city reported on his death. Montreal's *Gazette,* which appeared late in the day, gathered together those from the *Courier, Herald, Transcript,* and *Aurore des Canadas,* reproducing them in its editorial column, then adding comments at the end, along with a detailed description of the "Programme" for his funeral.[49]

Mills's prominence as head of the city, the respect with which he was widely held, and the poignancy of his death from typhus virtually effaced the widowed Hannah Lyman and their five children from these testimonials to a dead mayor. As Martin Pâquet has suggested in his study of the funerals of Canadian politicians, the public image of such deceased notables was detached from their corpse and joined the symbolic universe of the larger political community.[50] Press reports all stressed his ability to work constructively with political opponents and his sacrifice in caring for the sick immigrants. The *Aurore* described him as "intelligent and enlightened, liberal in his principles," and as having shown "himself always sincerely attached to the country of his adoption." One of the few reports that mentioned his family noted that he would carry to his tomb "the regrets of a mourning family, and his numerous friends." Similarly, the *Montreal Gazette* drew distinctions between Mills's public and private roles, casting the death of this "active and zealous public officer" as a "public loss: while an affectionate family circle has been bereft of its centre and head. Such events," it added, "are startling and mysterious."[51]

The sudden death of men in office threatened political continuity. Newspaper reports reminding readers of his final moments and of the sacrifice he had made of his life, like the more humble death notices, publicly announced what family members and those in the household were already experiencing – the separation of the deceased from the world of the living. General invitations to funerals evoked the wider ties between family and community. In the case of public figures like John Easton Mills, they reasserted political authority and continuity in their display of hierarchy and public order.[52]

Funerals and Burials

The bodies of husbands, wives, and children normally remained at home until their funeral and burial. Except in times of epidemics, or when the deceased's prominence led to the organization of a large and public funeral, Catholic, Protestant, and Jewish burials normally occurred one to two days after a death. When loved ones died in the Hôtel-Dieu or other institutions, family members were deprived of this final farewell period unless bodies were returned home. Particular rituals following deaths varied with class, religion, and ethnicity. Wives might wash and dress their husbands' bodies themselves, preparing them for visitors and burial, or call in neighbourhood women or family members skilled at laying out bodies. Some midwives saw to this task.[53] These intimate and final touches on the bodies of the dead have left few traces. Occasionally, inventories list costs to women who may have helped on such occasions.[54] By the 1860s, some funeral businesses were offering to do this task if requested.

Once the body was prepared, "family and friends and members of the community" visited, paid their respect to the surviving spouse and family, and "kept watch over the body until the funeral." The usual minimum of two days provided a time for friends and family to visit and pay their last respects, praying for their souls, farewells, and assurance that the deceased was truly dead.[55] Watching over the corpse was an old custom. It persisted throughout the nineteenth century in part to prevent body snatching by anatomists, but also to avoid live burial, a possibility fuelled by medical confusion, popular fear, rumours, stories, and the fiction writing of authors

like Edgar Allan Poe, who "graphically imagined the 'appalling and intoler-
able horror'" of burial alive in an 1844 short story titled "The Premature
Burial."[56]

Louis Ducharme was buried on 19 April 1834, two days after his death.
Within a week of his funeral, Scholastique had carefully recapitulated all
the expenses in greater detail than most widows. Funerals and burials for
those of all denominations were costly. They required the services of religious and secular men – ranging from priests and ministers through carters, grave diggers, beadles, and other church officials – as well as children's
choirs. Protestants normally paid for some of these services separately,
though the superintendents of the city's old Protestant cemeteries oversaw
and collected fees for the purchase of family lots or individual graves, the
grave digging, and the installation of headstones.[57] The Catholic parish of
Notre Dame, like other Catholic parishes, offered their parishioners pack-
age deals covering most of the necessary services at a range of preset prices.
It charged for every aspect of a funeral. Along with weddings and pew fees,
these were a major source of revenues for the parish and its religious and
lay workers.[58] Scholastique paid £2 9s. 2d. to the parish authorities and the
curé for the basic service and burial; £2 4s. 0d. to the beadle; a further 5s. so
the mourners could wear black arm bands; and 7s. 6d. in order to do the
way of the cross as part of the funeral. The coffin cost 10s.[59]

Usually, Catholic funeral corteges started at the deceased's home, then
proceeded to the church. After the ceremony, the priest, family, and friends
walked or went by carriage to the graveside, or in wintertime to the chapel
of the dead, where bodies were stored till the ground thawed. When Louis
Ducharme died, the main Catholic burial ground was located in Saint
Antoine ward, not far north of Saint Joseph suburb, where Scholastique
and Louis were residing when he died. Scholastique may or may not have
attended her husband's funeral. It would be a short walk from her home to
the cemetery if she wished to visit his grave. Over the next two decades,
Montrealers joined other citizens of Western cities in building new cemeteries further from the built-up inner city. Catholic, Protestant, and Jewish
cemeteries were relocated in new, separate areas in the more pastoral settings of the slopes of Mount Royal. The trip to the graves of husbands,
wives, children, and other loved ones for the burial or to honour their memories and mourn their loss would take more time or cost more money.[60]

Funerals, like mourning dress, varied dramatically with family wealth,
religious affiliation and belief, social status, and the personal preference of
the deceased and their kin. Unlike mourning clothing, which only widows
could claim from their deceased husbands' property, both spouses could
claim the expenses incurred for funerals. Legitimate costs included monies

paid for hiring people to sit with the corpse, dressing the body, and the cost of the church service, coffin, hearse, and burial.[61] This right was so fundamental that legislation in 1860 aiming once again to force the registration of wills and marriage contracts made it clear that expenses for last illnesses, funerals, and inventory making constituted a valid claim without registration.[62] Most of the husbands of the women in these two generations who became widows died during the time when historians have argued expensive, ostentatious funerals were considered customary, but when criticism of such funerals was also growing. Pat Jalland has described English middle-class families, some of whom paid hundreds of pounds for mourning clothes, black ostrich feathers, pages with wands, coaches, horses, and other paraphernalia.[63] All available evidence suggests that only a minority of Montrealers could afford or chose such pomp.

Executors, widows, and widows' relatives and friends probably made the funeral arrangements together. Ministers or priests might assist. When the deceased left a will, one of the first tasks of an executor was to see to the funeral arrangements and to carry out any wishes the deceased had expressed on the subject.[64] Hence, women chosen as their husbands' executors were officially entrusted with this responsibility. Eloi Beneche, as we saw, left the details of his funeral, masses, and the requiem to his executor and widow, the madam Rosalie Paquet. The newly widowed Euphrosine Mitresse Sansfaçon had more explicit instructions as executor of the cooper Jean-Baptiste Bergevin's will: Jean-Baptiste specified that he wanted his body buried in "the Montreal parish cemetery, in a grave of not less than ten feet in depth with a service of two bells, the body present on the nearest day possible following" his death, and that fifteen low Requiem masses should be said for the repose of his soul.[65]

Dr. Sutherland, like many elite and especially English-speaking testators, spared his widow, Catherine, the worries of arranging a funeral or acting as executor of his will, naming his only surviving son, Louis, and two city merchants as executors. He was as clear about his own funeral and burial as he was about how his widow should live and dress following his death. His will specified that he wanted only a simple funeral, a Church of England service, and to "be interred by the side of my son, William on my right hand and my daughter, Louisa on my left." The Protestant farmer Archibald Ogilvy also sought a simple funeral, stating in his will written in 1827 that "my body may be interred without any superfluous charges and expenses."[66] Most widows had no will to guide them. Many likely left such decisions to others.

Funerals and burials, like mourning clothes, sorted Montrealers starkly by class, status, and fortune. Marie Desormier had no money to pay the parish for funeral costs or a service when her labourer husband, Jacques

Paquet, died in 1854. The columns in the Catholic parish records that listed his funeral and burial costs were marked "gratis," as were those for most of the city's labourers and many construction workers, as well as their wives and children.[67] The rules of the parish were clear. The poor were to be buried free, and it was the *curé's* responsibility to make this known. But they received few other services. Marguerite Paris spent under £2 for the coffin and burial of her labourer husband, Joseph Guilbault, following his death in 1829.[68] The records of the parish council of Notre Dame show that the majority of craftsmen and small traders paid them between £1 and £2, or after the early 1860s, about $5.90, for the burial and service. A few paid only 8s. 4d., the fee for a burial alone. These prices secured the simplest of funerals. One pound ten shillings, the most common amount paid to the parish for such men's burials and funerals in the first half of the nineteenth century, was the set price for a service of the seventh order. In the parish's offerings, this was the lowest class available, though less could be paid for a simple burial without a service.

Just over £2 secured a sixth-order funeral. Scholastique Bissonnet paid £2 10s. to the parish, as well as a further £6 for other funeral-related costs for the funeral of her carpenter-turned-innkeeper husband, Louis Ducharme. This amount ensured that two bells were rung. At this level of service, the ornaments adorning the main alter were made of copper, rather than the silver used for higher classes of services. Ten children from the choir sang at the service along with four cantors, rather than the full children's choir of thirty. This price also covered the costs of digging the grave, but not the monies owed to *curés* and priests in attendance.[69] Coffins would have been extra too, procured in the early years of the century from local carpenters. In early-nineteenth-century Protestant cemeteries in Montreal, it cost £1 10s. to purchase a single grave. A lot could be purchased for £5 10s. Grave diggers charged 7s. 6d. for adults in the summer, more in winter. There were further charges if a tombstone was required. These payments and the additional monies owing the sexton and the superintendent had to be made before the grave could be occupied.[70]

The growing numbers of poor in the city posed problems to Catholics and Protestants alike, especially while the cemeteries were located within the confines of the lived city. All denominations faced the tricky question of whether the poor merited "an individual grave, a religious service at grave-side," or any kind of identification. Brian Young reports that during the 1820s, various Protestant churches set up funds to cover the burial of the poor, and some purchased specific lots in the city cemeteries for their parishioners. When space proved insufficient, Protestant trustees experimented with providing a "common winter pit," opening a cheaper cemetery site on Papineau Road to accommodate them. In 1833, they contemplated

securing ground just for the poor. When the new cemetery was constructed on Mount Royal in the 1860s, land was set aside specifically for
burying the poor.[71]

It was, as we saw in earlier chapters, in part to avoid a pauper's grave
that growing numbers of Catholic couples joined the Union des Prières
and that Montrealers of all faiths created and joined a range of mutual and
benevolent institutions. When Rose Galipeau's husband, the carpenter
François Lemay, died in 1852, the Union des Prières covered at least £1 9s.
6d. of the £2 5s. 4d. required for the ringing of one bell, his service, and
burial.[72] In 1872, the service and burial of Hermine Legris' husband,
Michel Julien, were paid for in this way.[73]

In contrast to these modest funerals, that organized for Jacques Genevay
following his death in February 1827 was lavish. Total costs came to over
£150. This was exorbitant by Montreal standards. This young, bilingual
Montrealer's family and friends sent him out of life in 1827 with as much
dash and disregard for debt as he seems to have lived it. They spent £3 for
funeral invitations. The service was held at St. Jacques Church, the recently completed church on St. Denis Street in the Saint Lawrence suburb
that served then as the parish cathedral and the episcopal palace.[74] They
owed the fabrique of the parish more than £25 for the service, burial,
and other costs alone – more than ten times the amount most artisans or
families in small trades paid for an adult burial. This amount secured a
funeral service of the first order, with four bells rung, the full choir of
thirty children singing and the four cantors, the best silver chandeliers
arrayed on the altars of the church, black coverings on the pews, and many
candles burning.[75]

Four adjutants accompanied Jacques-François-Louis Genevay's body to
his final resting place. The total of well over £150 local currency for her
mourning clothes, the service, the black crape and chenille, candles, digging the grave, and other expenses exceeds the £50 to £70 sterling that
the English reformer, Edwin Chadwick, suggested was usual for an ordinary middle-class funeral in England in 1843. These costs pale beside the
£500 to £1,500 sterling some members of the British aristocracy paid at
this time of expensive, ostentatious funerals.[76] Costs seem high given the
debts that hung over Genevay during his final illness. Family members
stepped in to help. Roughly a third of the funeral costs listed in the inventory of his goods appear to have been repaid by the husband of one of
Charlotte's sisters.[77]

Providing the commodities and services required for funerals became
good business in this city where deaths were so frequent. Montreal carpenters and joiners combined coffin making with general carpentry. In the
early decades of the century, a few took out advertisements in local papers,

discretely announcing their location, and noting that orders would be "attended to with dispatch," or "funerals furnished, with Hearses and all that is required, without any trouble to Customers."[78] When Susanna Moodie passed through the city in September 1832, after the worst of the cholera epidemic was past, she commented on the "sullen toll of the death-bell," the many notices placarded on the walls claiming that funerals would be "furnished at such and such a place, at cheapest rates," and the "exposure of ready-made coffins in the undertakers' windows" as signals that "death was everywhere."[79]

By mid-century, newspapers and city directories were carrying larger advertisements for undertakers and others providing for funerals, replete with visuals depicting caskets, hearses, and other funeral paraphernalia. George Armstrong, a cabinetmaker, upholsterer, and undertaker, married Margaret Longmore in October 1845 at Mountain Street Methodist Church. He was born in Ireland, as was Margaret. They married in 1845 when he was twenty-four and she was twenty-one. It was men of his generation who promoted the growing visibility and commercialization of the funeral business. By the 1850s, Armstrong was one of the most successful undertakers in the city. His advertisements in the *Gazette* announced that he furnished funerals "in any style," as well as carrying a variety of "Coffins, Crapes, etc.," along with the beds, mattresses, and other household furniture that filled his shop. As concern grew about the health problems that dead bodies caused in inner-city cemeteries, he began advertising "patent metallic burial cases." In 1858, he was successful enough to enlarge his shop. He then offered all styles of funerals "on application being made to him, by the friends of the deceased." By the 1860s, he could afford to include a picture of his substantial shop in his advertisement.[80] Marble cutters also advertised their skills at producing marble monuments, tombs, or gravestones, as well as chimney pieces. Advertisements aimed at Catholic and French-speaking Montrealers were similar, and competition among them heated up in escalating claims to superior services or cheaper funerals.[81] (See Figure 7.5.)

It was Armstrong's main competitor, Joseph Wray, who came to the home that Rebecca Conegan had shared with Sampson Brady just before 2 p.m. on 3 December 1852 to remove his body. Sampson had died three days earlier. As Rebecca adjusted to being a widow, at least seven men were officially involved in dealing with the arrangements that followed his death. Sampson had named three executors: his brother, a bookbinder from New York; Thomas Goodwin, a local "gentleman"; and James Adams, a Montreal grocer. Formally, the funeral arrangements were in their hands. Joseph Wray received nearly £9 for the services he provided, which included the coffin and the hire of horses. The funeral procession left their

CORBILLARDS OU CHARIOTS
Au No. 5, Rue St. George,
PRES DE LA RUE CRAIG.
———
M. ARSENE CHAPELEAU

INFORME ses amis et le public en général
qu'il a constamment chez lui, au No. 5, Rue St.
George, de MAGNIFIQUES CHARIOTS, ou
CORBILLARDS, qu'il livrera au plus bas prix
qu'en aucun place, avec un ou deux chevaux. Il
peut aussi fournir des BIERES, ou CERCUEILS,
de toute sorte, GANTS, CREPES, CIERGES,
&c., pour les services funèbres. Il fait aussi
savoir qu'il ensevelira tout homme ou enfant à
demande.
20 sept.—a

FIGURE 7.5   Competition in the funeral business, Montreal, 1850s-60s. M. Chapeleau informs his friends and the public in general that at his establishment at 5 St. George Street he always has magnificent carriages and coffins, and that he will deliver at the lowest price, with one or two horses. He can also furnish caskets or coffins of all sorts, gloves, crapes, candles, etc., for funeral services. He also wants it known that he will prepare and enshroud any men or children if requested. Note the decency of him specifying he will dress and lay out only the bodies of men and children. | "Corbillards ou Chariots" [Hearses or Carriages], *La Minerve,* 31 December 1858, 4.

house and proceeded to the American Presbyterian Church at the corner of St. James and McGill streets. There, two more men, Benjamin Workman and George Mathews, served as the witnesses of his death, overseen by the minister. Eventually Brady's body was interred in a family grave in the newly opened Protestant cemetery on the flanks of Mount Royal, though whether he was initially buried there or removed there after his brother William purchased the lot for £3 15s. 3d. in 1876 is unclear.[82]

Montreal's most elaborate funerals were for politicians, mayors, and other public figures. Mary Westcott's critique of Chief Justice Vallières de Saint-Réal's funeral in February 1847 was based both on its lavishness and the Catholic rituals it embodied.[83] She described it in great detail to her Protestant American father, tartly remarking that he

> died (not as he had lived) in the full glory of the Catholic faith and therefore received all the pomp and ceremony possible due to a good Catholic who was a dignitary of the land. Scores of priests in full costume with long trails, bearing silver incense cups. Scores of children bearing wax lights, and monks with silver bowls of holy water. All the judges, lawyers, &c. &c., many of the societies of which he was patron all in mourning, followed him to the church where the solemn funeral mass was said and he was taken in the vaults beneath Notre Dame. Half the town are in black and for 30 days, and yet who really cares that he is gone?[84]

The funeral held for Hannah Lyman's husband, John Mills, later that year after he died of typhus while mayor was an equally impressive testimonial to his public citizenship on the more local stage of urban politics. Kirsten Wood has argued that slave-holding Southern widows understood that "a husband's public service imposed certain civic obligations on his widow, as they had on his wife."[85] For the three widows of men who had been mayors, as well as prominent in other ways – Luce Perrault, Marie-Louise Lacroix, and Hannah Lyman – this meant that the city as a whole became spectators at their husbands' funerals, civic sharers of their grief. Widows of politicians experienced similar situations. As John Easton Mills had died on the job, his was a particularly prominent occasion. His death, as we saw, had been reported widely in many of the city's newspapers. So were the details of his funeral. An open invitation was extended to all citizens, both French and English, to "unite in the last melancholy testimony of respect for the deceased." Afterward, the evangelical Protestant paper the *Montreal Register* made a special point of noting that the procession included "men of all parties, political and religious," except "the Church of England." If Hannah or the children took part, this was not noted in any of the many reports of the funeral that appeared in the next few days.[86]

The funeral was held on a Monday afternoon, four days after his death. The journey began at their home, Belair Cottage, at the corner of St. Genevieve and Belmont streets. Although the papers had announced that it would begin at 2:00 p.m., it was closer to 2:30 when the funeral procession was ready to depart. The cortege partially retraced some of the route between Mills's home and his office on St. François Xavier Street.[87] It also

FUNÉRAILLES DE L'EX-MAIRE BERNARD A MONTREAL, LE 15 JUILLET

FIGURE 7.6   Funeral of the former mayor Aldis Bernard, Montreal, 15 July 1876. In this sketch of a Montreal mayor's funeral, the artist portrays women in roughly equal in numbers to men among the onlookers. Note the black mourning paraphernalia that decorates the horses and the carriage, and exemplifies the lavish funerals of the elite during this period. Bernard was mayor of Montreal between 1873 and 1875. The 1847 funeral of John Easton Mills was likely less lavish than this high Victorian one. | *L'Opinion publique*, 3 August 1876, 7. From the collection of the Bibliothèque et Archives nationales du Québec.

passed very close to several of the city blocks that he had been buying up in the 1830s and 1840s that had helped him achieve the rentier status that freed him up financially to take on the position of mayor. Shops were closed all along the route of the funeral procession.[88]

Like most funerals, Mills's was a very masculine affair, though women might take part in the crowd, as portrayed in the sketch of Mayor Aldis Bernard's 1876 funeral (see Figure 7.6). At the head were Mills's fellow members of the City Council, behind them the city's officers. Brothers from two friendly societies, the Odd Fellows and the Manchester Unity marched next, just in front of the pallbearers. They all wore white gloves and mourning badges on their arms. The pallbearers included some of the

city's leading merchants, politicians, and judges. Judges Samuel Gale and
Charles Dewey Day were among them. So were the merchants and politicians Peter McGill, George Moffatt, and Joseph Bourret. The governor
general had sent his carriage and one of his aides-de-camp. He followed
the mourners, with the commander of the British forces, the heads of
military departments, and officers of the garrison marching behind him.
Private citizens followed. Somewhere in the procession were members of
the Mechanics Institute. Mills had given generously to their library just
days before his death. Officers of the Champlain and St. Lawrence Railroad,
with which he had long been associated, also paid their respects. The *Courier*
suggested afterward that "no funeral ever took place in Montreal at which
there was so large an attendance." The hearse, the report concluded, was "a
new one ... from the manufactory of Mr. Baird" and "very elegant."[89]

The procession moved slowly east, then south down to Beaver Hall and
the American Presbyterian Church. The service opened with the choir
singing a hymn. Mr. Henry Wilkes delivered the main funeral address.
Words spoken "at most funerals and memorial services" were delivered,
then "lost to posterity."[90] Those preached at Mills's funeral, in contrast, were
captured permanently in print first in local newspapers and a year later as
a pamphlet. Wilkes stressed Mills's faith and his dedication to the "claims of
the suffering and dying," from whom he had "contracted the disease, the
effects of which are now before us – in an inanimate body, a bereaved and
weeping family, and a mourning city." Using the occasion to remind his
listeners of the importance of faith in Christ and of good works, he ended
by commending "the widow and the fatherless to that blessed God who is
the widows' judge and the father of the fatherless, in his holy habitation."[91]
After the service the mourners moved on foot and in carriages to the Old
Burying Ground in the heart of the expanding Saint Lawrence suburb.
There the Reverend Wilkes oversaw the burial. John's body would lie for
some years in easy walking distance of the family home.[92]

A mourning card including an image of John was printed as part of the
funeral process (see Figure 7.7). Visual reminders of the dead remained a
fairly elite privilege across the century, though such mourning cards, and
images or photographs, were part of the increasingly commercial paraphernalia of Victorian funerals promoted by undertakers.[93] Like his public
funeral, and the procession route that carved a semi-circle around the city
that he had shaped in so many ways, this mourning card enjoined the
whole city to share in grieving his loss through the words "Mourn
Hochelaga" engraved on it. In calling on Montreal's citizens to join in
mourning, it reasserted a sense of community among its people that had
been tested at the time of his election as well as during the typhus epidemic, and that might be tested again with his death.[94] By evoking the

JOHN EASTON MILLS
5ème Maire, 1847

FIGURE 7.7   Mortuary card produced for the funeral of Mayor John Easton Mills following his death in 1847 from typhus. | Archives de la Ville de Montréal, Gonds BM1, P1474.

Iroquois name of the village that Europeans first found in the place that became Montreal, it expressed Mills's historic significance, without acknowledging colonialism's impact on the colony's First Nations people. This connection to an Aboriginal past surfaces again in "A dirge for the Late J.E. Mills, esq," published with Wilkes' address. It cast Mills in the position of city patriarch, or of Indian chief:

> In sackcloth clothe the city,
> For her citizens are sad;
> Let Hochelaga's council-hall
> In mourning weeds be clad ;–
> For the chief of all her people,
> Sleeps now the sleep of death –

Man's last dread foe has chilled us
With his blighting, with'ring breath.

The poem proposes that the whole city don the weeds normally associated with widows.[95] Hannah's own grieving and mourning were thus sub-
sumed in the city's claim to mourn its dead mayor. Like less prominent
widows, she was positioned only in abstraction as a mother of fatherless
children, a nameless widow, a disembodied religious and social archetype,
in contrast to her departed husband, whose "manly form, full of life and
power ... moved about in its appropriate sphere of action, an object recognized by all, and loved by many."[96] Just as Mills's city councillors, the fire
companies, and members of the fraternal and other associations to which
he had belonged turned out in force to bid farewell to their former colleague and leader, so "the entire Montreal bar and most of the bench" es-
corted lawyer Adolphus Mordecai Hart's body from his home on Durocher
Street in the Golden Square Mile to the Mile End Railway Station from
whence his body was taken to Trois-Rivières. There, in the hometown of
his prominent family, he was given a Jewish burial. Constance Hannah
Hart began her year of full mourning; the bar of the city is reported to
have observed a month of mourning for their departed colleague.[97]

Such civic and public funerals often meant that officials rather than
family made the arrangements. And these could take some time. Marie-
Louise Lacroix did not say her final farewells to Charles-Séraphin's body
after he died at nearly eighty in 1876 until five days after his death, rather
than the usual two. Friends and relations were sent individual invitations,
but the *Montreal Gazette* and *La Minerve* also asked that "those not receiving an invitation should please consider" these notices as one. They were
invited to gather at his residence on St. Antoine Street. This was the mansion that the couple had opened up to the Jesuits to use as a novitiate after
they were permitted to return to Canada in 1843. After Marie-Louise and
Charles received the Prince on his 1860 tour of Canada as the city's mayor
and wife, they had renamed it the Prince of Wales Castle. Charles and
Marie-Louise's devotion and philanthropy were recognized in the large
number of Sulpicians and other priests and *curés* who accompanied his body
and participated in the service. Usually, death registers were signed by just
two people, often the church officials. Rodier's was witnessed by three
Sulpician priests, by the sheriff of Montreal, and by numerous family and
friends. After the service, his body was transported to the Catholic Notre-
Dame-des-Neiges Cemetery, on the other side of the mountain from the
Protestant and Jewish cemeteries.[98]

Routes taken, bells tolled, candles lit, churches chosen, the length and
class of services, and the locations and dimensions of graves were religious

and material currencies that sorted Catholic Montrealers at their death by class, wealth, faith, respectability, and gender. Different combinations of bells signalled to the wider city whether the Catholic dead were men, women, children, or priests. Harmonies of smaller bells tolled for women and girls, larger ones for priests and men.[99] Protestant and Jewish Montrealers had different but equally eloquent markers of social difference at death. Times of day and the routes from homes to churches to cemeteries also demarcated Catholics, Protestants, and Jews as much as their divergent religious rituals. Canadien and Irish Catholic widows' final farewells to their husbands' bodies began early, usually between 5:00 and 9:00 a.m.[100] The funeral for Irish Catholic immigrant Mary O'Leary's first husband, the Canadien painter Nicolas Venière, left their home at 7:00 a.m.[101] Pierre-Bernard Decousse's funeral procession began at 7:30 a.m. at the home and tavern in Jacques Cartier Square where he and Marie-Louise Genant had lived and worked since he ceased his trade as a master tailor. Only very prominent Catholic citizens' funerals began after 8:30 a.m. The prestige of Marie-Louise Lacroix and her husband, Charles-Séraphin Rodier, were signalled in part by the lateness of his funeral. It began at 9:00 a.m.[102]

Protestant and Jewish funerals were afternoon rituals. The body of Constance Hannah Hart's husband, Adolphus Mordecai Hart, left their home at 1:30 p.m., timed in part to allow time to catch the train to his family's hometown of Trois-Rivières. The funerals for Sampson Brady and Dr. William Sutherland, like that of John Mills, were scheduled to begin at 2 p.m. Across the century, most Protestant funerals in Montreal took place either at 2:00 or at 2:30 p.m.[103] Occasionally, they were held a bit later. The funeral of Margaret Jamieson's husband, William Moody, in August 1861 began at 4:00 p.m., the latest time we have found for funerals announced in newspapers. Perhaps that was to allow his fellow employees from the office of the *Montreal Herald* where he had long worked as a printer to attend. Moody was buried at the Mount Royal Cemetery, in a lot that he would eventually share with many of their children and other members of both his and her families.[104]

Gradually, Montrealers of all faiths who could afford it moved the remains of dead family members to the appropriate cemetery on the mountain, emptying the old cemeteries that had been dotted around the city. In Montreal, as elsewhere, reformers attacked urban cemeteries as public health dangers, manufactories "of Poison."[105] Promoters of the new rural cemeteries sold the romantic idea of gravestones in "extensive grounds, combining hill and dale, woodland and open land, laid out with taste, and carefully attended, with there a screen of evergreens, and there a bed of varied flowers."[106] After its opening in 1852, many of the city's prominent Protestant families disinterred deceased family members from the old and jumbled urban burial grounds and had them moved to the new "romantic setting" on the mountain.[107] John Mills's remains were moved away from what was described four years after his death as the "offensive appearance" and "foul air" of the Old Burying Ground.[108] Édouard-Raymond Fabre's body was moved to the Catholic Notre-Dame-des-Neiges Cemetery, which opened on the western side of the mountain in 1854. And although Adolphus Mordecai Hart's funeral was held in Trois-Rivières, his Montreal citizenship was eventually acknowledged in a grave erected for him and Constance in the Jewish cemetery, also on Mount Royal next to the Protestant cemetery. The emotional disruption and financial demands of such disinterments and reburials fell largely on the couples who married in the 1820s cohort and on the relatively small number whose marriages in the 1840s were dissolved by death within a decade.

These graves of such prominent Montrealers can be visited today. The lettering remains clear. Permanent and prominent, they are located in accessible sections of each cemetery, as befitted the status of such men. Their widows could readily command a carriage to visit their tombstones. Eventually, each of these widows joined their husbands, either in the grave or in the wording that linked them in death as in life. The graves of less wealthy Montrealers are hard to find. Few gravestones remain; moss, lichen, and time have blurred the wording of many that do. Sites have been reused. No traces remain of those who received a pauper's funeral. Working, middle-class, and elite widows visiting dead husbands' burial places might cross each other's paths in the cemetery, as they might on the streets of the city, but the geography of class and power expressed in the landscape of the dead meant they were unlikely to kneel in close proximity at their gravesides.

The black clothing that Scholastique Bissonnet and other widows donned signalled to the world that they were in mourning. Its style, elegance, and cost announced the wealth and status of their deceased husbands. Funerals, death notices, and obituaries similarly sorted Montreal widows more by the past status of their husbands than by their financial futures. These ritualized commemorations of death involved widows and those around them in decision making in the days following husbands' deaths. Such rituals were important markers of transitions.[109] They might offer widows comfort, space for dissemblance, or anguish for those unable to fulfill their desires for the departed for financial reasons or because of health regulations.

A husband's death heralded new legal autonomy for widows. Mourning customs contained that autonomy. In most of these early rituals of grieving, Scholastique Bissonnet, Hannah Lyman, Constance Hannah Hart, and the other women who outlived their husbands seem shrouded in a mantle as dark as their mourning clothes, despite the responsibilities some held for estates and organizing funerals. Widows entered a liminal space in which family, friends, and the wider community collaborated in a choreographed denial of the new legal autonomy and individuality they would assume as widows. This cultural shield that mourning rituals produced could be protective and supportive for some widows, constraining even claustrophobic for others.

For many new widows, dressing in mourning appropriate to their class and knowing that their husband would be buried in ways suitable to their religion and status were among their earliest challenges. Historians have presented the first year of widowhood as a time when widows were expected to retreat into the home to grieve except for the temporary distraction of funerals and business matters.[110] Here I have argued that widows were indeed anchored firmly in the shadows of their dead husbands in the early days following their deaths. Yet, these new widows could not remain out of sight. Wallowing in grief, even staying at home, were liberties few could afford to take. Within days of their husbands' burials, many turned to tasks that would make a legal difference to their status as lone mothers of minor children, or as heirs, as well as to their financial futures. The first twelve months of widowhood was a period of looking backward and looking forward. It is to some of the legal and money matters that Scholastique, Hannah, and other widows saw to in the first year of their widowhood that we turn next.

8

"Within a Year and a Day"
The First Year of Widowhood

Five days after the burial of her innkeeper husband, Louis Ducharme, Scholastique Bissonnet met with friends and relatives to choose a tutor for their children. Four days later, Notary Guy came to their home to make an inventory of their belongings.[1] Over the next few days, she met with the notary on several more occasions at her home and in his office. Dressed, presumably in her mourning clothes, and caring for her two young children, she may have found time to look back on her eight year marriage and grieve her dead husband. She also had to look forward and contemplate her future as family head and sole supporter of her offspring. As women refashioned their futures as widows, there were many decisions to make and legal matters to see to that obliged them to leave home and to interact with male officials. Under the Custom of Paris, the hour of a spouse's death set customary and legal clocks ticking that demarcated the first few days of widowhood from the early months and distinguished the first year and a day from what followed. Special rights and options that were available to widows, but not widowers, had to be exercised within legal deadlines.

Scholastique was careful, even precipitous, about respecting those deadlines. Her options as a new widow involved her in some decisions and actions that were less usual in common law jurisdictions.[2] Widows with minor children were best to ensure that a tutor was legally named for them, preferably shortly after their husbands' deaths. Those whose marriage had created a community of goods had the option of rejecting that community if its debts outweighed its assets. Widowers had no such option. However, to do so, widows had to arrange to have an inventory made of their property within three months of their husband's death. They had a further forty days to decide to accept or reject the community. Within this period, widows could live "with their servants," if they had them, at the expense of their husbands' succession. They could, as we saw, claim the costs of their mourning outfits, unless they had committed adultery. Men had no such option. Widows could also choose between legacies promised in husbands' wills and customary dower rights or dowers or other promises in their marriage contract. Dower before and after the changes made in 1841 existed only for widows. Men had no such claim. Nor was there any equivalent to curtesy, the privilege the English common law gave to men to use all their wives' real property until their own deaths. Those chosen as executors had a year and a day to complete their tasks.[3]

These are the topics of this chapter. It explores the diverse ways age, gender, class, wealth, custom, and religion shaped the tasks widows took on once their husbands' funerals were over. In so doing it adds to the work of other scholars who have examined the duties and actions of widows after husbands' deaths, and builds on earlier chapters in exploring the particularly rich and complex array of choices and situations that resulted from the mixture of legal, social, and cultural customs practised in nineteenth-century Montreal.[4] The many matters that Scholastique Bissonnet, Marguerite Paris, Caroline Campbell, Rebecca Conegan, Marie-Louise Genant, and other newly widowed women had to see to remind us that in the midst of the shock, grief, or relief that followed husbands' deaths, widows had many tasks to accomplish. Few newly widowed women performed these alone. Adult children, siblings, and other family members might protect, support, or scrutinize them. Those named as executors or tutors had more legal obligations than those who were not. But all widows had to play some part in the sets of negotiations and interactions that shaped their claims, their standards of living, and their futures as widows and often as single parents. Many also had to seek some form of paid labour, secure charity, or continue family businesses to support themselves and young children. These tasks had to be seen to during the time that etiquette marked out for widows as the initial period of deepest mourning, signalled to the wider world in their dull, black garments. After this first year, those following mourning mores could don lavender and lighter colours.[5]

Twelve months of loyalty, twelve months to complete a series of legal tasks, a minimum of twelve months of mourning. Law, social custom, and matters of family and property thus combined to mark this first year of widowhood as a special time in which widows negotiated their new identities and legal autonomy in the shadow of their deceased husbands. Legal autonomy might be, as Suzanne Lebsock has remarked, a "frightening prospect."[6] Yet, like the rituals of cleansing bodies, donning mourning attire, funerals and burials, the ritualized performances that the law demanded, may also have provided some women with structure and purpose in these early months. These ritualized repeated performances consolidated their new identities as widows.

Widows and Custody of Their Children

The friends and relatives of Scholastique Bissonnet and her children chose her as the tutor of her two minor children. Their decision was ratified before Judge George Pyke in Montreal's Court of King's Bench on 22 April 1834. Hannah Lyman, Rebecca Conegan, and Marie-Louise Genant were also selected as their children's tutors, as were most widows. Tutors were children's guardians. They were legally responsible for the care of minor children following a parent's death and had the authority to represent them in all civil acts. Such formal decisions were not necessary to make surviving mothers or fathers the tutors of their minor offspring, responsible for their share in family property. Many widows and widowers were probably quite content to claim tutorship of their minor children informally, saving the fees for the tutorship and inventory taking. Yet, Scholastique Bissonnet paid 7s. 6d. to the court for drawing up the act of tutorship and 12s. 6d. to Notary Guy for overseeing the naming of the tutor and sub-tutor. The same documents cost Marie-Louise Genant over £4, after her tailor-turned-innkeeper husband, Pierre-Bernard Decousse, died, nearly twenty years later.[7]

Avoiding such costs could pose problems later. Surviving parents of minor children whose marriage had created community property could not have an inventory of the couples' goods made unless a tutor had been formally appointed to represent their interests. Without an inventory taken within three months of a husband's death, widows could not take advantage of their right to reject an indebted community. They might also be accused of meddling in community property. Only an officially appointed tutor could act in court on the child's behalf. Such family councils appear to have been widely practised in rural areas before and after the Conquest. Jean-Phillipe Garneau found that in the rural region of Beaupré during the eighteenth century, such elections of tutors followed some three-quarters of the deaths of parents with minor children. In the very different urban context of nineteenth-century Montreal, not all residents would have been aware of the advantages of this custom, so foreign to the procedures of the English common law.[8] Some widows only learned the benefit of being formally appointed when they planned to remarry or when they sought to pursue a legal action on behalf of their children. Late in the century, this moment came for the widow Justine Wilhemy when she tried to sue a church official for embarrassing her son in front of the whole congregation during mass. The court held that, as she was not his formal guardian, she could not act on his behalf.[9]

In the official decision making about tutors, men held all the important roles. The meeting of family and friends occurred either before a judge or a notary. Scholastique met with at least six other people in Notary Guy's office to determine who was legally in charge of her children and their property. The law required the involvement of a minimum of seven people taken as equally as possible from the relatives and friends of each parent. They had to be over twenty-one and living in the same area. The only women eligible to participate were the mother and widows closely related to the minor children. Garneau insists convincingly on these rituals as masculine ceremonies of power that asserted the triple authority of the state, of men, and household heads.[10]

Family councils may have provided widows with much needed support in the early period of their grieving. But some widows surely faced them with trepidation. For the legal and social scripts that guided decision making varied depending on whether the surviving spouse was a widow or a widower. The office of tutor, as the feminist Marie Gérin-Lajoie would explain at the turn of the nineteenth century, was "essentially for males, only men of full age being qualified for it." The one exception was widows of minor children. Widows were "free to accept or refuse." Fathers could not refuse.[11] Would widows be chosen as their children's tutors? If yes, were they capable of the new tasks this thrust upon them? If not, would the tutor be someone they trusted? During these deliberations, the surviving parent was required to leave the room. Those chosen then swore on the bible in front of the notary or judge and family members and friends that they would fulfil their office faithfully. Even when chosen as their children's tutor, these were occasions of ongoing patriarchal and familial control, despite – and no doubt at times because of – widows' recent legal liberation.[12]

A family council needed good reasons not to assign the tutorship to the surviving parent. Court cases across the century confirmed the right of widows to be tutors unless they were proven unfit through misconduct or were unable to provide adequate support.[13] Records seldom note the reasons behind a family council's decision. So we must mostly guess at the family dynamics that left a minority of widows without official tutorship of their children and their property. In some cases, the widow was still a minor herself. In others, her capacity was in question, as with Maria Mitchell, to whose story we return shortly.[14] When two of Oliver Wait's brothers and five other male friends and relatives met to assign legal responsibility for the children of his two marriages, they selected Caroline Campbell as tutor for the four surviving children of their eight-year marriage, but not for the children born to Oliver and his first wife. Caroline was only twenty-five. The estate was sizable. Blended families could be complicated, and it was customary to keep the interests of children from separate marriage beds distinct. Those present selected Logan Fuller, Wait's son-in-law, as tutor for the four children from his first marriage who were still minors. They also appointed him curator of the property of his wife and Wait's other married daughter. Judge Reid ratified these choices made just nine days after Oliver's death while cholera still raged in the city.[15]

In addition to their responsibility for the care of their minor children, Scholastique Bissonnet, Caroline Campbell, and the other widows chosen as tutors were in charge of managing the children's property until they reached the age of twenty-one. They could not sell property without further permission from a family council. Family councils also appointed a subtutor. Always a male, he had to make sure the act of tutorship was registered, be present when the inventory of goods was made, and watch over the tutor's administration. He could remove the tutor, if he felt it was warranted. He was also meant to act for the minors whenever their interests appeared to be different from those of their tutor.[16] In this way, the law made it possible for widows to be their children's tutors and gave them considerable power in this position. At the same time, it ensured male supervision of their financial decisions. Scholastique Bissonnet shared the task with a "gentleman" named François Finchley. Children's uncles, especially on the dead father's side, were chosen most frequently as subtutors.[17] Both Caroline Campbell and Rebecca Conegan worked with their brothers-in-law as subtutors. This choice ensured that both sides of the family were keeping an eye on the futures and the property of orphaned children. Other subtutors were usually grandfathers, other relatives, family friends, or, as in Scholastique's case, local notables who accepted the position.

Maria Mitchell argued that the men who met and chose the tutor and subtutor for her children were "entire strangers." The day that Thomas slit his throat in late February 1859, a merchant, John O. Brown, and a neighbour George Horne took the children back to the Ladies' Benevolent Society. Maria spent the first three weeks of her widowhood in hospital recovering from the blows her husband inflicted on her and from their last shared heavy drinking spree. On 28 March, Brown called a meeting to choose a tutor for the children, apparently inviting Maria, though she would later deny it. The seven men chose Brown, whom others described as having helped the family with "articles of clothing and other things." They nominated a Mr. George Nunn, a painter, as the subtutor.[18] The children remained in the Protestant orphanage.

Maria was not happy with this decision. However bad a mother she had been, she was determined that Brown and his colleagues would not have the final word on her children's future. She visited them at the orphanage with one of her working-class friends and was shocked to discover that her eldest daughter had been sent into service outside the city.

When the matron refused to let her take her other children away, she returned at night, climbed over the wall, and "stole" them.[19] Perhaps she took them to the nuns, as the matron's journal suggested, or possibly back to her friend, Mary Peters' place. Maria then sought to have a say in their future. Working with Marcus Doherty, a young Catholic lawyer, they called a second meeting of friends and chose two Catholic men as the girls' tutor and subtutor.[20] Although their choice was sanctioned by the same officials, children could not have two sets of tutors. What happened to resolve this mistake is unclear. In early July, the five children were returned again to the orphanage.

Maria did not give up. In October, seven months after Brown had officially been designated as their tutor, Maria initiated a civil suit against him, again using Doherty as her lawyer. Her affidavit, signed on 25 October 1858, claimed she had been "wholly deprived of the keeping and comfort of her said five children; and that she is by law entitled to the custody of her said children in preference to all other persons whomsoever." Marcus Doherty must surely have taken on the case pro bono. Assisting a Catholic widow retrieve her children from Protestant control in a city in which religion was such a marker of difference may have outweighed any qualms he had about her character, and possibly advanced his visibility and career.[21]

Marcus Doherty and Maria did their best to produce a credible argument against the tutorship of Brown. Between October and November, they crafted a petition and found witnesses who would agree to sign affidavits and appear in court. Their affidavits sought to counter the image of Maria as a drunken mother. Her working-class friends Mary Eliza Peters, Bridget Halligan, and Mary's husband, Thomas Prendergast, gave evidence with care, painting a picture of an abused wife who was determined to make a new start and "perfectly able to direct how her children should be provided for."[22] Against their plausible tale of a battered wife struggling to pull her life together as a widow, Brown and his attorney Samuel Dorman produced compelling evidence from some of the city's leading medical professionals and law enforcers.[23] The chief of police, Moses Hayes, produced a listing of Maria's repeated arrests for being drunk. Robert Craik, chief surgeon at the Montreal General Hospital, as well as the coroner, argued that she had been very drunk when her husband beat her up. Other prominent Montrealers concurred in assessing her as a drunkard.

The judge who heard the case at the Superior Court of Lower Canada on 24 December 1858 was William Badgley. In 1858, Badgley was in his late fifties, just a bit older than Thomas Spiers had been at his death. He had six surviving children, one more than Maria and Thomas. It is unlikely that this very prominent conservative, solidly Anglican, ardently pro-British, ex-Member of the Canadian Legislative Assembly knew his fellow Freemason

Thomas Spiers well.[24] It is equally unlikely that he knew nothing of Maria's reputation or of the history of this tragic marriage prior to the trial. In colonial cities, as Kirsten McKenzie has argued, scandals spread readily and could undermine the "elaborate rituals of social distinction" so necessary to maintaining social boundaries.[25] Badgley made his judgment about the children's future two months later, on 28 February 1859, exactly one year after their father's suicide. It appears as a draft in the court documents and was later published at length in the *Lower Canada Jurist*. Badgley dismissed the petition with costs. Presenting her "notorious misconduct" as well established both before and after Brown took over as tutor, and her allegations against Brown as unproven, he concluded there was no "reason for setting aside this appointment for the purpose of making another, of another stranger." No charge of "moral or personal unfitness" had been made against Brown. He would remain the children's tutor.[26] Badgley's decision was in conformity with the Custom of Paris and, later, with the civil code. Once named, a male tutor normally held that position until death, unless he was found guilty of misusing funds or of immoral conduct.[27]

Maria never claimed she could support or raise her youngsters herself. Her actions suggest that her main goals were to secure access to them and have them raised as Catholics. Other widows no doubt turned to spirits to escape the challenges they faced. A few stiff drinks at home or too many glasses of wine at dinner might cause a few whispers and worries, especially over these decades when Canadians, like other North Americans, were rethinking "the place of booze in their daily lives."[28] Remedies ranging from laudanum and smelling salts offered widows other momentary or addictive escape, without necessarily tarnishing their respectability or capacity to mother children in others' eyes.[29] But Hayes's testimony about Maria ascribed an identity, not a cultural or culinary practice. Maria, in his testimony and that of other notable Protestant Montrealers, was a female drunkard. This, and the prominence of her opponents, weighed heavily against her claims as a widow and mother seeking to have a say in her children's future. In the ritualized ceremonies of choosing tutors, the judge and notary represented the state and the community in sanctioning the Council's choice. When those tutors were widows, these male actors publicly authorized a woman to step into the anomalous position of household head, under a set of gendered conditions, and under male surveillance. Maria's repeated drunkenness made her an effective example of bad mothering that justified refusing her that position.[30]

Taking an Inventory
As her children's tutor, Scholastique Bissonnet moved quickly to one of her first official tasks. Within four days of her appointment she invited

Notary Guy to the inn in the Saint Joseph suburb to make an inventory of the goods that she and Louis Ducharme had accumulated together. She and the subtutor had secured two local men to act as appraisers of their property – a master saddler and a local "bourgeois."[31] Making such inventories must have been emotionally and physically demanding for many widows, as it may also have been for the assessors and notaries who took part. Assessors were always men. Unlike the notary, they were not professionals. Some worked in the same profession as the deceased. Often they were men in trades like upholstery and cabinet making, or in branches of commerce that gave them some claim to know the current value of household goods. In these early decades of the century, they were frequently illiterate. Before mid-century they called out the worth of household items in a range of different currencies. The notaries appear to have converted them on the spot or later into either pounds, shillings, and pence or livres, sols, and deniers in the early years, or dollars in later ones.[32]

Not all widows needed to make sure such an inventory was made. If the couple's property had been kept separate, the executor would organize an inventory of only the deceased's estate. But women married in community property were wise to do as Scholastique did. An inventory legally identified what had belonged to the couple during their marriage and therefore what the survivor and the children, or the deceased spouse's heirs, had a claim to. Once completed and sworn under oath to be a true reflection of shared assets, that community was considered closed. If the survivor accepted it, a new community of property was created in effect between them and their children, and under their control and that of the subtutor.[33]

An inventory was redundant when spouses had promised each other the full ownership of all their goods in a will or marriage contract and there was no question of debts outweighing assets.[34] No inventory was needed if the community of goods had been dissolved through a separation of goods or of bed and board during the marriage. Nor was there any need to make one if a widow's adult children had already received their rightful share of the community and other property from their father. Similarly, if an inventory had been made shortly before the husband's death, or if all of a man's goods had recently been seized and sold, this onerous practice could be avoided.[35] The mathematics of poverty also made an inventory irrelevant for the propertyless, though the poor were meant to declare their penury. Still, for those widows who were unsure of the state of family finances, those sure that they were in bad shape, and those appointed tutors to young children whose interests and claims on half the community had to be established, an inventory was essential. It also was sensible for those contemplating remarriage.[36]

Scholastique fell into at least two of these situations: she had minor children, and the community owed significant sums. Notary Guy first asked her, in the presence of the four men and her two youngsters, to swear on the bible that she had not hidden anything. Other members of the household did the same. He then reminded her of her right to renounce the community of goods should she wish, as was usual when this was the marriage regime the couple had chosen. The retinue then scrutinized the domestic and work stock of the inn and home as they moved around itemizing the material goods that had been part of her married life and of the couple's livelihood. They began in what was identified as the entrance hall, working past several benches and a table and into the food preparation area of stoves, saucepans, tables, and chairs. The thirteen chairs painted yellow, other chairs, many tables, benches, beds, mattresses, chamber pots, bed linen, glasses, wine, brandy, flagons, and carafes that appear throughout the listing suggest that the family's living and sleeping spaces mingled with those of the guests in their inn and that productive work had not been banished from domestic space, as was increasingly true in middle-class homes.[37] Nothing was fancy. Most of the tables and chairs were old and painted. The mattresses were largely made of straw. Their most valuable single possession was a clock, estimated to be worth £4. There were no pictures on the walls. Scholastique's contributions to running the inn were reflected in tools among the beds and tables. A washing line, irons, washtubs, and the blue used to whiten sheets all hint at work she either did herself or oversaw.[38]

The itemized listing of the goods of Scholastique and her deceased innkeeper husband took up nine pages. Notary Guy's writing was small and neat. The inn that Marie-Louise Genant and Pierre-Bernard Decousse had been running looks more modest. Their belongings filled only four pages, though the notary's writing was larger. Notary Labadie required less than two pages to list the possessions of the former labourer Joseph Guilbault and Marguerite Paris following Joseph's death in 1830, while he could squeeze the list of the belongings of the former master painter Antoine Laurent and his widow, Émilie Monjean, onto one page, an inventory that took under two hours.[39]

Among the city's prominent and elite citizens, in contrast, some inventories extended over fifty pages and the listing process could take days. The list of Oliver Wait's belongings filled eleven pages. Those of his younger colleague, the grocer William Gay, took up fourteen. The listing of Hannah Lyman's and John Mills's community property took over seventy pages. That of the belongings that Édouard-Raymond Fabre was leaving in Luce Perrault's hands after his death in 1854 was equally long.[40] As Richard Bushman has argued, it is easy to assume from their apparent extensiveness that all a couple owned was covered in such listings. There were many reasons why this would not be true. Items might be given away, sold, or exchanged for rent or food during illnesses and following deaths.[41] Furthermore, in Montreal what had to be included in an inventory depended on marital regimes chosen and promises made in marriage contracts. Caveats aside, the past history of lived material inequalities still jump out from these documents, reverberating in the echoes of the footsteps of the notary, widow, heirs, and estimators. The differences of women's past standards of living as wives are evoked in the number of pages notaries filled, rooms visited, in upholstery and curtain fabrics, the kinds of carpets on the floor, and the type of wood of beds, chairs, tables, and other furniture. The domestic details of a widows' past life as a wife were translated in diverse currencies into the potential basis of her future as a widow, transcribed onto the page by the notary, sometimes diligently totalled at the bottom of every page, sometimes only on the final one.

The estimates that Notary Guy recorded of the property of Scholastique and Louis came to a total of £66 9s. 5d. in local currency. After itemizing the goods in the inn, they stopped for the day, agreeing to complete the process four days later. All was left in Scholastique's hands until the next meeting, with the subtutor's agreement. This they scheduled for 30 April. She swore to take good care of all these goods. Such breaks were normal. Often they were much longer. Determining monies owed and owing could take time. But Scholastique's situation was pretty simple. She was illiterate, but the couple had kept some records of their financial transactions. The shared work of husbands and wives that innkeeping required meant that this illiterate widow would have had a pretty clear idea of what they owed or were owed.[42]

When they met at 4 p.m. four days later as planned, they began by listing what people owed the couple. Almost all the names were male and most debts were for well under £1. Few were for over £10. William Irvine, the saddler, one of the assessors, owed them around £3. There was only one woman's name on the list of debtors. At 2s. 11d., her debt was among the smallest. These outstanding debts totalled £65 9s. 5d., but ten were marked as "doubtful." Scholastique and Louis' own debts included over £50 owing on rent and over £221 in unpaid accounts. There were also the funeral costs, the money Scholastique had borrowed from her mother for her mourning outfit, and the inventory to pay for. It was 8 p.m. when all these had been tallied. Scholastique declared there was nothing more to show them. She again swore to take good care of all and also declared that she understood the contents of the document.[43]

Choosing between Promises Made in Law, Marriage Contracts, and Wills

Mathematics, memories, and her legal obligations surely mingled as Scholastique contemplated her next move. Options had to be discussed with the subtutor. She may also have talked with her widowed mother. The law allowed forty days to "deliberate." It also allowed a widow to "continue to live in the house where she has been dwelling, and to use community money to pay living expenses, servants, etc., according to her rank in life," for the first three months beyond this period of deliberation.[44] Scholastique did not wait. The next afternoon she met again with Notary Guy. First she informed him that she had forgotten to disclose her dead husband's clothes. If she were suspected of hiding them, or any other of their goods, she could be deemed guilty of "meddling in the community." This eliminated a widow's right to renounce the community and obliged her to pay half the debts, as well as to give up her claims on the goods hidden or sold.[45]

How did Scholastique omit "to mention" her husband's clothes? Of all the family goods surveyed on the domestic inventory-taking tour, the trousers, shirts, hats, and coats that a dead husband had worn were surely the most powerful reminders of his absence – the hardest to forget. Scholastique was not alone in acting strangely about these intimate reminders of a departed spouse. Other widows left them till last, forgot them, or set them apart in some other way. And assessors and notaries appear to have accepted that recording clothing was sensitive territory. When the goods of Marie-Noflette Charland, another innkeeper's widow, were being listed, the whole process ceased for two and a half hours before the retinue of men turned to his shirts, vests, gloves, and trousers, as well as his books and music.[46] Notary Papineau waited a week between completing the listing of the furniture and other items in the bedroom that Charlotte Mount and Jacques-François-Louis Genevay had shared and turning to his clothing.[47] The very last possessions of Oliver Wait's that were listed were his clothes. Caroline Campbell had stuffed them all in a trunk some time between his death and the taking of the inventory. Frances Swift also placed her husband's clothes in a trunk some time between his murder in February 1827 and the inventory taking three months later.[48]

If envisioning the clothes that husbands could no longer wear on living bodies was painful for some grieving widows, others seem to have been more cavalier or pragmatic. Marie-Louise Jobin sold some of the clothing of her first husband, a master brewer, before the inventory was made.[49] Clothes carried diverse emotional significations. Margaret Reid, whose farmer husband died in 1850, explained that her husband's "clothes and

wearing apparel ... have and will be converted into clothing" for his surviving seven minor children.[50] Pragmatism? Or the sentimental recycling
of familiar fabric to clothe the bodies of her dead husband's offspring?

The clothes Scholastique Bissonnet had neglected to mention were of
minimal economic value. It took little time to appraise Louis' two hats,
several pairs of pants, old frocks, three shirts, one coat, and one pair of
boots. Their total value of £4 9s. was very close to the amount that
Scholastique's mother had lent her for mourning for herself and her two
children.[51] Oliver Wait's clothes, in contrast, were valued at £35; Jacques-
François-Louis Genevay's gold watch and chain alone were estimated as
worth £15.[52]

Scholastique had quickly resolved the dilemma that concealing her husband's clothing might have posed. The mathematics of her situation was
clear. Even collecting every penny of the £65 owed them and selling every
item listed in the inventory would have covered only half their debts. She
informed Notary Guy that she wished to renounce the community, thus
taking full advantage of the protection that the law offered widows whose
marriage, like hers, had created shared community property. Widows who
rejected the community could still claim the cost of their mourning
clothes and food and lodging for themselves and their children for the first
three months of mourning from the community assets before debts were
paid. In this way, even a husband who left family finances in debt remained
liable for his wife and children's support as they began their first three
months without him. The two assessors estimated that she and the children
could rightfully claim £12 10s. for food and rent from Louis' half of their
property for the three months following his death, as well as the costs of
the funeral and their mourning.[53]

Scholastique's fiscal future as a widow was not rosy. In rejecting the
community, widows did not lose their claim to a customary dower, until
that right was effectively eliminated in 1866. But recall that dower was
based on husbands' *propres* – any property husbands had owned when they
married or inherited. This was of little use to Scholastique, for Louis had
owned no such property.[54] Nor is there evidence that she had inherited
property of her own that she might draw on as a widow. In renouncing the
community, she was giving up her claim on all they had owned except her
own wearing apparel. Yet, she had acted expeditiously and made the only
sensible choice. Within two weeks of her husband's death, Scholastique
and her children's subtutor had ensured that she would receive three months'
support from her husband's share of their property and that she would not
have responsibility for an indebted estate. After that, unless she could expect to receive any assets when her widowed mother died, she would have
to find ways of supporting her two children on her own.[55]

The vast majority of widows who, like Scholastique Bissonnet, had married without making a marriage contract and whose husbands had made no will had one main choice when left with major debts. They could renounce their half of the shared community property, as she did, starting widowhood with virtually nothing instead of with debts, or possibly with a dower until the law changed. Or they could accept the community and allow creditors to seize their goods for the debts owing. The law exempted certain basic furnishings, clothing, and tools from seizure, so a widow might retain more belongings that way. Exemptions expanded over the century.[56] Calling in debts could be a lengthy and emotionally draining process. Scholastique chose the simpler solution. It left her with little else than the promise of three months' support.

Marguerite Paris made a different choice. Although her debts also outweighed the value of her household goods and any monies owing her, she chose not to reject their community after Guilbault died in 1830. As she reckoned out her future, the small house in the Saint Lawrence suburb that they had purchased during their marriage and which therefore was part of their community property promised shelter for her and her two daughters. Without it, she might end up alongside other labourers' widows on the streets, homeless, scavenging, stealing, or selling her body to survive.[57]

The options available to widows who had made marriage contracts establishing regimes other than community property depended on the wording of that contract and, if their husbands had made wills, on their provisions. Excluding property or keeping spouse's property separate meant that wealth and property accumulated by husbands during the marriage was their individual property. Men, as we saw, could do pretty well what they wished with their property in a will. Widows, or anyone else, could turn down a legacy offered in a will. But if their marriage contract excluded community property, rejected dower, and there was no will, or if they refused a legacy, intestacy provisions made it unlikely that widows would have a legitimate claim on their husbands' estates.[58] Only those with separate property of their own might start their widowhood with some assets.

Montreal widows therefore faced a range of different choices as they contemplated their future. Most had not made a marriage contract and their husbands had made no will. They accepted or rejected the community. When husbands wrote a will but had not made a marriage contract, widows could choose between what was offered in the will and their right at law to half the community and a customary dower, until after the transformations of dower law in 1866. And when there was both a marriage contract and a will, the promises of a marriage contract had to be honoured, though widows could choose whichever seemed most advantageous, and sometimes both.[59]

Laura Mower told Notary Doucet within a month of her husband's burial that she had decided to renounce the provisions of John Campbell's will, even though he had promised her all he owned. Given the £844 owed to creditors, compared to the £100 customers at his bookstore owed him, the annuity of £50 annually that he had mortgaged his property at the time of their marriage contract to provide must have seemed to promise a more stable basis for her future as a widow.[60] This was a choice she was legally entitled to make. The possibilities were set out clearly in the Custom of Paris, reaffirmed in 1866 in the new civil code, and reiterated in reported cases throughout the century.[61] Perhaps he had major debts. Perhaps she would never reclaim the promised £50, though this choice gave her a chance to rank among his creditors. Unlike dower, rejected in their marriage contract, an annuity did not give her a claim before all other creditors. But it did place her squarely among them. The wisdom of her earlier decision to keep her own property separate was clear. Whether or not she had made money by keeping a store, as she had planned when they married, his creditors had no claim on her own assets. Had she and John failed to make a marriage contract, as was true of so many immigrants, all of the property they both accumulated would have fallen into a community of goods and been susceptible to his creditors' claims.

Caroline Campbell was able to take advantage of both the promises that her affluent husband had made in their marriage contract and in his will. Together these ensured that she would have an annuity of £100 from Oliver's estate, roughly the income of a middling clerk.[62] At about £8 a month, this was double the total amount allowed Scholastique Bissonnet and her children for her first three months of widowhood. It was ten times the value of all the goods itemized in the home of the labourer's widow Marguerite Paris, which came to a total of around £11 when they were listed in 1830. Caroline also had property of her own. Because their marriage contract excluded community property without authorizing her to manage any separate property of her own, it had been managed by her husband during the marriage. She would control it following his death.[63]

Caroline was adequately provided for. Still, there were many other issues to resolve in the aftermath of Oliver's sudden death from cholera in 1832. His failure to name an executor in his will had to be resolved before anything could be done about her annuity or the legacies for the children of his two marriages. Five meetings in the courts, notarial offices, and at her home with judges, notaries, and other men resolved most outstanding issues.[64] Two days after she was chosen as her children's tutor and Logan Fuller as tutor of the children from Wait's first marriage, they both went to Notary Arnoldi's office to begin to sort out Oliver's business affairs. In contrast to the innkeepers' widows Marie-Louise Genant and Scholastique Bissonnet, it is unlikely that Caroline had any involvement in Oliver's business affairs. There were the seven minor children from her husband's two marriages to care for, and his affairs were complex. At least two major business contracts were outstanding when he died. Caroline and Logan Fuller agreed to give Joseph Ross, a Montreal trader who had been working with Wait, power of attorney. This would permit him to complete the canal construction that Wait had begun before his death, and to supply the 3,000 cords of wood Wait had promised to have delivered to Her Majesty's Fuel Yard in Quebec City. A day later, Caroline met with Notary Arnoldi for the third time, accompanied by James Wait, the subtutor for her own children. Arnoldi drew up a second power of attorney. This gave Logan Fuller full powers to call in all debts owing Oliver's estate and effectively act as executor. The business and non-business sides of settling Oliver's estate remained firmly in male hands.[65]

Eleven weeks later, Caroline and Logan Fuller took the fourth step in determining Oliver's estate. In early November, Notary Arnoldi came again to her home, this time to make an inventory. Like Scholastique Bissonnet and other widows, Caroline and the children were required to be present as men combed their home, itemizing its contents and evaluating their worth. But because this was not community property, the reason was different. Caroline had no claim on the property being enumerated beyond the promises of their marriage contract and Oliver's will. The document itself is entitled "Inventory of the Estate of the Late Oliver Wait," whereas the listing following Louis Ducharme's death is identified as the inventory of the goods of the community that existed between Louis Ducharme and Scholastique Bissonnet. In contrast to Scholastique Bissonnet's clear claim to £12 10s. from her husband's part of their property to support her and her children over the first three months of her widowhood, the £42 that Caroline Campbell had spent on herself and the children since Oliver's death three months earlier were listed as a debt she owed his estate.[66]

Itemizing Oliver's possessions took several days. The assessors she and her son-in-law chose included the businessman and politician Jacob De Witt, a prominent Montreal figure who, like Oliver Wait, was sympathetic to the Patriotes at this time. Oliver's material belongings were valued at nearly £600. Few widows had much, if any cash on hand. Caroline reported that there had been £263 15s. in Oliver's desk at the time of his death, a very large amount of ready cash. In the three months since his death, they had received additional money as rent on properties he owned, as well as from Joseph Ross, who had efficiently fulfilled his mandate to oversee Wait's contractual obligations.[67]

Once the contents of the house, stables, and yard had been assessed and the assets, liabilities, and Caroline's expenses since Oliver's death listed, Notary Arnoldi went back over the funeral expenses and itemized the bills paid since his death. Oliver Wait's succession was ready to settle. His will had established that once the money had been put aside to ensure Caroline's annuity, the rest of the estate should be divided among all his children "share and share alike."[68] Now, three months following his death, the basis of the fortune they would inherit was clear. As tutors to his minor children, Caroline, her brother-in-law James Wait, her step son-in-law Logan Fuller and the subtutors would be responsible for deciding what was best for the minor children until they reached adulthood.

Caroline had no grounds to contest her husband's will, or to reject the promises made there for anything better. As a canny businessman and a responsible husband, Oliver had secured her claims in contracts that were binding. The £100 annuity was reasonable, though at roughly the amount a minor clerk might expect to receive, living on it alone would have diminished her standard of living. There was no mention of it terminating should she decide to remarry. Wait had more than sufficient funds to ensure its payment.[69] Yet, the basis of her claim and the amount were less than they would have been had there been no marriage contract or will. Wait had carefully avoided the customary patriarchy that left widows half the accumulated wealth, as well as dower on half the estates owned when they married.

One final step liquidated his estate. Ten days after the inventory taking, Notary Arnoldi oversaw the public auction of Wait's goods. Over the two previous weeks, this sale had been announced at the doors of the parish church following the main Sunday service, as was required by law. Now, friends, relatives, and strangers came to their home, seeking bargains and quality goods. One by one the possessions that the law recognized as Oliver's were auctioned off to the highest bidder. The records of such sales in notaries' files indicate the names of the purchaser, the item sold, and the price. The earliest items were sold to prominent male neighbours and citizens: James Wait, Caroline's brother-in-law, purchased some cables; John Molson, the brewer, bought several kinds of sleighs; William Molson, his brother, purchased two hundred bundles of barley sheaves.[70]

Invisible in the earliest purchases, Caroline soon stepped to the fore. As a woman with some resources of her own who knew she would have a steady income, she was able to join in the bidding process or to request that someone else do so on her behalf. Hers was the sixth name listed when she "purchased" garden rakes and forks. Ten items later, she secured five washtubs, then a sofa and some of the rush-bottomed chairs that had

sat in their parlour and their dining room. As the sale continued she became the most frequent bidder. Her name is listed beside toys, bedding,
linen, a grey colt, a red bull, a black pony, kitchenware, a "house pump and
machine," various stoves, and boilers, as well as jelly cups, and many bushels
of celery, cabbages, and potatoes. By the end of the second and final day of
the sale, the notary's tally of the bids had reached £810 6s. Mrs. Wait's account, scribbled on the front of the document, totalled over £370. Caroline
had bought back for herself and her children nearly half the chattels considered to belong to her husband. This was the proportion that the law
offered widows whose marriage had created shared community property.
As a widow of means, she could participate actively and immediately in
the process of recuperating familiar and loved household goods that Sherry
Olson has shown much less privileged Montreal families also attempted
but over a longer time period.[71]

The image of this privileged widow in the early months of her mourning making sure she would have access to domestic treasures, necessities,
tools, and work animals in her new life as a widow is triply important.
First, it underlines the additional disruptions that even wealthy women
faced when a marital regime like separate property gave husbands control
over all family property.[72] Second, it complicates the idea of the first year of
widowhood as one of retreat into home and family. Caroline received a
crowd of prominent Montrealers to the home that was her husband's
property. She watched as they sought to purchase family assets that the law
saw as belonging to her husband. And she engaged in the purchasing process. Third, her history serves as a reminder that provisions in wills that contemporary historians have judged as unfavourable for women – annuities
or the use of property rather than full ownership – could offer significant
material security to widows. For some, though not Caroline, they could be
more generous than a promise of all their husbands owned.[73]

Jacques-François Genevay and the bookseller John Campbell had promised their wives all they owned. Yet, neither generous marriage contracts
nor wills could ensure that all wives with a foothold in Montreal's elite
society would face widowhood well provided for. Caroline could not avoid
the public sale of her husband's goods, undertaken to divide up his estate.
Yet, Oliver Wait's success as a major contractor and merchant meant that
she faced widowhood with the knowledge that she could count on a stable
income and sufficient finances to repurchase household items. She also had
the support of family members. Genevay's death, in contrast, left both his
widowed wife, Charlotte, and his widowed mother, in financial trouble.
How this son of a high-up government official made his living is not clear.
In most notarial records he is listed simply as "esquire." The inventory of

his goods, which began on 24 April 1827, indicated that he used one room of his dwelling as an apothecary. It was stocked with a range of medicines and medical books. The estate of 3,000 acres in Upper Canada and a further 2,300 in Lower Canada that Genevay and his mother inherited from his father remained unsettled at the time of his death. His mother had dower rights on that land, which Genevay should have ensured she was receiving. His desperate scramble during the final months of his life to settle some of his debts was not successful. The extent of his debts in this inventory is even more striking than the expensive mahogany furniture and lavish furnishings of their home.[74] There are so many debts, and to such prominent Montrealers, that Charlotte and Jacques' financial problems must have been common knowledge long before Jacques' death. Among others, he owed money to Robert Unwin Harwood, to Charles-Séraphin Rodier, and to Jacob De Witt.

Two weeks after Jacques-François Genevay's death, Notary Thomas Bedouin resigned as one of the executors because the "estate would be onerous and difficult to administer for several other reasons known to him." The remaining executor, the prominent lawyer Hugh Heney, had the will probated on 22 March.[75] On at least eight occasions between that day and 7 May, notices in La Minerve published Heney's request that anyone owing money or having a claim on Genevay's estate present themselves to Notary Papineau.[76] On 27 March, Heney and the two widows, Charlotte and Agathe Dumas, were joined by Charlotte's uncle, Dr. Henry Munro; Notary Papineau; and two assessors, the Montreal merchant Francis Badgley and Benjamin Berthelet, to whom they agreed to show all Genevay's possessions and papers. It took one day to itemize the goods in the dining room, parlour, vestibule, and Genevay's apothecary room. The next day they finished listing his tools, instruments, and the contents of the kitchen, laundry, courtyard, and outer buildings, and lastly, his bedroom.[77] The young couple had lived lavishly and beyond their means. Their dining room table and sideboard were made of mahogany. They were well equipped with silver, glass, and chinaware. Six sleighs and carriages of various kinds were valued at over £76. Their books suggest wide, if not very deep, reading interests. They included Homer, *Hoyle's Games, Romeo and Juliet, Ivanhoe,* as well as *Prononciation de la langue anglaise* and *Guide des Étrangers à Londres.* Two other books, *Bookkeeping Methodized* and *Tables Showing Interest at Six Percent,* suggest that they sought some resolution or clarity about their financial troubles from books. The assessed value of their possessions was similar to those of Oliver Wait – around £640.[78]

On the third day, starting again at 9 a.m., Charlotte, Agathe Dumas, and the four men turned their attention to the monies owing and owed. They were not finished by 5 p.m., but it was already clear that neither the tome on bookkeeping nor the book of interest rates had helped Jacques resolve his debts. Over £3,400 principal and interest were owing to the Bank of Montreal. He owed several major Montreal merchants around £300. Four days later, further debts were itemized, including for the doctors and their pew in the Catholic parish church. Although the amounts of many outstanding debts were still unknown, by the end of that day it was clear that over £4,500 was owing creditors. As the process of tallying debts continued, the older widow stepped in. Agathe Dumas proclaimed that although she had not kept regular track of her son's transactions as his legal tutor, she did have sufficient knowledge of the situation to declare that his debts outweighed what might come from his father's succession.[79]

Within a week, Charlotte explained to Notary Papineau that she wished to renounce the bequest in Jacques' will of all he owned after his debts were paid and claim the promises in their marriage contract instead. She swore she had not meddled at all in his goods, and signed her name clearly and firmly.[80] Recall that their marriage contract had stipulated that their property remain separate, and that she could live in one of his houses; take a furnished bedroom as her own, along with her clothing; and receive an annuity of £100. In choosing the promises of her marriage contract, Charlotte placed the burden of securing her support on her husband's widowed mother. That same day, Agathe leased out the house next to theirs, securing an annual income of £75 in quarterly payments.[81]

It took eight more months until, just four days before the end of Charlotte's first year as a widow, her mother-in-law arranged to pay the first installment of the monies that the marriage contract had stipulated would be paid the day she became a widow. By then, Charlotte was no longer living with her mother-in-law. She had gone to live among family in Saint Denis. She did not use her new legal capacity as a widow to act on her own behalf to lever payment from her widowed mother-in-law. It was her sister's husband, a notary, who acted officially as her procurer, going with Notary Kimber to the home of Agathe Dumas to secure her promise to pay the sum of £60 to cover the costs of Charlotte's mourning, her right to the furnishings of their bedroom, and three-quarters of the monies promised annually. Marie-Agathe promised to mortgage all her existing and future property to fulfill these obligations. The burden on this aging widow was softened somewhat by their stipulation that, should she be late with her payments, they would not seek interest.[82]

By the end of the year following her husband's death, Charlotte Mount's survival as a widow looked a bit more secure. It depended, however, on the ability of her twice widowed mother-in-law to deliver on the promises of their marriage contract. The financial stability of these two widows was inextricably linked – what one gained, the other lost. The records show few signs of Charlotte acting on her own as a widow. She left the city for good, and married again nine years after her first husband's death. That marriage lasted only from September 1836 until her death in 1838.[83]

Charlotte Mount cannot have been ignorant of the debts that hung over their marriage. Marie-Louise Genant, in contrast, likely had no idea that the marriage contract that she believed had settled her claims as a widow when she married in 1843 was invalid. That contract had rejected community property and allowed the survivor to take £50 as the *préciput* from the other's goods and to use all the goods that both owned after the death of the first spouse. The surviving spouse was to care for these as a "good father" would. However, if that spouse remarried, these goods were to return to the dead spouse's heirs, just as they would following the surviving spouse's death. The contract had also specified that an inventory of the goods should be made when the first spouse died. Marie-Louise did not do this during the first year of her widowhood. Some time between her husband's death in August 1852 and October 1853, she learned that the marriage contract was not valid because it had been signed by only one notary. This meant that the law, and hence community property, framed her claim on family assets. Whereas Scholastique Bissonnet and Caroline Campbell had been named as tutors to their minor children within several weeks of their husbands' deaths, Marie-Louise Genant attended to this after more than a year. In September 1853, a meeting of family and friends named her the tutor of her four children, aged between one and nine years. A month later, she arranged for Notary Mathieu and two evaluators to make an inventory of her goods, now understood to have been shared equally by the two, rather than separate. Once the inventory was complete, she was left in charge of all the shared possessions – half in her own right and the rest as the tutor of her four minor children.[84]

Although the disruption of a contract whose promises turned out to be unenforceable must have been disorienting, there were advantages to Marie-Louise in this retroactive change of marital regime. It left her as a widow and tutor in charge of all the couple's property and legal owner of half, whereas the marriage contract had promised her only the use of all of Pierre-Bernard's possessions until she remarried or died. But there were also disadvantages. It placed her own belongings in the community and hence accessible to debtors. Too much time had passed too for her to renounce the community had she wished to. Luckily, Marie-Louise faced widowhood with assets that outweighed debts. As we saw in Chapter 3, her and Pierre-Bernard's tavern was modestly stocked. Their debts were few. Those listed were for the laying out, burials, and funerals of one of her sons and of Pierre-Bernard. Still, together these amounted to over £27. Once settled, Marie-Louise's assets would diminish dramatically. But she had the stocked tavern and control over the community property. She could hope to build on her experience as a wife to secure some income, pay the rent, and support herself and the four surviving children.[85]

Errors of the kind that Marie-Louise experienced challenged the sanctity of contracts in which the parties' wishes were meant to be both paramount and binding. Over subsequent decades, notaries and legislators sought to shore up the validity of contractual agreements made in wills and marriage contracts in which such required procedures had not been followed. The professionalization of notaries also helped minimize many kinds of errors. From at least the mid-century on, legislators sought to render such family documents valid in cases of procedural errors, so as not to cause the "ruin of many families." In the early 1850s, William Badgley turned, with what the *Montreal Gazette* described as "his usual perseverance," to the question of making sure instruments transmitting property were as clear as possible. He sought unsuccessfully to pass a law that would make proof of probate anywhere in British possessions sufficient evidence of the legitimacy of a will written elsewhere, and to make wills written in English fashion in the colony valid with only two witnesses' signatures. Marie-Louise's problem was addressed directly in legislation in 1864 and in 1870, making most kinds of notarial acts valid when, as in her case, the second notary had not signed.[86] After the new Civil Code (1866) and Code of Civil Procedure (1867) came into in effect, legislators passed a series of laws to ensure the validity of wills and inventories. Legislation in 1875 made it clear that wills in which a witness could not sign his or her name were also valid.[87] Thus, legislation bolstered the legitimacy of these contracts that established claims on family property, giving primacy to testators' intentions and reinforcing the understanding that freedom of willing was a fundamental right of British subjects in this colony, as at home.

"Within a Year and a Day": Executors' Work and Time-Limited Claims

When Luce Perrault oversaw the inventory of the possessions in her home at the corner of St. Lawrence and Craig streets, she did so in four formal capacities: as the universal legatee in usufruct of all Édouard-Raymond Fabre's property; as the tutor of the three of their children who were still minors; as a widow promised a dower in her marriage contract; and as the executor of his will. Widows named by their husbands as executors faced an additional set of obligations beyond responsibility for the funeral. For a year and a day after the testator's death, or longer if this was provided for in the will, they were "seized of the goods of the testator" and responsible for rendering account of them.[88] Fabre, the very canny and successful businessman, had named Luce as his executor in the will he wrote in 1842. Apparently nothing in the subsequent twelve years altered his faith in her abilities enough to change that designation.[89] Kirsten Wood has wisely suggested that individual men made decisions based not on broad understandings of women's competence, but on the capacities of their own wives to manage their particular family property, and that such decisions are best understood when we know something about the marriage.[90] Fabre was meticulous about money matters. His affairs would have been in good order. Some estates were more onerous than others to deal with, and some women more capable or better aware of money and property issues. Charlotte Mount would surely not have appreciated being in charge of dealing with the massive debts left when Jacques-François Genevay died when even the competent notary Thomas Bedouin balked at that task.

Quebec law introduced one further level of complexity to executing wills. The processes involved for English-style wills and notarial wills were different. As widows appointed executors in notarial wills, Luce Perrault, Rosalie Paquet, and Laura Mower had to oversee "the estate as a prudent manager," ensure that an inventory was made, pay outstanding debts, and discharge legacies. They also had to be ready to render account of the estate to the heirs, if there were any.[91] Rosalie Paquet's responsibilities as executor of Eloi Beneche's will were probably minimal and hardly onerous for a woman used to running a brothel. There were no children to care for, no property to share, and hence no inventory needed to be made. When Beneche died in February 1846, Rosalie would have sought to collect any monies owed him, paid off any debts, then assumed control. She could simply take over all he owned, as promised in his will.[92] Édouard-Raymond Fabre left all he had to Luce Perrault to use during her lifetime, or until she remarried.[93] As executor and tutor, she oversaw the process of making the inventory of their goods. This began three months after his death on 24 October 1854 and was not completed until March 1855. She worked with Notary Papineau to call in debts. And once those were settled, their property was left in her hands. It was to be divided among his legitimate heirs upon her death.[94]

Those named executors in an English-style or holograph will had the additional responsibility of going to court to prove the wills' authenticity. Such a will normally transferred the deceased's property into the hands of the trustees for a year and a day, and frequently for an indeterminate period until all legacies had been settled. The widows Christina Dalyrmple, Jane Davis, Christiana McLeod, and Mary Jane Ross all went to court, appearing before judges and listening while male witnesses confirmed that the writing in the wills they had produced was indeed that of their dead husbands.[95]

These additional responsibilities may further explain why relatively few men writing English-style wills designated their wives as executors. So, as suggested earlier, does the fact that they were written predominantly by relatively wealthy Anglo-Protestant merchants, the men most likely to leave large and complicated estates.[96]

Thus, in Montreal there was a hierarchy or scale of difficulty and challenge that related not only to the state of the dead husband's estate but also to the instruments determining how an estate would be settled. English-style wills were potentially the most demanding. Notarial wills were less so. The promises of a marriage contract were sacred and were normally sorted out during the taking of an inventory or negotiated informally within families. Dowers could simply be taken up, as they officially began on the day of a husband's death. When no marriage contract or will dictated women's claims or bequeathed them with special authority, widows still frequently ended up settling estates. Those named as tutors did so in that capacity. All of these processes could and did go awry, so that in later years widows ended up in court competing with children for inheritances or dowers, making claims against executors, or charged with mishandling community property or an estate.[97]

The merchant-mayor husbands of Luce Perrault and Hannah Lyman both left their estates in good shape. The two men died at a time when much of their income came from investments, rather than daily earnings or profits. They had, in R.J. Morris' description of the middle-class property cycle, reached the "adult stage," in which unearned income was the major basis of family support, though the "break with business was often partial." Morris suggests that reaching this stage usually occurred when men were in their "early to mid-fifties."[98] Mills, as we saw, was fifty-one when he died of typhus in 1847; Fabre died of cholera at fifty-four. Both had been able to turn to city politics because their fortunes were already made. When middle-class women were widowed at this stage of the property cycle, they could well face a lesser decline in their standard of living than did widows of younger men. However, sudden deaths like those of John Mills or many of the cholera victims in 1832 could leave executors with numerous unsettled accounts.

Hannah Lyman did not take on these matters alone. Mills had employed a "confidential clerk" who saw to much of the bookkeeping at the bank on St. François Xavier Street. Following Mills's death, it was this clerk, Matthew Campbell, who carefully pulled together the various ledgers, daybooks, cashbooks, bills receivable, balance sheets, and other volumes in which Mills's business matters were recorded. Between Mills's death on 12 November and 1 December, Campbell brought everything up to date, balanced the books, and collected some of the monies owing. Hannah was not officially John's executor, for he had made no will. Her claims and her authority derived from her appointment as tutor of their minor children, and from her claim on the community property that resulted from their marriage.[99] By 29 November, she had appointed her nephew, William Lyman, to act as her attorney. That day and on two others, notices in the *Gazette,* the *Herald, La Minerve,* and the *Pilot* requested all those with claims against John's estate or indebted to him to "make payment without delay, at the late Office of the deceased." They were signed by William as "attorney to Mrs. Hannah Lyman Mills, Tutrix."[100]

Yet, as the city went through the process of replacing its "martyr mayor," Hannah could not avoid taking part in sorting out some of the financial matters interrupted by his death.[101] Two weeks after Mills's funeral, she visited Thomas John Pelton, the notary whom her husband had used frequently during the 1840s. He had been married just three years at this time, and he and Caroline Scott had three little girls. Hannah Lyman's first visit with Pelton was to protest a bill for £30 owed to her husband that had not been paid. Eleven days later, Pelton came to Belair Cottage, Hannah's home, at her request to make the inventory of the community property. Pelton and the assessors – an auctioneer, a cabinetmaker, and an upholsterer – were efficient. They itemized all the goods in the eleven rooms of the house, the passageway, and the cellar by 5 p.m. on the first day. At that point, the assessed value of the rosewood, satin damask-covered couches and chairs; mahogany and rosewood tables; piano; luxury Wilton carpets; dishes and silverware; and other possessions had reached over £814. At 10 a.m. the next morning, the men returned to assess the carriages, wagons, harnesses, saddles, and horses in the yard. That completed, with the tally of the shared family possessions reaching well over £1,100, the group proceeded to Mills's office on St. François Xavier Street, where they continued the inventory.[102]

Reviewing the many books, bonds, mortgages, obligations, promissory notes, bills, and active and passive debts took quite some time. Hannah joined the men once again on 7 December at John's office and then for three more days. By 4 p.m. on 10 December, Pelton had completed his work and Hannah swore that to the best of her knowledge there was nothing left to list. Over £18,000 was still owed to John's creditors, but Pelton estimated that the total value of the household furniture, bonds, cash, and other belongings came to nearly £45,000, without including significant land holdings in the city. Had John and Hannah chosen to keep their property separate, as so many of his peers in the merchant community did, Hannah might have had no claim on any of this. With no marriage contract and no will deeming otherwise, half these assets would belong to her. With the agreement of her married daughter's husband, all the goods were left in her "charge and possession."[103]

Employing the services of an attorney did not absolve Hannah from further actions. In early January, she returned again to Pelton's office – the second of at least six visits between November 1847 and April 1848. Each time she went accompanied by her son-in-law, the subtutor for her minor children. Each time she legitimated her actions in her own name, as having been Mills's wife "commune en biens," and as their minor children's tutor. And each time they sought to tidy up some unsettled aspect of the financial affairs of her husband.[104] April was the last time she appeared in Pelton's records. Five months after Mills's death, most money matters seem to have been sorted out. She could focus on rebuilding her life as a widow. Hannah was able to stay at Belair Cottage with her four minor children and to use the furniture and other goods that had graced their home during John's life.

Newly widowed women also stepped out from their homes, walking, hiring carters, or taking their carriages as they kept appointments in the offices of notaries and before judges in the courts for other reasons closely related to their financial futures as widows. Canny and scheming, asserting entitlements, or simply desperate, they sought legal ways to better ensure their standard of living and that of their children. Within twelve months of her husband's murder in 1872, the widow Gregoire appeared before Judge McKay seeking damages against the man who had killed him. She estimated the amount of support she was deprived of by his loss at $5,000. Her claim was accepted. Such civil claims could be made only within a year of the death.[105] Similarly, the heirs of men accidentally killed in duels could make claims on the surviving party, their seconds, or assistants for compensation for the family if they did so within twelve months.[106] Across the century, other widows sought and sometimes received compensation from employers when husbands were killed at work. Pilots' widows took advantage of the laws that set up funds to provide support to "Decayed Pilots" and their widows and children.[107] A widow of a checker who was killed on the wharf received $6,000 in compensation because the ship's captain was judged negligent.[108] Widows petitioned the legislature when benefit societies did not deliver on promises of weekly life rents that were to have been secured through small contributions during their marriages.[109]

Historians have not been wrong to focus on the first year of widowhood as a time of seclusion and grieving, symbolized by the black clothing widows donned. Yet, as women went from wife to widow, they had much to deal with in addition to the grief, worries, or relief that accompanied their husbands' deaths. Widows undertook a series of tasks, assessing and shaping the material bases of their future lives as widows. Legal clocks dictated the timing for naming tutors for minor children, taking inventories, renouncing indebted communities, and executing estates. To take full advantage of the special possibilities the law offered some widows, these had to be completed within a year and a day, the same period that etiquette marked out as that of deepest mourning. Anxious arithmetic and legal procedures thus cut into the early months of mourning.

Widows took on few of these tasks alone. Helped by kin, overseen by kin, constrained by kin, they moved between their homes, notaries' offices, and the courts. In all these spaces they interacted with men in official capacities from which women were excluded. Family members or friends might provide solace, but in the months following husbands' deaths, many widows also spent time with notaries, lawyers, judges, and male assessors of their property. Women could fulfill none of these tasks. Over the course of these interactions, the contours of widows' future lives were spelled out. Much was never put to paper, but much was.

Widows' rights, claims, and options in this first year of widowhood were framed by past imaginings about how the marriage would end. Provisions in husbands' wills, in marriage contracts, and in the law interacted with husbands' wealth to offer Montreal's widows diverse options and to promise different widows starkly varied futures. Both were shaped by cultural traditions and class concerns. Yet, no legal regime could change the mathematical reality that an estate with more debts than assets would not provide any support in widowhood. Widows' right to reject such a community meant that some started their widowhood with little rather than debts. Such widows could not wait until their mourning was over to seek ways to support themselves.

By the end of the first year, most women had a pretty clear idea of what their financial situation would be as widows, single mothers, and family heads. Neither Luce Perrault nor Hannah Lyman would experience major changes in their standards of living nor be obliged to find new housing. Both had minor children to raise, but Édouard-Raymond Fabre and John Easton Mills had successfully accumulated sufficient capital to attain that stage in the property cycle when they were able to live off their investments as rentiers. Scholastique Bissonnet, the innkeeper's widow, had ensured she did not begin her widowhood in debt, but she would have to rely on her own resourcefulness to support her two children. Three years after Louis' death, she remarried. So, as we saw, did the blind soap and candle manufacturer's widow, Rebecca Conegan, and Charlotte Mount, who had faced widowhood with massive debts and the challenge of collecting her promised support from her twice-widowed mother-in-law. With her one-room, one-storey wooden house, Marguerite Paris was quite privileged as a labourer's widow, though how she could support herself and her one daughter is unclear. She remained in the house on Vallée Street for at least three years after Joseph Guilbault's death in 1829, not far from one of the properties that Émilie Tavernier, the devout widow of the merchant Jean-Baptiste Gamelin, inherited along with their home when he died in 1827. For both these widows, ownership of real property offered more than shelter as they reshaped their lives as widows. Property also gave them the possibility of expressing their political beliefs and fulfilling other desires. It is to their experiences as widows and their involvement in colonial politics and institution building in the city that the next two chapters turn.

9

Widows' Votes

Marguerite Paris, Émilie Tavernier, Sarah Harrison, and the Montreal By-Elections of 1832

The poll had been open for six days when Marguerite Paris stepped up to proclaim her vote. Joseph Guilbault had died two and a half years earlier. Speaking loudly enough for the male officials at the poll to hear, this labourer's widow publicly declared that the Patriote candidate, Daniel Tracey, was her choice. It was 1 May 1832, the sixth day of voting in the by-election underway in Montreal West precipitated by the retirement of John Fisher.[1] The day before, election officials had moved the poll from the Hall of the American Presbyterian Church – an alien place for Roman Catholic Montrealers like Marguerite to enter – to a house behind it belonging to one of the Donegani brothers, supporters of the Patriotes.[2] The day after Marguerite voted, Sarah Harrison went to the polls and chose Stanley Bagg. She may well have been wearing mourning, for her husband the tinsmith, William Nelson, whom she had married in 1824, had died just six weeks earlier and it was only a month after she had arranged to have an inventory made of their goods.[3] Émilie Tavernier confirmed her family's close political ties to the Patriotes by choosing Tracey a week later. Sarah's vote so soon after her husband's death serves as a further reminder that some widows dealt with much more than their grieving and matters as-sociated with settling estates in the early months of their widowhood. Many had to secure incomes. Sarah was drawn into colonial politics, as were many other Montreal women in 1832.

Surely even the illiterate widow Marguerite Paris knew the hustings were particularly dangerous ground. The city's newspapers had reported fighting from the day the poll opened. Even Montreal's many citizens who, like her, could neither read nor write, would have known about the dis-order at the hustings. Just the day before she voted, the *Montreal Gazette*, the unabashed champion of businessman and establishment candidate Stanley Bagg, had reported the "most disgraceful riots and disturbances";

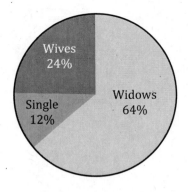

FIGURE 9.1 Marital status of women seeking to vote, Montreal West, 1832

Note: N = 215.
Source: Poll book, Montreal West 1832, transcribed and digitized by Nathalie Picard, "Women Voters, Lower Canada," database.

"several of our most respectable citizens have been most violently assaulted; beaten and otherwise maltreated."[4] The same day, *La Minerve,* equally un-wavering in its advocacy of Patriote candidate Daniel Tracey, the fiery Irish editor of the *Vindicator,* had described the insults and violence of drunken bullies who had seriously injured three of his supporters.[5]

In deciding to vote, these widows were stepping into a public space that was physically dangerous, and politically and culturally contested. It was watched and commented on by the journalists of the city's highly partisan newspapers, and it was occupied by men and some women of all ethnic, religious, and class backgrounds. Even approaching the poll would later be described as a perilous act.[6] This danger did not deter the widows Marguerite, Sarah, Émilie, and other women from seeking to participate. Over the twenty-three days of voting, some 215 women made it to the hustings and sought to express their political choice, a dozen or so did so twice. Most were widows, but married and single women braved the crowds as well (see Figure 9.1). Placing their bodies in this very public space, these women demonstrated that they did not accept the understand-ing that politics and the public sphere were for men alone, though histor-ians have shown such ideas were increasingly prevalent across the Western world by this period.[7] Nor was this election unique. Earlier that month, seventy-two women tried to vote in the by-election to determine repre-sentatives for the other Montreal seat, Montreal East. Furthermore, Nathalie Picard's research shows that women voted in at least fourteen other districts in Lower Canada between 1821 and 1844, that the numbers of female voters fluctuated, and that their presence was being noted and contested.[8]

This particular by-election is well known to Canadian historians.[9] It lasted twenty-three days, was marked by violence throughout, and ended in three deaths. Most historians have focused on it as a key moment in the making of Quebec nationalism and the lead-up to the rebellions. It was indeed a key moment in the production of divergent imaginings of nation in Lower Canada. It was also a critical event in the contestation of colonial rule. And, as in all such imaginings of identity and nation, understandings of gender, class, religion, and ethnicity interacted to shape and reshape practices and interpretations of the event. The presence of Marguerite Paris, Sarah Harrison, and Émilie Tavernier at the polls reminds us that during and after their first year of widowhood, Montreal women engaged with other residents of the city in many ways as they sought work or charitable assistance, took on benevolent activities, oversaw their children's upbringing, and reshaped their own lives. Their votes also remind us that politics mattered profoundly in Montreal during the 1830s to women as well as men. Women of the generation who married in the 1820s, were already widowed by the time of this by-election, and possessed or rented property of the required value were able to vote. In its wake, politicians eliminated women's right to vote.

This chapter builds on work by the Clio Collective, Fernand Ouellet, Nathalie Picard, and Allan Greer on Lower Canadian women's involvement in the politics of this period.[10] It joins international studies of the regendering of the public and private in the late eighteenth and nineteenth centuries and the growing body of literature exploring the complicated story of women's involvement in multiple publics, the print media, religious activism, and politics. Exploring the experiences of Marguerite, Émilie, and Sarah responds to Jane Rendall's plea that historians pay more attention to the ways some nineteenth-century women exercised their franchise rights.[11] By looking in detail at the widows who voted, at discussions in the press, and then exploring later investigations and debates, I seek to shed new light on the link between this election and the attempt to prevent women from voting in 1834, and their definitive exclusion in 1849.

Widows and Other Women at the Hustings

Marguerite Paris, Émilie Tavernier, and Sarah Harrison were three of 141 widows who walked up to the poll and attempted to vote in the 1832 Montreal West by-election. In contrast to the six weeks that had passed since Sarah's husband died, Marguerite had been a widow for thirty months, Émilie for over four years. They were not the only women who had married between 1823 and 1826 and had already lost their husbands who sought to vote in this by-election. So did Marguerite Gagnon, widow

of the mason Medard Labrie; Mary Howard, a shoemaker's widow; as well
as the more elite merchants' widows, Sarah Campbell and Anna Foster.
Women made up 14 percent of the citizens seeking to express their political
choice in this tumultuous by-election. This, Nathalie Picard reports, was
the highest proportion of women involved in any of the Lower Canadian
nineteenth-century elections for which she analyzed the poll books. Two
other widows from the 1820s marriage cohort, Amable Leduc and Émilie
Monjean, voted a few weeks earlier in the Montreal East by-election.
Women constituted over 9 percent of the voters in that by-election.

Marguerite, Émilie, Sarah, and the other women could imagine taking
part in elections because the law did not explicitly prevent them and because other women had done so in various elections since 1791. That year,
the Constitutional Act established the first elected Legislative Assembly
and set out the property requirements for "persons" eligible to vote. Only
political candidates were referred to specifically by the pronoun "he."
Persons admitted to vote had to be twenty-one years old, a "natural citizen
or subject" of His Majesty, and possess or rent land above a specified value.
That value was set pretty low. Urban voters had to own a house or land
with a minimum annual revenue of £5 11s. 1,5d. local currency or have
lived as a tenant for twelve months prior to the by-election in a dwelling
for which their rent was at least double that amount.[12] The resulting franchise was broader and more inclusive than in England or most other colonies of British North America. Catholics could vote and, after 1831, so
could Jews. Just south of Montreal, across the Saint Lawrence River, at least
twenty-seven First Nations women from Kahnawake voted in the 1825
election in Huntingdon County, where they helped elect Austin Cuvillier,
then a candidate for the Parti Canadien, the precursor to the Patriotes.
Cuvillier returns to the story of the 1832 by-election shortly, as a prominent opponent of Tracey.[13]

Under the broadest interpretation of election law, propertied widows,
single women, and wives recognized as having separate property should
have been eligible in all Lower Canadian elections if their property reached
the required value. In practice, allowing women to vote varied from region
to region and election to election.[14] It was a dubious, contested right. The
men appointed as returning officers had significant power to rule on questions of eligibility. Their mandate included running the election, naming
the clerk who would assist them, ensuring that notice of the election was
posted, determining the location of the poll, getting magistrates to call in
constables if they were needed to keep order, overseeing the taking of
oaths, entering all information in the poll book, and deciding whether
candidates' challenges to particular voters were valid. Jacques Viger later

told members of the House of Assembly investigating this by-election that as returning officer for the Montreal East by-election earlier in April 1832, he had systematically refused the vote of all married women. He also turned away all "persons in a state of inebriety."[15] Although Viger likened wives to drunks as being too readily influenced, he did not contest the right of widows or single women to vote.[16]

Conflict marked most of the twenty-three days that the poll was open. Election laws were based on the open voting methods of England. Officials chose the polling places, candidates addressed the crowd, and voters proclaimed their choices verbally. When one hour passed without anyone seeking to vote, the election was deemed over and the leading candidate had won. Blocking opponents from the polls was therefore one way to attempt to secure victory for the man who had the most votes at any moment.[17] Candidates and their supporters could verbally challenge the right to vote of those choosing their opponent. Laws forbidding wearing ribbons, cockades, and badges; hurling verbal insults; blocking; and buying drinks were frequently broken. In the rough politics of open voting, both sides engaged in verbal and physical intimidation. Assemblies in the predominantly male spaces of taverns, in which the champions of each candidate sought to recruit voters, released jostling and jeering bullies onto the streets. Violence became so much part of this election that the newspapers made a special point of remarking on the occasional peaceful day. They also reported on each day's voting tally. Such published counts informed the wider citizenry about who was ahead, much as opinion polls do today. In these nineteenth-century contests, the election campaign, the voting, and the publication of people's choices were concurrent, a potent mix that further fuelled violence.[18]

In this by-election, Stanley Bagg, who was closely linked to the colonial establishment, had the power to shape the running of the by-election in ways that Tracey could not. That the first poll opened in a Protestant church hall in this city in which Catholics were a majority and most Patriote supporters were Catholic was one powerful sign of his influence. As the by-election continued, he and his supporters drew on their close links to the justices of the peace, swearing in additional constables from among Tory supporters to maintain the peace. Some were known to be the bullies who intimidated Tracey supporters. On the second to last day of this longest election in the colony's history, as tempers and intimidation reached new heights, pro-Bagg magistrates called in the British troops garrisoned in the city. Among them was George Moffatt, the rabidly anti-French, anti-Catholic politician and merchant who would later take the lead in pushing aggressively for registry offices. At the time of this by-election, he had recently entered the Legislative Council, where his biographer reports he was "increasing the animosity" between Patriotes and Tories. "As one of the magistrates of Montreal, he approached the garrison for assistance in keeping order at the polls, and instructed the army to advance on a rioting mob."[19] By the end of that day, three men in the crowd, all Canadiens, had been shot by the soldiers. Canadiens quickly renamed the street "La rue du Sang" – the street of blood. In Patriote circles, the three murdered men became martyrs.[20]

All this was in the future when Marguerite Paris proclaimed her vote on 1 May, a relatively peaceful day, newspapers reported. The poll had opened at 8 a.m. Tracey was well ahead, with 296 votes to Bagg's 220. When she stepped up to name Tracey as her choice, Stanley Bagg contested her right to vote. Hence, this labourer's widow was required to publicly affirm the authenticity of her voting rights. She swore on the bible that she did indeed possess the requisite property qualifications. Her vote was accepted. The male polling clerk inscribed her name in the poll book, indicated that she lived on Vallée Street in the Saint Lawrence ward, put a tally mark under Tracey's name, and noted that Bagg had contested her right to vote. The returning officer, Mr. Saint George Dupré, then signed his name beside the entry.[21]

Women who considered voting could anticipate a series of contestations. The first was the very question of whether, as women, they should go to the poll. Early in the 1820s, an article in the *Montreal Gazette* had dismissed women's voting as "absurd and unconstitutional" and derided the "spiralling influence of women in Lower Canadian politics," predicting the dangers of a "petticoat polity" should women continue to vote. Shortly after the by-election, the same pro-bureaucratic paper reproduced a statement attributed to the popular English poet Mrs. Hemans. A woman, she argued, could "never with consistency appear in the forum or the pulpit – in the senate or at the poll ... without disparagement of her sexual character."[22]

The gender disorder that would result if women decided not only to vote but to claim a place in the Assembly was evocatively caricatured in an 1827 commentary in the *Quebec Mercury*. Women's presence, it suggested, would distract men from "the affairs of state." Alluding to high birth rates among Canadiennes, the English newspaper suggested that, "in this prolific country," frequent pregnancies would keep women away from their duties, so that the "business of the state must be neglected whilst these family concerns were going forward."[23] This image of a political institution both peopled and rendered empty by pregnant women evoked the desirability of the separation of home and politics, with the latter reserved for men. It again ignores the reality that single women, and especially widows, dominated among female voters, conflating all women with married women, as became so common in the nineteenth century.[24]

Such words fuelled the commonsense understanding that assimilated women in public with public women and potentially prostitutes. Such discursive genderings of the changing public sphere were contested. In 1828, a petition from Quebec City electors stressed women's intellectual equality with men, arguing that to vote was not a natural right of either men or women but based on their qualifications. The petition, reproduced in full in *La Minerve,* argued that under English law it was property, not the person, that was the basis of taxation and of representation, and that therefore the votes of widows with the proper qualifications were in all ways equal to those of men.[25]

Women's presence at the polls was sufficiently contested that it might risk tarnishing their respectability. Yet, they went in great numbers, braving the derision of rowdy male opponents of their candidate. They could anticipate the humiliation of having their right to vote denied by the returning officer. Or, like Marguerite Paris and Sarah Harrison, they might be forced to defend the authenticity of their claim against a challenge from their candidate's opponent and have to swear an oath attesting to their eligibility. These two relatively poor widows were not alone in having to make such a public affirmation. Six of every ten women who dared to present themselves during this by-election were either called upon by the opponent of their candidate to swear an oath about their qualifications or were not allowed to vote. Women were more likely to have their vote contested and somewhat more likely to be disqualified than men. More than one in ten women was either disqualified or refused to swear an oath and withdrew.[26]

Ambiguity about the propriety of women at the poll legitimated aggressive challenges to their claims. So did the suggestion voiced periodically in the press and later, that women were sought after by candidates because they were susceptible to being told how to vote. Ambiguity also secured protection. As the by-election drew to an end, the returning officer requested that Montreal's chief of police provide "six Constables with long Constable's staves, within the enclosure near the Hustings" to prevent anyone from getting too close unless they wished to vote or were accompanying "Ladies."[27] In this protective move he both recognized women's presence and furthered the understanding that women voters were unlike male voters.

How individual women were treated at the poll depended on a complex mix of political expediency, personal networks, the legitimacy of their claims, and gendered treatments in which some men sheltered some women

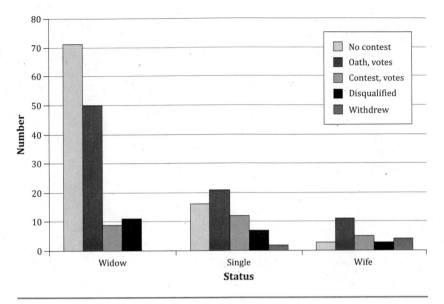

FIGURE 9.2   Contesting women's votes, Montreal West, 1832

Note: Seeking to vote, including repeat attempts, $N = 225$ (widow, $N = 141$; single, $N = 58$; wife, $N = 26$).

Source: Poll book, Montreal West 1832, transcribed and digitized by Nathalie Picard, "Women Voters, Lower Canada," database.

as they entered the hustings, while others engaged in hostile questioning. Women were not treated as a single category. Widows faced fewer challenges than married and single women. None withdrew, fewer were required to swear an oath, and a greater proportion voted successfully than other women. As women no longer obviously under the patriarchal power of fathers and husbands, their claim to vote on the basis of independence and ownership of property had greater resonance than that of single women or of wives whose property was separate from that of their husbands. At the poll what mattered was whether they were known to hold property or would swear that they did. Half the widows were able to vote without formal questioning. Only a quarter of the single women and half that proportion again of wives' attempts went uncontested (see Figure 9.2).

Marguerite Paris was suspect as a potentially fraudulent voter not just for her gender, but because of her poverty and status as a labourer's widow. The craftsmen's widows Sarah Harrison and Marguerite Gagnon faced similar challenges. No one contested the votes of the merchants' widows Anna Foster or Sarah Campbell, both of whom voted for Stanley Bagg, or that of Émilie Tavernier Gamelin for Tracey. Émilie's closest brother and former guardian, François Tavernier, was an ardent supporter of Papineau and the Patriotes. At some point during the by-election, he was arrested and charged with assaulting a Bagg supporter.[28] Émilie had close family ties to both Patriotes and to some of the notable Canadien families who had broken with Papineau and thrown their support behind Bagg and the Tories. Property, strong family connections, and her reputation as a devout Catholic widow working with the poor and elderly of the city likely guaranteed her immunity from harassment as she voiced her political choice.

Although the marriage contract of Émilie Tavernier and Jean-Baptiste Gamelin had provided that the two spouses' property should remain separate, it had also stipulated that should the surviving partner outlive any offspring, he or she could own and dispose of the other spouse's property as full owner.[29] Émilie faced widowhood with three small properties and initially one surviving son. He died. Her assets gave her the means to do what became her passion and eventually her profession – provide material, physical, and spiritual support to the poor. By the time of the by-election, Émilie was thirty and closely involved in many of the new ventures that the city's bourgeois Catholic women were organizing to care for orphans, redeemed prostitutes, the sick, and girls from the country seeking domestic work. In 1828, she had taken first one, then several frail widows into her home on St. Antoine Street.[30] Needing more space, she soon arranged to use a larger building, moving in 1830 to an old school at the corner of St. Lawrence and St. Catherine streets, close to where many of her relatives lived.[31]

At the time of the by-election, she had recently moved these elderly and infirm widows yet again, this time into a larger building that she rented in the Saint Lawrence suburb, at the corner of St. Catherine and St. Phillip streets. This dwelling was large enough to house herself and up to twenty women. She and the friends, relatives, and other women assisting her in this work and in other charitable enterprises regularly traversed the streets of the city. They collected food, clothing, and money for their poor from the city's citizens and visited others in their homes. The streets of the city were familiar to them, and Émilie and her colleagues would have been familiar figures on them.[32] Catholicism, like Protestantism, translated readily in this period "into a claim to enter the public world and contribute to the work which needed to be done," giving such women "license to enter the public arena" in "purposeful and empowering ways."[33]

A few days before Émilie Tavernier chose to vote, the poll was moved for the third time. The new location close to a building occupied by the Notre Dame Parish church wardens must surely have seemed a preferable place to the two earlier polls. It was very close to the new Catholic parish church, which was still under construction. It was also just six blocks south of her latest shelter for women on St. Phillip Street, and hence an easy

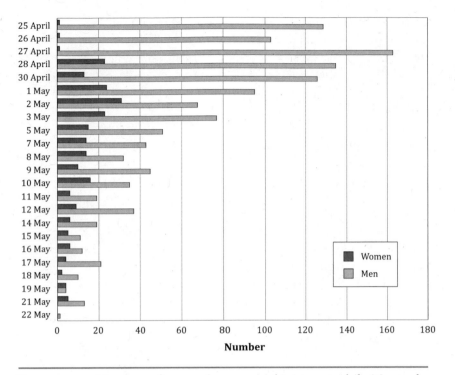

FIGURE 9.3 Numbers of men and women seeking to vote daily, Montreal West by-election, 1832

Note: N = 1,249 men and 233 women, including those who went to the poll more than once. No voting was held on Sundays.
Source: Livres d'élection de l'élection de 1832 à Montréal, quartier Ouest, Collection Charles Phillips, 1770-1957, P148, Bibliothèque et Archives nationales du Québec.

walk.[34] Some fifty-five people sought to vote the same day as Émilie Tavernier. Ten were women. The fifth voter that morning was a widow, so was the eighth. Twenty-one men then marched up to voice their choices. One Tracey supporter retired when his vote was objected to by Bagg. A male labourer's vote was contested. He left, but returned and voted. The nine men just ahead of Émilie all chose the Tory candidate, Stanley Bagg. They included John Campbell, the bookseller and husband of Laura Mower.[35] Following Campbell's vote for Bagg, the profoundly male face of the voters changed. Felicité Barbeau, a married woman, chose Stanley Bagg. Daniel Tracey demanded that she swear on oath that she did indeed own property. Two unmarried sisters, Charlotte and Marguerite Leduc, chose Tracey and faced the objections of his opponent. Over the rest of the day, four more women voted. Only Émilie's vote went uncontested.

The gender composition of voting citizens varied from day to day over the course of the election (see Figure 9.3). The very first day, Mrs. Isabella

McIntyre attempted to voice her choice but was turned away. No more women tried that day. On the third day, widow Elizabeth Summers voted for Stanley Bagg. On day six, when Marguerite Paris voted, she was one of twenty-three women approaching the hustings. A day later, female involvement peaked when twenty-nine women sought to vote. Women must have been highly visible that day, for they represented over a quarter of those seeking to vote. Some voted alone. Others, like Émilie Tavernier, voted with small clusters of women. They came from all parts of the electoral district – from the commercial streets of the old city and from the rougher streets of the suburbs of Saint Lawrence and Saint Joseph. Some were neighbours. In this relatively small colonial town, many would have known each other.

When the press mentioned women at the hustings, they represented them as the dupes of the candidates. Historians have not sufficiently critiqued the underpinnings of such claims. The patterns of their voting and their family histories make it hard to imagine that all or even many voted against their will. Few wives voted with their husbands, few daughters with their fathers. Politics was hardly a foreign world for many of these women. Political debates permeated the culture of the colony and of Montreal in this volatile period. Women regularly attended the sessions of the Legislative Assembly. Nathalie Picard has pointed out that many female voters were from Canadien families with long traditions of female voting. Evidence of this tradition in Émilie Tavernier Gamelin's own extended family is striking. The aunt who had raised her, Marie-Anne Tavernier Perrault, voted as a widow in 1820, as did Marie-Barbe Castonguay, Émilie's brother's wife and close friend. In the Montreal West election of 1827, her cousin, Agathe Perrault, the widow of Maurice Nowlan, had voted for Louis-Joseph Papineau and Robert Nelson. Agathe voted again in 1832, three days after her cousin Émilie. She too chose Tracey.[36]

Fernand Ouellet has argued that because women's votes in Lower Canadian elections apparently followed dominant trends, female voters were "swayed by pressure from the candidates."[37] Such analysis downplays the cultural importance of political conflicts in this period. It allows no place for women embracing familial traditions of passionate involvement in politics, or for couples' political interests constituting part of their "deep emotional attachment" to each other.[38] Neither Émilie Tavernier nor Agathe Perrault would have been swayed by any arguments Tory candidates might make. Their families were too intimately involved in the emerging Patriote movement. Nor does it seem likely that even a fairly poor widow like Marguerite Paris would have been tempted by money or other offers to vote against the party so strongly supported by the largely Canadien artisans, carters, and labourers of the Saint Lawrence suburb who were her neighbours and relatives.[39] Women supportive of the Patriotes might have been swayed to vote. It is highly unlikely they could be swayed in the opposite direction.

Similarly, given the growing identification of the Patriotes with a nationalism that embraced Irish Catholic supporters but represented the British as coterminous with the ruling elite, there was little space for most English-speaking widows to imagine voting for the Patriotes. This was not the widow Anna Foster's first election. In 1827, she was among the ninety widows who voted in the election that pitted the Parti Canadien candidates Louis-Joseph Papineau and Robert Nelson against the establishment candidates Peter McGill and John Delisle in Montreal West. The latter were her choice then, as was true of most of the widows with English names. When she voted on 16 May 1832, she again chose the establishment candidate, Stanley Bagg. Had Caroline Campbell owned the requisite property to vote, and chosen to do so, her choice would have been more interesting, given her husband's and father's places among the Irish and American supporters of the Patriotes. Her innkeeping father, William, was one of several English-speaking Patriote supporters who were roughed up by Bagg supporters just three days into the by-election. *La Minerve* reported that he received severe contusions.[40] In such heated times, open voting ensured that if reluctant women were encouraged to vote, it would be by those whose politics they shared. Personal politics forged in the crucibles of colonialism, empire, family discussions, and ethnic, religious, and class cultures and interests, rather than candidates' rhetoric or money, surely shaped most women's allegiances long before they reached the poll.

Still, both men and women were courted as voters. In the aggressive attempts of supporters on each side to ensure victory, candidates plied potential supporters with free drinks, dinners, and promises. They treated them in the taverns and hotels of the city and sought them out on the streets and in their homes, despite legislation that fined those seeking to influence voting.[41] The resulting intrusion of politics into domestic space would later be signalled by one leading figure in the by-election as evidence of an election gone awry. As a young man, the Montreal merchant Austin Cuvillier, who was married to Émilie Tavernier's cousin and godmother, Marie-Claire Perrault, had been a critic of colonial policy and a committed member of the Parti Canadien. He was among the moderate nationalists distancing themselves from Patriote politics in the years leading up to this 1832 by-election. By 1832, the break was complete. When some five hundred Montrealers met to determine who should be nominated to run in the by-election, Cuvillier's public nomination of Stanley Bagg in English was met with cries of "Parlez français!" He recommended Bagg "as a very respectable man," long established in the colony. Drawing on and furthering widely circulating stereotypes of the Irish as unruly and easily led by priests and others, and evoking well-known incidents in Tracey's short history in the colony, Cuvillier dismissed Tracey as an inappropriate choice. He had arrived too recently, he was too violent, and he was too prone to attacking "the private character of individuals."[42]

Cuvillier's new support of the colonial Tory elite made him a prime target of Patriote scorn during this by-election and afterward. When his wife, Marie-Claire Perrault, sought to vote for Bagg on 19 May, Patriotes responded to her not as any woman but as the wife of a Canadien who had chosen to defect from the "national" party.[43] Assimilating domestic and political subterfuge, *La Minerve* questioned the validity of the separation of goods that the couple had organized to protect their property from Cuvillier's creditors. *La Minerve* impugned Cuvillier's abilities as family provider and businessman by discussing his bankruptcy, and mused more broadly on the implications of separate property for a husband's marital authority. Could two spouses vote if they were properly separate as to goods? If the Cuvilliers' separation was not valid, did Marie-Claire "have the right that she was allowed to exercise?" If they were really separate as to property, why had she been the one who paid off some of his creditors? Her vote offered one more reason to critique the lack of independence of the returning officer, understood by all Patriotes to be controlled by Bagg and his supporters. Such tricky legal questions, the article suggested, were best left to jurists, and yet the "Returning Officer had not found this a tricky question. He decided Mme C. should vote without hesitation."[44] In this commentary, *La Minerve* linked voting by wives, rather than women in general, to broader questions of domestic and political disorder in the colony, to issues of nationalist loyalty, and to the disruptions caused by choices like separate property, which could be represented both as English in origin and of dubious propriety.

Later, Cuvillier sought to show that the Patriotes had been improperly canvassing for women's votes. At the investigation initiated by Patriote politicians, he demanded that a witness, Joseph Roy, confirm that he had called at Mrs. Nowlan's home in the Saint Lawrence suburb during the election. Cuvillier's knowledge of such a visit likely came from family gossip, for the Mrs. Nowlan he refers to can only have been his sister-in-law and Émilie Tavernier's cousin, Agathe Perrault, the widow Nowlan.[45] Joseph Roy agreed that he had visited her but denied that he was canvassing for Patriote votes. His account of that visit paints a powerful gendered picture of domestic intrusions during the campaign:

When I knocked at the door, a girl came to say, that Mrs Nolan was not at home. I said, Mrs Nolan conceals herself, to avoid troublesome people, tell her that I am not canvassing for the Election. The young girl began to laugh, and said, yes, Mrs Nolan is in the room, and keeps out of sight. I saw Mrs Nolan, to whom I repeated the same thing; she laughed, and told me how much she had been tormented by people who were looking for votes.[46]

Roy thus effectively counteracted Cuvillier's suggestions of impropriety through his claim to have been welcomed and to have shared laughter with Cuvillier's sister-in-law. This resonates as the shared laughter of shared politics with a widow who had supported Patriote candidates in earlier elections and may have already voted at the time of the visit, or knew she would do so shortly.

Despite the violence and the contestations of their right to be at the poll, more women voted in this by-election than in any other nineteenth-century Lower Canadian election, and they constituted a greater proportion of the voters.[47] Whether they came on their own initiative, reluctantly, or were bribed to do so, they placed their bodies in the contested streets and stepped out publicly to assert their political choices in considerable numbers. And if they possessed the required qualifications, they voted. A significant proportion of the women whose property qualified them to vote appear to have done so. Historians have estimated that somewhere between one in four and one in eight male family heads were eligible to vote in Lower Canadian elections of this period. About 60 percent of eligible male household heads voted in these two highly contested Montreal by-elections of 1832. The gendered nature of contemporary sources makes it a challenge to venture similar estimates for women. As the majority of voters were widows, I have made three rough measures of the extent to which widows who may have been eligible to vote in the two 1832 Montreal by-elections did so. Each suggests very high rates of engagement. The first is based on the women who married between 1823 and 1826. By the time the by-elections in Montreal East and West were over, on 22 May 1832, the widows Marguerite Paris, Émilie Tavernier, and Anna Foster were among at least forty-four women from this generation of marriages whose husbands had died. Seventeen of them had already remarried. Nine of the remaining twenty-seven, or one in three of those who were still widows, went to the poll in the by-elections. Most of the others would not have fulfilled the property requirements. Second, comparing the names of widows who voted in either of the two 1832 by-elections to those listed in the enumeration of property owners that Jacques Viger made later that year for the first anticipated Montreal city election suggests that around half the propertied widows voted.[48] Third, the enumerators for the 1831 census of Lower Canada identified 205 widows who were heading households in the city. They no doubt missed some, for Émilie Tavernier Gamelin, for example, was not listed as a household head. Of those enumerated, 135 were identified as property owners. Among the widows who voted in the two 1832 by-elections, 116 owned property. This suggests that over four of every five eligible, property-owning widows may have expressed their political choices that year.[49] These rough measures suggest that somewhere between one-third and four-fifths of eligible Montreal widows braved the public space and disorder of the hustings to elect either Patriote or Tory candidates in 1832.[50] Most of the widows and other female voters were property owners. In this city in which the vast majority of families rented their homes, women's claims to vote were more rooted in property owning than those of men.[51] Yet, because of the low franchise requirements, fairly meagre holdings legitimated the public voice of widows of modest means. The property on which Marguerite Paris staked her claim as a citizen was her one-room wooden house and lot on Vallée Street in the Saint Lawrence ward. This was property that she and her labourer husband, Joseph Guilbault, had succeeded in purchasing through their joint labours during their marriage and that formed the most significant part of the community property she had a claim on as his widow.[52] It had provided her and her daughter, Marie-Marguerite, with shelter in the three years since his death.[53] Jacques Viger valued it for taxation purposes as worth £116, or an annual revenue of just £7. Among the widows who had married between 1823 and 1826 and voted in 1832, only Amable Leduc, widow of the carter Charles Perrault, had property taxed at less. At £100, or an annual potential revenue of just £6, her property represented the lowest possible threshold for voting. About one in five of the city's widows assessed in 1832 owned properties worth as little as those of Amable and Marguerite. They lived mostly in the artisanal and working-class suburbs of Saint Lawrence, Saint Louis, and Saint Mary.

As widows of labourers, carters, and artisans, Marguerite Paris, Amable Leduc, and Sarah Harrison defy the hypothesis proposed by the political scientist Diane Lamoureux that most female voters in Lower Canada were owners of seigneuries.[54] Their modest properties pale beside those of the city's major male landowners or its wealthiest widows. In Viger's 1832 evaluation, the city's leading landholding widows came in roughly equal numbers from French- and English-speaking families. Eleven widows, all with land estimated as worth over £100 annually in revenues, owned nearly half the total value of all the widows' properties that he evaluated. When these widows voted, they chose Stanley Bagg. They included Marguerite Viger, whose husband, the merchant Pierre Berthelet, had died in 1830, leaving her with properties assessed as worth a revenue of over £800 annually – the highest amount for any Montreal woman in 1832. This elderly

Canadienne widow, who was born at the time of the Conquest, was in her early seventies when she went to the hustings in 1832. No one contested her vote.[55] Elizabeth Mittleberger, the widow of Thomas Oakes, a prosperous tinsmith, would have been closer to ninety. She was widowed in 1817, managed Thomas' business for some time, and in 1832 was listed as owning two properties on St. Paul and Notre Dame streets assessed as worth £320 annually in revenue.[56] Anna Foster Saddler's fortune was more modest. Her gentleman husband had left her with two properties in the Saint Anne suburb worth £55 and £8 in annual revenue.

Widows from the first marriage cohort who voted in the 1832 by-elections whose husbands had been masters and craftsmen in the artisanal trades based their claims on much more modest properties. Sarah Harrison, Mary Howard, and Sarah Campbell were renting their dwellings.[57] Émilie Monjean, who voted in Montreal East, had, as we saw, brought considerable real and moveable property into her marriage with the master painter Antoine Laurent. In 1832, her house on Sanguinet Street in the Louis suburb was assessed at a capital value of around £250, more than twice the worth of Marguerite Paris' small home. This difference underlines the large social and economic gap between these widows of a master craftsman and a labourer.[58]

Gender, Citizenship, and Election Coverage in the Press

All in all, nearly two hundred women successfully performed the act of citizenship in Montreal West by walking through supportive and hostile crowds, swearing to their legitimacy as voters, and pronouncing the name of the candidate of their choice. More tried. Over sixty other women voted in the election just weeks earlier in Montreal East. Yet, in the day-to-day election reports of Montreal dailies, the presence of these women at the poll was rarely mentioned. When women were referred to it was usually to discredit the masculinity and behaviour of the opposing side, or to deride their inability to find more appropriate electors. With the exception of the discussion of Marie-Claire Perrault Cuvillier's vote in *La Minerve,* newspaper reports never named individual women voters.

Conflicting political visions of citizenship that built on and produced divergent forms of ethnicity and masculinity took up the space of newspaper reports. In its support of Stanley Bagg and the established order, the *Gazette* claimed a vision of masculine citizenship rooted in independence, industry, integrity, respectability, honour, class hierarchy, and benevolence toward the poor. Supporters stressed that Bagg had been in the colony since his childhood, reminding readers of Tracey's recent arrival. They lauded his contributions to agriculture and commerce and his loyalty to his king, country, and the constitution – political language that Cecilia

Morgan has shown also represented all that was "both British and manly" about Upper Canadian Conservatives at the same time.[59] Conservatives belittled their opposition, representing Tracey and his largely Catholic supporters as uncontrolled, dishonest, and desperate – the kinds of rowdy, violence prone, lower-class men who did not deserve to exercise the vote and who could be easily swayed by the words of eloquent but misguided superiors, as they were by priests. These dismissals of Tracey's supporters frequently represented them as unruly Irishmen, rather than Canadiens, implying, for example, that many had recently arrived and to get through the winter had been dependent on charity given by just the kind of men they were opposing. The clothes on their bodies were read to critique the breadth of the franchise, and justify contesting their votes: "The appearance of the great majority is sufficient to cast a doubt upon their claim." Mistreatment of women was offered as further evidence of their misguided manliness: "Mr Bagg's friends, particularly the ladies, when at the poll, are hooted and hissed at, nay, even Mr Bagg himself has been assaulted and otherwise mistreated." Here surely was proof that "Tracey and his friends have disgraced themselves by their conduct so unworthy of BRITISH subjects, enjoying a free constitution."[60]

In the equally fanatical criticism of the Tories published daily in *La Minerve,* women's presence at the poll was linked with that of cripples, the elderly, and the infirm as evidence that Bagg had few voters left in reserve and was getting desperate.[61] Women's presence, by implication, could mean only that they were dragged to the poll. Patriote supporters asserted that they were working for the public interest, the public good, and the rights of the people. The "people," in the columns of *La Minerve,* included the Irish and frequently Americans, as well as Canadiens. At this point, its nationalist vision embraced all those who espoused the Canadien cause, including especially their fellow Catholics, the Irish.[62]

Patriote and Tory newspapers produced divergent characteristics of proper citizens but shared their representation as masculine. Women cannot have been invisible at the hustings, yet women as a category had little place in the competing understandings of citizenship articulated in the public sphere of assemblies, newspaper reporting, and pamphlet writing. In this formative period of Lower Canadian politics, as in the revolutionary politics of the eighteenth-century American colonies, France, or the constitutional politics of England, the citizen whose qualities were in the process of being elaborated discursively by Patriotes and Tories was male. The reason, imagination, and independence that historians have identified as key characteristics of the individual constructed in emerging liberal theory were the very opposite of the emotionality and dependence accorded to females or ascribed to political opponents. Widows and other women might vote, but the gendering of politics as masculine, that Allan Greer has so well described, limited their visibility in the press.[63]

There was one major exception. The public debate about the right of Austin Cuvillier's wife to vote, discussed above, points to the significance of loyalty as a critical theme in this election. Patriotes willingly integrated Irishmen like Tracey and his "compatriots, our adopted brothers," into their fold. They were understood to embrace similar political goals and to identify with a nationalism being built in opposition to the unjust implementation of British colonial rule. Much more troubling were Canadiens, like Cuvillier, who had "fallen into the trap" of supporting the bureaucracy, who had turned "Brutus" on their people. In the public rhetoric of the election, as reported in the columns of the press, Patriotes wavered between derision and anguish over how such men could be brought back into a party that sought to speak for all Canadiens. In public anguishing over transgressions from the boundaries of the imagined nation they were building, Austin Cuvillier was the name most frequently mentioned. That his wife tried to vote, that their marital and monetary affairs could be proclaimed suspect, all signalled both Cuvillier's perfidy and the unmanly way Stanley Bagg neglected no strategy to muster as many votes as possible.[64] This also further diffused the understanding that it was the Tories who relied on women as voters, and further delegitimized women at the hustings.[65]

Viger's Gaze: Producing Knowledge about Citizens

Widows and other women clearly voted. Yet, in the public press, citizens are largely presented as masculine. Women's presence denoted improper election behaviour or desperation for votes. This supports Greer's argument that in the 1830s the understanding that politics were male was sufficiently widespread to justify women's exclusion from the vote. Yet, neither Greer nor other historians have adequately explained why politicians decided in 1834 that the time had come to exclude women from voting. True, similar legislation had already been passed in England and some US states, and would eventually be passed in most of the other colonies of British North America, despite little evidence of women voting in those jurisdictions. Fernand Ouellet has suggested that the 1832 election played a role. Yet, his explanation that Papineau was upset because too many women had again for his opponent is insufficient. In transforming Papineau into the sole author of the bill, and in rooting the explanation in the actual act of women voting, rather than more generalized ideas, Ouellet has raised an important question: How did anyone know how many women voted for each candidate? The *Montreal Gazette* alluded disparagingly to Papineau's habit of lurking around the poll, and especially to his close surveillance during the coroner's subsequent investigation into the murders that brought the election to an end.[66] Papineau undoubtedly saw women voting, but he did not count the votes for each candidate by their gender. Daily tallies of the votes in the newspapers were never broken down by sex. Furthermore, if there was a connection between this election and the 1834 bill, why and how did women's vote, so invisible in the print media during the election, become visible?

The answer lies with Papineau's cousin, Jacques Viger.[67] At the time of the 1832 election, Viger was in his mid-forties. Few, if any Montrealers, knew the city's streets and people better than he did. No one showed a greater interest in accumulating such knowledge. Whereas his more famous cousins focused on the political future of Canadiens at the level of the colony, Jacques Viger's passion was the city – its past, its people, and its future. In 1813, he was named surveyor of Montreal's highways, streets, lanes, and bridges. His interest in the physical infrastructure of the city would continue throughout his life. In 1825, he published a document outlining potential improvements to the laws dealing with roads in Montreal. That same year, he and Louis Guy worked as the census commissioners for the whole island of Montreal. In that capacity, as Jean-Claude Robert suggests, many of "the details of his fellow-citizens' lives were known to him." Three years later, he drew on his intimate knowledge of the social geography of the city to advise his Patriote, politician cousins, Louis-Joseph Papineau and Denis-Benjamin Viger, on how best to allocate boundaries for the wards of the city and set the property qualifications low enough to ensure a Canadien majority in city elections.[68] He was, as we saw, the returning officer in the Montreal East by-election early in April 1832. After the Montreal West by-election, as politicians prepared a bill to incorporate Montreal, it was Viger who set out to assess the value of all property holdings in anticipation of the city's first municipal election, predicted for June 1832.[69] When that was finally held, in 1833, he was chosen as the city's first mayor.

During the twenty-three days of voting during the 1832 by-election, Jacques Viger observed very carefully and practised his "habit of collecting matters of history." His testimony to the House of Assembly after the election shows that he played multiple roles in diverse locations. He went to the hustings most days of the election. He acted as an intermediary between Papineau and his political adversaries. He repeatedly encouraged Benjamin Delisle, the high constable of the District of Montreal, to produce accurate lists of the constables sworn in, including those who were summoned but refused to appear. He eavesdropped on the whispered

FIGURE 9.4 Jacques Viger, nineteenth century. | Archives, Ville de Montréal, Fonds BM1, P2202-3.

conversations of Bagg supporters about hiring and paying bullies, asked questions, and offered advice.[70]

Jacques Viger appointed himself as official voyeur as he fixed his gaze on the electoral behaviour of the people of his city (see Figure 9.4). Like a growing number of men of his times, Viger sought to make sense of the world through counting and categorizing. One of his ways of mastering this unruly political event in which he had no official capacity was to watch closely, to listen, and to intervene. Another was to categorize people's involvement. He drew up a list of all the special constables sworn to maintain the peace during the election, annotated with his own comments and calculations. And, as he later explained to Austin Cuvillier, he had procured an entire copy of the poll book from "one of the writers in the Police Office of the Prothonotaries at Montreal." He then made additional transcriptions of the entire poll book, organizing each one differently so that he could see at a glance how and when every Montrealer had voted, and identify voters by their ethnicity and sex.[71]

The summary statistics that Viger produced from his analyses and transcriptions of this poll book have served as the basis of most published accounts of this election.[72] Much more interesting are his transcriptions. These allowed him to answer many questions that politicians later had about the election. One in particular highlights his interest in the issue of women voting. In the front of the leather volume containing one of his copies of the poll book, he inserted an alphabetical list of all the men and women who presented themselves at the hustings. On this list, he identified Tracey voters in black, those for Bagg in red, and those who were disqualified in blue. Widows and wives were cross-indexed by both their married names and their maiden names. Beside each name, he placed a number indicating their order in the voting. With this cross-referencing system, he could see at a glance how anyone had voted. In the days of open voting, this was not the shocking transgression of privacy it would seem today. It was, however, extremely useful to a man intent on knowing his city, its people, and their politics.[73]

His transcription of the poll book with which this alphabetical listing was bound listed all Montrealers presenting at the poll in the same order as the original poll book. However, he added information that was not required at the time of the voting. He assigned everyone an ethnicity, drawing for the latter on his own personal knowledge to designate them as Canadiens, Americans, or Irish – the groups understood to be the most likely Patriote supporters. The rest were simply listed as "English and others." The Scots, so prominent in Montreal's English-speaking community and economy, disappeared in his categories, absorbed, as Linda Colley has suggested occurred in the broader context of English politics and empire, into the category of British.[74]

As Viger transcribed names and added selected details on each citizen, slotting them into categories of his making, he picked up his red pen each time the voter was a woman. In the pages of this volume, the women, so barely visible in journalist's narratives of election events, jump off the parchment, their names inscribed in red rather than black ink (see Figure 9.5). Beside the name of any married men or woman whose spouse voted he indicated, also in red, what their polling number was. This colour-coding was part of his method of ensuring accurate counts. It also rendered the number of women voters, and their daily presence at the poll, highly visible. It was through his careful counting, based on these transcriptions, and his frequent observation of the poll that he legitimated his expertise at the investigations that followed the election.

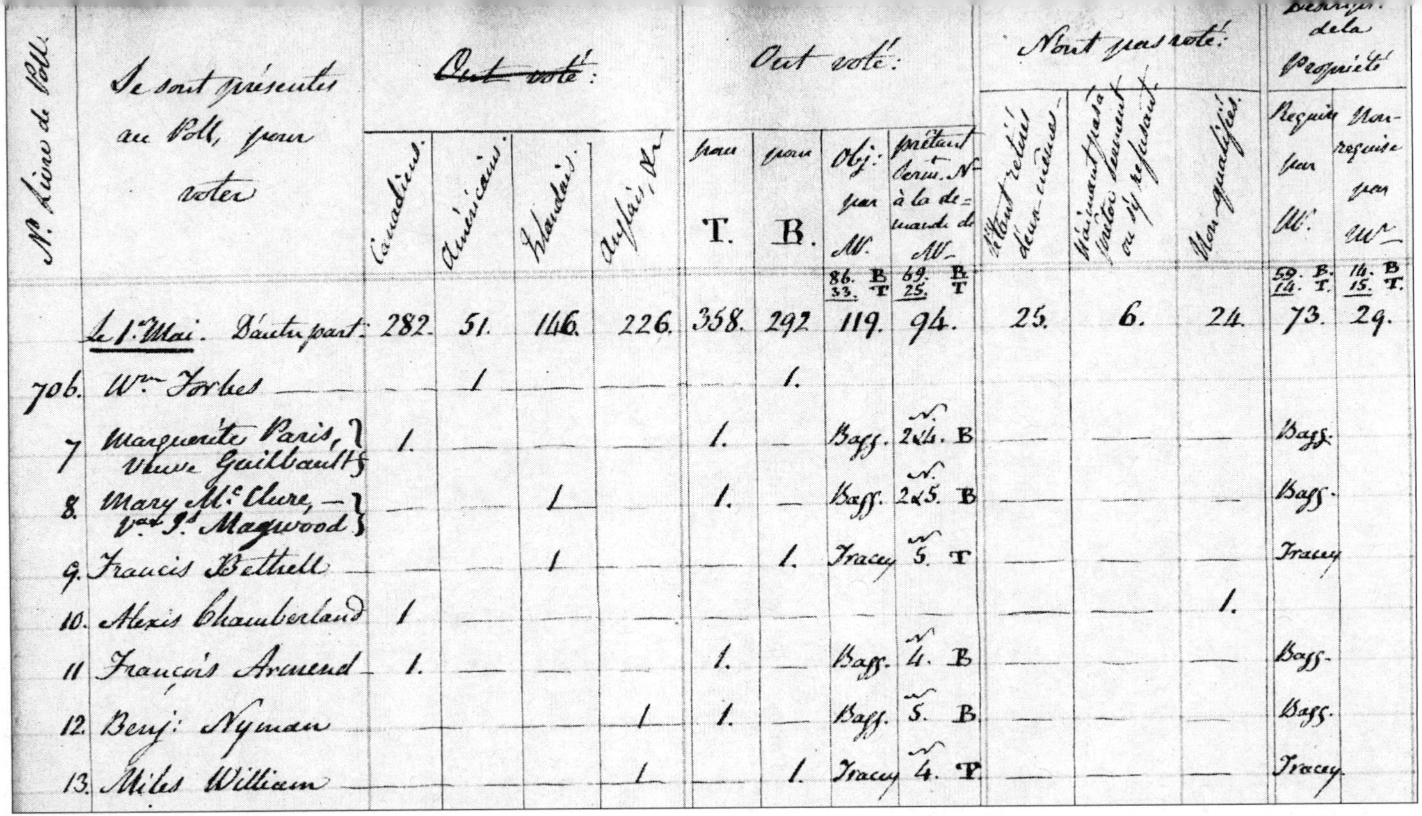

No. Livre de Poll	Se sont présentés au Poll, pour voter	Ont voté: Canadiens	Américains	Irlandais	Anglais, &c	Ont voté: pour T.	pour B.	Obj: par M.	prêtant Serm. N. à la demande de M.	N'ont pas voté: n'étant retenu deux...	n'ayant pas voulu prêter serment ou s'y refusant	Non-qualifiés	Description de la Propriété: Requis par M.	Non-requise par M.
								86. B / 33. T	69. B / 25. T				59. B / 14. T	14. B / 15. T
	Le 1er Mai. D'autre part:	282.	51.	146.	226.	358.	292	119.	94.	25.	6.	24.	73.	29.
706.	Wm Forbes		1				1.							
7	Marguerite Paris, veuve Guilbault	1.				1.		Bass.	N. 224. B				Bass.	
8.	Mary McClure, vve Js Magwood			1		1.		Bass.	N. 225. B				Bass.	
9.	Francis Bethell			1			1.	Tracey	N. 5. T				Tracey	
10.	Alexis Chamberland	1										1.		
11	François Arnaud	1.				1.		Bass.	N. 4. B				Bass.	
12.	Benj: Nyman				1	1.		Bass.	N. 5. B				Bass.	
13.	Miles William				1		1.	Tracey	N. 4. T				Tracey	

FIGURE 9.5 Marguerite Paris' vote (item 7) as transcribed by Jacques Viger, Montreal West, 1832. In this version of the poll book, Viger ascribes ethnicities to voters and wrote women into the record in red ink. His columns list everyone who presented at the polls, his ascription of their identity, who they voted for, who objected to their vote, whether they voted, and whether they were required to swear an oath or to describe the property on which their claim was based. | Centre d'archives de Montréal de Bibliothèque et Archives nationales du Québec, Livres d'élection de l'élection de 1832 à Montréal, quartier Ouest (extrait). Collection Charles Phillips, 1770–1957, P148.

From Red Ink, Redcoats, and the "Street of Blood" to Male Citizens

In his leather-bound volume, Viger with his red ink marked out female voters as different kinds of citizens. On the streets of the city, the shedding of Canadien blood brought this tumultuous election to a close, erasing for a while the memory of the significant number of widows and other women at the hustings. Before the violence escalated on 21 May and the riot act was read, the troops called in, and three Canadien men shot, Tracey was three votes ahead of Bagg. The day after, the political invective that already marked the journalism of the city newspapers reached new heights, carving harder lines of ethnic difference and hatred between both sides and telling two very different tales of the day's events. That morning the poll opened early. Only one male voter stepped up. Tracey was declared the winner. He, LaFontaine, and other Patriote politicians cautioned against expressing joy at his election and invited supporters to share in mourning the dead. Some three hundred people accompanied Tracey to his home "in profound silence." Bagg lodged an official protest against the result.[75]

Over the following days, newspapers across the colony reported on the event. In Montreal, the coroner's inquest began immediately and there were calls on all sides for further investigations. On 24 May, the public funeral of the three Canadiens attracted some five thousand people in this city of twenty-seven thousand. They were given a first-class service at the Notre Dame Parish church. Papineau and other Patriote politicians headed the funeral convoy to the cemetery. Whether women joined the crowd was not mentioned.[76] Nor are women visible in most of the many records generated by the events of 21 May. None testified at the coroner's inquest, which, after many adjournments resolved in September that there was no basis for a charge of murder against the colonel and the captain of the troops who had fired into the crowd.[77] Women may have attended the assemblies that met in parishes across the colony after church to discuss the "horrors" of 21 June; to deplore the actions of Canadiens like Austin Cuvillier, for having "ignominiously abandoned the mass of the Canadiens to serve in a party that is not worthy of their support"; to proclaim faithfulness to the King and disgust for the actions of the soldiers, magistrates, and Bureaucratic Party, as Patriotes called the Tories; and to announce special church services to pray for the souls of the three victims.[78] Yet, no female names appear among the lists of local notables reported in attendance at such meetings. Such public assemblies, such meetings of citizens to discuss the affairs of their country, to engage in rational discourse, were the very essence of the new kind of "bourgeois public" that the German scholar Jürgen Habermas has identified as typifying the politics of eighteenth- and nineteenth-century Western states. As with elections, women might attend and hang around the fringes, but such occasions were represented as resolutely male spaces.[79]

It is only in the evidence taken by the committee of the House of Assembly investigating the election that there is any mention of women as electors or as members of crowds at the hustings. And of the witnesses called, only Jacques Viger seemed interested in alerting the politicians to the question of women voting. He did so several times, despite soliciting little reaction initially. Early in January 1833, nearly a month after the investigations began, he answered a question about how frequently he attended the poll and whether he had observed that people were blocked from voting by informing his questioners that he had seen a great many women voting on both sides. The next day he used the data he had so carefully recorded to place women's voting in the public record. In authoritative, statistical detail, he reported that

> 225 women came to the Hustings, 26 of whom did not vote. There were 199 that voted; of whom 95 voted for Mr. Tracey and 104 for Mr. Bagg; that is to say 49 spinsters, 20 of whom voted for Mr. Tracey, and 29 for Mr. Bagg; 131 widows, 68 of whom voted for Mr Tracey, and 63 for Mr. Bagg; and 19 married women, 7 of whom voted for Mr. Tracey, and 12 for Mr. Bagg.

He then gave committee members his list showing the numbers of women who voted each day and informed them that "six married women voted ... jointly with their husbands." There was no immediate reaction to this information. The questioning turned to how the magistrates and members of the House of Assembly had voted. Viger could use his careful records to tell all.[80]

It was not until late January that women's votes attracted any interest. On 28 January, James Leslie, the main Patriote questioner, asked Viger whether he had allowed married women to vote during the Montreal East by-election. Viger replied that he had not. Four weeks later, Leslie wanted to know which women "were brought to vote toward the end of the hour, so as to feed the poll?"[81] At this point, widows, wives, and spinsters no longer appear as statistical categories. Giving evidence that he must have read from the red-ink transcription of the poll book, Viger started naming the women who had voted just after the returning officer proclaimed that the election would be over if no one voted in the next sixty minutes.[82] This was easy for him to do, for he had identified such moments in his transcription with little stars. He did not mention the many men who also voted at these critical moments, or the larger number of women who voted at other times in the day. He identified twenty-three women by name – less than 5 percent of the female voters. Fifteen of them were supporters of Bagg, thus reinforcing the accusation of Patriotes that Bagg's supporters were pulling women to the hustings to increase his chances.[83] Leslie also wished to know which married women had voted at the same time or at different times from their husbands. Again, Viger was able to be specific. He named six couples, including "Mary Wilson, who voted on the 19th May for Mr Bagg, wife of Alexander Nimmo, who had voted on 3 May for the same candidate ... Marie-Claire Perrault who voted on the 18th May for Mr Bagg; wife of Austin Cuvillier, Esquire, who had voted on the 18th for the same candidate."[84] Viger explicitly mentioned Mme Cuvillier twice – as a woman voting to prevent the poll closing and as a wife voting the same way as her husband. He did so without casting any obvious judgment. Yet, this publicity added to the broader discourse in newspapers and the assemblies throughout the province that had named Austin Cuvillier as the most prominent of the Canadiens wishing to "crush their compatriots" with their support for the Tories.[85]

Viger, with his careful lists, numbers, and tracking of citizens' votes, placed information about women's voting squarely on the floor of the Legislative Assembly, in the public record, and on the agenda of electoral reform in the colony. Less than a year later, the Patriote politician John Neilson picked up the issue, identifying a range of doubtful practices at recent elections that should be dealt with. These included whether women should vote, how oaths should be sworn, and how tension and struggles at the poll could be reduced. Not once was the possibility of a secret ballot raised, a method that would have avoided many of the electoral problems and that was already practised in most states south of the border.[86]

It was a few days later that Louis-Joseph Papineau rose in the Assembly, pronouncing:

> As to women voting, that is something it is right to destroy. It is ridiculous, nay odious to see wives dragged to the hustings by their husbands, girls by their fathers, often even against their wishes. The public interest, decency, the modesty of the sex demand that these scandals should not be repeated any more. A simple resolution of the Chamber would exclude such people from the right to vote.[87]

This widely quoted statement has been read by historians as a general expression of the new understandings of gender and citizenship the Patriotes were articulating. Allan Greer rightly notes how little sense it made, given that most female voters were widows. He also shows how well it reflected Rousseauian ideas about gender in which "sexual disorder on the part of women, as evidenced by political self-assertion, was considered deplorable." Yet, Papineau's words effected more than a representation of such views. They also continued the very personalized Patriote attacks on Cuvillier as a traitor to the Canadien cause and the critique of his wife's vote during the 1832 by-election as a signifier of both domestic and political instability. Papineau was explicitly impugning the honour of Cuvillier and his wife in referring to wives dragged to the hustings. And Cuvillier, who was present in the Assembly at the time, was well aware of it. So, no doubt, were other politicians. Cuvillier retaliated, expressing surprise that Papineau would "accuse the women who vote of immodesty" when he had seen him "receive their votes with pleasure" while a candidate. The debate was brief. The only exchange in the Assembly on this subject was between these two men. Under attack from Cuvillier, Papineau wriggled between his language of gendered citizenship and individual critique, finally asserting unconvincingly that his were "general and not individual reflections ... I was not accusing anyone." The debate went no further. The motion to insert a clause clarifying that voting was a male right into the wider electoral reform bill was passed without amendment.[88]

It was only because other parts of the wider bill were subsequently found unconstitutional that the question of women's right to vote remained unresolved.[89] After the discontent fuelled by the deaths during the 1832 by-election had mushroomed into rebellion, repression, rule by the appointed Special Council, and the amalgamation of the largely British province of Upper Canada with the mixed but largely French-speaking province of Lower Canada, the question was again addressed. In 1849, a year after American feminists had come together at Seneca Falls seeking greater rights for women, including the right to vote, politicians put the last nail in the coffin, removing the possibility of widows and other women voting in another omnibus electoral reform bill.

I have found no evidence that the clause excluding women in 1849 was even debated.[90] Nor have I found evidence of written protests from women. I hope others do. Some women had continued to vote between the time of the 1834 attempt to exclude them and 1849. In 1844, Agathe Perrault Nowlan voted again in a Montreal election, as she had done in 1827 and in 1832. Her cousin, Émilie Tavernier Gamelin, did not. Once again the widow Nowlan chose the reform candidate – and once again she was joined by a female relative, this time her widowed sister-in-law. Other voters that year included the widow Elizabeth Bland, who had married the trader Robert Noxon in 1825. The candidate she chose in the 1844 election was George Moffatt, the virulent anti-Canadien merchant, whom, as we saw in Chapter 4, spent years agitating to transform many aspects of the Custom of Paris, including curtailing widows' rights to dower. The new laws regarding dower, passed during the period of Special Council rule, would not have influenced her own claims as a widow. For, at the time of her marriage, she had signed a contract in which she agreed to bar dower in return for keeping her own property separate and the promise of a lump sum of £250 from her husband at his death.[91]

Marguerite Paris, Émilie Tavernier, and Sarah Harrison were among the widows who engaged in colonial politics. So did smaller numbers of single women and wives. Over two hundred women attempting to vote in this colonial city of some twenty-seven thousand inhabitants may seem small. Yet, the widows and other women who stepped up to the poll over the twenty-three days of voting between April and May 1832 made up 14 percent of the voters and may have included as many as four of every five eligible widows. The women who braved the hustings in 1832 were taking advantage of a right that growing numbers of Canadiennes and new-comers had embraced alongside British constitutional government, with its elected assembly, since 1791. They followed the legacy of Papineau's grandmother who, in 1809, in an earlier bitterly contested Montreal election, voted for Papineau's father. When asked for whom she wished to vote she is reported to have stated "For my son M. Joseph Papineau, for I believe that he is a good and faithful subject."[92]

Whether they responded to bribes because of their poverty or to nationalist pleas from family and friends, or chose to vote based on deeply held political convictions, these women exposed their bodies and reputations to the crowds at the hustings. Sarah's widow's weeds or Émilie Tavernier's reputation as devout and generous may have offered them particular protection as they moved through the crowds. Male relatives and political allies may have chivalrously cleared a path for others. Whether they arrived alone or in a group, timidly or with bravado, on foot or in a carriage, their very presence at the hustings contested the masculinization of public space and of politics and their near absence in the election reporting. As a widow in the early months of mourning, Sarah also transgressed and challenged the understanding that widows should withdraw into family and the home.

Their presence at the polls in such numbers helped seal their fate. Louis-Joseph Papineau was no doubt influenced by ideas about gender deriving from Rousseau and more broadly from the growing hold of the idea of separate spheres in the Anglo-American world, as Allan Greer and Nathalie Picard have argued. Yet, the diffusion of new understandings of citizenship does not explain the timing of their decision or help interpret the minimal exchanges that occurred in the 1834 debate in the House of Assembly, when the first attempt was made to exclude women. Critical, I have argued here, were two local notables. Jacques Viger played a key role as the modern producer of knowledge who gendered the records, made the numbers known, pinned them down in statistical tables, and entered them into the public record. He contributed more information about women voting in his testimony before the House of Assembly investigating the election than did any elected politician in the brief debates in the Assembly in 1834 or 1849. Important too, especially in interpreting the brief debate of 1834, was the reaction of the Patriotes to Canadiens like Austin Cuvillier who chose to support their enemies – the bureaucrats, Tories, "the English Party." As Patriotes struggled to articulate a new vision of nation, the disloyal challenged their claim to speak for the conquered nation, exposing the fragility and constructed character of ethnicity as a boundary marker. The line between the public embarrassment of Mme Cuvillier in the newspapers and the attempt by the Patriote-controlled Assembly to remove women's right to vote in 1834 was a direct one. Only constitutional errors in other sections of the bill prevented it from becoming law at that time. Patriotes deployed gender disorder in the Cuvillier household to underline the disorder of Canadiens opting to support their opponents.

By 1849, when the new bill to remove women's right to vote passed so quietly, the economic, political, and cultural context had changed. Owning property, or renting at a specified value, ceased to bestow citizenship rights on widows. In Montreal, it became less and less likely that a labourer's widow like Marguerite Paris would own or inherit real property. In the wake of the rebellions of 1837 and 1838, the Catholic Church gained a new hegemony over institutions and Catholic citizens. Patriotes became reformers and liberals. The divisions between Canadien and others hardened into a less ethnically inclusive strand of nationalism that idealized francophone, Catholic women's contribution to the nation as mothers of large families. And the numbers of Catholic women taking vows and working as teachers, nuns, and charity workers within religious orders increased dramatically. Protestant Montreal women, as we saw, also became heavily involved as lay charity workers.

Marguerite Paris, Sarah Harrison, and Émilie Tavernier were among the last generation of women able to vote in Quebec until the twentieth century. The women of the next generation who married in the 1840s would negotiate different ways to express their political beliefs and occupy public space. The last of the voting widows whose lives I have followed, Sarah Campbell, died in Montreal in 1884 at the age of eighty-three, after fifty-three years of widowhood. By that time, a new generation of Montreal women, Protestant and Catholic, English and French speaking, were organizing to change women's rights. A year later, the prime minister raised the issue of enfranchising widows and spinsters in federal elections. In the hundreds of pages of Hansard recording the debates, women's involvement in earlier elections was not mentioned. The battle for women's right to vote again in the Province of Quebec was long and difficult. Whereas early-nineteenth-century observers had commented on Quebec as a place where wives and widows had too much power, a century later, Québécoises were generally viewed as being behind the rest of the country. Qualified Quebec women could vote in federal elections after the First World War. In 1940, Quebec became the last Canadian province to allow women to vote in provincial elections.

Some of the widows who were active in the 1832 by-elections found other ways to shape their city and contribute to their communities. Key among them were Agathe Perrault and Émilie Tavernier Gamelin, whose work is explored in the following chapter.

10

Widow to Mother Superior
Émilie Tavernier Gamelin
and Catholic Institution Building

On 29 March 1844, Émilie Tavernier Gamelin donned a grey habit, a veil, and a white headband. This was the costume chosen for the newly formed religious order that would continue her work with widows and other elderly women. Simple and plain, it projected an image that reflected the vows of poverty, chastity, obedience, and commitment to serving the poor that she and six other novices made early that morning (see Figure 10.1). Bishop Bourget heard the vows of these first nuns in the first religious community to be founded in the colony, the first for which he could claim paternity.[1] Like the widow's weeds Émilie had donned seventeen years earlier, this dark costume identified her publicly as belonging to a particular category of women whose sexuality and behaviour were regulated by strong cultural, legal, and religious codes. Widow's mourning clothes announced the ongoing bonds of fidelity, dependence, and grieving that were expected to tie women to their dead husbands for at least a year. Émilie's new habit proclaimed her embrace of chastity and her commitment to serve the Lord and to obey the male hierarchy of the church that represented him on earth. It took courage to don this particular habit, the young Édouard-Charles wrote to his father, Édouard-Raymond Fabre, on hearing of her decision.[2]

Émilie Tavernier Gamelin's name is well known in Quebec. She is one of very few Canadian Catholics to have been beatified and proposed for sainthood.[3] Over the decades following her death, her life story has been told and retold in pamphlets, books, and institutional histories by Sisters of Providence and Catholic priests. Historians have acknowledged her significance with an entry in the *Dictionary of Canadian Biography,* and the journalist and historian Denise Robillard has written a detailed biography of her life.[4] More recently, a marvellous statue of her has been installed in the Berri-UQAM metro station, near where the Sisters of Providence

FIGURE 10.1   "Mère Gamelin," reproduction of a painting of Mother Émilie Tavernier-Gamelin, 1980, by Lawrence Williams. | Providence Archives, Sisters of Providence, Montreal.

Asylum and convent once stood (see Figure 10.2). Outside, the poor and homeless still seek support.

I retell her story in this chapter for several reasons. First, she is the only woman of these two generations of marriages who went from wife to widow to nun to mother superior – a trajectory of widowhood available only to Catholics. The choices she made thus provide an example of how religious belief and spirituality supported some women after their husbands' deaths. Furthermore, her choices as a widow and then a mother superior highlight the social and religious activism practised by elite Protestant, Catholic, and, later, Jewish Montreal women of these generations, already explored partially in Chapter 3. The institutions that they built increased

FIGURE 10.2 Statue of Émilie Tavernier Gamelin, Berri-UQAM metro station, Montreal. | Artist, Paoul Hunter; Bettina Bradbury photograph.

the range of options facing sick, senile, and struggling widows and other elderly women seeking shelter and support, and offered both Catholic and Protestant women new and prominent positions in the "business of benevolence."[5] Third, her work illuminates Jean H. Quataert's argument that the significance of women's involvement in institution building and benevolence transcended charity and the social sphere, contributing materially and symbolically to the contested cultural and political work of community and nation building.[6] Finally, her story offers instructive lessons about the timing of the religious revival, usually seen as beginning among Catholics in Quebec in the 1840s.[7] The chapter explores these themes, beginning with her religious activism and activities between 1832 and 1843, then investigating Bishop Bourget's role in reshaping her work, and finally exploring the challenges she faced as the mother superior of a new religious order.

Émilie Tavernier, 1827-43: Domestic Accommodations and Religious Activism

By the time of the Montreal by-election in April 1832, Émilie had occupied three different buildings as she sought to accommodate the growing number of infirm and elderly women she was sheltering. She began, as we saw, in the home she had shared with Jean-Baptiste Gamelin on St. Antoine Street during their short marriage. Soon, this domestic space was too small. In 1830, she rented out part of that house for £18, and with the help of the parish priest secured the use of the ground floor of an old school at the corner of St. Lawrence and St. Catherine streets. Soon she was sheltering ten elderly women there.[8] The school was sixteen or so blocks east and north from Émilie's home. She went there twice a day to talk, work, sing, read, and pray with her charges. The journey took time and energy. For a while she moved into the spacious home of her cousin, friend, and fellow voter, the widow Agathe Perrault Nowlan, convincing her at one point to shelter some of the women in her own home.[9]

There was a limit to providing institutional care within such domestic settings. It was two years later, in 1832, having "resigned herself to the sacrifice of her own home," that Émilie rented a building very close to that of Agathe on the corner of St. Catherine and St. Phillip streets. This L-shaped house was more spacious, and the architecture allowed her to balance her own private living space with the needs of the elderly poor and sick women (see Figure 10.3). There was room in one wing for about twenty women. She occupied the other wing. There she could pray in silence and retain some of the trappings of her bourgeois lifestyle.[10]

The women whom Émilie took in were ill and elderly. She was especially interested in helping those with dementia and other forms of mental illness, women who had no families or whose families could not deal with their infirmities. Accounts suggest they included women who had been homeless and women who had survived only by begging. Her biographer, Denise Robillard, reports that some Montrealers were initially highly critical of her work. They belittled her as extravagant and suggested she was wasting her resources. Above all, they questioned why a young, attractive,

FIGURE 10.3 Domestic accommodations: Buildings used by Émilie Tavernier to shelter elderly and senile women, 1828–43

(a) 1823–30, 3 St. Antoine, Jean-Baptiste Gamelin's house.

(b) 1830–31, St. Lawrence and St. Catherine streets, the schoolhouse.

(c) 1831–36, St. Catherine and St. Phillipe streets, the "L-shaped house."

(d) 1836–43, St. Catherine and St. Christophe streets. Initially known as the Yellow House, this building became known as Providence House as Émilie's work expanded.

Sources: (a) Artist unknown. Album chronologique, AG-Fa1.1, 1900, Providence Archives, Sisters of Providence, Montreal; (b)–(d) From Rose-de-Lima Tessier, *Vie de Mère Gamelin* (Montreal: Eusèbe Sénécal, 1900), 29, 90. Providence Archives, Sisters of Providence, Montreal.

bourgeois widow with suitors would choose to dedicate her time and energy to elderly and senile women rather than remarrying. Later, and especially after her death, supporters would assess her refusal of marriage more positively and describe her as creating a new family to replace the children she had lost.[11]

There were indeed parallels between managing these shelters and running a family home. She bore all the responsibilities of a family head combined with those of the bourgeois wife. Just as poor widows and many working-class wives scrambled and begged to support their children, Émilie cajoled, begged, and solicited support from friends and fellow citizens to secure furniture, food, clothing, and bedding for her widows. After her cousin Joseph Perrault died, she and Agathe purchased at least five old beds, a few mirrors, and other furniture at the sale of his goods, surely for her shelter.[12] Like any other household head, she had to find ways to pay the rent and the costs of heating through the long, cold Montreal winters. Like bourgeois wives, she oversaw discipline in the home, religious instruction, and the work of domestic employees, as well as of her charges. The complex cross-currents of authority relations between women of divergent class cultures and levels of mental and physical capacity made these challenging tasks. Émilie instituted rules about language and sought to impose regular periods of prayer and meditation.[13]

Unlike most housewives, she did not undertake these tasks alone or just with the help of children or servants. Émilie drew brilliantly on her family and class networks, and especially on other Catholics for support. In 1832, she created an Association of Charity Ladies specifically to assist her. They helped in seeking food from the city's hotels and market vendors, finding clothing, and raising money in various ways. Ties of gender, family, friendship, shared religious belief, and class fuelled their social engagement. At various times, those most closely involved included two of her first cousins, the voting widows Agathe Perrault Nowlan and Marie-Claire Perrault Cuvillier, and the wives of her two brothers, Julien and François – the midwife Marie-Barbe Castonguay and Sophie Cadieux, respectively. Her first cousin once removed, Luce Perrault, was also very active. As a publisher with major connections to leading newspapers, Luce's husband, Édouard-Raymond Fabre, was in a perfect position to help them with publicity.[14] Most of these women were, as we saw in the previous chapter, closely connected to the Patriotes of the period. For these women, radical dreams about new ways to provide for the poor were not separate from the new visions of nation that were being articulated in print and in public by their male Patriote relatives. They and the early Protestant pioneering builders of nineteenth-century charities were claiming new places for middle-class women in the changing culture, society, and class relations of their city, carving out Protestant and Catholic female sectors within a sphere of social engagement.[15] Men were involved in a range of ways. Formally and informally they promoted women's activities, assisted in funding them, and provided advice and legitimation. Printed pastoral letters, and circulars, like published sermons, were, as the American historian Anne Boylan has argued, critical in legitimizing and soliciting donations to women's activities in these early years of institution building.[16]

When cholera hit Montreal just three weeks after the Montreal West by-election, Émilie was among the women who built on their previous

work and their networks of kin, class, and religion, reinforcing the identification of female charitable work with two target groups: orphans and
widows. Émilie took charge of raising subscriptions for those sick with
cholera. She joined with sixteen other lay Catholic Charity Ladies in scour-
ing the city systematically, suburb by suburb, to determine who needed assistance. In this way, they mapped out the topography of poverty at the
height of the epidemic, identifying "172 widows and 520 orphans" in desperate need. In this female-run census-like operation they echoed the
footsteps and methods that Viger had used just months earlier when he
sought to identify the city's legitimate voters.[17] Protestant women also
took to the city streets, seeking donations to help destitute women and
children.[18] Thus, these women embraced modern ways of producing knowledge and surveying the city to establish the basis of their benevolence. They
held meetings, made resolutions, and responded to the request of the city's
Sanitary Committee to distribute monies received from the governor general to those in need. Émilie temporarily sheltered some of the orphans
with her elderly women.[19] In the midst of the dangers of cholera, both
Protestant and Catholic bourgeois women responded similarly, creating
enduring new institutions to shelter both widows and children, legitimating their own presence on the streets and their authority in this sphere of
action.

In the aftermath of the cholera epidemic, Émilie focused much of her
attention on her elderly women and the challenge of supporting them. A
hand-to-mouth existence and a professed faith in Providence's ability to
provide were among the main features of these years, as of later ones. Yet,
Émilie and the laywomen who worked with her also exhibited four characteristics that Anne Boylan has argued were shared by the most successful charitable Protestant groups in New York and Boston run by women
around this period. These, she suggests, "promoted ambitious institutional
projects (a refuge or asylum), served clients who could be deemed deserving, had access to wealthy supporters and enjoyed significant political
connections."[20] Émilie's work can be assessed fruitfully through these four
aspects.

Émilie's institutions became more and more ambitious as she increased
the number of women under her care. By 1836, there were some two
dozen women in residence in the L-shaped house on St. Philip Street. She
could fit no more. That year she convinced Antoine-Olivier Berthelet, one
of the city's leading businessmen and philanthropists, to visit her shelter.
Berthelet was of the same generation as the husbands who married during
the 1820s. His father was a merchant and a doctor, and in 1822 Antoine had
married well, taking Marie-Angelique Chaboillez, of the very prominent
merchant and fur-trading family, as his wife. Berthelet became one of the

most successful of those male Canadien elite of this generation who focused their economic strategies on the land market. In 1832, he was elected
to the Assembly for Montreal East. In his two years there, he, like Austin
Cuvillier, sided with the Tories. This assured his defeat in 1834. As he
reached rentier status and could live off the revenues of his accumulated
assets, his main focus became charitable work. Leon Polio aptly suggested
that he became Bishop Bourget's "minister of finance." He was more than
that. For he and his wife, like Émilie, also started a lay institution to shelter
needy Montrealers.[21]

Berthelet agreed to donate a building and to have it renovated for
Émilie's elderly women. It was two stories high and could house up to
thirty people. The donation deed affirmed his hopes for the success of
Émilie's establishment and its goal of supporting "old, infirm women,
incapable of supporting themselves by their own efforts." The building,
known then as the Yellow House, was to be used to further this project for
as long as Émilie remained in charge. If "death, illness, infirmity, absence"
or other reasons made this impossible, the deed gave his heirs the power to
pass it on to others undertaking similar work. In this trust-like arrangement, Berthelet witnessed his confidence in Émilie's religious and charitable undertaking but stopped short of giving her any real power over the
property itself, by placing it in the hands of a Sulpician priest.[22] The new
shelter was situated near the intersection of St. Hubert and St. Catherine
streets in what was then known as the Saint Louis suburb. It became
known as Providence House. This area was becoming a new hub of Catholic institutions. In the past, the city's main Catholic establishments had
been concentrated in the old city, within close distance of the Sulpicians'
seminary.[23] Soon after his appointment as Montreal's first bishop, in 1821,
Jean-Jacques Lartigue began building the St. Jacques Church as a new
cathedral at the corner of St. Denis and Mignonne streets, with his residence next door. Émilie's new refuge was four short blocks to the east –
"almost in the shadow of the Bishop's palace." Berthelet's donation thus
moved Émilie's base far east of her previous shelters and away from areas
that were increasingly dominated by Protestant residences and institutions.
Demonstrating a sound eye for the future potential of the area, Émilie arranged to purchase land directly beside that donated by Berthelet. Her
work was now geographically within the zone of her ally the bishop and
far from that of the Sulpicians, with whom the bishopric was in almost
constant conflict (see Figure 10.4). She was playing "a hand in altering the
map of the city and in defining its meaning," as Sarah Deutsch shows
women did in later nineteenth-century Boston.[24]

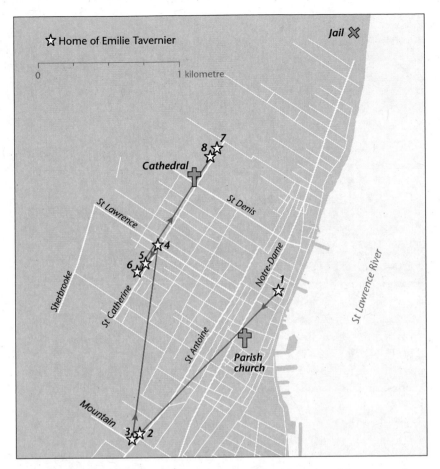

FIGURE 10.4   Locations of Émilie Tavernier's residences and homes, and Montreal's main Catholic institutions, 1800-51

1   1814-22: resided with her aunt, Marie-Anne Tavernier Perrault, St. Vincent Street.

2   1822-23: resided with her cousin, Agathe Perrault, 5 St. Antoine.

3   1823-30: home of Jean-Baptiste Gamelin, to which she moved when she married and where she took in her first elderly women, 3 St. Antoine.

4   1830-31: school used to house elderly women, St. Lawrence and St. Catherine streets.

5   1830+: home of her cousin, and co-charity worker, the widow Agathe Perrault Nowlan, St. Urbain and St. Catherine streets.

6   1831-36: sheltered up to twenty women, St. Phillipe and St. Catherine streets.

7   1836-43: "Providence House," sheltered up to thirty women, St. Catherine and St. Christophe streets.

8   1843-51: Providence Asylum, St. Catherine and St. Hubert.

Map: Sherry Olson/Eric Leinberger

Thus, Émilie secured a more substantial institution in part through her access to wealthy supporters, her ambitious project, and the particular appeal of the elderly and sick women as deserving of charity. Nor was she lacking in the fourth of the attributes that Boylan suggests characterized successful women's charitable enterprises: significant political connections.[25] Émilie and her charges moved into their new building in May 1836. A day after they were settled, Bishop Jean-Jacques Lartigue, long a close friend and confidante of Émilie, blessed the new institution and those residing there.[26] Outside Providence House, the conflicts between supporters of the colonial administration and the Patriotes escalated dramatically over the next two years. Lartigue's sensitivity to colonial injustice toward his people evaporated as Patriote ideology became more revolutionary and challenged the authority of colonial rule. By May 1837, Patriote committees were holding frequent assemblies in and around the city and calling for boycotts of British goods to further their claims for extended political rights. The governor banned public meetings. Young militant anglophone Tories aggressively displayed their Britishness and masculinity on the streets of Montreal in the paramilitary association the Doric Club. Patriote women formed their own association and, in September, Patriote males formed their own paramilitary group, the Fils de la Liberté. A month later, Émilie's brother François was at the head of one of three detachments of the Fils de la Liberté that marched close to Providence House as it filed past St. Jacques Church and Bishop Lartigue's palace protesting his edicts. In early November, the two groups clashed violently on the city streets. The governor banned military drills. Bishop Lartigue denounced insubordination to legitimate authority and threatened Patriotes with excommunication. When *curés* from the countryside asked Lartigue to request that the British government respect the rights of Canadiens, he declined, excommunicating those involved. As political difference turned first into open warfare outside the city and then to a series of military defeats, many of Émilie's family and friends were on the side opposite to her bishop and the Catholic hierarchy.[27]

François Tavernier, her brother, was among the Montrealers imprisoned in the leadup to the first rebellion. So too, as we saw, was Édouard-Raymond Fabre, along with other relatives and husbands of Émilie's friends and neighbours. François remained a prisoner until Durham released the prisoners in July 1838; he was imprisoned again the day before Christmas 1838.[28] The inside of a prison was familiar territory for Émilie. She and other Charity Ladies had been visiting women and sick and mentally ill prisoners, taking food, clothing "from the wardrobes of the rich," and words of encouragement. The authorities suspended all visits following the rebellions. Once again, Émilie's connections on both sides of the political divide, the growing acknowledgment of the importance of her charitable work, and her persuasive personality opened doors for her. She and some of her Canadienne friends and relatives were among the few Montrealers given permission to visit the Patriotes. She visited most days, usually with another widow, Marguerite Barsalou, the mother of a prominent Patriote, and sometimes with her cousin Agathe Perrault Nowlan, or with Sophie Gauvin, the wife of her cousin Julien Perrault. Other prominent Canadienne wives joined her at times. They included Adèle Berthelot, who had married Louis-Hippolyte LaFontaine in 1830. He was imprisoned briefly between November and December 1837, but with the outbreak of the rebellions he had begun to shed his earlier rabid anti-clericalism and militant pro-Patriote stand, and to demonstrate the skill at "political manoeuvre and compromise" that would lead him to political prominence in the 1840s.[29]

These women took out subscriptions in the city to raise money to help purchase tobacco, clothing, and soup and other food for the prisoners. Émilie carried letters and news back and forth between the prisoners and family members, consoled the men, prayed with them, and cajoled authorities into allowing her to take in the wife and children of at least one of the men before he was hanged for treason. This was exhausting work. In March 1838, she contracted typhoid fever and, close to death, wrote her will, leaving much to the institution she had founded and its elderly clients, but also significant property and possessions to her brother and other relatives. She recovered, convinced that she had further work to do in correcting some of her own impatience and lack of gentleness and charity, convinced also that her work should continue.[30]

In Patriote circles she became known as the "angel of the prisoners." For years, men recalled her visits with emotion. After her death, "un chroniquer" contributed to the eulogies of her life, recalling her visits as memories of those difficult years that would live for ever. The "citizens whom she visited and consoled" in their cells in the depths of the prison, he argued, became the major financial supporters of her work between then and her death.[31] This is an interesting claim, for Émilie's close links to the Patriotes preceded the rebellions, and the wives and sisters of male Patriotes were already closely involved in supporting her work as Charity Ladies. Furthermore, both before and after the rebellions, her supporters always included some Canadiens who had broken with the Patriotes.[32] The suggestion does, however, highlight how Émilie's compassionate support of the political prisoners during and after the rebellions further strengthened her identification with the Patriotes.[33] Moreover, if Providence House was indeed widely understood as closely linked to the Patriote cause, incorporating it into the power structures of the Church would hold significant appeal for ecclesiastical authorities.

Émilie's success in her early years of institution building was due to two further factors. The first was religious. From the time of her husband's death, Émilie had found consolation and spiritual sustenance in her faith and in meditating and praying to Mary, as the mother of sorrows. Religious faith, combined with her acute sense of what was necessary to achieve her goals, meant that she sought advice and approval from the male Catholic hierarchy for her projects. During the 1830s, she delicately juggled her ties to the Patriotes with her spiritual ties to the bishop, Jean-Jacques Lartigue. She also sought to maintain good relations with the wealthy Sulpicians, who could offer valuable financial support for work with the poor and sick of the city if they chose. Navigating the complicated relations between the seminary and the bishop was an ongoing challenge. Bishop Lartigue and Émilie had known each other since childhood, and they talked frequently.[34]

Without Émilie's own spiritual conviction that her work was important and institutional support, her project would likely have failed. Her actions surely support the argument of Eleanor Gordon and Gwyneth Nair that "religious belief could (and did) encourage a different even oppositional way of thinking which led to a questioning of separate spheres as formulated in terms of 'public' and 'private.'"[35] At the same time, her sense of what was needed and possible meshed with the dominant ethos of Catholic charity in which assisting the most needy of the poor was valued as a way to minimize time in purgatory, a step to personal salvation, and a Christian duty.[36]

Émilie's desire for a particular kind of religious lifestyle was a shared one, with parallels in earlier periods of Catholic revival. Like Jeanne Mance, the lay Catholic nurse, remembered as one of the founders of Montreal in the seventeenth century, and Catholic women in France at the time, Émilie, the widow Henriette Huguet-Latour, and several other of these pioneers initiated convent-like living arrangements for laywomen that served as the basis for engaged charitable works.[37] Such an alternative to marriage or taking the veil attracted young women for diverse reasons. In 1835, Émilie had been joined in her work by Madeleine Durand, a woman nine years younger than her who had learned nursing skills with the nuns at the cloistered Hôtel-Dieu and had some sewing skills garnered in local establishments. She offered to assist Émilie without remuneration for the rest of her life. More young laywomen would join in her project in the years to come.[38]

The second, final factor in Émilie's success in the years before 1844 was the property she had inherited when Jean-Baptiste Gamelin died. Her project was chronically underfunded. She had trouble securing the government grants that helped other Montreal charitable institutions, and the Sulpicians were at best erratic in providing financial help. Collecting in the streets and markets and running bazaars remained fundamental to the survival of her project. But Émilie also contributed her own assets. Without some property and financial assets she would not have been able to take in her earliest charges or purchase the property next to Providence House. In the years following Jean-Baptiste's death she carefully paid off monies owing on the apple orchard, rented out part of the St. Antoine house, and bought and sold land to fit her changing projects. Late in 1836, she sold the house on Vallée Street.[39]

Thus, between the time of her widowhood in 1827 and the end of the rebellions, Émilie created and oversaw the slow, steady growth of a successful lay enterprise caring for sick, elderly, and demented women with the close collaboration of Catholic, female family members and peers. As with Protestant women in Montreal and in other North American cities, the ambitious nature of Émilie's project, the deservingness of her clients, her access to wealthy supporters, and her significant political connections contributed to ensuring a fragile but enduring existence over those years. These complicated interrelationships would soon change.

Ultramontane Catholicism, Bishop Bourget's Dreams and Émilie Tavernier's Choices

On 29 March 1844 at six-thirty in the morning, Bishop Bourget went to Providence House to receive the professions of Émilie Tavernier and the six other women who had started their novitiate several months before her. The chapel was decorated for the occasion by the Charity Ladies. After the mass the seven novices marched in procession toward the altar, each following a young girl dressed in white, representing an orphan. These girls carried the different parts of the habits for the new nuns. As they walked forward, each novice supported one of the elderly women of the institution on her left arm. On their right, each held hands with a Charity Lady. Émilie was accompanied by the elderly widow Elizabeth Cadieux and by her cousin and godmother, Marie-Claire Perrault Cuvillier. The young girl representing an orphan was her niece. As in weddings, family members played central roles in this moment of transition. During the ritualized ceremony, Montreal's new bishop, Ignace Bourget, first formally consecrated the founding of the new community, then examined the seven novices and blessed their new habits. They retreated, then returned clad in their new costumes, received the bishop's blessing, and made their vows.[40]

The choreography and symbolism of this occasion marking these women's "symbolic removal from the path of ordinary women" were striking.[41] The virginal young girls dressed in white represented both the chastity that the new nuns would embrace and orphans as suitable future charges. The elderly women's prominent place in this pageantry reiterated the centrality of such women to Émilie's charitable work over the years since her husband's death. Indeed, among the elderly women attending the ceremony were some who had been among those she took into her home years earlier. During the ceremony, it was the elderly women accompanying the novices who placed the silver rings on their fingers, bidding them to remember that they were becoming servants of the poor. The equally visible placing of the Charity Ladies similarly acknowledged their indispensable involvement in creating and running the institution in the past, and underlined the ongoing importance of lay contributions to charity. Each Charity Lady handed the novice a gold cross, promising to work with the sisters in union and charity in the future.[42]

As with marriages, material contributions accompanied religious rituals. Émilie donated her last two pieces of property, each including a building, to the new religious order. Valued at £500, this was a much larger dowry than any other new Sister of Providence. In contrast to orders that drew their sisters from wealthy families, these women came mostly from modest origins. Of the six taking the veil with Émilie, one was admitted free; most gave dowries of from £15 to £25. Only one other contributed property valued at over £100.[43]

Émilie had spent twenty-three years of her life as a single woman, just four as a wife, fewer as a mother, and seventeen as a widow. Over her years of widowhood she had been actively engaged in religiously inspired charitable work. In this ceremony, she embraced one more fundamental transition in her social and legal identity. She became a nun. At the same time, Bishop Bourget gave her work canonical status, sealing its shift from a lay religious enterprise to one subject to the authority of the bishop and the male religious hierarchy of the city. The next day, Bourget met with the new sisters and explained the rules under which they would work, including how they should conduct elections for the official positions within the new order. The sisters elected Émilie as the community's first mother superior. Just a few years earlier, she and the Patriote canon Augustin-Magloire Blanchet had laughed together at the impossibility of such a transition in her life. He had then suggested that she was no more likely to become a nun than he was to be bishop.[44] Yet, in 1844, this was the choice that Émilie made. Her deep faith was never in question. How she would express it was. The changing political, social, and religious context of the years leading up to her decision and the success of her work with elderly women explain much about her choice. Exploring how this bourgeois widow navigated and shaped these transitional, post-rebellion years in the colony casts new light on old debates among religious and other historians of Quebec about these times.

Much had changed in her work, in Montreal, and in the colony between 1838 when Émilie was running Providence House and visiting imprisoned Patriotes and the day she took her vows in 1844. First, her work had continued to grow in size and complexity. The enumerator for the 1842 census noted that there were thirty-two people living in Mrs. Gamelin's household. The categories into which he was required to fit the residents of this dwelling that hovered between house and institution were broad ones. All were female, except for one elderly man. Nine were aged fourteen to forty-five, the rest were over forty-five. All were listed as Canadiennes and Catholic. He noted one black person in the column assigned for people of colour. Institutional records show fifty-two women there by 1843, at least two-thirds of them widows. Virtually all stayed until their deaths, which on average occurred almost ten years after their arrival.[45] Neither source indicates servants, probably because there were no paid domestics.[46] Denise Robillard suggests that the main caregivers were Émilie, Madeleine Durand, and one blind domestic assistant.[47]

Second, Émilie and the Charity Ladies embraced new money-raising activities whenever opportunities arose. Most days, she combined time with her charges and prayer time with trips into town, where she sought food and other supplies for her charges from the city's merchants and shopkeepers. The Charity Ladies visited the elderly often and assisted in money raising and securing other gifts. They held superbly successful bazaars at least once a year, selling products they had made or owned, as well as ones made by the elderly women.[48] They cultivated their relations with Montreal's wealthiest Catholics. This brought repeated donations, and knitted Providence House and its work further into the hearts and minds of the Catholics of the city. Yet, the financial situation was unremittingly precarious.

Émilie also hoped to persuade fellow Montrealers to bequeath legacies to her project in their wills. It was apparently in part to make this possible that she and the Dames de Charité decided that it was necessary to secure civil incorporation for their project.[49] Incorporation offered significant advantages, as Lori Ginzberg has argued, especially as it "was good business." In June 1841, shortly after elected government resumed, she arranged for two Patriote politicians, Denis-Benjamin Viger and Jules Quesnel, to present their petition for incorporation in the Assembly. In the previous several years, when Robert Unwin Harwood and other members of the Special Council were busy restructuring the colony's laws, such relatively mundane matters seldom made it to the table.[50] Yet, the ordinances that they instituted, and especially the Registry Ordinance, had contributed to growing uncertainty about the legal rights of married women. This could pose problems for some of the tasks taken on by the Charity Ladies. Furthermore, incorporation and the legal institutional status created through this process was increasingly understood as the safest framework for charitable associations, as well as for business enterprises.

The petition from Émilie Tavernier Gamelin and the other Charity Ladies was one of several such acts seeking to incorporate existing institutions that were agreed to one after another in the same session. Politicians agreed to incorporate the Ladies of the Roman Catholic Orphan Asylum of Montreal, the Ladies' Benevolent Society, and Émilie's Asylum for Aged and Infirm Women. Each act specified that all married women who were members of the corporation could undertake legal actions without the authorization of their husbands, "any Law, usage or custom to the contrary notwithstanding."[51] Such blanket authorizations liberated married women from their husbands' control only while acting for the corporation. As Lori Ginzberg has explained, "Corporate status circumvented married women's formal legal disabilities," bestowing "concrete, and often surprisingly broad, powers that were theoretically restricted to male or unmarried female citizens."[52] Yet, such acts concurrently reasserted wives' obligation to seek their husbands' permission in any other kinds of legal acts. Thus, the law legitimated one area of public action for wives who had already been heavily involved in such work, while recalling their legal subordination to their husbands. For Émilie and her cousin and friend Agathe Perrault as widows, or Madeleine Durand, who was single, this made no difference. The wives involved – the act explicitly named Marie-Claire Perrault, wife of Austin Cuvillier, Sophie Cadieux, Émilie's brother François' second wife, among others – were placed on the same legal footing in their membership as widows, single women, and men.[53] As prominent women with personal ties in the Legislative Assembly, Émilie, her co-workers, and her female relations were among the minority of women with access to legislators. Their new status as lady directors would soon be announced publicly in city newspapers giving notice of their meetings.[54]

At least six of the twelve women listed in the Act of Incorporation were Émilie's relatives. They included three from the generation of Émilie's parents on the Perrault side and three from her generation. Later that year, Bishop Bourget would describe her project as "one person's work."[55] It was not. These relatives, along with friends and other dedicated prominent women, inspired by their religious beliefs, had been crucial to this project that hovered somewhere between a family and an institution, between a lay religious community and an old-age home.

Neither the growth in the size and complexity of her work over the years, nor ongoing financial challenges, nor its civil incorporation on their own explain Émilie's decision to become a nun, though all are relevant. The fourth major change precipitating Émilie's decision was the radical regime change fostered in the wake of the rebellions, especially by the man who became Montreal's bishop in 1840. In April that year, Émilie's old friend and confidante, Jean-Jacques Lartigue, died. Four days later, his protegé, Ignace Bourget, was installed. Over the next four years he lauded her work, made it into a showcase model of charitable enterprise, and manoeuvred brilliantly to shape its direction. In the process he restructured Émilie's options. Bourget was installed as Montreal's second bishop while the Special Council was still sitting. From the moment of his inauguration, this astute manager, authoritarian regulator, and zealous Catholic moved quickly to occupy the vacuum left in the wake of Patriote defeat. In this climate he was able to build on the ultramontane ideas of his predecessor and apply them in a very different political context.[56] Like a right-wing government keen to establish its stamp from the very first days of its rule, Bourget extended Lartigue's initiatives and set out to reshape the morals and practices of his people.

Bourget drew inspiration from Rome and from the ultramontane version of Catholicism sweeping France. His was a conservative Catholicism, but modern and radical in its deployment of the print media, theology, and network and association building to increase his flock. His religiosity appealed to the emotions, the senses, and fear of damnation.[57] Poverty, promiscuousness, intemperance, and secularization were among the targets that fuelled his social interventions, as they did those of so many Protestant reformers of the times in Montreal and other North American and European cities. Sin and the promise of redemption through charitable work and charitable giving were among the carrots and sticks he deployed to draw Catholic Montrealers into an increasingly complex web of religious institutions and relations.

Émilie's work and reputation were critical to Bourget's early projects. Her experiment and the engagement of her female peers in this and other charitable initiatives offered a template for charitable work that might bind lay citizens, charity, and the Catholic hierarchy together in new ways. She was already working with a group that was among the most deserving of the poor. Furthermore, she had built up a rich network of support among the Catholic elite. Bourget was a farmer's son and not originally from the city. These men and women, socially Bourget's superiors, were in the habit of giving money to help fund the institution. He could maintain his insistence on the spiritual significance of the poor and poverty while securing the support of the rich.

Several aspects of Émilie's work troubled this new bishop. First, he was very aware of the minimal support she had for all the daily domestic and caring work involved. Providence House could not become the larger and more impressive project he was beginning to imagine without many more workers to care for the sick and elderly women. Second, there was little question about Émilie's religious inspiration and commitment to charitable work. She turned to her male Catholic superiors for spiritual guidance. But Émilie was also a strong-minded and determined woman whose enterprise was being run by laywomen. Furthermore, in the city and beyond, her initiatives had attracted a lot of personal attention. She was "becoming very popular in Montreal."[58] This might lead to vanity on her part. In Bourget's emerging view, such work should resound to the glory of the Catholic Church, not of particular individuals. He must also surely have considered both the pitfalls and the advantages of the association of her project with the Patriote milieu of her family and friends. Following his appointment as bishop, Bourget quickly pursued alternative possibilities. The history of the actions he took that transformed Émilie Tavernier Gamelin's life and work serves in many ways as a microcosm of the ways he reshaped his diocese and the practices of his parishioners.

Over the months after he became bishop, Bourget began forging instruments and practices that would further his broader goals. The new weekly journal, *Mélanges religieux,* spread his message. He invited the French bishop of Nancy, Mgr. Forbin-Janson, the ultramontane, anti-republican, messianic preacher then spreading his message among American Catholics, to hold retreats throughout the diocese of Montreal. These spurred lapsed Catholics into more active engagement and gave fervent Catholics renewed ways to express their faith. And with Forbin-Janson's help, he initiated temperance societies and other new associations to foster piety.[59] Then, in early May 1841, with a new, more bureaucratic structure in place to rule his diocese, he left to visit France and Rome to research ways to further his goals. It was while he was away on this long trip that the Association of Charity Ladies received its civil charter.

Bourget appears to have decided before leaving that the city's charitable enterprises should be run by nuns. In France he consulted widely, told people of Émilie's work, and tried to convince Sisters of Charity to come to Montreal. He visited convents where the sisters engaged in charitable work.[60] This was a time of intense female activist engagement in France, as in the United States and elsewhere. Hazel Mills has argued that French women's inspiration was religious but extended "far beyond the confines of the convent or parish church." Growing numbers of uncloistered congregations "spent the majority of their time in the community, teaching poor girls in charity schools, tending to the sick in hospitals or their own homes." Like Émilie and her fellow lay activists, both Protestant and Catholic, such engaged women became familiar figures on the streets of many communities. And, as in Émilie's case, some of them were initially lay communities created by like-minded women dedicated to helping the poor. Charity Ladies there too joined confraternities, held meetings for various pious reasons, and supported the work of religious orders. As in Montreal, these were often among the wealthiest wives and widows of the community.[61]

Observing the range of activities that sisters in congregations were undertaking in France added to Bourget's growing sense that nuns were the best workforce for such charitable endeavours. Equally appealing in the wake of the rebellions was the understanding that these French communities were successful counters to anti-clericalism and republicanism. He was surely also impressed by the massive increase in the numbers of women taking the veil. Mills suggests this was "the era of the nun" in France. There were around fourteen thousand nuns and novices in France in 1809. Four decades later, there were nearly five times that number.[62] In Bourget's colony, in contrast, recruitment of male and female Catholic personnel was minimal and had been falling for over a century. Marta Danylewycz reports that "the female religious population in Quebec hovered between 230 and 260" between the Conquest and the rebellions. The decline was particularly precipitous around Montreal and much of its hinterland over the early nineteenth century. Louis Rousseau and Céline Payette report that only 56 women and 38 men joined a religious order between 1830 and 1839. Between 1840 and 1844, the numbers increased to 108 women and 126 men and then to 226 women and 150 men in the following five years. Émilie and her fellow novices were among the first of these. Their ceremony signalled the beginning of a change that would make life as a nun a viable alternative to spinsterhood, marriage, and widowhood for thousands of women over the next eighty years.[63]

Fortified, inspired, and armed with new knowledge about practices and institutions in Europe, the ultramontane entrepreneur returned with a clearer sense of how he would engage the people of his diocese and transform many of their religious practices.[64] On the day of his return in the early fall of 1841, Bourget issued a circular to the clergy of his diocese, reporting on his voyage and inviting them to unite with him to implement his goals. He shared his desire to multiply the ways charity was exercised, to give a better Catholic education to boys and girls, and to bring reinforcements for this work. Begging was to be curtailed, and charitable giving extended, drawing on rules for charitable associations that he had secured from the Pope.[65] On 15 October, he invited the bishops of Boston and Kingston and Quebec's coadjutor to visit the elderly women and observe the quality of care given them at Providence House. The next week he visited again, praying with some of the elderly and meeting with Émilie

FIGURE 10.5   Mgr. Bourget, Émilie Tavernier, and the Charity Ladies, 1841. | Engraving by Edmond J. Massicotte. Providence Archives, Sisters of Providence, Montreal.

and the other Charity Ladies of the new corporation (see Figure 10.5). This was their first meeting as a corporation.

There is no indication that Bourget had shared any of his plans with Émilie or other Charity Ladies prior to his departure. He now revealed that the Daughters of Charity of Saint Vincent de Paul had agreed to come to Montreal from France to care for the elderly women. They would, he explained, require a larger building to house the sisters and their charges. The Charity Ladies were to raise sufficient funds to procure land and have a new building constructed to house the nuns. I have found no record of what these women thought of this news. They supported Agathe Perrault Nowlan when she moved that the new building retain the name "Providence," which had become so associated with their work.[66]

The next edition of Bourget's journal, *Mélanges religieux,* presented the project to create the new Providence Asylum run by religious sisters as "the cradle of an admirable undertaking," as if, as Denise Robillard suggests, this was a completely new enterprise. Eleven days after their meeting with Bourget, the laywomen of the corporation met again for their first general assembly. Previously, they had run their own meetings. Now the bishop presided. His assistant, Jean-Charles Prince, was present too, as was the Sulpician Bréguier dit Saint Pierre. They elected Émilie as the director of the new asylum. Her cousin, Agathe, was chosen as treasurer, a position that historians have noted was often assigned to widows, understood to be better able to manage finances than wives. Sophie Cadieux, her brother's wife, became secretary.[67] A few days later, Bourget sent Mgr. Forbin-Janson to visit Émilie and see her charitable work.[68]

Émilie and the Charity Ladies needed assistance to care for the growing number of elderly women inmates. The rapid movement of events surrounding their future demonstrates one thread in the "dynamism" and authoritarian control that René Hardy has argued Bourget brought to his episcopacy in general.[69] His assistance involved a major relinquishment of power for these women. Four days after Forbin-Janson's visit to Providence House, Bourget issued a mandement and pastoral letter seeking Montrealers' support of the Providence Asylum. He brilliantly set out the basis of his claims to oversee Émilie's work and by extension other charitable works, asserting his patriarchal role and claiming that, following the Scriptures, the care of widows and orphans was above all an obligation of bishops, but that such work was best delegated to faithful followers under episcopal supervision. Then he informed his readers that both the poor and the rich were particularly happy in French cities to whom God had given the present of Daughters of Charity of Saint Vincent de Paul. He represented the Charity Ladies' initiative in seeking incorporation as a sign that God's hand was at work, and described his meetings with the Ladies of Charity as if they were initiated by him alone.[70] Without naming either Émilie or Antoine-Olivier Berthelet, he described the work being undertaken by this establishment "founded in part by a rich resident of the city, and lead by a virtuous widow who had used up her modest fortune to satisfy the longing the Lord had given her to comfort elderly and infirm women." Bourget reported that new land had already been purchased and that construction would begin on an asylum large enough to house more elderly women, as well as the sisters who were expected to arrive shortly from France. He reminded Montrealers that contributing to the upcoming fundraising campaign promised well for the grace of their souls and for charitable works.[71]

Within two weeks, the fourteen Charity Ladies took to the streets to raise money for their new building, again dividing the city into sections as they had done during the cholera epidemic. As usual, they included Émilie and Agathe Perrault, as well as Adèle Berthelot, whose husband, Louis-Hippolyte LaFontaine, had recently taken up a seat in the new Assembly of the United Province of Upper and Lower Canada.[72] Bourget went door to door as well.[73] Montrealers responded well. This highly organized solicitation raised over £1,000. A month later, the women agreed to set up a subcommittee to oversee construction of the new building. Its members included their original benefactor, Antoine-Olivier Berthelet, and John Ostell. This Anglican immigrant from London, England, had arrived in the colony in 1834 and quickly established himself as a leading surveyor and architect. By 1841, he had already made a mark on the Catholic, Protestant, and civic architecture of the city. His works included the new custom house; the arts building for the new Protestant university, McGill; and the towers of the new Notre Dame Parish church. In January 1837, he had married into Émilie's extended family. His wife, Eleanor Gauvin, was her cousin, and the daughter of Marguerite Barsalou, another Charity Lady. Émilie's brother François Tavernier was the third member of the subcommittee.[74] She had visited him and his fellow Patriotes in prison. It was his turn to assist in this social project that was dear to the hearts of his wife, sister, and so many other relatives. Thus, the Charity Ladies and their friends and relations remained closely involved in funding and planning the new asylum, now under Bourget's direct supervision.

Geographically, the new asylum was even closer than its predecessor had been to the Bishop's Palace and St. Jacques Church – the cluster of buildings and personnel that historian Lucien Lemieux characterizes as the "hearth of ultramontanism in Quebec."[75] Ostell designed it. And, with consummate skill, Bourget turned it into an early jewel of his mandate. Construction began in the autumn of 1841. In May the following year, the first stone was blessed in a ceremony led by the bishop of Toronto and attended by the bishop of Kingston, as well as by many priests. The French-language newspapers of the city reported in detail on its progress. The bishop's paper, *Mélanges religieux,* dedicated attention to it in seven successive issues. *L'Aurore des Canadas* represented it as a national as well as a religious monument. Like the religiously inspired philanthropic institutions in nineteenth-century Germany that Jean H. Quataert has studied, the new asylum was becoming a "permanent memorial" that honoured communities of "patrons and clients," embedding "notions about charity and obligation, need and virtue as well as authority and responsibility."[76]

In the spring of 1843, one of the planned two four-storey wings opened. The chapel and second wing were completed gradually over subsequent years. Others were added later (see Figure 10.6).[77] Ostell's classical and very institutional architectural style contrasts sharply with the simplicity of Providence House, which the women left in May 1843, just a few months after Émilie and her fellow novices took the veil. Large and imposing in the streets of this socially mixed, predominantly Canadien suburb, it was an unmistakable symbol of Bourget's determination to provide for the poor

FIGURE 10.6 The Providence Asylum, ca. 1945. When the asylum opened in 1843, only part of the middle wing was complete. John Ostell was the architect. | Photographer unknown. Providence Archives, Sisters of Providence, Montreal, M2.38(09), AG-Ka1.1.

and to incorporate Émilie's work into a different structure of religious rule and a renewed and Catholic vision of nation and community.

What the place of Émilie would be in this new project remained unclear. She and the other Charity Ladies prepared for the arrival of the nuns from France. They implemented the new rules that the bishop deemed should regulate the daily lives of their elderly patients as well as their own activities as lay Catholic workers.[78] They continued to raise money, holding bazaars that furthered the visibility of the asylum, and enticed buyers and donors.[79] Quietly, they shared their anxiety about what the future would hold for Émilie and for themselves and this project to which they had dedicated so much time, energy, and emotion. By February 1842, Émilie's intense self-questioning had clarified her commitment to her work and to some aspects of her future. That month she privately vowed to be a servant to the poor, to give herself to God, and do what he wished of her. The vow specified that she would be "vigilant in conversation" and habits, and distance herself from luxury. Bourget retained a copy of this vow.[80]

The final impetus to Émilie's decision to take the veil came nearly a year later when Bourget learned that the French Daughters of Charity had committed to going to Algeria and Rome instead of Montreal. In the face of this serious setback, and with construction of the new convent underway, Bourget took a bold step: he decided to create a local community. All existing religious communities were offshoots of European orders. He can have had little doubt that some Canadiennes would respond to his call for novices.[81] Laywomen had shown impressive evidence of their commitment to charitable works and several women had already requested admission to the Providence Asylum as novices.[82] Quickly he set up a novitiate, chose seven women as the first novices, and placed them under the supervision of Canon Jean-Charles Prince. They included Madeleine Durand, who had been Émilie's main assistant for the previous eight years.[83]

Émilie continued to oversee the asylum's charitable work, but the spiritual direction of the novices was in Prince's hands. As the move to the new building took place in May 1843, she agonized further about her future, wondering and worrying about what she would gain and give up should she join the novices.[84] Canon Prince discouraged her from any such decision. By July, however, after intensive discussions and praying with Bishop Bourget and Bréguier dit St. Pierre, her confessor, she made the only decision that would allow her to conciliate her religious beliefs and continue to work with the elderly women in the new context of a religious community. She did not tell any of her friends or relatives that she had decided to become a nun. Perhaps she feared ridicule. Montrealers had reacted with curiosity and some derision when the first novices donned their new habit just two months earlier. After her death, Bourget claimed that she had always shuddered at the thought of wearing a nun's habit.[85]

For months, Bourget and Prince had been making arrangements for Émilie to travel to the United States to observe the ways nuns were running similar institutions there. In September 1843, she set off for New York, Boston, and Emmitsburg, Maryland, with Paul-Joseph Lacroix and her two widowed friends, relatives, and fellow Charity Ladies, Agathe Perrault Nowlan and Marguerite Barsalou Gauvin. They visited charitable institutions, prisons, and the Sisters of Charity. This order was founded by another widow, Elizabeth Seton, who had converted to Catholicism after the deaths of her husband and sister. Like Émilie, she initially founded a religiously inspired, lay community, working closely with relatives and likeminded women. As in Émilie's case, her project was ultimately integrated formally into the Church. The many parallels with Émilie's life and situation must have been striking to both Bourget and Émilie.[86]

In Emmitsburg, as in every other place that she visited, Émilie observed and asked questions. She sought out the latest theories about running prisons and institutions for the insane. Father Deluol, with whom Bourget had been corresponding to set up the visit, reported back that she had made good use of her time, listening to his advice and observing how the community there was run. Expressing his excitement at Bourget's news about the creation of a new community, he suggested that Mrs. Gamelin "would supply by practise what she does not bring of theory."[87]

Novice to Mother Superior

On her return, Émilie made her decision public and donned the new habit that the novices had prepared in her absence.[88] In assuming the clothing and the discipline of a nun, Émilie was acknowledging her submission to a new life script and to a new set of power relations. Although Bourget and Canon Prince were themselves novices in the training of novices, the preparation for taking the veil was more rigorous than anything Émilie might have learned when she planned to become a wife, or when she became a widow. And the obedience that she was expected to exhibit to her male superiors surpassed even that demanded of wives to their husbands. There were strict rules and schedules to follow, orders to obey, new devotions to learn, old habits to squash, and the ongoing work of the asylum to accomplish as well. Émilie was still in charge in many ways. She was also a novice. Her new submission to her superiors and their rules must have been particularly challenging. Soon after the novices took their vows, the asylum was integrated even more tightly into the Church's fold institutionally and through ongoing visits and spiritual supervision.[89]

Once Émilie had taken her vows in March 1844 and been selected as the first mother superior, she regained some of her former authority, but it was of a new and different kind. This transition from widow to mother superior was not an easy one for a forty-three-year-old woman to make. Perhaps if she had thrown herself into the work shortly after her husband's death, as the American widow Elizabeth Seton, whose order she had just visited, had done, it might have been easier. Émilie became a widow as a young woman aged twenty-seven, younger than some of the other women who took their vows alongside her. Over the intervening years of active social work, she took responsibility for running her life and her projects. She had always been aware of what she saw as her own failings – her love of the world, of luxury, of public recognition were all attributes that she sought to control.[90] Now, even more than before, others would be observing her closely, noting when she exhibited characteristics deemed unseemly in religious life. As mother superior she had to continue to oversee the growing numbers of elderly charges and to take the lead in all the new ventures they were encouraged to adopt. Spiritually and practically, she also had to set an example for the other sisters and for the novices.

Funding remained unpredictable. Bourget's insistence that rich Catholics give for the good of charity and their souls still involved fundraising. The numbers in the asylum grew, and the range of clients they took on expanded, so support was always needed. Sisters and charges alike continued to live on unused food or leftovers from hotels, on food donated by the sisters of the Congregation of Notre Dame, or by city merchants and shopkeepers. Sisters and those inmates who were able to do so fabricated a growing range of products and offered new services to augment resources. In addition to producing candles, soap, ornaments for churches, and goods to sell at bazaars, they began to make mattresses and clothes, to sew soutanes for priests, and to take in the washing from the Bishop's Palace around the corner. Along with the massive washing required to keep their elderly and sometimes incontinent charges clean, this washing, drying, and ironing kept sisters and able elderly women busy for much of every week. They also visited the sick, the poor, and the dying in their homes.[91]

In addition to their elderly charges, they fulfilled Bourget's dream of taking in orphans. By the end of 1844, fifty young girls were living with them.[92] Later in 1844, they also started taking in women pensioners. Unlike most of the elderly, infirm women, the pensioners paid for their board, sometimes in contractual agreements that promised care until their death in return for a sum of money. Those making significant contributions might secure their own living spaces. Among the first six pensioners, mostly single women, were several English-speaking Montrealers. They included Mary McCord, the unmarried daughter of John Samuel McCord, Montreal's prominent Anglican judge and future founder of the new Protestant cemetery. To the chagrin of this arch-Anglican family, she had converted to Catholicism. She worked with the Charity Ladies distributing soup to the poor. Life within this Catholic institution offered her, she wrote, the chance to "die in the Roman Catholic faith which I embraced with conviction and in the bosom of which I have had the good fortune to live." She shared her family's commitment to charitable giving. When she died, she left her wealth to a range of Catholic communities and institutions, including the Providence Asylum.[93]

Over the next few years, Émilie accepted further responsibilities. These included caring for aged and infirm priests. After Édouard-Raymond Fabre reported on the "giant steps" the institution was making to his son, Édouard-Charles, at the time he was contemplating becoming a priest, he joked that he might end his days there. The £50 that these priests each agreed to pay annually for nursing and domestic care helped stabilize the finances of the institution. As with other endeavours, it also added to the workload of the sisters and other staff. Two initiatives responded to the ever-increasing domestic labour requirements of this rapidly growing institution. First, the congregation began to accept women as *filles séculières,* women who did not take vows but lived in the institution and did domestic work. They also sheltered young women new to the city who were seeking work as domestics. While they awaited a placement, they honed their domestic skills helping the sisters and the *filles séculières* with the washing, cleaning, and other daily tasks.[94]

Two other ventures in 1846 extended the work of the Sisters of Providence geographically beyond Montreal. Several sisters began caring for mentally ill patients in an old farm at Longue-Pointe. And they agreed to take over the direction of an institution similar to theirs started by lay Charity Ladies across the river in La Prairie. Word of Émilie's work spread. In August 1849, she oversaw the opening of a third house in Saint Elizabeth, some sixty miles north of Montreal. In October, a fourth opened at Sorel, southwest of the city. In these towns, local Catholics sought schooling for their children and the social assistance for which the Sisters of Providence were becoming well known in the colony and beyond.[95] These were the first of a series of rapid geographical expansions that would eventually see the Sisters of Providence take part in the colonization of the Canadian and American West.

By 1850, the bishops of Oregon, Quebec City, and Toronto and a *curé* in New Brunswick had all wondered if Émilie could send Sisters of Providence to work in their communities. Bourget deflected such requests, insisting on the protocol that the Grey Nuns had to be approached first. The Sisters of Providence were created, he reminded his Toronto colleague, "only to gather the crumbs that fall from the tables of the old communities."[96] In his public pronouncements he waxed more and more eloquent about the communities of saintly women as a "ministry of women, elevated and sanctified by Our Lord ... to be the glory of the Church and the consolation of its poor."[97] Bourget blended public praise with a harsh and demanding rule over this new community and its mother superior. This, combined with geographical expansion and new responsibilities, added to the challenges Émilie faced daily as mother superior.

Of these projects, care of the mentally ill was an area in which Émilie was particularly keen to participate. Her long experience working with patients with dementia and other psychiatric disorders had convinced her that Montreal needed a better solution than sending them to Beauport, the only major mental asylum located far away, near Quebec City. Émilie determined to seek state support for this project, which she saw as a collective social responsibility. In 1848, her old friend's husband, Louis-Hippolyte LaFontaine, was back in power as attorney general and prime minister in the first Reform ministry following Lord Elgin's acceptance of responsible government.[98] Émilie requested that the government build and furnish an institution at Longue-Pointe, paying the Sisters of Providence £40 rent annually for their work until it was ready. She promised to provide enough sisters to care for up to thirty patients and sought support for two sisters and a priest to go to Boston and Baltimore to educate themselves about how the Americans were dealing with the insane. In preparation, Émilie returned to New York and Boston to visit the Sisters of Charity in May 1850. That same year, she supported the work of another sister who was learning the latest techniques for assisting children and elderly people who could not hear or speak. By 1851, classes for such children were being held at the asylum.[99]

These new undertakings were all added in the seven years after Émilie took her vows and assumed the administrative and spiritual responsibilities of a mother superior. In that period, the number of elderly women helped at any one time had increased from forty to around seventy. They included women who were blind, deaf, "mad," subject to fits, and more generally aged and infirm. By the early 1850s, there were also some seventy orphans in the asylum, thirty to forty women paying pensions, and around twenty aging priests. Nearly fifty women had taken their vows, and most years there were about fifteen novices and ten postulants.[100] Such giddy institutional growth and diversification would have been a challenge for any leader. Émilie was in charge of seeing that the diverse material and spiritual needs of these different women were attended to, and she cared profoundly about doing so. She sought to personally attend to the needs of each elderly woman and to each novice seeking to take her vows. Balancing the care of their charges with the rigid rules that their superiors imposed on them and on the institution was an ongoing challenge for the sisters.

When typhus hit the city in 1847 and cholera spread again in 1849, Sisters of Providence and the Grey Nuns were among those who cared for the sick in the immigrant sheds. Maintaining the schedule of prayer and care that was expected was virtually impossible. Many sisters fell sick and were cared for in the asylum by the orphans and Charity Ladies. Bishop Bourget applauded the sisters' sacrifices. Yet, nothing was more important to him and his coadjunct Prince than following the rules. The rules they had chosen to train the novices and set the daily rhythms of the congregation were in many ways better suited to contemplative orders than to the active, engaged social work that the Sisters of Providence espoused.[101] In their capacities as religious patriarchs of the congregations, these men insisted on overseeing the smallest infractions and criticizing personal failings. Mothers superior, sisters, and novices alike were expected to crush all spontaneity and public gaiety and to submit utterly to the wishes of their God, as translated by these two men. Sisters were caught between an authoritarian structure of rule and the need to be flexible in providing care.

Denise Robillard and other biographers have eloquently chronicled the conflict between Émilie's spirituality rooted in service to the poor, simplicity, and confidence in Providence and these harsh relations of rule. Both Prince and Bourget were new at overseeing the training of nuns. They worried about making mistakes; sought to eliminate popular songs, jokes, and fun; and demanded absolute obedience and submission. They mistrusted Émilie's past as a middle-class wife and mother and sought to eradicate memories of that time of her life that might muddy her vocation. They interpreted the very qualities of persistence and conviction that had led to her success as evidence of vanity and worldliness. At one point, Canon Prince required that she remove the painting of her and her husband made soon after their marriage from the new asylum, judging that she was too attached to it. Later, he insisted that she had to place locks of hair that she had saved from each of her three dead children out of her sight in the place were she would be buried. In retreats, confession, and pastoral visits, the two men highlighted her spiritual failings, while to outsiders they spoke of the project with pride.[102]

Émilie struggled with the conflicting impulses of her faith and spirituality, her desire to see her life work succeed, the challenges of the new demands for self-rule, and the need to set an example in the community. In her written self-examinations, she spoke of how hard she found the conduct of her superiors toward her. In her prayers, she worried about going mad or having to leave the community to save herself. At times she doubted her vocation. Yet, she always drew comfort and eventually calmness from meditating on the Good Mother of Seven Sorrows. She determined to govern with gentleness and charity toward the faults of others, as well as "blind obedience" to her superiors.[103]

Émilie's problems were not only with her superiors, though their rigidity accentuated them. A few of the sisters, trained in their religiosity by Prince and Bourget to interpret any deviation from prescribed patterns as cause for alarm, began to complain to the bishop about Émilie during the typhus epidemic. Resources were stretched thin, sisters were sick and dying, normal life was disrupted, and the workload for those in the asylum was heavy. Soon the bishop was mentioning "murmurs" in the community. From the accusatory letters of three of the sisters written behind Émilie's back, and his own interviews and observations in the community, Bourget began to develop a listing of irregularities and problems in the congregation. Between September and October 1847, he listed fifty-seven indictments: Émilie sought to keep too much control in her own hands; she desired the esteem of the world too much; there was so much work to do that religious observances were neglected; silences were not being observed; the novices were not being trained properly, nor kept sufficiently apart from the sisters; and so on. Handwritten first in September 1847, then elaborated over the next few months and presented to her later that year, these indictments precipitated a profound sense of failure in her. At one point, like a husband threatening separation, Bourget petulantly threatened to cut off relations with the congregation.[104]

Yet the bishop needed her work, and Émilie negotiated the conflict among herself, her superiors, and her beliefs deftly, drawing them back on side in the only way that was politically or religiously possible for a woman and a nun. She humbly accepted their critiques and promised greater humility, obedience, and self-searching. In her own reflections and resolutions, she critiqued her excessive concern with herself, her lack of fervour, and her excessive occupation "with the temporal needs of the House" over "the Spiritual." Complaints resurfaced again in April 1851, though this time Bourget appears to have responded wisely, consulting each nun privately, and following up with a ten-year overview of the community's growth and challenges.[105]

For years, Émilie had suffered from stomach problems. These years of dissension and the conflicting demands of overseeing the convent and caring for those in the asylum and for those suffering from poverty, typhus, cholera, and other illnesses in the city took their toll. Yet, in September 1851, Émilie insisted on visiting all the houses that she had founded outside the city, despite a new outbreak of cholera. On 22 September, in a gesture acknowledging both the difficulties she had been facing and her remarkable competence, Bourget allowed her to chair the council meeting without the supervision of a male religious superior. The next night, she fell ill with cholera. Within ten hours she was dead. To avoid the risk of contamination from cholera, there was no public funeral. Émilie was quickly buried the next day in the chapel of the Providence Asylum.[106]

Immediately after the hasty funeral service, Bishop Bourget spoke to the sisters about Émilie's life, using its example to teach the lessons he wished them to learn. He insisted on her virtues and acknowledged her strengths and contributions, as well as her spiritual faith, struggles, and pain over the discontent in the community. She was, he reminded them, a widow who might well have remarried yet chose instead to work with the most neglected of widows. He frankly outlined the difficult situation he had placed her in when she thought she could lead the new community yet remain "in the world." But he also portrayed her as a bourgeois woman who was used to being obeyed and had trouble with the required qualities of humility and obedience.[107] He was not wrong, of course. These were the critiques that Émilie had often made of herself. However, without those characteristics, it is hard to imagine how she could have overseen the dramatic expansion of her work or balanced the spiritual, administrative, and social challenges of her job. Without her bourgeois contacts, her political connections, and Montrealers' faith in her charity, she could not have secured the significant material support from elite Catholics that made the work possible.

In the twentieth century, Catholic authorities decided that Émilie's life as wife, widow, mother superior, and charity worker provided an instructive model of charity, humility, and simplicity demonstrated through a life lived in dedication to the needy, and initiated the process of sainthood.[108] Her widowhood is instructive for historians in other ways. She shared with religious widows of all beliefs the solace that faith offered in dealing with the death of loved ones.[109] Widows' disproportionate involvement in religion and in religious activities has been noted by historians of widowhood. Faith also offered widows the hope of reunification with dead husbands and children. When close to death in 1838, a vision convinced Émilie that her husband was "amongst the number of the blessed." For the rest of her life she struggled with her failings, in the hope that these would not prevent her eventually joining him.[110] Yet, Émilie practised her religious belief very differently from the inward-looking "conjugal spirituality" in France that Agnès Walch and Scarlett Beauvalet have described, in which Catholic widows engaged in ongoing spiritual, loving relationships with dead husbands, who became their intercessors with God for a final reunification. Nor do her choices mesh with the domestically focused piety that Marguerite Van Die argues supported evangelical women of the period, especially after family deaths.[111]

Émilie's was an engaged faith expressed through what the abbé Bourassa described as "charity in action" and the historian Jean Quataert has called "religion of the deed."[112] Her commitment to social activism was shared by other Catholic and Protestant widows, and by growing numbers of middle-class and elite women expressing their faith through good works. Widows were particularly prominent among the Catholic women of her time who reshaped the city's institutional landscape. Several others became nuns and even mothers superior in these years of rapid institution building.[113] Widowhood liberated some bourgeois women from both the authority and the domestic demands of husbands, allowing them to dedicate much of their time, energy, and often property to charitable work. In this work they built important community institutions and, as Ann Fior Scott and others have argued, also nurtured business and administrative skills and self-confidence.[114]

Historians of Protestantism have tended to associate such charitable initiatives with evangelical revivals. This ignores the parallel movements among Catholic women in France, Ireland, Quebec, and elsewhere. It also ignores the appeal that female Catholic charity could hold for Protestants.[115] Several years after Émilie's death, Anna Jameson, the English crusader for women's rights who had spent a short time in Upper Canada in the 1830s, published a book that argued that such "Sisters of Charity" were needed in all faiths. She spoke glowingly of the model that charity-oriented nuns offered, suggesting that benevolent Protestant women follow their example as a way to a "more equal and natural apportioning of the work that is to be done on earth."[116]

Émilie's faith and commitment to engaged, charitable work led eventually to her taking the veil. Life in a convent clearly offered an alternative to lay widowhood, just as Marta Danylewycz has argued it did to marriage or spinsterhood. In the history of Quebec and of Catholicism, this was a well-travelled trajectory, and one that Émilie was aware of as she reimagined her life. Her own patron saint, Émilie Césarée, had taken the veil after the death of her husband, St. Basile. In taking her vows, she echoed previous generations of widows whose choices had shaped the early colonial history of New France.[117]

Émilie's institution building occurred within a historically specific colonial and urban context. The timing "of a particular turn to philanthropic work in a society is a complicated matter," suggests Jean H. Quataert.[118] Jean-Marie Fecteau has called our attention to the ways "certain elements of the clerical elite" were able to "invent a specifically Catholic mode of management of the social in a modern world" in nineteenth-century Lower Canada/Quebec.[119] Historians of Catholicism in Quebec have debated about the roots of the expansion of religious involvement and transformation of devotional practices in the wake of the rebellions. Some have highlighted the visit of the bishop of Nancy in 1841 as key to accelerating changes in religious practices. Others have insisted on a more top-down campaign of social control and acculturation exemplified best in the person of Ignace Bourget after he became Montreal's bishop in 1840. Still others wisely seek to transcend this over-dichotomized debate. The timing of the religious activism of Émilie Tavernier and her contemporaries, both Protestant and Catholic, suggests it would be helpful for historians to pay more attention to the earlier years of the century. Montrealers and other Canadiens were practising their own version of devout social work well before the bishop of Nancy started his tour of charismatic preaching, or Bishop Bourget began instituting new devotional practices and associations. In the 1820s and 1830s, bourgeois, religiously inspired women and devout men initiated changes in the city's institutions and the delivery of social services that reflected their gender and class interests and their religious and political hopes.[120] The success of Émilie and the Charity Ladies during in the 1830s offered a template of the ways lay Montrealers could be drawn into the Church. But her individual success, its widespread recognition, and her close connections to the Patriotes also made her work troubling for Church authorities. Bourget needed such works to be part of his collective project, and he needed them to be seen as part of Canadien nation building. In diverse ways he struggled for paternity of the project. Like the leaders of other established denominations whom Anne Boylan describes as building on the "growth of women's collective activity," Bourget knew how to "employ womanpower in the cause of denominational ascendency."[121]

Several women's historians have underlined how the initiatives of Émilie Tavernier and other early-nineteenth-century institution builders were incorporated into the ultramontane project and have argued that laywomen were pushed aside in the process.[122] There is much truth in this interpretation. Yet, these arguments seem to me to minimize the ongoing involvement of laywomen, Catholic as well as Protestant, and to give short shrift to women's faith, belief, and spirituality. Émilie was swept into Bourget's ultramontane project, so that her only option if she wanted to remain centrally involved became to assume the habit of this new kind of nun. Her life story might well be read as a microcosm of the rise of ultramontanism in Quebec, with the new options and constraints it offered Catholic women. Yet, Émilie also embraced that transition with both pragmatism and piety, perhaps with more experience than theory, as the American bishop she visited had remarked to Bourget. And her new situation as a mother superior also offered her considerable power to implement her vision of caring for growing numbers of the elderly and infirm women of the city, as well as for orphans, the disabled, and the mentally ill.

Émilie's work left enduring institutions that continued to grow and expand geographically over the century following her death. It left significant architectural traces, national civic monuments, on the landscape of Montreal. Alongside her Catholic and Protestant peers she extended the range of institutional options available to elderly and infirm widows and other elderly of the city. The Sisters of Providence was the first congregation to focus explicitly on elderly and infirm women, and they remained known and sought after by the city's sick, lonely, and poor widows. In 1859, at age sixty, Marie-Anne Séné sought shelter, ten years after the death of her husband. So did Adelaide Bebel in 1872 at the age of seventy-three, eighteen months after she become a widow. We return to their stories in Chapter 12, after exploring the diverse ways other widows managed to support themselves and their children.

11

Patchworks of the Possible
Widows' Wealth, Work, and Children

"I hope dear Caroline that your future may be far more bright than your past has been and that you may have all the comfort in your children you can derive." This wish, with its acknowledgment of the difficulties of marriage breakdown, was sent to Caroline Scott by her uncle in 1861, around the time of her separation from the notary, Thomas John Pelton.[1] When Pelton died of heart disease at the age of forty-six two years later, in June 1863, Caroline faced widowhood with only a minimal claim at best on his estate, compared to Émilie Tavernier, Luce Perrault, or Hannah Lyman. Yet, she possessed significant privileges and personal strengths compared to Maria Mitchell, Marguerite Paris, and many other widows. She had some material wealth of her own, secured as her separate property at the time of her marriage.[2] Thomas Pelton had promised Caroline a one-time payment of £100 instead of a dower in their marriage contract, due within three months of his death, though whether she would ever secure this is unclear.

Furthermore, unlike Émilie Tavernier, Caroline had surviving offspring. And, in contrast to Maria Mitchell, who was "wholly deprived of the keeping and comfort" of her children following her failure to have a say in their futures, Caroline had retained authority over her six children.[3] Although her two youngest had not yet begun school when she became a widow, Carrie, her eldest, as we saw, was already earning as a teacher and sending home money. In contrast to Maria Mitchell, Caroline, like Émilie Tavernier, had a strong kin-based network. Her ties to her siblings and their spouses who lived in Montreal were especially close. Her own family and her relatives through marriage were solidly located in the city's professional middle classes. They supported her and her children emotionally, socially, and possibly financially, taking them into their homes for visits,

FIGURE 11.1   Mrs. Pelton, Montreal, ca. 1870. Caroline was around fifty-one when she had this photo taken. She had been a widow for six years. The image conveys her determination and resilience as a middle-class, middle-aged widow. Note her black clothing and white collar and cap. | William Notman, photographer, silver salts on paper mounted on paper, albumen process. McCord Museum, Notman Photographic Archives, I-42943.1.

arranging outings, and writing letters before, during, and after her separation and widowhood. At forty-five, Caroline was middle-aged and apparently healthy and resilient. Even before her husband died, the same uncle praised her "active cheerful mind under appalling difficulties" and her "glorious ability" to surmount difficulties.[4] Finally, her time as a separated wife had in many ways served as an apprenticeship in the single parenting and challenges of self-support that characterized the lives of most of the women who were widowed while they still had dependent children. The image of her shown in Figure 11.1, taken at William Notman's studio six years after she became a widow, captures her resilience and strength of character.

Caroline faced widowhood as a middle-aged, middle-class woman with hopes for a middle-class future for her children. She possessed more resources than most widows, yet no obvious means to secure a middle-class income. Lisa Wilson has suggested that for widows in colonial Philadelphia, retaining a middling status was less common than financial comfort or "real distress."[5] Caroline's location financially and culturally on the continuum between wealthy elite widows, whose husbands had successfully provided for their support, and poverty-stricken labourers' widows makes her history a useful entry point to explore the patchwork of possibilities that widows stitched together as they renegotiated their relationships with children, other family members, the city, and the economy as the gendered survivors of marriage in the years following their husbands' deaths.

Whereas the previous two chapters focused on widows exercising political rights and building charitable institutions, this one explores questions of family and economics. It explores aspects of the financial and family situations and the money-raising and residential choices and possibilities of Montreal widows that are visible in censuses, city directories, and family papers. I move between focusing a zoom lens on Caroline and other widows from the two generations of marriages who were still alive by the 1860s and using a wide-angle one to look more broadly at widows in the city, especially through the censuses of 1861 and 1881, to capture the diverse patchworks of practices that widows deployed to establish or support their children and themselves. By then, some of these women had been widowed for decades, some were newly widowed, and some were still married.

Widows' Assets: Children, Their Work, and Their Futures

Wives and widows who survived into the 1860s had married in an artisanal and commercial city. They grew old and negotiated widowhood in an increasingly modern, industrial, and expanding urban context.[6] Thomas John Pelton's death in 1863 added Caroline to the 3,400 or so Montreal women identified as widows on the sheets filled out by the census enumerators two years earlier. The census takers also identified some 1,060 widowers. This was the first time that a Canadian census had distinguished the widowed from the married or single population. By 1861, those women who, like Caroline, married in the 1840s were mostly in their forties and fifties. Those from the 1820s generation who were still alive were in their sixties and seventies. Even the controversial published results of the 1861

LATOUR.

3 Evans Mrs. S
3 Rice W., of Smith & Cochran
7 Wait George
8 Wilson W., messenger, bank
8 and 10 Wilson Mrs. William,
    boarding house
9 Stethem Wm. G., bookkeeper
9 Espied Arnold, upholsterer
11 Sowdon Frs. M., bookkeeper
12 Pelton Mrs., wid Thomas
12 Hogan J., commission merch.
14 Prior Mrs., wid James
15 McManus Francis, carpenter
16 Lemoine G. P.
17 Simpson G., carpenter and joi.
17 Smith Joseph, turner
18 Doyle Mrs., wid Jas., washer w
    Delsel James, carpenter
22 Smith Albert, cattle dealer
24 Lee Samuel, servant
    Hedge Mrs., wid Samuel, off
      Radegonde
    Yates John C., commission agt
25 De Lorimier Tancr. C., advoc.
25 Donaldson Wm., laborer, r
25 Kennedy James, coachman
27 Folsom John R., of Smith &
      Cochrane
27 Fitzgerald John, brassfinisher
29 Bulmer John, builder
    Veit F., jun., n Zion church
    Veit Frederick, professor of
      music, near Zion church
    Akin J., of Akin & Kirkpatrick

FIGURE 11.2   Caroline Scott Pelton, Latour Street listing, 1864-65. Note the ways widows are referred to by their husbands' names, and as "Mrs." or "wid," whereas men's occupations are listed. | Bibliothèque et Archives nationales du Québec, *Lovell's Montreal Directory,* 1864-65, 63.

census revealed that in Montreal, as elsewhere, widows vastly outnumbered widowers. This was largely because, as we saw in Chapter 6, men remarried more often and more quickly than women. Among women in their forties, as Caroline Scott was, around 14 percent were widows. Among those in their fifties, over a quarter were widowed, while widows predominated among those in their seventies and eighties. When the more reliable census was taken in 1881, Caroline had been a widow for nearly twenty years. The number of widows identified in Montreal had doubled to over 6,700. There were fewer than 2,300 widowers. Among women in their sixties, as Caroline was by then, 43 percent were widows and 43 percent were wives.

Among the women in their eighties, the age of most women from the first cohort of marriages who were still alive, over 70 percent were widows.[7]

Widows lived on virtually every street and city block, as the pages of the city's annual directories made clear (see Figure 11.2). Some sources and conventions made them more visible than widowers. No man was ever listed as a widower, or by his deceased wife's name in a census or city directory, as wives usually were. In their sheer numbers, widows were embodied reminders that life was uncertain, marriage fragile, and illness and death unpredictable. They remind us too that female-headed households are not new. Nor are many of the challenges that women face as, depending on their age, wealth, and other resources, they struggle to keep families together, to support themselves and their children, and to maintain dignity as women managing without men.[8]

Determining what resources widows had to live upon is challenging. As we have seen, promises made in marriage contracts and wills and widows' claims on community property or dower interacted with the wealth that individual men or collaborative couples had accumulated to set a baseline for widows' standards of living. These varied widely in their amounts and in the particular configurations of patriarchy that they structured. The liberal patriarchal practices of Montreal's elite left widows in vastly different situations. Constance Hannah Hart started widowhood with a lump sum of £1,000 – ten times that promised Caroline Scott. Oliver Wait had guaranteed Caroline Campbell an annual income of £100, whereas Catherine Farquhar was sheltered from both residential disruption and any need to earn additional income, given Dr. William Sutherland's bequests of $6,000 annually, a house to live in, carriages, and her $300 annual dress allowance. The collaborative patriarchy opted for most frequently by Canadien artisans in marriage contracts and wills left some widows who were the tutors of their minor children either with community property intact, if reduced once debts were paid, and, if properly registered, a stipulated dower. Others started with pretty well nothing when they chose to reject the community, as Scholastique Bissonnet did. The customary patriarchy of the law set the economic baseline of most widows' financial situations, given the shrinking proportions making marriage contracts.[9] Here too, what that meant for widows varied dramatically. Marguerite Paris was able to retain the one-room, wooden house that she and her husband had purchased during their marriage, and controlled it as owner of half and tutor to her daughter. This made her a rather privileged widow, but she would have to find other ways to deal with the issue that Olwen Hufton identified as critical years ago: how to make up for the loss of the deceased husband's earning capacity.[10] This was not a problem for Hannah Lyman. She also inherited half of all the property accumulated during her marriage with John Easton Mills and was officially responsible for the rest as her minor children's tutor. Mills's careful investments meant that Hannah and the children were able to live off income generated through a range of good investments and business decisions. She could turn to her business-savvy brothers for advice.[11]

Most widows had to supplement whatever assets they retained after their husbands' deaths. They countered fears of managing, of hunger, illness, losing their shelter or their children, and of being "driven into the streets," by pulling together their own particular patchworks of possibility, framed by their wealth, their health, their skills, and their family situation.[12] The visibility of income-generating or saving strategies varies. Most sources mask much about widows' work, investments, and other sources of support.[13] There is no simple way, as other historians have observed, to "determine exactly how rich or poor each widow was."[14] All but the very wealthy and the minority left with sufficient income to live upon stitched together a patchwork of practices rather than relying on any single source of support. They relied in part on resources and skills honed earlier as wives, but added new fabric and sewed new seams depending on what was possible for them.

Possibilities were financial, social, and cultural, shaped by customs rooted in class, religion, and culture. What Caroline Scott would envisage as possible was shaped by her middle-class values as well by as her financial needs. The liberal, patriarchal organization of property chosen by Caroline Scott and Thomas Pelton left Caroline in charge of her own separate property. She may or may not have received the lump sum offered instead of a dower in their marriage contract. That £100 was well below the £788 5s. that Gillian Hamilton has calculated was the average promised by professional husbands choosing separate property in these marriage contracts.[15] It was more than the annual wages of most labourers and, in the 1860s, around the amount a fairly skilled worker might have hoped to make yearly in this industrializing city. But this was not to be an annual income. It was a one-time payment. And Caroline was the widow of a professional, not a craftsman, skilled worker, or labourer. Just three months before Pelton's death, she had rented "a nice two story wooden house." It was costing her fully half that amount – "an immense £50 a year." She had found it impossible to secure anything suitable at the £30 she hoped to pay.[16]

In late 1861, while Caroline was a separated wife and not yet a widow, her letters to Carrie expressed her gratefulness to her daughter for money she sent. It arrived "quite safely yesterday afternoon," she reported and expressed her pleasant surprise "at the amount, only expecting about half that sum." She planned to use the money later that afternoon to pay the rent.[17] A few months later, she again thanked Carrie for a letter that included another "welcome enclosure," "just in time for the rent too." Gently acknowledging her dependence on her daughter's regular contributions, and sharing the worry about paying rent that so many widows experienced, she told Carrie, "I am always anxious when I do not receive your letter on Saturday, knowing you would not disappoint me if you could avoid it." Anxieties about paying the rent and indebtedness to landlords were not new for many women, but in the absence of a male breadwinner, they took on greater proportions.[18]

Letters were a vital link between Caroline and her eldest daughter after Carrie began teaching in the Ottawa district in 1861, probably after her father left Montreal. Carrie remained there for several years after his death in 1863. Caroline's letters reported in detail on the health and activities of Carrie's younger siblings, as well as of aunts, uncles, nephews, and cousins in Montreal and elsewhere. They transmitted motherly advice and cautionary tales for this young teacher in her first job. Their exchanges nurtured the emotional ties between this lone mother, the children at home, and Carrie, while providing the main medium through which Caroline continued the practical training for life and marriage that most middle-class mothers instilled on co-resident daughters once they completed their schooling.[19] She reminded her daughter to be "particular" about whom she went out walking with, yet also insisted that she did not wish her "to have less amusement than you have." Caroline supported her eldest's attempt to stay out of local quarrels, reminding her that as a teacher she was a "public character." She pushed her to improve her French and to sing in the choir, and mingled reports on local marriages, births, and deaths with accounts of her sewing, family outings, and card games.[20]

Carrie replied to her mother with news and with the money that helped pay the rent. Children's earnings, as historians have long shown, were critical components of working-class family economies and of widows' economic and support systems.[21] Caroline's cautious pleasure on receiving money from her daughter remind us that children's earnings were also important for many middle-class widows whose husbands died leaving insufficient assets to replace their lost incomes. The letters between Caroline and Carrie are powerful reminders too that the ties between widows and their children were emotional as well as financial. Children were sources of worry and of support, as Josette Brun observes in her study of widows in New France. Widows of all classes took on responsibility not just for the day-to-day oversight of surviving, dependent children but also for social reproduction in the long run – for what Quebec's prominent family historian Gérard Bouchard describes as transmitting advantages to the next generation. Some did so guided by provisions in wills and marriage contracts.

Most shouldered this responsibility alone or with the help of friends and kin. Husbands' deaths interrupted urban cycles of skill transmission as well as those of property accumulation.[22]

Urban widows faced a different array of challenges in overseeing their children's futures than those captured in Bouchard's rural model, in which success was measured by establishment on land. What constituted success for city children is slippery to assess. It varied with widows' individual dreams, their class position, their means, and their family situation. For some, especially early in the century, the lure of land ownership as security remained the ideal solution. In 1830, the soldier's widow Susanna Agnew was struggling to raise her four small children in Montreal on a pension of £36 and an additional £18 per annum. In a petition to the governor general, she shared her hope to leave the city before the children contracted bad habits and to establish them on land where they could develop "those habits of industry which alone in this country can render them independent." Expressing her concern about their future, especially should she too die, she requested "a grant of land, however small," to "build a small house and cultivate a garden, the produce of which, with land to support a cow and a few sheep." Home ownership offered an urban equivalent, as Richard Bushman has observed, though this was becoming harder to achieve. Even raising urban offspring through childhood "to puberty," as one of Caroline Scott's brothers put it, or to adulthood, should surely figure among the measures of successful reproduction in the city.[23] Securing food, shelter, and schooling suitable to their class, and marriage to a good provider or to someone socially equal or superior for girls, and a trade or profession for boys were others.

Caroline Scott and Thomas Pelton's children were aged two to seventeen when their father left them, two years older when he died. Godfrey, Caroline's only son, was fifteen when his father died. Caroline sought to provide him with the schooling and work experience that might allow him to achieve a middle-class lifestyle. One of her daughters, Maria, was frequently ill. But it was Godfrey's future that surfaced as of most concern in surviving family letters from these years. She tried to place him in the High School of Montreal, drawing on connections within the Anglican community to get a letter of recommendation from the bishop. Family members concurred that this would improve Godfrey's opportunities.[24] There is no evidence that he attended.[25] Two years later, Caroline reported to Carrie with delight that she had found him an "excellent situation" with Crathern and Caverhill, hardware and metal merchants. They were taking him on trial in March, and would engage him for five years if they were satisfied. They offered him £15 for the first year, then £10 each year after. Caroline expressed relief that he liked it "very much so far." It would, she reported, in words that hint at her anxiety about his future, be "the making of him."[26]

Thus, Godfrey Pelton began to move in those lower circles of the mid-nineteenth-century business world, where, with good placement and diligence, some young men might hope to work their way up. Godfrey apparently lived with his mother over the next fourteen years. The small amounts he received during his apprenticeship meant he could contribute only minimal amounts initially to the expenses of running the household. He was twenty-two when the 1871 census was taken. In 1873, aged around twenty-five, his name was listed for the first time in Lovell's city directory. It appeared below Caroline's. That year he was identified as a clerk, two years later as a commercial traveller. In 1876, he married and established his own, separate household. By 1877, all of Caroline's children except the second youngest had married. The girls' husbands were all merchants.[27] Over her first fourteen years of widowhood, with economic contributions from her children, some assets of her own, and moral and probably financial support from her own siblings, Caroline had overseen her children's establishment within the middling classes.

Elite widows, better endowed with annuities, dowers, or real property than Caroline Scott Pelton, and secure in the possession of homes and furniture, faced fewer financial worries and less fear of losing status. Such women, Suzanne Lebsock has suggested, were "free above all to invest in their children."[28] Yet, they were not immune to worries about their education, their health, and futures, or their failures and problems.[29] When Luce Perrault became a widow in 1854, her two eldest children were already established in their gendered paths. Hortense Fabre had been married to George-Etienne Cartier for eight years and given birth to three daughters. Cartier's parliamentary career was taking off as he went from backbencher to speaker to attorney general, then co-premier in 1857 with John A. Macdonald. Still, there was much to worry about in this apparently successful match that Fabre had approved of, even pushed, initially. The growing rift between this couple, so mismatched in their family cultures, ages, politics, and inclinations, was increasingly widely known. It must have pained Luce. Brian Young reports that during the 1850s, Hortense and Cartier rarely appeared in public together and that, by the 1860s, Cartier "rarely slept at the family home." By the end of that decade, he was living with Luce Cuvillier, and her presence at social functions was noted publicly. Luce Cuvillier was one of the daughters of Austin Cuvillier and Marie-Claire Perrault, the wife whose vote for Stanley Bagg had received such attention during the 1832 by-election. She was Luce Perrault's cousin. Édouard-Charles, Luce's eldest son, was ordained in 1854, just weeks after his father's death. The joy of him being made a canon likely mingled with

Luce's grieving. Twenty-two years later she would celebrate his appointment as the third bishop of Montreal when he replaced Ignace Bourget.[30]
Luce's children were widely spaced in age, as was common in these
generations. Her youngest daughter, Marie-Anne Hectorine, was born just
one year before Fabre's death. Gustave-Raymond was only twelve, and
Hector was twenty when they lost their father. Édouard-Raymond had
already encouraged Hector in his education at the new Collège de Montréal, and in his interest in the colony's politics.[31] Luce lived in comfort. In
1861, she had three live-in servants to assist in running her household. But
she would have to oversee the education and raising of her two youngest
without their father's controlling hand, though with loving support for
her and careful oversight from her eldest son.[32] Similarly, the children of
Hannah Lyman and John Easton Mills included one daughter, who was
already married; Elizabeth and John, who were in their teens; and Ada and
Alice, aged six and two respectively.[33] In 1841, Hannah and John had lost
two of their sons – George, nearly six, and Edwin, who was ten months
old, to scarlet fever. Within two years of her husband's death, his namesake
and her only remaining son also died of scarlet fever, at the age of eighteen,
just as he was beginning to make his way in the world. Hannah's mothering
as a widow would focus on the three surviving girls. She too was assisted
in some of this work by servants. In 1861, she was among the tiny proportion of Montreal widows employing four domestic servants.[34]
Constance Hannah Hart's children were all adults and pretty well established when she began her widowhood at the age of fifty-three, following
Adolphus Mordecai Hart's sudden death in 1879. Emile was working in
the Hart Brothers family business. Gerald was the general manager of
Citizens Insurance Company of Canada. Constance remained in the home
they had moved to on returning from the United States at the corner of
Durocher and Prince Arthur streets. Two years after she became a widow,
the census enumerator identified her as the head of a household that included these two sons, already in their thirties, and her two daughters –
Harriet, aged twenty-nine, and Miriam, aged twenty-six. There was one
live-in servant.[35] Perhaps with his mother's encouragement, Gerald continued his father's interest in historical issues and in writing. In the late
1880s and early 1890s, he published studies of the fall of New France and
the Quebec Act.[36] Historian, bibliophile, and numismatist, he also served as
the president of the Montreal Society for Historical Studies.
Work opportunities were changing in Montreal. Widows who had
married artisans in the 1820s might well have hoped to establish their children within their class.[37] As employers changed what they offered and expected of apprentices over these years, the chances of moving from
apprentice to master diminished.[38] By the 1860s, when the children of

couples married in the 1840s were reaching their twenties, industrialization had further transformed labour markets and life chances. Some widows who had married master craftsmen in the 1820s or 1840s successfully raised sons who took up work in the growing number of white collar, clerical, and commercial positions that industrialization and the expansion of commerce in the city opened up. Twenty years after Margaret Jamieson's printer husband, William Moody, died, she was living with one of her sons and a married daughter and son-in-law. The two men were both working as clerks.[39] The 1861 census captured Leocadie Paris four years after the death of her husband, Louis-Joseph Gauthier. This master carriage maker's widow, who had been left her all his goods in his will to use for as long as she remained a widow, and charged to raise, nourish, and support their children and have them reasonably educated, was then aged thirty-four. She occupied a two-storey stone house along with two other families and was sufficiently visible to be listed in the city directory that year, interestingly not as a widow but as "Gauthier, Mrs. L.J." at 93 St. Lawrence Street. Living with her were a thirty-four-year-old male, identified as a relative; her five children, aged five to thirteen; and a twenty-eight-year-old single woman, Emmerance Landry from Maskingongé. All the children were recorded as attending school. Leocadie apparently weathered this expensive period of the family life cycle and fulfilled Louis-Joseph's hopes successfully. She moved house a few times after his death but never moved far from the intersection of St. Lawrence and Dorchester Streets, where they lived when he died in what became known as Saint Louis ward. In 1866, her sons Édouard and Albert were both listed in the city directory for the first time. Both were clerks. Her name appeared in the directory every year listed before her children, and when the enumerator arrived in 1881 he recorded her as the household head. Three of her five children were still living with her in a house on a respectable block on St. Elizabeth Street just north of Craig Street. Nearby were middle-class widows living with their professional sons, and Charlotte Führer, who would later write a sensational memoir of her experiences as a midwife. Édouard was then twenty-seven and listed in the census as a clerk, in city directories as a commercial traveller. Albert was identified as a merchant in both sources. No occupation was indicated for her twenty-four-year-old daughter. Eugenie's "leisure" might be read as one sign of Leocadie's successful transition from master craftsman's wife to bourgeois widow. Another is that in this census, Emmerance Landry, by then forty-eight years old, was identified as a servant. Unless she had left and returned between these two censuses, this single woman had spent at least twenty of Leocadie's twenty-four years as a widow living in her household. The emotional content of relationships cannot be read from census data. "What matters," as Davidoff and colleagues argue, is that such relationships were ones "of *interdependence*." Some of Leocadie's success in transmitting advantages to the next generation was tied to this long-term relationship between mistress and maid, in which support and friendship likely blended with her authority as mistress of the house.[40]

Other children of craftsmen's widows ended up working in less-skilled jobs than their fathers had held. Hermine Legris' children were already in their twenties and established in a range of working-class occupations when her carpenter-turned-baker husband, Michel Julien died in 1872. Nine years later, the census enumerator recorded this woman who had dabbled in prostitution as a wife and lived separately from her husband – identifying herself as a widow in court and city records for years before her husband died – as living on St. Felix Street in Saint Antoine ward. Hers was one of three families within what was probably a triplex. He listed Hermine as aged seventy-two, and the head of a family that included her fifty-year-old unmarried son, Édouard, and thirty-four-year-old daughter Matilda. The incomes that Édouard and Matilda made as an unskilled labourer and dressmaker respectively likely helped support Hermine as she aged. It is likely that she also sewed, for the city directory lists her as a dressmaker over this period. Her thirty-two-year-old daughter, Sophie; her husband, François-Xavier Dionne, a watchmaker; and their four-year-old son were the second family in the dwelling. The third was headed by another widow, a woman in her fifties described in the census as a trader and in the city directory as selling stationery.[41] Thus, Hermine lived in close proximity to earning adult children, as well as to another widow. In the relations between generations, she may have had some power, for she retained control over whatever possessions remained from her marriage. The census shows us only some of the threads in the "dense tangle" of economic and emotional support, love and loyalty, or self-interest that linked widows like Hermine or Caroline Scott Pelton to their married children.[42]

Some sons and daughters of widowed parents continued to live with or near them, contributing to family finances by finding work, caring for their parents, and often delaying, missing out, or avoiding marriage themselves. Love, concern, the widow's control, or lack of other possibilities, along with financial need, could all contribute to these lengthy co-residences that have captured the attention of historians in a range of periods and places.[43] In the patchwork of provisions that Montreal widows stitched together, the economic contributions of children, and especially co-resident children past their teens, were a major component (see Figure 11.3).

Half the widows enumerated in Montreal in 1861 had offspring of any age living with them in their household. Widowers appear to have been better able to retain at least one child alive and at home. Close to two-

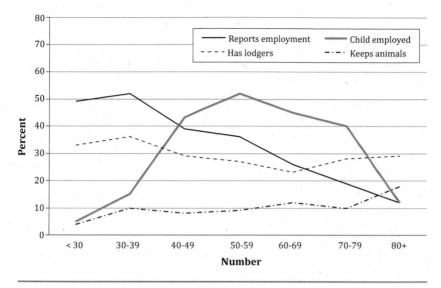

FIGURE 11.3 Percentage of Montreal widows (family heads only) reporting employment, working children, lodgers, or keeping animals, by widow's age, 1861

Note: Widows heading families, N = 1,395.
Source: 1861 Census, Montreal, database single parents.

thirds of widowers had co-resident offspring. Half the children in widows' households reported some kind of employment, compared to under four out of ten living with a widowed father. Widows under fifty living with offspring were much more likely to have a child earning some kind of income than were widowers. This difference increased as they moved into their fifties. Men's superior earning power and related standard of living would partially explain the difference, so clear in Figure 11.4. So would the continued co-residence of daughters who acted in their mothers' shoes for widowed fathers. In 1861, the likelihood of a widow living with an earning child increased steadily with age; for widowers it decreased. To be childless or to lose one's children through death, departure, or disagreement might relieve widows of the worries of supporting and raising them, but, as Maria Mitchell insisted, it also deprived them of their "keeping and comfort."[44]

The widely varied timing of husbands' deaths left some widows childless, some alone because children had already left home, and some assuming a new level of responsibility for surviving children at different stages in their education, work, and career development. Widows of labourers and other unskilled workers with children not yet of working age were the major clients of the city's orphanages. As we saw, it was to cater for the

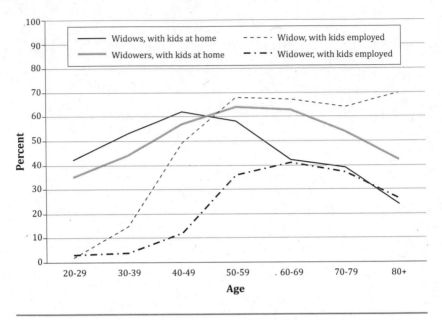

FIGURE 11.4   Percentages of Montreal widows and widowers (family heads only) with children living with them and the percentage whose offspring reported employment, by widow or widower's age

Note: Widows heading families, $N = 1,395$; widowers heading families, $N = 496$.
Source: 1861 Census, Montreal, database single parents.

children of widows, unable to raise them temporarily or permanently, that the Ladies' Benevolent Society was created. Janice Harvey reports that over the years between its opening in 1832 and the end of the century, the society sheltered 644 children of widows. Some of these widows had placed their children almost immediately following their husbands' deaths. Others, in the words of one widow, "struggled on and managed to keep them" until their own health gave way or their patchwork of money-raising and -saving possibilities failed.[45] The pattern was similar at the St. Alexis Orphanage, begun by the Sisters of Providence ten years after Émilie Tavernier Gamelin's death. The nearly five hundred girls whom that orphanage sheltered for periods ranging from days to years between 1860 and the end of 1884 included many widows' daughters.[46] At whichever stage widows relinquished or resumed major control of their children's lives, powerful hopes, emotions, and obligations tied them to their children. Depending on their own material situation, those who were not independent financially balanced their need for income against their desire to educate children and prepare them for suitable employment. And they balanced care of their youngsters against their own capacity to generate money.

THE RUN ON THE MONTREAL CITY AND DISTRICT SAVINGS BANK. THE MAYOR ADDRESSING THE CROWD.—FROM A SKETCH BY E. JUMP.

FIGURE 11.5 "The Run on the Montreal City and District Savings Bank: The Mayor Addressing the Crowd." In this sketch by E. Jump, women figure prominently among the bank customers concerned about the viability of bank stocks and dividends. | *Canadian Illustrated News,* 19 October 1872, 6, 16: 253. Library and Archives Canada, Record 1695.

Making Money: Widows' Visible Means of Support

Contributions from her children's earnings, her own separate estate, and possibly the lump sum from Pelton are three discernable threads in Caroline Scott Pelton's patchwork of support. She had sufficient money to invest a little, for within five years of her widowhood she owned three $100 shares in the Commercial Bank of Canada, and a $100 share in the Merchants' Bank of Canada, established by Hugh Allan and opened in 1864.[47] These were small investments. They would generate small returns if all went well. In 1877, the Merchants' Bank nearly collapsed, threatening such widows' dividends. Perhaps this scare led Caroline to look beyond the Montreal banks for greater security. By the 1880s, she owned two $100 shares in the Bank of Hamilton. But she had not lost faith in the Merchants' Bank. In 1885, she owned two additional shares.[48] Her visible investments in banks that year totalled $500, hardly enough to produce a sufficient income to live on. Caroline's were modest investments compared to those of most male shareholders, as they were to some of the other women who married in the 1840s and became widows. In 1885, Constance Hart held at least $1,200 worth of shares spread equally between the Merchants' Bank and the Bank of Toronto. Caroline and Constance were not exceptional in investing in bank stock. On the basis of such investments in Hamilton, Ontario, and Vancouver, British Columbia, Peter Baskerville has convincingly suggested that between the 1860s and 1930s, "investment in bank stocks was increasingly a women's sphere of activity," with widows the "most active investors."[49] The significance such assets might have for widows, and hence the potential dangers that bank failures could pose, is represented in the 1872 sketch shown in Figure 11.5, with its many anxious-looking women customers at the Montreal City and District Savings Bank.[50]

Constance had sufficient discretionary income as a relatively wealthy widow to lend significant amounts to her son Gerald. She owned the home at the corner of Durocher and Prince Arthur streets. The photo taken of her and a friend in the mid- to early 1890s (see Figure 11.6) shows that it was furnished lavishly with numerous chairs, sofas, paintings, and Victorian bric-a-brac. At some point in the early 1890s, Constance was attracted to the land boom that was occurring as people poured into Victoria, British Columbia. She purchased a vacant lot in an area just opening up for development, joining the growing number of Victoria women who were investing in land.[51]

Although Caroline Scott's means appear to have been relatively modest, I have found no indication that she took on any form of paid labour during her nearly forty years as a widow, except for taking in lodgers. In her interactions with the men working as census enumerators who called at her house in 1861, 1871, 1881, and 1891, she made no mention of having an occupation. Nor did the annual city directories ever indicate that she was employed.[52] In this too she was not alone. Over two-thirds of the widows living in Montreal in 1861 reported no visible means of support to the census enumerators. Three-quarters reported no employment twenty years later. This was the most significant difference between the family economies of widows and widowers, for most widowers whatever their age reported some kind of employment. The exceptions were largely men past their prime. The widows most likely to be involved in recognized employment were young. Among those aged between their twenties and forties, over four of every ten reported an occupation in both 1861 and 1881. After the age of fifty, the proportions reporting a job fell rapidly.[53] (See Figure 11.3.)

That few elite widows needed or chose to seek any kind of employment is not surprising. When elite and middle-class men lived long enough and were successful enough in investing to provide for either their own

FIGURE 11.6 "Mrs. Adolphus M. Hart and friend, in her drawing room, Montreal, QC, ca. 1895." Constance Hannah Hart at home, ca. 1893-95. Constance Hannah Hart *(right)*, surrounded by the family furniture, paintings, and other family belongings that she divided up carefully as she wrote a codicil to her will on the day she died in 1899, about four years after this photo is believed to have been taken. | Robert E.J. Summerhayes, photographer. McCord Museum, Notman Photographic Archives, MP-0000, 154.24

old age or for their widow, they fulfilled their provider role after their death, as before. Although Hannah Lyman and her children co-owned John Easton Mills's banking business and other assets following his death, and Hannah came from an active merchant family, running such businesses was increasingly frowned upon in the upper echelons of the middle classes as incompatible with "a life of propriety."[54] Overseeing households and their children's education, the obligatory social visiting with friends and family, and charity work all took time and energy.

Such widows continued to represent their dead husbands in private and in public. Naming practices reflect this. Hannah Lyman was usually listed in Lovell's directory as Mrs. J.E. Mills, widow, and occasionally as Widow J.E. Mills. Similarly, Luce Perrault was listed, following English custom, as Mrs. E.R. Fabre, though in 1865 she was referred to as Mrs. Lucy Fabre, widow of Édouard.[55] Thus, when some census enumerators wrote "widow," "Veuve Rodier," or "widow Gullen" in the column of the census designated for occupations, they were not just making a careless entry, placing a marital status where an occupation should have been. Rather, such a "permanent, almost professional description"[56] captured the ongoing bond that tied widows to their deceased husbands. It also can be read to signal the range of ways husbands' financial provisions and property continued to support some women in their widowhood. Other elite widows, faced with a census category that failed to capture the realities of their financial situation, claimed more specific bases of income while asserting their independence from paid labour by telling enumerators that they were "rentiers," "independent," or "bourgeois" – or asserting, as at least ten widows did in 1861, that their occupation was "lady."[57]

Even among widows who had not been left in any comfort, the realities of home responsibilities combined with the dismal lack of good work options for women, meant as Suzanne Lebsock and others have suggested, that most widows avoided paid work outside the home, making the best they could of the resources they commanded.[58] For Caroline Scott, this meant finding ways to save money rather than to earn it. With her one son and four daughters aged four through eighteen at home when she became a widow, she had plenty of hands to help. Caroline trimmed her own bonnets and sewed dresses for her daughters. She taught the girls to sew. They helped with the washing and making of preserves. One of Carrie's sisters described one such occasion, inviting her to imagine them

> sitting on the stairs of the kitchen porch with a large parcel of sugar (25 lbs) before us and a dish of raspberries on one side with a pair of scales in her hand into which I was putting the fruit assisted by Emma while Tiff the cat and kitten are looking on in amazement ... Mother says she will not make any more raspberry preserves this year. Fancy we have made 24!!!. I think they were only half a dollar per bucket!!

Lessons about thrift and domestic economy mingled with work and laughter. Godfrey was expected to learn basic domestic tasks. Caroline described him as adept enough at the age of fourteen to set the table and prepare at least part of the family tea.[59]

As Caroline pieced together ways of making and saving money, her thoughts turned to one of the most common ways that genteel and working-class widows alike could make a little money – exchanging space in their home and their own domestic labour for lodging. Although the enumerators of the 1861 census recorded only 52 widows as boarding house-keepers, there were 397 widows who headed their own homes and had at least one lodger or boarder in their household.[60] When Caroline took the financial risk in 1863 of renting a house for £50 a year, she confided to Carrie that the larger house would allow her to take in a married couple or "two ladies." Sharing her plans about the ways spaces would be used, she reported that she had decided the boarders could occupy the middle flat, while the family would have "a nice parlour, dining room and kitchen ... on the lower flat with two good attic bedrooms which I intend keeping for ourselves." Seven years later the house she was renting included a male and female border as well as one Irish Catholic servant. [61]

Middle-class widows like Caroline could afford to place discrete advertisements in city newspapers. "Four or five respectable gentlemen can be genteelly accommodated with BOARD and LODGING in a private house," announced one woman in 1842. "A WIDOW LADY residing in the vicinity of Place d'Armes Square can accommodate Two Gentlemen with a Private Sitting Room and Board," advertised another Montrealer in 1861 in the *Montreal Gazette*. Such announcements appeared frequently. Carefully crafted to assert the widows' respectability and gentility, and to protect their anonymity, most differed from Caroline's views about the ideal tenants in specifying that "gentlemen" were their desired clientele. Leonore Davidoff reminds readers that it was men without wives or mothers who normally paid someone to "look after or 'do' for" them, whether as servants, house-keepers, or landladies.[62] Word of mouth or signs in windows secured boarders for those unable to afford such advertisements.

Taking in boarders, or running a boarding house, as I have argued in earlier work, required space and the linen and labour power to provide for them. As young widows of craftsmen, Marie-Louise Genant and Margaret Jamieson both sought to make money this way as widows. Marie-Louise was used to running the tavern she had shared with the former master tailor Pierre-Bernard Decousse. At the time of his death in 1852, they possessed a significant amount of bedding and linen. Some assets remained after his long illness, death, and the sorting out of debts. The mistake in their marriage contract meant that half their shared community property was hers. As tutor to Marie-Louise, Sophie-Corine, Louis-Phillipe, and Charotte, she had full control over the whole property. For several years she continued to run the tavern in Jacques Cartier Square. She was listed as its keeper in the 1854 and 1855 city directories. After four years of residential stability, however, she began moving almost annually. She ran boarding houses on St. Lawrence Street, Fortification Lane, and then St. Jean Baptiste Street. In 1861, the census enumerator listed her as keeping a boarding house in a substantial four-storey stone dwelling. It was nine years since her husband had died. She was identified as thirty-seven. Her youngest daughter, Charlotte, had died several years earlier. Her three surviving children were between the ages of eleven and seventeen. None was identified as employed or as attending school. On census day, some nine boarders were staying in the four-storey stone house with her and her children. Two live-in servants assisted with the washing, cleaning, and general domestic care that made taking in that many boarders such a demanding task. The children surely helped too. Marie-Louise never appeared again in the city's directories.[63] When the 1881 census was taken she was aged fifty-six, listed no job, and was living in a small apartment with her eldest daughter, Marie-Louise, who was still single at age thirty-seven.[64]

Margaret Jamieson also decided to take in boarders some time after her printer husband, William Moody, died in August 1861, leaving her, like Caroline Scott Pelton, with six living children to raise. When she became a widow at the age of thirty-eight, her eldest son, William, was already eighteen and had probably been working for some time. Even Thomas, who by then was about sixteen, and David, at fourteen, may have been contributing to the family economy. The three girls were younger – Mary about twelve, Elizabeth eight, and Margaret only four years old. Twenty years later, in 1881, Margaret was listed in the city directory as keeping a boarding house at 43 St. Dominique – one street west of St. Lawrence Boulevard. When the census was taken that year, she was housing six boarders, all men in their twenties and thirties with respectable jobs – printers, tailors, a carriage maker, and a clerk. She was able to employ one servant, a fifteen-year-old French Canadian girl, to help her care for so many boarders.[65]

Living with her in addition to the six boarders were three of her five surviving children. One daughter, Margaret, had died in 1877 at the age of nineteen of consumption – the disease that killed so many young women in the city. Her third son, David, by then thirty and still single, was working as a clerk, and her two surviving daughters and their husbands all lived with her. Mary had married a Catholic Irishman who was listed as a jeweller. Elizabeth's husband described his origins as French and a clerk. They had a ten-month-old son. "One might consider the cornerstone of diversity to be the combination of ethnicities within the household itself," suggest Jason Gilliland and Sherry Olson, whose detailed work on the 1881

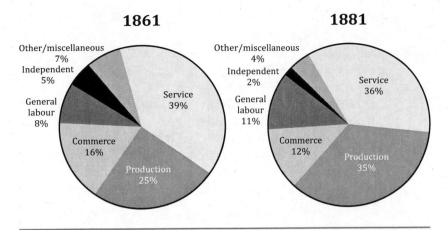

FIGURE 11.7   Major sectors of widows' employment, Montreal, 1861 and 1881

Note: Widows reporting employment, 1861, N = 962 of 3,404; 1881, N = 1,612 of 6,715. *Source:* Bettina Bradbury, Single Parents Montreal, 1861, database; Lisa Dillon, the 1881 Canadian Census Project and the North Atlantic Population Project, Montreal, 1881, database.

census shows that one person in ten was living in a household, including "someone of another group." This printer's widow's large household included Catholics, Presbyterians, and Anglicans, and people who claimed their origin as Scottish, Irish, English, and French Canadian.[66]

The other ways widows found to make money that they reported or census enumerators acknowledged were depressingly limited. The 1861 census returns included an occupation for 962 of the 3,404 women identified as widows. This was close to a third of the widows. Twenty years later, 1,612 – or only about a quarter of the 6,715 widows – were identified as having some visible means of support. As I have shown in earlier work, widows' reported engagement in paid labour was dramatically higher than that of the city's wives, under 4 percent of whom listed a job in either of these decades.[67] The jobs they listed were clustered in four main areas: service, sewing, varied businesses, and unskilled labour (see Figure 11.7). A few widows from both cohorts of marriages were working in most of these areas when the censuses of 1861 and 1881 were taken. Knowing something of their earlier and later lives helps contextualize what census takers reported about their work and families.

Service involved the largest number of widows. Over a quarter of the city's widows reporting a job were listed as servants, domestics, cooks, or charladies. The proportion was only slightly lower twenty years later. Like

Emmerance Landry, the servant who lived with Leocadie Paris during so much of her widowhood, widows plied their domestic skills in other people's homes in return for minimal pay and sometimes shelter.[68] As aids and maids, charwomen, servants, cooks, nurses, gardeners, and housekeepers, they cared for others, using skills understood as female, and remunerated accordingly.[69] Some widows advertised for such positions, especially in the early years of the century. In 1826, a "respectable English Woman, who has recently become a Widow," sought "the superintendence of a Gentleman's Family." She promised "references as to character."[70] Still other widows provided services as sick nurses, midwives, and wet nurses, caring for the sick, the dying, and the newborn. These widows ranged in age from their twenties through to their eighties. One woman seeking a housekeeping position in the city advertised herself as a "widow of a certain age."[71] In 1861, nearly two-thirds of the widows working in various kinds of domestic service lived and worked in other people's houses. This gave them shelter and meals but little time or space to themselves, and subjected them to the complicated class, gender, and authority relations inherent in domestic work.[72]

Employers rarely sheltered servants' children. Live-in domestic service created conflict between widows' mothering and their paid work. Widows working as "servants, laundresses and charwomen" dominated among the women placing their children with the Ladies' Benevolent Society. In 1861, Marie Gagné was listed as a cook in a bourgeois, three-storey wooden home that boasted three other servants and a cow, and housed a total of ten people. She had married a carpenter, Séraphin Bernard, in 1842 and was widowed at thirty, five years before the 1861 census was taken. If any of her children had survived, they resided elsewhere. The history of domestic service suggests that as a cook in a multi-servant household, she was likely better paid and not worked as hard as many servants.[73] Yet, her life was brief. One year later, in 1862, she died at the age of thirty-six. Her widowhood lasted six years.

Grace Telfer also found employment in service as a widow. She was among the minority of widows over the age of sixty who reported a job in 1861. She had migrated from Scotland and married John Thompson, a joiner, in 1823 at St. Gabriel Street Presbyterian Church. She was widowed at the age of forty-two in 1843. The 1861 census identified her as a housekeeper. This live-in position provided her with shelter and employment, but she was the only servant in a household with four boarders and a family of four. Work conditions in domestic service were frequently appalling, the work never-ending, and employers less and less willing to continue to provide shelter when their servants aged or fell ill. Homes for friendless and elderly women, like Émilie Tavernier's early asylums and later religious institution, responded in part to the need of such elderly or sick women. Grace Telfer Thompson did not work much longer as a domestic. In 1864, she too died, at the age of sixty-three. She had spent twenty-one years as a widow and twenty as a wife.[74]

Washing for others was another classic widows' task, undoubtedly employing more than the 86 widows in 1861 or the 138 in 1881 who reported this as their occupation. Housewives from the elite down to the better paid among the working classes tried to pass this hated task on to someone else. The choosiest employers sought references, and for genteel widows, offering them was important. "Washing and ironing done in a Superior manner, by a Woman who thoroughly understands her business," advertised one woman in a Montreal newspaper, noting that she could "produce the most satisfactory references as to character and ability.[75] But washing was heavy, physically demanding work. It required access to water, a stove to heat it on, large containers to wash in, and space to hang items out to dry. Marie Rachel Landkerker, who had married the mason Dominique Séné in 1826 and was widowed in 1857 at the age of fifty-three, made washing one basis of her living as a widow for at least some time during the early years of her twenty-six years of widowhood. She was one of nearly 9 percent of employed widows who told the census taker in 1861 that they worked as washerwomen. At that time, this daughter and widow of masons was boarding with non-relatives, apparently eking out a living day to day.[76]

Wifely skills – caring for the sick, newborn, and needy or diseased bodies as nurses, midwives, or wet nurses – offered other widows ways to secure some economic support. Among them in 1881 was Matilde Beauchamps, who had married the carter François-Xavier Leboeuf-Laflamme in 1842 at around the age of twenty-four. He died in 1874 when they were both fifty-six. For several years before his death, she described herself as a midwife and a widow to the men making Lovell's city directory. She continued to report this occupation for the rest of her life.[77]

By the 1880s, the transformation of industry, and particularly of the sewing industry, meant that work in production rivalled service as the main sector of recognized work for widows. Clothing production had been part of the vibrant artisanal economy of early-nineteenth-century Montreal. As Mary Anne Poutanen has shown, women were active as dressmakers and milliners at the time the first cohort of women were married. They ran their own shops, employing young women as apprentices to learn the trade. Dressmakers' shops are listed in all city directories across the century. Yet, by the 1860s, widows or married and single women running their own dressmaking businesses in their own homes or in well-publicized shops were a minority. Sweated labour characterized the industrial transformation of this major sector of Montreal's economy as it did elsewhere, and it was here that widows and their children were more likely to be found. Sewing, dressmaking, and other needle trades employed a quarter of the widows identified as working in 1861, including Anna Taylor, the mother of two and widow of the painter Charles Gall, who had died in 1847. As the job opportunities multiplied, so did the proportion of working widows who sewed for a living. In 1881, a third of Montreal's widows listing a job were in the needle trades, and production was as large a sector of employment of widows as service. Exploitative, exhausting, and poorly remunerated, its sweated labour offered many Montreal widows, as well as some working-class wives, pittances, which they could increase by involving their children in the work.[78]

The third major area in which Montreal widows reported making money was by running businesses. These ranged from profitable to pitiful, from legal to illegal, from hotels and saloons through market stalls and boarding houses. Historians writing about widows involved in businesses have tended to focus on the most prominent and successful women. In Canadian history, this has been particularly the case in studies of New France. Peter Baskerville has recently begun to fill this gap by exploring women's involvement in business in Hamilton, Ontario, and Victoria, British Columbia, mostly in the late nineteenth and early twentieth centuries. The subject deserves further study. I have no evidence that any of the widows from the two marriage generations became very prominent in business. The city certainly always boasted a few prominent widows who traded in land or ran successful businesses. Their visibility diminished over time. In the early years of the century, we saw that Widow Oakes was prominent among land speculators, and had in that capacity voted in the 1832 by-election. In the 1860s, the widow of one of Montreal's two major city directory publishers, Christina Mackay, continued the work of her husband for several years.[79] Most widows ran smaller, more fragile enterprises, heavy in their demands on the time, energy, and financial resources of their proprietors. Suzanne Lebsock has suggested that women who had helped with businesses as wives could when widowed, "carry on the business without missing a beat." Perhaps, and evidence certainly suggests that many, like Marie-Louise Genant, tried to do so.[80] My sense is that in Montreal in this period, few lasted long. Neither Hannah Lyman nor Luce Perrault stepped visibly into their husband's shoes, though Hannah and her children remained the owners of John Mills's impressive shop on St. François Xavier Street, as well as significant landowners.[81]

A few widows of craftsmen, skilled workers, and men in the lower ranks of commerce started up new businesses, managing to open small shops, produce independently at home, run market stalls, or truck their wares throughout the city, selling from door to door. Mary Hillock Robson, who

had married a salesman in 1844 and become a widow in 1847, reported in
1861 that she was running a fancy goods shop. City directories from 1861
to 1865 list her shop at 260 Notre Dame Street.[82] Clusters of widows had
stalls at the city's several markets. Among them were Elmire Chef Vas de
Bon Coeur, whose shoemaker husband, Henry Smallwood, died in 1874,
after they had been married for twenty-nine years. She was listed in the
1881 directory as selling vegetables at the Bonsecours Market. The census
enumerator that year simply recorded her as a trader. When he called, she
was living alone. A year later, she became one of the few widows in their
fifties to remarry. In a ceremony witnessed by illiterate sons of each new
spouse, she married, at the age of around fifty-five, a widower who listed
his occupation as potash maker.[83]

Casual unskilled work, picked up in a range of workplaces across the
city and translated to or by census takers simply as *journalière* or day labourer,
drew in growing numbers of widows in the later decades of the century.
Among them in 1861 were Marie Charpentier, the widow of a mason, and
Angèle Beaulieu, a confectioner's widow. Both had married in the 1840s.
Both were recorded as *journalière*. Marie became a widow after ten years
of marriage. In 1861, she had no children living with her. Angèle, who was
thirty-nine and described as illiterate, was raising four children. Her sixteen-
year-old daughter was working as a servant – possibly living elsewhere.
Two boys aged nine and ten were attending school, while a thirteen-year-
old daughter probably ran the household while her mother was out working.[84] A few other widows described forms of employment to census takers
that hint at the vast array of ways of making a living that are more readily
apparent in police records than in censuses. Despite widows' prominence
among prostitutes in the city, the only widow to describe herself as such
to the enumerator was the English-born, thirty-five-year-old widow Ann
Summers. She and all the other women in the brothel where she resided
were listed as prostitutes. This information bothered either the enumerator
or his superior, for their return was cosigned by Montreal's chief of police.
Other sex trade workers may, as Patrick Dunae suggests, have used coded
words, reporting themselves as seamstresses and possibly boarding house-
keepers. Faced with the intrusive questions of the census enumerator in
1881, the sixty-year-old widow Kate Charbonneau was blunt. She reported
her occupation as begging. She lived alone.[85]

Residential Histories: Autonomies, Dependencies, and Connections

Caroline Scott moved frequently as a widow. Such mobility might be interpreted as a sign of her struggle to secure adequate housing for herself
and the children. Yet, annual moves were common in this city of renters.

And moving was not a new experience for her. It repeated the peripatetic pattern of moving house that had characterized her years as a wife. When her husband left Montreal in 1861, the couple was renting a house owned by a widow at 126 St. Antoine Street, in the Saint Antoine suburb north-west of the old commercial city, for $100 a year. The house she pinned her money-raising hopes on at number 118 on the same street rented for $160 annually. She remained there for two years, then moved again, this time several blocks east to Latour Street. In 1863, this was a fairly respectable, newly established area, inhabited by a mixture of craftsmen, businessmen, and independent women.[86] Next door was a clergyman. Rebecca Conegan, the illiterate widow of the blind soap manufacturer, Sampson Brady, lived a few doors away with her new husband, the grocer Henry Benallick, whom she had married in 1853, a year after Sampson's death. The city directory for 1863-64 listed three other widows heading households on the same street, as well as several married women identified as household heads, who may have been widows or wives living apart from their husbands. Several houses away from Caroline's new dwelling, the widow Doyle took in washing and boarders. Caroline stayed there about three years, moved again, then moved at least four more times before the mid–1880s.[87]

Her mobility across the city contrasts with the residential stability of some more elite and well-provided-for widows. For her first twenty years of widowhood, Hannah Lyman Mills remained living in her and John's large, richly furnished home, Belair Cottage, at the head of St. Genevieve Street where, as we saw, she and John had set up house shortly after their marriage.[88] Constance Hannah Hart stayed on in the house on Durocher Street that she and Adolphus had purchased sometime after returning from the United States.[89] Catherine Farquhar remained for at least seven years at 667 Dorchester, the house that had been the couple's home when Dr. John Sutherland died in 1875. She fulfilled the condition of the codicil to his will that had allowed her $3,000 annually, provided she lived with their son and cooked his meals and did his washing until he was twenty-five. The city directory of 1881 is the last one that lists them both at that address. In the census listing later that year, Louis is identified as being thirty-one and married. He and his twenty-one-year-old wife were keeping their own house. They had two servants but no children. His widowed mother disappears from the records.[90]

Not all elite wives remained in the homes they had dwelled in as wives. Wealthier widows might move voluntarily, not wanting to remain in a home with difficult memories, seeking to lease the family home to generate additional revenues, or preferring to live with married sons and daughters. Within a year of Édouard-Raymond Fabre's death, Luce Perrault left their "nine-room home at the corner of Craig and St. Lawrence" streets,

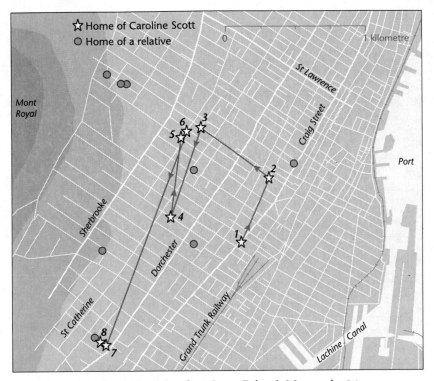

FIGURE II.8   The widow Caroline Scott Pelton's Montreal, 1862-99
  1 1863: 118 St. Antoine Street.
  2 1864-66: 13 Latour Street.
  3 1867-70: 34 Aylmer Street.
  4 1871-75: 102 Stanley Street.
  5-6 1876-83: 11 Burnside Place, with Godfrey, then Maria.
  7-8 1884-88: 14 then 12 Fort Street.

moving her two younger children just one block west to a house at the corner of Craig Street and St. Charles Borromé. They remained there for five more years, then when Marie-Anne Hectorine was about seven and Gustave-Raymond around nineteen, they moved again, this time some eight blocks east and north to Lagauchetière, the street constructed in the space where the city walls had once stood. Unlike Caroline Scott, Luce did not move again. She remained in this second home as a widow until her death many decades later.[91]

Reasons for moving varied dramatically. Frequent relocations were a common experience among the wives of Montreal's labourers, carters, and men who fell ill or were unemployed. As Lisa Wilson observes, "Most women who had experienced this kind of nomadic existence during marriage continued to do so after its dissolution."[92] Yet, as historians Tony Ballantyne and Antoinette Burton have suggested of transnational migrations, mobility may also be read "as a constitutive factor in the social life of sentiment and its multiple articulations."[93] Although Caroline Scott Pelton's frequent moves contrast with the continuity of home that marked the widowhood of Constance Hannah Hart, her reasons for moving were never purely financial. Her move to Latour Street placed her a very short walk away from the house of Mary Ann and Dr. Robert Godfrey, her sister and brother-in-law and their children, facilitating the visiting and joint outings of sisters and cousins that were part of their family life. The timing of her next major move coincided with Carrie's return to Montreal around 1867. The house Caroline rented on Aylmer Street in 1867 was close to the school in which Carrie was teaching. The house at 102 Stanley Street to which Caroline and Carrie moved in 1871 was a few blocks further west but still within easy walking distance of the school. It was also larger and more expensive. Rent on the house on Aylmer Street was $220 a year. The new place on Stanley Street cost $280, a very high rent in Montreal at that time, but she needed space. Godfrey still lived with her, as did the younger children. The move followed the 1871 marriage of Maria, her third daughter, to Jacob Beall. This couple moved in with her at some point over the next few years. After her second daughter, Charlotte Jane, married John Williamson Mackedie in 1872, the newlyweds took up residence next door to Caroline and Maria.[94] Peter Gossage has shown that in Saint Hyacinthe a minority of newly wed couples moved in with the parents of one spouse. In Caroline Scott's middle-class family, some moved in, others made sure they were living in close proximity, exemplifying Gilliland and Olsen's argument that "intense socialization of the extended family produced an overlapping of kinship and neighbourhoods" across the city.[95]

With her co-resident son and son-in-law both working as clerks, Caroline had assistance in paying the rent. Living with Maria and her husband and proximity to her other children made it possible to share meals, sociability, and care. Sickly as a child, Maria likely remained so as a wife. She and Jacob had no children. Caroline, by then in her early fifties, could assist when needed, seeking, as Kirsten Wood argues Southern widows did, "to help their families as much as they were helped." This cohabitation of Caroline, daughter, and son-in-law continued over subsequent years, modified around 1884 when Maria's husband died, and transformed again in 1888 by Maria's early death at the age of forty-one.[96]

In 1874, Carrie, then aged thirty-one, married the forty-two-year-old merchant John Sharpe Shearer, a partner of John Mackedie, her sister Charlotte's new husband.[97] On that occasion, one of her uncles explicitly acknowledged the significant role Carrie had played as the eldest daughter of a widow. In the letter he sent with a wedding present, he told her how he and his wife had "*always admired* with delight your dutiful and loving devotion to you Mother and *family* & I most trust that you may be long spared in health and happiness to extend to the future sharer of your joys and sorrows the same unselfishness and affection that has ever character-ized your industrious and cheerful life."[98] Within a year of their marriage, the couple also took up residence on Stanley Street. Two years later, Godfrey married. He and his new wife set up house at 11 Burnside Place. Although this couple stayed there only about three years, until 1884 one or another member of the family rented the same dwelling. After Maria's husband died, Caroline and her newly widowed daughter moved, this time to the western limits of the city, to Fort Street, just south of Sherbrooke Street and east of Atwater. A few years later, Godfrey and his wife and children moved onto the same street.[99] (See Figure 11.8.)

As Caroline's children reached maturity, they reshaped their residential relations, constructing new cartographies of kinship, clustering with or close to their widowed mother, moving frequently in tandem, and some-times trading houses. Over the years, they zigzagged westward, roughly following the trajectory of so many English-speaking Montrealers. Their moves frequently took them into recently constructed areas, where they rented solidly respectable houses from the men who had built them, who often lived nearby. Caroline Scott and her children did not have a family home to remain in after Thomas John Pelton died, as Hannah Lyman, Catherine Farquhar Sutherland, or Constance Hannah Hart did, but they were far from on the street. Indeed, without the responsibility of owning a home, Caroline was able to adjust her residential situation to the needs of her children, choosing propinquity to different offspring and living with them, depending on their needs and hers. Hers was not the downward spiral of a struggling widow. Most of her moves took her into homes that cost more rather than less to rent.[100]

Throughout this time, Caroline was usually recognized in city director-ies and census enumerations as the head of her family and household, with her name preceding those of Godfrey or her son-in-law. It is tempting to read a sense of her growing independence and autonomy in the changing ways her public persona was announced to the world in the city director-ies between 1868 and the mid-1870s. Initially, she was listed as "Pelton, Mrs. Widow J." In the mid-1870s, her name appeared as "Pelton, Mrs. Caroline, widow, T.J."[101] Similarly, Catherine Farquhar, who was identified as "Sutherland, Mrs. Wid. Dr. Wm" in the first two years of her widow-hood, began to appear as "Sutherland, Catherine, Wid. Dr. Wm" several years later.[102] As women fought for rights to property and a say in society, such subtle changes in the public naming of widows recognized new, if limited, forms of personhood in their first names, without releasing widows from their ongoing connections to their dead husbands in both the label of widow and their surnames.

Caroline Scott Pelton's age, and her own health, determination, and resources as a middle-class widow, allowed her to maintain her independence and head her own household until well after her children reached adulthood. The census enumerators' listings for 1861 suggest that only four of every ten Montreal widows were recognized as the head of their own household then. Two decades later, this increased to well over half of all widows.[103] In 1861, a further third were living in families that were headed by their children, parents, or other kin; around a sixth boarded with families, who may have been relatives or strangers; and some 5 percent had, like Grace Telfer, found work and shelter as live-in domestics. The other 4 percent were listed in institutions when the census was taken, though more would pass days, weeks, and even months in the different institutions of the city. We return to such women in the next chapter.

How census enumerators decided who was the head of the household in widows' households like that of Caroline Scott Pelton in 1881, which included married children, is not always clear. That year her son-in-law Jacob Beall was described as the family head. Enumerators were meant to list heads and spouses first, then children, followed by other kin, including parents.[104] The normative assumption of male headship must surely have overridden some widows' claims as household heads when they lived with adult sons. Usually such recognition had some basis in the authority relations of domestic rule as translated to the enumerator by those who answered their questions. Figure 11.9 shows that widows in their forties were most likely to be recognized as heading a household, especially when they were living with their children. This was true for about 45 percent of the three-quarters of widows in their forties who were living with offspring, but of only 8 percent of those who lived apart from or had no offspring. Most of those living without offspring lived with kin, boarded, or worked as servants. As widows aged, the proportions heading families or households dropped, slowly for those with children, and remained low for those without.

Class, the ability to retain children in the household, and age interacted to influence whether widows would head their own households. Among the women who married in the 1820s or 1840s, were widowed by 1861 or 1881, and can definitely be identified in those censuses, seven out of ten widows from the elite and middle class were considered household heads. In contrast, five of every ten craftsmen's widows and less than one in ten women whose husbands had been labourers or unskilled workers were

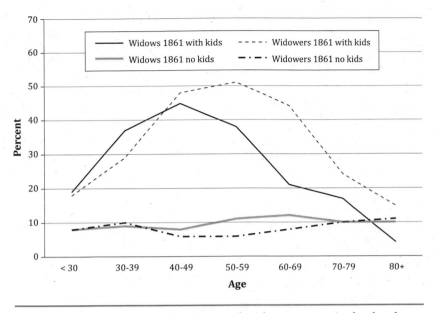

FIGURE II.9 Percentages of widows and widowers recognized as heads of households, by their age and whether they had co-resident children

Note: Widows, 1861, N = 1,395; 1881, N = 6,715.

Source: Bettina Bradbury, Single Parents Montreal, 1861, database; Lisa Dillon, the 1881 Canadian Census Project and the North Atlantic Population Project, Montreal, 1881, database.

listed as household heads.[105] However resourceful they were, few property-less, urban widows of unskilled men who did not have sons of earning age were able to muster the resources necessary to rent a dwelling. Some time after Marie Desormier became a widow in her early sixties, she moved in with a couple in their late forties, probably her daughter and son-in-law. The man was a labourer, as her husband, Jacques Paquet and father had been. Marie was typical of the city's poorer widows who, when captured at all in the censuses, were residing with relatives, friends, or strangers. Such widows of the unskilled would predominate in what Wally Seccombe has described as the "movement of dependants, the very young and the elderly," out of households when death took away "the primary breadwinner's earnings." Such moves contributed to the major increase in patterns of co-residence that accompanied industrialization. These were also the women who were most likely to turn to the city's charitable institutions, as we will see in the next chapter.[106]

As striking as the location of labourers' widows in the homes of relatives and strangers in the census is the absence of their children, especially when contrasted with the lengthy co-residences of adult children with mothers who were elite or middling widows, like Caroline Scott. Living with children, young or adult, and heading a household were interrelated. "The proportion of elderly widows who headed households," reports historian Lisa Dillon, "was smaller in the absence of children than in their presence."[107] Over 60 percent of all Montreal widows living with offspring in 1861 were listed as the head of their family, compared to a little over 20 percent of those without.[108]

Remaining a household head was also inseparable from the class backgrounds of widows, and this is invisible in most census enumerations. Poorer widows lost their offspring through deaths and departures. Again, the patterns among the widows of the two marriage cohorts identifiable in the 1861 census are suggestive, though the numbers are very small. Although 72 percent of the middle class and elite widows were living with offspring, this was true of only 57 percent of widows of craftsmen and of only 22 percent of the widows of unskilled men.[109] Kirsten Wood observes in her study of Southern slave-holding widows that "childlessness exacerbated the insecurities" of widowhood.[110] Similarly, R.J. Morris insists that class made a difference to the "ability to keep children alive."[111] Yet, the absence of children in many of these widows' lives is not just a result of failure to conceive, bear fetuses to term, or children's deaths. Some had borne no children. And many, unlike Wood's privileged slaveholders or the middle-class families in England whom Pat Jalland and Morris have studied, simply did not have the resources to raise children or to keep them at home as they reached adulthood. Their children were scattered in orphanages, working in other people's houses, or running their own fragile family economies.[112]

Caroline Scott and other widows stitched together patchwork quilts of practices out of cloth they inherited from their time as wives. Their designs and fabric varied dramatically, shaped first by the revenue potential of their inheritances and diverse claims on family property, then by the range of possible money-raising and -saving possibilities that suited their class, finances, temperament, and family situations. Designs depended too on their age and health when they became widows and over the years. Possibilities changed as widows and their children aged and as industrialization and the building of an array of institutions transformed work and charitable options.

Husbands' legacies shaped widows' lives for better and worse, richer and poorer, in sickness and in health, and long after their deaths. Yet widows' inheritances included more than the promises made in marriage contracts and wills, or the results of the balance of assets and debts tallied in inventories. What we can see of Caroline Scott's life as a widow reminds us that housing, character, class, values, reputations, linkages to kin, colleagues, fellow citizens, and especially, surviving children constituted critical elements of the estates that women worked with as they reshaped their lives as widows. As a widow, Caroline seems to have been remarkably successful. In contrast to elite and middle-class widows whose husbands had achieved rentier status before their deaths and promised significant annuities, lump sums, or their entire estates in marriage contracts and wills, her marriage contract offered her little. I have found no evidence that her own separate property would suffice to support herself and her six children, though clearly she possessed some means. As a new widow she did not benefit from the assistance of servants, as Catherine Farquhar and Hannah Lyman did. Her residential moves contrast dramatically with the residential stability of those widows following their husbands' deaths. Yet, for her, frequent moves were neither new nor negative. She seems to have purchased some bank stock, secured better and better housing, consistently headed her own household, and lived either with or within blocks of Carrie, Maria, or Godfrey and their spouses over her thirty years as a widow.

The legacies of craftsmen's and labourers' widows were often little more than the sweat equity and "creativity and tenacity" they had already exercised as wives.[113] Starting their widowhood with little if anything, they took in washing or boarders, found work in the expanding sewing industry, or took any kind of day labour that was going. Children's wages, charity, and crime were other possibilities that shaped the patchworks of poor widows as they sought to feed and shelter themselves and any surviving children. Illiteracy and poverty meant that the widows of labourers were the most likely to disappear in the tracking among sources on which these life stories are built. Were there systematic records of the Montrealers who used soup kitchens or sought outdoor relief and other forms of charitable aid, these widows would surely be among the major clients.

Aging, infirmity, and illnesses revealed the weaknesses and the strengths of widows' patchworks. Some bore up well, sheltering women through disease and decline to a dignified death. Others wore thin, frayed, or were sundered as previous support systems and practices fell apart. Widows' final illnesses, aging, challenges, and deaths are the subject of the next and last chapter.

Final Years, Final Wishes
Care, Connections, Old Age and Death

Caroline Walker had been sick "and weak in body" for at least two months when she decided to change the provisions of her previous will. It was September 1841. Thirteen years earlier, this daughter of a prominent family of judges and politicians was widowed after just two years of marriage to her lieutenant husband, Thomas Marshall Harris. Her two surviving sons, James and Thomas, were in their early teens as she again thought carefully about her final wishes. The will she had made two months earlier carefully detailed the property she was bequeathing to them. She did not seek to change those provisions. Rather, she had decided not to give all her clothing to her cousin, Louisa Walker, as that will promised. Now, sure that death was near, she registered her gratitude to another widow "whose extreme kindness and unremitting attention to me during my present illness is beyond commendation deserving of the dearest thanks of myself and my children."[1]

In recognition of the care her "esteemed friend, Eliza McKenzie Gordon, widow of the late George Smith," had given her over the preceding months, she bequeathed Eliza £50 and all her wearing apparel.[2] This was no mean gift. £50 was half the sum the notary Thomas Pelton had promised Caroline Scott when they married around that time. More significantly, Caroline Walker probably owned a considerable wardrobe. When she married in 1826, clothes valued at £100 were a major component of the substantial £324 worth of clothing, jewellery, and household goods designated as her separate property. These signalled her status among the colony's elite. They included one riding habit, ten white dresses, three silk dresses, one canton crape, two gauze dresses, one lace dress, three coloured dresses, six nightgowns, five slips, five petticoats, twenty caps, twelve nightcaps, six lace caps, four pairs of corsets, twelve pairs of cotton stockings, six pairs of silk stockings, twenty pocket handkerchiefs, ten pairs of shoes, ten pairs of gloves, eight muslin collars, and eight frills.[3] Over the intervening fifteen years, some of these may have worn out, been discarded as fashions changed, or replaced with attire more suitable to her persona as widow and mother, rather than wife. Still, the widow Eliza's caregiving was graciously acknowledged in clothing and cash. Caroline Walker died two weeks later. She was forty-one years old. Her body was buried in her family's plot.

Constance Hannah Hart decided to make adjustments to a previous will on the very day she died. Like Caroline Walker, she was not seeking to change the major provisions of her will. Rather, her codicil reflected family discussions and distributed loved family mementos as she wished. She wanted Gerald, her second son, who had lived with her at various times during her widowhood, to have "his china clock and his pictures, as well as any of the ornaments he wishes to keep." Emile, her eldest son, was to have her rocking chair and clock, as well as the use of "Aunt Emily's chair whilst he lives." After his death it was to pass to Miriam. She wanted her daughter Harriet to receive Aunt Frances' chair and a book by Byron. All four children were to share the proceeds from the sale of her "bedroom set of three pieces as well as my spring bed and mattress" and the rest of her furniture. Miriam was to have her "spirit cabinet," dinner set, and the other things she was leaving. The final sentence in her codicil read: "God bless you all and keep you from trouble."[4] Constance was buried two days later in Montreal's Jewish cemetery on Mount Royal, as she requested.

The changes that these two privileged widows made to their wills appear to fit the argument made by Suzanne Lebsock and others that nineteenth-century American and English women demonstrated a degree of what she calls personalism in their wills that would have been unusual in men's wills. Some have interpreted such individualized bequests as evidence of women's culture and sensibility, different from that of men.[5] I explore this interpretation later in the chapter. Here, I want to insist instead that Caroline's and Constance's changes of mind highlight the importance of thinking seriously about care, caregiving, and caring in widows' final years and final wishes. Most widows were used to being caregivers. The majority had raised children and nurtured them through childhood illnesses. Many had provided support to their husbands in their final illnesses. Widows played central roles in their own extended families and neighbourhoods, visiting the ill and acting as friends, nurses, caregivers, and layers out of bodies. Their own illnesses posed different challenges, especially if they were alone or had only minor children. As a widow with dependent children, Caroline Walker worried about her children's future and, more immediately, their care during her illness. And she had needed nursing herself – hence her gratefulness to Eliza. Constance's change of mind, in contrast, demonstrates how profoundly she cared about the distribution of family heirlooms.

Issues of care and caring – for ailing and aging bodies and about family property – are at the heart of this final chapter. It focuses on the last years of the lives of some of the widows whose marriages began in the 1820s and 1840s and on their different pathways to death. It explores how particular widows' health, age, wealth, class, religion, and connectedness to family, kin, faith, and fellow citizens shaped their ability to secure care, their residential options, the decisions they made about any property they owned, and the public acknowledgment of their deaths in newspaper announcements and obituaries, as well as their funerals, burials, and final resting places.

Final Illnesses, Caring, and the Causes of Death

Senility, paralysis, debility, or livers, bones, brains, and bodies weakened by age, years of poor diets, bad habits, or long-term illnesses challenged the diverse patchworks of support that widows stitched together. "Tending to the bodies of the infirm and elderly" placed new and different strains on the family support networks that had allowed some privileged widows to maintain autonomy through their widowhood and past the "shady side of fifty."[6] At forty-one, Caroline Walker was a relatively young widow. Married at twenty-six, widowed at twenty-eight, she had spent thirteen years as a single mother and widow. Widows whose age of death we have been able to determine died at an average of just under seventy, though the age range was considerable. Over half lived into their seventies. Significant numbers died in their eighties and nineties (see Figure 12.1).

Inconsistent and idiosyncratic as the recording of causes of deaths were, they hint at the challenges some widows would have faced in their final years and at the care they might have needed. The card in the Mount Royal Cemetery that records the details of Margaret Jamieson Moody's burial indicates that this printer's widow and boarding house-keeper died of "senile debility" in 1904. She was eighty years old. Like her husband, the former city mayor and merchant Charles-Séraphin Rodier, Marie-Louise Lacroix was described as dying of "debility" when she died three years after him, in 1879, at age eighty-four. Hermine Legris, the carpenter-turned-baker's widow, was listed as dying of old age in 1896 at the age of eighty-eight. Such diseases of old age – recorded as debility, general debility, senility, or simply "old age" – were the reasons given for the deaths of about a third of the 172 widows for whom we have any such details.[7] Dropsy, apoplexy, or paralysis were reported for a further 15 percent of the widows. Caroline Scott Pelton died of pneumonia. As Sarah Walker

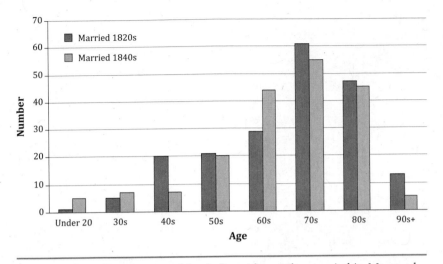

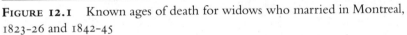

FIGURE 12.1   Known ages of death for widows who married in Montreal, 1823-26 and 1842-45

Note: Women widowed from 1823 to 1826 marriages whose age at death was known, *N* = 197; from 1842 to 1845 marriages, *N* = 385. Ages were not routinely given on death certificates and were reported less reliably before the 1850s, which skews the age distribution shown here toward older widows.

Source: Parish registers, marriages and deaths, Montreal, 1823-1915, complemented with information on age from obituaries or censuses.

Radenhurst headed into her seventies, after nearly fifty years as a widow, she struggled with bronchitis. Such pulmonary- or respiratory-related. illnesses, including tuberculosis, ended the lives of a further 15 percent of these widows. Margaret Logan, the second wife of Andrew White, the contractor who died during the cholera epidemic of 1832, had reached eighty-four years old when she died of breast cancer in 1872. Hers was among the 6 percent of deaths attributed to some form of cancer. Sarah Young, widow first of the labourer-turned-carter Samuel Allen and then of another carter, John Neil, and Amable Leduc, one of the widows who voted in the Montreal East by-election of 1832, were among the smaller number whose deaths were diagnosed as the result of cirrhosis of the liver or other liver problems. Accidents and lack of adequate care killed others. The twice-widowed Rebecca Conegan died at the age of sixty-nine of a fractured skull two years after the death of her second husband.[8] What lay behind the death of Sophie Demers, the remarried widow of a voyageur, which was attributed to "abuse" in 1865, or that of Harriet Shay, the widow of a merchant who suffocated in 1866, remains a mystery, as we have found no records of coroners' investigations for those dates.[9] Different illnesses and debilities related to aging posed diverse challenges to widows and to those caring for them.

Aging and Infirm Bodies and Residential Adjustments

Constance Hannah Hart, as we saw, remained in the Hart family home on Durocher Street following Adolphus' death in 1879 until at least 1892. The census enumerators in both 1881 and 1891 identified her as the head of her household, as did city directories and tax rolls. These sources indicate that Emile or Gerald or both of them lived with her at times during this period and that she usually had the assistance of a general servant. Their names always followed hers. It was there that at some point in the early 1890s the photographer Robert E.J. Summerhayes took the photo of her receiving a friend and surrounded by the chairs that featured in her codicil, as well as her extensive collection of furniture, paintings, and Victorian bric-a-brac reproduced in the previous chapter (see Figure 11.6). After 1893, however, when she was around sixty-seven, this Jewish widow disappeared from listings in the city directories, though she was still identified as the house's owner in the city's annual property rolls. In 1894, her house was rented out. A year later, her son Gerald was noted as living there, along with a medical doctor. Like so many elderly widows who had been heading up their own households, Constance either changed her living situation as she aged or was no longer recognized by information gatherers as heading her household. She may have moved to her daughter Miriam's home. Miriam had married Alfred Belasco, a commercial traveller, in 1888 and lived down the street and around the corner on Prince Arthur.[10] Constance Hannah Hart resurfaces in the documents that I have been able to locate when she decided to write her will in May 1898, and again that year when she added the codicil, then died, on 13 December.[11]

Like Constance and Caroline, most widows adjusted their living situations as they aged and faced diverse illnesses, patterns of decline, and changing needs for care.[12] Among widows enumerated in the city in 1861, the overall results of such adjustments are clear in the rapid decline in the proportion of older widows who headed their own families as they passed from their fifties into their sixties and seventies. About three out of every ten Montreal widows in their fifties were living with sons, daughters, or other relatives. Among those in their sixties, the age of most of the women who had married between 1823 and 1826, over four out of ten were with kin, whereas among widows older than eighty, over half resided with relations. Some secured live-in or daily caregivers. These might include children, nurses, domestics, or, as in Caroline Walker's case, a faithful friend. A few sought institutional assistance (see Figure 12.2).

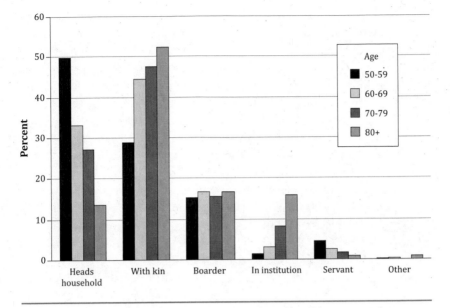

FIGURE 12.2   Residential situations of widows over fifty, Montreal, 1861

Note: Widows over fifty, N = 1,989.

Source: 1861 Census, Montreal. Database single parents.

Historians have tended to interpret such moves as evidence of elderly men's or women's "loss of control over their own home," or the end of their autonomy.[13] Later in the century, the early pioneer doctor and worker for the rights of women Elizabeth Smith Shortt would express her horror at the idea of ending her life dependent on her children or others. Scholars reading the letters and diaries of widows report a similar "discomfort with dependence," though its expression comes mostly from propertied and literate widows.[14] Yet, for many elderly women and men, moving in with children offered access to care they could no longer secure in their own home. Ongoing connection to kin, and especially to their children through bonds of affection, duty, or the power to control their inheritances, enabled them to secure care from relations that might see them through their final years. Moving into the home of an adult child might signal privileged access to care. It might also lead to neglect and abuse. Yet access to such shelter and care must surely be seen as a potential asset, rather than simply as evidence of failure to sustain autonomy.[15] What mattered were the quality of relationships, care, and standards of living.

Hannah Lyman was in her late sixties when she moved out of the home where she had spent her married years and the first two decades of her widowhood following John Mills's death in 1847. In 1867, her two youngest daughters, Alice Stiles and Ada Maria, married the Redpath brothers, George and John respectively. Both couples were moving to England and marrying there, so Hannah sold the family home and moved with them. Two years later, Alice died, leaving two young daughters. Ada Maria and John returned to Montreal.[16] Hannah did not. When the English census was taken in 1881, this American-born, Montreal-raised, elite widow was heading up an all-female household in Camberwell, Surrey, that included her two orphaned granddaughters, Alice Mary and Alice Ethel Redpath, then aged eleven and twelve, as well as her eldest daughter, Mary, then aged fifty-two. There was no sign of Mary's husband. Hannah was eighty-one. She had outlived her husband, her four sons, and her youngest daughter. As she approached her own death, a live-in nurse, a cook, a parlour maid, and a housemaid provided her and family members with a level of home care available only to the elite. She died a year later.[17]

Caroline Scott's tightly knit web of links with her adult children included, as we saw, periods of co-residence with her son, Godfrey Pelton, as well as with her daughter Maria and her husband. When Caroline and her newly widowed daughter, Maria, took up residence on Fort Street in 1884, Caroline was sixty-six. The two widows moved onto a block that had recently been developed with respectable, three-storey, grey stone dwellings and rented number 11 for $220 annually. The year that Caroline turned seventy, Maria died.[18] Directory listings suggest that Caroline remained in the house on Fort Street until her own death in 1900 at the age of nearly eighty-two.[19] Godfrey was living just up the street for most of that time, and Carrie and John Shearer continued to be within walking distance. Care could be shared among rather than within households (see Figure 11.8).

For the elderly of all class backgrounds, family was the most effective welfare institution, and there are traces of similar residential adjustments among all but those poorest of widows whose lives fade out of most sources.[20] Following her husband's death in 1874, the midwife Matilde Beauchamps, widow of the carter-turned-tin roofer François-Xavier Leboeuf-Laflamme, seems to have moved back and forth among three or four addresses either on St. Lawrence Street or around the corner on Lagauchetière. Sometimes she was living alone, at others with one or another of her two married daughters. When the census taker called in 1881, she was recorded as living with her daughter Matilde, her son-in-law, and their children as well as his widowed mother. She was sixty-two. A year later Matilde died, probably having spent the previous eight years of her life caring for and being cared for by kin, and insisting to the end on her identity as both midwife and widow to census takers and the makers of city directories.[21]

When Hermine Legris, the joiner, baker, and labourer's widow, died in 1896 after twenty-four years as a widow, the death notice in the newspaper reported that she died at home. She was eighty-seven years old. She too had spent some of her declining years living with several of her children, married and unmarried. In 1891, she was living with her widowed daughter Sophie, then aged forty and working as a dressmaker, and Sophie's son, thirteen-year-old Charles. In 1894, she was residing with this grandson.[22] Such ongoing connections to kin who were financially able and also willing to provide shelter or care offered the best chance of dying at home or in the homes of children or other kin with some level of material, emotional, and religious care and support. These were privileges that were difficult for poorer widows to sustain.

Institutional Encounters

Unconnected widows, strangers to the city, widows without living children, those who had no relations or who had bruised and severed links to friends and relations through excessive drinking, difficult mental illnesses, or senility, or whose families lacked financial and emotional resources, died on the city streets and in institutions.[23] In April 1875, Rosalie Paquet, then aged sixty-five and long past her life as one of the city's prominent madams, went to the General Hospital of the Grey Nuns, the order with the longest history of providing for Montreal's poor and needy. Her stay there was brief. Under a month later, she left. On the day of her departure, the labourer's widow Adelaide Bebel arrived. Three years earlier, Adelaide had turned to Émilie Tavernier Gamelin's order, the Sisters of Providence, seeking help at the age of seventy-three, a year and a half after she became a widow. When Adelaide arrived at the Asylum for Aged and Infirm Women, run by the Sisters of Providence, in 1872, Marie-Anne Séné had resided there for thirteen years. She entered in 1859, thirty-five years after her marriage and ten years after her husband, the joiner Antoine Hurtubise, died. In contrast to Adelaide, Marie-Anne never left. For the next twenty-six years she remained an inmate of the asylum that continued to expand upon Émilie Tavernier's determination to provide shelter for "friendless" widows.

Rosalie, Adelaide, and Marie-Anne were three of the many widows who turned to the growing number of Catholic and Protestant institutions in Montreal that offered care and shelter. Among the women of these two generations of marriages studied here, we have identified twenty-three, almost all Canadiennes, who definitely spent some time in an institution run by the Grey Nuns or the Sisters of Providence. More would have found shelter elsewhere. They represent around 6 percent of the Canadienne widows of the two generations combined. I have not consulted the records of the institutions that housed elderly Irish Catholic women, and the information recorded by the Protestant Benevolent Society makes identifying specific widows difficult.[24] No such institutions existed for the Jewish population until late in the century.[25] The choices these aging widows made and the details of the establishments they entered offer hints about the complicated range of motivations and challenges that led some elderly women to seek institutional care, embrace it, reject it, or lose the capacity to depart. The traces of their final years suggest the very different relationships that individual widows developed with particular institutions.[26]

Historians studying such institutions, the charitable networks of Montreal, the province, and indeed, the Western world, have analyzed them in a range of ways. Huguette Lapointe-Roy's pioneering 1987 study identified the diverse Catholic actors who reshaped charity provision in the city, giving brief histories of some institutions and of the numbers of people assisted. Her work revealed little about the people who used them or about their broader cultural and social significance.[27] Jean-Marie Fecteau's rigorous exploration of how liberalism offered the liberty to be poor and minimal charitable aid in order to motivate the poor to struggle for their own improvement is convincing. Yet, Fecteau does not address how the liberty to be poor was different for men and women.[28] Nor does the care of elderly men or women, long past the age at which they might be expected to internalize new forms of behaviour, fit readily into interpretations stressing moral regulation, the regulation of the self, or social control as the prime motivation for institution building.[29] Janice Harvey's research, as earlier chapters show, has been fundamental in demonstrating the goals and practices of the two major Protestant institutions run by women: the Ladies' Benevolent Society and the Protestant Orphan Asylum, to which Maria Mitchell's children were taken. Harvey has argued convincingly that the ladies sought to turn their charges into independent individuals, educated according to their station in life but with the necessary skills to survive. Yet, this argument also surely applies more readily to young women and the children they sheltered than to the aging women, who constituted a relatively small fraction of their clientele.[30]

It was New Year's Day 1859 when Marie-Anne Séné joined the elderly and sick women in the Providence Asylum. "Mother Gamelin" had died five years earlier. The community had continued to expand rapidly since Émilie's death. That year the river froze early. Proponents of a House of Industry reminded Montrealers of the large number of men and women, young and old, who were saved from freezing to death on the streets by admission to the prison.[31] Had Marie-Anne needed firewood to keep warm, she could have secured some from the depots for the poor run by

FIGURE 12.3 "Issuing Wood to the Poor." Note the prominence of women, possibly widows, in this 1872 representation of the poor seeking firewood, as well as the paradox of progress and neediness the artist relays. Elderly widows would have had trouble going to seek their own firewood. | Artist unknown. Musée du Château Ramezay, Montreal, No. 1998.3018.

the Sisters of Providence, the Grey Nuns, the Society of Saint Vincent de Paul, or from municipal authorities. Protestant charities also distributed wood to the needy. Widows of good character were considered the most deserving of the city's poor and predominated among those receiving charitable aid.[32] Figure 12.3 suggests how widows with children figured discursively and visually as "the poor," requiring help and deserving firewood. Wood, bread, flour, peas, beans, and sometimes clothing, blankets, or a stove were among the main forms of aid in kind offered by the Sulpicians, other religious orders, and the growing number of Protestant charities. From the 1840s on, lay Charity Ladies and men determined widows' eligibility for aid by visiting them in their homes and issuing certificates. Securing assistance usually required visiting the depots set up to distribute wood, food, and sometimes clothing and presenting the certificates. Furthermore, apart from bread, most foodstuffs distributed required preparation and cooking, work that was difficult for the elderly, the ill, or the incapacitated.[33] There were soup kitchens.[34] However, accessing those meals required either physical mobility or sending someone to collect the food. Visits by charity givers brought scrutiny and temporary relief, but for some men or women confined at home as bodies and minds weakened with age or illness, or facing homelessness on the streets with no one to care for them, institutional support must have seemed an appealing option.

Residential possibilities for Catholic elderly, weak, and sick men and women expanded dramatically over the century. The main options between the 1840s and 1870s were run by the Sisters of Providence, the semi-cloistered nursing sisters at the Hôtel-Dieu, and the Grey Nuns. All orders expanded the space available in existing institutions, created new ones, and added facilities for Irish Catholics over these years. Separate institutional options for elderly Protestant men or women remained more limited than for Catholics, leading one Protestant Montrealer to recommend in 1863 that Protestants take "a leaf out of the book of the Roman Catholics" regarding charitable institutions. The Protestant Montreal General Hospital provided for some of the city's poor when they were sick. The Protestant Ladies' Benevolent Society was created specifically to assist widows and orphans. An 1871 description highlighted the "aged widow," alongside the "deserted wife, the forsaken child, the deformed, the infirm, the paralysed, the blind," and "the incurable invalid," among its inmates.[35] Yet, only 189 women older than fifty entered in the years between the 1830s and the end of the century. Most of their inmates were children.[36] Other possibilities of refuge for Protestant women were the various servants' homes created across the century: denominational homes like the Anglican Church Home, begun in 1855; homes run by the growing number of national societies; the Houses of Industry and Refuge that were initiated on several occasions; or, after 1874, the Woman's Christian Temperance Union–initiated Home for Friendless Women.[37] Women whose lives had spun out of control or who were completely indigent might also try committing a crime, or simply begging the police to put them in jail for a while, as fair numbers did in the first half of the century. In every census year, widows were among the inmates enumerated in the city's prisons, hospitals, asylums, and, when it existed, the Protestant House of Industry.[38]

When Marie-Anne Séné entered the Providence Asylum in 1859, a sister inscribed her name in their large register, indicated that she was Antoine Hurtubise's widow, that he had been a joiner, and that Marie-Anne was a Canadienne, a Montreal resident, and sixty years old. Hers was the 303rd name in the register. The numbering of the women admitted began in

1830, soon after Émilie Tavernier sheltered the first group of elderly women in her home. The Sisters of Providence recorded marital status more consistently than did the Grey Nuns. If the person arriving said she was married or widowed, both orders usually listed the names of the spouse. Their reasons for seeking shelter were rarely recorded. Occasional notations identified particular women as "idiots," epileptic, paralyzed, blind, or having pulmonary problems. One elderly woman, their chronicles reported, was dumped outside the asylum on an early December night with her name and age pinned to her clothes. She begged them to let her stay, though there was no bed available.[39] Reasons were recorded quite frequently at the Ladies' Benevolent Society. The majority of its older women were described as destitute or aged. Related reasons included that they were homeless, helpless, starving, could not support themselves, or had family problems, or that their caretakers could not support them anymore. Edgar-André Montigny has convincingly argued that in Ontario, many families provided "amazing" care for aged and senile relatives before turning to asylums.[40]

Marie-Anne Séné may have depleted her financial resources over her first ten years of widowhood. She had benefited from the most generous provisions a husband could offer a widow. The day before he died in mid-January 1849, Antoine Hurtubise wrote a will leaving all of his belongings to her. They may have been minimal, but she was able to provide Charles with a decent funeral. She paid over £2 for his funeral service, as well as an additional 15s. for the cart and a further 15s. for the coffin and other sundry expenses.[41] Perhaps the Providence Asylum attracted some women who preferred the idea of shelter in an institution with only female residents. In the public imagination, Émilie's project was more closely associated than others were with the care of elderly women and specifically with widows. In Bishop Bourget's public pleas for support, he insisted on the importance of the help given to elderly women "who had no children to assist them."[42] As far as I can tell, neither Marie-Anne, Adelaide Bebel, nor Rosalie Paquet had any surviving children. Yet, Marie-Anne Séné had more personal reasons to turn to the Sisters of Providence. Her life story and that of the institution were closely intertwined. She and her two sisters, Agathe and Émilie, moved to Montreal some time before her marriage with Antoine Hurtubise in 1823. Agathe had helped Émilie Tavernier care for the elderly women housed at the Yellow House in the 1830s.[43] In 1844, Agathe became one of the founding seven Sisters of Providence, taking her vows immediately after Émilie Tavernier. Marie-Anne's sister Émilie was among the second group of women who took their vows as Sisters of Providence. She died before Marie-Anne arrived as an inmate.[44] Marie-Anne would surely have attended the ceremonies when her two sisters took their vows and probably attended her youngest sister's funeral. For her, then, this was not an unfamiliar place. Her move to an institution meant maintaining family ties, not breaking them.

Although Marie-Anne Séné's close family links in the institution were special, she shared much with the other inmates. Most of the widows whom she joined in the rooms for the poor were also the widows of un-skilled workers, especially of labourers as Adelaide Bebel was, or of men like her husband, who came from the crafts and especially the volatile construction trades.[45] The smaller numbers of wives using the asylum came from similar backgrounds. The class backgrounds of the twenty-three widows from the 1820s and 1840s cohorts of marriages who definitely spent some time among the poor cared for by the Sisters of Providence or the Grey Nuns were similar. Most of their husbands had been unskilled or craftsmen.[46] After his visit in the early 1840s, the Patriote Jean Girouard suggested that such women might "otherwise have died from misery or want of care."[47]

At sixty, Marie-Anne was somewhat younger than most women were when they first arrived. Her widowed companions averaged just under age seventy on their arrival, though women entered anywhere from their twenties to over age a hundred.[48] More than six of every ten of the women with whom Marie-Anne shared her food and prayers had also made the transition from wife to widow at least once. Thus, Marie-Anne joined a community of women, roughly united in their old age, class backgrounds, Catholicism, infirmities, and the experience of having been both wife and widow. Over time, more married women also found shelter there. Single women without children to turn to as they aged were a smaller proportion of the inmates, but overrepresented in relationship to their part in the city's population.[49]

Moving to such asylums did not relieve the elderly women from work. For able inmates in the asylums of the Grey Nuns and Sisters of Providence, as in Protestant institutions, work, like prayer, was not optional. Inmates' work helped run the institutions and the products of their labour raised money. In the 1840s, Girouard described women preparing rags to make carpets, some "with the only fingers that remain to them." Others knitted, making bags, while "those who cannot work pray."[50] Over subsequent decades work included sewing and washing, and making priests' soutanes, shoes, wax statues of Jesus, and other religious decorations for use in churches and to sell in the community. At the Providence Asylum in par-ticular, such labour continued to be critical to raising the money needed to run the institution. The sisters embraced new ideas and projects, adapting their methods to the changing technologies of production in an industrial-izing city, taking advantage of the religious paraphernalia that ultramon-tane Catholicism required, and developing new products. The printing of a thousand catechisms from their printing shop, a modern laundry and soap-making workshop, and fabricating hundreds of small reliquary as well as diverse medicines were but a few of their initiatives in the 1870s. That decade, Bishop Bourget allowed the sisters to add corset making to their productive ventures. In 1877, they modernized their laundry, adding steam-run washing machines and a huge dryer. By the 1880s, their income from making pine gum syrup counterbalanced cutbacks in support from the Sulpicians.[51]

Marie-Anne became a long-term resident in a complex economic and religious community, closely integrated into the hierarchy, struggles, and power structures of the Catholic Church. Inside, the unravelling of the days, months, and years were marked by work; strict timetables; religious rituals; the birthdays of patron saints, of Montreal's bishops, and of Émilie Tavernier; and by diverse festive occasions. The rhythms for the inmates were similar to those of the sisters. The newness of the congregation, its ongoing growing pains, friction, and particularly close links to the bishop, as well as Émilie's legacy, all shaped the ambience and material details of daily life. Unlike the Grey Nuns, who received fairly steady funding from the Sulpicians and from the government, the Providence Asylum received erratic amounts of government funding and continued to rely largely on gifts, legacies from the wealthy, and its own efforts.[52] Thanking Providence for gifts of money, bread, butter, and other foodstuffs at common prayers was a routine requirement for the sisters, the elderly, and the other inmates alike.[53]

Not all inmates were poor. Elite women also joined these institutions, entering, as we saw, as paying pensioners. At the Providence Asylum they included members of the prominent LaFontaine, Arnoldi, and Delisle families, women whose husbands had been well-known Patriotes; women who had been closely involved as Charity Ladies; and relatives of Émilie Tavernier. Among them were Marie-Adelaide Comte, widow of the Patriote Pierre Damour, as well as Émilie's cousin and friend who had worked so closely with her in creating the institution, the widow Agathe Perrault Nowlan. Some, as mentioned earlier, made contracts similar to those that aging rural couples made with their children, offering property, goods, or sums of money in return for care, treatment, and the promise of a mass or funeral upon their deaths.[54] Their quarters varied with their class and contribution. Most had a room, some several. A few brought their servants. Some arrived with daughters; most came alone. Some stays were short. Some came and went, while others remained for decades until their death.

They came for physical and spiritual reasons, attracted to the care they might receive but also to the religious atmosphere and the convent-like way of living. In 1851, Bishop Bourget expressed his satisfaction that people who had lived in lovely houses, with the best society, would content themselves with a small room, away from their kin, and live and work with the poor. Some were demanding. Like non-paying inmates, some came because of dementia or lost their faculties as they aged. Others threw themselves into the spiritual and social relations of the institution, making decorations and donating money during their time there, as well as leaving it money, linen, clothing, and other goods in their wills. [55]

The chronicling nun of the St. Joseph Hospice, which opened in 1844 and closed in 1909, recorded that some of these pensioners were sick, tired, suffering from sore legs, or sensing the need to prepare for their death. One woman with eye cancer wanted to save her family the work involved in caring for her and "to be closer to her Lord." The presence of these middle-class and elite women who could afford to pay for care at home and who in many cases were still closely connected to grown children and relatives is a good reminder that it was not just poverty that pushed women into Catholic institutions of care. Personal connections to the project, the religious atmosphere and rituals, their own spirituality and faith, and the heightened chance that a priest would be present to provide the final sacraments might also have attracted them. [56]

In their chronicles, the Sisters of Providence distinguished between "our Lady Pensioners" and "our dear old women" or "[our] infirm old ladies," generally using the possessive pronoun with affection, incorporating poor and rich differently into the enterprise. In the discursive strategies of the Catholic hierarchy, the poor, elderly inmates and their infirmities held a special place. As elderly women they were embodied reminders of the imminence of death for all and of the importance of charitable works to individual salvation. As widows they symbolized the deserving poor. The more decrepit, senile, and loathsome they were, the greater the charity involved in caring for them, or in giving to support those who did. When the Grey Nuns and Sisters of Providence received important visitors, those elderly who could leave their beds appeared in the carefully choreographed public presentation of their work – lined up explicitly in contrast to the orphans, children at the other end of life. On such occasions, the elderly stepped bodily into the church's discourse on death, confirming by their presence in a Catholic institution the crucial importance of a good Catholic death, and legitimating the broader role of the Church in the religious and political economy of Montreal. [57]

Such visits were not unusual, since asylums for the elderly, like institutions for the mad, featured regularly among the tourist sites of bishops, high-up clergy, governors, and more lowly visitors to the city. Neither the poor nor the pensioners were cut off from the outside world. Visits linked them to the hierarchy of the Catholic Church and introduced them to a range of prominent contemporary personalities from in and outside Canada. On holidays and feast days, celebrations were held both in and outside. Both the Grey Nuns and Sisters of Providence organized special suppers periodically for the inmates. On these occasions, lay charity workers normally served the meals, reversing class relations for the evening and demonstrating their compassion for those whose very infirmities reinforced the merits of their benevolence. Marie-Anne Séné would have attended many of these over her nearly three decades in residence with the Sisters of Providence. Theirs were fairly small, intimate affairs. In the early days of Émilie Tavernier's work, her sister-in-law had held a special dinner for the elderly women in honour of her daughter's marriage at which the newly wed couple served the meal.[58] At least three times between 1869 and 1884, while Marie-Anne Séné was in residence, Luce Cuvillier hosted. Her involvement underlines the ongoing familial links among the supporters of Émilie's work. Luce followed in the footsteps of her mother, Marie-Claire Perrault, who had accompanied Émilie when she took her vows and been so active among the earliest Charity Ladies. In the 1860s, Luce's widely known affair with the prominent federal politician George-Etienne Cartier did not prevent her from serving as president of the Charity Ladies' Association. She hosted one such dinner the year before Marie-Anne Séné died, serving all the elderly women with the help of seven sisters. After dinner she sat "among these good old ladies and told them stories while giving them tobacco."[59]

In placing herself in the asylum, Marie-Anne was agreeing to abide by the regulations that governed the religious, material, and social aspects of daily life. Probably the religious culture appealed to her. When another equally long-term resident died, the chronicles reported that she had given "herself to the community," wording that evokes both the giving up of self that marriage involved for women and the vow to serve God that nuns made.[60] In both cases it serves as a reminder that such a religious institutional life might appeal to some laywomen as they aged and faced diverse infirmities, or to women who wanted to embrace a religious life without becoming nuns. That a significant number of women might seek to live "away from the world" was explicitly recognized by one benefactor who died in 1882 and left her house to serve that purpose.[61]

Some poor inmates resented the rules, the rituals, their objectification, or the food and care. Feigning sickness or taking to their beds were possible expressions of resistance. Some were asked to leave. More registered their dissatisfaction by choosing to, though the viability of that choice depended on their state of health and alternative options. Adelaide Bebel stayed only twenty-four days with the Sisters of Providence in 1872.[62] In the homelike atmosphere of the early years, before Émilie's work was incorporated officially in the church, virtually all her elderly charges had stayed until they died. For these elderly widows it was "a quiet place to die."[63] Between Émilie's vocation and her death, and especially in the years after that, more and more chose to depart or were requested to do so.[64]

Marie-Anne Séné stands out for the length of her institutional residence. Between 1828 and 1891, only six other women remained as long or longer than her. Over half died or departed within two years or less. The average stay was a little over four years.[65] Deaths remained a pretty frequent experience, so that in addition to the organized religious rituals that punctuated their days and months, the inmates spent time praying for dying women and attending their funerals. Of the 135 women who joined Marie-Anne over her twenty-six years in residence, eighty-nine died before she did. She was intimately familiar with the culture of institutional Catholic deaths.

Institutions varied in the demographic features of the clientele, the atmosphere of the congregation, the care they offered, and the background of the sisters.[66] When Rosalie Paquet and Adelaide Bebel chose to seek shelter with the Grey Nuns in 1875, this congregation had been expanding the number of their institutions taking in elderly, sick, and poor men and women, as well as the numbers they were sheltering for over a decade. Their charges included men as well as women, were more diverse in their ages, and younger on average than those with the Sisters of Providence. They were also less likely to remain until their deaths. There too, the proportions leaving rather than dying increased over time.

The history of the Grey Nuns was as long as that of the Sisters of Providence was short. Opened initially in 1692, the General Hospital had cared for elderly, infirm, and poor women since the widow Marie-Marguerite Dufrost de Lajemmerais took over its management in 1747.[67] By the 1870s, their institutions taking in elderly men and women included their General Hospital, Saint Patrick House and the Saint Bridget Asylum for Irish Catholics, the Saint Joseph Hospice, the Saint Charles Hospice, and the Nazareth Asylum, most of whose inmates were blind.[68] Two years before Adelaide Bebel and Rosalie Paquet arrived, the sisters had moved all their inmates out of the stately three-storey Mother House on Wellington Street, close to the port, to an immense, new four-storey convent and asylum that took up a large city block on Dorchester Street in the northwestern part of the city.[69] (See Figure 12.4.)

It was to this large and rather grim building that Adelaide Bebel and Rosalie Paquet went in 1875. Neither embraced institutional life permanently or avoided it completely. Over these final years of her life, Adelaide moved in and out of shelters at least four times. Nine months after her three-and-a-half-month stay among the poor in the General Hospital of

FIGURE 12.4 The General Hospital of the Grey Nuns, Dorchester Street (now Boulevard René-Lévesque), Montreal. This is the main front entrance of the complex set of buildings constructed for the Grey Nuns that took up a full city block. | Archives de la Ville de Montréal, Fonds Gariepy, G-1486.

the Grey Nuns, she went to the Grey Nuns' Saint Joseph Hospice on Cemetery Street. After nearly a year there, the sisters transferred her to their Saint Charles Hospice for elderly and infirm men and women. She remained there for four months. At the age of seventy-eight she departed again. I have found no further traces of her life, nor any sign of her death.

Rosalie Paquet was sixty-five years old and had been a widow for nearly thirty years when she entered the Grey Nun's General Hospital. Like so many of the women who ended up in such shelters, she left few visible traces of her years of widowhood in the city's directories over her years of widowhood. This contrasted with her visibility in her days as a young madam.[70] How this aging woman, probably suffering from sexually trans-mitted diseases, was received by the sister who recorded her entrance is no more visible today than are most other aspects of her life.[71] She stayed only twenty-four days. In contrast to Adelaide, however, her death was clearly registered. Rosalie died three years later, in January 1878, at the St. Jean de

Dieu Lunatic Asylum at Longue-Pointe, the asylum that fulfilled Émilie Tavernier's hope of providing a new kind of specialized and humane care for the insane. Émilie died without seeing this project come to fruition, but in 1873, the Sisters of Providence had opened this large, modern asylum at the eastern end of Montreal Island. Between 1873 and 1889, they transferred at least thirteen of their elderly women there.[72] The Grey Nuns may have done the same. Their registers provide little information on transfers. It is possible that Rosalie was transferred directly there from their asylum.

On arrival, Marie-Claude Thifault reports, inmates were obliged to wash and surrender their clothes. They were issued with new garments deemed suitable to their previous station in life. Their names were registered, as were details of their illness as described by the doctor who oversaw their admission. What Rosalie wore on entry, or what clothes were considered suitable for her, and what the doctors wrote about her state of body or mind are all protected by privacy legislation. Here she spent her last days, possibly her last years, struggling, perhaps with the dementia that might hit any man or woman as he or she aged, but more likely suffering from the bodily weakness, confusion, disorder, or personality changes and dementia that characterize the secondary and tertiary stages of syphilis. It was half a century since her first arrest for involvement in a disorderly house at the age of sixteen, in 1827, and over thirty years since she had married Eloi Beneche, in 1843. There were no reliable means of avoiding sexually transmitted diseases. Before the use of penicillin, only those with the strongest immune systems were likely to escape its awful impact. And yet, Rosalie lived until she was nearly seventy, entering this asylum in her late sixties. There was little chance of a cure for her at the St. Jean de Dieu asylum or elsewhere. Therapy there, Thifault suggests, was an illusion for most patients. Control, chaos, care, or comfort within an institution that was much more like a prison than the asylum of the Grey Nuns that she had left were the promises of Rosalie's final dwelling place.[73]

Nuns, doctors, and paid asylum workers watched over the inmates at all times of day and night. Thifault describes the crowd of marginal and marginalized women circulating the same corridors, eating at the same dining hall, using the same toilets, and sharing living spaces, losing all privacy. Yet, for Rosalie, some of this was surely not so new. Privacy was a luxury that many poor and working-class women could not afford. Living among marginal and marginalized women had started early in her life. Sharing living spaces, beds, and toilets might also remind her of earlier times running brothels. Many inmates remained connected to family members, and some returned home permanently or temporarily.[74] Rosalie had no children. She died as she had lived much of her life, among women marginalized for their behaviour. Whereas her co-workers in the early-nineteenth-century Montreal sex trade had often died young and on the streets, she died elderly and with some level of physical and religious comfort and care, thanks in part to Émilie Tavernier's conviction that such women should not be left to fend for themselves on the streets.[75]

Final Possessions, Final Wishes

The clothes that Rosalie Paquet relinquished on entering the St. Jean de Dieu asylum may have been the last things she possessed apart from her own body. As an institutionalized inmate, that too risked passing into the hands of anatomy professors and their medical students. To face death in full possession of one's faculties, body, clothing, and any property was a privilege that Constance Hart and Caroline Walker shared with only some widows. For propertied widows, impending death provoked reflection on the future of children, friends, family possessions, and belongings. In conversations with children, friends, doctors, or priests, they might pass on their own wishes about their deaths, their funerals, or the dispersion of their property. Caroline Walker and Constance Hart were among the relatively few who, blessed with clarity, literacy, and some property, recorded their final wishes in formal wills.

Constance wrote shakily as she spelled out her final wishes regarding her ornaments, clocks, pictures, chairs, and copy of Bryon on 13 December 1898. She had probably been sick since at least May of that year, when she made a notarial will. Since then, she had clearly been discussing the final disposition of her property with her four grown children. The codicil began with the sentence, "As I have just made a new will and Lalla thinks I have not done her justice." Constance was determined to control the distribution of these domestic family items that carried sentimental meaning for her and her children and linked generations of the Harts through material objects. Suzanne Lebsock argued in 1984 that women's wills were characterized by a degree of "personalism" unmatched in those written by men. Men in early-nineteenth-century Petersburg, Virginia, divided estates equally, she reports, whereas women tended to play favourites. They chose daughters over sons, and generally recognized the "inequalities of love, loyalty and need within families." Lebsock considered this part of a broader "distinctive women's value system or culture."[76]

Other historians have also noted the different patterns of male and female bequests. R.J. Morris suggests that the testators whose wills he analyzed in Leeds, England, conceptualized property and its transmission in three ways. "Cash economy capitalists" dominated among male will makers. Such men directed their executors to have virtually all their goods and real property valued and sold and invested to provide an annuity to their widow, and to divide the rest equally among their children. The second group, real estate people – or "urban peasants" – listed items of real property and allocated them in bundles to their heirs, thus keeping land within the family and shaping family geographies within the urban landscape. The third category, "things people," were mostly women. Widows were much more likely than either spinsters or males to "detail specific things and allocate them to specific friends and relatives." "Silver, especially silver marked with initials, was often a carrier of family identity"; so were plate, beds, and bedding.[77]

One problem with Lebsock's link between women's bequests and the idea of a women's culture was, as Lisa Wilson has noted, that she does not acknowledge that most women giving bequests were widows, so that the distribution of most family property had often already occurred through husbands' wills.[78] This is a fair critique, but it needs to be developed further, as well as placed in the context of common law practices and rules of inheritance. It was relatively rare in common law jurisdictions for married women to make wills until after the passage of married women's property acts late in the century. As marriage made husbands the owners of most of their wives' property, they controlled its distribution, whether in gifts to their children when they married, at other moments, or in their wills. So, except for widows who had inherited a full estate outright, most widows were distributing only property not already accounted for and only property that was theirs to control. Morris is careful, reminding readers that "widows could only devise what was theirs outright," usually possessions, yet he often lumps widows and single women together as "women," despite their very different legal rights.[79]

The Quebec legal context offers an interesting contrast to common law jurisdictions because of the community property provisions of the Custom of Paris, the custom of giving children gifts across their life cycles, and the ease with which separate property could be established in marriage contracts. Montreal widows were more likely than those in common law jurisdictions to have property of their own, as their half of community property, as their separate property, or as a bequest from their husband. The small numbers of widows' wills we have found, and the serendipitous searching strategy that located them, require modest claims here. Still, zooming in on these few widows' wills in some detail, in the context of what we know about their individual lives, offers hints about wider practices. These merit further study.[80]

We have found twenty-eight wills written by women who married in the 1820s or 1840s and became widows. Sixteen were written while the women were still wives, twelve as widows. Not surprisingly, English-style wills are overrepresented because they are easier to locate, so most were the wills of the widows of merchants, high-ranking army men, public servants, or professionals. A few were the widows of craftsmen and men in small businesses.[81] All twelve women who wrote their wills as widows and had living children gave most of their belongings and property to their children. Most sought a rough equality, but unlike men, who tended to adhere to the liberal principle of giving all an equal part, these widows appear to have privileged equality of outcome. As the surviving spouse, often in full control of all remaining property, they exhibited a mixture of "personalism" and a commitment to functional equality. Some compensated for daughters' inequality as single women, widows, or wives, as historians have noted female testators did elsewhere. Some acknowledged the particular contributions or situations of specific sons or daughters. Others compensated for husbands who had made unequal distributions.[82] Still others factored in loans and earlier donations. Several, like Caroline Walker, also used their wills to acknowledge the contributions that other women – daughters, friends, or servants – had made caring for them over the years or during illness and incapacity. Marie-Louise-Josephte Chartier de Lotbinière asked her children not to abandon "little Rose Daly."[83] Mary-Jane Ross left £100 in recognition of Mrs. Mary White's faithful service.[84] A few widows, like other testators, used their wills to set out their wishes about their funerals, to assert their religious faith, or to encourage particular forms of behaviour among their children. The wills of this small number of Montreal widows spanned Morris' three categories rather than fitting neatly into any of them.

The property that Caroline Walker could devise in her own will comprised her own separate property and what remained of their belongings. Her husband's will had bequeathed her all his moveable property, and placed his immoveable property in his father's hands to divide equally between their two sons. Caroline's will was similar to his, apart from her gifts to the widow Eliza Gordon. She owned considerable property outside Montreal. She wanted that land and the rest of her estate to go equally to both boys.[85] Mary Lloyd's wishes were similar. She sought equality regardless of gender. She and her former husband, the merchant William Snowden, partially fit but also confound Morris' definition of an "urban peasant," or "real estate person." This emigrant from New Glasgow had married in Montreal in 1823. Her and William's marriage contract excluded community property, and gave William full control over the administration of her goods. They lived outside the city for much of their marriage, but her children moved back there, and after she became a widow in 1857 she joined them. In 1863, she purchased a plot in the Mount

Royal Cemetery and had her husband's body moved there. The will she made in 1865 conveys the authority of someone with complete knowledge of and control over her estate. She placed her considerable land holdings outside Montreal, along with one Montreal lot, in the hands of her trustees to sell within ten years, requesting that they divide the proceeds equally among her two daughters and four sons. In this provision she fits Morris' category of a cash economy capitalist. She also owned six adjacent lots on St. Antoine Street in Montreal, each with a three-storey shop, dwelling, and stables either under construction or complete. She left each of her children one, explicitly providing that on lots where a shop was not yet completed, or if one was destroyed before her will came into effect, the executors were to have it repaired or completed. In this way, like Morris' urban peasants, her bequests shaped the familial geography and ownership patterns of a city block. She also provided her husband's living brother with sufficient income annually to live at the level of comfort to which he was accustomed. To her only unmarried daughter she left all her clothing apparel and jewellery, plates, furniture, and other household effects, thus acknowledging how that daughter's needs differed from those of her married sister.[86]

The elite widow Sarah Walker Radenhurst also made special provisions for her daughter Helen, who had never married. Sarah had been widowed for nearly fifty years when she sat down to write her will at the age of seventy-six in July 1879. By then her daughters Eliza Ann and Helen Radenhurst were well into adulthood. Eliza Ann had married Thomas Roe, a Quebec-born Protestant trader of Irish origin. In recognition of Helen's singleness, and perhaps of the ways her own widowhood had discouraged Helen from marrying, Sarah bequeathed all of her bedroom furniture, including the stove, to her. She divided the rest of her bank stocks and furniture equally between the two girls, stipulating that they should share the interest during their lifetimes and that the survivor should take the capital.[87]

Constance Hart's wishes in her codicil appear to fit the personalism that Lebsock identifies with women, or they suggest that she was a "things" testator, according to Morris' categories. She also made special provisions for a widowed daughter. Yet, she too sought a rough equality of outcome among her children once the emotionally loaded family possessions had been parcelled out. When she called the notaries John Redding and Lewis Hart to draw up her will in May 1898, six months prior to the codicil, she lucidly explained her wishes. She had made major loans to Gerald. Forgiving those were her legacy to him, along with the family paintings. Emile was to have the property she had purchased in British Columbia. She wanted her house sold for as good a price as possible, and specified that $3,000 of the proceeds was to go to her daughter Miriam, possibly to pay back a loan. Any further proceeds from the sale of her home and furniture were to be shared equally among all except Gerald. Her two daughters were to share her jewellery and clothes. All else that she owned was to be divided among Emile, Miriam, and Harriet, with the latter, who was a widow, receiving a double share. In Morris' terms, Constance was a cash economy capitalist, a things person, and a real estate person rolled into one.[88] Her decisions left one son owning a piece of land on the far western coast of the country; her other son well established and debt free; family mementos, including paintings, chairs, and ornaments, allocated to specific children; and her other things and primary residence sold and distributed to her offspring in ways that recognized past contributions and current needs.

None of these widows showed any commitment to primogeniture. Indeed, Catherine Wade wrote her will to counteract the possibility that residence in Upper Canada following her 1825 Montreal marriage, and her husband's death there, might mean his possessions would all go to her eldest son. They had moved when the question of abolishing primogeniture provoked heated debates in and outside the Legislative Council and Assembly. Her will provided that, should Ontario law require that all her husbands' possessions go to one child, her own estate was to be divided equally between the other two. Her preference was for all her belongings except her wardrobe and clothing apparel to be shared equally. These were to go to her only daughter. Clothes were the most intimate of the "female things" that Morris argues women cared about "when allocating property."[89]

The few wills of widows from the crafts, small commerce, or labouring communities reflect the egalitarian spirit found in their marriage contracts. When Elizabeth Parslow decided to write her will in 1898, it was fifty-five years since her piano maker husband, John Stephenson, had died. They had made no marriage contract. Two of her three children had lived to adulthood. Her one daughter, Sarah, aged about forty-nine, was also a widow. Elizabeth's will was simple and reflected the spirit of most men's wills. It gave all she had to the children, to be shared equally. Elizabeth Lang, a peddler's widow, was an exception in giving all to her daughters and nothing to her sons.[90]

This small number of widows' wills suggests the importance of seriously considering age, marital status, past family histories, and personal idiosyncrasies alongside gender in examining wills. Many of these widows offered their daughters special bequests of clothing, jewellery, or personal and domestic items, and larger portions of their estates than their sons.[91] Mostly, they balanced acknowledgment of care they had received, assistance to daughters who were widowed or single, and adjustments for support already received in order to promote a rough equality in outcomes that recognized gender and other individual differences.[92]

Final Moments: Death, Funerals, and Burials

Constance Hart's will dealt first with her faith and her body. "I desire," she wrote, "that my body be buried in a quiet and unostentatious manner and according to the rites of the Jewish persuasion."[93] Widows' final wills scripted the partition of remaining property and sometimes the desired details of funerals and burials. Final illnesses and deaths produced diverse narratives of their lives. Shared over dead bodies, recorded at times in family letters and papers, and publicized in condensed form in death notices, obituaries, or tombstone inscriptions, these produced particular, partial identities and histories out of the rich complexities of lives lived. Widows' deaths, funerals, and burials – like those of the husband or husbands, and in so many cases children whom they had outlived – initiated diverse final journeys and produced varied records, resting places, and memorials.

The details of Émilie Tavernier's death have been repeated and reworked in successive biographies and hagiographies since 1851, taking on narrative stability as a classic Catholic "good death" story in which she moves from foundress to heroine to future saint.[94] Her death from cholera was, as we saw, fairly sudden. Accounts describe her as sufficiently lucid to make her last confession to Mgr. Prince and receive the "Holy Viaticum." She retained "consciousness till the last minute. Bishop Bourget administered the final rites, then all the sisters came to see her and she bade them farewell. She is said to have summoned all her energy to call on her fellow nuns to make humility, simplicity, and charity the basis of their perfection, insisting on charity as the most important virtue. At four in the afternoon she died, pressing the Crucifix to her breast.[95] After her death, the elderly inmates were described as inconsolable. One is reported to have run into the streets proclaiming, "The mother of the poor is dead." The news of her death was spread further by the tolling of the funeral bell and word of mouth. Later accounts describe the poor hastening "thither from all parts, invading the avenue, and the corridor near to the chapel, begging that they might be allowed to see the body of their Mother ... to kiss her feet."[96] No one was allowed near. Religious ritual had governed her death, but health regulations would shape her burial. A sister placed her in a coffin and covered her body with lime. Had there been a public funeral, it might have rivalled those of some of the city's prominent men and produced a different narrative of her final moments. When one of their sisters died in 1850, the procession included some fifty carriages, most sisters, inmates, and pensioners, as well as numerous Montrealers. But by 1851, the risk of spreading cholera at such events was well established. Émilie's body was taken to the chapel crypt, near to the resting places of Sisters of Providence who had died before her. Waiting the usual two days was out of the question. Mgr. Prince presided over the funeral the next morning, and her body was lowered into the chapel crypt.[97]

In the days and months that followed, *Mélanges religieux,* the newspaper that the bishop directed, published a series of celebratory accounts of her many works, thanking God for sending "such a heroine to our city, such an example to our century."[98] The accounts lauded her work with the poor, the insane, and the elderly. Some reminded readers of her close association with the imprisoned Patriotes at the time of the rebellions.[99] Some were reprinted in *La Minerve.* I have found no mention of her death in the *Montreal Gazette.*

Marie-Anne Séné died of "old age" over thirty years later, on 1 March 1885. She was eighty-six and had spent most of her sixties and all of her seventies and eighties in the Sisters of Providence Asylum for Aged and Infirm Women. Over her twenty-six years as an inmate, her sister Agathe, Mother Zotique, came and went, moving among posts in various institutions in and beyond Montreal. She returned for part of her retirement.[100] As a long-term resident, Marie-Anne could be pretty sure that she would receive the final sacraments before her death, and die with the support that this community that she had made hers and her religious faith offered her.[101] Yet, she did not leave the details of her death and burial to providence. She also joined a prayer union, and the fabrique records indicate that it contributed some $800 to her funeral, covering the digging of the grave, a carriage, and a range of other expenses. That she had retained ongoing connections to the broader Montreal community is suggested by the fact that her death and funeral were announced in *La Minerve,* which informed Montrealers that her funeral service would be held in the Providence chapel at seven in the morning three days after her death.[102]

This chapel, linked to the charitable work of Émilie Tavernier and the Sisters of Providence, was the location of the funeral services of several other Catholic widows who had married in the 1820s or 1840s and been inmates, pensioners, or linked to the institution through charitable work or the Patriote movement of the 1830s. The mass held at the first-class funeral in the chapel for Émilie's cousin and friend Agathe Perrault Nowlan, in 1871, was led by her great-nephew, M. Édouard Fabre, son of Luce Perrault and Édouard-Raymond. Fabre, who became Montreal's third bishop five years later, presented Agathe's life as having fulfilled the two main virtues of widowhood in taking good care of her household and doing good works. He made no mention of her active involvement in elections.[103] Six years later, Marie-Adelaide Comte, widow of the Patriote Pierre Damour, died after fracturing her femur. Her first-class funeral was held in the chapel too, as were those of many of the women pensioners.[104] Luce Perrault lived longer than any other widow from the 1820s generation of marriages whose deaths we have been able to determine. A week after her funeral was held, in 1904, the mother superior of the Sisters of Providence announced that an early-morning service would be sung in their chapel for the repose of her soul. Friends and relatives were invited. Four days later, the funeral for Stephanie de Lorimier, one of the daughters of the Patriote François-Marie-Thomas Chevalier de Lorimier, whom Émilie Tavernier had visited in prison before he was hung following the rebellions, was also held there.[105] The link between the Providence Asylum and the Patriotes thus endured.

A funeral service in a cathedral, church, chapel, or synagogue associated with one's family, friends, and faith, followed by burial in a family plot, were dignified endings that fulfilled the widespread desire to avoid the anatomist's knife or the indignities of a pauper's internment and that fuelled Montrealers' involvement in so many groups providing burial insurance and other ways to finance funerals.[106] If the choice to spend their final time in an institution procured Marie-Anne Séné and other inmates religious attention at their death and a decent funeral, this was not true of all institutionalized individuals. Madness made it unlikely that Rosalie Paquet or many other inmates at the St. Jean de Dieu asylum would receive the final sacraments in a lucid state. Worse, in the words of the 1872 revisions to the law, which provided anatomy schools with bodies for dissection, "the bodies of persons found dead and publicly exposed, or of those who, immediately before death, have been supported by any public institution receiving aid from the provincial government," were to be delivered to the medical schools unless a close relative claimed them "within the usual period for interment." I have seen no evidence of what happened to Rosalie's body, or of where she was buried. The official registration of her death in the institution's register is witnessed by two illiterate men and a doctor. Those of other inmates were signed by a doctor who explicitly identified himself as the anatomy inspector, a clear indication of the final fate of their bodies.[107] As Julie-Marie Strange suggests, these "lonely dead enter our histories only rarely, usually in the guise of cadavers ... or paupers whom nobody owned."[108]

Their deaths produced no obituaries, no death notices, no funeral invitations, and no commemorations on tombstones, though they might appear in the photographs of anatomy students at work or circulate in jokes about corpses and their identity.[109] The deaths of widows connected to family and friends, in contrast, were normally reported in daily and religious newspapers, friends and family were invited to their funerals, some joined husbands in cemeteries, and their lives and deaths might be memorialized on cemetery headstones. Obituaries and death notices in the city's newspapers are among the last traces many of these widows left. As with the death notices for husbands who died before their wives, they offer sparse hints about the social and cultural relations of their final journeys and the meanings made of their lives by those who survived them. The very placement of death notices in the public spaces of newspaper columns signalled widows' ongoing connectedness in the city and the assumption of those placing them that their death was of interest to a community of family and friends who might not learn about it in other ways.

Caroline Scott Pelton died on 8 December 1900. Her ongoing connectedness to her children is reflected in the careful way her age was recorded when her death was registered. She is listed as eighty-one years, eleven months, and eight days old. Married at the age of twenty-five in 1843, she had passed twenty years of her life as a wife, several of them separated from her husband, then nearly double that time as a widow. The announcement of her death in the *Montreal Gazette* two days later was a simple one, as were those for most of these widows. It stated that she had died "at her late residence" at 80 Fort Street on the 8th, the widow of T.J. Pelton, and that her funeral was to be a private one. In this brief announcement, her age was given as eighty-two. Even in this sparse recounting, paid for by the word, there is a narrative of her life and of her success as a wife who outlived her husband. She, like about half of the widows whose death notices we have found, had died in a home represented as hers – not on the streets, not alone or with strangers, and not in an institution.[110] She had succeeded in living into her eighties and had died in close contact with kin who cared about her sufficiently to organize a funeral and to announce her death publicly. In linking Caroline Scott the widow to her dead husband, Thomas John Pelton, as was conventional in such notices, her survivors collapsed the history of their estrangement prior to his death into her long widowhood.

Little was unusual about this death notice, except the private funeral. Only four of the eighty death notices we have found for the widows of these two generations of marriages that mentioned funerals stipulated that the funeral would be private. These were all late in the century and held for widows who, like Caroline, were Protestant and of the 1840s cohort of marriages. This public assertion to the right to private grieving suggests changes that would accelerate in the twentieth century as dealing with death and grief were privatized and pushed out of sight. Most notices of widows' deaths followed fairly standard formulas and conventions, as did those of husbands or wives. These varied little across the century. Frequently, their name and age, their dead husbands' name, and sometimes where they had died was all that was said about the widows.[111] Wording and content varied somewhat with cultural and religious customs. Three-quarters of those we have found identified the widows by their maiden name, as well as listing that of their dead husband, thus embracing the Canadien tradition of using women's maiden names, as well as their married ones. Recall that when husbands died, their widows were usually nameless. Scottish customary nomenclature lingered. Rebecca Conegan's death notice identified her as the "relict of the late Sampson Brady," that of Mary Lloyd as the "relict" of William Snowden.[112]

Luce Perrault's death in February 1904 led to the publication of several articles in the Montreal daily newspaper *La Patrie*. She was reported to have died in her home on Lagauchetière Street. This was the house Luce had moved to as a widow in 1861 with her youngest children. Her daughter Marie-Anne Hectorine and her new husband, the hardware merchant L.J.A. Surveyer, had moved in with her between 1875 and 1876. They and their growing family lived with her for the rest of her life. When she died, aged ninety-two, she had outlived her husband by fifty years; her son, Édouard-Charles; her daughter Hortense, as well as Hortense's prominent husband, George-Etienne Cartier. One article identified her as "the mother of the first archbishop, Mgr. Fabre," daughter of the late Julien Perrault and Euphrosine Lamontagne; sister of M. Chas Perrault, an elected representative in 1837, as well as of Louis Perrault and Adolphe Perrault; and wife of Édouard-Raymond Fabre, "who 50 years ago was mayor of Montreal." Longer than the usual brief death notices, and including a photo, it also recognized her individually as one of the founders of the Providence Asylum, a cousin of Madame Gamelin, and involved in many religious and benevolent associations. This photo presents her as an alert, kindly looking, elderly woman, still dressed in what appear to be widow's weeds, staring straight at the camera and holding a book (see Figure 12.5). Prominent, literate, and benevolent, she was reported to have died piously around 7 p.m. A second, smaller column on the same page identified her as "one of the last and most distinguished survivors of a brilliant generation" and "allied to several men who played considerable and sometimes tragic roles in our history. She counted in her immediate family some of our most distinguished compatriots." Both notices conveyed condolences to the family, suggesting they were written by journalists or friends. "We bow with profound respect before her coffin," one concluded, "and we offer the family the homage of our most sincere condolences."[113]

Mme FABRE MEURT A 92 ANS

La mère du premier archevêque de Montréal décédée hier soir.

FIGURE 12.5   Luce Perrault, "Mme Fabre." Luce Perrault Fabre outlived her husband, the former Patriote, bookseller, and mayor Édouard-Raymond Fabre, by fifty years. She was one of the few women of these two marriage cohorts whose death led to a report on her life, as opposed to a brief death notice. Note that the subtitle links her to her son, the former archbishop. | *La Patrie*, 27 February 1904. From the collection of the Bibliothèque et Archives nationales du Québec.

Prominent English-speaking families and army families also often related widows' genealogies, identified the regiments to which their husbands had belonged, or highlighted their transnational lives by linking them back to their birthplaces. The notice of Caroline Walker's death linked her first to her prominent family, as the "daughter of the late Hon. Judge Walker and Granddaughter of Major Hughes," only then mentioning her husband. Like the headstones of the elite McCord family that Brian Young has analyzed, prominent English Montrealers linked their histories back to post-Conquest times, claiming their place in the genealogy of occupation and the history of the colony.[114] The notice of Sarah Walker's death in 1880 listed her as the widow of William Radenhurst, Captain of Her Majesty's Canadian Fencibles, and mentioned her brother, Joseph. The notice for the Irish Protestant widow Margaret Lawlor highlighted her place as wife and mother, and also the fifty-seven years she had spent in the Montreal since leaving her native home in Queen's County, Ireland. As with some other transnational families, this notice explicitly asked papers in the United States and Ireland to copy the notice.[115] Thus, in the notices of their deaths, widows were relocated historically and globally within the genealogies, politics, economy, and history of the city in ways that continued to link their lives to those of husbands, fathers, and male ancestors.

As with other death notices, most notices of widows' deaths served to announce the time and trajectory of funeral routes to living "friends and family," inviting them to participate.[116] As discussed earlier, these wide-open public invitations made death a community affair, the very opposite of the private event envisaged by Caroline Scott Pelton's family. When Marie-Louise Lacroix, widow of the politician and merchant Charles-Séraphin Rodier, died in 1879, the notice published in both the *Montreal Gazette* and *La Minerve* explicitly invited those not receiving an invitation to consider the announcement one. Much more common was a formulaic phrase, "Family and friends are invited to attend." From these sparse announcements we can conjure up a picture of the final journey some widows' bodies took across the city they had lived in and shaped as wives and widows.[117]

Marie-Louise Lacroix's funeral route retraced that of her husband's three years earlier. As the widow of a former mayor, public citizen, and benefactor, it was important that her funeral reflect the prominent civic role he had played.[118] Mourners were invited to gather at 9 a.m. at her residence on St. Antoine Street. This was the mansion that the Rodiers had opened up to the Jesuits in 1843 after their return to Canada to use as a novitiate and renamed the Prince of Wales Castle.[119] The funeral then proceeded east to Le Gesù, the Jesuit-run church that had opened in 1865 on Bleury Street. After the service, her body was transported to the Notre-Dame-des-Neiges Cemetery. There her body joined her husband's.

Friends and family gathered early in the morning for Catholic widows, as for all Catholics, and later for Protestants.[120] Most widows' bodies left the place they died, transported first to a local church, chapel, or synagogue for a service, then on to a Catholic, Protestant, or Jewish cemetery. There they were buried, many alongside the bodies of husbands and children whom they had outlived. Constance Hart's grave stands prominently today in the Jewish cemetery on Mount Royal, her name and those of her children linked in the stone engraving to Adolphus Hart's career and to the prominent Hart family of whom they were part. Margaret Logan White, who died in 1872, was buried in the Protestant Mount Royal Cemetery alongside her daughter, who had died at eighteen, some sixteen years earlier. After the private funeral in December 1900, Caroline Scott's body joined that of her daughter Maria Louisa, whom, as we saw, had died in 1888 at the age of forty-one. Her father-in-law, Joshua Pelton, who had been sexton of the old Protestant cemeteries in the city, then worked as the agent in the city for the Mount Royal Cemetery Company, had purchased the large plot prior to his death in 1863, the same year as her husband, Thomas Pelton, died. Caroline was laid to rest alongside the man from whom she had separated forty years earlier, her father-in-law, and many other relatives.[121]

Widows also died, in institutions as we saw, on the streets, and alone in their homes or with strangers, ending up buried in paupers' graves. Elizabeth Hall outlived the blacksmith she had married in 1845 rather late in life by nine years. When she died in 1857, no one was able to pay for a funeral or for her burial. She was interred in the poor ground of the Protestant cemetery. Two Catholic women of similar class origins, Amable Leduc and Hermine Legris, the carpenter-turned-baker's widow, in contrast, took advantage of the expansion of Catholic institutions to avoid such a demeaning end by joining a prayer union. Their contributions and involvement secured a decent burial and service for Amable when she died of a liver problem in 1873, and for Hermine when she died of "old age," at eighty-eight in 1896.

Death separated these Montreal widows into Catholic, Protestant, and Jewish cemeteries, located from mid-century onward on different slopes of Mount Royal, far above the industrializing, growing city below. In their deaths, as over their married and widowed lives, the traces they left varied with their wealth, class, and religious and national customs and individual circumstance. Luce Perrault and Édouard-Raymond Fabre's grave, like that of John Easton Mills and Hannah Lyman's family or that memorializing Constance and Adolphus Hart, still stand prominently in the main parts of each respective cemetery, testifying to their importance as citizens. The graves and plots of widows from more modest backgrounds and their husbands and children, stand in more distant sections, determined in part by cost, in part by when the grave was purchased. Others lie without memorials, names, or links to family members, once buried in common graves, in the poor or free grounds, and in sections long since reused.

Connections to children and kin and their ongoing caring continued to make a difference after their deaths, ensuring that some were memorialized on headstones, their lives and deaths retold anew. Even husbands and wives not buried together were often reunited in the memorializing family work that produced the inscriptions. Epitaphs united widows and their former husbands, whether both bodies were in the grave together or not. John Easton Mills was interred in the old Protestant burial ground after the huge civic funeral that followed his death from typhus in 1847 while mayor. In 1854, Hannah Lyman had his body and that of their son moved to part of the large family plot her brother Benjamin had purchased in the new cemetery. Hannah died and was buried in England. The Mills family grave mentions both parents, as well as children who died before them, relocating their memories regardless of where they died. Similarly, although Adolphus Hart's body lay in his family's hometown of Trois-Rivières, his name and Constance's are united in the genealogy on the family gravestone. In these landscapes of grief, those relatives left alive and able to afford to "reconstruct the family unit in stone" shaped long-lasting family stories that might complement or compete with the more complicated ones told around deathbeds, or at funerals and wakes.[122]

Conclusion

Widows lived in every city, town, village, rural, and First Nations community of Canada in the nineteenth century. They dwelled on every street of colonial cities. The possibility that women would outlive their husbands haunted individuals, produced melodramatic tales in popular culture, and shaped economic and cultural practices. The death of a husband left young mothers to raise children on their own – the equivalent of single mothers, divorced women, and some widows today. Deaths later in life left some elderly women bereft of emotional and financial support, and others well provided for. Husbands' deaths left some widows deeply grieved, some relieved. And yet, there are few Canadian studies of nineteenth-century widows' lives.[1] *Wife to Widow* begins to remedy that. Many questions about widowhood deserve further exploration.

Wife to Widow has focused on the lives of women who became widows in Canada's major nineteenth-century city, Montreal, and on negotiations and renegotiations of patriarchy in their individual lives, in the laws that framed marriage and widowhood, and in the politics of the period. I have done so by following the lives of two generations of women from their marriages in that city in the 1820s and 1840s to the deaths of their husbands, then through their widowhood to their own deaths, weaving their life histories into legal practices, political debates, and aspects of the history of Montreal, the colony, and the wider world. The collective genealogies resulting from this process provided information on general demographic patterns and legal and cultural practices, and served as the basis of the individual biographies traced in the book's chapters. The women followed here appear as wives and widows, as individuals, and as statistics. I have used their real names. These were an essential component of the tracing process. To un-name them, or rename them fictitiously, as some historians are required to do by privacy legislation, would have stripped away their identities in much the same way as nineteenth-century naming customs often did. These biographies and tracings were a central part of the story told here. They allowed aspects of the lives of Marguerite Paris, the labourer's widow who voted in the 1832 by-election; Rebecca Conegan, who married the soap maker who went blind; and Maria Mitchell, whose drunken and abusive husband eventually slit his own throat, to enter the historical record. They and other women whose lives have appeared here in fragments deserve to have their names remembered.

The stories of their marriages and experiences as widows highlight the diversity of their lives, as well as the many ways they negotiated patriarchy as nineteenth-century women. The diverse traces of their lives left in the records consulted here show us "patriarchy at work" in these women's institutional encounters.[2] As they became wives, male priests or ministers ensured that details were recorded as required by denominations and the state. Marriage contracts were drawn up by male notaries, as were notarial wills. Male judges or justices sanctioned decisions about who would be chosen as widows' children's tutors. Male editors received and wrote obituaries and death notices and ran the city's newspapers, while male census enumerators and information collectors for city directories recorded details of their lives. Male grave diggers and undertakers carried husbands' bodies away, as they did those of their children and those of the widows. Women, whether single, married, or widowed, negotiated a patriarchal system in their interactions with the wider world.

Women who became widows shared only a few characteristics. They were gendered female, they married, and their husbands died before them. The social category of widow is a product of heterosexual marriage and of a particular gendered demography of death. Widowhood liberated women from the legal restrictions the law imposed on wives. It did not liberate them from the wider constraints and power relations of class, gender, ethnicity, or religion that structured interactions in and outside marriage. Widow was also a cultural category, produced and shaped through popular culture, custom, and law in ways very different from that of widower. Wives who became widows negotiated their new identity through a limited set of cultural understandings of widowhood, stereotypes, and representations. Merry or inconsolable; the poor deserving widow; the black widow who had buried several husbands; the faithful widow wearing black until her own death; or the unfaithful, lusty widow jumping into men's beds – these were some of the discursive representations that shaped understandings of the category and might attach too readily to an individual widow's actions.

Wives who became widows remained firmly linked to the memories, names, and fortunes of their dead husbands. Mourning dress, naming practices, legal definitions of sexual loyalty that extended into the first year of widowhood, and provisions in wills that were conditional on remaining unmarried all scripted widowhood in ways that individual women might embrace or resist and that varied little across the nineteenth century. Black mourning clothes signalled their entry into the status of widow, their loyalty to their dead husband, and their dependence on him. This was recognized in the Custom of Paris, which allowed the value of mourning clothes to be taken from husbands' property. Naming practices perpetuated that link, usually identifying widows only by their husbands' surnames and often by the men's given names as well. They appeared in city directories and other sources as "Widow Pelton," "Veuve Gamelin," or the "relict of the late Sampson Brady." Thus, widows lived in many ways as embodied traces of their former husbands, whose identity persisted in their names and their widow's weeds. Dead husbands' success or failure as providers also marked all widows' lives in multiple and diverse ways, shaping their standards of living and possible places of residence.

Beyond these shared characteristics, widows were a diverse group. Age, life cycle status when they were widowed, class, wealth, individual character, health, religious and political beliefs, generation, decisions, choices, and sheer luck divided them. Marriages in Montreal involved immigrants, newcomers from rural areas, and long-time residents whose family histories dated back to before the Conquest. Most couples' choices reasserted differences of religion, ethnicity, and class, as men and women usually married spouses of similar backgrounds. There were exceptions. The Scottish immigrant Robert Unwin Harwood was not alone in marrying into a Canadien seigneurial family and hence facilitating his insertion in local elite society. The Irish Catholic Maria Mitchell married an Irish Protestant against her friends' advice. And several Irish Catholic women married French Canadian spouses.[4]

Age gaps of ten, fourteen, even twenty-five years were not uncommon, and when, as was usual, the husband was older, these compounded the legal and social inequality marriage imposed on wives. Some of their husbands died within several months of their marriages, a few after as long as sixty years. Émilie Tavernier married at the age of twenty-three, became a widow after just four years of marriage at the age of twenty-seven, and remained a widow for fifteen years before taking the veil in 1844. Rosalie Paquet, who started working in Montreal's sex trade at sixteen, married at thirty-two. She lost her sex trade partner after just three years of marriage. Rosalie remained a widow, slipping out of sight until her final years, when she sought shelter first with the Grey Nuns and later, possibly involuntarily, in the St. Jean de Dieu asylum for the insane, run by the Sisters of Providence, where she died in her late seventies. The average marriage lengths we have been able to calculate of twenty-three years for the generation who wed in the 1820s and twenty-seven years a generation later hide massive variations. Some widows remarried quickly, though never in the proportions that men did. Remarrying widows in Montreal, as elsewhere, were mostly under forty years of age. Most women remained widows till their deaths. Those deaths came days, months, even decades later, so the lengths of their widowhood were equally varied. Yet, the majority of widows whose lives and deaths we have been able to trace lived into old age, dying in their seventies, their long lives contrasting with those of wives who died before their husbands, who only reached forty-five or forty-six on average.

These women married in a period when, historians argue, "companionate marriage" based on affection and romantic love were increasingly understood as the best basis for marriage.[3] *Wife to Widow* has not sought to probe the intimacies and emotional content of these marriages. I have argued here that the term "companionate patriarchy" better captures men's continued dominance and authority within marriage at this time. All brides entered a patriarchal institution. In marrying they agreed to their future subordination as wives. Husbands were considered the seigneurs, chiefs, and lords of that relationship. That subordination was social, cultural, and legal. In Montreal, the particular property-related contours of that subordination could be negotiated more readily than in common law jurisdictions because of the variety of legal traditions and the availability of notaries. I have suggested that in Montreal, companionate patriarchy took three main forms, though there were variations and the lines between them were not rigid. Customary patriarchy regulated marriages and widowhood when couples did not make marriage contracts or wills. This was the regime determined by the Custom of Paris and chosen deliberately or in ignorance by a growing majority of couples marrying in Montreal. Collaborative patriarchy was created in marriage contracts that chose community property, often twinned either with a specified dower or some other provision for widowhood, and frequently accompanied by the promise that the survivor could use the entire community property prior to his or her death or remarriage, or take full ownership. Wills also offered similar provisions. This was mostly a Canadien choice, and one that remained the preference of couples from the artisanal and crafts community in both generations. It built on long-standing cultural and legal traditions in the colony and recognized the collaboration of partners that was essential to functioning family economies in that community.

A more liberal patriarchy was created in marriage contracts that re-jected community property, usually opted to keep wives' property separate, and promised lump sums, annuities, or other alternatives to dower. Among the couples marrying during the 1820s, this was largely the choice of rela-tively wealthy Anglo-Protestant couples and was often accompanied by flourishing denunciations of the Custom of Paris. By the 1840s, Canadien merchants were also making this choice, which could protect some family goods from creditors and allow wives to control their own property, if they owned any. Close to a century later, in 1927, the Quebec feminist Marie Gérin-Lajoie argued that most couples were choosing separate property in order to protect women's moveable property. She warned that this re-gime could rarely offer a widow anything as advantageous as community of goods did, and argued for a rethinking of husbands' powers of control within that regime.[5] This shift to separate property was one thread in the forging of a new, liberal patriarchy.

These different choices meant that wives who became widows had a range of different claims on property accumulated during marriages. These transcended the simple dichotomy between English and French law that Charles-Élzear Mondelet, writing as M. had presented in 1841. Yet, as the most virulent, anti-Custom of Paris, pro-British, nineteenth-century Tories asserted repeatedly, and as more recent generations of feminists have argued, property regimes matter. Community property, established via the law or in a marriage contract, acknowledged wives' ownership of half the property accumulated during marriage. It thus offered wives who became widows a much greater claim on property accumulated during a marriage than did the common law rules of husband and wife in England, most other settler colonies, and the United States. Widows with young children were usually chosen as tutors, so those married under this regime retained control of the other half until their children reached adulthood. In addi-tion, until customary dower was eliminated, they would receive half of their husbands' other property to use, then pass on to their children if they had any. Such provisions could minimize disruptions, leaving homes, fur-niture, and other belongings in widows' hands as they sought to compen-sate for the loss of their dead husbands' incomes.

Liberal patriarchy in which wives' property was kept separate from hus-bands' placed full power over all other property accumulated during a marriage in the husband's hands. He might bequeath it to his wife. He might not. In the absence of a will, widows could count only on their own separate property, or any promises made in a marriage contract. The combination of freedom of willing and separate property left husbands free to leave widows pretty well penniless if they wished. Most did not. Good husbands provided both in life and after death. Convincing men that providing for wives and children demonstrated their manliness and individual responsibility was a significant thread of the liberal project. Men's freedom of willing was a further thread in the forging of a new, liberal patriarchy.

The details of wives' claims on property mattered and made a difference. So too did the wealth that a couple or a husband had accumulated. The combinations of provisions in wills and contracts with differential abilities to save during marriages, early deaths, and long illnesses meant women faced widowhood with widely divergent property bases and potential incomes as widows. Mostly these reflected the class position and assets of their husband, as well as his age when he died. On every visible measure of widows' wealth – value of housing owned or rented, promises in wills, residential location in the city, or bank stocks purchased – it is the wide diversity of widows' situations that is striking. Class and wealth made a difference. The widows of two prominent merchants and mayors, Hannah Lyman and Luce Perrault, began their widowhood with significant economic resources built up over the years by their husbands, despite the relatively young deaths of John Easton Mills at fifty-one and Édouard-Raymond Fabre at fifty-four. Neither widow was obliged to move out of their family home immediately following their husbands' deaths, though Luce would move later. Both had married children as well as minor children when they became widows. Both benefited from the assistance of more than two servants to run their households.

Wealthy men, in control of all their accumulated wealth, might bequeath their wives considerably less than half their assets and yet leave them in comfort, sometimes with considerable autonomy. A spouse's right to half the accumulated community assets was a fair one and not very different from contemporary family law. Yet, half of zero is zero. The Custom of Paris offered wives married in community property the right to renounce an indebted estate. This possibility allowed some widows of both generations to commence their new lives without debts – and for some, with a dower. But unless there was property they had inherited or kept out of that community in a marriage contract, it left them with little else. This was Scholastique Bissonnet's situation once the goods she shared with her innkeeper husband had been tallied. How she supported herself and her two children for three years is unclear. She then remarried.

In addition to the diverse lengths of women's marriages and widowhood, widows' divergent property claims, and the range of assets the widows could command, their individual characters, beliefs, and choices varied too. After losing her children as well as her husband, Émilie Tavernier chose to dedicate her life to sheltering less-fortunate widows. Caroline Scott, the middle-class notary's widow, had few obvious financial resources but was rich in connections to kin and chose to maintain close relations with her children. She succeeded in raising her six children to adulthood, and benefited from the wages her daughter Carrie earned as a teacher, and later from the earnings of her son and son-in-law. During her widowhood of thirty-seven years, she lived in close residential proximity to all her children. Hermine Legris, whose husband seems to have moved between baking, joining, and day labouring, as well as in and out of her home, spent her final years as a widow moving between the homes of several of her children and a grandson.[6] Maria Mitchell, in contrast, faced widowhood with the reputation of being a drunkard and bad mother. This Catholic immigrant from Ireland never claimed that she could raise her six children on her own. However, with the assistance of a young Irish Catholic lawyer and her working-class friends, she chose to fight to have a say in their future, and sought unsuccesfully to get them out of the control of the Protestant men who had swooped in on them and taken them to a Protestant orphanage after Thomas Spiers beat her up one last time.

Long-term close residential links with children was a privilege that only some wealthier widows could sustain. Labourers' widows of both generations seem especially likely to have been childless, to have lost contact with surviving children, or to have had insufficient resources to share residential space. Childless widows sought live-in work as cooks and domestic servants. Some ended up on the streets. And like Adelaide Bebel and Rosalie Paquet, some sought shelter in institutions for the elderly. The work of Émilie Tavernier in creating such shelters, along with the growing number of spaces offered by the Grey Nuns, other Catholic orders, and some Protestant charities, expanded the options for poor, senile, sick, elderly women and men at a time when the state offered no support in old age. Those sheltered had to conform to religious rules and rhythms and work if bodily able to do so.

Renegotiations of patriarchy, gender, and the nature of the marriage contract occurred at the level of these women's individual lives and couples' choices. They were also integral to the broader transformations of the law and the politics of the period. The changes to dower were integral to the broader reformulation of patriarchy and capitalism in the colony. As the Collective Clio pointed out years ago, widows lost an *ancien régime* right – one that guaranteed them the use of a portion of their husbands' property for their widowhood. For the growing numbers of urban widows whose husbands owned little beyond their community property, this was a meaningless right. In agricultural families, in contrast, dower could be significant. On the land-rich prairies, women fought for dower rights in the early twentieth century.[7] Dower had placed a gendered lien on land, constraining its transfer. The Registry Ordinance and subsequent legislation freed up land as a commodity that could be more readily bought and sold.[8] Curtailing dower along with provisions of lump sums or generous annuities to widows also liberated capital for investment and credit. Limitations to dower increased the amount and type of property that men could bequeath in a will. Here was a further thread in the forging of new capitalist relations, patriarchy, and a liberal order in which males emerged freer to accumulate and dispose of most of their property as they wished.

The Collective Clio suggested in its pioneering survey of Quebec women's history that the curtailing of dower and women's loss of the vote were twin aspects of the defeat of Quebec women's traditional rights during the 1840s. I have built on their insights here. The choices of Marguerite Paris, Émilie Tavernier, Sarah Harrison, and the other women, mostly widows, to go to the hustings in Montreal in 1832 and in other Lower Canadian elections show that women did take advantage of a law that made property rather than gender the basis of voting rights. Although Tory, English merchants pushed for changes to dower initially, Patriote politicians were in agreement by the late 1830s. And eliminating women's voting was, as Allan Greer has noted and I have explored in more detail here, the work of Patriotes and bourgeois Canadiens. Leading them in the Assembly was the Patriote leader Louis-Joseph Papineau, armed, I have suggested, with detailed names and numbers provided by his cousin, Jacques Viger, Montreal's first sociologist and mayor. Here was a further thread in the renegotiating of patriarchy in the period. The vote became a gendered right, held by some but not all males, and deemed suitable for those in control of their selves, their passions, and their property. Women who married in the 1820s and their contemporaries were able to take advantage of that right if they held the required property. Subsequent generations would not until feminists achieved voting rights for women municipally, federally, and eventually, provincially, when Quebec became the last province to give women the vote in 1940.

Émilie Tavernier shared a vision of different forms of citizenship for women with other middle-class and elite Catholic and Protestant women of her generation. She too voted in 1832. It was in their shared desire to forge new ways to care for the growing numbers of marginalized peoples of the city that these women contributed most obviously to building a new realm of social engagement within the changing colony. The dynamism and utopian vision of Catholic and Protestant women, especially the contemporaries of the women who married in the 1820s, was central to creating new collective, charitable institutions where women sought to assist orphans, widows, the elderly, pregnant mothers, and others. In performing the work of benevolence they deployed their class privilege and negotiated patriarchy within their denominations. Theirs were some of the lay initiatives that laid the groundwork and then fuelled the rise of ultra-montanism, as well as protestant activities.

Jean-Marie Fecteau has painted a compelling picture of the ways Quebec ultramontanism built on the freedom liberalism offered to religious and benevolent institutions in the civil sphere to deal with poverty. But Quebec bishops, and especially Bishop Bourget, built on existing examples. As Fecteau suggests, the Catholic Church structured a particular form of modernity within the logic of liberalism.[9] Émilie's spiritual and personal struggle to provide care for elderly women was enriched by her own char-acter, connections, and spirituality. Her dreams were both furthered and constrained by Bourget's incorporation of her project within the new ultra-montane order. She thus negotiated both the patriarchal institution of the Catholic Church and the more personal implementation of that vision by Bourget in which increasingly paternity of the Sisters of Providence would be accorded to him, not her. The flourishing of ultramontanism offered fewer leadership positions to laywomen in the generations that followed Émilie. More and more Quebec women would make the choice my col-league Marta Danylewycz highlighted years ago between marriage and taking the veil.[10] Yet lay women remained active in many ways.

Changing choices in individual marriage contracts; the curtailing, then elimination of dower through legislation and the related expansion of the amount of property men with property could dispose of in their wills; and changes in married women's rights were intertwined with broader political, institutional, and legal changes. Some were sanctioned in the Civil Code of 1866 and subsequent transformations of jurisprudence and legis-lation. These continued the process accelerated by the Registry Ordinance and its provisions regarding dower that made Quebec civil law more lib-eral, capitalism-friendly, and closer to the English common law.[11] Political changes led to the acceptance of responsible government, in which both voters and politicians were unquestionably male. The economic transform-ations that accompanied intensified exchange in a world economy and the consolidation of industrial capitalism accelerated as the colonies of British North America joined to become the new nation of Canada in 1867.

Since the last of these women died, more than a century of feminist interventions and other changes have reshaped women's rights as well as the protection that the state offered to the poor, the sick, and the elderly. Concern about the ability of widows with young children to combine good mothering with income generation led to feminist campaigns for widows' or mothers' pensions in most Western countries. These were in-stituted in Canadian provinces between 1916 and the 1940s. Quebec was among the last provinces to do so, in 1937. After the Second World War, different levels of government in Canada began to lay the groundwork of a welfare state, providing old-age pensions, which offered some buffer to the elderly poor; support to some unemployed – especially men – through unemployment insurance; providing welfare and income support for some men and women who were unable to earn; providing health care for all; and regulating the starkest inequalities between male and female wages. Over recent decades, much of this "welfare state" has been undermined or dismantled.

The question of wives' claims on property accumulated during a marriage was publicly addressed in jurisdictions of the English common law when nineteenth- and early-twentieth-century feminists sought to improve property rights for married women. Legislation in Canada's common law provinces instituted the liberal regime of separate property between the 1870s and 1880s, as in most other common law areas of North America and the British Empire. Given women's unequal ability to earn, save, or accumulate, this could not counter gender inequality. In English Canada, it was the case of one Alberta woman, Irene Murdoch, that became pivotal in feminist mobilizing to change that law in the 1970s. When she and her husband divorced, she sought compensation for the skilled work, heavy labour, and contributions to their cattle ranch that she had made. These included running it "single-handed for about five months" every year. The Supreme Court did not accept her claim to half the ranch on the basis of her contributions. Instead, she was initially awarded a $200 monthly allowance. Later she was awarded a much larger lump sum. Feminist pressure following this case led legislators in the common-law provinces to change family law to recognize that women's child rearing and domestic and other labour contributed to family wealth, and to give them a claim to it when marriages dissolved through death or divorce. In Quebec, the old regime of community property was modified in 1969.[12] New laws there as elsewhere could not ensure that most women were left wealthy following separation, divorce, or death. As with the widows studied here, their fortunes would always be linked to those of their divorced or dead partners and constrained by their capacity to earn. But new family property laws did recognize that women's labour in the home, and raising children should earn them a significant share in the accumulated wealth of the couple, as community property in Quebec had long done.

Marguerite Paris, Émilie Tavernier, Caroline Scott, and the other women whose lives I have followed here from wife to widow were born over two hundred years ago. They lived at a time when major economic transformations were underway and when questions of marriage law and the claims of husbands, wives, and others on property were debated as part of wider concerns about politics, citizenship, the law, and colonialism. The liberal version of patriarchy that was taking hold over this period increased the power of some men to save, exchange, and bequeath their property, curtailing earlier socially guaranteed rights like dower. Immigration separated some Montrealers from the potential support of other family members. Death was unpredictable, both because epidemics struck periodically and because a range of other diseases killed children, wives, and husbands at all ages. They lived at a time when gender inequality was understood to be normal, and when poverty was either seen as the individual's fault or the proper domain of charitable interventions.

The challenges they faced as they negotiated their lives as wives and widows, shaping and shaped by the laws and politics of their times, were specific to their individual situations, and to that time and place. Since then, women's legal rights as individuals, wives, or widows have been transformed. Marriage and parenthood are options that may be chosen or rejected by heterosexual or same-sex couples. Although current wars are producing new generations of young widows, widowhood is widely understood as something that occurs in later life. Yet, many of the issues raised in their lifetimes have returned to the public agenda. We too live in a time of dramatic economic transition in which the bases of wealth are changing, the distances between rich and poor increasing, and major crises in the system challenge the established fiscal and political order of things. Partners' claims on property accumulated during relationships – dwellings, pensions, and other wealth – when couples divorce or separate or one dies are again a major issue of public and private concern – complicated by the divergent claims of those in recognized heterosexual, common law, or same-sex partnerships or marriages.

Like them, we also live in a time when individuals or family members are assuming much of the onus of providing for old age, illness, separation, or divorce. Many more women today take on paid work and earn over a much longer period of their life cycle, and some are extraordinarily successful. Yet, women, and especially racialized and immigrant women, remain less likely than men to have accumulated adequate work-based pensions for their old age. On wages that still average seventy cents on the dollar earned by men, personal savings are impossible for many. Single mothers – whether unmarried, separated, divorced, or widowed – head the poorest families in the nation. Many immigrants live far from family support systems. More women live alone than in the past. And women generally outlive men. Elderly widows, single women, and divorcées face the "shady side of fifty" with financial means as divergent as those of Montreal's nineteenth-century widows. Placing the onus on individuals' capacity to save will only exacerbate the inequalities of the wider system in which individuals' earning power is constrained by their race, gender, class, immigration status, age, health, and ability.

Notes

Introduction

1 *L'Aurore des Canadas,* 18 December 1840, my translation; Hall, "Of Gender and Empire," 46, 51; Levine, "Why Gender and Empire?" 1-13.

2 Stoler, *Race and the Education*; Perry, *On the Edge*; Pickles and Rutherdale, *Contact Zones*; Van Kirk, *Many Tender Ties.*

3 McDowell, *Gender, Identity and Place,* 4.

4 Stoler, *Carnal Knowledge,* 7 (quote); Perry, *On the Edge*; Levine, *Prostitution, Race and Politics.*

5 Generations vary dramatically and people married and remarried at all ages. A few people married or remarried in both of these periods. I use "generation" and "cohort" interchangeably.

6 Normand and Hudon, "Le contrôle," 196; Garneau, "Une culture"; Greenwood, *Legacies of Fear*; Kolish, *Nationalismes*; Morin, "La perception"; Normand, "La codification de 1866."

7 Vinet, *Pseudonymes québéçois,* 329, lists "un citoyen," "un libre electeur," "spectateur," and "M." as some of the pseudonyms used by Charles Mondelet (1801-75); Fauteux, *Pseudonymes canadiens,* also identifies Judge Mondelet as the "M." who wrote in *La Revue de legislation* and in *La Revue Canadienne,* 94; Elizabeth Nish "Charles-Elzéar Mondelet," *Dictionary of Canadian Biography,* online version (hereafter cited as *DCB*).

8 In the 1820s and 1840s, some Jewish marriages were registered in Protestant churches.

9 Jalland, *Death*; Jalland, *Women, Marriage*; Noel, *Family Life*; Ward, *Courtship*; Ward, *A Love Story*; Wilson, *Life after Death*; K.E. Wood, *Masterful Women.*

10 Hewitt, "Compounding Differences," citation at 322; Wrigley, "Family Reconstitution," 96-159; Stone, "Prosopography."

11 Dechêne, *Habitants and Merchants*; Dépatie, "La transmission du patrimoine au Canada"; Dépatie, "La transmission du patrimoine dans les terroirs"; Dessureault, "Parenté et stratification"; Gossage, *Families in Transition.*

12 Bouchard, *Quelques arpents d'Amérique.*

13 Burgess, "Work, Family and Community."

14 Olson, "Feathering Her Nest"; Olson, "Pour se créer un avenir," 357-89; Olson and Thornton, "The Challenge of the Irish," 331-62; Olson and Thornton, "La

croissance naturelle," 191-30; Olson and Thornton, "Familles montréalaises," Olson and Thornton, "Le raz de marée irlandais."

15 Since completing most of this research, many instruments have been digitized. The geographer Sherry Olson and historian Robert Sweeny have digitized some Montreal tax evaluation rolls, censuses, and other nominal records for this period. Lisa Dillon and others have made a digitized version of the 1881 census. They have generously shared some of their databases with me. The 1881, 1891, and 1901 censuses of Canada can now be searched through the Library and Archives Canada website. The Bibliothèque et Archives nationales du Québec, Montreal branch (hereafter cited as BAnQM), has digitized the cross-references to Protestant marriages, deaths, and births for much of this period, though their indexes miss some people we found in our tracings. For the period stretching from the earliest occupation of New France up until 1800, it is now possible to locate the entire Catholic population in the database made by demographers at the Université de Montréal.

16 These were central concerns in the social mobility literature of the 1980s. Most mobility studies used computer programs to link names. As our numbers were smaller, the spellings of French and English names extremely variable, and our method different, we linked names manually, seeking specific individuals, as genealogists do. We gave up on most John Smiths.

17 Many notaries' indexes are now available on the BAnQM website. This would have facilitated our research.

18 Émilie Tavernier Gamelin is the only widow of these two cohorts of women who has been written about extensively, initially by Catholic writers, more recently in a biography that has been translated into several languages. Giroux, *Une Heroïne du Canada*; Bourassa, *Madame Gamelin*; Tessier, *Vie de Mère Gamelin*, translated by Sadlier as *Life of Mother Gamelin*; Anon., *Biographies de la mère Gamelin*; Robillard, *Émilie Tavernier-Gamelin*.

19 Hewitt, "Compounding Differences," 322.

20 Nootens, *Fous, prodigues et ivrognes*.

21 We developed strict rules about trustworthy matches, and I have kept only those whom we are certain were correctly linkaged in the numbers used throughout.

22 Bouchard and La Rose, "Réglementation." The Lower Canadian civil code formalized in 1866 required almost as much information as did Catholic rules, thus transforming Catholic tradition into standard practice.

23 Doolittle, "Close Relations?" 548, suggests that "women's frequent lack of a life-long surname marks them as particularly elusive in the search for kin, but also signifies their lesser importance in the construction of family."

24 Notre Dame Parish, Marriage registration, 10 July 1826; Death registration, 17 April 1834; Remarriage registration, 1 February 1837; Death registration, 10 July 1895.

25 Zion Congregational, Marriage registration, 7 November 1844; Death registration, 8 July 1854; Remarriage registration, 24 January 1856.

26 Thanks to Alan Stewart for suggesting this source.

27 Young, *Respectable Burial*.

28 Lot Records B: 217, Death Registration, Ownership Records, Individual Deaths, Mount Royal Cemetery records (hereafter cited as MRC).

29 Bouchard and La Rose, "Réglementation," describe the required content of marriage registers.

30 Of the 759 Catholic marriages between 1823 and 1825, we know that 216 women definitely became widows, 211 men definitely became widowers, 141 lack sufficient information, and 191 disappear. For the 579 Protestants over those years, we

know for sure only that 69 women and 43 men were widowed; the outcome is unclear for 144, and 323 were untraceable or disappeared.

31 Brun, *Vie et mort.* Under English common law, in contrast, widowers could claim curtesy – a "life interest in his wife's lands." Holcombe, *Wives and Property,* 22; Chambers, *Married Women*; Bradbury et al., "Property and Marriage," 9-39.

32 Greer, *The Patriots,* 294-331.

33 Ibid., 352-53.

34 Watt, "Authoritarianism," i, 1; Greer, *The Patriots,* 357; Young, "Positive Law, Positive State," 50-63.

35 Collective Clio, *L'histoire des femmes,* 164-65; Pateman, *The Sexual Contract,* 7; Stanley, *From Bondage to Contract.*

36 Fecteau, *Nouvel ordre,* 273; Greer, "1837-38"; Watt, "Authoritarianism," 7; Greer, *The Patriots.*

37 Sweeny, "The 1825 Manuscript Census" lists a total of 22,354 individuals. Bernard, Linteau, and Robert, "La structure professionnelle," 386, report 22,540 inhabitants. Scholars basing their reports on Viger's calculations report 26,154. Marsan, *Montreal in Evolution,* 143.

38 McKenzie, *Scandal in the Colonies,* 49-50.

39 Williams, *The Road to Now.*

40 J.M. Duncan, *Travels,* 2: 155; Finch, *An Englishwoman's Experience,* 381-82, describes Kahnawake women embroidering moccasins and going to Montreal and Lachine at times to buy alcohol. Patricia Todd, "James D. Duncan," *DCB.* The spelling then was usually Caughnawaga.

41 Linteau and Robert, "Propriété foncière," 56-57; Bernard, Linteau, and Robert, "La structure professionnelle"; Tulchinsky, *Taking Root.*

42 Sweeny, "Making a Bourgeois Town"; Marsan, *Montreal in Evolution.*

43 Olson and Thornton, "Ethnic Partition," 162; Sweeny, "Making a Bourgeois Town."

44 Bernard, Linteau, and Robert, "La structure professionnelle"; Lewis, *Manufacturing Montreal*; Tulchinsky, *The River Barons.*

45 Olson and Thornton, "Ethnic Partition"; Olson and Thornton, "The Challenge of the Irish"; Sweeny, "Internal Dynamics."

46 Poutanen, "'To Indulge'"; Senior, *British Regulars in Montreal*; Senior, *Roots of the Canadian Army.*

47 Rousseau with Payette, "Le recrutement de l'élite," 201.

48 Courville, ed., *Population et territoire,* 10-11, 81-84; Bradbury and Myers, eds., *Negotiating Identities,* 1-21; Jenkins, *Montreal Island*; Lewis, *Manufacturing Montreal*; Linteau, *Histoire de Montréal*; Marsan, *Montreal in Evolution*; Rumilly, *Histoire de Montréal,* 5 vols.

49 Bock, "Women's History"; Curtis, *The Politics of Population*; McPherson, Morgan, and Forestell, eds., *Gendered Pasts,* 1-11; Parr, *Labouring Children,* vii-xxii; Pierson, "Experience, Difference," 79-106; J.W. Scott, *Gender and the Politics,* 28-50.

50 Bonnell and Hunt, eds., *Beyond the Cultural Turn*; Sewell, "The Concepts of Culture," 47. Inspirations included Demos, *The Unredeemed Captive*; Nathalie Zemon Davis, *Women on the Margins*; Ulrich, *A Midwife's Tale*; Backhouse, *Petticoats and Prejudice*; Backhouse, *Colour-Coded.*

51 For example, Rowbotham, "The Trouble with Patriarchy"; J.W. Scott, "Gender: A Useful Category of Analysis."

52 Cited in Bennett, *History Matters,* 55.

53 Backhouse, "'Pure Patriarchy.'"

54 Riley, *"Am I That Name?"*; Nootens, "Un individu"; Bradbury and Myers, *Negotiating Identities,* 4; Hall, *Civilising Subjects,* 16.

55 Hewitt, "Compounding Differences," 322.

56 Davidoff, "Regarding Some 'Old Husbands' Tales,'" 257; Duncan, ed., *Body Space*; Blunt and Rose, eds., *Writing Women and Space*; Landes, ed., *Feminism*; McDowell, *Gender, Identity and Place*; Rendall, "Women and the Public Sphere"; Sandwell, "The Limits of Liberalism."

57 Blom, "The History of Widowhood"; Bell and Yans, eds., *Women on Their Own*; Bremmer and Van Den Bosch, *Between Poverty*; Hardwick, *The Practice of Patriarchy*; Hufton, "Women without Men"; Lebsock, *The Free Women*; McCants, "The Not-So-Merry Widows"; Scadron, *On Their Own*; Wilson, *Life after Death*; K.E. Wood, *Masterful Women*; Wulf, *Not All Wives*.

58 On the period of New France, see Brun, *Vie et mort*; Dechêne, *Habitants and Merchants*; Gauvreau, *Québec*; Plamondon, "Une femme d'affaires." On rural areas, see Cohen, *Women's Work*; Nanciellen Davis, "Patriarchy from the Grave"; Gagan, *Hopeful Travellers*; and Elliott, *Irish Migrants,* who offers a nuanced analysis.

59 On provisions in wills and laws of inheritance, see Darrow, *Revolution in the House*; Hardwick, *The Practice of Patriarchy*; Lebsock, *The Free Women*; Shammas, Salmon, and Dahlin, *Inheritance in America*; Wilson, *Life after Death*. On widows as businesswomen, see Baskerville, *A Silent Revolution?*; Gamber, "Gendered Concerns"; S.I. Lewis, "Business Widows." On the situations of poor widows, see Bradbury, "Mourir chrétiennement"; Dillon, *The Shady Side*; McLean, "Single Again"; Stewart, "The Elderly Poor."

60 Basch, *In the Eyes of the Law*; Chambers, *Married Women*; Davidoff and Hall, *Family Fortunes*; Girard, "Married Women's Property"; Girard and Veinott, "Married Women's Property Law"; Holcombe, *Wives and Property*; Goody, Thirsk, and Thompson, eds., *Family and Inheritance*; Hardwick, *The Practice of Patriarchy*; Lebsock, *The Free Women*; Morris, *Men, Women and Property*; Nazzari, "Widows as Obstacles"; Rogers, "Money, Marriage, Mobility"; Shanley, *Feminism, Marriage*; Stanley, *From Bondage to Contract*; Staves, *Married Women's Separate Property*.

61 Boylan, *The Origins*; Ginzberg, *Women*; Noel, "'Femmes Fortes'"; Noel, "Women and Social Welfare"; Prochaska, *Women and Philanthropy*; Quataert, *Staging Philanthropy*; A.F. Scott, *Making the Invisible,* 283; Varty, "'A Career'"; Varty, "The City."

62 Davies, "'Services Rendered'"; Little, *"No Car, No Radio"*; Skocpol, *Protecting Soldiers and Mothers*; Strong-Boag, "'Wages for Housework.'"

63 Clarke, *Struggle for the Breeches*; Cott, *Public Vows*; Greer, *The Patriots*; Hufton, *Women and the Limits*; Landes, *Women and the Public Sphere*; Ryan, *Women in Public*; J.W. Scott, *Only Paradoxes to Offer.*

64 Collective Clio, *L'histoire des femmes,* 164-65.

65 Hall, *Civilizing Subjects*; Hall, "Of Gender and Empire"; Levine, "Why Gender and Empire?"; Stoler, *Carnal Knowledge*; Stoler, *Race and the Education.*

66 Davidoff et al., *The Family Story,* 17; Doolittle, "Close Relations?" Excellent recent Quebec studies include Fahrni, *Household Politics*; Nootens, *Fous, prodigues et ivrognes*; Petitclerc, *"Nous protégeons l'infortune."*

67 Cott, *Public Vows*; Dupâquier, ed., *Marriage and Remarriage*; Gagnon, *Mariage et famille*; Gossage, *Families in Transition*; Ward, *Courtship.*

68 Dillon, *The Shady Side*; Grau, "Residence Patterns of Aged Widows."

69 Davies, *Into the House of Old*; Dillon, *The Shady Side*; Haber and Gratton, *Old Age*; Snell, *The Citizen's Wage*; Troyanksi, *Old Age.*

70 Ariès, *The Hour*; Gagnon, *Mourir*; Gauvreau, *Québec*; Gauvreau, Gervais, and Gossage, *La fécondité des québécoises*; Hartog, *Man and Wife*; Houlbrooke, ed., *Death, Ritual and Bereavement*; Jalland, *Death*; Kselman, *Death and the Afterlife*; Pelling and Smith, eds., *Life, Death*; Richardson, *Death, Dissection*; Strange, *Death, Grief and Poverty.*

71 Bouchard, *Quelques arpents d'Amérique*; Greer, *Peasant, Lord and Merchant*.

72 Cohen, *Women's Work*; Nanciellen Davis, "Patriarchy from the Grave"; Gagan, *Hopeful Travellers*.

73 Baskerville, *A Silent Revolution?*; Morris, *Men, Women and Property*; Shammas, Salmon, and Dahlin, *Inheritance in America*, 7; Stobart and Owens, eds., *Urban Fortunes*, 1.

74 Brierley, "La notion"; Brierley, "Co-Existence of Legal Systems"; Brierley, "The English Language Tradition"; Brisson, *La formation*; Brisson and Kasirer, "The Married Woman in Ascendance"; Fyson, *Magistrates, Police, and People*; Kolish, *Nationalismes*; Morel, *Un exemple*; Morel, *Les limites*; Normand and Hudon, "Le contrôle"; Morel, "L'émergence du nouvel ordre"; Young, *The Politics of Codification*; Benton, *Law and Colonial Cultures*; Nazzari, "Widows as Obstacles."

75 Garneau, "Une culture"; Garneau, "Droit et 'affaires de famille'"; Garneau, "Le rituel"; Nootens, *Fous, prodigues et ivrognes*.

76 Fecteau, *La Liberté du pauvre*; Fecteau, *Nouvel ordre*; Feretti, *Brève histoire*; Feretti, *Entre voisins*; Hardy, *Contrôle social*; Perin, *Ignace de Montréal*; Rousseau and Remiggi, eds., *Atlas historique*; Young, *George-Etienne Cartier*; Young, *In Its Corporate Capacity*; Young, *The Politics of Codification*.

77 Brah, *Cartographies of Diaspora*, 16.

78 Davidoff and Hall, *Family Fortunes*, 179.

Chapter 1: Marriage Metropole

1   Marsan, *Montreal in Evolution*, 101.

2   Ibid.

3   Repertory of Vital Events, 1621-1799, The Research Program in Historical Demography, http://www.genealogie.umontreal.ca/.

4   Ibid. All marriages, births, and deaths cited were located in the registers and/or indexes conserved at the BAnQM, unless otherwise indicated.

5   http://www.familysearch.org/. The birth of their daughter, Matilda, was registered at Christ Anglican Church in Montreal in 1834, folio 30. None of their other children's births was registered there.

6   Marriage registration, 13 November 1845, Christ Anglican Register; Forrest and Jourdain, Marriage contract, Notary Gibb, 13 November 1845, BAnQM (all notarial acts cited were at the BAnQM unless otherwise indicated); Marsan, *Montreal in Evolution*, 131-33; Georginna Forrest and family fonds, Finding Aid, R2953-0-5-E, Library and Archives Canada (hereafter cited as LAC); Deaths of individuals whose last name was Jourdain are listed in the Notre Dame Parish register that goes back to the seventeenth century in 1748, 1751, and 1758. On her father and brother especially, see "Captain Alfred Forrest," in J.B. Mansfield, ed., *History of the Great Lakes*, vol. 2, http://www.linkstothepast.com/marine/captainsF.php.

7   *London Gazette*, 2 September 1836; Ester, passenger list, February 1833, ozs, 64126, sh: 179, http:/www/blaxland.com/ozships/alpha. My thanks to Jane Watson of the Jourdain family for this information. McKenzie, *Scandal in the Colonies*, 1.

8   C.H. Currey, "Dowling, Sir James (1787-1844)," *Australian Dictionary of Biography* (Melbourne: Melbourne University Press, 1977), 1: 317-20. http://www.adb.online. anu.edu.au/; Ester, passenger list, September 1833, ozs, 63940, sh: 194, http://www.blaxland.com/ozships/alpha.

9   New South Wales Registry of Births, Deaths and Marriages, V83542 90/1835; V1835176 126/1835.

10 McKenzie, *Scandal in the Colonies*, 1, 54, 56.

11 *London Gazette*, 2 September 1836.

12 Thomas, *Comparative Advantages*, 21.

13 M.A.C. Jourdain to Georginna Forrest, June 1864, Forrest fonds, R2853-0-5-E, LAC.

14 Creighton, *The Empire of the Saint Lawrence*; Young, *In Its Corporate Capacity*; Burgess, "Work, Family and Community"; Sweeny, "Internal Dynamics"; Tulchinsky, *The River Barons*; Lewis, *Manufacturing Montreal*. As a site of confluence and conflict, see Olson and Thornton, "Familles montréalaises"; Courville, ed., *Population et territoire*, 7-11.

15 Brah, *Cartographies of Diaspora*, 16.

16 Lester, *Imperial Networks*; Ballantyne and Burton, eds., *Bodies in Contact*; Courville, Robert, and Séguin, *Atlas historique*; Courville, ed., *Population et territoire*; Courville, *Quebec*.

17 Brah, *Cartographies of Diaspora*, 16, 14, 182, 183, quotations at 182.

18 Gagnon, *Mariage et famille*, 60-61.

19 Rome, "Benjamin Hart and 1829," 16-23; Bouchard and La Rose, "Réglementation," 515-34.

20 Olson and Thornton, "Familles montréalaises"; Bernard, Linteau, and Robert, "Les tablettes statistiques," 11, 14; Bernard, Linteau, and Robert, "La structure professionnelle."

21 Bouchard and La Rose, "Réglementation," 515-34.

22 The information available about brides' fathers and husbands' parish and domicile included in the Catholic marriage registers for husbands and wives with French names suggests that in the 1820s, 81 percent of the 516 Canadienne wives' fathers and 57 percent of the 312 husbands came from Montreal; 11 percent of bride's fathers and 22 percent of grooms came from elsewhere on Montreal Island or parishes to the north; 5 percent and 8 percent came from parishes to the south or east of Montreal respectively; and 3 percent and 6 percent from Quebec City or Trois-Rivières. In the 1840s, 80 percent of the 50 percent sample of 466 wives and 67 percent of the 494 husbands were from Montreal; 11 percent of brides' fathers and 15 percent of grooms from the island or parishes to the north; 5 percent and 9 percent from parishes to the south and east; and 4 and 5 percent from Quebec City or Trois-Rivières. Men came from a larger number of parishes and geographic areas of the colony.

23 Courville, ed., *Population et territoire*, 11-12.

24 Frederick H. Armstrong, "Charles-Séraphin Rodier," *DCB*.

25 Inventory, J.F.L. Genevay, 27 March 1827, Notary Joseph Papineau.

26 This information is not available for most Protestant couples and difficult to find from contemporary sources. The few brides whose origins we know of generated death records or obituaries that cited their place of birth. None of the censuses prior to 1851 listed wives independently, which would have allowed checking ages and birthplaces. The 1851 census for most of Montreal has not survived. By 1861 and after, many were dead.

27 Marjory Campbell, "John Gregory," *DCB*; Gerald Tulchinsky, "John Forsyth," *DCB*; Brown, "Diverging Identities," 195-206; Van Kirk, *Many Tender Ties*.

28 Alfred Dubuc and Robert Tremblay, "John Molson Jr.," *DCB*; Denison, *The Barley and the Stream*; Bettina Bradbury, "Anne Molson," *DCB*; Ken Cruikshank, "Sir David Lewis Macpherson," *DCB*.

29 Brian Young, with Gerald Tulchinsky, "Sir Hugh Allan," *DCB*.

30 *La Minerve*, 19 April 1827. In this large advertisement, he expresses his recognition of his clients at his Hotel St. Mary and indicates that he had just opened a boarding house with spacious rooms, good food, and good stables on St. Gabriel Street.

31 Lyman, ed., *Genealogy*, 33; Tulchinsky, *The River Barons*, 110.

32 Marriage registration, 12 December 1844.

33   One hundred and eighty-seven women with non-French names married in Notre Dame, the Catholic parish church, between 1823 and 1826. Thirty-three of their fathers were indicated as being from Montreal and four more as domiciled there. Most of the rest were from counties in Ireland. However, 40 of the brides were identified as from Montreal and 130 as domiciled there. Quite how to interpret the use of these categories, for immigrants especially, is not clear, but this does suggest that many women came without their parents. A generation later, only fifty-four fathers of the 363 non-French (largely Irish Catholic) brides were listed as from Montreal, the rest as from elsewhere, while 85 percent of the brides were identified as domiciled in the city.

34   Marriage registration, Notre Dame Parish, 17 November 1823, 8 February 1825.

35   Akenson, *The Irish in Ontario*, 21-22; Cousens, "The Regional Variation," 15-30.

36   Among the 89 brides where fathers' parishes in Ireland were listed between 1823 and 1826, 42 were from Ulster, 16 from Munster, 28 from Leinster, and 3 from Connacht. Among the 125 grooms whose father's location was noted, 45 fathers came from Ulster, 36 from Munster, 40 from Leinster, and 4 from Connacht. Between 1842 and 1845, fathers' locations were noted for 259 brides: 76 from Ulster, 81 from Munster, 60 from Leinster, and 42 from Connacht. The 261 listings for grooms' fathers included 65 from Ulster, 97 from Munster, 58 from Leinster, and 41 from Connacht.

37   Akenson, *The Irish in Ontario*, 22.

38   Ibid., 23.

39   Beaudoin, "Quelques observations."

40   Gagnon, *Mariage et famille*, 112-13.

41   On this anti-Catholicism, see Colley, *Britons Forging the Nation*.

42   Marriage contract, de Lotbinière and Harwood, 13 December 1823, Notary Doucet; Marcel Hamelin, "Michel-Eustache-Gaspard-Alain Chartier de Lotbinière," *DCB*; John Thompson, "Robert Unwin Harwood," *DCB*.

43   J.K. Johnson, "John Munro," *DCB*; "Selected Families and Individuals," http://www.rootsweb.ancestry.com/; Marriage contract, Mount and Genevay, 5 February 1823, Notary Papineau; "A Return of the Numbers of Acres of Crown Lands granted to Executive Councillors and their Families," 195, Appendix B, Durham, *Report*.

44   Gagnon, *Mariage et famille*; Gossage, *Families in Transition*, 91, found thirty-five dispensations among the 921 couples in the three cohorts of marriages that he studied in Saint Hyacinthe. He suggests that dispensations increased later in the century.

45   On Wilkes, see Noel, *Canada Dry*, 69-70, 83-85; Philippe Sylvain, "Henry Wilkes," *DCB*.

46   Mitchell v. Brown, Superior Court Montreal, 28 February 1859, no. 849, TP111 S2, SS2, SS1, 1858, BAnQM.

47   Gagnon, *Mariage et famille*, 179-80, cites proximity to forbidden times, poor roads, couples coming from parishes far from each other, and fear of a charivari or malicious argument against the marriage as reasons.

48   Ibid., 83, 137; Marriage registration, 7 November 1824, Christ Anglican Register; Marriage registration, 8 February 1825, Notre Dame Parish.

49   Gossage, *Families in Transition*, 91.

50   Van Die, *Religion, Family and Community*.

51   Bernard, Linteau, and Robert, "La structure professionnelle"; Olson and Thornton suggest that many grooms not indicating an occupation were general labourers, "Ethnic Partition," 157-200. Many immigrants likely had no idea how they would make a living.

52 Compare with the six categories used by Olson and Thornton, "Ethnic Partition," 176: merchants, professionals, clerks, skilled, semi-skilled, and labourers. How best to capture class, status, and so on has, of course, been a source of huge debate among historians and sociologists. I have used large groupings because of small numbers.

53 Olson and Thornton, "Ethnic Partition," 178.

54 On the sailors and soldiers in Montreal, see Poutanen, "'To Indulge'"; Senior, *British Regulars in Montreal*; Senior, *Roots of the Canadian Army*.

55 Leprohon, *Antoinette de Mirecourt*. It was translated into English a year later as *Antoinette de Mirecourt, or, Secret Marrying and Secret Sorrowing*.

56 In the 50 percent sample for the 1840s, eighty-five brides married men in the lower ranks; eleven married men above the rank of lieutenant.

57 Talbot, *Five Years' Residence*, 283.

58 Tosh, *A Man's Place*, 13.

59 Very close to the 62 percent that Olson found in the 1842 census. Olson and Thornton, "Ethnic Partition," 18.

60 Burgess, "Work, Family and Community."

61 Ibid.

62 Lease, Easton to Decousse, 3 February 1843, Notary Pelton.

63 Copartnership, 21 October 1844, Notary Belle.

64 *Lovell's Montreal Directory* (hereafter *Lovell's*), 1843-44.

65 Ward, *A Love Story*; Tosh, *A Man's Place*, 57.

66 Gerald Tulchinsky, "Jedediah Hubbell Dorwin," *DCB*; John Witham, "Andrew White," *DCB*; Sweeny, with Hogg and Rice, "Les relations ville/campagne," 346-47.

67 "Report from the special committee appointed to enquire into the manner in which juries in criminal matters have been drawn in Lower Canada" (Quebec: Nelson and Cowan, 1830), Canadian Institute for Historical Microreproductions, 901314 (hereafter cited as CIHM).

68 Forty from the 1820s, thirteen from the 1840s.

69 Marguerite Jean, "Émilie Tavernier," *DCB*; Bradbury, "Anne Molson," *DCB*; J.C. Stockdale, "Rosanna Eleanora Mullins," *DCB*.

70 Bernard, Linteau, and Robert, "La structure professionnelle"; Robert, "Les notables de Montréal."

71 Young, with Tulchinsky, "Sir Hugh Allan," *DCB*; Thompson, "Robert Unwin Harwood," *DCB*.

72 Armstrong, "Charles-Séraphin Rodier," *DCB*.

73 Clotilde Painchaud, "Alexis Painchaud," *DCB*.

74 Young, with Tulchinsky, "Sir Hugh Allan," *DCB*.

75 Borthwick, *History and Biographical Gazetteer*, 520.

76 Tulchinsky, *The River Barons*, 10, 13, 101, 114-16; Gerald Tulchinsky, "Thomas Workman," *DCB*.

77 Sweeny, "Les relations ville/campagne," 346-47; Pierre Landry, "Stanley Clark Bagg," *DCB*; Witham, "Andrew White," *DCB*.

78 Jean Benoit, "Joseph Barsalou," *DCB*.

79 Robillard, *Émilie Tavernier-Gamelin*, 79-83.

80 Jean-Louis Roy, "Édouard-Raymond Fabre," *DCB*.

81 Gossage, "La Marâtre"; Gossage, "Tangled Webs."

82 Bouchard, *Quelques arpents d'Amérique*, 172. Rounded percentages for the Catholic marriages of the 1820s and 1840s respectively were: both single 79 percent, 83 percent; single wife, widowed husband 11 percent, 9 percent; husband single, wife widowed 6 percent, 4 percent; and both widowed 4 percent, 3 percent. These

compare with rates reported for the Saguenay, 1842–51, of 86 percent, 10 percent, 3 percent, and 2 percent, and in Saint Hyacinthe, 1854–61, of 72.5 percent, 15.6 percent, 1.7 percent, and 7.1 percent. Bouchard, *Quelques arpents d'Amérique,* 172; Gossage, *Families in Transition,* 92.

83 Robillard, *Émilie Tavernier-Gamelin,* 41, 49; Notre Dame parish, Marriage registration, 27 October 1833; St. Gabriel Street Presbyterian Church, Marriage registration, 14 August 1824; Notre Dame parish, Marriage registration, 12 September 1825.

84 Of 501 Canadienne brides who were marrying for the first time, 278 (56 percent) had two living parents in the 1820s, as did 227 (49 percent) of the 468 in the 1840s sample. Among the 171 Irish-Catholic brides, 89 (52 percent) of those marrying in the 1820s, and only 132 (39.5 percent) of the 334 marrying for the first time in the 1840s, had two living parents. On the post-famine, see Beaudoin, "Quelques observations," 140–45.

85 Erickson, "Emigration from the British Isles"; Guinnane, *The Vanishing Irish,* 104. This merits further research, as it would be one more indicator of the similarities of pre- and post-famine migration that historians have been exploring.

86 Guinnane, *The Vanishing Irish,* 17, stressed the significance of individual decisions to migrate and to marry in arguing against Malthusian explanations of Irish depopulation after the famine.

87 Robillard, *Émilie Tavernier-Gamelin,* 41, 51–52.

88 Ibid., 67, 86–86.

89 Ibid., 51.

90 Dupâquier, ed., *Marriage and Remarriage.*

91 For the traveller's account, see Shirreff, *A Tour through North America,* 99, 350.

92 Gossage, *Families in Transition,* 105.

93 Unlike Gossage, *Families in Transition,* I did not start with censuses that give age information. Nor could we usually make estimates based on multiple age declarations as Gossage did. Marriage registers indicated only whether the bride and groom were minors or majors. Age information here is based largely on death registers and obituaries, sometimes from censuses. I could estimate the year of birth for 393 brides marrying in the 1820s (376 for the first time) and for 404 (380 first time) from the 1840s. We found information for 287 men (267 first marriages) for the 1820s and 354 (337 first marriages) for the 1840s. Standard deviations of 5.9 and 6.4 for new wives in the 1820s and 1840s and of 7.1 and 8.3 for the grooms point to the wide variation around these averages.

94 Ward, *Courtship,* 58. Of the 212 couples marrying in the 1820s and the 237 couples in the 1840s for whom we could determine the birth dates for both bride and groom, age gaps ranged from 0 to 32, with 65 percent falling between 0 and 7 years. In four out five of these cases, the husband was older than the wife. Only one couple had a greater age difference than Émilie Tavernier and Jean-Baptiste Gamelin.

95 *Montreal Gazette,* 7 February 1821; *La Minerve,* 21 November 1833; *Montreal Gazette,* 27 February 1836, 16 January 1846; Fyson, *Magistrates, Police, and People,* 175; Marriage Register, Christ Anglican Church Cathedral.

96 *Montreal Gazette,* 7 February 1821; *La Minerve,* 21 November 1833; *Montreal Gazette,* 27 February 1836, 16 January 1846; Palmer, "Discordant Music," 28; Greer, "From Folklore to Revolution," 35–55; http://www.rawbw.com/. Death registration, Christ Anglican Church, 1834, folio 14; Death registration, American Presbyterian Church, 1842, folio 11.

97 Fyson, *Magistrates, Police, and People,* 175; Longmore, *The Charivari,* stanzas 144, 174, 179. Bentley, *Early Long Poems on Canada,* convincingly argues, following

Mary Lu Macdonald, that this tale is based on the marriage of the merchant Tous-
saint Pothier and Anne-Françoise Bruyères Burton, who married in 1820 and fit
the ages and marital status of the couple in the poem. http://www.uwo.ca/
english/canadianpoetry/.

98 Gossage, *Families in Transition,* 97.
99 Ibid., 105.
100 Poutanen, "Women Arrested in Montreal"; Poutanen, "'To Indulge,'" 62-64;
  Marriage registration, 28 February 1843, Notre Dame Parish.
101 Among the 759 Catholic 1820s marriages, 449 (59 percent) published three banns,
  82 (11 percent) published two, and 202 (27 percent) published one. Only 24 (3
  percent) published none. Among the 870 Catholic couples sampled between 1842
  and 1845, percentages were similar.
102 Beaubien, *Traité sur les lois civiles,* 1:27, 33-34; Crémazie, *Manuel des notions utiles,* 86;
  Gagnon, *Mariage et famille,* 189.
103 "Marriage Bonds and Licences," LAC, http://www.collectionscanada.gc.ca/.
104 Marriage registration, 4 June 1823, Notre Dame Parish; Marriage contract, 4 June
  1823, Notary Doucet; Robillard, *Émilie Tavernier-Gamelin,* 86; Rousseau, "Les passages," 149.
105 Robillard, *Émilie Tavernier-Gamelin,* 86, reports that the event was noted in the
  Gazette Canadienne, Montreal Herald, Canadian Courant, Montreal Advertiser, and *Spectateur Canadien.*
106 Ward, *Courtship,* 106-7.
107 Abraham Joseph Diaries, 1 September 1839; Fanny David Joseph Diaries, 28 June
  1877, R5374-0-4-E, Abraham Joseph Collection, LAC.
108 Gossage, *Families in Transition,* 95, reports that Mondays and Tuesdays remained
  the usual day of weddings in Saint-Hyacinthe until close to the end of the century.
  Rousseau, "Les passages," 149, reports that in four of five parishes reporting to
  Bishop Bourget in 1846, marriages were on Tuesdays rather than Mondays.
109 Beaubien, *Traité sur les lois civiles,* 1: 36-37; Crémazie, *Manuel des notions utiles,* 87.
  Between 1823 and 1826, twenty-nine women married men in the army; 76 per-
  cent of them disappeared. Between 1842 and 1846, there were ninety-three such
  marriages and eighty-one (86 percent) disappeared. On Whyte, see *Montreal Gazette,* 28 May 1840, cited in Leprohon, *Antoinette de Mirecourt,* xxxiv. After her widowed mother died, she sought her part in the estate of her father. *Lower Canada
  Jurist,* 1874.
110 Burke, *A Genealogical and Heraldic Dictionary,* 1456; *Montreal Gazette,* 28 May 1840,
  cited in Leprohon, *Antoinette de Mirecourt,* xxxiv.
111 Burgess, "Work, Family and Community," 341.
112 Cruikshank, "Sir David Lewis Macpherson," *DCB.*
113 R.I.K. Davidson, "George Monro," *DCB.*
114 Bradbury, "Anne Molson," *DCB.*
115 Young, with Tulchinsky, "Sir Hugh Allan," *DCB.*
116 "Take Me Home," *Montreal Transcript and Commercial Advertiser* (hereafter *Montreal
  Transcript*), 23 August 1842; "Maxims to Marry By," *Montreal Gazette,* 28 January
  1826; "The Ruined Tradesman," *Family Herald,* 21 December 1859.
117 Our research strategy meant we did not follow wives who moved with their husbands into Montreal.
118 Crémazie, *Manuel des notions utiles,* 87, suggested that wives were not obliged to
  follow husbands out of the province, whereas Beaubien, in *Traité sur les lois civiles,*
  1:37, argues that they could not be obliged to move beyond the boundaries of Her
  Majesty's possessions. See also Brah, *Cartographies of Diaspora,* 16.
119 Mitchell v. Brown, Superior Court Montreal, 28 February 1859.

120 Durham, *Report on the Affairs of British North America*, 14.
121 Pateman, *The Sexual Contract*.

Chapter 2: Companionate Patriarchies

1 Marriage contract, Campbell and Wait, 14 August 1824, Notary Jobin.
2 Stanley, *From Bondage to Contract*, 1, 209; Pateman, *The Sexual Contract*, 7.
3 *Montreal Gazette*, 4 January 1826, 4 March 1826, 7 December 1826, 24 January 1831, 23 September 1846, 10 December 1851.
4 Lebsock, *The Free Women*, 17-18; Pateman, *The Sexual Contract*, 7; Stanley, *From Bondage to Contract*; Beaubien, *Traité sur les lois civiles*, 1:47 (my translation).
5 Darrow, *Revolution in the House*, 113; Shorter, *The Making*; Stone, *The Family*; Trumbach, *Rise of the Egalitarian Family*; Ward, *Courtship*.
6 Lebsock, *The Free Women*, 32.
7 Darrow, *Revolution in the House*, 57.
8 Hardwick, *The Practice of Patriarchy*, 18; occasionally costs appeared on documents. Most marriage contracts made by Notary Doucet during the 1820s cost 15 s., a few were 5s., some as much as 25s. Notary Doucet, 1823-26.
9 K.M. Brown, *Good Wives*, 297.
10 Doucet, *Fundamental Principles*, 262-66; Beaubien, *Traité sur les lois civiles*, 2:287-91.
11 Across late-eighteenth- and nineteenth-century Europe, many local customs were eliminated or modified, creating codes as part of the reformulation of nation states. On France, see Yver, *Egalité entre héritiers*; Darrow, *Revolution in the House*; on Scotland, see McCrum, "Inheritance and the Family," 149-71.
12 Holcombe, *Wives and Property*; Basch, *In the Eyes of the Law*; Chambers, *Married Women*.
13 Evidence, Samuel Gale, 8 May 1828, 26 June 1828, British Parliamentary Papers, *Reports from Select Committees*, 23, 266; Kolish, *Nationalismes*.
14 Evidence, Denis-Benjamin Viger, 10 June 1828, British Parliamentary Papers, *Reports from Select Committees*, 145; *La Minerve*, 2 February 1837.
15 J. Duchesnay to Perrault the elder, 1 October 1788, cited in Kolish, *Nationalismes*, 255.
16 Hall, "Of Gender and Empire," 46.
17 Dechêne, *Habitants and Merchants*, 419-20; Trudel, *Histoire de la Nouvelle-France*, 3: 417-34; Landry, *Orphelines en France*, 147; Greer, *Peasant, Lord and Merchant*, 54.
18 Early analyses in Bradbury et al., "Property and Marriage."
19 Armstrong, "Charles-Séraphin Rodier," *DCB*.
20 Basch, *In the Eyes of the Law*; Bradbury, "From Civil Death"; Holcombe, *Wives and Property*; Shanley, *Feminism, Marriage*; Staves, *Married Women's Separate Property*; Chambers, *Married Women*.
21 Bradbury, "'In England.'"
22 Bradbury et al., "Property and Marriage," 15.
23 *La Minerve*, 1 February 1836.
24 *La Minerve*, 2 February 1837; Doucet, *Fundamental Principles*, 2:264, art. 225; Gérin-Lajoie, *La Communauté Légale*, 5-6.
25 Bertrand et uxor v. Pouliot, *Quebec Law Reports* 4 (1878), 8; Desjardins v. Chretien, *Lower Canada Jurist* 15 (1871), 56; Smith et vir v. Chrétien, *Lower Canada Jurist* 23 (1879), 8; La Corporation de Quebec v. Walsh, *Quebec Law Reports* 10 (1884), 23.
26 Less than 4 percent of the 398 labourers made contracts in the two generations combined. When a widower married a single woman, 15 percent did so; among merchants of both generations, 63 percent made a contract, whereas 80 percent did so when the husband was a widower.

27 Marriage contract, Campbell and Wait, 14 August 1824, Notary A. Jobin. The marriage register lists her as aged seventeen, the contract as sixteen.

28 Hardwick, *The Practice of Patriarchy,* ix.

29 Inventory, Genant and Decousse, 20 September 1853, Notary Mathieu.

30 Robillard, *Émilie Tavernier-Gamelin,* 47, 48, 50.

31 Marriage contract, Tavernier and Gamelin, 4 June 1823, Notary Doucet.

32 Marriage contract, Genant and Decousse, 16 July 1843, Notary Valotte.

33 Marriage contract, de Lotbinière and Harwood, 13 December 1823, Notary Doucet.

34 Marriage contract, de Lotbinière and Harwood, 13 December 1823, Notary Doucet; Doucet, *Fundamental Principles*; Jacques Boucher, "Nicolas-Benjamin Doucet," *DCB*. Doucet was the primary notary for forty-five (19 percent) of the contracts made by these couples.

35 I counted those present at sixty-seven of the contract-signing occasions. Hardwick, *The Practice of Patriarchy,* 61, reports an average of twelve witnesses in early-modern Nantes.

36 Marriage contract, Mower and Campbell, 14 January 1826, Notary Doucet; *Lovell's,* 1843-44.

37 Marriage contract, Forrest and Jourdain, Notary Gibb, 13 November 1845; M.A.C. Jourdain, Washington Village, to Georginna Forrest, June 1864, Forrest fonds, LAC.

38 Diefendorf, "Widowhood and Remarriage," 393.

39 Marriage contract, Campbell and Wait, 14 August 1824, Notary Jobin.

40 Ibid; Marriage registration, 14 August 1824.

41 Marriage contract, Smith and Allan, 11 September 1844, Notary W. Ross.

42 Young with Tulchinsky, "Sir Hugh Allan," *DCB*.

43 E. Ranvoye, Quebec, to L. Duvernay, Trois-Rivières, 9 February 1826, Ludger Duvernay collection, LAC; Noel, *Family Life,* 69.

44 Darrow, *Revolution in the House,* 59.

45 Marriage contract, Campbell and Wait, 14 August 1824, Notary Jobin.

46 Marriage contract, Mower and Campbell, 1 January 1826, Notary Doucet.

47 Marriage contract, White and Gay, 24 May 1826, Notary Griffin; Marriage contract, Hart and Hart, 12 December 1844, Notary Crawford; Marriage contract, Dufau and Charpentier, 29 June 1823, Notary Doucet.

48 Evidence, John Neilson, British Parliamentary Papers, *Reports from Select Committees,* 1828, 82.

49 Marriage contract, Legris and Julien, 4 September 1825, Notary Doucet; McCord, *The Civil Code,* art. 1384, s. 2. Among the 177 couples choosing community property in a marriage contract between 1823 and 1826, around 21 percent of husbands and 17 percent of wives placed such goods in the community compared to 15 percent of husbands and 9 percent of wives of the 55 couples a generation later.

50 Marriage contract, Monjean and Laurent, 22 November 1824, Notary Ritchot; Purchase, 21 April 1824, cited in Inventory, Monjean and Laurent, 7 April 1834, Notary Labadie; Evaluation roll, 1832. The inventory describes her selling one of the lots during their marriage for £200, while the evaluation roll of 1832 set the worth of the remaining lot at £100. A wide range of currencies was used in early-nineteenth-century Quebec. I have converted 24 livres anciens cours to £1 local currency in the early decades and £1 local currency into Cdn$3.33 from the 1860s on. See Hamilton, "Property Rights," 86; McCullough, *Money and Exchange,* 292.

51 E. Ranvoye, Quebec, to L. Duvernay, Trois-Rivières, 9 February 1826, also cited in Noel, *Family Life,* 63.

52 Since the husband administered the community and became the owner of all the moveables entering it, including those from which his *propres fictifs* might be taken, the clause of réalisation had little meaning when applied to his property because he became liable to himself for the moveables realiseés. Réalisation improved the position of a wife who renounced the community in favour of claiming her matrimonial rights, including her *propres fictifs*. Around 40 percent of husbands who chose community property in a contract in each generation, and 50 percent of wives made this choice. My thanks to Alan Stewart for clarifying these practices. See Bradbury et al., "Marriage and Property," 20.

53 Marriage contract, Dufau and Charpentier, 29 June 1823, Notary Doucet.

54 Evidence, Denis-Benjamin Viger, 10 June 1828, British Parliamentary Papers, *Reports from Select Committees*, 145.

55 Marriage contract, Rea and Smith, 15 November 1825, Notary Doucet.

56 Marriage contract, Tavernier and Gamelin, 4 June 1823, Notary Doucet.

57 Marriage contract, Perrault and Fabre, 8 May 1826, Notary Mondelet. My translation.

58 Darrow, *Revolution in the House,* 67. Clearly, attributing intent retroactively to a contract as we did here is tricky. Our interpretation of the contracts suggests that in the 1820s generation, among the 68 Anglo-Protestants grooms, 9 chose community property, 28 (41 percent) chose and established separate property, 24 (35 percent) sought separate property but established exclusion, and 7 (10 percent) sought to exclude community. In the 1840s generation, there were fewer mistakes. Among the 42 Anglo-Protestant and Jewish grooms, 2 (5 percent) chose community, 36 (36 percent) chose separation, 3 (7 percent) mistakenly chose exclusion, and 1 (2 percent) sought exclusion.

59 McCord, *The Civil Code,* arts. 1416-17; Wilson v. Pariseau and Simard, *Lower Canada Jurist* 1 (1857), 164-66.

60 Bradbury et al., "Property and Marriage." Intent did not interest the judges.

61 Marriage contract, Rea and Smith, 15 November 1825, Notary Doucet.

62 Marriage contract, Smith and Allan, 11 September 1844, Notary Ross.

63 Gordon Burr, "Andrew Allan," *DCB.*

64 Marriage contract, Mower and Campbell, 14 January 1826, Notary Doucet.

65 Tremblay, "La société Montréalaise," 59, reports that 4 of the 1,032 marriage contracts passed on the Island of Montreal between 1750 and 1770 did not create community property. Cardin and Desmarais, "Les contrats de mariage," 50, found 8 of a sample of 70 Montreal contracts between 1801 and 1812 were not in community; 7 of these were in English.

66 *La Minerve,* 1 October 1832, 2 February 1837.

67 Marriage contract, Westcott and Papineau, Notary D.E. Papineau, 25 August 1845.

68 Grimké, *Letters on the Equality*; Thompson, *Appeal of One Half.*

69 *La Minerve,* 14 May 1832, 5 May 1833; *Montreal Gazette,* 31 December 1833, cited in Heaman, "Taking the World," 604.

70 Lebsock, *The Free Women,* 85.

71 In the name-based sample created by Sherry Olson, most traders became "insolvent" at least once, but it was untimely death that magnified the impact of such an episode on the family. Oslon, "Feathering Her Nest"; Morris, *Men, Women and Property.*

72 Lebsock, *The Free Women,* 57; Shammas, Salmon, and Dahlin, *Inheritance in America.*

73 Marriage contract, Torrance and Stephenson, 20 July 1826, Notary Bedouin.

74 Marriage contract, de Lotbinière and Harwood, 13 December 1823, Notary Doucet.

75 Marriage contract, Tavernier and Gamelin, 4 June 1823, Notary Doucet; Marriage contract, Perrault and Fabre, 8 May 1826, Notary Mondelet; Marriage contract, Genant and Decousse, 16 July 1843, Notary Valotte.

76 Davidoff and Hall, *Family Fortunes*; Smith, *Ladies of the Leisure Class*; McKenna, *A Life of Propriety*.

77 Lebsock, *The Free Women*, found that "before the 1840s, only 14.3 percent (6/42) ... empowered the woman to sell her property; from 1841 to 1860, that figure jumped to 62.3 percent (33/53)," 76. For later in the century in Canada, see Baskerville, *A Silent Revolution?*

78 Morris, *Men, Women and Property*, 262-63.

79 McKay, "The Liberal Order Framework"; Sandwell, "The Limits of Liberalism"; Fecteau, *La Liberté du pauvre*.

80 Darrow, *Revolution in the House*, 254.

81 Young, "Getting Around Legal Incapacity."

82 Doucet, *Fundamental Principles*, 2:266, art. 234, 235, 236.

83 Benjamin et al. v. Clarke et vir, *Lower Canada Jurist* 3 (1860), 121; Laviolette, and Martin, *Lower Canada Jurist* 5 (1861), 211; McCormick et Buchanan, *Revue Légale* 2 (1870): 733; Perreault et al. ès qual. v. Charlebois et vir *Montreal Law Reports, Superior Court* 6 (1890), 311; *Legal News* 13 (1890): 284; Métrissé et al. v. Brault, *Lower Canada Jurist* 4 (1860), 60; *Lower Canada Reports* 10 (1860), 157. An act to amend art. 210 of the civil code, 1875, c. 24, Statutes, Quebec Statutes, 1867 onward (hereafter cited as SQ) modified that article to read: "The separation renders the wife capable of suing and being sued, and of contracting, for all that relates to the administration of her property; but for all acts and suits tending to alienate her immoveable property, she requires the authorization of her husband, or upon his refusal the authorization of a judge:" *Montreal Law Reports, Superior Court* 6 (1890), 311; *Legal News* 13 (1890): 284.

Chapter 3: Marriage Trajectories

1 Marriage contract, Farquhar and Sutherland, 1 October 1844, Notary Guy; *Montreal Gazette*, 20 March 1841; Morris, *Men, Women and Property*, 260-63; Bushman, *The Refinement of America*, 19.

2 Marriage contract, Farquhar and Sutherland, 1 October 1844, Notary Guy; *Classic Encyclopedia*, s.v. "Charles James Lever," http://www.1911encyclopedia.org/.

3 Davidoff and Hall, *Family Fortunes*, 272; Hardwick, *The Practice of Patriarchy*, 73. Morris, *Men, Women and Property*, 49-50, reports that making testamentary inventories had faded in England but not Scotland by the early nineteenth century.

4 K.M. Brown, *Good Wives*, 297; Greer, *Peasant, Lord and Merchant*, 74; Dechêne, *Habitants and Merchants*, 242; Inventory, Paris and Guilbault, 3 March 1830, Notary Labadie; Birth registration, Notre Dame Parish, 12 September 1826, 19 July 1827.

5 A.M. Stewart, "Settling an 18th-Century *Faubourg*"; Robillard, *Émilie Tavernier-Gamelin*, 95; Sale, Vallée, and Guilbault, 12 April 1828, cited in Inventory, Paris and Guilbault, 3 March 1830, Notary Labadie. Linteau and Robert, "Propriété foncière"; Sweeny, "A Partial Tax Roll, 1832"; Sweeny, "The 1832 By-Election."

6 A.M. Stewart, "Settling an 18th-Century *Faubourg*"; Ward, *History of Domestic Space*, 8-14, 24; Inventory, Paris and Guilbault, 3 March 1830, Notary Labadie; Darrow, *Revolution in the House*, 176.

7 Burgess, "Work, Family and Community."

8 Marriage contract, Legris and Julien, 4 September 1825, Notary Doucet.

9 Marriage contract, Monjean and Laurent, 22 November 1824, Notary Ritchot; Inventory, Monjean and Laurent, 7 April 1834, Notary Labadie.

10 Sweeny, "A Reconstituted Tax Roll, 1825"; Sweeny, "A Partial Tax Roll, 1832."

11 Inventory, Monjean and Laurent, 7 April 1834, Notary Labadie; Bushman, *The Refinement of America,* 228; Marriage contract, Monjean and Laurent, 22 November 1824, Notary Ritchot.

12 *Lovell's,* 1842-43, 1844-45, 1848; Lease, Easton to Decousse, 3 February 1843, Notary Pelton; Marriage contract, Genant and Decousse, 16 July 1843, Notary Valotte.

13 Burgess, "Work, Family and Community"; Ruddel, *Les apprentis artisans.*

14 *Lovell's,* 1843-52; Marriage contract, Genant and Decousse, 16 July 1843, Notary Valotte; Inventory, Genant and Decousse, 20 September 1853, Notary Guy; *La Minerve,* 14 August 1852.

15 Partnership agreement, Brady, Brady, and Darling, 21 October 1844, Notary Belle; *Lovell's,* 1843-44, 1845-46; Sale, Mrs. Darling and William Brady to Mr. Sampson Brady, 21 July 1852, Notary Smith; *Lovell's* 1848 lists the factory at 62 St. Charles Barrommé Street, while "Mrs. Brady," is listed at Lagauchetière, near Panet; Inventory, Conegan and Brady, 26 February 1853, Notary Smith.

16 Marriage contract, Forrest and Jourdain, 13 November 1845, Notary Gibb.

17 Birth, Death, Marriage registrations, Montreal parishes.

18 Power of attorney from Logan Fuller and Caroline Campbell to Joseph Ross, 23 August 1832; from Caroline Campbell, James Wait, and Louis Laporte (sic), 24 August 1832, Notary Arnoldi.

19 Rev. Royal Robbins, *The World Displayed in Its History and Geography, Embracing a History of the World from the Creation to the Present Day* (New York: W.W. Reed, 1831).

20 Inventory, Oliver Wait, 10 and 12 November 1832, Notary Arnoldi.

21 J.L. Roy, *Édouard-Raymond Fabre,* 21, 24, 36-39, 54-59; *Lovell's,* 1843-54.

22 Bushman, *The Refinement of America.*

23 Tulchinsky, "Jedediah Hubbell Dorwin," *DCB*; Witham, "Andrew White," *DCB*; *La Minerve,* 16 August 1832.

24 Inventory, Paris and Guilbault, 3 March 1830, Notary Labadie; Sweeny, "A Partial Tax Roll, 1832."

25 Poutanen, "Women Arrested in Montreal"; Poutanen, "'To Indulge.'"

26 I identified 6 of the 1,338 women who married between 1823 and 1826 in Poutanen's transcription of sex trade-related offences, "Women Arrested in Montreal." Of these, all but Rosalie Paquet and Hermine Legris were married to labourers when they were arrested, or would marry a labourer later.

27 Hufton, "Women without Men"; Stansell, *City of Women.*

28 Poutanen, "Women Arrested in Montreal"; *Lovell's,* 1842-46.

29 *Lovell's* and *Mackay's,* 1843-61; Necrologies, Fabrique of the Parish of Notre Dame, Montreal (hereafter cited as FPNDM); Census, 1871, Saint Antoine ward, Section b: 3, p. 71, household 180.

30 BAnQM, Quarter Sessions, Queen v. Charles Smith, 19 June 1843; affidavit of Agnes Kirkpatrick, and 20 June 1843, Affidavits of Ann Coynne, Sarah Johnston, cited in Pilarczyk, "'Justice in the Premises,'" 339-40; Marriage Registration, 12 May 1842; Death registration 9 July 1845; Montreal *Gazette,* 10 July 1845; Marriage Registration, 15 April 1847.

31 Marriage registration, 11 October 1824; Quarter Sessions, Marie-Anne Landreville v. Vincent Labelle, 18 July 1837, cited in Pilarczyk, "'Justice in the Premises,'" 347.

32 Nootens, *Fous, prodigues et ivrognes,* 26-27.

33 Pilarczyk, "'Justice in the Premises,'" 237, 262, quote at 239. In police and criminal records he found 487 complaints against husbands for domestic violence between 1825 and 1850, and 84 against wives.

34 Deposition 13, Prendergast, Halligan, 18 December 1858, Mitchell v. Brown, 28 February 1859, Superior Court, dossiers, BAnQM.
35 *The Pilot*, 20 November 1849, and *Montreal Transcript*, 22 November 1849, cited in Pilarczyk, "'Justice in the Premises,'" 315; Harvey, "To Love, Honour and Obey."
36 Extract from St. George's Chapel Parish Register; Deposition, Chief of Police, Montreal, 22 March 1858, Mitchell v. Brown, 1859, Superior Court, dossiers, BAnQM.
37 *Montreal Witness*, 3 March 1858; *Lovell's*, 1848, 1852, 1853, 1854.
38 Tosh, *A Man's Place*, 4; Tosh, "What Should Historians Do?" 186; Davidoff and Hall, *Family Fortunes*, 229-34; Morris, *Men, Women and Property*.
39 *Mackay's*, 1856-57, 408; *Starke's*, 1858, 108; Elizabeth Gibbs, "William Badgley," *DCB*; *Montreal Witness*, 3 March 1858; *Mackay's*, 1858.
40 Harland-Jacobs, "All in the Family," 454.
41 Ibid., 454, 456, 457; Clawson, *Constructing Brotherhood*; Carnes, *Secret Ritual and Manhood*.
42 Fecteau, *La Liberté du pauvre*, 245; Taylor, *Sources of the Self*, 13, 395-400.
43 Tosh, "What Should Historians Do?"; *Mackay's*, 1856-57.
44 Mitchell v. Brown, *Lower Canada Jurist* 3 (1859), 113-14; Mitchell v. Brown, 28 February 1859; Deposition 13, Prendergast, Halligan, 18 December 1858, Mitchell v. Brown, 28 February 1859, Superior Court, dossiers, BAnQM; Pilarczyk, "'Justice in the Premises,'" 229-30.
45 Mitchell v. Brown, *Lower Canada Jurist* 3 (1859); Mitchell v. Brown, 28 February 1859, Superior Court, dossiers; Ladies' Benevolent Society Register; Harvey, "The Protestant Orphan Asylum," 149, 172, 177; Ladies' Benevolent Society, *Matron's Journal*, vol. 2, 24 May 1858, p. 29, 3 July 1858, 36; Ladies' Benevolent Society Register, cited in Harvey, "The Protestant Orphan Asylum," 194.
46 Harvey, "The Protestant Orphan Asylum," 152.
47 Deposition 13, Prendergast, 18 December 1858, Mitchell v. Brown; Extract from St. George's Chapel Parish Register; Deposition, Chief of Police, Montreal, 22 March 1858, Mitchell v. Brown, 1859, Superior Court, dossiers, BAnQM; Tutorship, John O. Brown, BAnQM.
48 Inventory, Conegan and Brady, 26 February 1853, Notary James Smith.
49 Dissolution, partnership Brady, Brady and Darling, 1 February 1851, Notary James Smith.
50 Morris, *Men, Women and Property*, 256.
51 Files, Notary Pelton, 1842-56; Evidence, T.J. Pelton, 15 July 1851, Appendix Q.Q., *Journals of the Legislative Assembly of the Province of Canada* (hereafter cited as *JLAPC*).
52 Marsan, *Montreal in Evolution*, 256; Davidoff and Hall, *Family Fortunes*; Morris, *Men, Women and Property*, 27; MacLeod, "Salubrious Settings," 52-53, 111.
53 MacLeod, "Salubrious Settings," 116; Banker, 30 St. François Xavier, house Bellaire Cottage, head Genevieve St.; *Lovell's*, 1844-45, 1845-46.
54 MacLeod, "Salubrious Settings," 86, 124, Tables 2 and 3; Tulchinsky, "Thomas Workman," *DCB*.
55 MacLeod, "Salubrious Settings," Table 3.
56 Sweeny, "Structure out of Change."
57 Birth registration, 2 June 1845, 29 December 1847, 27 April 1848, 17 July 1850, Christ Anglican Church, BAnQM; Mount Royal Cemetery, burial records, lot C207; Will, Sutherland, probated 16 February 1875.
58 Sweeny, "Structure out of Change"; Morris, *Men, Women and Property*, 172; Sweeny, "A Reconstituted Tax Roll, 1825"; Sweeny, "A Partial Tax Roll, 1832"; *Lovell's* 1852 and 1854 list them at 21 Great St. James Street. From 1864 to 1881, they were identified as being on Dorchester.

59 *Lovell's,* 1843-66.
60 Young with Tulchinsky, "Sir Hugh Allan," *DCB.*
61 Ibid.; MacLeod, "Salubrious Settings," 229; Census, 1871, Saint Antoine ward, section 106:7, household 127.
62 *Lovell's,* 1844-57.
63 *Lovell's,* 1844-55.
64 Hardwick, *The Practice of Patriarchy,* 6.
65 Files, Notary Pelton, 1842-56; Evidence, T.J. Pelton, 15 July 1851, Appendix Q.Q., *JLAPC; Lovell's,* 1855-1861; Birth Registration, St. George Anglican Church, 20 November 1859; Census, 1861, Montreal, folio 5096.
66 T.J. Pelton, Knowlton, to Carrie Pelton, Montreal, 4 June 1861, Pelton Papers, McGill University Archives (hereafter cited as McGA).
67 Caroline Scott to Carrie Pelton, Montreal, 4 October 1861; Caroline to Carrie, Montreal, 1 November 1861; Caroline to Carrie, 5 March 1863, Pelton Papers, McGA.
68 Hardwick, *The Practice of Patriarchy,* 110.
69 D. Rome, "Adolphus Mordecai Hart," *DCB*; Adolphus M. Hart, *Uncle Tom in Paris; or, Views of Slavery Outside the Cabin* (Baltimore: William Taylor, 1854). The full text is available through Stephen Railton and the University of Virginia, http://www.iath.virginia.edu/utc/.
70 *Lovell's,* 1844-80; MacLeod, "Salubrious Settings."
71 Rome, "Adolphus Mordecai Hart," *DCB*, reports, in contrast, that they had three daughters and two sons.
72 Morris, *Men, Women and Property,* 29.
73 A Montreal Lady, *Household Recipes or Domestic Cookery* (Montreal: A.A. Stevenson, 1865), 7; Driver, *Culinary Landmarks,* 93; Census, 1881, Saint Antoine ward, division 4, p. 58.
74 Rome, "Adolphus Mordecai Hart," *DCB.*
75 Birth registration, Elvira Ellen Anne, born 11 November 1846, baptized 18 April 1847, folio 13; Birth registration, Charles Duffell Edward, born 29 July 1849, baptized 13 February 1850, folio 3; Death registration, Charles, 16 February 1851, folio 5; Birth registration, Bertha, born 11 July 1851, baptized 19 August 1851, folio 4, (all Christ Anglican Church); MRC; US Census, 1881, NA no. T90560, Boston, Suffolk, MA, p. 431D, online.
76 M.A.C. Jourdain to Georginna Forrest, 13 June 1858, 1 July 1858, 25 April 1860, 6 June 1864, Forrest fonds, LAC.
77 M.A.C. Jourdain to Georginna Forrest, 10 July 1864, 2 June 1863. Forrest fonds, LAC.
78 M.A.C. Jourdain to Georginna Forrest, 14 August 1864, Forrest fonds, LAC.
79 US Census, 1881, NA no. T90560, Boston, Suffolk, MA, p. 431D; M.A.C. Jourdain to Georginna Forrest, 10 July 1864, Forrest fonds, LAC.
80 M.A.C. Jourdain to Georginna Forrest, 14 August 1864, Forrest fonds, LAC; Morris, *Men, Women and Property,* 44.
81 Robillard, *Émilie Tavernier-Gamelin,* 87-89; on deputy husbands, see K.E. Wood, *Masterful Women,* 18.
82 Cott, *The Grounding*; Harvey, "The Protestant Orphan Asylum," 118-19.
83 Will, McDonnell, probated 13 February 1836; *Lovell's,* 1842; An Act to Incorporate the Ladies of the Protestant Orphan Asylum of the City of Montreal, 7 Vict., c. 52, 1843, Canada East.
84 An Act to Incorporate the Ladies' Benevolent Society of Montreal, 4 and 5 Vict., c. 66, 1841, Canada East; An Act to Incorporate the Protestant Infants' Home of Montreal," 34 Vict., c. 56, 1870, Canada.
85 *Lovell's,* 1890-91.

86 Harvey, "The Protestant Orphan Asylum," 120-43.
87 Robillard, *Émilie Tavernier-Gamelin*, 96.
88 Greer, *The Patriots*; Bernard, *Les rébellions de 1837-38*.
89 Roy, "Édouard-Raymond Fabre," *DCB*; J.L. Roy, *Édouard-Raymond Fabre*, 21, 24-26; Harvey, "Le leadership féminin"; Young, *George-Etienne Cartier*, 29.
90 Richard Chabot, "Édouard-Étienne Rodier," *DCB*.
91 Ibid.; Bernard, *Les rebellions de 1837-38*, 102-3.
92 *La Minerve*, 16 August 1832; see Chapter 9.
93 Papineau to Perrault, 7 January 1839, Perrault fonds, LAC, cited in J.L. Roy, *Édouard-Raymond Fabre*, 119.
94 Chabot, "Rodier," *DCB*; Nootens, *Fous, prodigues et ivrognes*, 124-25.
95 F. Noel, *Family Life*.
96 LaFontaine to Goldie, 12 December 1838, reproduced in Aubin, ed., *Louis-Hyppolyte La Fontaine*, 2; Roy, "Édouard-Raymond Fabre," *DCB*.
97 Chabot, "Rodier," *DCB*; Nootens, *Fous, prodigues et ivrognes*, 124-28.
98 J.L. Roy, *Édouard-Raymond Fabre*, 157-59, 169.
99 Ibid., 24; the next mayor's wife was referred to as "The Lady Mayoress," *Montreal Gazette*, 12 December 1851.
100 J.L. Roy, *Édouard-Raymond Fabre*, 24.
101 Fabre to Julie Bossange, 12 June 1846, cited in J.L. Roy, *Édouard-Raymond Fabre*, 33.

Chapter 4: "Dower This Barbarous Law"

1 Marriage contract, 13 December 1823, Notary Doucet.
2 Government House to Harwood, 16 July 1839; copy of appointment from Register's Office of the Records at Quebec, 3 August 1839; Harwood Papers, McGill Rare Books (hereafter cited as McGRB).
3 An Ordinance to Prescribe and Regulate the Registering of Titles to Lands, Tenements and Hereditaments, Real or Immoveable Estates, and of Charges and Incumbrances on the same; and for the alteration and improvement of the law, in certain particulars, in relation to the Alienation and Hypothecation of Real Estates, and the Rights and Interest acquired therein, Lower Canada (hereafter Registry Ordinance), 1841, c. 30, *Ordinances made and passed by the administrator of the government and Special Council for the affairs of the province of Lower Canada*, 1838-41 (hereafter cited as *LCO*); Bradbury, "Debating Dower," 56-78; Watt, "Authoritarianism."
4 Collective Clio, *L'histoire des femmes*, 164-65.
5 The lack of attention is perhaps in part because of its particularly obtuse title. On this, and for a detailed critique of the ordinance, see Crémazie, *Rapport de J. Crémazie*, 2; Young, "Positive Law, Positive State," 50-63; Perrault, "Le Conseil Spécial, 1838-1841," and Watt, "Authoritarianism," are exceptions.
6 Collective Clio, *L'histoire des femmes*, 164-65. Kolish describes earlier debates about registration but passes briefly over the Ordinance in *Nationalismes*.
7 Doucet, *Fundamental Principles*, 2:270; Armstrong, *A Treatise on the Law*, 36-38; Beaubien, *Traité sur les lois civiles*, 3:6-10; Loranger, *De l'incapacité*.
8 Salmon, *Women and the Law*, 142; Loranger, *De l'incapacité*.
9 Salmon, *Women and the Law*, 17-18; Staves, *Married Women's Separate Property*, 5.
10 Hall, "Of Gender and Empire," 51.
11 Evidence, J. Stephen, 24 June 1828, British Parliamentary Papers, *Reports from Select Committees*, 1828, 244; Greenwood, *Legacies of Fear*, 35-37, 186; Kolish, *Nationalismes*; Normand and Hudon, "Le contrôle," 171-201; Nazzari, "Widows as Obstacles," describes similar objections in Brazil.
12 Hall, *Civilizing Subjects*, 16; L.H. LaFontaine to Edward Ellice, 17 April 1838, in Aubin, ed., *Louis-Hyppolyte La Fontaine*, 2: 44.

13 J. Duchesnay to Perrault the elder, 1 October 1788, cited in Kolish, *Nationalismes,* 255; Evidence, John Neilson, 24 May 1828, British Parliamentary Papers, *Reports from Select Committees,* 81.

14 4 February 1823, 68, and 3 March 1823, 165, *Journals of the House of Assembly of Lower Canada* (hereafter cited as *JHALC*); Badgley, *Remarks on Register Offices,* 14; Evidence, Samuel Gale, 13 May 1828, British Parliamentary Papers, *Reports from Select Committees,* 29-30.

15 An 1829 bill in the Legislative Council that simplified the procedure for discharging other kinds of hypothecs was amended by the House of Assembly to clarify that it would have no impact on dower. 7 March 1829, *JHALC*; An Act to Provide for the more effectual extinction of secret incumbrances on lands, than was heretofore in use in this Province, 1829, c. 20, s. 14, Statutes, Lower Canada, 1791-1838 (hereafter cited as SLC).

16 Bills were introduced in the Legislative Council in 1817, 1819, 1821, 1822, 1823, 1824, 1825, 1827, and 1828, then again frequently during the early 1830s. *Journals of the Legislative Council of Lower Canada* (hereafter cited as *JLCLC*), 1810-37. On these, see Kolish, "Le Conseil Législatif"; *Gazette de Québec,* 24 December 1822; *Montreal Herald,* 8 March 1826; J.-E. Roy, *Histoire du notariat,* vol. 2, ch. 36.

17 Gerald Tulchinsky, "George Moffatt," *DCB*; Perrault, "Le Conseil spécial, 1838-1841," 143.

18 Kolish, "Le conseil législatif," 228; Kolish, *Nationalismes*; "Report of the Special Committee to whom was referred the Petition of certain Inhabitants of the City and District of Montreal, respecting the state of Law regarding the creation of incumbrances upon Real Estate in this Province, and praying for the establishment of Register Offices therein," November 1835-March 1836, Appendix F, *JLCLC,* 1836.

19 *JLCLC,* 1835-36, 263, 293, 326.

20 Moffatt and Badgley to Lord Glenelg, 15 April 1838; Badgley Papers, folder 10, McGA; Badgley, *Remarks on Register Officers,* 45-46, 25-29.

21 Moffatt and Badgley to Durham, 9 April 1838, Badgley Papers, folder 10, McCord Museum of Canadian History Archives (hereafter cited as MMA); Tulchinsky, "Moffatt," *DCB*.

22 Greer, *The Patriots,* quotations at 131, 210; Kolish, *Nationalismes,* 207; McKay, "The Liberal Order Framework"; Sandwell, "The Limits of Liberalism"; Normand and Hudon, "Le contrôle"; Linteau and Robert, "Propriété foncière."

23 *La Minerve,* 1 February 1836, 10 November 1836; Kolish, *Nationalismes,* 207-8.

24 *Le Populaire,* 21 August 1837; Greer, *The Patriots,* 285, 287.

25 Young, *The Politics of Codification,* 41.

26 *Montreal Gazette,* 6 March 1838.

27 *La Minerve,* 14 August 1837; Letter to the editor, *Le Populaire,* 30 April 1838, signed "un vrai Réformiste" and reproduced from the *Gazette de Québec.*

28 The quotation in the title of this section comes from *Debates of the Legislative Assembly of United Canada* (hereafter cited as *DLAUC*), 21 June 1847, 364.

29 Perrault, "Le conseil spécial, 1838-41," 138; Watt, "Authoritarianism."

30 Henderson, "Uncivil Subjects."

31 Government House to Harwood, 16 July 1839, Harwood Papers, McGRB.

32 Sweeny, "A Partial Tax Roll, 1832." His property on St. Hubert Street was close to the eastern section of the old city, where they had resided earlier. It was assessed as worth an annual revenue of £92; Sweeny, "Internal Dynamics," 157-58; Agreement, George Stacey and Harwood, 8 September 1826, Notary Griffin.

33 Partage, Chartier de Lotbinière, 19 January 1829, Notary Joseph Papineau. The choice of these two men underlines the small size and intimate linkages of

the elite in this colonial city. As explained in Chapter 1, Henry Munro was also the uncle of Charlotte Mount, who married Genevais. Paul-Joseph Lacroix was the father of Marie-Louise Lacroix, who married the Montreal merchant Charles-Séraphin Rodier in 1825.

34 "Measurement of the Stone of the House of R.U. Harwood, esquire at Vaudreuil," 22 November 1830, Harwood Papers, McGRB; Thompson, "Harwood," *DCB.*

35 Thompson, "Harwood," *DCB.*

36 Edward Hale to Eliza Hale, 10 January 1840, 9 June 1840, McGA.

37 Thompson, "Harwood," *DCB; JHALC,* 1834, 311, 318.

38 The first tutor chosen by family members for Chartier de Lotbinière's three daughters was the Patriote leader Louis-Joseph Papineau. Marie-Louise's cousin, Charlotte Mount's second husband, Louis Lacoste commanded the 1st Battalion in the Chambly Militia and was imprisoned for his role in the rebellions. H.J. Morgan, *The Canadian Parliamentary Companion.*

39 Harwood to Judge Badgley, 15 April 1839, Harwood Papers, McGRB.

40 Hamelin, "Michel-Eustache-Gaspard-Alain Chartier de Lotbinière," *DCB*; Harwood to Major Goldie (n.d.); Copy of appointment from Register's Office of the Records at Quebec, 3 August 1839, Harwood Papers, McGRB.

41 Young, "Positive Law, Positive State"; Greer, *The Patriots,* 357.

42 Edward Hale to Eliza Hale, 7 June 1840, 9 June 1840, Hale Papers, MMA.

43 Lord Durham was interested in this question. See "Report from Mr. Turton, on the Establishment of a Registry of Real Property for Lower Canada," Appendix E, Durham, *Report.*

44 Baker, "Law Practice and Statecraft," 51, 63, claims William Badgley authored this bill. I have found no evidence to support that claim. Contemporaries referred to Stuart as the author, as have several historians. *Le Canadien,* 30 October 1840; *Montreal Gazette,* 27 September 1847; Bonner, *Essay on the Registry Laws,* 16; Young, *The Politics of Codification,* 45; Evelyn Kolish, "James Stuart," *DCB.*

45 *Journals of the Special Council of the Province of Lower Canada* (hereafter cited as *JSCLC*), 5 November 1840-9 February 1841; Elizabeth Gibbs, "Dominique Mondelet," *DCB,* suggests incorrectly that he was appointed in 1838 but "never attended a meeting or participated in its activities." Watt, "Authoritarianism," 33-35; Edward Hale to Eliza Hale, 11 June 1840, 16 June 1840, Hale Papers, MMA.

46 Watt, "Authoritarianism," 32; Louis-Philippe Audet, "Edward Hale," *DCB*; Peter Deslauriers, "Jules-Maurice Quesnel," *DCB*; Peter Deslauriers, "Samuel Gerrard," *DCB*; Dubuc and Tremblay, "John Molson," *DCB*; Marthe Faribault-Beauregard, "Joseph-Édouard Faribault," *DCB*; Gibbs, "Dominique Mondelet," *DCB*; Kolish, "Sir James Stuart," *DCB*; Carman Miller, "Charles Dewey Day," *DCB*; Jean-Claude Robert, "Barthelemy Joliette," *DCB*; Robert Sweeny, "Peter McGill," *DCB*; Thompson, "Harwood," *DCB*; Tulchinsky, "George Moffatt," *DCB*; Young, *The Politics of Codification,* 84-95.

47 Peter McGill, John Molson, George Moffatt, Dominique Mondelet, and Barthélemy Joliette.

48 Peter McGill, John Molson, Charles Dewey Day, and George Moffatt. Constitutional Association of Montreal, Annual Report, 31 December 1838, folder 9, Badgley Papers, MMA.

49 Marion Phelps, "Paul Holland Knowlton," *DCB.*

50 Gibbs, "Dominique Mondelet," *DCB*; Nish, "Charles-Elzéar Mondelet," *DCB.*

51 Miller, "Charles Dewey Day," *DCB.*

52 Dominique Mondelet married Harriet Munro in 1832. She died in childbirth in 1837. Edward to Eliza Hale, 9 June 1840, 2 June 1840, Hale Papers, MMA.

53 Young, *The Politics of Codification*. Edward Hale to Eliza Hale, 30 April 1840, Hale Papers, MMA. Day was born in Quebec City and spent from 1823 to 1828 in India as private secretary to Lord Amherst, his uncle. At the time of the rebellions, he was settled in the Eastern Townships; sessions were behind closed doors, "Rules and Orders," *JSCLC*, 20 April 1838; Audet, "Hale," *DCB*; Bonner, *Essay on the Registry Laws*, 12.

54 Kolish, "Le conseil législatif," 217-30.

55 Bonner, *Essay on the Registry Laws*, 16-20, 37; *Le Jean Baptiste*, 20 November 1840.

56 Registry Ordinance, s. 21, 1841, *LCO*.

57 Customary dower is only mentioned in ss. 35 and 37, those dealing with how wives could relinquish dower rights on land or stipulating that dower would only be on property held by the husband at this death. On this, see Crémazie, *Rapport de J. Crémazie*, 3-5.

58 24 December 1840, *JSCLC*; Bonner, *Essay on the Registry Laws*, 17-18; Registry Ordinance, s. 1.

59 Registry Ordinance, s. 34-35; Crémazie, *Rapport de J. Crémazie*; Badgley, *Remarks on Register Offices*.

60 Registry Ordinance, s. 34-35; Holcombe, *Wives and Property*, quotation at 42; Staves, *Married Women's Separate Property*, 135; Bradbury, "From Civil Death," 43, 61.

61 Some of the wording of this section of the Registry Ordinance is very close to that of the English Fines and Recoveries Act passed nine years earlier in England.

62 *JSCLC*, 18 December 1840.

63 An Act for the Amendment of the Law Relating to Dower, England, 1833, c. 55, s. 4; Staves, *Married Women's Separate Property*, 112.

64 17 February 1845, 21 June 1847, *DLAUC*. An Act for the more easy barring of Dower, 1833, c. 4, facilitated barring dower in Upper Canada. The Registry Ordinance applied only to Lower Canada. Shammas, Salmon, and Dahlin, *Inheritance in America*, 85-86, report that it was only by the 1890s that over two-thirds of the pre-1850s states had abolished dower.

65 21 June 1847, *DLAUC*, 364; J.I. Little, "Lewis Thomas Drummond," *DCB*.

66 *JSCLC*, 18 December 1840.

67 Carole Pateman argues that "accounts of the rise of contract do not tell the whole story – half is missing ... the one that tells how a specifically modern form of patriarchy is established." *The Sexual Contract*, xi. She does not consider the ways men and later women reshaped the marriage contract as determined by the law of the land, thus establishing diverse modern forms of patriarchy.

68 Mackay, "The Liberal Order," 623.

69 *Le Canadien*, 4 November 1840; *Le Jean Baptiste*, 17 November 1840, 14 December 1840; *Le Canadien*, 2 November 1840.

70 The reform alliance under Baldwin and LaFontaine won overwhelmingly in the election of the winter of 1847-48.

71 LaFontaine, *Analyse de l'Ordonnance*, 107.

72 Crémazie, *Rapport de J. Crémazie*, 4.

73 Ibid., 10.

74 An Act to amend the Act and Ordinance therein mentioned, relative to the Registration of Titles to and Incumbrances upon Real Property in Lower Canada, 1845, c. 27, *LCO*.

75 Civil Code of Lower Canada, *First, Second and Third Reports* (Quebec: George E. Desbarats, 1865), 65; Morin, "La perception," 38-40.

76 Art. 2116, Civil Code. An Act to order the registration of customary dowers and servitudes in certain cases not provided for by the law, 1880, c. 16, SQ, extended

art. 2116 to dowers created before 1 August 1866, giving two years to register them. This period was extended to 1 May 1884, in An Act to amend the Act 44-45 Victoria, chapter 16 to extend the delay for registering the customary dowers and servitudes mentioned therein and to provide for more efficient publication of the Act, 1883, c. 25, SQ, and again, in An Act to amend the Act 44-45 Victoria, chapter 16, to extend the delay for registering the customary dowers and servitudes mentioned therein, 1884, c. 15, SQ, which extended the final deadline to 1 January 1885.

77 Cited in Greenwood, *Legacies of Fear,* 186.

78 These statements derive from our survey of all cases reported in the nineteenth-century law journals of Lower Canada. Law journals reported sixty-one cases between 1810 and 1891 that touched on dower.

79 Panet v. Larue, *Lower Canada Reports* 2 (1852), 83.

80 Forbes v. Legault, *Lower Canada Reports* 6 (1856), 100-1. The préciput was a specified value or amount, agreed to in a marriage contract, that the survivor could take from the community property. It was usually half the value of a specified dower.

81 Dessaint v. Ladrière, *Quebec Law Reports* 16 (1890), 277-80; Chambers, *Married Women,* 6, argues cogently about the dangers of relying on reported cases but also makes the point that they served an educative role. It is in this sense that I draw on them here.

82 Cavanaugh, "The Limitations," 198-225; McCallum, "Prairie Women," 19-34; Gérin-Lajoie, *La Communauté Légale,* 10, 21.

83 The issue of the priority of claims was critical. It was addressed again and again in subsequent legislation, as was the period allowed for registration. By 1852, hypothecs registered prior to 1844 ranked from the date of creation; those registered after ranked from the date of their registration. Bonner, *Essay on the Registry Laws*; An Act to amend the Act and Ordinance therein mentioned, relative to the Registration of Titles to and Incumbrances upon Real Property in Lower Canada, 1845, c. 27, Statutes, Province of Canada (hereafter cited as SPC); An Act to extend and amend the provisions of chapters 36 and 37 of the Consolidated Statutes for Lower Canada, with respect to the Registration of Titles to and the removal of incumbrances upon real estate in Lower Canada, 1862, c. 11, SPC; An Act to order the registration of customary dowers and servitudes in certain cases not provided for by the law, 1880, c. 16, SQ; An Act to amend the Act 44-45 Victoria, chapter 16 to extend the delay for registering the customary dowers and servitudes mentioned therein and to provide for more efficient publication of the Act, 1883, c. 25, SQ; An Act to amend the Act 44-45 Victoria, chapter 16, to extend the delay for registering the customary dowers and servitudes mentioned therein, 1884, c. 15, SQ.

84 Normand and Hudon, "Le contrôle," 196.

85 Holograph Will, Robert Unwin Harwood, probated 2 May 1863.

Chapter 5: Imagining Widowhood and Death

1 *Family Herald,* 7 March 1874, 2 May 1874.

2 Bouchard, "Sur les rituels," 123-39.

3 *Montreal Transcript,* 21 November 1846.

4 *Montreal Register,* 14 December 1848.

5 Mary Westcott-Papineau, Montreal, to James Westcott, Saratoga Springs, 25 or 26 December 1847, Westcott-Papineau Papers, LAC; Louise Sarah Hay married Augustin Cuvillier, son of the prominent auctioneer and Marie-Claire Perrault, on 16 March 1837. She died on 17 December 1847; Death registration, Notre Dame Parish.

6   Mary Westcott-Papineau, Montreal, to James Wescott, Saratoga Springs, 21 February 1847, Westcott-Papineau Papers, emphasis in original; James Lambert with Jacques Monet, "Joseph-Rémi Vallières de Saint-Réal," *DCB*; Davidoff and Hall, *Family Fortunes.*

7   28 July 1847, *JLAPC*; An Act to make provision for the subsistence of the Widow of the late Honorable Joseph Rémi Vallières de St. Réal, 1847, c. 36, Statutes, Province of Canada, 1841-66 (hereafter cited as SPC).

8   *Montreal Gazette,* 1 March 1826, 24 January 1831, 9 May 1846, 9 June 1846, 11 June 1851. For example, petition of Mrs. J.M.K. Gregory, widow, 20 November 1854, *JLAPC*, 1290; 22 November 1854, 1349; Skocpol, *Protecting Soldiers and Mothers*; Kessler-Harris, "Independence and Virtue," 6.

9   Davies, "'Services Rendered'"; Little, *"No Car, No Radio"*; Strong-Boag, "'Wages for Housework,'" 24-34. Quebec was among the last provinces to make provisions in 1937.

10   Marriage contract, de Lotbinière and Harwood, 13 December 1823, Notary Doucet; Will, Harwood, probated 2 May 1863.

11   Marriage contract, Scott and Pelton, 5 January 1843, Notary Gibb; Marriage contract, Hart and Hart, 12 December 1844, Notary Crawford.

12   Marriage contract, Mower and Campbell, 11 January 1826, Notary Doucet.

13   Marriage contract, Rea and Smith, 15 November 1825, Notary Doucet; Marriage contract, Smith and Allan, 11 September 1844, Notary Ross; Marriage contract, Campbell and Wait, 14 August 1824, Notary Jobin.

14   Morris, *Men, Women and Property,* 236-37, citing the will of Samuel Firth, 1832.

15   Marriage contract, Legris and Julien, 4 September 1825, Notary Doucet; Brun, *Vie et mort,* 76-77.

16   Marriage contract, Monjean and Laurent, 22 November 1824, Notary Ritchot.

17   Marriage contract, Tavernier and Gamelin, 4 June 1823, Notary Doucet; Marriage contract, Perrault and Fabre, 8 June 1826, Notary Mondelet.

18   Marriage contract, Genant and Decousse, 16 July 1843, Notary Valotte.

19   Marriage contract, Legris and Julien, 4 September 1825, Notary Doucet; Marriage contract, Tavernier and Gamelin, 4 June 1823, Notary Doucet; Marriage contract, Perrault and Fabre, 8 June 1826, Notary Mondelet.

20   Lebsock, *The Free Women,* 44-47; Shammas, Salmon, and Dahlin, *Inheritance in America*; Wilson, *Life after Death,* 47, 185.

21   Marriage contract, Perrault and Fabre; 8 June 1826, Notary Mondelet; Marriage contract, Hart and Hart, 12 December 1844, Notary Crawford, Marriage contract, Campbell and Wait, 14 August 1824, Notary Jobin; Marriage contract, Scott and Pelton, 5 January 1843, Notary Gibb.

22   Marriage contract, de Lotbinière and Harwood, 13 December 1823, Notary Doucet; Will, Harwood, probated 2 May 1863.

23   Evidence, Samuel Gale, 22 July 1828, British Parliamentary Papers, *Reports from Select Committees,* 1828, 28, 201.

24   Dechêne, *Habitants and Merchants,* 244-45, argues that peasants could give land to one child, whereas moveables had to be divided equally.

25   Morel, *Les limites*; Darrow, *Revolution in the House,* 5-10; Traer, *Marriage and the Family,* 171.

26   Staves, *Married Women's Separate Property,* 112.

27   J.R. McCulloch, *A Treatise on the Succession of Property Vacant by Death* (London: 1847), 10, cited in Morris, *Men, Women and Property,* 94.

28   *South African Advertiser and Mail,* 11 October 1866, 3 September 1866, 1 July 1871; Bradbury, "'In England.'"

29   Morel, *Les limites,* 8, 30-37; Garneau, "Une culture," 119.

30 Kolish, *Nationalismes,* 211; An Act to Explain and amend the Law respecting Wills and Testaments, 1801, c. 4, SLC; Bradbury, "Debating Dower," 56-78.

31 A.D. Smith, *Nationalism and Modernism,* 170-98; Kolish, *Nationalismes.*

32 In the 1830s, very public coverage of the contestation of M. Forretier's will by his daughter and son-in-law, Denis Benjamin Viger, promoted the understanding that "a will cannot go against morality." He used much of his dead wife's half of their community property during his widowhood, then sought to bequeath the remainder as he wished, specifying that anyone disagreeing with his decisions should be cut off. "Exposé," *La Minerve,* 21 April 1831. André Morel, *Les limites,* 40-41, 55-57, stresses the immorality of the possibility that men could give beyond their family, including to concubines, in his critique of the anglicization of Quebec law.

33 Will, Wait, 12 August 1832, Notary Arnoldi.

34 Marriage contract, Campbell and Wait, 14 August 1824, Notary Jobin.

35 *L'Aurore des Canadas,* 18 December 1840; An Act to explain and amend the Law respecting last Wills and Testaments, 1801, c. 4, SLC; Champagne, "La pratique testamentaire," 9; Sirois, *Forme des testaments,* 147; Owens, "Property, Will Making."

36 Gérin-Lajoie, *A Treatise,* 149.

37 Doucet, *Fundamental Principles,* 2:art. 289; Notary Glackmeyer explained the process in Evanturel and Evanturel, *Quebec Law Reports* 1 (1875), 74, 144-52; Evanturel v. Evanturel, *Lower Canada Reports* 16 (1866), 353. Will, Wait, 12 August 1832, Notary Arnoldi.

38 Champagne, "La pratique testamentaire," 79-80; Sirois, *Forme des testaments,* 147.

39 Will, Genevay, probated 22 March 1827; Marriage contract, Mount and Genevay, 5 February 1823, Notary Papineau; Inventory, Genevay, Notary Joseph Papineau, 27 March 1827. Heney's mother was Canadienne, his father English. Jacques L'Heureux, "Hugues Heney," *DCB.*

40 An Act to amend the law of Lower Canada as to the Execution of Wills in the English Form, 1864, c. 42, SPC.

41 Beaubien, *Traité sur les lois civiles,* 2: 58-66, 326; Student Note Books, 1850s, Lawyers' Papers, MG 4166, box 10, no. 79, McGA.

42 Morris, *Men, Women and Property,* 92, found that in Leeds between 1830 and 1834, some 10 percent of adult male and 3.5 percent of adult female deaths led to probate as a result of a will. Until a repertory of Montreal wills in notary's files and probated wills is made, no such estimate is possible for Montreal. In our serendipitous searching, we have found wills for 16 percent of the husbands who married in the 1820s and died before their wives and for 6 percent for those marrying in the 1840s. Our research strategy favoured the first cohort, so this suggests relatively high rates of will making. In the early stages of this study, researchers made a listing of all the wills listed in the files of notaries whose last names fell between A and G for the years leading up to 1840. Hence, the greater number of wills and testaments for the 1820s generation.

43 Darrow, *Revolution in the House,* 57; Morris, *Men, Women and Property,* 77-78. We also located the will of one husband made after his remarriage, of one made before his marriage, and of three women who became widows, then married again, and wrote these wills as wives.

44 Morris, *Men, Women and Property,* 80. Of these seventy-seven wills, sixteen were English-style wills; thirteen of these were made by elites in English.

45 Champagne, "La pratique testamentaire," 70-76. Twenty-four of the forty husbands writing in English made notarial wills, as did all thirty-six husbands writing in French; one wrote a holograph will.

46 Margaret White was born around 1807, as was Caroline Campbell. Oliver Wait appears on the list of Gay's creditors in Inventory, Gay, 31 August 1832, Notary Griffin.

47 Thirty-two of the thirty-four Canadien husbands' wills we found made notarial wills, as did all five Irish testators and twenty-three of the thirty-eight Anglo-Protestant or Jewish husbands.

48 All twenty-five of the Canadienne wives whose wills we have found made them with a notary, as did seven of the nine Anglo-Protestant or Jewish women. Twelve Canadienne women and three others signed with an X.

49 Of the seventy-six husbands, twenty-two (29 percent) were ill, as were eight (24 percent) of the thirty-four wives, and two (17 percent) of the twelve widows.

50 Of the sixty men's wills where we also know the date of their death, five (8 percent) wrote them on the day they died, seven (12 percent) in the week before. Some 42 percent were made within the year preceding their deaths. In Leeds, Morris found longer intervals, possibly because the process of probating wills makes it easier to find them than in Montreal. Morris, *Men, Women and Property,* 91.

51 Will, Mower, 19 September 1836; Will, Campbell, 19 September 1836, Notary Doucet. Laura's will precedes that of John, so I assume hers was made first. Noo-tens, *Fous, prodigues et ivrognes,* 158-59. In Chapleau v. Chapleau, *Legal News* 1 (1878): 473-74, a will written by a man suffering from delirium tremens was deemed invalid.

52 Twenty-six of the thirty-four wives' wills we found were made concurrently with their husbands'. This was true of nineteen of twenty-five made by Canadienne wives and seven of nine made by English-speaking Protestants.

53 On Quebec, see Parent and Postolec, "Quand Thémis rencontre Clio." On the American states, see Wilson, *Life after Death,* 33. Narret, *Inheritance and Family Life,* 7, reports that the Dutch mutual will disappeared more quickly after the English took over New York than did community property.

54 Darrow, *Revolution in the House,* 78.

55 Wills, Campbell and Mower, 19 September 1836, Notary Doucet; Wills, Gauthier and Asselin, 19 June 1832, Notary Belle.

56 Will, Bergevin, 10 July 1848, Notary Labadie.

57 Will, Gauthier, 24 May 1852, Notary Belle.

58 Dissolution of the partnership of Brady, Brady and Darling, and Will, Sampson Brady, 1 February 1851, Notary Smith; Will, Hannah, 16 November 1842, Notary E. Guy; Will, Hammond, 15 April 1846, Notary Ross.

59 Wills, Campbell and Mower, 19 September 1836, Notary Doucet; Will, Eloi Beneche, 6 February 1846, Notary Vallée; Will, Genevay, 24 February 1827, probated 22 March 1827.

60 Bouchard, *Quelques arpents d'Amérique,* 294-95; Will, Harwood, probated 2 May 1863.

61 Will, Wait, 12 August 1832, Notary Arnoldi.

62 Thirty-nine men (51 percent) named their wives as the sole executor; a further five named their wives with someone else. Thirty-six of these men promised their wives all they had to use or to own.

63 Lebsock, *The Free Women,* 36-42, quotation at 42; Wilson, *Life after Death,* 45-48.

64 Marriage contract, de Lotbinière and Harwood, 13 December 1823, Notary Doucet; Will, Harwood, probated 2 May 1863.

65 Will, Sutherland, probated 16 February 1875.

66 Ibid.

67 Marriage contract, Farquhar and Sutherland, 10 January 1844, Notary Guy.

68 Will, Sutherland, probated 16 February 1875.

69 Will, John Smith, probated 9 March 1872; Morris, *Men, Women and Property*, 149.
70 Bradbury, *Working Families*, 93; Bradbury, "Canadian Children," 280.
71 Rogers, "Money, Marriage, Mobility," 33, fn28.
72 Will, Wait, 12 August 1832, Notary Arnoldi; Will, John Smith, probated 9 March 1872; Will, Sutherland, probated 16 February 1875; Will, McIntosh, 10 November 1832, Notary Doucet; Will, McDonnell, probated 13 February 1836; Morris, *Men, Women and Property*, 148-49, 369, quotation at 80.
73 Will, Rodier, 10 December 1831, Notary Bedouin; Will, Rodier, 22 January 1876, and Codicil, 27 January 1876, Notary Decary.
74 Will, Beneche, 6 February 1846, Notary Vallée. Twenty-four of thirty-one (78 percent) of Catholic husbands married in 1823-26 mentioned God. All seven married 1842-46 whose wills we found did so. Thirteen of twenty-six and six of twelve respectively of Protestant husbands did so. Cliche, "L'évolution des clauses religieuses," 365-88.
75 Stearns, *Old Age in European Society*, 42, 121; Petitclerc, *"Nous protégeons l'infortune,"* outlines initiatives in Montreal and Quebec City, especially from the 1850s.
76 Richardson, *Death, Dissection*; Strange, *Death, Grief and Poverty*. Legislation in 1872 legitimated making the corpses of people found dead, or those supported in provincially funded institutions prior to their death, available for the study of anatomy, partially to control body snatching. An Act to amend chapter 76 of the Consolidated Statutes of Canada, respecting the practice of Physic and surgery, and the Study of Anatomy, 1872, c. 29, SQ.
77 *Montreal Gazette*, 17 January 1821; *Montreal Register*, 27 January 1848; *Montreal Witness*, 3 March 1858.
78 Necrologies, Lemay, 6 April 1833, FPNDM.
79 Hardy, *Contrôle social*, 76-77: Rousseau, "Les associations voluntaires paroissiales," 176.
80 Necrologies; Julien, 24 October 1872; Legris, 6 December 1896, FPNDM.
81 A fire closed the fabrique archives after we completed searches for the 1820s cohort. The details about burials varied across time. We found information on 291 wives and 246 husbands married 1823-26. Overall, 77 (27 percent) and 51 (21 percent) respectively had some or all their funeral costs covered by a prayer union. From the 1860s on, between four and six out of ten of the burials of this generation of spouses were paid for in part or fully by a prayer union in each decade.
82 Necrologies, Lemay, 20 January 1852, FPNDM.
83 Rousseau, "Les associations voluntaires paroissiales," 176; Caulier, "Des confréries pour l'élite," 178-83.
84 Petitclerc, *"Nous protégeons l'infortune,"* 17, 20. Acts of incorporations in the 1850s and 1860s included ones for the Benevolent Society of Notre Dame de Bonsecours, at Montreal, 1855, c. 234, SPC; the society called the Union of St. Joseph of Montreal, 1856, c. 131, SPC; the St. Antoine Association of Montreal, 1861, c. 119, SPC; the Association St. François Xavier de Montreal, 1862, c. 96, SPC; the society called La Caisse de Bienfaisance de Temperance, section St. Jacques, of the City of Montreal, 1865, c. 110, SPC.
85 Petitclerc, *Nous protégeons l'infortune*, 40.
86 These included acts incorporating the Montreal Decayed Pilots Fund, 1839, c. 19, LCO; Certain Charitable Philanthropic and Provident Associations, and for the effectual protection from fraud and misappropriation of the funds of the same, 1850, c. 32, SPC; the Canadian Society of Joiners and Carpenters of Montreal, 1858, c. 74, SPC; the French Canadian Butchers' Benevolent Society of Montreal Canada, 1864, c. 147, SPC; the Society of Canadian Artists, 1870, c. 59, SC; and the Quebec Civil Service Mutual Benefit Society, c. 36, SC.

87   Included were acts incorporating the Members of the British American Friendly Society of Canada, 1854, c. 64, SPC; St. George Society of Montreal, 1860, c. 14, SPC; and English Workingmen's Benefit Society of Montreal, 1869, c. 83, SQ; see also Leitch, "Importance of Being 'English'?"; Fecteau, *La Liberté du pauvre,* 69.

88   Fecteau, "La dynamique sociale," 508, 495; Fecteau, *La Liberté du pauvre.*

89   An Act for incorporating certain Charitable Philanthropic and Provident Associations, and for the effectual protection from fraud and misappropriation of the funds of the same, 1850, c. 32, SPC.

90   Inventory, Smith and McMillan, 27 January 1862, Notary Labadie.

91   Petitclerc, *"Nous protégeons l'infortune,"* 37-46; An Act to incorporate the Provident Life Assurance and Investment Company incorporated, 1855, c. 211, SPC; An Act to Secure to Wives and Children the Benefit of Assurances on the Lives of their Husbands and Parents, 1865, c. 17, SPC; An Act to amend the Act of 29th Vict. c. 17 relating to Life Assurance, 1869, c. 40, SQ; An Act to extend the provisions of the act of the late Province of Canada, 1870, c. 21, SQ; An Act to consolidate and amend the law to secure to wives and children the benefit of assurances on the lives of their husbands and parents, 1878, c. 13, SQ.

92   Cohen, *Women's Work,* 49, 161; Nanciellen Davis, "Patriarchy from the Grave"; Gagan, *Hopeful Travellers,* 55-56, 89-90. Other rural historians have found that most husbands left most of the property remaining when they wrote a will to their widows. Elliott, *Irish Migrants*; Little, *Crofters and Habitants,* 117-18; Bouchard, *Quelques arpents d'Amérique,* 294.

93   Pateman, *The Sexual Contract,* 2.

94   Goody, Thirsk, and Thompson, eds., *Family and Inheritance*; K.E. Wood, *Masterful Women,* 29-31; Morris, *Men, Women and Property.*

95   Morris, *Men, Women and Property,* 10; McCrum, "Inheritance and the Family," 157; Evidence, J. Stephen, 24 June 1828, British Parliamentary Papers, *Reports from Select Committees,* 1828, 244.

Chapter 6: Diverse Demographies

1   Will, Oliver Wait, 12 August 1832, Notary Arnoldi; Death registration, American Presbyterian Church, 12 August 1832; MRC, Death registration, 12 August 1832; *La Minerve,* 13 August 1832.

2   Bradbury, "Mourir chrétiennement."

3   F. Noel, *Family Life,* 300-9; Jalland, *Death*; Ariès, *The Hour,* 441-74; McManners, *Death and the Enlightenment.*

4   Protest, Smith against Genevay and Agathe Flemming, 8 September 1826; Transport, J.F.L. Genevay to P. Drolet, 27 September 1826; Procuration, Dame Agathe Dumas and Genevay to Dominique Mondelet, 5 October 1826; Procuration, Dame A. Dumas and F. Genevay to J.S. McCord, 7 October 1826, Notary Doucet.

5   Inventory, Genevay, 27 March 1827, Notary Joseph Papineau; *La Minerve,* 26 February 1827; Procuration by Genevay to Henry Mount, 1 February 1827, Notary Doucet.

6   Charles Roland, "John Stephenson," *DCB.* We have located forty-one inventories made following either the death of a husband or a wife. Of these, thirty-one were made following a husband's death.

7   Jalland, *Death,* 77-81.

8   Inventories are easier to locate for Montrealers dying before 1840, thanks to Christian Dessureault's index.

9   Inventory, Community, Paris and Guilbault, 3 March 1830, Notary Labadie.

10   Jalland, *Death,* 77-82; *The Lancet,* 26 October 1861, cited in ibid., 99.

11 McPherson, *Bedside Manners*, 27-29; Chroniques de l'Asile de la Providence, Maison-Mère (hereafter cited as Chronicles), 1, 1844, 1861, n.p., Providence Archives, Sisters of Providence (hereafter cited as PASP); Ancien Journal, 1, 1847, Archives of the Sisters of Charity of Montreal (Grey Nuns) (hereafter cited as ASGM); Lapointe-Roy, *Charité bien ordonnée*, 234-44.

12 Caroline Pelton to Carrie Pelton, Montreal, 13 August 1861, Pelton Papers, McGA.

13 Little, *Love Strong as Death*, 182-84.

14 Will, Wait, 12 August 1832, Notary Arnoldi.

15 Poutanen, "Women Arrested in Montreal"; *Lovell's* 1844-45, 1845-46; Will, Beneche, 6 February 1846, Notary Vallée.

16 McManners, *Death and the Enlightenment*; Kselman, *Death and the Afterlife*, 88, 97; *Montreal Gazette*, 4 March 1872.

17 Jalland, *Death*, 23-35, quotation at 23; McManners, *Death and the Enlightenment*, 234-45; *Montreal Weekly Witness*, 15 February 1859; Young, "Death, Burial," 109.

18 Rousseau, "Les passages," 150; Jalland, *Death*, 17; Ariès, *The Hour*; Kselman, *Death and the Afterlife*, 90-91.

19 Perin, *Ignace de Montréal*, 100; Rousseau, "Les passages," 150.

20 Rousseau, "Les passages"; Quigley, *The Corpse*, 51.

21 Chapleau v. Chapleau, *Legal News* 1 (1878): 473-74; Malo et vir et Migneault, *Revue Légale* 2 (1870): 186; Gagnon, *Quand le Québec*; Rousseau, "Les passages," 150; Bradbury, "Mourir chrétiennement"; Bradbury, "Elderly Inmates."

22 Will, Bergevin, 10 July 1848, Notary Labadie; *La Minerve*, 11 December 1848.

23 Ariès, *The Hour*; Ariès, *Western Attitudes*; McManners, *Death and the Enlightenment*. Bouchard draws upon interviews of elderly people in the Saguenay region of Quebec in "Sur les rituels."

24 Coroners' Reports, 1831-47, 1855, 1863, 1866-68, BAnQM; Painchaud, "Alexis Painchaud," *DCB*; Rome, "Adolphus Mordecai Hart," *DCB*.

25 *La Minerve*, 11 December 1848; *Montreal Gazette*, 10 July 1852, 24 September 1860, 24 September 1888, 14 January 1889, and 4 January 1890; *La Minerve*, 19 March 1852.

26 Most death notices, as we will see in the following chapter, mention little more than the age, occupation (for men), and death date of the deceased. A few give more details of their lives or deaths. Among the 113 death notices found for men from these two marriage cohorts, Joseph Lecour's is the only one that mentions a Christian death explicitly, whereas 7 of the 151 women's did so.

27 *La Minerve*, 1 December 1842.

28 Death registration, Charles Cousineau, 7 January 1871, necrologies, FPNDM.

29 Bilson, *A Darkened House*, 23-25.

30 *JLCLC*, 1831-32: 225; Sendzik, "1832 Montreal Cholera Epidemic," 11.

31 Alexander Hart to Moses Hart, 19 June 1832, Hart Papers, cited in Bilson, *A Darkened House*, 185; Tulchinsky, "Benjamin Workman," *DCB*; Thomas Brown, "Joseph Workman," *DCB*; Joseph Workman, "Medical Dissertation on Asiatic Cholera," University of McGill College, 25 May 1835, cited in Sendzik, "1832 Montreal Cholera Epidemic," 7.

32 Quoted in Bilson, *A Darkened House*, 24.

33 *Canadian Courant*, 16 June 1832; *La Minerve*, 14 June 1832; *Canadian Courant*, 7 August 1832.

34 Workman, "Medical Dissertation," 11-12, quoted in Sendzik, "1832 Montreal Cholera Epidemic," 2.

35 Will, White, probated 17 July 1832; Bilson, *A Darkened House*, 23-25.

36 Will, White, probated 17 July 1832; Witham, "Andrew White," *DCB*; Bilson, *A Darkened House,* 23-25; *La Minerve,* 12 July 1832.

37 Robert, "The City of Wealth," argues that mortality rates were higher among French Canadians than other groups. Small numbers and the difficulty of tracing Protestants and Irish Catholics complicate comparisons for the husbands and wives followed here. Using cases where the men's death dates are certain, as well as ones for whom we are not sure if it is a proper match but know that a man of that name and ethnicity/religion died on that day, which is the case for most of the Irish Catholics, suggests that 5 percent (17 of 319) of Canadienne wives of the 1823-26 marriage cohort died between June and the end of 1832, as did 8 percent (4 of 53) of Irish Catholics and 4.5 percent (5 of 110) of Protestant wives. For husbands the figures were 7 percent (20 of 290), 6 percent (4 of 65) and 12 percent (15 of 125) respectively. Among those whose identities we are certain about from this cohort, 7 percent of Canadienne wives, 0 percent of Irish Catholics, and 9 percent of Protestant wives definitely died during the epidemic, as did 6 percent, 11 percent, and 6 percent respectively of the men.

38 *Montreal Gazette,* 21 August 1832, cited in Ouellet, *Lower Canada, 1791-1840,* 139.

39 *La Minerve,* 5 August 1832; *Montreal Gazette,* 2 July 1832; Sendzik, "1832 Montreal Cholera Epidemic," 11-13, 41; Bilson, *A Darkened House,* 44-45.

40 Tulchinsky, "George Moffatt," *DCB*; Sendzik, "1832 Montreal Cholera Epidemic," 37-44.

41 Sendzik, "1832 Montreal Cholera Epidemic," 44; Bilson, *A Darkened House,* 42.

42 Sendzik, "1832 Montreal Cholera Epidemic."

43 Landry, "Stanley Clark Bagg," *DCB*; list of members of the Constitutional Association, 1837, *Montreal Transcript,* 14 January 1843; Tulchinsky, *The River Barons,* 13, 110, 143; Marsolais, Desrochers, and Comeau, *Histoire des maires,* 44-49.

44 Rumilly, *Histoire de Montreal,* 2:301-9; Tulchinsky, *The River Barons,* 110.

45 Marsolais, Desrochers, and Comeau, *Histoire des maires,* 44-49; Collard, *Montreal,* 122-29; Chronicles, 1, May 1847, PASP; Ancien Journal, 1. Notes sur l'Hôpital Générale des Soeurs Grises de Montréal depuis sa fondation jusqu'en 1857 (1688-1857), 491-517, ASGM.

46 Collard, *Montreal,* 120-30; *Montreal Register,* 18 November 1847.

47 *Montreal Register,* 18 November 1847; Wilkes, *Death in the City,* 10-14. The Earl of Elgin, then governor general, is said to have written to Earl Grey, "This day the Mayor of Montreal died, a very estimable man who did much for the immigrants and to whose firmness and philanthropy we chiefly owe it that the Immigrant sheds were not tossed into the river by the people of the Town during the summer." Cited in Collard, *Montreal,* 128; "Death of the Mayor," *Montreal Register,* 18 November 1847.

48 Inventory, Community, 30 November 1847, Notary Pelton.

49 J.L. Roy, *Édouard-Raymond Fabre,* 41.

50 We know that thirty-two wives were widowed prior to 1832, and at least twenty-three in 1832 out of the total of 204 known death dates for couples where husbands died first. Forty-two husbands lost wives prior to 1832, twenty-six during that year out of 206 certain death dates for wives who died first among those marrying 1823-26.

51 Coroners' Reports, 5 January 1834, 26 August 1847, BAnQM.

52 *La Minerve,* 1 February 1827.

53 Mitchell v. Brown, 28 February 1859, Superior Court, dossiers, BAnQM; *Montreal Witness,* 3 March 1858.

54 We located and recorded the causes listed for two hundred men's deaths in the records of the fabrique, Protestant cemetery records, coroners' records, and

occasionally parish registers. The main ones were heart related (18), TB (18), pulmonary (13), dropsy (18), paralysis (14), apoplexy (8), cancer (7), accidents (9), suicide (3), old age (23), and debility or senility (20). Landry and Lessard, "Les causes de décès," 512, note that causes were mentioned for only 2 percent of deaths in New France/Lower Canada between 1625 and 1799.

55 Robillard, *Émilie Tavernier-Gamelin*, 95.
56 Will, Beneche, 6 February 1846, Notary Vallée; Death registration, 12 February 1846, PND.
57 Will, Sutherland, probated 16 February 1875.
58 Burgess, "Work, Family and Community."
59 Will, O'Leary, 9 February 1830, Notary Ritchot; Will, Cadotte, 9 February 1830, Notary Ritchot.
60 Hardwick, *The Practice of Patriarchy*, 130-31; Lebsock, *The Free Women*, 26-27, found 56 percent of women widowed under age thirty, 30 percent of those aged thirty-one to forty, and 9 percent of those over forty remarried. Remarriages were much higher (73 percent) among poorer women than the middling (50 percent); Dupâquier, ed., *Marriage and Remarriage*.
61 This may also be a result of more rigorous searching for remarriages in Antonin Loiselle's index of French Canadian marriages for the first cohort, BAnQM.
62 Bremmer and Van Den Bosch, *Between Poverty*, 4; Bouchard, *Quelques arpents d'Amérique*, 292-93; Gossage, *Families in Transition*, 92.
63 K.E. Wood, *Masterful Women*, 151.
64 Bremmer and Van Den Bosch, *Between Poverty*, 6; Führer, *The Mysteries*, 71-72.
65 *La Minerve*, 17 December 1855.
66 Will, McDonnell, probated 13 February 1836.
67 Edward Bensley, "Andrew Fernando Holmes," *DCB*; Lorne Sainte Croix, "Benjamin Holmes" *DCB*.
68 Sylvestre Cartier to George-Etienne Cartier, 22 January 1849, cited in Young, *George-Etienne Cartier*, 27, fn35.
69 An Act to Incorporate the Managers of the Ministers' Widows' and Orphans' Fund of the Synod of the Presbyterian Church of Canada in connection with the Church of Scotland, 1847, c. 36, SPC; An Act to amend An Act and incorporate the managers of the Ministers' Widows' and Orphans' Fund of the Synod of the Presbyterian Church of Canada, in connection with the Church of Scotland, and amendments thereto, 1875, c. 61, SQ; An Act to incorporate the Congregational Ministers' Widows' and Orphans' Fund Society, 1860, c. 146, SPC; An Act to extend the provisions of the Act of the late Province of Canada (23 Vict.) entitled An Act to incorporate the Congregational Ministers' Widows' and Orphans' Fund Society, 1872, c. 70, SC.
70 On his close ties with the British and Foreign Bible Society, see Sylvain, "Henry Wilkes," *DCB*; Noel, *Canada Dry*.
71 J. Wood, *Memoir of Henry Wilkes*, 104-5.
72 Ibid., 112; Noel, *Canada Dry*, 64, 70.
73 J. Wood, *Memoir of Henry Wilkes*, 147.
74 K.E. Wood, *Masterful Women*, 153.
75 Donation, Susanna Holmes to Susan and Ann Martha McDonnell, 10 December 1847, Notary Gibb.
76 Morris, *Men, Women and Property*, 261; Lebsock, *The Free Women*, 77-85.
77 J. Wood, *Memoir of Henry Wilkes*, 147-48.
78 *Montreal Gazette*, 27 September 1850.
79 Gagnon, *Mariage et famille*, 150.

80   MRC; Will, Brady, 1 February 1851, Notary Smith; Inventory, Community, Conegan and Brady, 6 February 1853, Notary J. Smith.
81   K.E. Wood, *Masterful Women,* 150.
82   Will, Andrew White, probated 17 July 1832; Will, William Gay, 14 August 1832, Notary Doucet; The shop contents appear in Inventory, Gay, 31 August 1832, Notary Griffin; McKenna, *A Life of Propriety;* Davidoff and Hall, *Family Fortunes.*
83   Death registration, St. Gabriel Street Presbyterian Church, 1834, 26; MRC; Will, Margaret White, 25 June 1841, Notary Doucet; Inventory, Gay, 31 August 1832, Notary Griffin. The 1832 evaluation role lists James Carsuel (sic) as owning property on Campeau Street in Saint Mary's ward valued at £6 annually, and on Perthius Street in Saint Louis ward. She may have rented one of these. Their place on St. Paul was valued at £90 annual rent or revenue. Sweeny, "A Partial Tax Roll, 1832."
84   Marriage registration, Saint Paul's Presbyterian Church, 26 January 1833; Will, Margaret White, 25 June 1841, Notary Doucet; *Montreal Gazette,* 27 April 1841.
85   Will, Margaret White, 25 June 1841, Notary Doucet.
86   K.E. Wood, *Masterful Women,* 151-52.

Chapter 7: In the Shadow of Their Husbands

1   Inventory, Bissonnet and Ducharme, 26 April 1834, Notary Guy; M.L. Taylor, *Mourning Dress,* 127; *La Minerve,* 17 April 1834; Necrologies, 17 April 1834, FPNDM.
2   Will, Sutherland, probated 16 February 1875.
3   Butler, "Performative Acts," 270-82.
4   Bradbury, "Widows Negotiate the Law," 120-48.
5   Hillerman, "'Chrysalis of Gloom,'" 91; Reveley, "Black Trade in New Orleans."
6   Wilson, *Life after Death,* 12. Later she discusses the many actions widows took on as they began their widowhood. Jalland, *Death,* 210, 213, 217. Later nineteenth-century advice manuals advised that others should step in for all immediate members of the bereaved family, for example, Maud C. Cooke, *Social Etiquette or Manners and Customs of Polite Society* (London, ON: McDermid and Logan, 1896), 323.
7   Kete, *Sentimental Collaborations,* 22.
8   Deposition, Moses J. Hays, Chief of Police, 21 December 1858, Mitchell v. Brown, Superior Court, dossiers, BAnQM.
9   M.L. Taylor, *Mourning Dress,* 126; Reveley, "Black Trade in New Orleans."
10   Quotation from http://www.fashion-era.com/.
11   Eliza M. Lavin, *Good Manners* (New York: Butterick, 1888), 145-47, cited in Hillerman, "'Chrysalis of Gloom,'" 96.
12   Jane Austen wrote to her sister after the death of her sister-in-law, saying, "I am to be in bombazeen and crape," cited in M.L. Taylor, *Mourning Dress,* 126.
13   Hillerman, "'Chrysalis of Gloom'"; Masson and Reveley, "When Life's Brief Sun"; http://www.fashion-era.com/.
14   K.E. Wood, *Masterful Women,* 98; "Mourning and Funeral Usages," 17 April 1886 (electronic edition), *Harper's Bazaar,* http://www.victoriana.com/library/harpers/.
15   Michel de Lorimier, "François-Marie-Thomas Chevalier de Lorimier," *DCB.*
16   Ibid.; Roquebrune, *Testament of My Childhood,* 22.
17   McCord, *The Civil Code,* art. 1368; Hillerman, "'Chrysalis of Gloom,'" 23-26; M.L. Taylor, *Mourning Dress,* 134.
18   Jalland, *Death,* 300-5.
19   McCord, *The Civil Code,* art. 1368. This right was not spelled out explicitly in any clauses of the Custom of Paris. It was in the Quebec Civil Code of 1866. There the precedents cited include Pothier. It appears in France's Napoleonic

Code. Inventories from before 1866 assumed the wife's mourning would be taken from community property, if marriage created one, otherwise from the husband's estate. This right was upheld throughout the century. Dessaint v. Ladrière, *Quebec Law Reports* 16 (1890), 277; *Legal News* 14 (1891).

20 Marie-Louise Jobin spent £3 4s. 2d. for clothes and £1 8s. 7d. on other mourning expenses when her blacksmith husband died in 1823; Marie-Noflette Charland owed the dry goods merchant Ducondu £2 9s. 4d. for crape, gloves and ribbons; *Montreal Gazette*, 30 June 1831, cites agricultural labourers' wages in Upper Canada at 2s. 6d. to 3s. a day with board, carpenters and masons at 7s. 6d. without board. In Montreal, they were around 2s. 6d. daily without board, or a maximum of around £39 a year for eight months of work. Personal communication with Robert Sweeny.

21 Inventory, Paris and Guilbault, 3 March 1830, Notary Labadie.

22 Inventory, Conegan and Brady, 26 February 1853, Notary Smith; Inventory, Radenhurst, 7 June 1830, Notary Arnoldi; Inventory, Genevay, 7 June 1830, Notary Papineau.

23 Inventory, Charland and Letourneaux, 2 April 1834, Notary Lorimier. For more on this couple, see Bradbury, "Itineraries of Marriage."

24 Inventory, Bissonnet and Ducharme, 26 April 1834, Notary Guy; M.L. Taylor, *Mourning Dress*, 127; *La Minerve*, 18 June 1827 (my translation); *Lovell's*, 1861, 255.

25 Howarth, "Professionalizing the Funeral Industry," 122; *Lovell's*, 1862-63, 1863-64, 123.

26 Inventory, Conegan and Brady, 26 February 1853, Notary Smith.

27 Judge Robert McKay benchbook, re. Larue et vir v. Desautels, 30 December 1872, Torrance Bench Books, Lawyers' Papers, manuscript group (hereafter cited as MG) 4166, box 7, no. 52, McGA; Dessaint v. Ladrière, *Quebec Law Reports* 16 (1890), 277; *Legal News* 14 (1891).

28 Beaubien, *Traité sur les lois civiles*, 3: 32; Doucet, *Fundamental Principles*, art. 237; McCord, *The Civil Code*, art. 1338-83; Student Note Books, 1850s, Lawyers' Papers, MG 4166, box 10, no. 79, McGA.

29 Inventory, Dufresne and Mallette, 6 April 1833, Notary Labadie.

30 Mushira Eid distinguishes death notices from obituaries in her *The World of Obituaries*; *La Minerve*, 17 April 1834.

31 F. Noel, *Family Life*, 203.

32 Bouchard, "Sur les rituels," 128.

33 Petitclerc, *"Nous protégeons l'infortune,"* 11, describes all members of the Union St. Joseph going together to accompany the deceased's family in the funeral procession.

34 "You are invited to attend the funeral of François Trudeau, Esquire, which will take place Wednesday, the 23rd of this month, at 8:15 a.m. The funeral procession will depart from his home on St. Denis Street for the Parish Church and then to the burial ground," was the message on the invitation following the death of Angelique Locke's husband in 1849 (my translation). 21 May 1849, Funeral Invitations, Montreal, 1849, 30, LAC; *La Minerve*, 21 May 1849. After Mrs. McCord's death in 1822, Thomas McCord sent out two hundred similar invitations. It cost him £1 10s. for the carriage and letters. McCord Family Papers, MMA.

35 We found 272 death notices of men and women from these two cohorts and can identify a rough class position for 248. Of these, only 33 were for men or the wives or widows of men who were unskilled at the time of their marriage, 101 were involved in crafts, 13 in various forms of small trade, and 79 were professionals, merchants, or other members of the elite and middle classes.

36 Eid, *The World of Obituaries*.

37 *Montreal Transcript*, 10 December 1846; *La Minerve*, 20 October 1836.

38 *La Minerve,* 2 April 1857.
39 *La Minerve,* 14 August 1852.
40 *La Minerve* and *Montreal Gazette,* 5 February 1876.
41 Of the seventy-nine death notices we have found for men who died before their wives, only eight mention that the man left a spouse, or a spouse and children.
42 *Montreal Gazette,* 13 July 1848. Of the fifty-eight death notices we found for wives who died before their husbands, forty-seven identified them as "wife of" or "épouse de," with their husbands' name; a further six, all married in the 1840s, indicated they were the "beloved" wife of. Only four made no mention of the husband.
43 Eid, *The World of Obituaries,* 121-22.
44 The obituary of Marguerite Barsalou, the widow of Patriote Joseph Gauvin, highlighted her visits to the Patriotes in prison. *La Minerve,* 5 March 1856.
45 Eid, *The World of Obituaries;* Kselman, *Death and the Afterlife,* 5.
46 *La Minerve,* 13 August 1832, 16 August 1832.
47 *La Minerve,* 26 February 1827.
48 Kete, *Sentimental Collaborations,* xv, 17.
49 *Montreal Gazette,* 15 November 1847, reproduced excerpts from the *Courier, Herald,* and *Montreal Transcript,* 1, 4, 17 November 1847, respectively. The Baptist *Montreal Register,* 18 November 1847, carried a long description of the funeral. I found no description in *La Minerve.*
50 Pâquet, "Le deuil comme consensus," 76.
51 "Death of the Mayor of Montreal, J.E. Mills, Esqu.," *Montreal Gazette,* 15 November 1847.
52 Pâquet, "Le deuil comme consensus," 74-76.
53 Bouchard, "Sur les rituels," 129, found that until the 1920s or 1930s, family members in the Saguenay normally washed their dead.
54 Führer, *The Mysteries of Montreal;* Quigley, *The Corpse,* 52; Inventory, Wait, 10 November 1832, Notary Arnoldi, included among funeral expenses £5 3s. 9d. owed to a Mrs. Mathewson; Inventory, Radenhurst, 7 June 1830, Notary Arnoldi, lists £4 owing to a Mrs. Telfer under funeral expenses, alongside much more substantial expenses.
55 Laderman, *The Sacred Remains,* 24-31; Noel, *Family Life,* 200.
56 Bouchard, "Sur les rituels," 128-30; Behlmer, "Grave Doubts," 214.
57 Inventory, Bissonnet and Ducharme, 26 April 1834, Notary Guy; Young, *Respectable Burial,* 9.
58 "Salaires et tarifs, 1825," box 23, file 22; "Tarifs de l'union des prières de N. D.," 15 October 1879, box 81, file 33; "Tarif des services, 1895," box 57, file 14, FPNDM; J.-G. Landry, "Les finances," 100-1.
59 Inventory, Bissonnet and Ducharme, 26 April 1834, Notary Guy; Necrologies, Louis Ducharme, 19 April 1834, FPNDM. The records of the fabrique list only the £2 9s. 2d. paid for the service and burial.
60 Young, *Respectable Burial.*
61 This right was upheld throughout the century for widows, whether their marriage created a community of goods or separate property. See Dessaint v. Ladrière, *Quebec Law Reports* 16 (1890), 277; *Legal News* 14 (1891).
62 An Act Respecting the Registration of titles to or Charges upon Real Estate, 22 Vict., c. 56, 1860, SQ.
63 Jalland, *Death,* 195-96.
64 Will, Rodier, 10 December 1831, Notary Bedouin; Will, Rodier, 22 January 1876, Notary A.-C. Décary; Will, Campbell, 19 September 1836, Notary Doucet; Student Note Books, 1850s, Lawyers' Papers, MG 4166, box 10, no. 79, McGA; Gérin-Lajoie, *A Treatise,* 163.

65 Will, Beneche, 6 February 1846, Notary Vallée; Will, Bergevin, 10 July 1848, Notary Labadie.
66 Will, Sutherland, probated 6 February 1875; Will, Ogilvie, 25 November 1827, Notary Jobin.
67 Necrologies, Jacques Paquet, 31 July 1854, FPNDM.
68 Salairs [sic] et tarifs, 1825, box 23, file 22; Inventory, Paris and Guilbault, 3 March 1830, Notary Labadie, records that she paid 15 francs for the coffin and a further 20 francs for the funeral. In the 1820s, a five-franc piece was worth 4s. sterling (35 francs = 28s. sterling, or about £1 13s.). McCullough, *Money and Exchange,* 93. Interestingly, no charge appears in the columns of the fabrique. Necrologies, 3 November 1829, Joseph Guilbault, FPNDM.
69 Salairs [sic] et tarifs, 1825, box 23, file 22; Tarifs, Inhumations dans l'Église, FPNDM; J.-G. Landry, "Les finances," 100-1.
70 Rules and Regulations, Old Book (n.d.), MRC.
71 Young, *Respectable Burial,* 8, quotation at 54.
72 Necrologies, François Lemay, 22 January 1852, FPNDM.
73 Necrologies, Michel Julien, 24 October 1872, FPNDM.
74 Inventory, Genevay, 27 March 1827, Notary Joseph Papineau.
75 Salairs (sic) et tarifs, 1825, box 23, file 22; Causel du séminaire sur sepulture de 1821-30, box 33, file 5, FPNDM.
76 "Report on the Practice of Internment in Towns," 1843, quoted in Jalland, *Death,* 194, 195-96. McCullough, *Money and Exchange,* 109, reports the exchange rate in 1850 as 1.4s. 4d. sterling to £1. 0s. 0d.
77 Inventory, Genevay, 27 March 1827, Notary Joseph Papineau.
78 *Montreal Transcript,* 4 October 1836; *Montreal Gazette,* 2 January 1856.
79 Moodie, *Roughing It,* 42.
80 Young, *Respectable Burial,* 9, 55; *La Minerve,* 15 February 1859; *Montreal Gazette,* 2 January 1856, 15 December 1858, 3 January 1858, 2 January 1861, 23 February 1861, 1 March 1861.
81 *Montreal Gazette,* 17 July 1856, 18 April 1856; *La Minerve,* 31 December 1859.
82 Inventory, Conegan and Brady, 26 February 1853, Notary Smith; Sampson Brady, Brady lot, MRC; *Montreal Gazette,* 3 December 1852.
83 Lambert with Monet, "Joseph-Rémi Vallières de Saint-Réal," *DCB.*
84 Mary Westcott-Papineau to James Westcott, Saratoga Springs, 21 February 1847, Mary Eleanor Westcott-Papineau fonds, LAC.
85 K.E. Wood, *Masterful Women,* 106.
86 *Montreal Register,* 18 November 1847; Wood, *Memoir of Henry Wilkes,* 131-32.
87 *Montreal Gazette,* 15 November 1847, 17 November 1847; *Montreal Register,* 18 November 1847, including material from the *Courier; Lovell's,* 1844-45, 1845-46.
88 Inventory, Lyman and Mills, 30 November 1847, Notary Pelton; *Montreal Gazette,* 17 November 1847.
89 *Montreal Transcript,* reproduced in Wilkes, *Death in the City,* 17; *Montreal Gazette,* 15 November 1847, 17 November 1847, including material from the *Courier.*
90 *Montreal Transcript,* reproduced in Wilkes, *Death in the City,* 17-18; "Funeral of the Late Rev. Dr. McGill," *Montreal Gazette,* 12 February 1856; "The Late Mrs Bethune," *Montreal Gazette,* 30 January 1866; Jumonville, "Wastebasket and the Grave," 103.
91 Wilkes, *Death in the City,* 6, 14.
92 Young, *Respectable Burial,* 7; An Act to Vest in the Mount Royal Cemetery Company, the Old Protestant Burial Grounds, in the City of Montreal, 1872, 36 Vict., c. 67, QS.

93 Curl, *Victorian Celebration of Death,* 15; Pike and Armstrong, eds., *A Time to Mourn,* 67-90, 169-70.

94 http://www2.ville.montreal.qc.ca/; Wells, *Death and Society,* 9, speaks to the ways public funerals reasserted community.

95 Wilkes, *Death in the City,* 18-19; Men, women, and children wore specific kinds of mourning clothing, but the word "weeds" is usually reserved for widows. Its roots lie in Old English.

96 Wilkes, *Death in the City,* 4-5, 6, 14; *Montreal Register,* 18 November 1847; Wood, *Memoir of Henry Wilkes,* 131-32; http://www2.ville.montreal.qc.ca/.

97 Rome, "Adolphus Mordecai Hart," *DCB.*

98 *La Minerve,* 5 February 1876; *Montreal Gazette,* 5 February 1876; Armstong, "Charles-Séraphin Rodier," *DCB;* Radforth, *Royal Spectacle,* 5-6; Death registration, 3 February 1876, Notre Dame Parish; Necrologies, 8 February 1876, FPNDM.

99 Tableau des droits et usages de la paroisse de Montréal, 1829-30; Deliberations d'assemblées de marguilliers, 1778-1833, 1834-77, 1878-1929, FPNDM.

100 Of the sixty-seven Catholic announcements of funerals for the men and women of these generations that we have found in the city's newspapers that indicated a time, two began before 6:00 a.m., six between 6:00 and 6:45 a.m., twenty-five between 7:00 and 7:45 a.m., nineteen between 8:00 and 8:45 a.m., and just two at 9 a.m. Only three Catholic funerals occurred in the afternoon. All were between 2:00 and 2:30 p.m. and for Irish Catholics.

101 *La Minerve,* 26 September 1829.

102 *Montreal Gazette,* 7 February 1876; *La Minerve,* 5 February 1876. He died on the 3rd. The funeral did not take place until the 8th.

103 Among the thirty-two Protestant funerals we have found announced in city newspapers where the time of the funeral is given, one started at noon, nine at 2:00 p.m., thirteen at 2:30 p.m., seven at 3:00 p.m., one at 4:00 p.m., and one at 5:00 p.m.

104 *Montreal Gazette,* 16 August 1861; Lot B: 728, MRC.

105 *Montreal Gazette,* 24 February 1851; Young, *Respectable Burial.*

106 *Montreal Gazette,* 10 February 1851.

107 Young, *Respectable Burial,* 30-32, quotation at 32; Young, "Death, Burial."

108 *Montreal Gazette,* 3 February 1851.

109 Yeoh, "The Body after Death," 240-55.

110 Wilson, *Life after Death,* 12; Jalland, *Death,* 210, 213, 217.

Chapter 8: "Within a Year and a Day"

1 Inventory, Bissonnet and Ducharme, 26 April 1834, Notary Guy.

2 Davidoff and Hall, *Family Fortunes;* Holcombe, *Wives and Property;* Lebsock, *The Free Women;* Wilson, *Life after Death;* K.E. Wood, *Masterful Women.*

3 Doucet, *Fundamental Principles,* art. 237; Beaubien, *Traité sur les lois civiles,* 2: 58-66, 326; McCord, *The Civil Code,* art. 246-66; Student Note Books, 1850s, Lawyers' Papers, MG 4166, box 10, no. 79, McGA; Holcombe, *Wives and Property,* 22; Garneau, "Le rituel," 45-56.

4 The work of other scholars include K.E. Wood, *Masterful Women,* 15, 29, 31; Lebsock, *The Free Women,* 37-40, 120-25; Shammas, Salmon, and Dahlin, *Inheritance in America;* Lisa Wilson, *Life after Death.*

5 Doucet, *Fundamental Principles,* art. 297; M.L. Taylor, *Mourning Dress,* 136.

6 Lebsock, *The Free Women,* 120.

7 Inventory, Bissonnet and Ducharme, 26 April 1834, Notary Guy; Inventory, Genant and Decousse, 20 September 1853, Notary Mathieu.

8 If community property was not closed by making an inventory overseen by the tutor and heirs, children retained a claim on further acquisitions of the survivor. Brun, *Vie et mort*; Garneau, "Le rituel," 47; Garneau explains the disadvantages of not closing a community in "Droit et 'affaires de famille,'" 534-35. *Legal News* 2 (1879): 270, describes a widow obliged to repay the amount of an obligation her husband had made because she had neither closed nor renounced the community and was judged to have "meddled" in it.

9 Wilhemy v. Brisebois, *Revue Légale* 12 (1884): 424.

10 Beaubien, *Traité sur les lois civiles*, 2:58-66; McCord, *The Civil Code*, art. 249-71; Garneau, "Droit et 'affaires de familles.'"

11 Ferrière, *Dictionnaire de droit*, 326-31; Gérin-Lajoie, *A Treatise*, 71.

12 Garneau doubts the comfort argument in "Les rituels," fn33.

13 Ex parte Grace Ham, *Legal News* 6 (1883): 115; Lafrance v. Blain, *Lower Canada Jurist*, 33 (1889): 12, maintained that when fathers were dead, "the mother has the same rights and privileges with regard to minor children as did the father, including the right to send them to work"; Sébastien and Brien dit Durocher, *Revue Légale* 20 (1891): 620.

14 Tutorship, children of Oliver Wait, 21 August 1832, Notary Arnoldi. Of the thirty inventories, tutorship, or other documents we have located for women who definitely became widows and had not remarried that mention tutorships, two of the women had no minor children, twenty-three widows (77 percent) were chosen as the sole tutor, one with someone else, and three had no official role. The latter included one pregnant woman, one widow who was still a minor, and Maria Mitchell. This information comes mostly from inventories. Some were found searching the Actes de tutelles, clôture d'inventaires, curatelles, CV 601, S1, BAnQM.

15 Inventory, Wait, 10 November 1832, Notary Arnoldi.

16 Beaubien, *Traité sur les lois civiles*, 2:58-66; McCord, *The Civil Code*, art. 249-71.

17 Inventory, Bissonnet and Ducharme, 26 April 1834, Notary Guy.

18 Tutelle, John O. Brown, 24 March 1858; Defendant's answer to petition, 29 October 1858, Mitchell v. Brown, 28 February 1859, Superior Court, dossiers, BAnQM.

19 Cited in Harvey, "The Protestant Orphan Asylum," 194.

20 "Doherty, Hon. Marcus," in Anon., *Canadian Men and Women*, 276; Tutelle, John O. Brown, 24 March 1858.

21 Gordon, *The Great Arizona*, 284-306. In this small-scale conflict, Doherty played a role similar to the prominent Catholic lawyer Eugene Ives, who agreed to represent the Sisters of Charity in New York after local Anglo-Protestants in Arizona sought to keep the Catholic orphans they had sent out away from the Catholic Mexican-American families to whom they had been promised.

22 Affidavits, Mary Eliza Peters, Thomas Prendergast, Bridget Halligan, 18 December 1858, Mitchell v. Brown, 28 February 1859, Superior Court, dossiers, BAnQM.

23 *Starke's*, 1859, 56, reports that S.W. Dorman was appointed to the judiciary in November 1850, two and a half years after Marcus Doherty.

24 Young, *The Politics of Codification*, 60, 82, 89; Nish, "William Badgley," *DCB*; Backhouse, *Petticoats and Prejudice*, 34-35; *Mackay's*, 1856-57.

25 McKenzie, *Scandal in the Colonies*, 66.

26 Draft of Judgement, 28 February 1859, document 32, Mitchell v. Brown, 28 February 1859, Superior Court, dossiers, BAnQM; Maria Mitchell v. John A. Brown, *Lower Canada Jurist* 3 (1859), 113.

27 Beaubien, *Traité sur les lois civiles*, 1: 69. When widows who were tutors remarried, this position normally passed to their new husband.

28 Heron, *Booze,* 51; Warsh, ed., *Drink in Canadian History.*
29 Warsh, *Moments of Unreason.*
30 Gordon, *The Great Arizona,* 309: Gordon, *Heroes.*
31 Inventory, Bissonnet and Ducharme, 26 April 1834, Notary Guy.
32 Code of Civil Procedure of Lower Canada, 1866, art. 1304-14, 363-67.
33 Crémazie, *Manuel des notions utiles,* 92-93, 134-35; McCord, *The Civil Code,* art. 660-711.
34 In the forty-nine wills we have found written by husbands who died before their wives, ten of the husbands gave all their goods in full ownership. Of these, six were Canadiens, one Irish Catholic, and three Anglo-Protestants or Jews. Provisions in a will seem to have overridden the claims the law gave children to a *légitime* – a portion of their parents' estate. Morin, "La perception," 21.
35 McCord, *The Civil Code,* art. 1310-43. In Pichette v. O'Hagan, the Superior Court decided Hagan could not sell property his children inherited from their mother as their tutor, even though she had so authorized him in her will, overturning the lower court's decision. *Montreal Law Reports,* Superior Court, 2 (1886), 384; Cardin and Dickinson, "Les inventaires de biens," 132.
36 Doucet, *Fundamental Principles,* 2:art. 240, states that if a surviving spouse with minor children remarries without having an inventory made, the children can demand community of all the property, both moveables and immoveables.
37 Inventory, Bissonnet and Ducharme, 26 April 1834, Notary Guy; Davidoff and Hall, *Family Fortunes,* 159.
38 Inventory, Bissonnet and Ducharme, 26 April 1834, Notary Guy. They owed Rose Leonard 12s. 6d., possibly for assisting with the washing.
39 Inventory, Genant and Decousse, 20 September 1853, Notary Mathieu; Inventory, Guilbault and Paris, 3 March 1830, Notary Labadie; Inventory, Monjean and Laurent, 7 April 1834, Notary Labadie.
40 Inventory, Wait, 10 November 1832, Notary Arnoldi; Inventory, Gay, 31 August 1832, Notary Griffin; Inventory, Mills and Lyman, 30 November 1847, Notary Pelton; Inventory, Fabre, 25 October 1854-31, March 1855, Notary E.E. Papineau, also reproduced in J.L. Roy, "Edouard-R. Fabre," Appendix B.
41 Bushman, *The Refinement of America,* 228.
42 Inventory, Bissonnet and Ducharme, 26 April 1834, Notary Guy.
43 Ibid.
44 Gérin-Lajoie, *A Treatise,* 59.
45 Inventory, Bissonnet and Ducharme, 26 April 1834, Notary Guy; Student Note Books, 1850s, Lawyers' Papers, MG 4166, box 10, no. 79, McGA; Gérin-Lajoie, *A Treatise,* 59.
46 Inventory, Charland and Letourneux, 2 April 1834, Notary Lorimier.
47 Inventory, Genevay, 27 March 1827, Notary Papineau.
48 Inventory, Wait, 10 November 1832, Notary Arnoldi; Inventory, Watson, 25 April 1827, Notary Bedouin.
49 They had married in 1809 and he died sometime before February 1823. In November 1824, she remarried with Joseph Renaud, a blacksmith. Inventory, Jobin and de Launay, 14 February 1823, Notary Jobin.
50 Inventory, Reid and Hannah, 30 January 1850, Notary Smith.
51 Inventory, Bissonnet and Ducharme, 26 April 1834, Notary Guy.
52 Inventory, Wait, 10 November 1832, Notary Arnold; Inventory, Genevay, 27 March 1827, Notary Joseph Papineau.
53 Inventory, Bissonnet and Ducharme, 26 April 1834, Notary Guy.

54 See Chapter 5.
55 Inventory, Bissonnet and Ducharme, 26 April 1834 and addenda, 1 May 1834, Notary Guy. McCord, *The Civil Code,* art. 1351-52.
56 Kimberly Boara and Ulric Shannon, "With Their Husbands Buried and Their Hands Tied: Widows and Debt in Montreal, 1845-1865," unpublished research essay, McGill University, Department of History, 1997. An Ordinance to exempt certain articles from seizure in satisfaction of debts, 1839, 2 Vict., c. 28, SLC; An Act to exempt certain articles from seizure in satisfaction of debts, 1860, 23 Vict., c. 25, SPC; Code of Civil Procedure of Lower Canada, art. 556, set out exempt items, including beds and bedding; ordinary wearing apparel used by the debtor and family members; basic kitchen utensils, including a stove and pipes; chairs; one table; looms; ten books; thirty days' worth of fuel and food; a few animals; and work tools.
57 Inventory, Paris and Guilbault, 3 March 1830, Notary Labadie; Poutanen, "Bonds of Friendship," 25-58.
58 Intestacy law placed spouses fifth after children, parents, nephews and nieces, grandparents, and collateral kin. Gérin-Lajoie, *A Treatise,* 149; Morel, *Un exemple,* 12.
59 See Chapter 5. After 1866, the civil code required that the marriage act itself be registered if a customary dower was to be recognized. Contests about marriage contracts signed prior to these dates continued. Symons v. Kelly, *Lower Canada Jurist* 21 (1877): 251. Widows who were named as heirs in a will could not also claim customary dower. Question 8, Student Note Books, 1850s, Lawyers' Papers, MG 4166, box 10, no. 79, McGA.
60 Will, Campbell, 19 September 1836, Notary Doucet; Marriage contract, Mower and Campbell, 14 January 1826, Notary Doucet; Inventory, Campbell, 19 December 1836, Notary Doucet.
61 McCord, *The Civil Code,* art. 1342; St. Aubin versus Dame Lacombe, *Montreal Law Reports,* Superior Court, 2 (1886), 110.
62 Lower Canada, appendix to vol. 43, *JHALC,* Appendix U, the civil list for that year indicates public servants' salaries: inspector of the general public accounts, £300; his clerk, £100; clerk of the Crown in Chancery, £100; chief justice of Montreal, £1,300; puisne judges, £900; messenger of the Legislative Council, £32 8s.; doorkeeper, £25.
63 Inventory, William Campbell, 13 July 1832, Notary Doucet; Marriage contract, Campbell and Wait, 14 August 1824, Notary Jobin; Inventory, Wait, 10 November 1832, Notary Arnoldi.
64 Tutorship of the children of Oliver Wait, 21 August 1832, Notary Arnoldi.
65 Power of Attorney from Logan Fuller and Caroline Campbell to Joseph Ross, 23 August 1832; from Caroline Campbell, James Wait, and Louis Laporte [sic] to Logan Fuller, 24 August 1832, Notary Arnoldi.
66 Inventory, Wait, 10 and 12 November 1832, Notary Arnoldi.
67 Ibid.; Jean-Claude Robert, "Jacob De Witt," *DCB.*
68 Inventory, Wait, 10 and 12 November 1832, Notary Arnoldi; Will, Wait, 12 August 1832, Notary Arnoldi.
69 In their marriage contract, Wait explicitly stated that the £50 annuity was to come from principal worth £833 6s. 8d., which was to revert to the children on her death. Civil List, Appendix U, vol. 43, *JHALC,* 24 January 1834.
70 Procès verbal of Sale of Moveable effects belonging to the estate of the late Oliver Wait, 22 November 1832, Notary Arnoldi.
71 Ibid.; Olson, "Feathering Her Nest."

72   André Morel neglects this in *Un exemple*, 6-7, and *Les limites*, 53-56.

73   Lebsock, *The Free Women*, 47; Shammas, Salmon, and Dahlin, *Inheritance in America*, 115; Wilson, *Life after Death*, 185.

74   Inventory, Genevay, 27 March 1827, Notary Joseph Papineau; Will, Genevay, probated 24 February 1827.

75   Renunciation, Thomas Bedouin, as executor of the estate of J.F.L. Genevay, deceased, 16 March 1827, Notary Kimber; L'Heureux, "Hugues Heney," *DCB*. At this time, Heney was working with Louis-Joseph Papineau and other members of the assembly criticizing the actions of Governor Dalhousie. He would later criticize the Patriotes and was appointed a commissioner for administering the oath of allegiance after the rebellions.

76   *La Minerve*, 22 March 1827, 2 April 1827, 5 April 1827, 12 April 1827, 16 April 1827, 19 April 1827, 26 April 1827, 7 May 1827; Inventory, Genevay, 27 March 1827, Notary Joseph Papineau.

77   Inventory, Genevay, 27 March 1827, Notary Joseph Papineau.

78   Ibid.

79   Ibid.

80   Renunciation, by Charlotte Mount, widow of the former Jacques-François-Louis Genevay, 5 May 1827, Notary Kimber.

81   Marriage contract, Mount and Genevay, 5 February 1823, Notary Papineau; Lease, Mrs. Agathe Dumas, Widow Flemming, to Charles Brookes, 5 May 1827, Notary Kimber; Renewal of Lease, 8 February 1828, Notary Kimber.

82   Obligation, Widow Dumas to Widow Genevay, 25 February 1828, Notary Kimber.

83   Her second husband married again, returned to politics, and became a senator. Louis-Philippe Audet, "Louis Lacoste," *DCB*.

84   Marriage contract, Genant and Decousse, 16 July 1843, Notary Valotte; Inventory, Genant and Decousse, 20 September 1853, Notary Mathieu; *Lovell's*, 1852, 1853, and 1868.

85   Marriage contract, Genant and Decousse, 16 July 1843, Notary Valotte; Inventory, Genant and Decousse, 20 September 1853, Notary Mathieu; *Lovell's*, 1852, 1853, 1854, 1855-56.

86   "The Law of Evidence," *Montreal Gazette*, 8 August 1851; An Act to render valid certain Deeds passed before Notaries now deceased, 1864, 27-28 Vict., c. 44, Statutes, Province of Canada, Canada-East, 1841-66; An Act to render valid certain Notarial Acts, 1870, 33 Vict., c. 23, SQ.

87   An Act to render valid certain Notarial Acts, 1870, 33 Vict., c. 23, SQ; An Act to render valid certain Inventories, 1872, 36 Vict., c. 23, SQ; An Act to render valid certain Notarial Instruments, 1875, 38 Vict., c. 23, SQ; An Act to render valid certain notarial deeds, 1879, 42-43 Vict., c. 36, SQ. This act only covered acts passed between the passage of the new civil code in 1866 and this legislation. It was specifically to deal with divergences from the processes required by s. 843.

88   Crémazie, *Manuel des notions utiles*, ss. 474, 135; Student Note Books, 1850s, Lawyers' Papers, MG 4166, box 10, no. 79, McGA. Morris reports that in England, in contrast, probate had to be organized within six months of a death because of probate and legacy duties, which to the best of my knowledge did not exist in Lower Canada/Quebec. Morris, *Men, Women and Property*, 83.

89   Will, Fabre, 17 March 1842, Notary D.E. Papineau; Inventory, Fabre, 25 October 1854-31 March 1855, Notary D.E. Papineau.

90   Lebsock, *The Free Women*, 42; Wilson, *Life after Death*, 26, 48; K.E. Wood, *Masterful Women*, 32.

91   Gérin-Lajoie, *A Treatise*, 163.

92 Will, Beneche, 6 February 1846, Notary Vallée.
93 Will, Fabre, 17 March 1842, Notary D.E. Papineau.
94 Inventory, Fabre, 25 October 1854-31, March 1855, Notary E.E. Papineau.
95 Will, Skakel, probated 15 October 1846; Will, Smith Tylee, probated 13 April 1866; Will and Codicil, Steward, probated 9 February 1852.
96 In the fifty wills we have found written by men who died before their wives, twenty-one of the men chose their wife alone and four chose their wife and someone else as their executor. Nineteen of the former and two of the latter were notarial or holograph wills. Stated differently, eighteen (53 percent) of men writing notarial wills chose their wife, compared to only 2 (13 percent) in English-style wills. Some 70 percent of the twenty-three Canadien husbands of widows whose wills we have found named their wife alone or with someone else as executor, compared to only 33 percent of the three Irish Catholics and 33 percent of the twenty-four Anglo-Protestant testators.
97 Hatchette v. Cahill, *Revue Légale* 6 (1874), 532; Hebert v. Rossignol, *Legal News* 10 (1887), 5; Ross et vir v. Ross et vir, *Legal News* 5 (1882): 197.
98 Morris, *Men, Women and Property,* 149.
99 Tutelles, 24 November 1847. She was appointed as tutrix on 17 November, five days after his death. Inventory, Mills, 30 November 1846, Notary Pelton; *Montreal Gazette,* 29 November 1847.
100 *Montreal Gazette,* 29 November 1847; Lyman, ed., *Genealogy,* 31. William (b. 1839, d. 1869) was the son of William Lyman, Hannah's eldest brother, by his third wife, Caroline Williams.
101 Marsolais, Desrochers, and Comeau, *Histoire des maires,* 44. The chapter on Mills is entitled "John Easton Mills, le maire martyr." Mills was replaced by Joseph Bourret. In 1849, Édouard-Raymond Fabre succeeded him.
102 Inventory, Mills, 30 November 1847, Notary Pelton.
103 Ibid.
104 Hannah Lyman protest against Basile Roy, 19 November 1847; Annulation of transport by Alexander Courtenay, 7 January 1848; Protest against David Handyside, 22 March 1848; Protest against Joseph Snapp, 23 March 1848; Promissory Note, City Bank, 25 March 1848; Protest against D. and W. Macfarlane, 11 April 1848, Notary Pelton.
105 Judge Robert McKay benchbook, no. 52, re. Gregoire v. Pinsonnault, Practice Court, 3e division, 30 November 1872, MG 4166, McGA.
106 An Act for compensating families of persons killed by accident, and for other purposes, therein mentioned, 1847, 10 and 11 Vict., SPC.
107 An Ordinance re. decayed pilots, 1839, c. 19, *LCO*; Lelièvre et al. v. Baillargeon et La Maison de la Trinité, *Lower Canada Reports* 3 (1853), 520.
108 Byrd v. Corner, *Legal News* 6 (1883): 364.
109 Belisle v. L'Union St. Jacques, *Lower Canada Jurist* 15 (1871), 212; Petitclerc, *"Nous protégeons l'infortune,"* 150-56; Bradbury, *Working Families,* 186-87.

Chapter 9: Widows' Votes
1 Picard, "Les femmes," and Picard, "Women Voters," have been invaluable to me in writing this chapter, as were Robert Sweeny's computerized version of one transcription of the poll book by Jacques Viger; Sweeny, "The 1832 By-Election," and Sweeny, "A Partial Tax Roll, 1832." The electoral district of Montreal West covered the western half of the city, stretching from Saint Lawrence Street to the city's western boundary and south to the Saint Lawrence River.
2 For the three poll locations, see MacGregor, *British North America,* 2:192-93; Viger's transcription of the poll books, box 1, Phillips, P148, BAnQM.

3 Sarah rented on St. Paul Street. Her marriage contract had promised her £250 instead of dower and all their community property. But Nelson had not lived long enough to acquire much property. MRC, Death registration, 14 March 1832; Marriage contract, Harrison and Nelson, 6 November 1824, Notary Cadieux.

4 *Montreal Gazette,* 30 April 1832; Senior, *Redcoats and Patriotes,* 7.

5 Landry, "Stanley Clark Bagg," *DCB; La Minerve,* 30 April 1832.

6 Rumilly, *Histoire de Montreal,* 2: 83-84.

7 Davidoff, "Regarding Some 'Old Husbands' Tales'"; Davidoff and Hall, *Family Fortunes;* Greer, *The Patriots,* 197-207; Landes, ed., *Feminism;* Rendall, "Women and the Public Sphere"; Ryan, *Women in Public.*

8 Greer, *The Patriots;* Picard, "Les femmes." Picard's database shows that 14 women voted in Montreal elections in the late eighteenth century. In Montreal East, 102 women tried in 1820, 6 in 1824, 2 in 1827, 72 in 1832, and 2 in 1844, while in Montreal West, 111 sought to vote in 1827, 225 in 1832, 10 twice, and 1 in 1844. In 1844, 9 women voted in the new riding of Montreal Centre. Overall, between 1820 and 1844, she has found evidence of 950 women seeking to vote throughout the province. Over half were in Montreal.

9 Galarneau, "L'élection partielle"; Galarneau, "L'élection pour le quartier Ouest"; Ouellet, *Lower Canada, 1791-1840,* 226-29; Senior, *British Regulars in Montreal;* Boileau, *Le 21 Mai 1832;* Jackson, *Riot That Never Was.*

10 Collective Clio, *L'histoire des femmes,* 163-64, interprets the loss of the vote as part of the "defeat of the traditional rights of women" but does not link it to this election. Ouellet, *Lower Canada, 1791-1840,* 226-29; Greer, *The Patriots;* Picard, "Les femmes."

11 Clarke, *Struggle for the Breeches;* Gordon and Nair, *Public Lives;* Hufton, *Women and the Limits of Citizenship;* Klein, "A 'Petticoat Polity?'"; Klinghoffer and Elkis, "'The Petticoat Electors'"; Rendall, "Women and the Public Sphere," 484-85; Landes, *Women and the Public Sphere;* J.W. Scott, *Only Paradoxes to Offer.*

12 An Act to amend ... and to regulate elections, 1822, c. 4, s. 8, 10, SLC, uses the word "person," whereas An Act to continue for a further limited time and amend certain Acts ... relating to the trail of controverted Elections, 1825, c. 32, s. 16, states "any person ... claiming the right to vote" may be required to take one or more oaths "before he is admitted to vote." The French wording implies no gender. £1 Quebec currency in this period was worth about $3.33 dollars.

13 Picard, "Les femmes," 72-73; Constitutional Act, 1791; Garner, *The Franchise and Politics,* 74-75; Riddell, "Woman Franchise in Quebec." Historians estimate that between one in four and one in eight family heads could vote. See DeBrou, "Widows and Tenants," 6; Ouellet, *Lower Canada, 1791-1840,* 25.

14 Picard, "Les femmes."

15 28 January 1833, *JHALC.* The poll book indicates that seventy-two women voted, fifty-three were identified as widows, no marital status was given for seventeen, and one was described as separated from her husband.

16 28 January 1833, *JHALC;* Picard, "Women Voters."

17 *Montreal Gazette, La Minerve,* 25 April-25 May 1832; Galarneau, "L'élection pour le quartier Ouest," 33.

18 *Montreal Gazette, La Minerve,* 25 April-25 May 1832; Galarneau, "L'élection pour le quartier Ouest," 33; Senior, *Redcoats and Patriotes,* 7, states the poll could be closed after thirty minutes; Lower Canada, 40 George III (1800), c. 1, s. 11, cited in Picard, "Les femmes," 42, specified an hour. An Act to repeal and consolidate the laws relating to the Election of Members ... and the duty of Returning Officers, 1825, c. 33, s. 12, SLC, specified that polls had to be open for eight hours each day between 8 a.m. and 5 p.m. "unless otherwise determined by the unanimous consent of the Candidates"; Fredman, *The Australian Ballot,* 2-3.

19 Landry, "Stanley Clark Bagg," *DCB*; Tulchinsky, "George Moffatt," *DCB*.
20 This name continues to be evoked in history texts, popular histories, and on the World Wide Web, as a reminder of British brutality during this election. Boileau, *Le 21 Mai 1832*.
21 Poll book, Montreal West, 1832, BAnQM.
22 *New Brunswick Royal Gazette*, 20 June 1820, citing the *Montreal Gazette*, 25 April 1820, cited in Klein, "A 'Petticoat Polity?'" 71; *Montreal Gazette*, 31 December 1833, cited in Heaman, "Taking the World," 604.
23 *Quebec Mercury*, 14 August 1827.
24 Wulf, *Not All Wives*, 1.
25 Petition of Pierre Faucher, Romain Robitaille et al., electors in the City of Quebec, 3 December 1828, reprinted in *La Minerve*, 22 December 1828.
26 One transcription, along with Viger's statistical summaries, is housed in the Viger-Verreau fonds, file 10, box 45, P32, Les archives du Séminaire de Québec (hereafter cited as ASQ). Here I draw on Picard, "Women Voters," and another Viger version of the poll book in the papers of a Montreal antique bookseller, Charles Phillips, Livres d'élection de l'élection de 1832 à Montréal, quartier Ouest, Collection Charles Phillips, 1770-1957, P148, BAnQM. My thanks to Anna Shea for finding this. Here, Viger lists a total of 1,533 people presenting to the returning officer: 1,308 men and 225 women. Of these, he reports that 129 and 26 were disqualified, which would make the rate of disqualification for men 10 percent and 11.5 percent for women. Numbers listed as disqualified in Bradbury, "Widows at the Hustings," in Bell and Yans, eds., *Women on Their Own*, Table 4.1, p. 85, were incorrectly transcribed.
27 H. St. George Dupré to Benjamin Delisle, 15 May 1832, cited in *JHALC*, 20 December 1832, 36.
28 Appendix, Evidence of Austin Cuvillier, *JHALC*, 9 January 1833, 101.
29 Marriage contract, Tavernier and Gamelin, 4 June 1823, Notary Doucet.
30 Robillard, *Émilie Tavernier-Gamelin*, 101-4.
31 Sadlier, trans., *Life of Mother Gamelin*, 29.
32 Robillard, *Émilie Tavernier-Gamelin*, 101-4; Boylan, *The Origins*, 14, 138.
33 Gordon and Nair, *Public Lives*, 3, 4.
34 Robillard, *Émilie Tavernier-Gamelin*, 104; Jenkins, *Montreal Island*, 285; MacGregor, *British North America*, 2: 192-93.
35 On Laura Mower, see Chapters 2 and 5.
36 Picard, "Les femmes," 94-101; Richard Chabot, Jacques Monet, and Yves Roby discuss the 1827 election in "Robert Nelson," *DCB*; Picard, "Women Voters."
37 Ouellet, *Lower Canada, 1791-1840*, 25, 226.
38 F. Noel, *Family Life*, 109-10, 127-28.
39 France Galarneau, "Daniel Tracey," *DCB*.
40 *La Minerve*, 30 April 1832; Sweeny, "The 1832 By-Election."
41 An Act to repeal certain Acts, 1825, c. 33, s. 25, SLC, set a fine of £10 for anyone attempting to influence votes; Hamelin and Hamelin, *Les moeurs électorales*, 44.
42 *La Minerve*, 16 April 1832. Tracey had publicly criticized Cuvillier.
43 *La Minerve*, 24 May 1832; Ouellet, *Lower Canada, 1791-1840*, 226-29.
44 *La Minerve*, 21 May 1832.
45 Agathe Perrault was also the aunt of Luce Perrault Fabre.
46 Evidence, Mr. Joseph Roy, 1833, Appendix, 15, *JHALC*.
47 Picard, "Les femmes," 73.
48 Sweeny, "A Partial Tax Roll, 1832." Viger identified most widows only by their husbands' names. Émilie Tavernier was listed as Gamelin, Vve. Yet, Émilie Monjean was listed only as Émilie Monjean, with no indication she was a widow. Such

inconsistencies complicate searching for specific women. Viger did not cover the whole city. His roll includes the eastern wards of the city – Saint Mary and Saint Louis – and the eastern part of the old city, where he identified thirty, twenty-eight, and nine widows respectively; Saint Lawrence ward fell into each riding, with thirty propertied widows; in Saint Anne ward he listed only six propertied widows, and twelve in the western part of the old city. He did not enumerate the two most westerly wards, Saint Antoine and Saint Joseph, otherwise known as the Recollet suburb. The total number of women identified as widows with enough property to be listed came to 115. Some 141 widows sought to vote. However, many of the women who voted qualified as renters, not landowners. I am reasonably sure that 66 widows listed on the roll voted. Nine did so as "heirs." So, 57 of the 115 voted or about half. Sweeny, "A Partial Tax Roll, 1832"; voting women from Picard, "Women Voters."

49   Groupe de recherche sur la société montréalaise, Université du Québec à Montréal, "Montreal Census 1831." This digitalized version of the census made these calculations possible. Fifty-three widows voted in the Montreal East by-election, of whom 35 owned property. Eighty-one of the 129 widows who voted in the Montreal West by-election owned property.

50   Sweeny, "A Partial Tax Roll, 1832"; and count of the numbers of widows heading households enumerated in the census of 1831.

51   Of the 198 women who voted in the Montreal West by-election, 128 (65 percent) were recorded as owning property. In the Montreal East by-election, 47 (65 percent) of the 72 women and 35 of the 53 (66 percent) widows were recorded as owning property. When Jacques Viger calculated similar proportions for all the Montreal West electors, in contrast, he found that only 53 percent were proprietors. Nathalie Picard, "Women Voters"; Jacques Viger, Statistique de l'élection, ASQ, Viger-Verreau fonds, reproduced in Galarneau, "L'élection pour le quartier," Table 8.

52   Inventory, Paris and Guilbault, 3 March 1830, Notary Labadie.

53   Bradbury, "Itineraries of Marriage," 108-15.

54   Lamoureux, Citoyennes? 41.

55   Pierre Berthelet, http://www.vieux.montreal.qc.ca.

56   Campbell, A History of the Scotch Presbyterian Church, 77; Sweeny, "A Partial Tax Roll, 1832."

57   Picard, "Women Voters."

58   Marriage contract, Monjean and Laurent, 22 November 1824, Notary Ritchot; Inventory, Monjean and Laurent, 7 April 1834, Notary Labadie; Sweeny, "A Partial Tax Roll, 1832"; the inventory indicates she sold one lot during their marriage for £200. The tax roll of 1832 assessed the other at £100.

59   Montreal Gazette, 16 April 1832; Morgan, Public Men, 56.

60   Montreal Gazette, 16 April 1832, 30 April 1832, 5 May 1832, 17 May 1832.

61   La Minerve, 3 May 1832.

62   For example, La Minerve, 16 April 1832, 30 April 1832, 26 April 1832, and, for an earlier formulation, 23 April 1827, "French Canadians don't tend to exclusive power, they don't hold a national hatred against the English, and as soon as an inhabitant of this country shows they are really a citizen, there is no longer any difference," cited in Monière, Ludger Duvernay, 64, my translation.

63   Pateman, The Sexual Contract; Davidoff, "Regarding Some 'Old Husbands' Tales'"; J.W. Scott, Only Paradoxes to Offer; Greer, The Patriots.

64   La Minerve, 26 April 1832, 14 May 1832, 21 May 1832.

65   One hundred and five women voted for Bagg, ninety-three for Tracey.

66   Ouellet, Lower Canada, 1791-1840, 25-26, 226; Montreal Gazette, 24 May 1832, citing the Montreal Herald.

67 Jean-Claude Robert, "Jacques Viger," *DCB*; Sweeny, "Making a Bourgeois Town"; Evidence, Jacques Viger, 25 January 1833, *JHALC*, Appendix 1832-33; Livres d'élection.

68 Robert, "Jacques Viger," *DCB*.

69 The Act of Incorporation received royal assent in June 1832 and was put into effect a year later. Jenkins, *Montreal Island*, 289.

70 Evidence, Jacques Viger, 30 January 1833, *JHALC*, quotation at 200; Appendix, 1832-33, *JHALC*, 11, 36, 39-40, 63, 298-311; Robert, "Jacques Viger," *DCB*; Curtis, *The Politics of Population*.

71 Evidence, Jacques Viger, 30 January 1833, *JHALC*, 200; Liste Alphabétique des personnes qui se sont présentées au Poll du Q.O. de Montréal, pour voter, en 1832, Livres d'élection.

72 Ouellet, *Lower Canada, 1791-1840*, 376, suggests the poll book had disappeared; Galarneau, "L'élection partielle," is based on Viger's calculations, not the poll or Viger's transcriptions.

73 Livres d'élection.

74 Ibid.; Colley, *Britons Forging the Nation*; Colley, "Britishness and Otherness," 309-29.

75 *La Minerve*, 24 May 1832.

76 *La Minerve*, 28 May 1832; Courville, *Population et territoire*, 11.

77 Galarneau, "L'élection pour le quartier Ouest," 142-43.

78 *La Minerve* reports the following assemblies: 31 May 1832 on St. Athanase; 7 June 1832 on St. Remy; 14 June 1832 on Chambly; 25 June 1832 on St. Hyacinthe; 5 July 1832 on Deux Montagnes; 12 July 1832 on St. Benoit. Note how similar assemblies would be critical to the buildup of Patriote support in 1837. Greer, *The Patriotes*, 146-49.

79 Blunt and Rose, eds., *Writing Women and Space*; Davidoff, "Regarding Some 'Old Husbands' Tales'"; Duncan, ed., *Body Space*; Eley, "Nations, Publics"; Landes, ed., *Feminism*; Rendall, "Women and the Public Sphere"; Sandwell, "The Limits of Liberalism."

80 Evidence, Jacques Viger, 25 and 26 January 1833, Appendix, 1832-33, *JHALC*.

81 Evidence, Jacques Viger, 28 January 1833, 23 February 1833, Appendix, 1832-33, *JHALC*.

82 Livres d'élection.

83 *La Minerve*, 3 May 1832.

84 Evidence, Jacques Viger, 23 February 1833, Appendix, 1832-33, *JHALC*.

85 *La Minerve*, 14 May 1832, 16 April 1832, 21 April 1832. In St. Remy, the Assembly resolved, "as part of the county that Austin Cuvillier represents, [to] thank him for the good he has done until last year, and refuse in the future to give him the honour to represent us, because he has ignominiously abandoned the mass of the Canadiens to serve in a party that is not worthy of their support." *La Minerve*, 7 June 1832, my translation.

86 *La Minerve*, 3 February 1834, citing debate, 27 January 1834; Fredman, *The Australian Ballot*, 20-21.

87 *La Minerve*, 3 February 1834, my translation.

88 Greer, *The Patriots*, 202; *La Minerve*, 3 February 1834, citing debate, 27 January 1834, my translation.

89 Act to regulate ... contested Elections of Members, 1834, c. 28, SLC; Picard, "Les femmes," 58.

90 Picard, "Les femmes," 59; Cleverdon, *The Woman Suffrage Movement*, 158, 216; Collective Clio, *L'histoire des femmes*; An Act to repeal certain Acts therein mentioned, and to amend, consolidate, and reduce into one Act, the several Statutory

provisions now in force for the regulation of Elections of Members to represent the People of this Province in the Legislative Assembly thereof, 1849, c. 27, s. 46, SPC; Gibbs, ed., *Debates,* 1849, 6 March, 13 March, 16 March, 17 April, 18 April.

91 See Chapter 5 and Bradbury, "Debating Dower," 56-78; Marriage contract, Bland and Noxon, 31 December 1825, Notary O'Keefe; Picard, "Women Voters."

92 Cited in Picard, "Les femmes," 33, 67, 96.

Chapter 10: Widow to Mother Superior

1 Cause d'Émilie Gamelin, folder 484, Archives Soeurs de la Providence, Cause Émilie Gamelin (hereafter cited as PASP-CEG); Robillard, *Émilie Tavernier-Gamelin,* 83; Gray, *The Congrégation de Notre-Dame,* 23-24. In 1828, Marie-Clotilde Raizenne, a Grey Nun, moved to Upper Canada, where she headed up the Congrégation de l'Enfant-Jésus. Robert Scollard, "Marie-Clotilde Raizenne," *DCB.*

2 E.C. Fabre, Paris, to E.R. Fabre, Montreal, 13 November 1843, folder 458, PASP-CEG.

3 Others canonized or beatified include Marguerite Bourgeoys 1620-1700, who founded the Congrégation de Notre-Dame; Marguerite d'Youville, 1701-71, who founded the Grey Nuns; André Bessette, founder of Saint Joseph Oratory in Montréal; Mother Marie Léonie Paradis, who founded the Little Sisters of the Holy Family; Kateri Tekakwitha, Mohawk Christian.

4 In contrast to other chapters, this one relies heavily on secondary literature in combination with my research, and especially on Robillard, *Émilie Tavernier-Gamelin.* I am grateful to Sister Thérèse Frigon, who built up the archive supporting her beatification, for letting me consult its documentation.

5 Ginzberg, *Women,* 36; Boylan, *The Origins;* Ginzberg, *Women;* Hewitt, *Women's Activism;* Luddy, *Women and Philanthropy;* Prochaska, *Women and Philanthropy;* Quataert, *Staging Philanthropy;* Danylewycz, *Taking the Veil;* Errington, *Wives and Mothers;* Harvey, "The Protestant Orphan Asylum"; Morgan, *Public Men;* Varty, "'A Career'"; Varty, "The City."

6 Quataert, *Staging Philanthropy,* 5-6, 11.

7 Feretti, *Brève histoire;* Ferretti, *Entre voisins;* Hardy, *Contrôle social;* Lemieux, *Histoire du catholicisme québécois;* Rousseau and Remiggi, eds., *Atlas historique;* Rousseau, "À l'origine"; Rousseau and Remiggi, "Le renouveau religieux"; Sylvain and Voisine, *Histoire du catholicisme québécois;* Voisine and Hamelin, *Les Ultramontains.*

8 Chronicles, 1, 1827-28, n.p., PASP; Robillard, *Émilie Tavernier-Gamelin,* 101; Lapointe-Roy, *Charité,* 70; *La Minerve,* 30 April 1829, announced that the house was for rent.

9 Chronicles, 1, n.p., 1828-64, 1828, PASP; Bourassa, *Madame Gamelin,* 23.

10 Sadlier, trans., *Life of Mother Gamelin,* quotations at 29, 172; Robillard, *Émilie Tavernier-Gamelin,* 100-3, 186; *Mélanges Réligieux* (hereafter cited as *MR*), 10 October 1851.

11 Robillard, *Émilie Tavernier-Gamelin,* 102-3; *MR,* 7 October 1851.

12 Succession Sale, Joseph Perrault, 20-22 October 1831, folder 128, PASP-CEG.

13 Bourassa, *Madame Gamelin,* 30.

14 Robillard, *Émilie Tavernier-Gamelin,* 104; Boylan, *The Origins,* 140.

15 Riley, *"Am I That Name?"* 46, 49, 51.

16 Gilles Chaussé and Lucien Lemieux, "Jean-Jacques Lartigue," *DCB;* Noel, "Women and Social Welfare," 270, 274; Boylan, *The Origins,* 21, 139-40.

17 Robillard, *Émilie Tavernier-Gamelin,* 108; 13 August 1832, folder 144, PASP-CEG.

18 Harvey, "The Protestant Orphan Asylum," 81-82; Noel, "Women," 272; Bilson, *A Darkened House,* 45-46; Pearse and Mitchel, *Montreal Ladies Benevolent Society,* 9-25.

19   Lapointe-Roy, *Charité bien ordonnée*, 87; Daveluy, *L'Orphelinat Catholique*; *La Minerve*, 5 July 1832; Robillard, *Émilie Tavernier-Gamelin*, 107-8; Bilson, *A Darkened House*, 44; Huguet-Latour, *Annuaire de Ville Marie*, 88, dates the founding of the Catholic orphanage as 18 July 1832.

20   Boylan, *The Origins*, 175.

21   Léon Pouliot, "Antoine-Olivier Berthelet," *DCB*; Linteau and Robert, "Propriété foncière"; Sweeny, "A Partial Tax Roll, 1832." On rentiers, see Morris, *Men, Women and Property.*

22   Donation, Antoine-Olivier Berthelet to J. Bte. Bréguier St. Pierre, 2 September 1836, Notary Bedouin.

23   Young, *In Its Corporate Capacity*; Marsan, *Montreal in Evolution*, 144, 153, 157.

24   Sale, Sophie Labée to Émilie Tavernier, 28 August 1832, Notary Lukin; Robillard, *Émilie Tavernier-Gamelin*, 110-11, 119; Bourassa, *Madame Gamelin*, 30; Deutsch, *Women and the City*, 4.

25   Boylan, *The Origins*, 175.

26   Robillard, *Émilie Tavernier-Gamelin*, 111.

27   Ibid., 120-25; Bernard, *Les rébellions de 1837-38*; Greer, *The Patriots*; Laporte, *Patriotes et Loyaux*, 143-46, 241-42; Harvey, "Le leadership féminin."

28   Laporte, *Patriotes et Loyaux*, 146; Robillard, *Émilie Tavernier-Gamelin*, 120-25.

29   Robillard, *Émilie Tavernier-Gamelin*, 125-28; Institut Providence, *Notes historiques*, 4; Jacques Monet, "Sir Louis-Hippolyte LaFontaine," *DCB*; *L'Opinion publique*, 4 March 1880, 1.

30   Robillard, *Émilie Tavernier-Gamelin*, 125-33.

31   "Charité de la Mère Gamelin," *MR*, 28 October 1851.

32   Charles S. Rodier to Mgr. Bourget, 1 January 1843, Sisters of Providence, ACAM. Rodier sent £25 to Émilie through Bishop Bourget, congratulating the latter on having "established" the new asylum.

33   Boylan, *The Origins*, 175.

34   Lapointe-Roy, *Charité bien ordonnée*, 22, 29; Robillard, *Émilie Tavernier-Gamelin*, 103-4.

35   Gordon and Nair, *Public Lives*, 4.

36   Fecteau, *La Liberté du pauvre*, 297-99.

37   Marie-Claire Daveluy, "Jeanne Mance," *DCB*; Mills, "'Saintes Soeurs,'" 139-41.

38   Danylewycz, *Taking the Veil*; Robillard, *Émilie Tavernier-Gamelin*, 109.

39   Dates of the purchase and sale of the five properties in folder 1038, PASP-CEG; Robillard, *Émilie Tavernier-Gamelin*, 119; Sale, Tavernier to Leclaire, 6 August 1841, Notary Bedouin.

40   Deliberations, Council, 29 March 1844, folder 484, PASP-CEG; Institut Providence, *Notes historiques*, 24; Robillard, *Émilie Tavernier-Gamelin*, 183-85; Sadlier, trans., *Life of Mother Gamelin*, 93-107; *MR*, 22 April 1844, E.R. Fabre to E.C. Fabre, 8 April 1844, folder 502, PASP-CEG.

41   Gray, *The Congrégation*, 23.

42   Sadlier, trans., *Life of Mother Gamelin*, 105-6; Robillard, *Émilie Tavernier-Gamelin*, 183-85; Canonical examination of Widow Émilie Gamelin, 28 March 1844, Sisters of Providence, ACAM.

43   Financial archives, account books containing entries of dowries, pensions, and other revenues of the Asylum for Aged and Infirm Women, folder, 485, PASP-CEG; D'Allaire, *Les dots des religieuses.*

44   Robillard, *Émilie Tavernier-Gamelin*, 154.

45   "Registre des femmes vieilles et infirmes de l'Asile de la Providence de Montréal, 1831-1963," PASP.

46 Canada, Census of 1842, Montreal, Saint Mary ward, p. 531; Curtis, *The Politics of Population*, 55-56.

47 Robillard, *Émilie Tavernier-Gamelin*, 141.

48 Ibid., 191.

49 This is suggested in ibid.

50 Ginsberg, *Women*, 48; *LCO*, 1838-40, Indexes. The major exception incorporated the Bank of Montreal.

51 An Act to Incorporate the Ladies of the Roman Catholic Orphan Asylum of Montreal, 1841, c. 62; An Act to Incorporate the Ladies' Benevolent Society of Montreal, 1841, c. 6; An Act to Incorporate the Montreal Asylum for Aged and Infirm Women, 1841, c. 67, Statutes, Province of Canada, Canada-East, 1841-66.

52 Ginzberg, *Women*, 50.

53 Pastoral letter, 8 November 1841, *Mandements*; suggested this empowered the women to legally hold funds that would produce £1,000 annually to support the elderly women. At 6 percent, this would have required a capital of £16,600, an unlikely amount.

54 *Montreal Gazette*, 4 November 1841, 2.

55 Pastoral letter, 6 November 1841, *Mandements*; Institut Providence, *Notes historiques*, 5. The women a generation older were the siblings Marie-Claire Perrault Cuvillier and her sister, the widow Agathe Perrault Nowlan, as well as Euphrosine Lamontagne Perrault, the second wife of their brother, Julien-Isidore. Relatives of Émilie's generation included Euphrosine's daughter, Luce Perrault Fabre; Sophie Cadieux Tavernier, François' wife; and Marie-Angélique Cuvillier, daughter of Marie-Claire. The others were Madeleine Durand, her long-time assistant; Mrs. Paul-Joseph Lacroix; Mrs. Maurice Delisle; Mrs. Charles S. Delorme; and Miss Thérèse Berthelet, daughter of their major benefactor.

56 Perin, *Ignace de Montréal*.

57 Sylvan, "Ignace Bourget," *DCB*. Fecteau convincingly insists on the modern way in which ultramontane Catholicism in Quebec took advantage of the political vacuum after the rebellions to dominate civil association and the social sphere. Fecteau, *La Liberté du pauvre*, 266-67; Perin, *Ignace de Montréal*, 99-103, highlights the sensual and emotive appeal.

58 Bourassa, *Madame Gamelin*, 31; *L'Aurore des Canadas*, 25 August 1840, 11 December 1840.

59 Hardy, *Contrôle social*, 71-77, 118-20; Dionne, *Mgr de Forbin-Janson*, 1895.

60 Circular to the clergy of the Diocese of Montreal, 23 September 1841, *Mandements*, 1:149-55; Robillard, *Émilie Tavernier-Gamelin*, 138-40.

61 Mills, "Saintes Soeurs," 139.

62 Sylvain, "Bourget," *DCB*; Mills, "'Saintes Soeurs,'" 139; Langlois, "Les effectifs des congrégations féminines"; Langlois, *Le catholicisme au féminin*.

63 Rousseau with Payette, "Le recrutement de l'élite," 201. Danylewycz, *Taking the Veil*, 17, reports that the 1851 census enumerated 650 nuns in the Province of Quebec, representing 1.4 percent of unmarried women over the age of twenty; in 1881 there were nearly 4,000 and in 1921 over 13,500 representing 9 percent of single females over the age of twenty.

64 Voisine with Beaulieu and Hamelin, *Histoire de l'Église Catholique*, 45-47; Sylvain, "Ignace Bourget," *DCB*.

65 Circular to the clergy of the diocese of Montreal, 23 September 1841, *Mandements*, 1:149-55; Sylvain, "Bourget," *DCB*, reports he was away 3 May to 23 September 1841.

66 *MR*, 15, 22, October 1841; Register of official acts of the Corporation, 27 October 1841, folder 258, PASP-CEG; Robillard, *Émilie Tavernier-Gamelin*, 141-42; Institut Providence, *Notes historiques*, 5.

67 *MR*, 22 October 1841; Robillard, *Émilie Tavernier-Gamelin*, 142.

68 Voisine, with Beaulieu and Hamelin, *Histoire de l'Église Catholique*, 46-47.

69 Hardy, *Contrôle social*, 67.

70 Pastoral letter to the clergy and faithful of the city and parish of Montreal to recommend to their charity the Providence Asylum for elderly and infirm women, 8 November 1841, *Mandements*, 1:167-75; Robillard, *Émilie Tavernier-Gamelin*, 146-48.

71 Robillard, *Émilie Tavernier-Gamelin*, 146-48; Pastoral letter, 8 November 1841, *Mandements*, 1:167-75.

72 Monet, "La Fontaine," *DCB*. Opposition was widespread in Lower Canada, so he accepted the offer of running in York, later Toronto, one of the two seats won by Robert Baldwin, who became one of his few close friends.

73 Chronicles, 1, 1841, n.p., PASP; Actes officielles de la Corporation, 1:22 November 1841, 15; Bourassa, *Madame Gamelin*, 47.

74 Robillard, *Émilie Tavernier-Gamelin*, 148, 156; Bourassa, *Madame Gamelin*, 42; Ellen James, "John Ostell," *DCB*. Marguerite Barsalou was the wife of the prominent Patriote Joseph Gauvin.

75 L. Lemieux, *Histoire du catholicism québécois*, 115.

76 Quataert, *Staging Philanthropy*, 22-23; Lemieux, "Le dynamisme religieux," 2, insists on the interrelationship of politics and religion.

77 Robillard, *Émilie Tavernier-Gamelin*, 156, 166-67; Institut Providence, *Notes historiques*.

78 Chronicles, 1, 1843, n.p., PASP.

79 Robillard, *Émilie Tavernier-Gamelin*, 149, 153-56; Institut Providence, *Notes historiques*, 9.

80 Vow of chastity, Widow Gamelin, 20 February 1842, Sisters of Providence, ACAM; Robillard, *Émilie Tavernier-Gamelin*, 153-54.

81 Circular to Montreal clergy, 16 February 1843, *Mandements*, 1:230.

82 *MR*, 46, 5, 1843, cited in Institut Providence, *Notes historiques*, 13; Request for admission to the novitiate from Miss Mathilda Saucier, 28 March 1842, Sisters of Providence, ACAM.

83 The others were Marguerite Thobodeau, Agathe Séné, Emélie Caron, Victoire la Rocque, Delphine Payement, and slightly later, Justine Michon. The first two were from Montreal, the others came from nearby parishes. Institut Providence, *Notes historiques*, 10.

84 Sadlier, trans., *Life of Mother Gamelin*, 78-79; Robillard, *Émilie Tavernier-Gamelin*, 160; Jean, *Émilie Tavernier*, DCB.

85 Chronicles, 1:33, PASP; Sadlier, trans., *Life of Mother Gamelin*, 80-81; Robillard, *Émilie Tavernier-Gamelin*, 162. Funeral speech of Mgr. Bourget, 24 September 1851.

86 Boylan, *The Origins*, 118-23; Danylewycz, *Taking the Veil*, 41; Elizabeth Seton was also beatified.

87 Robillard, *Émilie Tavernier-Gamelin*, 172-75; Deluol of Emmitsburg to Bourget, 27 September 1843, Sisters of Providence, ACAM.

88 Gamelin to Fabre, 8 October 1843, folder 440, PASP-CEG; Sadlier, trans., *Life of Mother Gamelin*, 92-93; Robillard, *Émilie Tavernier-Gamelin*, 175-76; Bourassa, *Madame Gamelin*, 57-58.

89 Robillard, *Émilie Tavernier-Gamelin*, 166, 177, 180; Chronicles, 1, 1843, n.p., PASP. The new rules for the sisters set 4:30 a.m. as time to get up, first prayers at 5:00 a.m., then half an hour of meditation, then work. Mass was to be at 6:00 a.m.; breakfast for the infirm and work began at 7:00 a.m., the Sisters were to breakfast at 7:30 a.m. Services for the poor were at 11:15 a.m. and again at 6:30 p.m.

90 "Notes on my third retreat, which began on the 5th April, 1848, by Father Tellier," cited in Sadlier, trans., *Life of Mother Gamelin*, 246-49.

91 Robillard, *Émilie Tavernier-Gamelin,* 179-80, 202; Chronicles, 1, 1841, May 1843, n.p., PASP; Bourget to Harkin, 15 April 1845, file 579, PASP-CEG; Gagnon, *Plaisir d'amour;* Sadlier, trans., *Life of Mother Gamelin,* 95, 108, 126.

92 In November 1841, Bourget described their mission as care of the infirm in the asylum, teaching young girls, visiting the poor and sick in their homes, giving help to prisoners, and preparing the dying for their deaths. Institut Providence, *Notes historiques,* 7, Chronicles, 1, 1844, n.p., PASP, reports that orphans were admitted on 1 May 1844.

93 Will, Mary McCord, 23 February 1845, Notary Lacombe, box 352, McCord Family Papers, cited in Young, "Death, Burial," 111; Chronicles, 1, 1844, n.p., PASP. Other women listed were mesdemoiselles White, Burroughs, Halo, Masson, and Moran. Chroniques, 1, 2, 3, 4, PASP.

94 Danylewycz, *Taking the Veil,* 76-77; Robillard, *Émilie Tavernier-Gamelin,* 208, 215-20; E.R. Fabre to E.C. Fabre, 24 December 1844, no. 586, PASP-CEG.

95 Robillard, *Émilie Tavernier-Gamelin,* 269, 270-72; Sadlier, trans., *Life of Mother Gamelin,* 207, 223, 227; Institut de la Providence, *Histoire des Filles,* 2:199.

96 Bourget to de Charbonnel, bishop of Toronto, 18 November 1850, cited in Robillard, *Émilie Tavernier-Gamelin,* 287.

97 Circular of the bishop for the religious communities, 8 December 1850, *Mandements,* 2:148; Robillard, *Émilie Tavernier-Gamelin,* 286.

98 Monet, "La Fontaine," *DCB.*

99 Robillard, *Émilie Tavernier-Gamelin,* 277-78; 281-83; 289-90.

100 Institut Providence, *Notes historiques,* 32, for 1845 cites the numbers of elderly as forty, orphans fifty, and around twelve pensioners, religious and lay, in 1845; Robillard, *Émilie Tavernier-Gamelin,* 295.

101 Institut Providence, *Notes historiques,* 35; Bourget sought a French copy of the rules used by the Sisters of Charity, founded by Elizabeth Seton at Emmmitsburg, and L.-R. Deluol sent an "old manuscript" in French back with Émilie in 1843. 26 April 1843, Sisters of Providence, ACAM; this is described as the constitution of St. Vincent de Paul in Institut Providence, *Notes historiques,* 19. Robillard, *Émilie Tavernier-Gamelin,* 185-86, reports that in setting up the earliest set of rules, Bourget drew on those developed for the semi-cloistered nuns of the Hôtel-Dieu, which were written in 1688.

102 Robillard, *Émilie Tavernier-Gamelin,* 177, 186, 228; Notes on second retreat, begun 18 March 1847, file 734 PASP-CEG; Sadlier, trans., *Life of Mother Gamelin,* 170-72; On retreats, see Gray, *The Congrégation,* 43.

103 Robillard, *Émilie Tavernier-Gamelin,* 263, 264, 280; Notes on third retreat, 5-13 April 1848, file 808, PASP-CEG, and reproduced in Sadlier, trans., *Life of Mother Gamelin,* 232, 244-59.

104 Remarks on the Sisters of Charity, 26 September 1847, no. 847-13; Sister Vincent to Mgr. Bourget, n.d., 1847, no. 847-14; Sister La Conception to Bourget, September 1847, no. 347-17; Sister Vincent to Mgr. Bourget, 2 October 1847, no. 847-22; Draft letter of irregularities, 13 October 1847, Sisters of Providence, ACAM.

105 Citation from notes on third retreat, 5-13 April 1848, file 808, PASP-CEG (my translation); Robillard, *Émilie Tavernier-Gamelin,* 243-50, 292-94. Gray, *The Congrégation,* 108-13, points to the conflicts and difficulties mothers superior could face; the range of sources of "potential disharmony" within convents, including social distance; the formation of cliques; and the challenges of sustaining discipline.

106 Sadlier, trans., *Life of Mother Gamelin,* 232; Robillard, *Émilie Tavernier-Gamelin,* 305, 24 September 1851.

107 Robillard, *Émilie Tavernier-Gamelin,* 305.

108 This began in 1981. She was declared "venerable" in 1993 and beatified in 2001 following the medical approval of a miraculous cure.
109 Wilson, *Life after Death,* 19.
110 Bremmer and Van Den Bosch, *Between Poverty,* 2; Retreat notes, 1846, file 657, PASP-CEG, from PASP, A3, 1-3; "On my third retreat, which began on the 5th April, 1848, by Father Tellier," reproduced in Sadlier, trans., *Life of Mother Gamelin,* 45-46.
111 Walch and Beauvalet, "Le veuvage"; Van Die, "'A Woman's Awakening.'"
112 Bourassa, *Madame Gamelin,* 7; Quataert, *Staging Philanthropy,* 15.
113 Widow Angelique Blondeau initiated many new charitable ventures, including the first Association des Dames de la Charité, which began in 1827. Henriette Huguet-Latour Duncan began sheltering repentant prostitutes in 1830 but stopped when she remarried. The widow Marie-Rosalie Cadron Jetté began sheltering single pregnant women in 1840. Bourget incorporated her work in 1848, as the Sisters of Miséricorde. Their first mother superior, Sister Sainte Jeanne de Chantal, was a wealthy widow. Danylewycz, *Taking the Veil,* 20, 47, 80; Andrée Désilets, "Marie-Rosalie Cadron," *DCB.* The first Jewish women's such organization, the Ladies' Hebrew Benevolent Society of Montreal, was created much later, in 1877.
114 A.F. Scott, *Making the Invisible,* 283; Boylan, *The Origins,* 172-73.
115 Ryan, *Cradle of the Middle Class,* 186-91; A.F. Scott, *Making the Invisible,* 281.
116 Jameson, *Sisters of Charity,* 13, 17.
117 Claudette Lacelle, "Marie-Marguerite Dufrost de Lajemmerais," *DCB*; Hélène Bernier, "Marguerite Bourgeoys," *DCB.*
118 Quataert, *Staging Philanthropy,* 39.
119 Fecteau, *La Liberté du pauvre,* 281.
120 Rousseau, "À l'origine," 71-92; Rousseau and Remiggi, "Le renouveau religieux"; Lemieux, *Histoire du catholicisme québécois*; Hardy, "À propos du réveil religieux"; Hudon, *Prêtres et fidèles,* 13, 47, wisely remarks that the tepidity of the faithful before 1840 remains to be demonstrated; Hubert, *Sur la terre*; Perin, *Ignace de Montréal,* 96-103; Désilets, "Marie- Rosalie Cadron," *DCB*; Jean, "Eulalie Durocher," *DCB*; Lemieux, "Le dynamisme religieux," 2-4.
121 Boylan, *The Origins,* 7.
122 Collective Clio, *L'histoire des femmes,* 234-35; Noel, "Women and Social Welfare"; J. Noel, "Femmes Fortes."

Chapter 11: Patchworks of the Possible

1 W.G. Scott to Caroline Scott Pelton, 27 January 1861, Pelton Papers, McGA.
2 Marriage contract, Scott and Pelton, 1 May 1843, Notary Gibb.
3 On Maria Mitchell, see Chapter 8.
4 W.G. Scott to Caroline Pelton, 27 January 1861, Pelton Papers, McGill University Archives (herafter McGA).
5 Wilson, *Life after Death,* 99.
6 Around 73 percent of the women who became widows who had married between 1823 and 1825 and for whom we definitely know the husbands' death date were widows by 1860, as were 31 percent of the 209 who had married between 1842 and 1846. For men who outlived their wives the equivalent percentages were similar: 75 percent of the 207 married in the 1820s and 43 percent of the 228 from the 1840s.
7 Curtis, *The Politics of Population;* Dillon, The 1881 Canadian Census; 43 percent of women in their sixties, 63 percent of those in their seventies, and 73 percent of those in their eighties were reported widowed; Dillon, *The Shady Side,* 147, 161,

shows 47 percent of women over 65 in Canada in 1871 as widows compared to 22 percent of men and 50 percent of women, and 23 percent of men in 1901.

8   Wilson, *Life after Death*, 1-4; Stansell, *City of Women*; Bradbury, "Single Parenthood," 211-17.

9   The 69 percent of the women who married 1823-26 whom we know became widows and 85 percent of those marrying in 1842-45 had no marriage contract.

10 Hufton, "Women without Men," 1-22; 355-75; Wilson, *Life after Death*, 66.

11 Tutelle, Minors John Mills, 24 November 1847, no. 795, Tutelles, 1658-1882, BAnQM; Morris, *Men, Women and Property*, 149, 156.

12 Caroline Pelton to Carrie Pelton, Montreal, 1 November 1861, Pelton Papers, McGA; quotation from Jane Livingstone to Civil Secretary, 3 March 1837, 504: 19-19a, Civil Secretary Records, LAC, RG 2 A1, shares her worry that her landlord might force a sale of all her furniture to collect his debts and that she and her children would be "driven into the streets" because of the debts she owed him.

13 Wulf, *Not All Wives*, 130; Baskerville, *A Silent Revolution?*

14 Lebsock, *The Free Women*, 26; Wilson, *Life after Death*, 28-29; Wulf, *Not All Wives*, 130.

15 Hamilton, "Property Rights," 88.

16 Caroline Pelton to Carrie Pelton, Montreal, 5 March 1863, Pelton Papers, McGA.

17 Caroline Pelton to Carrie Pelton, Montreal, 4 September 1861, Pelton Papers, McGA.

18 Caroline Pelton to Carrie Pelton, Montreal, 5 March 1863, Pelton Papers, McGA.

19 Smith-Rosenberg, "The Female World," 11, 16.

20 Caroline Pelton to Carrie Pelton, Montreal, 4 October 1861, 25 August 1867, Pelton Papers, McGA.

21 Bradbury, *Working Families*; McLean, "Single Again," 127-50.

22 Brun, *Vie et mort*, 69-74; Bouchard, *Quelques arpents d'Amérique*, 159, 163; Morris, *Men, Women and Property*.

23 Petition, Susanna Agnew, widow of John Agnew, late Quarter Master of His Majesties 71 Regt. of Light Infantry, Lower Canada Land Papers, RG 1, L3L, vol. 29, Microfilm no. C2504, 159491-92, LAC; Bushman, "Family Security"; W.G. Scott to Carrie Pelton, 11 June 1861, Pelton Papers, McGA.

24 W.G. Scott to Caroline Pelton, 27 June 1861, Pelton Papers, McGA.

25 Thanks to Mary Anne Poutanen for searching the records for me.

26 Caroline Pelton to Carrie Pelton, 5 March 1863, Pelton Papers, McGA.

27 *Lovell's*, 1873-82; Marriage registration, Maria Louisa Pelton and James Beale, St. George Anglican Church, 1871; Marriage registration, Charlotte Jane Pelton and John MacKedie, St. George Anglican Church, 1872; Marriage registration, Caroline Henrietta Pelton and John Shearer, St. George Anglican Church, 1874; BAnQM.

28 Lebsock, *The Free Women*, 159.

29 Nootens, *Fous, prodigues et ivrognes*, deals with profligate sons later in the century.

30 Young, *George-Etienne Cartier*, 31-35; 56-60; J.L. Roy, *Édouard-Raymond Fabre*; Bonenfant, "Sir George-Etienne Cartier," *DCB*.

31 J.L. Roy, *Édouard-Raymond Fabre*, 34.

32 Census, 1861, Montreal, folio 14891; Young, "Édouard-Charles Fabre," *DCB*.

33 Tutelle, Minors John Mills, 17 November 1847, 1658-1882, no. 771, BAnQM.

34 Of widows heading a family in 1861, 9 percent had one servant, 3 percent had two, and less than 2 percent listed three or more.

35 Census, 1881, Montreal, Saint Antoine ward, division 4, p. 58; *Lovell's*, 1881.

36 Hart, *Fall of New France*, 1888; Hart, *The Quebec Act, 1774*; Rome, "Adolphus Mordecai Hart," *DCB*; Hart Family Papers, 2611-2-5, McGA.

37 Darrow, *Revolution in the House,* 154.
38 Burgess, "Work, Family and Community"; Poutanen, "'For the Benefit'"; Ruddel, *Les apprentis artisans*; Sweeny, "Internal Dynamics."
39 Census, 1881, Montreal, Saint Louis ward, division 1, p. 66.
40 Census, 1861, folio 11254; Census, 1881, Montreal, Saint Louis ward, division 6, p. 2; *Lovell's,* 1848-96; Führer, *The Mysteries*; Davidoff et al., *The Family Story,* 161, emphasis in original.
41 Census, 1881, Montreal, Saint Antoine ward, 9, 1; *Lovell's,* 1881-82, identifies her as living at no. 8 Mountain Street, Saint Antoine ward, with Hermine Barron. The previous year, her daughter, Sophie, was listed as a widow at this address.
42 Davidoff et al., *The Family Story,* 7.
43 Dillon, *The Shady Side,* esp. 162-67; Bradbury, *Working Families,* 205.
44 Affidavit, 25 October 1858, Mitchell v. Brown, 28 February 1859, Superior Court, dossiers.
45 Harvey, "The Protestant Orphan Asylum," 158-59; On Catholic orphanages, see Lapointe-Roy, *Charité bien ordonnée,* 172-81; Bradbury, "The Fragmented Family."
46 Bradbury, "The Fragmented Family," 109-28. Of the 574 children identified in their registers between 1860 and 1884, 49 (10 percent) were definitely the daughters of widows; a further 141 (29 percent) were brought in and returned to their mothers, some of whom were widows. Such institutions also helped widowers, relieving them of the care of children while they worked; 166 fathers, 15 of whom were identified as widowers, left their children there for varying lengths of time. The average stay for daughters of widows was twenty months, of those identified as mothers seventeen months, and fourteen for fathers, Register, Orphans, Saint Alexis Orphanage, PASP.
47 *Trade Review,* 8 November 1867, 677; Canada, Sessional Papers, no. 12, 1868.
48 Canada, Sessional Papers, no. 10, 1884, and no. 17, 1885; Young with Tulchinsky, "Sir Hugh Allan," *DCB.*
49 Baskerville, *A Silent Revolution?* 79, 86.
50 Canada, Sessional Papers, no. 17, 1885.
51 Will, Constance Hart, 4 May 1898, Notary Reddy; Baskerville, *A Silent Revolution?* 104-5 and personal communication.
52 Census, 1861, 1871, 1881, 1891, Saint Antoine ward, Montreal; *Lovell's,* 1842-90.
53 Bradbury, *Working Families,* 195-97; Dillon, *The Shady Side,* 171, reports 12 percent of elderly widows in Ontario and Quebec listed an occupation in 1901.
54 McKenna, *A Life of Propriety*; Davidoff and Hall, *Family Fortunes.*
55 *Lovell's,* 1857, 1861, 1863.
56 Aitken-Swan, *Widows in Australia,* 1.
57 Bradbury, Single Parents Montreal, 1861.
58 Lebsock, *The Free Women,* 193.
59 Caroline Pelton to Carrie Pelton, [?] September 1862, no. 975, 1; Sister to Carrie, n.d., no. 975, 10; Pelton Papers, McGA.
60 Bradbury, Single Parents Montreal, 1861.
61 Caroline Pelton to Carrie Pelton, Montreal, 5 March 1863, Pelton Papers, McGA; Census, 1881, Montreal, Saint Antoine ward, 12, 38.
62 *Montreal Transcript,* 23 August 1842; *Montreal Gazette,* 12 June 1861; Davidoff et al., *The Family Story,* 159.
63 Inventory, Genant and Decousse, 20 September 1853, Notary Mathieu; *Lovell's,* 1845-70; Census, 1861, Montreal, folio 961.
64 Census, 1881, Hochelaga district, Longue Pointe, division O, 19.
65 *Lovell's,* 1881; Census, 1881, Montreal, Saint Louis ward, 1, 66.
66 Ibid.; Gilliland and Olson, "Residential Segregation," 45.

67   Bradbury, Single Parents Montreal 1861; Bradbury, *Working Families.*
68   Lacelle, *Urban Domestic Servants.*
69   Wulf, *Not All Wives,* 133-47; K.E. Wood, *Masterful Women,* 84; Lebsock, *The Free Women,* 150-90; Anderson, *Family Structure*; McLean, "Single Again"; Wilson, *Life after Death,* 63-65.
70   *Montreal Gazette,* 21 April 1826.
71   *La Minerve,* 24 October 1827, 29 October 1827.
72   In 1861, only 26 percent of such workers headed their own family, compared to 53 percent of all the city's widows. Of the 381 widows in this sector, 64 percent were residing in their employers' homes or in institutions in which they appear to have worked.
73   Harvey, "The Protestant Orphan Asylum," 159; Census, 1861, Montreal, folio 4103; Lacelle, *Urban Domestic Servants;* Davidoff et al., *The Family Story,* 162, 175.
74   Marriage registration, 21 December 1823, St. Gabriel Street Presbyterian Church; Census 1861, folio 10975; Death registration, 24 November 1864.
75   Strasser, *Never Done,* 104-12; Bradbury, *Working Families,* 156-58; *Montreal Transcript,* 23 August 1842.
76   Census, 1861, Montreal, folio 12690.
77   Census, 1881, Montreal, St. Louis ward, division 4, 137; *Lovell's,* 1869-83. See also Führer, *The Mysteries of Montreal; Lovell's,* 1842-81.
78   Poutanen, "'For the Benefit'"; Census, 1861, folio 9892; Steedman, *Angels of the Workplace*; McIntosh, "Sweated Labour."
79   *Mackay's,* 1861-62, names widow Christina Mackay as owner.
80   Plamondon, "Une femme d'affaires"; Baskerville, *A Silent Revolution?*; Lebsock, *The Free Women,* 191; S.I. Lewis, "Business Widows," 115-39; Gamber, "Gendered Concerns."
81   The 1860 city evaluation role listed her house on St. Genevieve as worth $3,000, and the adjoining ground, orchard, and partially completed house at $36,000. Rôles de valeur locative – feuilles de routes (hereafter cited as RVL), Saint Antoine ward, Archives de la ville de Montréal (hereafter cited as AVM).
82   Census, 1861, folio 15183; *Lovell's,* 1849-67.
83   Census, 1861, folio 12774; Sweeny, "Lovell's 1880-81"; Census, 1881, Montreal, Saint Mary's ward, 5, 10.
84   Census, 1861, folio 14204.
85   Dunae, "Sex, Charades"; Census, 1881, Montreal, Hochelaga district, Saint Jean Baptiste Village, 1, 90.
86   RVL, 1862-63; 1866-67, Saint Antoine ward, Latour Street, AVM.
87   Mackay's, 1861-64; *Lovell's,* 1843-90.
88   *Lovell's,* 1843-70; Inventory, Mills, 30 November 1847, Notary Pelton.
89   Rome, "Adolphus Mordecai Hart," *DCB; Montreal Gazette,* 24 March 1879, 14 December 1898; MacLeod, "Salubrious Settings," 218: RVL, 1863-67, 1876, 1884, AVM; *Lovell's,* 1863-97.
90   Will, William Sutherland, probated 16 February 1875, BAnQM; *Lovell's,* 1846-87; Census, 1881, Saint Antoine ward, 3, 23.
91   *Lovell's,* 1843-1904.
92   Wilson, *Life after Death,* 61.
93   Ballantyne and Burton, eds., *Moving Subjects,* 9.
94   RVL, 1862-1900, AVM; *Lovell's,* 1862-1900; Census, 1871, Montreal, Saint Antoine ward, 12:15, hh 38. They were first recorded as living with her when the 1874-75 city directory was organized. The latter rent placed them among the top 7.1 percent of tax roll households, according to Gilliland and Olson, "Residential Segregation," 35.

95   Gossage, *Families in Transition,* 122; Gilliland and Olson, "Residential Segregation," 46.
96   Census, 1881, Saint Antoine ward, 4, 30; Pelton grave, MRC; K.E. Wood, *Masterful Women,* 67; Smith-Rosenberg, "The Female World," 11.
97   Marriage registration, Saint George's Anglican Church, 1874; Shearer, Mackedie, and Co., *Lovell's,* 1872-73 − 1874-75.
98   N. [?] Scott to Caroline Pelton, Montreal, 29 December 1873, Pelton Papers, McGA, emphasis in original; Census, 1881, Saint Antoine ward, 4, 30.
99   *Lovell's,* 1861-94.
100   RVL, Saint Antoine, 1862-63 − 1884, AVM.
101   *Lovell's,* 1864-65; 1868-75.
102   *Lovell's,* 1875-76 − 1882.
103   Bradbury, Single Parents Montreal, 1861; Dillon, The 1881 Canadian Census Project.
104   Dillon, *The Shady Side,* 58; Census 1881, Montreal, Saint Antoine ward, H, 4, p. 30, household 144.
105   I could definitively identify only forty-seven widows from these two generations in the 1861 census. Of ten middle-class and elite widows, seven were heads, as were ten of the twenty-three widows of craftsmen, but one of the nine unskilled workers' widows.
106   Census, 1861, folio 13,563; Seccombe, *Weathering the Storm,* 65; Ruggles, *Prolonged Connections,* 3-6.
107   Dillon, *The Shady Side,* 169.
108   Of the 1,708 widows we identified as living with their children in 1861, 1,051 were heads, compared to 344 of the 1,696 without co-resident children.
109   It is frustratingly difficult to identify widows definitively across time in censuses because of the ways their names are reported. Eight of the eleven elite and middle-class widows, thirteen of the twenty-three craftsmen's widows, and two of the seven labourers' widows from both cohorts definitely identified in the 1861 census were living with offspring.
110   K.E. Wood, *Masterful Women,* 143.
111   Morris, *Men, Women and Property,* 258.
112   Darroch, "Families, Fostering"; Jalland, *Death*; Wood, *Masterful Women.*
113   K.M. Brown, *Good Wives,* 297; Wulf, *Not All Wives*; Wilson, *Life after Death,* citation at 113.

Chapter 12: Final Years, Final Wishes
1   Will, Caroline Walker, probated 21 October 1841.
2   Ibid.
3   Marriage contract, Walker and Harris, 5 June 1826, Notary Griffin.
4   Codicil, Constance Hannah Hart, probated 4 April 1899.
5   Lebsock, *The Free Women,* 115, 135; Wilson, *Life after Death,* 22.
6   Davidoff et al., *The Family Story,* 7; Grau, "Residence Patterns of Aged Widows," 157-73; Dillon, "Women and the Dynamics of Marriage," 447-83; Dillon, *The Shady Side.*
7   We located causes of 172 widows' deaths in the records of the fabrique, the Protestant cemetery records, the coroners' records, and occasionally parish registers.
8   Among these 172 widows, 31 percent were recorded as dying of old age, senility, or debility; 15 percent of lung-related diseases, including consumption or tuberculosis; 8 percent of a heart problem; 7 percent of "dropsy"; 6 percent each of "paralysis" and cancer; and 5 percent of some kind of accident.

9 Thanks to Darcy Ingram, who transcribed some Montreal coroners' reports. Those he found were for 1830-47, some in 1849, 1863, and 1867 to 1868, and June to December 1866. Coronors inquests, BAnQM.

10 Census, 1881, Saint Antoine ward, division 4, p. 58; Census, 1891, Montreal, Saint Antoine ward, district 172, household 21; 118 Durocher Street, Saint Antoine ward, RVL, 1861-1890, AVM; *Lovell's,* 1879-98. Constance was at 118 Durocher Street at the Prince Arthur end. Miriam lived at 314 Prince Arthur, between Durocher and Suter.

11 Will, Hart, 4 May 1898, Notary J.F. Reddy; Codicil, Hart, probated 4 April 1899.

12 Dillon, *The Shady Side,* 154-63; Stavenuiter, "Last Years of Life," 223.

13 Dillon, *The Shady Side,* 163, 167-72; Fauve-Chamoux, "La femme seule," 212; Bradbury, *Working Families,* 206.

14 Stotts-McLaren, "Becoming Indispensable"; K.E. Wood, *Masterful Women,* 146.

15 Wulf, *Not All Wives,* 87; Seccombe, *Weathering the Storm,* 67.

16 Lyman, ed., *Geneaology,* 32-35; MacLeod, "Salubrious Settings," 218. On Ada Maria and her mysterious death in 1901, see "The Redpath Mansion Mystery," http://www.canadianmysteries.ca/.

17 British Census, 1881, folio 0669/47, p. 34.

18 Burnside Place, Saint Antoine ward, 1875, 1876; Fort Street, 1884-90, RVL, AVM.

19 From 1878, *Lovell's* listed her daughter before her in the street listings. *Lovell's,* 1878-89. I have not found Caroline in the 1891 census.

20 Gratton, "New History of the Aged," 12.

21 *Lovell's,* 1874-83; Census, 1881, Saint Louis ward, 4, 137.

22 Census, 1881, Saint Antoine ward, 9, 1; Census, Montreal, 1891, Saint Antoine ward, 269; *Lovell's,* 1891-95.

23 S. Stewart, "The Elderly Poor," 219; Stavenuiter, "Last Years of Life"; Montigny, "'Foistered upon the Government.'"

24 In the 1820s generation, 206 Canadiennes definitely became widows, 145 from the 1840s did. Fourteen women from cohort 1 and nine from cohort 2 definitely spent time with one of these two orders. As Protestant institutions usually listed women by their married names and seldom indicated their marital status, correct identification is very difficult.

25 *Jewish Encyclopedia,* Cyrus Adler and Clarence I. de Sola, "Canada," http://www.jewishencyclopedia.com.

26 Bradbury, "Mourir chrétiennement."

27 Lapointe-Roy, *Charité bien ordonnée.*

28 Fecteau, *La Liberté du pauvre*; Bradbury, "Review: La Liberté."

29 Hardy, *Contrôle social*; Fecteau, *La Liberté du pauvre*; Strange and Loo, *Making Good.*

30 Harvey, "The Protestant Orphan Asylum"; Harvey, "Le réseau charitable"; Harvey, "Les églises protestantes," 51-68.

31 Registre des femmes, 1859, PASP; *La Minerve,* 28 December 1858, 5 January 1859.

32 Goose, "Poverty, Old Age and Gender."

33 Lapointe-Roy, *Charité bien ordonnée,* 229-69; *Report of the Annual Meeting of the Montreal Protestant House of Industry and Refuge* (hereafter cited as MPHIR), 1872, reports 303 cords of wood were given to the needy, "principally widows with families," 12.

34 Lapointe-Roy, *Charité bien ordonnée,* 229-69, 276-77, 281-83; MPHIR, 1871-89.

35 Cited in Harvey, "The Protestant Orphan Asylum," 77.

36 Ladies' Benevolent Society, database.

37 Harvey, "The Protestant Orphan Asylum," 322, lists the Protestant charities across the century. On the national societies, see Leitch, "Importance of Being 'English'?"

38 Poutanen, "'To Indulge'"; Census, Montreal, 1861, 1881.

39 Registre des femmes, 1830-59, PASP; Chronicles, 4:165-66, PASP.

40 Reasons were registered for only 80 of 189 women over age fifty admitted to the Ladies' Benevolent Society, 1838-99. Forty-four (55 percent) were described as destitute, or destitute and aged; nine as unable to work or support themselves; seven as homeless; four as helpless, two as starving; and two had caretakers who could no longer look after them. Montigny, "'Foistered upon the Government,'" 812.

41 Will, Antoine Hurtubise, 17 January 1849, Notary Martin; Necrologies, Hurtubise, 18 January 1849, FPNDM.

42 Pastoral letter from the bishop of Montreal, *Mandements*, January 1850, 82.

43 Anon., *Biographies de la mère Gamelin*, 126-27.

44 Institut Providence, *Notes historiques*, 24-27, 36, 94; Agathe Séné took the name Sister Zotique. Émilie Séné seems to have died 13 December 1849; Bourassa, *Madame Gamelin*, 58; Sadlier, trans., *Life of Mother Gamelin*; Canonical examinations, Sisters of Providence, file 844-12, ACAM; Anon., *Biographies de la mère Gamelin*, 126-31.

45 Registre des femmes, 1830-91, PASP. The Sisters of Providence recorded occupations for the husbands of 122 of 304 women identified as widows. Of these, forty-five (37 percent) appear unskilled; thirty-six of them labourers; forty-one (34 percent) were in a range of crafts, including twenty-one in construction; twenty-six (21 percent) were in agriculture. Only nine (7 percent) were widows of elite or middle-class men.

46 Unskilled 8; crafts 7; agriculture 1; elite 2; lower commerce 1; unknown 4.

47 Jean Girouard to his wife, November 1844, reproduced in *MR*, 21 November 1851; Sadlier, trans., *Life of Mother Gamelin*, 42-43.

48 Registre des femmes, 1830-91 ($n = 486$), PASP.

49 Bradbury, "Mourir chrétiennement," 152.

50 *MR*, 21 November 1851, translated in Sadlier, trans., *Life of Mother Gamelin*, 42.

51 Chronicles, 2, August-September 1871, November 1871; Chronicles, 3, 1877, 141; Chronicles, 4, 1881, 37-40, PASP; Project to make corsets, 26, 28, 29 April 1875, Sisters of Providence, ACAM. Pine gum syrup was used to break fevers and for other ailments.

52 Chronicles, 1, 2, 3, 4, PASP; Quebec, *JLAPC*, 1855-91. The Sisters of Providence received an annual subsidy of $350 in 1855-57, $1,400 in 1858-61, $1,000 in 1862, $1,120 in 1864-74, and $784 in 1889-91.

53 Chronicles, 1, 2, 3, 4, PASP.

54 Pension agreement, Brazeau, 2 September 1844, folder 531; Donation, 12 July 1850, Campagnard, file 975, PASP-CEG; Will, Nowlan, 14 August 1849, Notary D.-E. Papineau.

55 Chronicles, 4, 37, describes the death of an eighty-three-year-old widow who had been a pensioner for twenty-five years, PASP; 30 August 1851, Sisters of Providence, ACAM.

56 Missions fermées, Canada, vol. 1, Hospice Saint-Joseph, 1-70, quotation at 42-43, PASP; *La Minerve*, 12 April 1877.

57 Bradbury, "Mourir chrétiennement," 159-63; Chronicles, 3, 1877, 133, and 4, 1883, 175, PASP.

58 Chronicles, 1, 2, 3, 4, PASP; Sadlier, trans., *Life of Mother Gamelin*, 32.

59 Chronicles, 2, 3, 4 December 1869, January 1883, January 1884, and Registre des Dames de la Charité, 6 October 1862, 19 November 1864, PASP; Young, *George-Etienne Cartier*, 31-33, 56-60.

60 Bradbury, "Mourir chrétiennement"; Chronicles, 2, February 1871, PASP.

61 Chronicles, 4, 1882, 70, PASP.

62 Registre des femmes, PASP.

63 Cook, "A Quiet Place to Die."

64 Fifty of the initial fifty-two elderly inmates. Registre des femmes, PASP.

65 Among the 430 women who entered between 1830 and 1891 for whom dates of entry and departure are clearly recorded, 26 percent remained for under a year; 19 percent for twelve to twenty-three months, 23 percent for two to four years, 21 percent for five to nine years, and the remaining 13 percent for ten or more years.

66 Langlois, *Le catholicisme au féminin*, 71; Danylewycz, *Taking the Veil*.

67 Lacelle, "Marie-Marguerite Dufrost de Lajemmerais," *DCB*.

68 Ancien Journal, 1, 1688-1857, 538-39; Chroniques Hospice St. Joseph, 1854-92; Registre d'admission des pauvres et orphelines, 1854-1907, Hospice St. Joseph, ASGM, AN1; Lapointe-Roy, *Charité bien ordonnée*, 168-69; Huguet-Latour, *Annuaire de Ville Marie*, 1863, 66-70.

69 Ancien Journal, 3, 1870, 197-220, ASGM.

70 Registre des pauvres, ASGM; *Lovell's*, 1842-61; Canada, Census of 1861, folio 10252.

71 Bradbury, "Mourir chrétiennement."

72 *MR*, 21 October 1851; Death register, 22 January 1878, NDM; Thifault, "L'enfermement asilaire."

73 Thifault, "L'enfermement asilaire," 10, 63, 74, 94, 208, 213, 215.

74 Ibid., 190.

75 On the demise of her co-workers, see Poutanen, "Bonds of Friendship." Thifault, "L'enfermement asilaire," xii, 62, argues that care and living conditions deteriorated during the 1920s.

76 Codicil, Constance Hannah Hart, probated 4 April 1899; Lebsock, *The Free Women*, xi, 112, 130-35, quotations at xi, 135.

77 Morris, *Men, Women and Property*, 128-36, quotations at 128-29.

78 Wilson, *Life after Death*, 37.

79 Morris, *Men, Women and Property*, 136.

80 Systematic comparisons of widows' and widowers' wills, along with those of their spouses, would better reveal gendered differences than just comparing men's and women's. On single women's wills, see Renaud, "Une place à soi?"

81 As noted earlier, finding notarial wills in Montreal is challenging without any central alpabetized registry. The list of probated wills makes such wills easier to find.

82 Chused, "Married Women's Property"; McCrum, "Inheritance and the Family," 165; Green, "Independent Women," 218-19.

83 Holograph will, Louise de Lotbinière, probated 16 October 1869.

84 Will, Mary-Jane Ross, probated 15 April 1885.

85 Will, Harris, probated 28 November 1828; Will, Caroline Walker, probated 21 October 1841.

86 Will, Mary Lloyd, and Codicil, 16 February 1867, probated 15 March 1867. She purchased a two-hundred-foot plot, paying 30 cents a foot. She died 17 November 1866. MRC.

87 Will, Sarah Walker, probated 28 January 1880.

88 Lebsock, *The Women*, 112-44; Morris, *Men, Women and Property*, 128-32; Will, Constance Hart, 4 May 1898, Notary Reddy, Palais de Justice, Montreal; Codicil, Hart, probated 4 April 1899.

89 Will, Catherine Wade, probated 15 November 1844; Morris, *Women, Men and Property*, 239.

90 Will, Elizabeth Parslow, probated 7 September 1898; Will, Elizabeth Lang, 13 May 1889, Notary Brodie.
91 Lebsock, *The Free Women,* 135.
92 Morris, *Men, Women and Property,* 109; Darrow, *Revolution in the House,* 9-11.
93 Will, Constance Hart, 4 May 1898, Notary John Reddy, Palais de Justice, Montreal.
94 Chronicles, 1, September 1851, PASP; Giroux, *Une Heroïne du Canada;* Bourassa, *Madame Gamelin;* Tessier, *Vie de Mère Gamelin* (1900), citations from Sadlier, trans., *Life of Mother Gamelin,* 229-35; Anon., *Biographies de la mère Gamelin;* Institut de la Providence, *Histoire des Filles de la Charité,* vols. 1-2 (1928-40); Robillard, *Émilie Tavernier-Gamelin;* "Mother Émilie Tavernier," http://www.providence.org/phs/archives/.
95 Sadlier, trans., *Life of Mother Gamelin,* 233-34; "Mother Émilie Tavernier," http://www.providence.org/phs/archives/; Bradbury, "Mourir chrétiennement"; Kselman, *Death and the Afterlife,* 89-95.
96 Sadlier, trans., *Life of Mother Gamelin,* 234; Robillard, *Émilie Tavernier-Gamelin,* 305.
97 Robillard, *Émilie Tavernier-Gamelin,* 304-5; Sadlier, trans., *Life of Mother Gamelin,* 234-35; *MR,* 26 September 1851.
98 *MR,* 30 September 1851.
99 *La Minerve,* 25 September 1851, 2 October 1851; *MR,* 26 September 1851, 30 September 1851, 7 October 1851, 10 October 1851, 21 October 1851, 28 October 1851, 21 November 1851; *Le Moniteur Canadien,* 26 September 1851.
100 Anon., *Biographies de la mère Gamelin,* 125-46.
101 Bradbury, "Mourir chrétiennement," argues that dying a Christian death with the full Catholic rites was a feature attracting women to such institutions.
102 Necrologies, Marie-Anne Séné, 4 March 1885, FPNDM; *La Minerve,* 2 March 1885. Of 133 Catholic widows from the 1820s marriages for whom we have details on their funerals from the records of the fabrique, fifty-three (40 percent) had contributed to a prayer union, which paid some of their funeral expenses.
103 Chronicles, 2, 1871, PASP.
104 Chronicles, 3, April 1877, 89, PASP; *La Minerve,* 12 April 1877.
105 *La Patrie,* 27 February 1904, 7 March 1904.
106 Strange, *Death, Grief and Poverty,* 138; Petitclerc, *"Nous protégeons l'infortune."*
107 An Act ... respecting the practice of Physic and surgery, and the Study of Anatomy, 1872, c. 29, Quebec; Young, *Respectable Burial,* 13; Rankin, "Anatomically Incorrect"; Death registration, St. Jean de Dieu Asylum, 25 January 1878, BAnQM. Many institutions sought to evade this outcome for their residents. Encouraging payment to burial societies, or, as in Marie-Anne Séné's case, the prayer union, was one way. Petitclerc, *"Nous protégeons l'infortune."*
108 Young, *Respectable Burial,* 13; Strange, *Death, Grief and Poverty,* 61.
109 Young, *Respectable Burial,* 13. See also the photos in Rankin, "Anatomically Incorrect."
110 Death registration, MRC; *Montreal Gazette,* 10 December 1900. We found ninety-three death notices for wives who became widows. Seventy-four indicated where the widow had died: thirty-eight (51 percent) indicated it was their residence, twenty-seven (37 percent) at a son or daughter's (usually identified as her son-in-law's), one with other relatives, and six (8 percent) in institutions. The numbers are small and uneven, but a higher percent of the nineteen Protestant widows (68 percent compared to 44 percent) were listed as dying in their own residence, whereas a higher proportion of the fifty-five Catholics were with children (39 percent compared to 32 percent of Protestants) or in institutions (11 percent compared to none).

111   The exception was the Baptist *Montreal Register* which during the 1840s and 1850s frequently featured narratives of the deaths of Montrealers and people across the globe that taught good evangelical living and dying.

112   *Montreal Gazette,* 19 November 1866, 21 October 1889, 23 November 1876.

113   *La Patrie,* 27 February 1904.

114   *Montreal Gazette,* 6 October 1841; Young, "Death, Burial."

115   *Montreal Gazette,* 21 January 1880; *La Minerve,* 28 February 1884; *Montreal Gazette,* 6 January 1898.

116   Only seven of the ninety death notices for widows gave no details about the funeral, two announced that it was to be private, and thirty-one gave details but listed no time.

117   *La Minerve* and *Montreal Gazette,* 15 April 1879.

118   Ibid.

119   Armstrong, "Charles-Séraphin Rodier," *DCB;* Radforth, *Royal Spectacle,* 5, 264.

120   Among the thirty-nine funerals announced for Catholic widows where the time was indicated, three were at 6 a.m., ten at 7 a.m., eighteen at 8 a.m., seven at 9 a.m., and only two in the afternoon. Among the thirteen Protestant notices indicating a time, all but two were in the afternoon.

121   Young, *Respectable Burial,* 33-34; Lot F: 325, MRC.

122   Strange, *Death, Grief and Poverty,* 163.

Conclusion

1   On First Nations widows, see Carter, *Importance of Being Monogamous.*

2   Walby, *Patriarchy at Work.*

3   Stone, *The Family;* Ward, *Courtship.*

4   Gilliland and Olson, "Residential Segregation," 45, point to higher "out" marriage among Irish-Catholic women.

5   Gérin-Lajoie, *La Communauté Légale,* 18.

6   *Lovell's,* 1894-95.

7   McCallum, "Prairie Women."

8   Normand and Hudon, "Le contrôle," 196.

9   Fecteau, "La dynamique sociale," 496-98; Fecteau, *La Liberté du pauvre,* 63, 146, 343.

10   Danylewycz, *Taking the Veil.*

11   Morin, "La perception," 9, 10, 18.

12   Prentice et al., *Canadian Women,* 439-40; Collective Clio, *L'histoire des femmes,* 528.

Bibliography

Archival Collections

Archives de l'archeveché de Montréal (ACAM)
Soeurs de la Charité de la Providence de Montréal, Fonds 525-106.

Archives de la Ville de Montréal (AVM)
Fonds du Service des finances et du contrôle budgétaire, Fonds VM2.
  Rôles d'évaluation foncière.
  Rôles de valeur locative – feuilles de routes.

Archives du Séminaire de Québec (ASQ)
Fonds Viger-Verreau Fonds, P32.

Archives of the Sisters of Charity of Montreal (Grey Nuns) (ASGM)
Ancien Journal, 1: Notes sur l'Hôpital Général des Soeurs Grises de Montréal, 1688-1857.
Ancien Journal, 2, 1857-67.
Ancien Journal, 3, 1867-77.
Circulaire Mensuelle, adressée aux diverses maisons de l'Institut, 1, 1877-80.
Circulaire Mensuelle, 2, 1881-83.
Circulaire Mensuelle, 3, 1884-87.
Circulaire Mensuelle, 4, 1882-92.
Chroniques Hospice Saint-Joseph, 1854-92, L10/H4.
Registre d'admission des pauvres, 2, 1797-1854, G6/IR3.
Registres d'admission des pauvres et des orphelins, 3, 1854-90, G6/IR5.
Registre d'admission des pauvres et des enfants trouvés, 1834-1945, G6/IR9.
Registre d'admission des pauvres et des orphelins (Hospice St. Joseph), 1854-1907, L10/T6.
Registre no. 1, Hospice St. Charles à Montréal, 1877-94, L35/R1.

Bibliothèque et Archives nationales du Québec à Montréal (BAnQM)

Judicial District of Montreal
Clôtures d'inventaires, CV601.
Dossiers, 1859. Ex Parte Maria Mitchell en destitution de tutelle, Petitioner v. John O. Brown, tutor, Superior Court, Montreal, 28 February 1859, no. 849, TP11, S2, SS2, SSS1, 1858.

Dossiers des tutelles et curatelles, CC601, S1-2.
Enquêtes du coroner, 1831-47, 1855, 1863, 1866-68, TL 32, S26, SS1.
Greffes des notaires, 1823-1904, CN601.
Registers of Births, Deaths, and Marriages, 1823-1910, CE601.
Testaments, CT601.

Private Papers
Collection Charles Phillips, 1770-1957, Fonds P148.
  Livres d'élection de l'élection de 1832 à Montréal, quartier Ouest.
  Listes des témoins entendus relativement à l'enquête sur les événements qui se
  sont produits lors de l'élection de 1832 à Montréal.

Genealogical Research Instruments
Loiselle Index of Catholic marriages celebrated in Quebec, Ontario, New Brunswick, and New England.

Judicial District of Bedford
Testaments, tutelles et curatelles, 1858-78, CT502, S58, SS2.

Fabrique of the Parish of Notre Dame (FPND)
Necrologies, 1823-26.

Library and Archives Canada (LAC)
Census returns, Montreal, 1831, 1842, 1861, 1871.
Census online, Montreal, 1881, 1891, 1901, http://www.collectionscanada.gc.ca/
  census/.
Civil secretary papers, RG 2 A1.
Duvernay, Ludger, collection, 1814-52, R6204-0-8-F.
Forrest, Georginna, and family fonds, 1849-89, R2953-0-5-E.
Funeral invitations collection, 1790-1856, Microfilm H-1807.
Hoyle, Robert, fonds, 1826-44, R2734-0-8-E.
Joseph, Abraham, fonds, R5374-0-4-E.
  Fanny David Joseph diaries.
  Abraham Joseph diaries.
Westcott-Papineau, Mary Eleanor, fonds, 1810-89, R4386-0-7-E.

McCord Museum (MMA)
Badgley family fonds, 1801-1929, P195.
Bagg, Abner, and Stanley fonds, 1810-45, P070.
Hale, Edward, fonds, P036.
Hart family fonds, 1760-1909, P013.

McGill Rare Book Department (McGRB)
Griffin, Frederick papers, 1827-76, Large mss., CM68.B224.
Harwood, Robert Unwin papers, 1823-53, De Lery Macdonald Papers, CH215.
  S193 a and b, CH213.S191.
Lyman-Corse Family Papers, 1815-91, CH404.002.9, CH258.S235, CH371.S331,
  CH275.Bd234.

McGill University Archives (McGA)
Hart family papers, 1820-1972, MG 2018.
Pelton, Caroline Henrietta, papers, 1842-1905, MG 2020.

Mount Royal Cemetery, Archives (MRC)
Alphabetical listing of burials
Listing by lot numbers
Plot owners

Providence Archives, Sisters of Providence, Montreal (PASP)
Archives de la Cause d'Émilie Gamelin
Chroniques de l'Asile de la Providence, Maison-Mère, 1, 1828-64, n.p., typewritten.
Chroniques de la Maison-Mère, 2, 1864-72.
Chroniques de la Maison-Mère, 3, 1876-81.
Chroniques de la Maison-Mère, 4, 1881-86.
Registre des femmes vieilles et infirmes de l'Asile de la Providence, 1830-91.
Registre pour les orphelines de l'orphelinat St. Alexis, 1860-1884.
Registre des vieillards et infirmes de l'Asile de la Providence, 1849-91.

Government Publications
British Parliamentary Papers. *Reports from Select Committees on the Civil Government of Canada and the affairs of Lower Canada with Minutes of Evidence.* Presented to the House of Commons. (1828) Shannon, Ireland: Irish University Press, 1968.
Canada. Journals of the Legislative Assembly of the Province of Canada, 1841-66.
—. Provincial Statutes of Canada, 1841-66.
—. Statutes of Canada, 1867-1901.
Lower Canada. Code of Civil Procedure of Lower Canada from the amended roll deposited in the Office of the Clerk of the Legislative Council as directed by the Act 29-30 Vict. Chap. 25, 1866.
—. Journals of the House of Assembly, 1791-1837.
—. Ordinances made and passed by the administrator of the government and Special Council for the affairs of the province of Lower Canada, 1838-41.
—. Provincial Statutes of Lower Canada, 1791-1837.
Quebec. Statutes, 1867-1901.

Law Reports
Legal News, vols. 1-14, 1878-91.
Lower Canada Jurist, vols. 1-35, 1857-91.
Lower Canada Reports, vols. 1-17, 1851-67.
Montreal Law Reports, Court of Queen's Bench, vols. 1-7, 1885-91.
Montreal Law Reports, Superior Court, vols. 1-7, 1885-91.
Quebec Law Reports, vols. 1-17, 1875-91.
Revue de législation et de jurisprudence et collection de décisions des divers tribunaux du Bas Canada, vols. 1-3, 1845-48.

Newspapers
L'Ami du Peuple, de l'Ordre et des Lois
L'Aurore des Canadas
Le Canadien
La Minerve
Montreal Daily Witness
Montreal Gazette
Montreal Register
Montreal Transcript and Commercial Advertiser

Other Sources

Aitken-Swan, Jean. *Widows in Australia*. Sydney: Council of Social Service of New South Wales, 1962.

Akenson, Donald. *The Irish in Ontario: A Study in Rural History*. Montreal/Kingston: McGill-Queen's University Press, 1984.

Anderson, Michael. *Family Structure in Nineteenth Century Lancashire*. Cambridge, UK: University Press, 1971.

Anon. *Biographies de la mère Gamelin et de ses six compagnes fondatrices de l'Institut des filles de la Charité servates des pauvres dites Soeurs de la Providence de Montréal*. Montreal: Sisters of Providence, 1918.

Anon. *The Canadian Men and Women of the Time: A Handbook of Canadian Biography*. Toronto: W. Briggs, 1898.

Ariès, Phillipe. *The Hour of Our Death*. Translated by Helen Weaver. New York: Knopf, 1981 [1977].

–. *Western Attitudes toward Death: From the Middle Ages to the Present*. Baltimore: Johns Hopkins University Press, 1974.

Armstrong, James. *A Treatise on the Law Relating to Marriages in Lower Canada*. Montreal: John Lovell, 1857.

Aubin, Georges, ed. *Louis-Hyppolyte La Fontaine: Correspondance générale*. Vol. 2, *Au nom de la loi: Lettres de Louis Hyppolyte La Fontaine à divers correspondants 1728-1847*. Montreal: Les Éditions varia, 2003.

Backhouse, Constance. *Colour-Coded: A Legal History of Racism in Canada, 1900-1950*. Toronto: Osgoode Society for Canadian Legal History/University of Toronto Press, 1999.

–. *Petticoats and Prejudice: Women and Law in Nineteenth-Century Canada*. Toronto: Women's Press, 1991.

–. "'Pure Patriarchy': Nineteenth-Century Canadian Marriage." *McGill Law Journal* 31 (1986): 264-312.

Badgley, William. *Remarks on Register Offices*. Montreal: Herald Office, 1836.

Baker, G. Blaine. "Law Practice and Statecraft in Mid Nineteenth Century Montreal: The Torrance-Morris Firm, 1848-1868." In *Essays in the History of Canadian Law*, Vol. 4, edited by Carol Wilton and David H. Flaherty, 45-91. Toronto: Osgoode Law Society and University of Toronto Press, 1981.

Ballantyne, Tony, and Antoinette Burton, eds. *Bodies in Contact: Rethinking Colonial Encounters in World History*. Durham, NC: Duke University Press, 2005.

–, eds. *Moving Subjects: Gender, Mobility, and Intimacy in an Age of Global Empire*. Urbana: University of Illinois Press, 2009.

Basch, Norma. *In the Eyes of the Law: Women, Marriage and Property in Nineteenth Century New York*. Ithaca, NY: Cornell University Press, 1982.

Baskerville, Peter. *A Silent Revolution? Gender and Wealth in English Canada, 1860-1930*. Montreal/Kingston: McGill-Queen's University Press, 2008.

Beaubien, Henry des Rivières. *Traité sur les lois civiles du Bas-Canada*. 3 vols. Montreal: Ludger Duvernay, 1832.

Beaudoin, Philippe. "Quelques observations sur les mariages irlandais dans la paroisse de Notre-Dame de Montréal (1840-1861)." *Études ethniques au Canada/ Canadian Ethnic Studies* 30, 1 (1998): 140-57.

Behlmer, George K. "Grave Doubts: Victorian Medicine, Moral Panic, and the Signs of Death." *Journal of British Studies* 42, 2 (April 2003): 206-35.

Bell, Rudolph M., and Virginia Yans, eds. *Women on Their Own: Interdisciplinary Perspectives on Being Single*. New Brunswick, NJ: Rutgers University Press, 2008.

Bennett, Judith. *History Matters: Patriarchy and the Challenge of Feminism.* Philadelphia: University of Pennsylvania Press, 2006.

Bentley, D.M.R. *Early Long Poems on Canada.* London, ON: Canadian Poetry Press, 1993.

Benton, Lauren. *Law and Colonial Cultures: Legal Regimes in World History, 1400-1900.* Cambridge: Cambridge University Press, 2002.

Bernard, Jean-Paul. *Les rébellions de 1837-38: Les Patriotes du Bas-Canada dans la mémoire collective et chez les historiens.* Montreal: Boréal Express, 1983.

Bernard, Jean-Paul, Paul-André Linteau, and Jean-Claude Robert. "La structure professionnelle de Montreal en 1825." *Revue d'histoire de l'Amérique française* 30, 3 (December 1976): 383-415.

–. "Les tablettes statistiques de Jacques Viger (1825)," Groupe de recherche sur la société montréalais au 19ᵉ siècle, Report 1972-73. Montreal: Department of History, Université du Québec à Montréal.

Bilson, Geoffrey. *A Darkened House: Cholera in Nineteenth-Century Canada.* Toronto: University of Toronto Press, 1980.

Blom, Ida. "The History of Widowhood: A Bibliographic Overview." *Journal of Family History* 16, 2 (April 1991): 191-210.

Blunt, Alison, and Gillian Rose, eds. *Writing Women and Space: Colonial and Postcolonial Geographies.* London: Guildford, 1994.

Bock, Gisela. "Women's History and Gender History: Aspects of an International Debate." *Gender and History* 1, 1 (1989): 7-30.

Boileau, Gilles. *Le 21 Mai 1832 sur la Rue du Sang.* Montreal: Editions de Meridien, 1999.

Bonnell, Victoria E., and Lynn Hunt, eds. *Beyond the Cultural Turn: New Directions in the Study of Society and Culture.* Berkeley: University of California Press, 1999.

Bonner, John. *An Essay on the Registry Laws of Lower Canada.* Quebec: John Lovell, 1852.

Borthwick, John Douglas. *History and Biographical Gazetteer of Montreal to the Year 1892.* Montreal: Lovell, 1892.

Bouchard, Gérard. *Quelques arpents d'Amérique: Population, économie, famille au Saguenay, 1838-1971.* Montreal: Boréal Express, 1996.

–. "Sur les rituels de la mort au Saguenay (1860-1920)." *Folklore canadien – Canadian Folklore* 14, 1 (1992): 123-39.

Bouchard, Gérard, and André La Rose. "Réglementation du contenu des actes de baptême, mariage et sepulture au Québec des origines à nos jours." *Revue d'histoire de l'Amérique française,* March 1981: 515-34.

Bourassa, L'Abbé G. *Madame Gamelin et les origines de la Providence: Lecture faite à la cloture du bazar annuel de l'Asile de la Providence.* Montreal: 1892.

Boylan, Anne M. *The Origins of Women's Activism: New York and Boston, 1797-1840.* Chapel Hill: University of North Carolina Press, 2002.

Bradbury, Bettina. "Canadian Children Who Lived with One Parent in 1901." In Sager and Baskerville, *Household Counts,* 247-301.

–. "Debating Dower: Patriarchy, Capitalism and Widows' Rights in Lower Canada." In Myers et al., *Power, Place and Identity,* 56-78.

–. "The Fragmented Family: Family Strategies in the Face of Death, Illness and Poverty, Montreal, 1860-1885." In *Childhood and Family in Canadian History,* edited by Joy Parr, 109-28. Toronto: McClelland and Stewart, 1982.

–. "From Civil Death to Separate Property: Changes in the Legal Rights of Married Women in Nineteenth-Century New Zealand." *New Zealand Journal of History* 29, 1 (1995): 40-66.

–. "'In England a Man Can Do as He Likes with His Property': Competing Visions of Marriage and Inheritance in Nineteenth-Century Quebec and the Cape Colony." Submitted for publication.

–. "Itineraries of Marriage and Widowhood in Nineteenth-Century Montreal." In *Mapping the Margins: Families and Social Discipline in Canada, 1700-1975*, edited by Nancy Christie and Michael Gauvreau, 103-140. Montreal/Kingston: McGill-Queen's University Press, 2004.

–. "Mourir chrétiennement: La vie et la mort dans les établissements catholiques pour personnes âgées à Montréal au XIXᵉ siècle." *Revue d'histoire de l'Amérique française* 46, 1 (Summer 1992): 143-75.

–. "Review: La Liberté du pauvre." *Bulletin d'histoire politique* 15, 2 (Winter 2007): 239-44.

–. "Single Parenthood in the Past: Canadian Census Categories, 1891-1951 and the 'Normal' Family." *Historical Methods* 33, 4 (2000): 211-17.

–. Single Parents Montreal, 1861. Database.

–. "Widows Negotiate the Law: The First Year of Widowhood in Early Nineteenth-Century Montreal." In Bradbury and Myers, *Negotiating Identities*, 120-48.

–. *Working Families: Age, Gender and Daily Survival in Industrializing Montreal.* Toronto: McClelland and Stewart, 1993.

Bradbury, Bettina, Peter Gossage, Evelyn Kolish, and Alan Stewart. "Property and Marriage: The Law and the Practice in Early Nineteenth-Century Montreal." *Histoire sociale/Social History* 26, 51 (1993): 9-39.

Bradbury, Bettina, and Tamara Myers, eds. *Negotiating Identities in Nineteenth- and Twentieth-Century Montreal.* Vancouver: UBC Press, 2005.

Brah, Avtar. *Cartographies of Diaspora: Contesting Identities.* London: Routledge, 1996.

Bremmer, Jan, and Lourens Van Den Bosch. *Between Poverty and the Pyre: Moments in the History of Widowhood.* London: Routledge, 1995.

Brierley, John E.C. "The Co-Existence of Legal Systems in Quebec: 'Free and Common Soccage' in Canada's 'pays de droit civil.'" *Cahiers de droit* 20 (1979): 277-87.

–. "The English Language Tradition in Quebec Civil Law." *L'actualité terminologique/Terminology Update* 20, 6. Ottawa: Secretary of State, 1987.

–. "La notion de droit commun dans un système de droit mixte: Le cas de la Province de Québec." In *La Formation du droit national dans les pays de droit mixte*, edited by Faculté de droit et de science politique, 103-18. Aix-Marseille: Presses universitaires d'Aix-Marseille, 1989.

Brisson, Jean-Maurice. *La formation d'un droit mixte: L'évolution de la procédure civile de 1774 à 1867.* Montreal: Themis, 1986.

Brisson, Jean-Maurice, and Nicholas Kasirer. "The Married Woman in Ascendance, the Mother Country in Retreat: From Legal Colonialism to Legal Nationalism in Quebec Matrimonial Law Reform, 1866-1991." In *Canada's Legal Inheritances*, edited by J. Guth DeLloyd and W. Wesley Pue, 409-23. Winnipeg: Canadian Legal History Project, 2001.

Brown, Jennifer. "Diverging Identities: The Presbyterian Métis of St. Gabriel Street, Montreal." In *The New Peoples: Being and Becoming Métis in North America*, edited by Jacqueline Peterson and Jennifer S. Brown, 195-206. Winnipeg: University of Manitoba Press, 1985.

Brown, Kathleen M. *Good Wives, Nasty Wenches, and Patriarchs: Gender, Race, and Power in Colonial Virginia.* Chapel Hill: University of North Carolina Press, 1996.

Brun, Josette. *Vie et mort du couple en Nouvelle-France: Québec et Louisbourg au XVIIIᵉ siècle*. Montreal/Kingston: McGill-Queen's University Press, 2006.

Burgess, Joanne. "Work, Family and Community: Montreal Leather Craftsmen, 1790-1831." PhD diss., Université du Québec à Montréal, 1986.

Burke, Sir Bernard. *A Genealogical and Heraldic Dictionary of the Landed Gentry of Great Britain and Ireland*. London: Harrison, Pall Mall, 1863.

Bushman, Richard. "Family Security in the Transition from Farm to City, 1750-1850. *Journal of Family History* 6 (1981): 238-56.

–. *The Refinement of America: Persons, Cities, Houses*. New York: Knopf, 1992.

Butler, Judith. "Performative Acts and Gender Constitution: An Essay in Phenomenology and Feminist Theory." In *Performing Feminisms: Feminist Critical Theory and Theatre*, edited by Sue-Ellen Case, 270-82. Baltimore: Johns Hopkins University Press, 1990.

Campbell, Robert. *A History of the Scotch Presbyterian Church, St. Gabriel Street, Montreal*. Montreal: W. Drysdale, 1887.

Cardin, Martine, and Guy Desmarais. "Les contrats de mariage au Bas-Canada: Étude préliminaire." *Cahiers d'histoire* 3, 2 (Spring 1983): 45-63.

Cardin, Martine, and John A. Dickinson. "Les inventaires de biens après décès et la civilisation matérielle dans les plaines de Cäen et de Montréal, 1740-1780." In *Sociétés villageoises et rapports villes-campagnes au Québec et dans la France de l'ouest XVIIᵉ et XXᵉ siècles*, edited by François Lebrun and Normand Séguin, 131-40. Trois-Rivières: Centre de recherche en études Québécoises, Université du Québec à Trois-Rivières, 1987.

Careless, J.S. *The Union of the Canadas: The Growth of Canadian Institutions, 1841-1857*. Toronto: McClelland and Stewart, 1967.

Carnes, Mark C. *Secret Ritual and Manhood in Victorian America*. New Haven, CT: Yale University Press, 1989.

Carter, Sarah. *The Importance of Being Monogamous: Marriage and Nation Building in Western Canada to 1915*. Edmonton: University of Alberta Press, 2008.

Caulier, Brigitte. "Des confréries pour l'élite: Le cas de Notre-Dame de Montréal." In Rousseau and Remiggi, *Atlas historique*, 178-79.

Cavanaugh, Catherine. "The Limitations of the Pioneering Partnership: The Alberta Campaign for Homestead Dower, 1909-25." *Canadian Historical Review* 74, 2 (June 1993): 198-225.

Chambers, Lori. *Married Women and Property Law in Victorian Ontario*. Toronto: University of Toronto Press, 1997.

Champagne, Claude. "La pratique testamentaire à Montréal, 1777-1825." *Cahiers de Thémis* 1 (January 1972): vi-98.

Creighton, Donald. *The Empire of the Saint Lawrence*. Toronto: Macmillan, 1956.

Chused, Richard, H. "Married Women's Property and Inheritance by Widows in Massachusetts: A Study of Wills Probated between 1800 and 1850." *Berkeley Women's Law Journal* 2 (Fall 1986): 42-88.

Clarke, Anna. *The Struggle for the Breeches: Gender and the Making of the British Working Class*. Berkeley: University of California Press, 1997.

Clawson, Mary Ann. *Constructing Brotherhood: Class, Gender, and Fraternalism*. Princeton, NJ: Princeton University Press, 1989.

Cleverdon, Catherine L. *The Woman Suffrage Movement in Canada*. Edited by Ramsay Cook. Toronto: University of Toronto Press, 1974 [1950].

Cliche, Marie-Aimée. "L'évolution des clauses religieuses traditionelles dans les testaments de la région de Québec au XIX siècles." In *Religion Populaire, Religion de clercs?* edited by Benoit Lacroix and Jean Simard, 365-88. Quebec: Institut Québécois de Recherche sur la Culture, 1984.

Cohen, Marjorie. *Women's Work, Markets and Economic Development in Nineteenth Century Ontario.* Toronto: University of Toronto Press, 1988.

Collard, Edgar Andrew. *Montreal: The Days That Are No More.* Toronto: Doubleday, 1978.

Collective Clio. *L'histoire des femmes au Québec depuis quatre siècles.* 2nd ed. Montreal: Le Jour, 1992.

Colley, Linda. *Britons Forging the Nation 1707-1837.* London: Pimlico, 1992.

Cook Sharon. "A Quiet Place to Die: Ottawa's First Protestant Old Age Homes for Men and Women." *Ontario History,* 81, 1 (1989): 25-40.

Cott, Nancy. *The Grounding of Modern Feminism.* New Haven, CT: Yale University Press, 1987.

–. *Public Vows: A History of Marriage and the Nation.* Cambridge, MA: Harvard University Press, 2000.

Courville, Serge, ed. *Population et territoire.* Sainte-Foy, Quebec: Presses de l'Université Laval, 1996.

–. *Quebec: A Historical Geography.* Translated by Richard Howard. Vancouver: UBC Press, 2008.

Courville, Serge, Jean-Claude Robert, and Normand Séguin. *Atlas historique du Québec: Le pays laurentien au XIXe siècle; Les morphologies de base.* Sainte-Foy, Quebec: Presses de l'Université Laval, 1995.

Cousens, S.H. "The Regional Variation in Emigration from Ireland between 1821 and 1841." *Transactions of the Institute of British Geographers* 37 (December 1965): 15-30.

Crémazie, Jacques. *Manuel des notions utiles sur les droits politiques, le droit civil, la loi criminelle et municipale, les lois rurales.* Quebec: J. and O. Crémazie Libraires-Éditeurs, 1852.

–. *Rapport de J. Crémazie, écuier, nommé en vertu de l'acte 4 Vict. chap 30, pour visiter les bureaux d'enregistrement de Québec et de Gaspé.* Montreal: Desbarats and Derbishire, 1846.

Curl, James Stevens. *The Victorian Celebration of Death.* Stroud, Gloucestershire: Sutton, 2000.

Curtis, Bruce. *The Politics of Population: State Formation, Statistics, and the Census of Canada, 1840-1875.* Toronto: University of Toronto Press, 2001.

D'Allaire, Micheline. *Les dots des religieuses au Canada français, 1639-1800: Étude économique et sociale.* Montreal: Hurtubise HMH, 1986.

Danylewycz, Marta. *Taking the Veil: An Alternative to Marriage, Motherhood, and Spinsterhood in Quebec, 1840-1920.* Toronto: McClelland and Stewart, 1987.

Darroch, Gordon. "Families, Fostering and Flying the Coop: Lessons in Liberal Cultural Formation, 1871-1901." In Sager and Baskerville, *Household Counts,* 197-246.

Darrow, Margaret. *Revolution in the House: Family, Class and Inheritance in Southern France, 1775-1825.* Princeton, NJ: New Jersey Press, 1989.

Daveluy, Marie-Claire. *L'Orphelinat Catholique de Montréal.* Montreal: Le Devoir, 1919.

Davidoff, Leonore. "Regarding Some 'Old Husbands' Tales': Public and Private in Feminist History." In *Worlds Between: Historical Perspectives on Gender and Class,* edited by Leonore Davidoff, 227-67. Oxford: Blackwell, 1995.

Davidoff, Leonore, Megan Doolittle, Janet Fink, and Katherine Holden. *The Family Story: Blood, Contract, and Intimacy, 1830-1960.* London: Longman; New York: Addison Wesley Longman, 1999.

Davidoff, Leonore, and Catherine Hall. *Family Fortunes: Men and Women of the English Middle Class, 1780-1850.* Chicago: University of Chicago Press, 1987.

Davies, Megan. *Into the House of Old: A History of Residential Care in British Colum-bia.* Montreal/Kingston: McGill-Queen's University Press, 2003.

–. "'Services Rendered, Rearing Children for the State': Mothers' Pensions in British Columbia, 1919-1931." In *Not Just Pin Money: Selected Essays on the His-tory of Women's Work in British Columbia,* edited by Barbara K. Lathan and Rob-erta J. Pazdro, 249-63. Victoria: Camosun College, 1984.

Davis, Nanciellen. "Patriarchy from the Grave: Family Relations in 19th Century New Brunswick Wills." *Acadiensis* 13, 2 (1984): 91-100.

Davis, Nathalie Zemon. *Women on the Margins: Three Seventeenth-Century Lives.* Cambridge, MA: Harvard University Press, 1995.

DeBrou, David. "Widows and Tenants on the Hustings: Estimating Voter Turn-out in Early Nineteenth-Century Quebec City." Paper presented at the annual meeting of the Canadian Historical Association, Queen's University, June 1991.

Dechêne, Louise. *Habitants and Merchants in Seventeenth-Century Montreal.* Montreal/Kingston: McGill-Queen's University Press, 1992.

Demos, John. *The Unredeemed Captive: A Family Story from Early America.* New York: Random House, 1994.

Denison, Merrill. *The Barley and the Stream: The Molson Story – A Footnote to Can-adian History.* Toronto: McClelland and Stewart, 1955.

Dépatie, Sylvie. "La transmission du patrimoine au Canada (XVIIe-XVIIIe siècles): Qui sont les défavorisés?" *Revue d'histoire de l'Amérique française* 54, 4 (Spring 2001): 557-70.

–. "La transmission du patrimoine dans les terroirs en expansion: Un exemple canadien au XVIIe siecle." *Revue d'histoire de l'Amérique française* 44, 2 (Autumn 1990): 171-98.

Dessureault, Christian. "Parenté et stratification: Parenté et stratification sociale dans une paroisse rurale de la vallée du Saint-Laurent au milieu du XIXe siècle." *Revue d'histoire de l'Amérique française* 54, 3 (Winter 2001): 411-48.

Deutsch, Sarah. *Women and the City: Gender, Space, and Power in Boston, 1870-1940.* New York: Oxford University Press, 2000.

Diefendorf, Barbara, B. "Widowhood and Remarriage in Sixteenth-Century Paris." *Journal of Family History* 7, 4 (Winter 1982): 379-95.

Dillon, Lisa. The 1881 Canadian Census Project and the North Atlantic Popula-tion Project. Database. Version 2003-01-28 15:28:00. Montreal: Department of Demography, Université de Montréal, 2003.

–. *The Shady Side of Fifty: Age and Old Age in Late Victorian Canada and the United States.* Montreal/Kingston: McGill-Queen's University Press, 2008.

–. "Women and the Dynamics of Marriage, Household Status, and Aging in Vic-torian Canada and the United States." *History of the Family* 4, 4 (December 1999): 447-83.

Dionne, Narcisse-Eutrope. *Mgr de Forbin-Janson: Évêque de Nancy et de Toul; Sa Vie – Son Oeuvre en Canada.* Quebec: Léger Brousseau, 1895.

Doolittle, Megan. "Close Relations? Bringing Together Gender and Family in English History." *Gender and History* 11, 3 (November 1999): 542-54.

Doucet, Nicolas Benjamin. *Fundamental Principles of the Laws of Canada as they existed under the natives, as they were changed under the French kings, and as they were modified and altered under the Dominion of England.* 2 vols. Montreal: John Lovell, 1841.

Driver, Elizabeth. *Culinary Landmarks: A Bibliography of Canadian Cookbooks, 1825-1949.* Toronto: University of Toronto Press, 2008.

Dunae, Patrick A. "Sex, Charades and Census Records: Locating Female Sex Trade Workers in a Victorian City." *Histoire sociale/Social History* 42, 84 (2009): 267-98.

Duncan, John Morison. *Travels through Part of the United States and Canada in 1818 and 1819.* Vol. 2. Glasgow: University Press, 1823.

Duncan, Nancy, ed. *Body Space: Destabilizing Geographies of Gender and Sexuality.* London: Routledge, 1996.

Dupâquier, Jacques, ed. *Marriage and Remarriage in Populations of the Past/Mariage et remariage dans les populations de passé.* London: Academic Press, 1981.

Durham, John George Lambton, Earl of, Charles Buller, and Edward Gibbon Wakefield. *Report on the Affairs of British North America.* Toronto: R. Stanton, 1839.

Eid, Mushira. *The World of Obituaries: Gender across Cultures and Over Time.* Detroit: Wayne State University Press, 2001.

Eley, Geoffrey. "Nations, Publics, and Political Cultures: Placing Habermas in the Nineteenth Century." In *Habermas and the Public Sphere,* edited by Craig Calhoun, 289-339. Cambridge: Massachusetts Institute of Technology, 1992.

Elliott, Bruce. *Irish Migrants in the Canadas: A New Approach.* Montreal/Kingston: McGill-Queen's University Press, 1988.

Erickson, Charlotte. "Emigration from the British Isles to the USA in 1831." *Population Studies* 35, 2 (July 1981): 175-97.

Errington, Jane. *Emigrant Worlds and Transatlantic Communities: Migration to Upper Canada in the First Half of the Nineteenth Century.* Montreal/Kingston: McGill-Queen's University Press, 2007.

–. *Wives and Mothers, Schoolmistresses and Scullery Maids: Working Women in Upper Canada, 1790-1840.* Montreal/Kingston: McGill-Queen's University Press, 1995.

Fahrni, Magda. *Household Politics: Montreal Families and Postwar Reconstruction.* Toronto: University of Toronto Press, 2005.

Fauteux, Aegidius. *Pseudonymes canadiens.* Montreal: G. Ducharme, 1938.

Fauve-Chamoux, Antoinette. "La femme seule et son travail." *Annales de Demographie historique,* 1981: 207-13.

Fecteau, Jean-Marie. "La dynamique sociale du catholicisme québécois au XIXe siècle: Eléments pour une réflexion sur les frontières et les conditions historiques de possibilité du '"social."' *Histoire sociale/Social History* 35, 70 (November 2002): 497-515.

–. *La Liberté du pauvre: Crime et pauvrété au XIXe siècle québécois.* Montreal: VLB éditeur, 2004.

–. *Un nouvel ordre des choses: La pauvreté, le crime et l'État au Québec, de la fin du XVIIIe siècle à 1840.* Outremont, Quebec: VLB éditeur, 1989.

Feretti, Lucia. *Brève histoire de l'Église catholique au Québec.* Montreal: Boréal, 1999.

–. *Entre voisins: La société paroissiale en milieu urbain, Saint-Pierre Apôtre de Montréal, 1848-1930.* Montreal: Boréal, 1996.

Ferrière, Claude de. *Dictionnaire de droit et de pratique.* Paris: Veuve Savoye, 1771.

Finch, Marianne. *An Englishwoman's Experience in America.* 1853. repr. New York: Negro Universities Press, 1979.

Fredman, L.E. *The Australian Ballot: The Story of an American Reform.* East Lansing: Michigan State University Press, 1968.

Führer, Charlotte. *The Mysteries of Montreal: Memoirs of a Midwife.* 1881. Edited by Peter Ward. Vancouver: UBC Press, 1984.

Fyson, Donald. *Magistrates, Police, and People: Everyday Criminal Justice in Quebec and Lower Canada, 1764-1837.* Toronto: Published for the Osgoode Society for Canadian Legal History by University of Toronto Press, 2006.

Gagan, David. *Hopeful Travellers: Families, Land, and Social Change in Mid-Victorian Peel County, Canada West.* Toronto: University of Toronto Press, 1981.

Gagnon, Serge. *Mariage et famille au temps de Papineau.* Quebec: Presses de l'Université Laval, 1993.

–. *Mourir, hier et aujourd'hui.* Quebec: Presses de l'Université Laval, 1987.

–. *Plaisir d'amour et crainte de Dieu: Sexualité et confession au Bas-Canada.* Sainte-Foy, Quebec: Presses de l'Université Laval, 1990.

–. *Quand le Québec manquait de prêtres.* Sainte-Foy, Quebec: Presses de l'Université Laval, 2006.

Galarneau, France. "L'élection partielle du quartier-ouest de Montréal en 1832: Analyse politico-sociale." *Revue d'histoire de l'Amérique française* 32, 4 (March 1979): 565-84.

–. "L'élection pour le quartier Ouest de Montréal en 1832: Analyse politico-sociale." MA thesis, Université de Montréal, 1978.

Gamber, Wendy. "Gendered Concerns: Thoughts on the History of Business and the History of Women." *Business and Economic History* 23 (Fall 1994): 129-40.

Garneau, Jean-Philippe. "Une culture de l'amalgame au prétoire: Les avocats de Québec et l'élaboration d'un langage juridique commun au tournant des XVIIIᵉ et XIXᵉ siècles." *Canadian Historical Review* 88, 1 (March 2007): 113-48.

–. "Droit et 'affaires de famille' sur la Côte-de-Beaupré: Histoire d'une rencontre en amont et en aval de la conquête britannique." *Revue juridique, Thémis* 34, 2 (2000): 519-61.

–. "Le rituel de l'élection de tutelle et la représentation du pouvoir colonial dans la société canadienne du XVIIIᵉ siècle." *Bulletin d'histoire politique* 114, 1 (Autumn 2005): 45-56.

Garner, John. *The Franchise and Politics in British North America, 1755-1867.* Toronto: University of Toronto Press, 1969.

Gauvreau, Danielle. *Québec, une ville et sa population au temps de la Nouvelle-France.* Sillery, Quebec: Presses de l'Université du Québec, 1991.

Gauvreau, Danielle, Diane Gervais, and Peter Gossage. *La fécondité des québécoises, 1870-1970: D'une exception à l'autre.* Montreal: Boréal, 2007.

Gentleman's Magazine, n.s., 28 (July-December 1842).

Gérin-Lajoie, Marie. *La communauté légale.* Montreal: Impr. des Sourds-Muets, 1927.

–. *Traité de droit usuel.* Montreal: Librairie Beauchemin, 1910.

–. *A Treatise on Everyday Law.* Montreal: John Lovell and Son, 1902.

Gibbs, Elizabeth, ed. *Debates of the Legislative Assembly of United Canada, 1841-67.* 13 vols. Montreal: Presses de l'École des hautes études commerciales, 1970-1993.

Gilliland, Jason, and Sherry Olson. "Residential Segregation in the Industrializing City: A Closer Look." *Urban Geography* 31, 1 (2010): 29-58.

Ginzberg, Lori G. *Women and the Work of Benevolence: Morality, Politics and Class in the 19th-Century United States.* New Haven, CT: Yale University Press, 1990.

Girard, Philip. "Married Women's Property, Chancery Abolition, and Insolvency Law: Law Reform in Nova Scotia, 1820-1867." In *Essays in the History of Canadian Law.* Vol. 3, *Nova Scotia,* edited by Philip Girard and Jim Phillips, 80-127. Toronto: Osgoode Society for Canadian Legal History/University of Toronto Press, 1990.

Girard, Philip, and Rebecca Veinott. "Married Women's Property Law in Nova Scotia, 1850-1910." In *Separate Spheres: Women's Worlds in the 19th-Century Maritimes,* edited by Janet Guildford and Suzanne Morton, 67-92. Fredericton: Acadiensis Press, 1994.

Giroux, Henri. *Une Heroïne du Canada: Mme Gamelin et ses Ouevres.* Montreal, 1885.

Glenn, Patrick H., ed. *Droit québécois et droit français: Autonomie, concordance*. Cowansville, Quebec: Éditions Yvon Blais, 1993.

Goody, Jack, Joan Thirsk, and E.P. Thompson, eds. *Family and Inheritance: Rural Society in Western Europe, 1200-1800*. Cambridge: Cambridge University Press, 1978.

Goose, Nigel. "Poverty, Old Age and Gender in Nineteenth-Century England: The Case of Hertfordshire." *Continuity and Change* 20, 3 (2005): 351-84.

Gordon, Eleanor, and Gwyneth Nair. *Public Lives: Women, Family and Society in Victorian Britain*. New Haven, CT: Yale University Press, 2003.

Gordon, Linda. *The Great Arizona Orphan Abduction*. Cambridge, MA: Harvard University Press, 1999.

–. *Heroes of Their Own Lives: The Politics and History of Family Violence*. New York: Penguin Books, 1988.

Gossage, Peter. *Families in Transition: Industry and Population in Nineteenth-Century Saint-Hyacinthe*. Montreal/Kingston: McGill-Queen's University Press, 1999.

–. "La Marâtre: Marie-Anne Houde and the Myth of the Wicked Stepmother in Quebec." *Canadian Historical Review* 76, 4 (December 1995): 563-97.

–. "Tangled Webs: Remarriage and Family Conflict in 19th-Century Quebec." In *Family Matters: Papers in Post-Confederation Canadian Family History*, edited by Edgar-André Montigny and Lori Chambers, 355-76. Toronto: Canadian Scholars Press, 1998.

Gratton, Brian. "The New History of the Aged: A Critique." In *Old Age in Bureaucratic Society: The Elderly, the Experts, and the State in American Society*, edited by David Van Tassel and Peter N. Stearns, 3-29. New York: Greenwood Press, 1986.

Grau, Antonia Gomila. "Residence Patterns of Aged Widows in Three Mediterranean Communities and the Organization of the Care." *History of the Family* 7 (2002): 157-73.

Gray, Colleen. *The Congrégation de Notre-Dame, Superiors, and the Paradox of Power, 1693-1796*. Montreal/Kingston: McGill-Queen's University Press, 2007.

Green, David R. "Independent Women, Wealth and Wills in Nineteenth-Century London." In Stobart and Owens, *Urban Fortunes*, 195-222.

Greenwood, F. Murray. *Legacies of Fear: Law and Politics in Quebec in the Era of the French Revolution*. Toronto: University of Toronto Press, 1993.

Greer, Allan. "1837-38: Rebellion Reconsidered." *Canadian Historical Review* 76, 1 (March 1995): 1-18.

–. "From Folklore to Revolution: Charivaris and the Lower Canadian Rebellion of 1837." In *Historical Perspectives on Law and Society in Canada*, edited by Tina Loo and Lorna R. McLean. Toronto: Copp Clark Longman, 1994.

–. *The Patriots and the People: The Rebellion of 1837 in Rural Lower Canada*. Toronto: University of Toronto Press, 1993.

–. *Peasant, Lord and Merchant: Rural Society in Three Quebec Parishes, 1740-1840*. Toronto: University of Toronto Press, 1985.

Grimké, Sarah. *Letters on the Equality of the Sexes and the Condition of Women*. Boston: Isaac Knapp, 1838.

Groupe de recherche sur la société montréalaise, Université du Québec à Montréal. *Montreal Census, 1831*. Database.

–. *Montreal Census, 1842*. Database.

Guinnane, Timothy W. *The Vanishing Irish, 1850-1914*. Princeton: Princeton University Press, 1997.

Haber, Carole, and Brian Gratton. *Old Age and the Search for Security: An American Social History*. Bloomington: Indiana University Press, 1993.

Hall, Catherine. *Civilising Subjects: Metropole and Colony in the English Imagination, 1830-1867.* Chicago: University of Chicago Press, 2002.

–. "Of Gender and Empire: Reflections on the Nineteenth Century." In Levine, *Gender and Empire,* 46-76.

Hamelin, Jean, and Marcel Hamelin. *Les moeurs électorales dans le Québec de 1791 à nos jours.* Montreal: Les Éditions du Jour, 1962.

Hamilton, Gillian. "Property Rights and Transaction Costs in Marriage: Evidence from Prenuptial Contracts." *Journal of Economic History* 59, 1 (March 1999): 68-103.

Hardwick, Julie. *The Practice of Patriarchy: Gender and the Politics of Household Authority in Early Modern France.* University Park: Pennsylvania State University Press, 1998.

Hardy, René. "À propos du réveil religieux dans le Québec du XIXe siècle: Le recours aux tribunaux dans les rapports entre le clergé et les fidèles." *Revue d'histoire de l'Amérique française* 48, 2 (1994): 187-212.

Hardy, René. *Contrôle social et mutation de la culture religieuse au Québec, 1830-1930.* Montreal: Boréal Express, 1999.

Harland-Jacobs, Jessica. "All in the Family: Freemasonry and the British Empire in the Mid-Nineteenth Century." *Journal of British Studies* 42 (October 2003): 448-82.

Hart, Gerald Ephraim. *The Fall of New France.* Montreal: W. Drysdale, 1888.

–. *The Quebec Act, 1774.* Montreal: Gazette Printing Co., 1891.

Hartog, Hendrik. *Man and Wife in America: A History.* Cambridge, MA: Harvard University Press, 2000.

Harvey, Janice. "Les églises protestantes et l'assistance aux pauvres à Montréal au XIXe siècle." *Études d'histoire religieuse* 69 (2003): 51-68.

–. "Le leadership féminin dans les associations privées de charité protestantes au XIXe siècle à Montréal." In Tardy et al., *Les Bâtisseuses de la Cité,* 65-78.

–. "The Protestant Orphan Asylum and the Montreal Ladies' Benevolent Society: A Case Study in Protestant Child Charity in Montreal, 1822-1900." PhD diss., McGill University, 2001.

–. "Le réseau charitable protestant pour les enfants à Montréal: Le choix des institutions." *Revue d'histoire de l'enfance "irrégulière" – Le temps de l'histoire* 5 (September 2003): 191-204.

Harvey, Kathryn. "To Love, Honour and Obey: Wife-Battering in Working-Class Montreal, 1869-79." *Urban History Review/Revue d'histoire urbaine* 19, 2 (1990): 128-40.

Heaman, E.A. "Taking the World by Show: Canadian Women Exhibitors to 1900." *Canadian Historical Review* 78, 4 (December 1997): 599-631.

Henderson, Jarett. "Uncivil Subjects: Metropolitan Meddling, Conditional Loyalty, and Lord Durham's 1838 Administration of Lower Canada." PhD diss., York University, 2010.

Heron, Craig. *Booze: A Distilled History.* Toronto: Between the Lines, 2003.

Hewitt, Nancy A. "Compounding Differences." *Feminist Studies* 18, 2 (Summer 1992): 313-26.

–. *Women's Activism and Social Change: Rochester, New York, 1822-1872.* Ithaca, NY: Cornell University Press, 1984.

Hillerman, Barbara Dodd. "'Chrysalis of Gloom': Nineteenth Century American Mourning Costume." In *A Time to Mourn: Expressions of Grief in Nineteenth-Century America,* edited by Martha V. Pike and Janice Gray Armstrong, 91-106. New York: Stoney Brook Museum, 1980.

Holcombe, Lee. *Wives and Property: Reform of the Married Women's Property Law in Nineteenth-Century England*. Toronto: University of Toronto Press, 1983.

Houlbrooke, Ralph, ed. *Death, Ritual and Bereavement, 1500-1940*. London: Routledge, 1989.

Howarth, Glennys. "Professionalizing the Funeral Industry in England 1700-1960." In *The Changing Face of Death: Historical Accounts of Death and Disposal*, edited by Peter C. Jupp and Glennys Howarth, 120-34. New York: St. Martin's Press, 1997.

Hubert, Ollivier. *Sur la terre comme au Ciel: La gestion des rites par l'Église catholique du Québec fin XVIIe-mi XIXᵉ siècle*. Sainte-Foy, Quebec: Presses de l'Université Laval, 2000.

Hudon, Christine. *Prêtres et fidèles dans le diocèse de Saint-Hyacinthe, 1820-1875*. Sillery, Quebec: Septentrion, 1996.

Hufton, Olwen. *Women and the Limits of Citizenship in the French Revolution*. Toronto: University of Toronto Press, 1991.

—. "Women without Men: Widows and Spinsters in Britain and France in the Eighteenth Century." *Journal of Family History* 9, 4 (Winter 1984): 355-75.

Huguet-Latour, L.A. *Annuaire de Ville Marie: Origine, utilité, et progrès des institutions Catholiques de Montréal*. Montreal: Senecal, 1863.

Institut de la Providence. *Histoire des filles de la Charité, servantes des pauvres, dites Soeurs de la Providence*. 4 vols. Montreal: Providence, Maison Mère, 1925-30.

—. *Notes historiques sur l'Institut des Soeurs de la Charité de la Providence*. Montreal: Providence, Maison Mère, 1893.

Jackson, James. *The Riot That Never Was: The Military Shooting of Three Montrealers in 1832 and the Official Cover-Up*. Montreal: Baraka Books, 2009.

Jalland, Pat. *Death in the Victorian Family*. New York: Oxford University Press, 1996.

—. *Women, Marriage and Politics, 1860-1914*. Oxford: Clarendon Press, 1986.

Jameson, Anna. *Sisters of Charity, Catholic and Protestant and the Communion of Labor*. Boston: Ticknor and Fields, 1857.

Jenkins, Kathleen. *Montreal Island: City of the Saint Lawrence*. New York: Doubleday, 1966.

Jumonville, Florence M. "The Wastebasket and the Grave: Funeralia in the South." *Southern Quarterly* 31, 2 (Winter 1993): 98-118.

Kessler-Harris, Alice. "Independence and Virtue in the Lives of Wage-Earning Women: The United States, 1870-1930." In *Women in Culture and Politics*, edited by Judith Friedlander, Blanche Wiesen Cook, Alice Kessler-Harris, and Carroll Smith-Rosenberg, 3-17. Bloomington: Indiana University Press, 1986.

Kete, Mary Louise. *Sentimental Collaborations: Mourning and Middle-Class Identity in Nineteenth-Century America*. Durham, NC: Duke University Press, 2000.

Klein. Kim. "A 'Petticoat Polity?' Women Voters in New Brunswick before Confederation." *Acadiensis* 26, 1 (1996): 71-75.

Klinghoffer, Judith Apter, and Lois Elkis. "'The Petticoat Electors': Women's Suffrage in New Jersey, 1776-1807." *Journal of the Early Republic* 12, 2 (1992): 159-93.

Kolish, Evelyn. "Le conseil législatif et les bureaux d'enregistrement (1836)." *Revue d'histoire de l'Amérique française* 35, 2 (September 1981): 217-30.

—. *Nationalismes et conflits de droits: Le débat du droit privé au Québec: 1760-1840*. LaSalle, Quebec: Hurtubise, 1994.

Kselman, Thomas A. *Death and the Afterlife in Modern France*. Princeton, NJ: Princeton University Press, 1993.

Lacelle, Claudette. *Urban Domestic Servants in Nineteenth-Century Canada.* Ottawa: Environment Canada – Parks, 1987.

Laderman, Gary. *The Sacred Remains: American Attitudes toward Death, 1799-1883.* New Haven, CT: Yale University Press, 1996.

LaFontaine, L.-H. *Analyse de l'Ordonnance du Conseil Spécial sur les bureaux d'hypothèques, suivie du texte anglais et français de l'ordonnance; des lois relatives à la création des ci-devant bureaux de comtés; et de la loi des lettres de ratification.* Montreal: Louis Perrault, 1842.

Lamoureux, Diane. *Citoyennes? Femmes, droit de vote et democratie.* Montreal: Remue-menage, 1989.

Landes, Joan B., ed. *Feminism, the Public and the Private.* New York: Oxford, 1998.

–. *Women and the Public Sphere in the Age of the French Revolution.* Ithaca, NY: Cornell University Press, 1988.

Landry, Jean-Guy. "Les finances de la fabrique." In Rousseau and Remiggi, *Atlas historique,* 97-105.

Landry, Yves. *Orphelines en France, pionnières au Canada: Les Filles du Roi au XVIIᵉ siècle.* Montreal: Lemeac, 1992.

Landry, Yves, and Rénald Lessard. "Les causes de décès aux XVII et XVIII siècles d'après les registres paroissiaux québécois." *Revue d'histoire de l'Amérique française* 48, 4 (Spring 1995): 509-26.

Langlois, Claude. *Le catholicisme au féminin: Les congrégations françaises à supérieure générale au XIXᵉ siècle.* Paris: Éditions de cerf, 1984.

–. "Les effectifs des congrégations féminines au XIXᵉ siècle: De l'enquête statistique à l'histoire quantitative." *Revue d'histoire de l'Église de France* 60 (1974): 44-63.

Lapointe-Roy, Huguette. *Charité bien ordonnée: Le premier réseau de lutte contre la pauvrété à Montréal au 19ᵉ siècle.* Montreal: Boréal, 1987.

Laporte, Gilles. *Patriotes et Loyaux: Leadership régional et mobilisation politique en 1837 et 1838.* Sillery, Quebec: Septentrion, 2004.

Lebsock, Suzanne. *The Free Women of Petersburg: Status and Culture in a Southern Town, 1784-1860.* New York: W.W. Norton, 1984.

Leitch, Gillian. "The Importance of Being 'English'? Identity and Social Organisation in British Montreal, 1800-1850." PhD diss., Université de Montréal, 2007.

Lemieux, Lucien. *Histoire du catholicisme québécois: Les années difficiles (1760-1839).* Vol. 2, Book 2. Montreal: Boréal, 1989.

Lemieux, Raymond. "Le dynamisme religieux des cultures francophones: Ouverture ou repli?" In *Religion, secularisation, modernité: Les expériences francophones en Amérique de Nord,* edited by Brigitte Caulier, 1-32. Sainte-Foy, Quebec: Presses de l'Université Laval, 1996.

Leprohon, Rosanna. *Antoinette de Mirecourt, or, Secret Marrying and Secret Sorrowing.* 1864. Edited by John C. Stockdale. Ottawa: Carleton University Press, 1999.

Lester, Alan. *Imperial Networks: Creating Identities in Nineteenth-Century South Africa and Britain.* London: Routledge, 2001.

Levine, Philippa, ed. *Gender and Empire.* Oxford: Oxford University Press, 2004.

–. "Why Gender and Empire?" In Levine, *Gender and Empire,* 1-13.

–. *Prostitution, Race and Politics: Policing Venereal Disease in the British Empire.* New York: Routledge, 2003.

Lewis, Robert. *Manufacturing Montreal: The Making of an Industrial Landscape, 1850-1930.* Baltimore: Johns Hopkins University Press, 2000.

Lewis, Susan Ingalls. "Business Widows in Nineteenth-Century Albany, New York, 1813-1885." In Bell and Yans, *Women on Their Own,* 115-39.

Linteau, Paul-André. *Histoire de Montréal depuis la Confédération*. Montreal: Boréal, 2000.

Linteau, Paul-André, and Jean-Claude Robert. "Propriété foncière et société à Montréal: Une hypothèse." *Revue d'histoire de l'Amérique française* 28, 1 (June 1974): 45-65.

Little, J.I. *Crofters and Habitants: Settler Society, Economy, and Culture in a Quebec Township, 1848-1881*. Montreal/Kingston: McGill-Queen's University Press, 1991.

–. *Love Strong as Death: Lucy Peel's Canadian Journal, 1833-1836*. Waterloo, ON: Wilfrid Laurier University Press, 2001.

Little, Margaret. *"No Car, No Radio, No Liquor Permit": The Moral Regulation of Single Mothers in Ontario, 1920-1997*. Toronto: Oxford University Press, 1998.

Longmore, George. *The Charivari: Or Canadian Poetics; A Tale, after the Manner of Beppo*. 1824. Edited by Mary Lu Macdonald. Ottawa: Golden Dog Press, 1977.

Loranger, Louis. *De l'incapacité légale de la femme mariée*. Montreal: Senecal, 1899.

Lovell's Montreal Directory, 1843-1910. Montreal: John Lovell's. http://bibnum2.banq.qc.ca/bna/lovell/index.html.

Luddy, Mary. *Women and Philanthropy in Nineteenth-Century Ireland*. Cambridge: Cambridge University Press, 1995.

Lyman, Arthur, ed. *Genealogy of the Lyman Family in Canada: Ancestors and Descendants of Elisha Lyman*. Montreal: Beaver Hall Press, 1943.

MacGregor, John. *British North America*. Vol. 2. Edinburgh: William Blackwood; London: T. Cadell, 1833.

Mackay, Robert W. Stuart. *Montreal Directory*. Montreal: Lovell and Gibson, 1842-54.

Mackay, Christina. *Montreal Directory*. Montreal: Owler and Stevensson, 1855-62.

MacLeod, Roderick. "Salubrious Settings and Fortunate Families: The Making of Montreal's Golden Square Mile, 1840-1895." PhD diss., McGill University, 1997.

Mandements, lettres pastorales, circulaires et autres document publié dans le diocèse depuis son érection. Montreal: J. Chapleau and Sons, 1869-1952. Canadian Institute for Historical Microreproductions no. 93391-93405.

Marsan, Jean-Claude. *Montreal in Evolution*. Translated by Arnaud de Varent. Montreal/Kingston: McGill-Queen's University Press, 1981.

Marsolais, Claude-V., Luc Desrochers, and Robert Comeau. *Histoire des maires de Montréal*. Montreal: VLB éditeur, 1993.

Masson, Ann, and Bryce Reveley. "When Life's Brief Sun Was Set: Portraits of Southern Women in Mourning – 1830-1860." *Southern Quarterly* 27, 1 (Fall 1988): 33-56.

McCallum, Margaret. "Prairie Women and the Struggle for a Dower Law, 1905-1920." *Prairie Forum* 18, 1 (Spring 1983): 19-34.

McCants, Anne E.C. "The Not-So-Merry Widows of Amsterdam, 1740-1782." *Journal of Family History* 24, 4 (October 1999): 441-667.

McCord, Thomas. *The Civil Code of Lower Canada together with a synopsis of Changes in the Law, references to the reports of the commissioners, the authorities as reported by the commissioners*. 2nd ed. Montreal: Dawson Brothers, 1873.

McCrum, Ann. "Inheritance and the Family: The Scottish Urban Experience in the 1820s." In Stobart and Owens, *Urban Fortunes*, 149-71.

McCullough, A.B. *Money and Exchange in Canada to 1900*. Toronto: Dundurn Press; Charlottetown: Parks Canada, 1984.

McDowell, Linda. *Gender, Identity and Place: Understanding Feminist Geographies*. Cambridge, UK: Polity Press, 1999.

McIntosh, Robert. "Sweated Labour: Female Needleworkers in Industrializing Canada." In Mitchinson et al., *Canadian Women*, 142-71.

McKay, Ian. "The Liberal Order Framework: A Prospectus for a Reconnaissance of Canadian History." *Canadian Historical Review* 81, 4 (December 2000): 617-45.

McKenna, Katherine M.J. *A Life of Propriety: Ann Murray Powell and Her Family.* Montreal/Kingston: McGill-Queen's University Press, 1993.

McKenzie, Kirsten. *Scandal in the Colonies: Sydney and Cape Town, 1820-1850.* Melbourne: Melbourne University Press, 2004.

McLean, Lorna. "Single Again: Widows' Work in the Urban Family Economy, Ottawa, 1871." *Ontario History* 83, 2 (June 1991): 127-50.

McManners, John. *Death and the Enlightenment: Changing Attitudes to Death among Christians and Unbelievers in Eighteenth-Century France.* Oxford: Clarendon Press, 1981.

McPherson, Kathryn. *Bedside Manners: The Transformation of Canadian Nursing, 1900-1990.* Toronto: Oxford University Press, 1996.

McPherson, Kathryn, Cecilia Morgan, and Nancy M. Forestell, eds. *Gendered Pasts: Historical Essays in Femininity and Masculinity in Canada.* Toronto: Oxford University Press, 1999.

Mills, Hazel. "'Saintes Soeurs' and 'Femme Fortes': Alternative Accounts of the Route to Womanly Civic Virtue, and the History of French Feminism." In *Wollstonecraft's Daughters: Womanhood in England and France, 1780-1920*, edited by Clarissa Campbell Orr, 133-50. Manchester: Manchester University Press, 1996.

Mitchinson, Wendy, Paula Bourne, Alison Prentice, Gail Cuthbert Brandt, Beth Light, and Naomi Black, eds. *Canadian Women: A Reader.* Toronto: Harcourt, Brace, 1996.

Monière, Denis. *Ludger Duvernay et la révolution intellectuelle au Bas Canada.* Montreal: Quebec Amerique, 1987.

Montigny, Edgar-André. "'Foistered upon the Government': Institutions and the Impact of Public Policy upon the Aged, the Elderly Patients of Rockwood Asylum, 1866-1906." *Journal of Social History*, Summer 1995: 817-35.

Moodie, Susanna. *Roughing It in the Bush or Life in Canada.* Edited by Carl. F. Klinck. Toronto: McClelland and Stewart, 1983 [1852].

Morel, André. "L'émergence du nouvel ordre juridique instauré par le Code civil du Bas-Canada." In *Le nouveau code civil: Interprétation et application*, 49-63. Montreal: Thémis, 1993.

–. "Un exemple de contact entre deux systèmes juridiques: Le droit successoral du Québec." *Annales de l'Université de Poitiers* 4-5 (1963-64): 1-13.

–. *Les limites de la liberté testamentaire dans le droit civil de la Province de Québec.* Paris: R. Pichon and R. Durand-Auzia, 1960.

Morgan, Cecilia. *Public Men and Virtuous Women: The Gendered Languages of Religion and Politics in Upper Canada, 1791-1850.* Toronto: University of Toronto Press, 1996.

Morgan, Henry J. *The Canadian Parliamentary Companion.* Montreal, 1871.

Morin, Michel. "La perception de l'ancien droit et du nouveau droit français au Bas-Canada, 1774-1866." In Glenn, *Droit québécois et droit français*, 1-41.

Morris, R.J. *Men, Women and Property in England, 1780-1870: A Social and Economic History of Family Strategies amongst the Leeds Middle Class.* Cambridge: Cambridge University Press, 2005.

Myers, Tamara, Kate Boyer, Mary Anne Poutanen, and Steven Watt, eds. *Power, Place and Identity: Historical Studies of Social and Legal Regulation in Quebec.* Montreal: Montreal History Group, 1998.

Narret, David. *Inheritance and Family Life in Colonial New York City.* Ithaca, NY: Cornell University Press, 1992.

Nazzari, Muriel. "Widows as Obstacles to Business: British Objections to Brazilian Marriage and Inheritance Laws." *Comparative Studies in Society and History* 37, 4 (October 1995): 781–802.

Noel, Françoise. *Family Life and Sociability in Upper and Lower Canada, 1760-1870.* Montreal/Kingston: McGill-Queen's University Press, 2003.

Noel, Jan. *Canada Dry: Temperance Crusades before Confederation.* Toronto: University of Toronto Press, 1994.

–. "'Femmes Fortes' and the Montreal Poor in the Early Nineteenth Century." In Mitchinson et al., *Canadian Women,* 68-85.

–. "Women and Social Welfare in the Montreal Region, 1800-1833: Preliminary Findings." In *Changing Roles of Women within the Christian Church in Canada,* edited by Elizabeth Gillan Muir and Marily Färdig Whiteley, 261-83. Toronto: University of Toronto Press, 1995.

Nootens, Thierry. *Fous, prodigues et ivrognes: Familles et déviance à Montréal au XIXᵉ siècle.* Montreal/Kingston: McGill-Queen's University Press, 2007.

–. "Un individu 'éclaté' à la dérive sur une mer de 'sens'? Une critique du concept d'identité." *Revue d'histoire de l'Amérique française* 62, 1 (2008): 35-68.

Normand, Sylvio. "La codification de 1866: Contexte et impact." In Glenn, *Droit québécois et droit français,* 43-62.

Normand, Sylvio, and Alain Hudon. "Le contrôle des hypothèques secrètes au XIXᵉ siècle: Ou la difficile conciliation de deux cultures juridiques et de deux communautés ethniques." *Recueil de droit immobilier,* 1990: 171-201.

Olson, Sherry. "Feathering Her Nest in Nineteenth-Century Montreal." *Histoire sociale/Social History* 33, 65 (2000): 1-35.

–. "Pour se créer un avenir: Stratégies de couples et stratégies de recherche." *Revue d'histoire de l'Amérique française* 51, 3 (1998): 357-89.

Olson, Sherry, and Patricia Thornton. "The Challenge of the Irish Catholic Community in 19th Century Montreal." *Histoire sociale/Social History* 35, 70 (November 2002): 331-64.

–. "La croissance naturelle des Montréalais au XIXᵉ siècle." *Cahiers de démographie du Québec* 30, 2 (Autumn 2001): 191-230.

–. "Ethnic Partition of the Work Force in 1840s Montréal." *Labour/Le Travail* 53 (2004): 157-200.

–. "Familles montréalaises du XIXᵉ siècle: Trois cultures, trois trajectoires." *Cahiers québecois de démographie* 21, 2 (Fall 1992): 51-75.

– "Le raz de marée irlandais à Montréal." In *Les chemins de la migration en Belgique et au Québec XVIIᵉ-XXᵉ siècles,* edited by Yves Landry, 69-80. Louvain: Academia, 1995, 69-80.

Ouellet, Fernand. *Lower Canada, 1791-1840: Social Change and Nationalism.* Toronto: McClelland and Stewart, 1980.

Owens, Alastair. "Property, Will Making and Estate Disposal in an Industrial Town, 1800-1857." In Stobart and Owens, *Urban Fortunes,* 79-107.

Palmer, Bryan. "Discordant Music: Charivaris and Whitecapping in Nineteenth-Century North America." *Labour/Le Travail* 3 (1978): 5-62.

Pâquet, Martin. "Le deuil comme consensus: Les rituels funéraires des responsables politiques au Canada et au Québec, 1868-2000." *Bulletin d'histoire politique* 14, 1 (Autumn 2005): 73-88.

Parent, France, and Geneviève Postolec. "Quand Thémis rencontre Clio: Les femmes et le droit en Nouvelle France." *Cahiers de droit* 36, 1 (March 1995): 293-318.

Parr, Joy. *Labouring Children: British Immigrant Apprentices to Canada, 1869-1924.* 2nd ed. Toronto: University of Toronto Press, 1994.

Pateman, Carole. *The Sexual Contract.* Stanford, CA: Stanford University Press, 1988.

Pearse, N.C., and Mrs. Alister Mitchel. *History of the Montreal Ladies' Benevolent Society, 1815-1920.* Montreal: The Society, n.d. [1920?].

Pelling, Margaret, and Richard M. Smith, eds. *Life, Death, and the Elderly: Historical Perspectives.* London: Routledge, 1991.

Perin, Roberto. *Ignace de Montréal: Artisan d'une identité nationale.* Montreal: Boréal, 2008.

Perrault, Antonio. "Le Conseil spécial, 1838-1841." *Revue du Barreau* 3 (1943): 130-44, 213-30, 265-74, 299-307.

Perry, Adele. *On the Edge of Empire: Gender, Race, and the Making of British Columbia, 1849-1871.* Toronto: University of Toronto Press, 2001.

Petitclerc, Martin. *"Nous protégeons l'infortune": Les origines populaires de l'économie sociale au Québec.* Montreal: VLB éditeur, 2007.

Picard, Nathalie. "Les femmes et le vote au Bas-Canada de 1792 à 1849." MA thesis, Université de Montréal, 1992.

–. Women Voters, Lower Canada. Database.

Pickles, Katie, and Myra Rutherdale, eds. *Contact Zones: Aboriginal and Settler Women in Canada's Colonial Past.* Vancouver: UBC Press, 2005.

Pierson, Ruth. "Experience, Difference, Dominance and Voice in the Writing of Canadian Women's History." In *Writing Women's History: International Perspectives,* edited by Karen Offen, Ruth Pierson, and Jane Rendall, 79-106. Bloomington: Indiana University Press, 1991.

Pilarczyk, Ian Christopher. "'Justice in the Premises': Family Violence and the Law in Montreal, 1825-1850." PhD diss., McGill University, 2003.

Plamondon, Lilianne. "Une femme d'affaires en Nouvelle-France: Marie-Anne Barbel, veuve Fornel." *Revue d'histoire de l'Amérique Française* 31, 2 (September 1977): 165-86.

Poutanen, Mary Anne. "Bonds of Friendship, Kinship, and Community: Gender, Homelessness, and Mutual Aid in Early Nineteenth Century Montreal." In Bradbury and Myers, *Negotiating Identities,* 25-48.

–. "'For the Benefit of the Master': The Montreal Needle Trades during the Transition, 1820-1842." MA thesis, McGill University, 1985.

–. "'To Indulge Their Carnal Appetites': Prostitution in Early Nineteenth-Century Montreal, 1810-1842." PhD diss., Université de Montréal, 1996.

–. Women Arrested in Montreal, 1809-1842. Database.

Prentice, Alison, Paula Bourne, Gail Cuthbert Brandt, Beth Light, Wendy Mitchinson, and Naomi Black. *Canadian Women: A History.* 2nd ed. Scarborough, ON: Thomson Nelson, 1996.

Prochaska, F.K. *Women and Philanthropy in Nineteenth-Century England.* Oxford: Oxford University Press, 1980.

Quataert, Jean H. *Staging Philanthropy: Patriotic Women and the National Imagination in Dynastic Germany, 1813-1916.* Ann Arbor: University of Michigan Press, 2001.

Quigley, Christine. *The Corpse: A History.* Jefferson, NC: McFarland and Co., 1996.

Radforth, Ian. *Royal Spectacle: The 1860 Visit of the Prince of Wales to Canada and the United States.* Toronto: University of Toronto Press, 2004.

Rankin, Matthew. "Anatomically Incorrect: Body Snatching in the Nineteenth Century." *Beaver* 82, 5 (October-November 2002): 28-32.

Renaud, Catherine. "Une place à soi? Aspects du célibat féminin laïc à Montréal à la fin du 19ᵉ siècle." MA thesis, Université de Montréal, 1994.

Rendall, Jane. "Women and the Public Sphere." *Gender and History* 11, 3 (November 1999): 475-88.

Report of the Annual Meeting of the Montreal Protestant House of Industry and Refuge. Montreal: House of Industry and Refuge, 1864-1879.

The Research Program in Historical Demography, Repertory of Vital Events, 1621-1799. *http://www.genealogie.umontreal.ca/.*

Reveley, Bryce. "The Black Trade in New Orleans: 1840-1880." *Southern Quarterly* 31, 2 (Winter 1993): 119-22.

Richardson, Ruth. *Death, Dissection and the Destitute.* London: Routledge and Kegan Paul, 1987.

Riddell, William Renwick. "Woman Franchise in Quebec a Century Ago." *Royal Society of Canada,* 3rd Series (1928): 85-99.

Riley, Denise. *"Am I That Name?" Feminism and the Category of "Women" in History.* Minneapolis: University of Minnesota, 1988.

Robert, Jean-Claude. "The City of Wealth and Death: Urban Mortality in Montreal, 1821-1871." In *Essays in the History of Canadian Medicine,* edited by Wendy Mitchinson and Janice Dickin McGinnis, 18-37. Toronto: McClelland and Stewart, 1988.

–. "Les notables de Montréal au XIXᵉ siècle." *Histoire sociale/Social History* 8, 15 (May 1975): 54-76.

Robillard, Denise. *Émilie Tavernier-Gamelin.* Montreal: Éditions du Méridien, 1988.

–. "Marguerite Lacorne, conseillère de Jacques Viger." In Tardy et al., *Les Bâtisseuses de la Cité,* 57-64.

Rogers, Nicholas. "Money, Marriage, Mobility: The Big Bourgeoisie of Hanoverian London." *Journal of Family History* 24, 1 (January 1999): 19-35.

Rome, David. "Benjamin Hart and 1829." *Canadian Jewish Archives,* n.s., 24 (1982): 16-23.

Roquebrune, Robert de. *Testament of My Childhood.* 1858. Translated by Felix Walter. Toronto: University of Toronto Press, 1964.

Rousseau, Louis. "À l'origine d'une société maintenant disparue: Le réveil religieux montréalais de 1840." In *Religion et culture au Québec: Figures contemporaines du sacré,* edited by Y. Desrosier, 71-92. Montreal: Fides, 1986.

–. "Les associations voluntaires paroissiales." In Rousseau and Remiggi, *Atlas historique,* 175-77.

–. "Les passages de la vie." In Rousseau and Remiggi, *Atlas historique,* 145-52.

Rousseau, Louis, with Céline Payette. "Le recrutement de l'élite." In Rousseau and Remiggi, *Atlas historique,* 199-212.

Rousseau, Louis, and Frank Remiggi. "Le renouveau religieux montréalais au XIXᵉ siècle: Une analyse spatio-temporelle de la pratique pascale." *Studies in Religion/Sciences Religieuses* 21, 4 (1992): 431-54.

–, eds. *Atlas historique des pratiques religieuses: Le Sud-Ouest du Québec au XIXᵉ siècle.* Ottawa: Presses de l'Université d'Ottawa, 1998.

Rowbotham, Sheila. "The Trouble with Patriarchy." *New Statesman,* December 1979.

Roy, Joseph-Edmond. *Histoire du notariat au Canada depuis la fondation de la colonie jusqu'à nos jours.* 4 vols. Lévis, Quebec: Revue du notariat, 1900-2.

Roy, Jean Louis. "Édouard Raymond Fabre, Bourgeois Patriote du Bas-Canada, 1799-1854." PhD diss., McGill University, 1971.

–. *Édouard-Raymond Fabre, libraire et Patriote canadien, 1799-1854: Contre l'isolement et la sujétion.* Montreal: Hurtubise, 1974.

Ruddel, David-Thiery. *Les apprentis artisans à Québec, 1660-1815.* Montreal: Presses de l'Université du Québec, 1977.

Ruggles, Steven. *Prolonged Connections: The Rise of the Extended Family in Nineteenth-Century England and America.* Madison: University of Wisconsin Press, 1987.

Rumilly, Robert. *Histoire de Montreal,* 5 vols. Montreal: Fides, 1970-74.

Ryan, Mary. *Cradle of the Middle Class: The Family in Oneida County, New York, 1790-1865.* New York: Cambridge University Press, 1981.

–. *Women in Public: Between Banners and Ballots, 1825-1880.* Baltimore: Johns Hopkins University Press, 1990.

Sadlier, Ann T., trans. *Life of Mother Gamelin: Foundress and First Superior of the Sisters of Charity of Providence, by a Religious of Her Institute.* Montreal: House of Providence, 1912.

Sager, Eric, and Peter Baskerville, eds. *Household Counts: Canadian Households and Families in 1901.* Toronto: University of Toronto Press, 2007.

Salmon, Marylynn. *Women and the Law of Property in Early North America.* Chapel Hill: University of North Carolina Press, 1986.

Sandwell, Ruth. "The Limits of Liberalism: The Liberal Reconnaissance and the History of the Family in Canada." *Canadian Historical Review* 84, 3 (September 2003): 423-50.

Scadron, Arlene. *On Their Own: Widows and Widowhood in the American Southwest, 1848-1939.* Urbana: University of Illinois Press, 1988.

Scott, Ann Fior. *Making the Invisible Woman Visible.* Urbana: University of Illinois Press, 1984.

Scott, Joan Wallach. "Gender: A Useful Category of Analysis." *American Historical Review* 91, 5 (December 1986): 1053-75.

–. *Gender and the Politics of History.* New York: Columbia University Press, 1988.

–. *Only Paradoxes to Offer: French Feminists and the Rights of Man.* Cambridge, MA: Harvard University Press, 1996.

Seccombe, Wally. *Weathering the Storm: Working-Class Families from the Industrial Revolution to the Fertility Decline.* New York: Verso, 1993.

Sendzik, Walter. "The 1832 Montreal Cholera Epidemic: A Study in State Formation." MA thesis, McGill University, 1997.

Senior, Elinor Kyte. *British Regulars in Montreal: An Imperial Garrison, 1832-1854.* Montreal/Kingston: McGill-Queen's University Press, 1981.

–. *Redcoats and Patriotes: The Rebellions in Lower Canada, 1837-38.* Ottawa: Canada's Wings, 1985.

–. *Roots of the Canadian Army: Montreal District, 1846-1870.* Montreal: Society of the Montreal Military and Maritime Museum, 1981.

Sewell, William H. Jr. "The Concepts of Culture." In Bonnell and Hunt, *Beyond the Cultural Turn,* 35-61.

Shammas, Carole, Marylynn Salmon, and Michel Dahlin. *Inheritance in America from Colonial Times to the Present.* New Brunswick, NJ: Rutgers University Press, 1987.

Shanley, Mary Lyndon. *Feminism, Marriage, and the Law in Victorian England, 1850-1895.* Princeton, New Jersey: Princeton University Press, 1989.

Shirreff, Patrick. *A Tour through North America: Together with a Comprehensive View of the Canadas and United States, as Adapted for Agricultural Emigration.* Edinburgh: Oliver and Boyd, 1835.

Shorter, Edward. *The Making of the Modern Family.* New York: Basic Books, 1975.

Sirois, Joseph. *De la forme des testaments.* Montreal: Wilson and Lafleur, 1907.

Skocpol, Theda. *Protecting Soldiers and Mothers: The Political Origins of Social Policy in the United States.* Cambridge, MA: Belknap Press, 1992.

Smith, Anthony D. *Nationalism and Modernism: A Critical Survey of Recent Theories of Nations and Nationalism.* London: Routledge, 1998.

Smith, Bonnie. *Ladies of the Leisure Class: The Bourgeoises of Northern France in the Nineteenth Century*. Princeton, NJ: Princeton University Press, 1981.

Smith-Rosenberg, Carroll. "The Female World of Love and Ritual: Relations between Women in Nineteenth-Century America." *Signs* 1, 1 (1975): 1-29.

Snell, James G. *The Citizen's Wage: The State and the Elderly in Canada, 1900-1951*. Toronto: University of Toronto Press, 1996,

Stanley, Amy Dru. *From Bondage to Contract: Wage Labor, Marriage, and the Market in the Age of Slave Emancipation*. New York: Cambridge University Press, 1998.

Stansell, Christine. *City of Women: Sex and Class in New York, 1789-1860*. Urbana: University of Illinois Press, 1987.

Starke's Montreal Pocket Almanac and General Register for 1858. Montreal: J. Starke, 1858.

Stavenuiter, Monique. "Last Years of Life: Changes in the Living and Working Arrangements of Elderly People in Amsterdam in the Second Half of the Nineteenth Century." *Continuity and Change* 11, 2 (1996): 217-41.

Staves, Susan. *Married Women's Separate Property in England, 1660-1833*. Cambridge, MA: Harvard University Press, 1990.

Stearns, Peter N. *Old Age in European Society: The Case of France*. London: Croom Helm, 1977.

Steedman, Mercedes. *Angels of the Workplace: Women and the Construction of Gender Relations in the Canadian Clothing Industry, 1890-1940*. Toronto: Oxford University Press, 1997.

Stewart, Alan M. "Settling an 18th-Century *Faubourg*: Property and Family in the Saint-Laurent Suburb, 1735-1810." MA thesis, McGill University, 1988.

Stewart, Stormie. "The Elderly Poor in Rural Ontario: Inmates of the Wellington County House of Industry, 1877-1907." *Journal of the Canadian Historical Association*, 3, 1 (1992): 217-33.

Stobart, Jon, and Alastair Owens, eds. *Urban Fortunes: Property and Inheritance in the Town, 1700-1900*. Aldershot: Ashgate, 2000.

Stoler, Ann Laura. *Carnal Knowledge and Imperial Power: Race and the Intimate in Colonial Rule*. Berkeley: University of California Press, 2002.

–. *Race and the Education of Desire: Foucault's History of Sexuality and the Colonial Order of Things*. Durham, NC: Duke University Press, 1995.

Stone, Lawrence. *The Family, Sex and Marriage in England, 1500-1800*. New York: Harper and Row, 1977.

–. "Prosopography." *Daedalus* 100 (1971): 46-79.

Stotts-McLaren, Sheryl. "Becoming Indispensable: A Biography of Elizabeth Smith Shortt (1859-1949)." PhD diss., York University, 2001.

Strange, Carolyn, and Tina Loo. *Making Good: Law and Moral Regulation in Canada, 1867-1939*. Toronto: University of Toronto Press, 1997.

Strange, Julie-Marie. *Death, Grief and Poverty in Britain, 1870-1914*. Cambridge: Cambridge University Press, 2005.

Strasser, Susan. *Never Done: A History of American Housework*. New York: Pantheon Books, 1982.

Strong-Boag, Veronica. "'Wages for Housework': Mothers' Allowances and the Beginnings of Social Security in Canada." *Journal of Canadian Studies* 14, 1 (Spring 1979): 24-34.

Sweeny, Robert. *The 1825 Manuscript Census of Montreal*. Database. St. John's: MUN, 1997-2002.

–. *The 1832 By-Election, Montreal West*. Database.

–. "Internal Dynamics and the International Cycle: Questions of the Transition in Montreal, 1821-1828." PhD diss., McGill University, 1985.

–. Lovell's Alphabetical Listing of 1880-81 of Montreal. Database. St. John's: MUN, 2003.

–. "Making a Bourgeois Town: Old Montreal; 1800 to 1850." Paper presented at the International Committee of Historical Sciences Meeting, Sydney, Australia, July, 2005.

–. A Partial Tax Roll for the City and Suburbs of Montreal, 1832. Database. St. John's: MUN, 2002.

–. A Reconstituted Tax Roll of Montreal, 1825. Database. St. John's: MUN, 1997-2002.

–. "Structure out of Change: Montreal Doctors 1819-1845." Unpublished paper, n.d.

Sweeny, Robert, with Grace Hogg and Richard Rice. *Les relations ville/campagne: Le cas du bois de chauffage*. Montreal: Groupe de recherche sur l'histoire des milieux d'affaires de Montréal, 1988.

Sylvain, Philippe, and Nive Voisine. *Histoire du catholicisme québécois: Réveil et consolidation*. Vol. 2, Book 2. Montreal: Boréal, 1991.

Talbot, Edward Allan. *Five Years' Residence in the Canadas: Including a Tour through Part of the United States of America, in the year 1823*. Vol. 2. London: Longman, 1824.

Tardy, Évelyne, Francine Descarries, Lorraine Archambault, Lyne Kurtman, and Lucie Piché, eds. *Les Bâtisseuses de la Cité*. Montreal: Association canadienne-française pour l'avancement des sciences, 1993.

Taylor, Charles. *Sources of the Self: The Making of the Modern Identity*. Cambridge, MA: Harvard University Press, 1989.

Taylor, Mary Lou. *Mourning Dress: A Costume and Social History*. London: George Allen and Unwin, 1983.

Tessier, Rose-de-Lima. *Vie de Mère Gamelin, fondatrice et première supérieure des Soeurs de la Charité de la Providence par une religieuse de son institut*. Montreal: Eusèbe Senécal, 1900. Translated by Anna T. Sadlier as *Life of Mother Gamelin: Foundress and First Superior of the Sisters of Charity of Providence, by a Religious of Her Institute*. Montreal: House of Providence, 1912.

Thifault, Marie-Claude. "L'enfermement asilaire des femmes au Quebec: 1873-1921." PhD diss., University of Ottawa, 2002.

Thomas, Rolph. *Comparative Advantages between the United States and Canada for British Settlers*. London: Smith Elder, 1842.

Thompson, William. *Appeal of One Half of the Human Race, Women, Against the Pretensions of the Other Half, Men, to Retain Them in Political and Thence in Civil and Domestic Slavery*. 1825. Reprint, London: Virago, 1983.

Tosh, John. *A Man's Place: Masculinity and the Middle-Class Home in Victorian England*. London: Yale University Press, 1999.

–. "What Should Historians Do with Masculinity? Reflections on Nineteenth-Century Britain." *History Workshop Journal* 38 (1994): 179-202.

Traer, James F. *Marriage and the Family in Eighteenth Century France*. Ithaca, NY: Cornell University Press, 1980.

Tremblay, Yves. "La société Montréalaise au début du Régime Anglais." MA thesis, University of Ottawa, 1970.

Troyanksi, David G. *Old Age in the Old Regime*. Ithaca, NY: Cornell University Press, 1989.

Trudel, Marcel. *Histoire de la Nouvelle-France: La seigneurie des Cent-Associées, 1627-1663*. Montreal: Fides, 1983

Trumbach, Randolph. *The Rise of the Egalitarian Family: Aristocratic Kinship and Domestic Relations in Eighteenth-Century England*. New York: Academic Press, 1978.

Tulchinsky, Gerald, J.J. *The River Barons: Montreal Businessmen and the Growth of Industry and Transportation, 1837-53*. Toronto: University of Toronto Press, 1977.

–. *Taking Root: The Origins of the Canadian Jewish Community*. Toronto: Lester, 1992.

Ulrich, Laurel Thatcher. *A Midwife's Tale: The Life of Martha Ballard, Based on Her Diary, 1785-1812*. New York: Vintage Books, 1991.

Van Die, Marguerite. *Religion, Family and Community in Victorian Canada: The Colbys of Carrollcroft*. Montreal/Kingston: McGill-Queen's University Press, 2005.

–. "'A Woman's Awakening': Evangelical Belief and Female Spirituality in Mid-Nineteenth-Century Canada." In Mitchinson et al., *Canadian Women*, 49-78.

Van Kirk, Sylvia. *Many Tender Ties: Women in Fur-Trade Society, 1670-1870*. Winnipeg: Watson and Dwyer, 1980.

Varty, Carmen Nielson. "'A Career in Christian Charity': Women's Benevolence and the Public Sphere in a Mid-Nineteenth-Century Canadian City." *Women's History Review* 14, 2 (2005): 243-64.

–. "The City and the Ladies: Municipal Politics and Female Benevolence in Mid-Nineteenth Century Hamilton, Canada West." *Journal of Canadian Studies* 38, 2 (Spring 2004): 151-71.

Vinet, Bernard. *Pseudonymes québeçois*. Quebec: Éditions Garneau, n.d.

Voisine, Nive, with André Beaulieu and Jean Hamelin. *Histoire de l'Église Catholique au Québec (1608-1970)*. Montreal: Fides, 1971.

Voisine, Nive, and Jean Hamelin. *Les Ultramontains canadiens-français: Études d'histoire religieuses présentées en hommage au professeur Philippe Sylvain*. Montreal: Boréal Express, 1985.

Walby, Sylvia. *Patriarchy at Work: Patriarchal and Capitalist Relations in Employment*. Cambridge, UK: Polity, 1986.

Walch, Agnès, and Scarlett Beauvalet. "Le veuvage: Une expérience de spiritualité conjugale; Trois témoignages de veuves catholiques (1832-1936)." *Histoire, économie et société* 14, 4 (1995): 609-25.

Ward, Peter. *Courtship, Love and Marriage in Nineteenth-Century English Canada*. Montreal/Kingston: McGill-Queen's University Press, 1990.

–. *A History of Domestic Space: Privacy and the Canadian Home*. Vancouver: UBC Press, 1999.

–. *A Love Story from 19th-Century Quebec: The Diary of George Stephen Jones*. Peterborough, ON: Broadview Press, 1989.

Warsh, Cheryl Lynn Krasnick, ed. *Drink in Canadian History*. Montreal/Kingston: McGill-Queen's University Press, 1993.

–. *Moments of Unreason: The Practice of Canadian Psychiatry and the Homewood Retreat, 1883-1923*. Montreal/Kingston: McGill-Queen's University Press, 1989.

Watt, Steven. "Authoritarianism, Constitutionalism and the Special Council of Lower Canada, 1838-1841." MA thesis, McGill University, 1997.

Wells, Robert V. *Death and Society in an American Community, 1750-1990*. Cambridge: Cambridge University Press, 2000.

Wilkes, Henry. *Death in the City: Address at the funeral of the late John Easton Mills, Esq., mayor of the city of Montreal, delivered in the American Presbyterian Church, November 1847*. Montreal: J.C. Becket, 1848.

Williams, Dorothy. *The Road to Now: A History of the Blacks in Montreal*. Montreal: Vehicule Press, 1997.

Wilson, Lisa. *Life after Death: Widows in Pennsylvania, 1750-1850*. Philadelphia: Temple University Press, 1992.

Wood, John. *Memoir of Henry Wilkes, D.D.: His Life and Times*. Montreal: Grafton and Sons, 1887.

Wood, Kirsten E. *Masterful Women: Slaveholding Widows from the American Revolution through the Civil War.* Chapel Hill: University of North Carolina Press, 2004.

Wrigley, A. "Family Reconstitution." In *An Introduction to English Historical Demography from the Sixteenth to the Nineteenth Century,* edited by D.E.C. Eversley, Peter Laslett, and E.A. Wrigley, 96-159. New York: Basic Books, 1966.

Wulf, Karin. *Not All Wives: Women of Colonial Philadelphia.* Ithaca, NY: Cornell University Press, 2000.

Yeoh, Brenda S.A. "The Body after Death: Place, Tradition and the Nation-State in Singapore." In *Embodied Geographies: Spaces, Bodies and Rites of Passage,* edited by E.K. Teather, 240-55. London: Routledge, 1999.

Young, Brian. "Death, Burial and Protestant Identity in an Elite Family: The Montreal McCords." In Bradbury and Myers, *Negotiating Identities,* 101-19.

−. *George-Etienne Cartier: Montreal Bourgeois.* Montreal/Kingston: McGill-Queen's University Press, 1981.

−. "Getting Around Legal Incapacity: The Legal Status of Married Women in Trade in Mid-Nineteenth Century Lower Canada." *Canadian Papers in Business History,* vol. 1, edited by Peter Baskerville, 1-16. Victoria: Public History Group, University of Victoria, 1989.

−. *In Its Corporate Capacity: The Seminary of Montreal as a Business Institution, 1816-1876.* Montreal/Kingston: McGill-Queen's University Press, 1986.

−. *The Politics of Codification: The Lower Canadian Civil Code of 1866.* Montreal/Kingston: McGill-Queen's University Press, 1994.

−. "Positive Law, Positive State: Class Realignment and the Transformation of Lower Canada, 1815-1866." In *Colonial Leviathan: State Formation in Mid-Nineteenth-Century Canada,* edited by Allan Greer and Ian Radforth, 50-63. Toronto: University of Toronto Press, 1992.

−. *Respectable Burial: Montreal's Mount Royal Cemetery/L'histoire du cimetière Mont-Royal.* Montreal/Kingston: McGill-Queen's University Press, 2003.

Yver, Jean. *Egalité entre héritiers et exclusion des enfants dotés: Essai de géographie coutumière.* Paris: Sirey, 1966.

Index